Expositions of the Psalms

Augustinian Heritage Institute, Inc.

THE WORKS OF SAINT AUGUSTINE
A Translation for the 21st Century

Part III – Books
Volume 18:
Expositions of the Psalms
73-98

THE WORKS OF SAINT AUGUSTINE
A Translation for the 21st Century

Expositions of the Psalms
73-98

III/18

translation and notes by
Maria Boulding, O.S.B.

editor
John E. Rotelle, O.S.A.

New City Press
Hyde Park, New York

Published in the United States by New City Press
202 Cardinal Rd., Hyde Park, New York 12538
©2002 Augustinian Heritage Institute

Cover picture (paperback): From the hymnal of the choir books of the
Augustinian Monastery of the Holy Savior (San Salvatore), Lecceto, Italy:
The Heavenly Jerusalem. Artist: Attributed to Filippo degli Agazzari, O.S.A.

Library of Congress Cataloging-in-Publication Data:

Augustine, Saint, Bishop of Hippo.
    The works of Saint Augustine.

    "Augustinian Heritage Institute"
    Includes bibliographical references and indexes.
    Contents: — pt. 3, v .15. Expositions of the Psalms, 1-32
—pt. 3, v. 1. Sermons on the Old Testament, 1-19.
— pt. 3, v. 2. Sermons on the Old Testament, 20-50 — [et al.] — pt. 3,
v. 10 Sermons on various subjects, 341-400.
    1.   Theology — Early church, ca. 30-600.   I. Hill,
Edmund.   II. Rotelle, John E.   III. Augustinian
Heritage Institute.   IV. Title.
BR65.A5E53   1990   270.2   89-28878
ISBN 1-56548-055-4 (series)
ISBN 1-56548-167-4 (pt. 3, v. 18)
ISBN 1-56548-166-6 (pt. 3, v. 18: pbk.)

We are indebted to Brepols Publishers, Turnholt, Belgium,for their use of the Latin critical text
of *Enarrationes in Psalmos I-CL*, ed. D. Eligius Dekkers, O.S.B. et Johannes Fraipont,
Corpus Christianorum Latinorum XXXVIII-XL (Turnholt, 1946) 1-2196.

Nihil Obstat:John E. Rotelle, O.S.A., S.T.L., Censor Deputatus
Imprimatur: + Patrick Sheridan, D.D., Vicar General
            Archdiocese of New York, July 22, 1999

The *Nihil Obstat* and *Imprimatur* are official declarations that a book or pamphlet is free of doctrinal or
moral error. No implication is contained therein that those who have granted the *Nihil Obstat* and
Imprimatur agree with the contents, opinions or statements expressed.

Printed in the United States of America

Contents

Why our prayer seems to be rejected — 270; Verses 16-19. The Church suffers and endures, until its hope is fulfilled — 270

Exposition 1 of Psalm 88

Verse 1. Understanding for the weak made strong — 273; Verses 2-3. The mercy and the faithfulness of God — 273; Verses 4-5. The promises to Abraham's seed. Confidence in preaching is based on God's word — 275; Verse 6. The newly-made "heavens" proclaim the Lord's wonders — 277; Verse 7. Preachers of truth are rain-bearing clouds, but none equal the Lord. We are children of God, but the only-begotten is unique — 278; Verses 8-9. The diffusion of God's truth and mercy — 280; Verses 10-11. The sea is tamed and the sea-monster wounded — 281; Verses 12-14. Creation and redemption: all is God's gift — 282; Verse 15. God's mercy and truth forestall the future judgment — 283; Verses 16-17. Delighting in grace, God's people walks in the light of his countenance — 284; Verses 18-19. Exalted and upheld in God — 285; Verses 20-24. God's promise to David, and to Christ, the son of David — 285; Verses 25-28. Our response to God's mercy and faithfulness — 286; Verses 29-30. The new covenant and our inheritance — 287

Exposition 2 of Psalm 88

A link with the preceding sermon — 289; Verses 31-35. Sin, punishment, the far-reaching promise of mercy, and the abiding covenant — 289; Verses 36-38. Eternal life for the body as well as the soul — 292; Verses 39-46. Disappointment and calamities instead of the fulfillment of the promises — 294; The coming of the Anointed One is only deferred — 296; Verses 47-49. The fulfillment in Christ is already suggested in the psalm — 297; Christ's resurrection foreshadowed — 299; Verses 50-52. Believers have still had to suffer hardship and insult — 299; Verse 53. The unfailing blessing of the Lord. Concluding exhortations — 301

Exposition of Psalm 89

Verse 1. The role of Moses — 303; Verse 2. The eternity of God is our refuge — 303; Verses 3-6. The transience of human life, contrasted with God's eternal, immutable being — 305; Verses 7-10. Death is the punishment for sin, but an abbreviated life is not necessarily a sign of God's anger — 307; Spiritual interpretations are offered for the seventy and eighty years — 308; Verses 11-12. What it means to attain true understanding of God's anger, and knowledge of his right hand — 309; Verse 13. Long-suffering — 311; Verses 14-15. The promise of morning — 312; Verses 16-17. Works and the one work — 313; Conclusion: the psalm goes under the name of Moses for a special reason — 314

Exposition 1 of Psalm 90

What it means to imitate Christ, particularly when we are tempted — 315; Verses 1-3. Dwelling safely and humbly within the help of the Most High — 317; Verse 4. Sheltered under the wings of incarnate Wisdom — 319; Verses 5-6. God's shield in our warfare; the dangers from different weapons — 320; Verse 7. No one can afford to be complacent. Christ identifies himself with his hard-pressed members — 323; Verse 8. The insight that comes from faith — 327; Verses 9-12. Hasty conclusion: we must leave the rest for tomorrow — 328

Exposition 2 of Psalm 90 329

Augustine reiterates his teaching on the whole Christ, head and members; this is the key to understanding in all the psalms — 329; Verses 1-8. Recapitulation of yesterday's explanation of the early verses. God will protect us even in the heat of persecution if we trust in him, not in ourselves — 331; Verses 9-12. Our lofty refuge: Christ was tempted to empower us when we are tempted — 333; Hunger: the temptation to conjure bread out of stones — 336; Another temptation: the lust for power — 337; How did the angels bear up the Lord? Stumbling on the stone means falling foul of the law — 339; Verse 13. The devil, whether savage or insidious, will be defeated — 341; Verses 14-16. Deliverance and eternal life — 342

Exposition of Psalm 91 345

Faith, hope, and charity in our time of endurance — 345; Verse 1. The title: the Sabbath of the heart — 346; Verse 2. Confess to the Lord that your sins are your work, your good deeds his — 347; Verses 3-4. Praise in light and darkness, with deeds and words — 349; Verse 5. Any good we do is of God's making; the evil is from ourselves. The temptation to be scandalized at the prosperity of the wicked — 350; Verse 6. The deep, high wisdom of God — 352; Verses 7-8. If you covet temporal glory, you may perish eternally — 354; Verses 9-10. Who are God's hidden enemies? — 354; Verse 11. The Church's ever-green youth — 355; Verses 12-13. The prospect of judgment. Palm trees and cedars — 356; Verses 14-16. Be tranquil, and proclaim God's just dealing — 357

Exposition of Psalm 92 360

Verse 1. The sixth day and the sixth age — 360; Beauty and strength are the Lord's apparel, and both are required by an apostle — 362; A meditation on the Lord's girdle: the incarnation and humility — 363; There is a movable world, and a stable, immovable world — 365; Verse 2. God's throne in humble souls. Christ's eternal birth — 366; Verses 3-4. The loud voice of the rivers — 368; Verse 5. Christ has conquered the world — 370

Exposition of Psalm 93 372

The scope of this psalm: a corrective to people who believe God's dispositions to be unjust — 372; Verse 1. The title points us to the stars — 375; The serenity of the high stars, reflected in the forbearance of the saints — 377; The unrolled book of the sky symbolizes scripture, which we must read now, and fix our hearts in now, but not for eternity — 379; The universal fairness of God's punitive judgments — 381; Verse 2. Retribution will fall only on the proud — 383; Verses 3-4. The psalm is therapeutic. Why is God so patient? — 385; Verses 5-7. Two deluded assessments — 387; Verses 8-11. The all-wise Lord is instructing you, and offering you understanding — 388; Verses 12-13. The humility of a sinner is more acceptable to God than the complacency of one who lives virtuously — 390; Verse 14. Temporary suffering is chastisement, not rejection — 393; Verse 15. Rectitude of heart: Christ prefigured our weakness in his agony — 394; Verses 16-17. The just person, beset by temptation, finds help in the Lord — 398; Verses 18-19. Confess your instability, and you will walk triumphant — 399; Verses 20-21. The labors and suffering of the righteous are God's educative tools. Labor is the price of rest — 400; Verse 22. The positive effect of the discipline begins to appear — 405; Verse 23. God brings good results from the actions of bad people, but the wicked are requited according to their intentions — 405; Augustine sums up his reflections and concludes the sermon — 407

praying and fasting for its persecutors — 469; Verses 3-4. God's name is terrible and holy. Judgment and justice in human beings are his creation — 472; Verse 5. How can we worship the Lord's footstool? Christ's flesh is meant — 474; Verses 6-8. The privileges of Moses, Aaron and Samuel, who prophesied of Christ — 476; Moses, Aaron, and Samuel were nonetheless punished, and in this they foreshadowed all faithful disciples — 477; Verse 9. The stone hewn from the mountain fills the earth — 481; Conclusion: the life-giving rain must find receptive soil — 483

Exposition of Psalm 73

A Sermon to the People

Verse 1. The synagogue, still intent on old promises, seeks understanding

1. The title of this psalm is *Understanding for Asaph*. Now the name, Asaph, means "Congregation" in our language, and "Synagogue" in Greek. We need therefore to investigate what it was that the synagogue was trying to understand. But first of all we need to investigate what the synagogue itself was, because that is the necessary starting-point if we are to find out what it was that the synagogue understood.

Now any congregation can be called a "synagogue" if the word is used in a general sense. We can speak of a congregation of cattle just as well as of one formed of human beings; but the congregation in question here cannot be composed of animals, since understanding has been mentioned. This is clear from the stricture passed against humans who, though of high dignity, undervalued the understanding implanted within them: human beings failed to understand how they were honored; they were no better than the foolish beasts, and became like them (Ps 48:13.21(49:12.20)). We have no need, then, to prove at length that the psalm does not envisage a congregation of cattle; there is no occasion to labor the point. But since the congregation is one of human beings, we must try to understand exactly who these humans are. Clearly they are not the people who failed to understand how they were honored, and were no better than the foolish beasts, and became like them. We have here a congregation of people who do understand. This can be inferred from the title written over the psalm: *Understanding for Asaph*.

It is therefore the voice of an intelligent congregation that we are to hear. But the name "synagogue" is properly applied to the congregation of Israelites, so much so that whenever we hear "synagogue" we automatically think of the Jewish people, and no other. We should be prepared, then, to listen to the voice of this people in the present psalm. But of what sort of Jews, what sort of Israelites? Not the voice of the straw, but perhaps that of the grain;[1] not the voice of the branches that were broken off,[2] but perhaps that of branches consolidated in place. *For not all who spring from Israel are Israelites*, says scripture, but *it is*

---

1. See Mt 3:12.
2. See Rom 11:17.19-20.

through Isaac that posterity will be reckoned to Abraham. *It is not the children of Abraham's flesh who are children of God; it is the children of the promise who are accounted Abraham's descendants* (Rom 9:6-8).

There are certain authentic Israelites, then, one of whom was the man of whom it was said, *Look, there is a true Israelite, in whom there is no guile* (Jn 1:47). In saying this I am not referring to the fact that we are all Israelites inasmuch as we are Abraham's progeny: this is certainly the case, for it was to the Gentiles that the apostle said, *You are the descendants of Abraham, his heirs according to the promise* (Gal 2:29). In this sense all of us who follow our father Abraham along his path of faith are Israelites. But this is not what I mean here in speaking of Israelites. In the present context we must understand the term "Israelites," in the sense intended by the apostle when he said, *I am myself an Israelite, sprung from the stock of Abraham, of the tribe of Benjamin* (Rom 11:1). We must try to understand here what the prophets meant when they said that *a remnant shall be saved.*[3]

The voice to which we must listen in this psalm is that of the remnant that was saved; we must let the synagogue speak to us, that synagogue which had received the Old Covenant, and was intent on its material promises, and was therefore sent staggering. What else but this unsteady gait is evoked in another psalm, the title of which also includes Asaph? What do we hear there? *How good God is to Israel, to those of straightforward hearts! Yet my feet had all but slipped.* Then as though to reply to our question, "What sent your feet slipping?" it continues, *My steps very nearly slid out of control, because I envied sinners, seeing the peace that sinners enjoy* (Ps 72(73):1-3). Relying on those promises of God which were associated with the Old Covenant, the psalmist expected prosperity on earth, and observed that the godless enjoyed it in plenty. He saw that people who did not worship God had at their command ample supplies of those very things which he expected God to give; and as a result his feet slithered, for it looked as though his service of God had been pointless. *Look, they are sinners,* he complained, *yet they have won abundant wealth in this world. So I said, To no purpose have I justified my heart* (Ps 72(73):12-13). You can see how nearly his feet had slid out of control when he was brought to the point where his soul asked itself, "Why should I bother to serve God? Look at that fellow over there: he does not serve God, but he gets on well; I serve him, and have a hard grind. And even if I were well off, why should I think my prosperity a consequence of serving God, when the person who does not serve him is equally fortunate?" The psalm I have quoted immediately precedes the one we are concerned with today.

---

3. Rom 9:27; compare Is 10:22.

The Old Covenant and the New: the same commandments, different signs and promises

2. Not by any contriving on our part, but by God's dispensation, it has most opportunely happened that we have just heard in the gospel, *The law was given through Moses, grace and truth came through Jesus Christ* (Jn 1:17). If we compare the Old Covenant and the New, we find that the sacred signs[4] are not the same, nor are the promises the same; but most of the commandments are the same. We are commanded, just as the Israelites were, *You shall not kill, you shall not commit adultery, you shall not steal, honor your father and your mother, you shall not bear false witness, you shall not covet your neighbor's property, you shall not covet your neighbor's wife.*[5] Whoever does not keep these commandments goes astray, and will be quite unworthy to receive[6] God's holy mountain, of which scripture speaks: *Lord, who will sojourn in your tent, and who will take rest on your holy mountain? One with clean hands and pure heart* (Ps 14(15):1; 23(24):4). If we examine the commandments we find that they are all common to Old and New Testaments alike, or at any rate that there are very few in the gospels not already articulated by the prophets.

The commandments are the same, then; but the sacred signs[7] are not the same, and neither are the promises. It is easy to see why the commandments are the same, because they are our guidelines for serving God. But the sacred signs are different, because while some sacred signs bestow salvation, others foretold and promised the Savior. The sacraments of the New Covenant give salvation; those of the Old Covenant were promises of the Savior who was to come. You, then, Christian, since you already hold the things that were promised, since you already have your Savior, why do you seek those signs which did no more than promise him? I say, "You already hold the good things that were promised," not because we have already received eternal life, but because Christ has already come, Christ who was proclaimed in advance through the prophets. The sacred signs have been changed; they have been made simpler, fewer, more conducive to salvation, more appropriate and efficacious.

Why are the promises not the same? Because what was promised of old was the land of Canaan, a rich, fertile land flowing with milk and honey; what was promised was a time-bound kingdom; what was promised was prosperity in this world, many children, and the subjugation of Israel's enemies. All these bless-

---

4. *Sacramenta*, here and later in this section. See note at Exposition of Psalm 67,16. The term for Augustine covers words, actions, events, and institutions which under either dispensation signify the grace hidden within them and offered to believers. It is therefore wider than, though it includes, the sacraments of the Christian Church. Compare his reflections on *sacramenta* in his Exposition 2 of Psalm 68,6 and Exposition of Psalm 77,2.

5. See Ex 20:12-17; Dt 5:16-21.

6. Variant "ascend."

7. *Sacramenta*.

ings are aspects of earthly happiness. Why was it necessary for them to be promised first? Because *it is not the spiritual that comes first. The animal body comes
first, and what is spiritual afterwards*, scripture tells us. *The first man was from
the earth, earthly, but the second man is from heaven, heavenly. As the earthly
man was, so are the earthlings; as the heavenly man is, so too are the heavenly
ones. As we have borne the image of the man of earth, so too let us bear the image
of him who is of heaven* (1 Cor 15:46-49). The Old Covenant bears the image of
the earthly man; the New Covenant bears that of the man from heaven. But in
case anyone might gather from this that the earthly person was created by some
power other than that which created the man from heaven,[8] God willed to
demonstrate that he is the creator of them both by showing himself as the author
of both Testaments, promising earthly gifts in the Old, and heavenly blessings in
the New.

But what about you—how long will you go on behaving as though you were
still the earthly person? How long will you persist in relishing only the flavors of
earth? Just because childish things are given to a child, toys to divert a childish
mind, does that mean that we should not pluck them out of the hands of an
adolescent, so that he or she may handle something more useful, something
more suited to maturer years? Of course not. You know this yourself, for you
give nuts to your own child when he or she is little, but a book when the child
grows bigger. So too did God through the New Covenant dash those things like
childish toys from the hands of his sons and daughters, so that he could give them
something more useful as they matured; but this does not mean that he is not to
be acknowledged as the donor of those earlier gifts. On the contrary: he gave
both. But while *the law was given through Moses, grace and truth came through
Jesus Christ* (Jn 1:17). Grace, because what was formerly commanded through
the written code is now fulfilled through charity; and truth, because what was
promised earlier is now given to us.

All this Asaph understood. Clearly, all the blessings that were promised to the
Jews have been taken away. Where is their kingdom now? Where is the temple?
Where the anointing? Where is any priest? Are there any prophets left among
them? Since the coming of him whom the prophets foretold, none of these things
has existed in that nation. It has lost its earthly privileges, but does not yet seek
heavenly gifts.

The self-defeating folly of attachment to earthly goods

3. You, then, must not cling to earthly goods, even though God gives them.
This does not mean that, because we are forbidden to cling to them, someone
other than God is the giver. Not at all. God himself gives these things. However,

---

8. As held by Manichees and others.

if you hope for some good thing from him, do not overestimate its importance if it is something he gives likewise to a person who is not good. If such gifts of God were very important in his eyes, he would not give them to bad people. He wills to give such things to the wicked also, in order that good people may learn to seek something different from him, something he does not give to evildoers.

But the hapless Jews clutched at their earthly blessings. They would not put their confidence in him who made heaven and earth, who had given them these earthly goods, who had granted them temporal deliverance by snatching them from captivity in Egypt, who had parted the sea, led them through, and sunk their pursuing enemies beneath its waves. They refused to rest their confidence in him who, as he had given earthly gifts to them in their childhood, would certainly have given them heavenly gifts as they grew up. Instead, driven by fear of losing what they had received, they killed the giver.

We say this, brothers and sisters, so that you, as people who belong to the New Covenant, may learn not to be attached to earthly things. To the Jews the New Covenant had not been revealed, yet they were inexcusable in their determination to cling to the goods of this world. How much more inexcusable are we if we pursue worldly things, when to us the heavenly promises of the New Covenant have been revealed! Call to mind, brothers and sisters, the anxiety voiced by Christ's persecutors: *If we leave him alone like this, the Romans will come, and sweep away our land and our nationhood* (Jn 11:48). Listen to that! Fearful of losing privileges that belonged to earth, they killed the King of heaven. And what happened to them? They lost even their earthly holdings. In that place where they slew Christ, they themselves were slaughtered. Attempting to avoid the loss of their land, they killed the giver of life; the result was that they were killed themselves and lost the land. Both events happened at the same season, so that from the coincidence of time the Jews might be left in no doubt why they suffered so terribly; for their city was sacked as they were keeping Passover, when the whole nation, numbering many thousands, had gathered to celebrate the festival.[9] God made use of evil men, though he is good; he used unjust agents, though he himself is just and acted justly. He wreaked vengeance on them in such a way that many thousands of Jews perished and their city was destroyed.

In our psalm Asaph's understanding mind bewails these disasters. In his lament his intelligence is evident: he discerns the difference between earthly and heavenly things, and between Old and New Testaments, so that you may see what you must pass through, what you may expect, what you must leave behind, and what you must cling to. He begins with a question.

4. *Why, O God, have you cast us off, even to the end?* He says, *You have cast us off, even to the end*, because he speaks in the name of the Jewish people, and in the name of that assembly which is properly called the synagogue. *Why, O God,*

---

9. See Josephus: *Jewish War* VI,9,3. The city fell to Titus and his legions at Passover, A.D. 70.

have you cast us off, even to the end? He is not reproaching God, but he asks, "Why? What is the reason? Why have you done this? What have you done? *You have cast us off, even to the end.*" What does *to the end* mean? Until the end of the world, perhaps; or could it mean that you have cast us upon Christ, who is the end, the goal, for everyone who believes?[10] But *why, O God, have you cast us off, even to the end? Your mind is angry with the sheep of your flock.* Why is it angry with the sheep of your flock, if not because we kept on clutching at earthly things, and refusing to acknowledge our shepherd?

Verse 2. The staff, the snake, and Christ

5. *Be mindful of your congregation, which you made your own from the beginning.* This cannot be the Gentiles speaking, can it? Did God make the Gentiles his own from the beginning? No; he made Abraham's descendants his own, the Israelite people who according to the flesh derived from the patriarchs, though the patriarchs are our ancestors too, for we became their children not by carnal descent but by imitating their faith.

What happened to those whom God made his own from the beginning? *Be mindful of your congregation, which you made your own from the beginning. You redeemed the staff of your inheritance.* He called this congregation "the staff of God's inheritance." To understand why, we need to look back at an event which occurred at the outset, when God willed to make this congregation his own by rescuing it from Egypt. We need to recall what kind of sign he gave to Moses. Moses said to God, *"What sign am I to give them, to make them believe that you sent me?" And God said to him, "What are you carrying in your hand?" "A staff." "Throw it on the ground." He dropped the staff on the ground, and it turned into a snake. Moses was terrified. Moses fled from it. And the Lord said to him, "Catch hold of its tail." He caught it, and it reverted to its original form. It was a staff again, as it had been a staff to begin with.*[11] What is the meaning of this episode? It did not happen without good reason. Let us put our question to the letter God has sent us.[12]

To what did the snake's persuasion lead men and women? To death.[13] So death derives from a snake. Now, if death comes from a snake, the staff in the guise of a snake symbolizes Christ in death. This is why the Lord commanded Moses to erect a bronze serpent in the desert, when the people were being bitten and killed by serpents; Moses was to instruct the people that anyone who had

---

10. See Rom 10:4.
11. See Ex 4:1-4.
12. *Litteras Dei.* Augustine uses this expression to designate scripture in his Exposition 2 of Psalm 90,1; Exposition of Psalm 149,5; and elsewhere. It is found also in John Chrysostom, *Hom. 2 on Genesis* 2; and was used by Pius XII in his encyclical *Div. Affl. Spiritu*, 5, in 1943.
13. See Gn 3:4.5.

been bitten, and then looked at the bronze serpent, would be healed.[14] This was done, and people who had been bitten by the snakes were cured of the poisonous wounds by looking at the bronze serpent. To be cured by a serpent is certainly a strange mystery! What does it mean—to be healed of snakebite by gazing at a snake? It symbolizes being saved from death by believing in one who died. Yet *Moses was terrified, and fled from it.* And what is the meaning of that, brothers and sisters, that Moses ran away from the snake? What else could it represent, than events that we know about from the gospel? Christ died, and the disciples were terrified, so they abandoned the hope in which they had lived until now. But what was Moses told to do? *Catch hold of its tail.* Why the tail? It means, "Grasp what comes at the end." God's promise, *You shall see my back* (Ex 33:23), suggests the same truth. First it became a snake, but when its tail was held it became a staff; so too the one who was killed subsequently rose again.

Another interpretation is to take the snake's tail as the end of the world. For the present the Church marches on in its mortal condition. Its members come and go, passing away through death as though through the snake, since death was sown by the snake. But at the end of the world we, like the snake's tail, are taken back into God's hand. We are then endowed with unshakeable firmness as his kingdom, so that the psalm's prophecy, *you redeemed the staff of your inheritance*, may be verified in us.

But we must remember that the synagogue is speaking here. The staff of God's inheritance is more obviously redeemed among the Gentiles; but for the Jews there is hidden hope, because of those of their race destined to believe in the future, and of those who believed at the time when the Holy Spirit was sent, empowering the disciples to preach in the tongues of all nations.[15] Several thousands of Jews believed then, even from the ranks of those who had crucified Christ. They had been close at hand when the Spirit was given, and so firmly did they believe that they sold all their possessions and laid the proceeds at the feet of the apostles.[16] But all this was hidden from the psalmist; and because the redemption of God's staff was to be more conspicuous among the Gentiles, he specifies whom he meant when he said, *You redeemed the staff of your inheritance.* He was not referring to the Gentiles, among whom this was to be more evidently the case. To whom then? *Mount Zion.*

But Mount Zion can itself be understood in different ways. *The mountain on which you dwelt*: this means the place where the first people of God lived, where the temple was built, where sacrifices were solemnly offered, where everything was provided that was then needful to promise Christ's coming. But a promise

---

14. See Nb 21:6-9; Jn 3:14.
15. See Acts 2:4.
16. See Acts 4:34-35.

becomes redundant when the reality is given. Before the time for the fulfillment, the promise serves a necessary purpose, for without it the persons to whom the promise was made might forget what they had been promised, and die from lack of expectancy. It is essential that their expectancy should be kept up if they are to be ready to accept the fulfillment when it comes, so they cannot afford to neglect the promise. Prophetic types were therefore not superseded throughout that era, so that when the day should come, the shadows might be chased away. *Mount Zion, the mountain on which you dwelt.*

Verses 3-4. Pagan attack on the holy place

6. *Raise your hand against their arrogance, even to the end.* As you cast us off even to the end, so now *raise your hand against their arrogance, even to the end.* Whose arrogance is meant? The arrogance of those by whom Jerusalem was overthrown. But who were they? The rulers of the Gentiles, obviously; and it was indeed to their advantage that his hand was raised against them *even to the end,* for they have now come to know Christ, Christ who is *the end of the law, bringing justification to everyone who believes* (Rom 10:4). What a blessing the psalmist was wishing upon them! He speaks as though in anger; he seems to be uttering a curse; yet we could wish for nothing better than the implementation of it. Or, rather, let us be glad that in Christ's name it is already being implemented. Those who wield the scepter today submit to the wood of the cross, and already the prophecy of another psalm is coming true: *all the kings of the earth will worship him, and all nations will serve him* (Ps 71(72):11). On the foreheads of kings the representation of the cross is more highly prized than the jewels set in their crowns. *Raise your hand against their arrogance, even to the end.*

How great a devastation has the spiteful enemy wrought among your holy things! Among things sacred to you—in your temple, in your priesthood, among all the holy signs established at that time—*how great a devastation has the spiteful enemy wrought!* It was truly an enemy who did this, for the Gentiles responsible were at that time worshipers of false gods. They adored graven images and served demons, yet they successfully inflicted great harm on the holy things of God. How could they ever have had the power to do it, unless they were given permission? And when would they have been given God's permission? Only when those holy things, once the bearers of the promise, were no longer necessary, because he who had promised was now offering himself to us, to have and to hold. This is why the psalm could lament, *How great a devastation has the spiteful enemy wrought among your holy things!*

7. *Those who hated you boasted.* Remember who they were, and what they were like at that time, the Gentiles who destroyed the temple and the city of God: they were servants of demons, servants of graven gods; and *they boasted.*

In the midst of your solemn festival. Recall what I said earlier: Jerusalem was overthrown as the very same festival was being celebrated during which they had crucified the Lord. As the Jews had then gathered to do their savage work, so they gathered again this time, but to perish.[17]

Verse 5. God can make use of the actions of evildoers to further his good plans

8. *They set up their signs, their emblematic signs, and knew not.* They had insignia, and they set them up in the temple: their standards, their eagles, their dragons, their Roman emblems;[18] and perhaps too their statues, which they had placed in the temple on a previous occasion.[19] They had been given "signs" by the soothsayers who served their demons; and such oracles too may be meant when the psalm speaks of *their signs.*

And they knew not. What did the pagans not know? That *you would have no power over me, had it not been given you from above* (Jn 19:11). They did not know that the power they had to afflict, and capture, and destroy the city was not some honor conferred on them; rather their impiety was like an axe in God's hand. They had become the tool of a wrathful God, not the realm of a God at peace with them. God often acts in this respect in the same way as humans do. Sometimes an angry parent will seize a stick lying about—some kind of branch perhaps—and beat his son with it; but then he throws the branch into the fire, and keeps an inheritance safe for his son. In the same way God sometimes employs bad people for the amendment of good people; and through the short-lived power he allows to those who are to be condemned in the long run, he effectively disciplines those who are destined for freedom. How should we apply the principle in the present context? You do not suppose, surely, brothers and sisters, that the discipline imposed on the Jewish people was of a nature to destroy them completely? How many of them came to believe later; how many more will believe in due course? There is straw and there is grain—different materials, but the threshing sledge goes to work on them both. Under the same sledge some is crushed, some purified. How great a good has God done for us through the evil

---

17. See note on 3 above. Augustine is uniting in a single perspective the destruction of the city in A.D. 70 by the armies of Titus, which occurred when many Jews were present for Passover, and the earlier destruction by Nebuchadnezzar in June-July 587, which is the probable background to the present psalm; see 2 Kgs 25:9. Augustine's tendency to see the one in terms of the other is particularly marked in the next section.
18. Clearly it is A.D. 70 now.
19. Pontius Pilate, procurator of Judea A.D. 26-36, had upset the Jews by bringing standards and shields into the temple. This may be the allusion here; but Augustine could also be thinking of the desecration of the temple in 167 B.C., when Antiochus IV Epiphanes set up the statue of Olympian Zeus on the altar for burnt offerings, the "abomination" referred to in Mt 24:15; see Dn 9:27; 11:31; 1 Macc 1:59.

act of the traitor Judas! Indeed, how great is the good conferred on believing gentiles through the savagery of the Jews! Christ was slain so that he might hang there on the cross for anyone bitten by the serpent to look at. So too, perhaps, had the attackers heard from their gods that they were to go to Jerusalem and capture it. When they had taken the city and destroyed it, no doubt they told themselves that the feat had been achieved by their demons. *They set up their signs, their emblematic signs, and knew not.* What did they not know? They were *as though obeying a decree from on high*; for had the command not been issued from heaven, the barbaric gentiles would never have been licensed to commit such outrages against the Jewish people. But the order was given them from above, as the Book of Daniel indicates: *From the time you began to pray a word has gone forth* (Dn 9:23).

This same truth was pointed out by the Lord to Pilate, who was full of self-importance and set up his signs, his pagan signs. He demanded of Christ, *Have you no answer to make to me? Are you unaware that I have the power either to put you to death or to release you?* (Jn 19:10). But the Lord's reply punctured this inflated fellow, leaving him like a collapsed balloon: *You would have no power over me, had it not been given you from above.*

We can read this psalm-verse in the same light. *They set up their signs, their emblematic signs, and knew not.* Knew not what? That they were *as though obeying a decree from on high.* Could they possibly have known how such an order had been issued from heaven, to bring these events about?

Verses 6-8. The destruction of Jerusalem

9. Now that we have considered the overthrow of Jerusalem let us run through the next verses swiftly, for they are quite straightforward, and it is not pleasant to dwell upon the punishment of enemies. *They hacked down all her doors together with axes, like trees in a wood; they felled her with pick and battering-ram*; that is, by plotting, and relentlessly.[20] *They felled her with pick and battering-ram.*

10. *They burnt your holy place with fire; they defiled the tabernacle where your name dwelt on earth.*

11. *They said in their hearts, the whole tribe of them with one accord....* What did they say? *Come on; let us rid the earth of all the festivals of the Lord.* The words, "of the Lord," are inserted by the speaker, Asaph, in his own name. Obviously the raging attackers would not have called the one whose temple they were demolishing "the Lord." *Come on; let us rid the earth of all the festivals of the Lord.*

---

20. The two implements mentioned are the *dolabrum* and the *fractorium.* Augustine is perhaps punning on the similarity of the former word to *dolus,* guile, when he speaks of "plotting"; but the reference could also be to *in idipsum,* here translated "together."

Verses 9-10. The Jews complain that signs and prophecy are withdrawn

What has Asaph to say? What does Asaph's understanding²¹ make of all this? Does he gain nothing from the discipline imposed on him? Is his depraved mind not corrected? Everything that was part of the old order has been overthrown. Nowhere have the Jews any priest, nowhere an altar, nowhere a sacrifice, nowhere a temple. Can they not realize, then, that something else has come to take the place of all they lost? Would this regime of signs have been superseded, unless what it promised had come?

Let us see how Asaph's understanding is getting on now; let us see whether he is profiting from all the distress. Listen to what he says: *We have not seen the signs we used to see, there is no prophet now,*²² *and still he will not recognize us.* Those Jews who say that they are not yet recognized—in other words, they are still in captivity, not yet set free—are still looking for Christ to come. Well, of course, Christ is still to come, but he will come as judge. At his first coming he came to call; at his second he will come to distinguish. He will come again because he has already come, and that he will come has been plainly revealed; but he will come then from on high. He was once there in front of you, O Israel! He lay there helpless and you tripped over him, so you were dashed against him; but if you want to avoid being crushed by him, honor him when he comes from above; for thus it was foretold by a prophet: *Anyone who trips over this stone will be bruised by it, and anyone on whom it falls will be crushed.*²³ In his littleness he bruises you, but in his greatness he will crush you. You do not see now the signs you used to see, nor have you any prophet now; and you admit, *Still he will not recognize us.* That is because you still do not recognize him. *There is no prophet, and still he will not recognize us.*

But a prophetic sign is there: the conversion of the Gentiles

12. *How long is the enemy to scoff at you?* Shout away, like someone forlorn and abandoned, shout like the sick person you are, the patient who chose to kill your physician when you might have been healed by him. He still does not recognize you? But look what he has done, he who does not recognize you. Those to whom no tidings of him were brought shall see him, and those who

---

21. See the psalm's title.
22. Jewish tradition held that prophecy had fallen silent after Malchy; see 1 Mc 4:46; 9:27; 14:41. But if the psalm was inspired by the events of 587 B.C. the cessation lamented was something temporary.
23. Lk 20:18; compare Is 8:14-15.

have never heard of him will understand;[24] yet you go on lamenting, *There is no prophet, and still he will not recognize us.* Where is your understanding?[25]

The adversary profanes your name everlastingly. But there is a reason why the adversary is permitted to profane your name everlastingly; it is this: that you, Lord, may be provoked to anger and rebuke him,[26] and in rebuking recognize him for ever. Or we could take this phrase, *in finem* to mean "until the end." Until what end? Until you come to acknowledge him, until you cry out to him, until you seize the tail and are gathered into God's kingdom.

Verse 11. Another sign: the leprous hand

13. *Why do you turn your hand away everlastingly, your right hand from your bosom?* This is an allusion to another sign given to Moses. Earlier we heard of the sign concerning his staff; now we have that of his right hand. After displaying the prodigy of the staff, God gave him another sign. *"Put your hand into your bosom." And he put it there. "Now bring it out." He brought it out, and found it white* (Ex 4:6), that is, unclean; for whiteness on the skin is a sign of leprosy, not the glow of health. God's inheritance, his own people, became unclean when thrust out away from him. But what did God command next? *"Draw it back[27] into your bosom." He drew it back, and it returned to its original color* (Ex 4:7). "And so," asks Asaph, "when will you do likewise? How long will you keep your right hand thrust out far from your bosom, so that it remains out in the cold and unclean? Call it back; let it regain its proper color and acknowledge its Savior." *Why do you turn your hand away everlastingly, your right hand from your bosom?*

That is the cry of a blind person, one who fails to understand; but God does what he does.[28] Why did Christ come? *Blindness has fallen upon part of Israel, until the full tally of the Gentiles comes in, and so all Israel may be saved* (Rom 11:25-26). Observe the Gentile advance guard, Asaph, and at least follow, if you have not managed to take the lead. Christ did not come in vain, nor was he slain to no purpose. The grain did not fall into the ground pointlessly, but in order to rise again vastly multiplied.[29] The serpent was raised up in the desert to heal anyone venomously bitten. Pay attention to what was done, and do not deem his coming meaningless, or he may find you graceless when he comes again.

---

24. See Is 52:15; Rom 15:21.
25. The faith of the Gentiles is itself the sign the Jews should be able to see, especially as it was foretold by their own prophets.
26. Either the Gentile adversary, representing all the Gentiles, or the Jews.
27. Literally "call it back."
28. Variants: "God has done this"; "God has done what he does."
29. See Jn 12:25.

Verses 12-13. Salvation on earth: Asaph begins to understand

14. Asaph has understood. After all, the psalm is entitled, *Understanding for Asaph*. So what does he say? *"God is our king from before time was made, and he has wrought salvation in the midst of the earth*. On the one hand we lament, *There is no prophet now, and still he will not recognize us*; but on the other we confess, *God is our king from before time was made*, because he is the Word who exists from the beginning, through whom all the ages came to be; and *he has wrought salvation in the midst of the earth*. What did he do, our God who is *our king from before time was made*—what did he do? He *wrought salvation in the midst of the earth*; yet here am I, still crying out like one forsaken. He has done his saving work in the midst of the earth, but I have remained earth and nothing more."

Asaph has understood very well; the psalm is promoting *understanding for Asaph*. Why did all these things come to pass? What kind of salvation has Christ wrought? He has taught men and women not to cling persistently to temporal things, but to desire those of eternity. *God is our king from before time was made, and he has wrought salvation in the midst of the earth*. "While we are wailing, *How long, O Lord, is the enemy to scoff at you? For ever? How long will the adversary profane your name? How long will you hold your hand away from your bosom?*—while we are complaining thus, *God is our king from before time was made, and he has wrought salvation in the midst of the earth*, and we are asleep! The Gentiles are wide awake, but we are snoring; and in our nightmares we think he has abandoned us." *He has wrought salvation in the midst of the earth*.

15. Come now, Asaph, apply yourself to understand. Tell us what kind of salvation God has wrought in the midst of the earth. After the earthly things that for you represented salvation had been overthrown, what did he do? What did he promise? *In your strength you gave stability to the sea*. The Jewish nation was like dry land, separated from the waves; the Gentiles in their harsh saltiness were the sea.[30] They lapped around the dry land on every side and—wonderful to behold—*in your strength you gave stability to the sea*, while the earth remained dry, thirsting for your showers. *In your strength you gave stability to the sea; you shattered the heads of the dragons in the water*. Through water you smashed the heads of dragons, which represent the proud claims of the demons by whom the Gentiles were possessed, because through baptism you set free the people who had been the demons' prey.

---

30. Augustine meditates on the stormy sea as an image of the world, particularly the Gentile world, in his Exposition of Psalm 64,9, and *Confessions* XIII,17,20.

Verse 14. The chief dragon is devoured

16. What else is to come, after the shattering of these dragons' heads? There is more, because the dragons have a leader, and he is the primordial dragon, and the most powerful. When Christ wrought salvation in the center of the earth, what did he do with this leader? Listen: *you broke the dragon's head in pieces.* Which dragon is meant here? By "dragons" in the plural we understand all the demons who fight under the command of the devil; so who but the devil himself can be meant by the singular dragon whose head was broken to pieces? What did Christ do to him? *You broke the dragon's head in pieces.* Its head represents the beginning of sin; and on this head the curse was laid, that Eve's descendant would watch for the head of the serpent.[31] The Church is warned to avoid the beginning of sin, and what else is the beginning of sin, but the serpent's head? We are told that *the starting-point of all sin is pride* (Sir 10:15). The dragon's head was thus broken in pieces when the devil's pride was smashed.

The Lord who wrought salvation in the center of the earth dealt with the devil, then; but what did he do with him? *You gave him to the Ethiopian peoples to eat.* What does that mean? How am I to interpret *Ethiopian peoples*? Obviously as "all nations." Now Ethiopians are black, and it is fitting that black people should stand for the Gentiles. People who were formerly black, and they most especially, are called to faith, so that scripture can say to them, *You were darkness once, but now you are light in the Lord* (Eph 5:8). These black people are called indeed, but not destined to remain black, because from them is formed the Church, of which scripture says, *Who is this who comes up, made white?* (Sg 8:5, LXX). What of the black bride? She tells us: *I am dark-skinned but beautiful* (Sg 1:4).

Now in what sense have the Ethiopians been given the dragon to eat? I think it would be easier to understand if they were said to have been given Christ as their food; but Christ was the food by which they would be consummated in perfection, whereas the devil was something they were to consume. The point of this comes out in the story of the calf which the unfaithful, apostate people worshiped. They went after the gods of the Egyptians, forsaking him who had freed them from enslavement to the Egyptians; and from this episode a great mystery was set in train. Moses was furious with the Israelites who venerated and worshiped the idol. Inflamed with zeal for God he was determined to visit such temporal punishments upon them as would scare them away from the risk of eternal death. He banished the calf's head from their midst by flinging it into the fire; then he ground it to powder, mixed it with water, and gave it to the people to drink.[32] Thus was established a great sacred sign.[33] How mighty was

---

31. See Gn 3:15.
32. See Ex 32:19-20.
33. *Sacramentum.*

that prophetic wrath, proceeding from a mind not disturbed but illuminated! What did he do? First of all, throw it into the fire, so that it melts until its shape is unrecognizable. Then pound it into little pieces so that it gradually vanishes. Then sprinkle it into water and give it to the people to drink. What does this procedure suggest? Surely that the worshipers of the devil had become his body, as Christ's faithful become so truly his body that to them it can be said, *You are Christ's body, and his limbs* (1 Cor 12:27). Now the body of the devil had to be consumed, and this needed to be done by Israelites, for it was from the people of Israel that the apostles sprang, and the primitive Church. Moreover, Peter was given a command with regard to the Gentiles, *Slaughter and eat* (Acts 10:13). What did *slaughter and eat* mean? Slay what they are, and turn them into what you are. So in the one story we have *Slaughter and eat*; in the other, "Pound it into pieces and make them drink"; but both point to the same sacred mystery. It was necessary, absolutely necessary, that what had been the devil's body should be transformed by faith into the body of Christ. This is how the devil is consumed, as he loses his members.

The same mystery is hinted at in another story about Moses and a snake. The magicians performed a feat comparable to his, hurling their staves to the ground and conjuring dragons out of them; but the dragon produced by Moses swallowed the staves of all the wizards.[34] We should discern the devil's body in these too. This is what happens: he is devoured by the Gentiles who have come to believe; he is given as food to the Ethiopian peoples.

Another way in which we can understand the statement, *you gave him to the Ethiopian peoples to eat*, is this: they all bite him now. Bite him—in what sense? By rebuking and blaming and accusing him. This can be called biting, for the metaphor is plainly used in scripture, though in the context of a prohibition: *if you bite and try to eat each other, take care that you are not gobbled up by one another* (Gal 5:15). What is meant by *bite and try to eat each other*? You go to law with one another, you disparage each other, you hurl insults at each other. But notice also that the devil is being gnawed away by bites of this kind. Is there anyone, even a pagan, who when angry with his slave does not call him "Satan"? That is an instance of the devil being given away as food! A Christian says it, a Jew says it, a pagan says it. This last worships the devil, yet uses his name as a curse.

---

34. See Ex 7:12.

Verse 15. The difference between fountains and torrents, strength and weakness

17. Now let us look at the remaining verses. Pay close attention, brothers and sisters, I implore you; it is a great pleasure for us to listen to the words that are coming, because what we hear in them is known to us as realized throughout the world. When these words were spoken, the realities did not yet exist; they were promised, but not yet brought to pass. But now—what joy overwhelms us when we see the prophecies we read in the Bible being fulfilled in our world![35] Let us see what God has done, he who *has wrought salvation in the midst of the earth*, as Asaph understood.

You burst open fountains and torrents to gush with the clear water of wisdom, and pour forth the riches of faith, and drench the salt-bound Gentiles. So would their irrigating flood convert all unbelievers to the sweetness of faith.

You burst open fountains and torrents. There may be some distinction here; or they may both be one, inasmuch as the fountains spread their water so widely that rivers were formed: *you burst open fountains and torrents*. But if a distinction is implied, we could understand it like this: in some people God's word becomes *a fountain of water springing up to eternal life* (Jn 4:14). Others hear the word, but do not have the strength to lead good lives; nonetheless they do not keep the word to themselves, but speak out, and they become torrents. What I mean is that torrents are, strictly speaking, streams that do not flow perpetually. (I am aware that in our translations we sometimes find a river improperly called a "torrent," as in the psalm where it is said, *They will be inebriated by the rich abundance of your house, and you will give them the full torrent of your delights to drink* (Ps 35:9(36:8)), where the torrent in question is one that will never dry up.) But torrents, properly so called, are rivers which disappear in summer,[36] though in the winter rains they flood and run swiftly. Similarly you may see a person who is thoroughly faithful, one who will persevere to the end and never forsake God in any temptation, one who endures all kinds of affliction, not in the cause of any falsehood or error, but for the sake of the truth. Whence does such a person draw that vigorous life? It must derive from the word which has become in him or her *a fountain of water springing up to eternal life*. Another person welcomes the word, preaches it, does not keep silent about it, and flows along smoothly; but summer will show whether this one is a fountain or a torrent. All the same, the earth is watered through both of them by him who *wrought salvation in the midst of the earth*. Let the fountains gush and the torrents flow. *You burst open fountains and torrents*.

---

35. A clear instance of Augustine's conviction of the actuality of the psalms, a conviction he expected his audience to share. See the Introduction in Volume 1.
36. Possibly he is thinking of the association of *torrens* with the verb *torreo*, to heat or scorch.

18. *You dried up the rivers of Etham.* In one instance he makes fountains and torrents burst forth; in the other he dries up rivers. As the waters flow on one side, so do they dry up on the other. *The rivers of Etham,* says the text. What is Etham? The word is Hebrew; how is it to be interpreted? "Strong," or "robust." Who is the strong, robust one, whose rivers are dried up by God? Who else but the dragon? This must be right, for the gospel tells us, *No one can get into a strong man's house and carry off his implements, unless he has tied up the strong man first* (Mt 12:29). The "strong one" is he who trusts in his own strength and abandons God; he is the "strong one" who said, *I will set my throne in the north; I shall be like the Most High.*[37] But from the cup of his own perverted strength he offered human beings a drink. Strong did they aspire to be, believing that they would become gods by eating the forbidden food. Adam became so strong that he deserved to be taunted, *Look, Adam has become like one of us!* (Gn 3:22). The Jews who relied on their own righteousness were similarly "strong": *they failed to recognize the righteousness that comes from God, and by seeking to set up a righteousness of their own, they did not submit to God's righteousness* (Rom 10:3).

Humankind has dissipated its strength, and is left like the tax-collector, weak, helpless, standing far off, not daring to lift his eyes to heaven, but beating his breast and praying, *Lord, be merciful to me, a sinner* (Lk 18:13). Such a person is infirm, and confesses his infirmity. He is not strong, he is parched earth. He needs to be irrigated by the fountains and torrents. But those others, who presume on their own virtue, are still "strong." Let their rivers be dried up; let the teachings of the heathen do them no good, the magical arts of soothsayers and astrologers profit them nothing; for the rivers of the "strong man" have run dry. *You dried up the rivers of Etham.* Let their teaching wither from drought, and let people's minds be flooded with the gospel of truth.

Verse 16. Both day and night, both spiritual and carnal persons, belong to God

19. *The day is yours, and the night is yours.* Surely everyone knows this? He made them, for all things were made through the Word.[38] But to him who *wrought salvation in the midst of the earth* are these words now addressed: *the day is yours, and the night is yours*; so evidently we are meant to glean from them something that has to do with the salvation he has wrought in the midst of the earth.

The day is yours. Who are "the day"? Spiritual persons. *And the night is yours.* Who are these? Carnal folk. *The day is yours, and the night is yours.* Let

---

37. Is 14:13-14. See a note on this passage at Exposition of Psalm 59,10.
38. See Jn 1:3.

the spiritually-minded speak of spiritual things to spiritual people, for scripture says, *We speak wisdom among the perfect, interpreting spiritual truths to people possessed of the Spirit* (1 Cor 2:6.13). The carnally-minded are not yet capable of this wisdom; as scripture again says, *Not as spiritual persons could I speak to you, but only as carnal* (1 Cor 3:1). Thus when Spirit-possessed persons speak to others of their kind, *day speaks the message to day*; but when even carnal persons do not conceal by silence that faith in Christ crucified of which even little ones are capable, *night imparts knowledge to night* (Ps 18:3(19:2)). *The day is yours, and the night is yours.* Spiritual persons belong to you, and carnal persons belong to you. You enlighten the former with immutable wisdom and truth; you console the latter by your manifestation in the flesh, as the moon consoles the night.[39]

The day is yours, and the night is yours. Do you wish to hear about the day? See if you are capable of it; stretch your mind up as far as you possibly can. Let us test whether you belong to the day; let us see whether there is trembling in your demeanor. Can you gaze upon that truth you heard just now in the gospel: *in the beginning was the Word, and the Word was with God; the Word was God* (Jn 1:1)? You cannot think of words except as transient sounds. Can you take in the idea of the Word, which is not a sound, but God? Did you not hear the gospel say that *the Word was God*? But you can think only of words within your own experience, so when you hear, *All things were made through him*, you know that those who shape words were themselves made by him, made by the Word. So what must this Word be like? Do you understand, you carnal creature? Answer me: do you understand? No, you do not. You still belong to the night, and you need the moon if you are not to die in the darkness; for there are sinners around, people of whom a psalm says, *Sinners have bent their bows to shoot those of honest heart when the moon is darkened* (Ps 10:3(11:2)). When Christ's body was taken down from the cross and laid in the tomb, it was as though darkened, and his killers scornfully exulted. He had not yet risen, and though the disciples were people of honest heart, the moon was not visible, so they were the target of unbelievers' arrows.

This is why we beg you, Lord, to descend in your gracious mercy. Remain with the Father, from whom you descend, but come down to us, so that not only may the day speak the message to the day, but night may also impart knowledge to night, for *the day is yours, and the night is yours.* You were in the world, and though the world was made by you, the world did not know you; yet in your gracious mercy descend to us. Let the night too receive its consolation; yes, let it receive the consolation of which scripture says, *The Word was made flesh, and dwelt among us* (Jn 1:14). *The day is yours, and the night is yours.*

---

39. The moon is ever changing, and so provides the contrast with "immutable wisdom and truth."

You perfected sun and moon. The sun represents Spirit-filled persons, the moon stands for the carnal. Let no one who is still carnal be given up as hopeless, but let the carnal too be made perfect. *You perfected sun and moon*: the sun, which means a wise person, and the moon one who is unwise, but whom you have not abandoned. Scripture affirms that *A wise person abides like the sun, but a fool is changeable like the moon* (Sir 27:12). Does it mean that because the sun is unchanging and *a wise person abides like the sun*, another who is still carnal, still foolish, and *changeable like the moon*, is therefore to be forsaken? No, indeed. What would become of the apostle's reassurance, *I owe a debt to both wise and foolish* (Rom 1:14)? *You perfected sun and moon.*

Verses 17-19. Re-creation through grace and repentance

20. *You made all the ends of the earth.* Surely he did that in the beginning, when he established the earth? Yes, but how did he, who *wrought salvation in the midst of the earth*, create the ends of the earth? How else, but in the way of which the apostle speaks, *by grace we have been saved, through faith, and this is not our own doing but the grace of God. It does not come from works, lest anyone boast* (Eph 2:8-9)? Were there no good works on our part, then? There were, but how were they accomplished? By the grace of God. Read on, and let us see this stated: *We are his own handiwork, created in Christ Jesus for good works* (Eph 2:10). This is how he who *wrought salvation in the midst of the earth* also *made all the ends of the earth.*

Summer and spring—both are your creation. Summer represents those afire with the Spirit.[40] You made them, says the psalm. But you also made the new-born lambs[41] in the faith, and they are the spring. *Summer and spring—both are your creation.* Let none of them boast as though they had not received your grace. *Both are your creation.*

21. *Remember this creation of yours.* What creation is meant? We shall see. *The enemy has accused the Lord.* O Asaph, now that you understand, bewail your former blindness! *The enemy has accused the Lord.* Members of his own race said of Christ, *This man is a sinner; we do not know where he comes from, though we know that God spoke to Moses; this man is a Samaritan* (Jn 9:24.29; 8:48). *The enemy has accused the Lord, and a senseless people has provoked your name.* In earlier days Asaph was that senseless people, but that was before there was any *understanding for Asaph.* The same change was described in the psalm that preceded this one. What did that say? *I became like a beast in your presence, yet I was always with you* (Ps 72:23(73:22-23)), because he did not run after the gods and idols of the Gentiles. Beast-like, he did not know; but as a man

---

40. Or "fervent spirits."
41. Or "new shoots," "new bread," etc.

he came to know later, for he said, *I was always with you* even though *like a beast*; and what did he declare afterward in that psalm—which, remember, was a psalm of Asaph? *You grasped the hand of my right hand. You led me by your will, and you have taken me up in glory* (Ps 72:24(73:23-24)). He says, *By your will*, not in any righteousness of mine; by your gift, not by my endeavor.

The same movement is traced in the present psalm: *the enemy has accused the Lord, and a senseless people has provoked your name.* So they all perished, did they? By no means. Some of the branches were broken off, but enough remained for the wild olive to be grafted in.[42] The root remains firm; and even from the branches that were broken off for their unbelief there were some who were called back through faith. The apostle Paul himself was broken off because he did not believe, but through faith later restored to the root.[43] But unquestionably *a senseless people* did *provoke your name* when they said, *If he is the Son of God, let him come down from the cross.*[44]

22. Well, Asaph, now that you have understood, what have you to say? *Do not fling to the beasts a soul that confesses to you.* I acknowledge my fault, says Asaph, because, as another psalm says, *I perceived my sin, and did not cloak my unrighteousness* (Ps 31(32):5). Why do you say that? Because when the Israelites were marveling at the gift of tongues, Peter charged them with having killed Christ, who had been sent for their sake. *On hearing this they were pierced to the heart, and asked the apostles, What shall we do? Tell us.* The apostles replied, *Repent, and let every one of you be baptized in the name of the Lord Jesus Christ, and your sins will be forgiven* (Acts 2:37-38). Through this repentance confession has been made, and so now the prayer can be offered, *Do not fling to the beasts a soul that confesses to you.* Why does it speak of "confessing to you"? Because *I was reduced to bitterness when the thorn stuck fast in me* (Ps 31(32):4). They were pierced to the heart. These people who had been boastful in their savagery were now bitterly repentant.

Do not fling to the beasts a soul that confesses to you. What beasts are these? Obviously the beasts whose heads were shattered in water. The devil is called a beast, a lion, and a dragon; so the psalm prays, "Do not hand over to the devil and his angels a soul that confesses to you. Let the serpent devour me if I still hanker for the tastes of earth, if I still long for earthly things, if I remain fixed in the promises of the Old Testament now that the New has been revealed. But now that I have laid aside my pride, and resolved to give no credit to my own righteousness, but only to your grace, let the proud beasts have no power over me." *Do not fling to the beasts a soul that confesses to you.*

---

42. See Rom 11:17.
43. Thus is answered the question Augustine posed at the beginning of the section: What creation?
44. See Mt 27:40.

Do not forget the souls of your poor servants for ever. We were rich, we were strong. But you *dried up the rivers of Etham.* No longer do we set up our own righteousness; we acknowledge your grace. We are poor; hear us, your beggars. We no longer dare to raise our eyes to heaven, but beat our breasts, saying, *Lord, be merciful to us sinners.*[45] So, Lord, *do not forget the souls of your poor servants for ever.*

Verses 20-21. The promises of the New Covenant for the poor in spirit

23. *Call to mind your covenant.* Give what you have promised: we have written evidence to back up our claim, and we are waiting for our inheritance. *Call to mind your covenant*—but not the old one. I am not asking for the land of Canaan, or for the subjugation of enemies in this world, or for carnal fertility and numerous children, or for earthly riches, or for any temporal well-being. But call to mind that covenant in which you promised us the kingdom of heaven. I have come to know this covenant for what it is.

Asaph has acquired understanding now; he is a beast no longer, but sees the truth of what was prophesied: *Lo, the days are coming, says the Lord, when I will conclude with the house of Israel and the house of Judah a new covenant, not like the covenant that I established with their ancestors* (Jer 31:31-32). *Call to mind your covenant, for darkened people, people of wicked houses, have taken their fill of the earth.* They are called people of wicked houses because their hearts are wicked. Our hearts are our houses, and those who are pure of heart find it pleasant to live in them. *Call to mind your covenant,* though, and let the remnant at least be saved,[46] because the many, who have thoughts only for this earth, have grown dark in taking their fill of it. Dust has clogged their eyes and blinded them, and they have themselves become the dust which the wind sweeps away from the face of the earth.[47] *Call to mind your covenant, for darkened people, of wicked houses, have taken their fill of the earth.* By giving all their attention to the earth they have grown dark; another psalm says of them, *Let their eyes be dimmed so that they cannot see; bend their backs over permanently* (Ps 68:24(69:23)). They have *taken their fill of the earth,* these *darkened people, people of wicked houses,* so called because they have wicked hearts. Our hearts are our houses, as we said before; and it is pleasant for us to dwell in them if we cleanse them from sin. But if an evil conscience is there, it repels the person who is ordered to enter his house, like the man who was told to carry his pallet because his sins had been forgiven: *Pick up your sleeping mat and go into your house* (Mk 2:11), the Lord told him. Carry your flesh, and go into your healed

---

45. See Lk 18:13.
46. See Rom 9:27.
47. See Ps 1:4.

conscience. *Darkened people, people of wicked houses, have taken their fill of the earth*; they are darkened because full of earth. Who are these darkened ones? Those who have wicked hearts, whom the Lord will requite as their hearts deserve.

24. *Do not let a humble person be turned away in shame*, for it is the earth-bound who are shamed by their pride. *The needy and poor one will praise your name.* You see from this how sweet poverty must be, brothers and sisters; you see how the poor and needy are especially close to God. But it is the poor in spirit who are meant, for theirs is the kingdom of heaven.[48] Who are the poor in spirit? The humble, those who tremble at God's words, who confess their sins, and rely on no merits or righteousness of their own. When they do anything good, they praise God; when they do wrong, they accuse themselves. *Upon whom shall my spirit rest, but upon the humble, peaceable person, the one who trembles at my words?* (Is 66:2). Clearly Asaph has understood now. He no longer clings to the earth, no longer demands the things promised under the Old Covenant. He has become your beggar, your pauper; he thirsts for your rivers because his own have dried up. Now that he has become this sort of person let him not be cheated of his hope. With hands outstretched before you he sought you in the night; let him not be disappointed.[49] *Do not let a humble person be turned away in shame; the needy and poor one will praise your name.* Confessing their sins they will praise your name; longing for your eternal promises they will praise your name. It is not those swollen with temporal goods who will praise you, not those who are exalted and inflated with their own righteousness. No, not those: who then? *The needy and poor one will praise your name.*

Verse 22. Faith in the promises of the unseen God, and in our ultimate resurrection

25. *Arise, O Lord, and vindicate my cause.* I seem to have been deserted, because I have not yet received what you promised, so my tears have been bread to me day and night, as every day I hear the taunt, "Where is your God?"[50] And because I cannot show them my God, they jeer at me for being on a wild-goose chase. Nor is it a pagan only who mocks me like this, or a Jew, or a heretic; sometimes it is a fellow-Catholic who grimaces when God's promises are preached, or our future resurrection is foretold. Moreover such a person, even though bathed already in the water of eternal salvation and a bearer of Christ's sacrament, may perhaps say, "Have you seen anyone come back to life?" or "Since I buried my father I haven't heard him speaking from the grave! God gave a law to

48. See Mt 5:3.
49. See Ps 76:3(77:2).
50. See Ps 41:4(42:3).

his servants for a limited time, and it is on this time that they must concentrate;[51] for has anyone come back from the underworld?" What am I to do with such doubters? Can I show them what they do not see? No, I cannot; for God is under no obligation to make himself visible for their benefit. Let them go on like that if they want to; let them behave so, and argue in those terms. They try to change God for the worse because they are unwilling to change themselves for the better. God exists: let anyone who is able, see him, and anyone who is unable to see, believe. But what of those who are able to see him—do they see him with their eyes? Of course not! He who said, *Blessed are the pure of heart, for they shall see God* (Mt 5:8), was not pointing to the sun or the moon.[52] But an unclean heart is not even disposed to faith, whereby it might believe in what it cannot see. "I don't see," it will say, "so why should I believe?" Oh, so you can see your soul, can you? How foolish you are! Your body can be seen, but does anyone see your soul? And since the only thing that can be seen is your body, why aren't you a candidate for burial?

He is perplexed because I asked him the question, If the only thing that can be seen is your body, why aren't you being buried? But he has an answer ready; he is shrewd enough to reply, "Because I am alive." But how do I know that you are alive, if I can't see your soul? How can I know? "Because I talk, because I walk, and do things." Stupid still! From your bodily activities I acknowledge a living person; but from the activities of created things you cannot acknowledge their Creator!

Now it is possible that the one who maintains, "Once I'm dead, I shall no longer exist," is a person of some education, and he has learned this from a crazy fellow named Epicurus, a so-called philosopher, but in truth a lover of futility rather than a lover of wisdom.[53] Philosophers themselves dubbed him "the Pig,"[54] because they held that a "philosopher" who held bodily pleasure to be the supreme good deserved to be called a pig wallowing in the mire of the flesh. So perhaps it is from this man that our educated objector has learnt to say, "Once I'm dead, I shall no longer exist."

Let the rivers of Etham be dried up, and these pagan doctrines wither away; let the green shoots of Jerusalem spring up; let those see who have the capacity to see, and those who are unable to see believe with their hearts. All these things

---

51. *Dedit legem ad tempus servis suis, ad quod se avocent.* On this reading the antecedent of the relative pronoun must be *tempus*; but a variant is *quam*, of which the antecedent would be *legem*: "… to this law they must betake themselves."

52. An allusion to Manichean beliefs.

53. The Greek thinker Epicurus (342-270 B.C.) held that the senses were the sole criterion of truth, and pleasure the goal of human existence. Prudence, being the means of attaining this goal, was the principal virtue. He denied the possibility of life after death. His doctrines were influential, the best known of his subsequent disciples being the Roman Lucretius; others are referred to in Acts 17:18. The doctrines of Epicurus are Augustine's target throughout this section.

54. See Horace, *Ep.* 1,4,16.

which we now see occurring throughout the world, this salvation God has wrought in the midst of the earth, did not yet exist when the prophecies were spoken. But they were foretold at that time, to be demonstrably realized now; and yet the fool can go on saying in his heart, *There is no God* (Ps 13(14):1; 52(53):1). Woe to those with twisted hearts, for what is still outstanding will come, just as those other things which were non-existent when predicted have come to pass since then. Can we suppose that God has brought into being all he promised, with the sole exception of judgment day, and that on this point alone he has deceived us? When Christ was not on earth, God promised him, and the promise was fulfilled. A virgin had never given birth; God promised, and it happened. There had been no shedding of the precious blood, by which the edict condemning us to death was deleted;[55] he promised, and it was carried out. Flesh had never arisen to eternal life; he promised, and fulfilled his promise. The Gentiles had not yet come to believe; God promised, and it happened. It had never been known for heretics, fortified by the name of Christ, to fight against Christ; God foretold it, and so they have. The idols of the Gentiles had not yet been abolished from the earth; he foretold it, and they were. Since he foretold all these things, and brought them to pass, is it likely that he lied to us about one thing only—the day of judgment? Unquestionably it will come, as all these other things have come. All of them were once future events, and were prophesied in advance as to come later, as in due course they did. And the day of judgment will also come, my brothers and sisters.

Let no one say, "It will never happen," or, "Yes, it will come, but it is a long way off." The day when you must depart this life is very near. Let the primordial deception be enough. If we had not the strength to abide by the Lord's precept at the beginning, let us at least be corrected by that example. When Adam was told, *If you touch that, you will certainly die*, he had no precedent of human falling to deter him. Then the serpent sidled in and said, *No, of course you will not die*.[56] The serpent was trusted; God was scorned. The serpent was trusted, the fruit was eaten, and humans died. Is it not obvious that God's threat was realized, rather than the enemy's promise? Unquestionably it is so; we know it. From that day we have all been liable to death, so let us at least be warned by experience to be wary. Still today the serpent never tires of whispering in our ears, "You surely don't think that God is going to damn great crowds of people, and save only a few?" What else is this suggestion but another way of phrasing the original one: "Disobey the commandment; you will not die"? As it was then, so is it now. If you act on the devil's suggestion and spurn God's command, the day of judgment will come, and you will discover that God meant what he said when he threatened, and that the devil's promise was false.

---

55. See Col 2:14.
56. See Gn 2:17; 3:4.

Arise, O Lord, and vindicate my cause. You died, you were despised; and still they say to me, *Where is your God?* (Ps 41:4.11(42:3.10)). *Arise, O Lord, and vindicate my cause.* He who will come to judge is no other than he who rose from the dead. It was prophesied that he would come; he came, and was spurned by the Jews when he walked about on earth, as he is spurned by bogus Christians now while he reigns in heaven. *Arise, O Lord, and vindicate my cause.* Let me not perish, for I have believed in you. Let me not be deceived in my hope; let me receive what you have promised, because I have believed in what I have not seen. *Vindicate my cause.*

Remember the taunts against you, flung at you all day long by an imprudent person. Christ is still insulted, for vessels of wrath[57] are never lacking *all day long*, or, in other words, to the end of this age. People still say, "The Christians preach rubbish"; they still say, "It is idle to talk of rising from the dead." But *vindicate my cause; remember the taunts against you.* What taunts? Those *flung at you all day long by an imprudent person.* Is someone who talks like that prudent?[58] Prudent means "looking ahead." If a prudent person sees ahead it can only be with faith, for with our bodily eyes we can scarcely see further than where to put our feet *all day long.*

26. *Do not ignore the voice of those who plead with you*—the voice of those who groan, and look for what you promised under the New Covenant, and walk in the light of that faith—*do not ignore the voice of those who plead with you.* Yet still unbelievers say, "Where is your God?" *Let the pride of those who hate you ever rise up before you*; and do not ignore their pride either. No, it is not ignored. It is certain that God will either punish them or correct them.

---

57. See Rom 9:22.
58. Possibly another reference to Epicurus.

Exposition of Psalm 74

A Sermon to the People

Verse 1. The inviolability of God's promises

1. This is a psalm which applies the remedy of humility to the tumor of pride, but comforts the humble in their hope. By this double action it ensures that none shall arrogantly presume on themselves, and that no humble person shall despair of God; for God's promise is authoritative, certain, fixed, unshakeable, and trustworthy. It admits of no doubt at all, and it is the comfort of the afflicted. And comfort is sorely needed, for *human life on earth is all temptation* (Jb 7:1), scripture warns us. This does not imply that we should aspire to a prosperous life, and think that the only thing to be avoided is a life beset with troubles. Not so, for both kinds require caution: the one lest it corrupt us, and the other lest it crush us. Whatever our fortunes in this world, no one must look for refuge anywhere but in God, or seek any other joy than that of his promises. Many people are beguiled by a life that seems to abound in all sorts of good fortune; but God never lets anybody down.

When a person is converted to God, he or she finds a new kind of delight, and different joys, for pleasures are changed, not taken away. None of the things that give us joy in this life are definitively ours, but our hope is so certain that it is more worth having than all the pleasures of the world; as scripture bids us, *delight in the Lord*. But in case you might take that to mean that you already have what he has promised, it immediately adds, *And he will grant you your heart's desire* (Ps 36(37):4). If you do not yet see your heart's desire realized, why should you delight in the Lord? Because you are absolutely certain of the one who has promised, and by promising he has put himself in your debt.

The title of the present psalm offers us an assurance, so that our hope-filled prayer may remain steady, and we may be led into the good things God has promised. *Do not cancel it at the end*, says the title. What does *do not cancel it* mean? Deliver what you promised. But when? *At the end*. That is the mark on which our spiritual eye must be trained: *the end*. Let everything else we encounter on the road pass us by, so that we may reach the end. Let the proud revel in their present prosperity; let them be swollen with honors, aglitter with gold, surrounded with servants, hemmed about with obsequious clients—all these things pass away, transient as a shadow. When the end comes, all those who now hope in the Lord will rejoice, but upon the proud will come a sadness without end. When the reward which the proud deride is granted to the humble, then will the conceit of the proud turn to mourning. Theirs will be the lament familiar to us from the Book of Wisdom. Beholding the glory of the saints who, while humiliated here, bore up bravely, who, when flattered here, did not countenance it, the proud will exclaim, *These are the people we once held in derision!* They will ask themselves, *What good has our pride done us, or what benefit has come to us from our vaunted wealth? All these things have passed away like a shadow* (Wis 5:3.8-9). Because they put their trust in destructible things, their hope will be destroyed; but our hope will then give way to fulfillment.

From the heart[1] of our faith we have prayed, *Do not cancel it at the end*; we pray that God's promise may remain for us inviolable, firm, and certain. Have no fear that any powerful agent may invalidate the promises of God. He will not annul them himself because he is truthful, and there is no one more powerful than he who could make his promise void. Let us be completely confident about God's promises, then, and sing the words with which the psalm opens.

Verse 2. Confession and invocation

2. *We will confess to you, O God; we will confess to you and call upon your name.* Do not call upon him until you have confessed to him; confess first, and then call upon him. Remember that in calling upon him you are calling him into yourself;[2] for what else is calling upon him but calling him in? If he is invoked by you—or, in other words, if he is invited into you—to whom is he coming? He does not approach a proud person. He is most high, certainly, but no exalted person can reach him. When we want to reach something high up, we usually stretch upward, and if we still cannot reach it we look for something like scaffolding or ladders, so that by raising ourselves we can get to it. The opposite is the case with God. He is on high, but it is the lowly who reach him. Scripture tells us, *The Lord is close to those who have bruised their hearts* (Ps 33:19(34:18)); and the bruising of the heart is piety and humility. Heart-bruised persons are angry with themselves; they own themselves in the wrong, and hope thereby to find God well disposed to them; they constitute themselves as their own judges, that they may have God as counsel for the defense.

So then, God is invoked, and he comes. To whom? Not to a proud person. Listen to another text: *The Lord is most high, and he looks on the lowly; but whatever is exalted he knows from afar* (Ps 137(138):6). Although *the Lord is most high*, it is not on the lowly that he looks from a distance; on the contrary, he knows from afar anything that is exalted. Perhaps the proud might be tempted to rejoice that they will go unpunished, since the psalm says that the Lord looks on

---

1. Variant: "With the mouth."
2. The point is clearer in Latin: *invocare* = to "call upon, invoke"; *vocare ... in* = to "call into."

the lowly. They might suppose that the Lord, whose home is in the high places, is unaware of their swaggering. But the psalm strikes terror into them: he sees you, he knows you, though from afar. Those to whom he draws near he renders blessed; but you arrogant folk, you exalted people—you will not go unpunished, because he knows you. But you will not be blessed, because he knows you only from afar. Take care what you are doing, then, for if he is looking at you he will not overlook your behavior.[3] It would be much better for you that he should overlook and pardon, than that he should know your conduct and look at it. What does overlooking imply? That he does not know something. But how could he not know? Only in this sense: that he decides not to take cognizance of it; for we speak of someone taking cognizance of what he intends to proceed against and punish. Listen to a believer praying that God will overlook what he has done: *Turn your face away from my sins* (Ps 50:11(51:9)). But what if he turns his face away from you—what will you do then? That is a grievous matter; you would have reason to fear that he is deserting you. But then, if he does not turn his face away, he is taking cognizance, isn't he?

No, because God is wise enough, and powerful enough to turn his face away from the sinner while not turning it away from the one who is confessing the sin. This is why scripture says in one place, *Turn your face away from my sins*, and in another, *Do not turn your face away from me* (Ps 26(27):9). First the psalmist begs, "Turn away from my sins," and then, "Do not turn away from me." Confess to him, and then call upon him, for by confessing you cleanse the temple into which he is to come when called upon. Confess, then invoke. May he turn his face away from your sins, but not turn it away from you; may he turn his face away from what you have made of yourself, but not turn away from what he made. He made you, a human being; what you made is your sins. Confess, then, and call upon him. Say to him, *We will confess to you, O God, we will confess to you.*

The purpose of repetition

3. This repetition is a confirmation of the sentiment just expressed, and it ensures that you do not regret having made your confession. It is not to some cruel master that you have confessed, not to an avenger, not to one who will revile you; so confess without anxiety. Hearken to the exhortation in another psalm: *Confess to the Lord, because he is good* (Ps 105(106):1; 106(107):1). What does that mean—*because he is good*? Why are you afraid to confess? He is good, and he forgives anyone who confesses. You may well be afraid to confess to a human judge, for he may punish you for what you have confessed; but do not

---

3. Augustine is punning on *agnoscere*, to "know, recognize, perceive," and *ignoscere*, to "pardon, forgive, overlook."

be afraid of confessing to God. Render him propitious by confessing your sin, for you will not leave him in ignorance by denying it. *We will confess to you, O God, we will confess*; and, confident now, *we will call upon your name*. We have emptied our hearts in our confession; you have struck fear into us, but cleansed us. Confession humbles us: draw near to the humble, since you distance yourself from the proud.

In many scriptural texts it is made clear to us that repetition reinforces a declaration. This is why the Lord says, *Amen, amen*, and why in certain psalms we find *May it be! May it be!*[4] One "May it be!" would have sufficed to express the meaning, but an extra "May it be!" is added for emphasis. Moreover, you know the story about Pharaoh, King of Egypt. Joseph had been thrown into prison because of his steadfast purity, and Pharaoh had a dream. We are all familiar with it. He saw seven sleek cows eaten by seven gaunt beasts; and then again seven rich ears of grain devoured by seven meager ears. How did Joseph interpret this? He declared, you remember, that these were not two separate dreams, but a single vision. *One interpretation applies to both*, he said; *but the fact that you saw it twice serves as a confirmation.*[5] I have reminded you of this anecdote lest you think that the repetition of words in sacred discourse is a sign of any tendency to verbosity. Repetition is frequently used for emphasis. *My heart is ready, O God, my heart is ready* (Pss 56:8(57:7)); 107(108):1); and again, *Hold out for the Lord, act manfully; let your heart be strengthened, and hold out for the Lord* (Ps 26(27):14).

There are innumerable examples of this mode of speech throughout the scriptures; it is enough for us to remind you of these few, and you will observe others for yourselves. So now turn your attention to the substance of the verse: *we will confess to you, and we will call upon you*. I have explained why confession precedes invocation: when you call upon God, you are issuing an invitation to him. If you are high and mighty he does not wish to come when called upon. If you are high and mighty you will be in no state to confess; but neither will you withhold from God the knowledge of your sins. Your confession teaches him nothing, but cleanses you.

Christ and his Church speak as one person

4. So now the speaker has confessed, and has called upon God—or, rather, many have confessed, and called upon God; and now all speak as one person, saying, *I will recount all your wonders*. This person has by confessing emptied himself of all that is bad; then by invoking God he has filled himself with good things; and now by recounting God's wonders he has given a name to the good

---

4. See Pss 71(72):19; 88:53(89:52). The Latin is *Fiat, fiat*.
5. See Gn 41:25-32.

things that fill him. But notice this, brothers and sisters: at the time when confession was made there were many voices: *We will confess to you, O God, we will confess to you and call upon your name.* Many are the hearts that confess, but one is the heart of all who believe. Why is that so—that there are many hearts confessing, but only one heart among believers? People confess a great variety of sins, but all confess the same faith. Therefore when Christ has begun to dwell in our inmost being through faith,[6] when we have confessed and invoked him, and he has begun to take possession of us, then is formed the whole Christ, head and body, one from the many. From now on, listen to the words of Christ. When the psalm began with *We will confess to you, O God, we will confess to you and call upon your name*, that did not sound as though he were speaking. But now we begin to hear the utterance of the head. However, whether the head speaks or the members speak, Christ is speaking. He speaks in the person of the head and in the person of the body; but what did scripture say? *They will be two in one flesh. This is a great mystery*, says Paul, *but I am referring it to Christ and the Church* (Gn 2:24; Eph 5:31-32). And the Lord himself affirms in the gospel, *They are two no longer, but one flesh* (Mt 19:6). To make it perfectly clear that there are in some sense two persons involved, but that these two are one through being joined in wedlock, they speak as one person through Isaiah; yet what they say is, *He has adorned me like a bridegroom with his wreath, and decked me like a bride with her jewels* (Is 61:10). The head is the bridegroom, the body is the bride; and they speak as one. Let us listen to this speaker, and in him speak as ourselves. Let us be his members, so that this voice may be ours as well. *I will recount all your wonders*, he says. So Christ is preaching himself, telling the good news of himself even through his members, those who already belong to him. Through them he can attract others, who will be joined to the members through whom his gospel has been spread. One body is to be formed, under one head, living one life in one Spirit.

Verse 3. Time, judgment, and the incarnation

5. Now, what does he say? *When my time comes, I will pronounce righteous judgments.* When will he pronounce righteous judgments? When his time comes.[7] That time is not yet. Thanks be to his mercy, he first preaches justice, then gives righteous judgments on the basis of his preaching. If he willed to judge us before preaching, would he find anyone worthy of acquittal? Or anyone who deserved to be absolved? No, indeed; but now is the time for preaching, and

---

6. See Eph 3:17.
7. *Cum acceperit tempus*, literally, "when he has received time" or "when he has made time his own." Augustine plays on this literal meaning of the phrase in the second half of this section.

so he announces, *I will recount all your wonders.* Listen as he recounts them, listen as he preaches, for if you scorn him his warning is there for you: *When my time comes, I will pronounce righteous judgments.* "At present," he says, "I forgive the sinner who confesses; but in the future I will not spare anyone who scorned me." *I will sing to you of your mercy and justice, O Lord* (Ps 100(101):1), declares another psalm. *Mercy and justice:* mercy for this present era, but justice later; for by this mercy sins are pardoned, but by this justice sins are punished. Is it your hope that you will have nothing to fear when he punishes sins? Then love him now, while he pardons them. Do not refuse him, do not be self-important, do not say, "I have nothing for which I need his forgiveness."

If you are minded to take that line, listen to what else this verse implies. *When I receive time as my own, I will pronounce righteous judgments.* Did Christ "receive time"?[8] Did the Son of God "receive time"? No, the Son of God did not receive time, certainly, but the Son of Man received time; and they are one and the same: the Son of God through whom we were created, and the Son of Man through whom we were created anew. The man was taken up by God; God was not taken by the man. Humanity was ennobled, but godhead was in no way degraded. The Son of God did not cease to be what he was, but he took to himself what he was not.[9] What was he? *Being in the form of God he deemed it no robbery to be God's equal:* these are the words of the apostle. And what did he take to himself? *He emptied himself, and took on the form of a slave* (Phil 2:6-7). And as he took to himself the form of a slave, so did he also take time to himself. Was he changed thereby? Was he diminished? Was he left the poorer? Did he fall or decline by accepting it? Far be it from us to think so. What does the text mean, then—*he emptied himself, and took on the form of a slave*? He is said to have emptied himself because he took to himself what was lower, not because he degenerated from his equality with God.

Well, then, brothers and sisters, what does he mean by saying, *When I receive time as my own, I will pronounce righteous judgments*? He "received time" as Son of Man; he governs all times as Son of God. Listen to a passage in the gospel which shows how, as Son of Man, he received the time for judging: God *has given him authority to pass judgment, because he is the Son of Man* (Jn 5:27). As Son of God he never received authority to judge, because he was never without it. But as Son of Man he received time: the time for being born and suffering, the time for dying and rising and ascending, and likewise the time for coming again

---

8. See preceding note; the Latin is the same, but the translation has been altered to reflect the different interpretation Augustine is putting on it here. For him, time is a dimension of created being; see notes at Exposition of Psalm 38,7; Exposition of Psalm 76,8.
9. These sentences closely resemble the statement of orthodox belief in the incarnation formulated by Pope Leo in his "Tome" to Flavian in A.D. 449, and adopted by the Council of Chalcedon in A.D. 451.

and judging. Moreover, his members can, in him, make the same statement, for he will not judge without them, as he promises in the gospel: *You too will sit upon twelve thrones, judging the twelve tribes of Israel* (Mt 19:28). The whole Christ—the head and the saints who are his body—claims, *When I receive time as my own, I will pronounce just judgments.*

Verse 4. The unstable earth, and the strengthening of its pillars

6. What next? *The earth has melted away.* If the earth has melted,[10] what can have caused it to melt but our sins? This is why they are called delinquencies.[11] To be "delinquent" is to be "deliquescent" like a liquid leaking down from the stable framework of virtue and righteousness; for a person sins through an appetite for what is lower. As we are strengthened by love[12] for what is higher than ourselves, so too we drip down and are deliquescent through greed for things below. But our merciful and forgiving God takes note of the melting away of natural things through the sins of men and women. He is the forgiver of sins, not yet the judge who demands their punishment, and so he observes this state of flux and says, *The earth has melted away, and all its inhabitants.* The earth itself has melted away in the persons of falling earth-dwellers: the second phrase is not an additional idea, but an explanation. You might have asked, "How has this melting away of the earth happened? Were its foundations undermined, so that some part of the earth sank, and slid into the abyss?"[13] No: "earth" means *all its inhabitants.* "I found the earth full of sins," says God, "and what did I do? *I strengthened its pillars.*"

What pillars did he strengthen? He calls the apostles "pillars." The apostle Paul speaks in this way of his fellow-apostles: they *were reputed pillars*, he says (Gal 2:9). But what use would those pillars have been, if the Lord had not strengthened them? When the earth shook even the pillars tottered, for all the apostles lost hope during the Lord's passion. But the pillars who tottered at the Lord's passion were given new hope by his resurrection. The foundation-stone of the building cried out through his pillars; the architect himself cried out through all those pillars; for one such pillar was the apostle Paul, who demanded, *Do you presume to interrogate Christ, who speaks through me?* (2 Cor 13:3).

---

10. *Defluxit.* In the following lines Augustine makes the connections between *defluo,* to "run down, melt away," and *delinquo,* to "fall short, commit an offense," whence derives *delictum,* "a sin, offense."
11. *Delicta.*
12. *Caritate.*
13. The biblical cosmology is assumed throughout this section: below the earth lay the vast abyss, but the earth rested on pillars built by God. Its stability should therefore have been assured, but sin destabilized the created order.

So then, says Christ, "I strengthened its pillars. I rose again, and proved to them that death is not to be feared. I showed those frightened disciples that not even the body perishes in death. My wounds terrified them, but my scars put new strength into them." Our Lord Jesus Christ could have risen unscarred. Would it have been difficult for one so powerful to restore his bodily frame to such integrity that no trace whatever should remain of the wounds that had been there? He had the power so to heal it that no scar would show; but he willed instead to keep the evidence that would strengthen the quaking pillars.

Verse 5. Listen to the healer

7. We have heard what he cried out through those pillars, my brothers and sisters; we have heard it already, because never a day passes when they are silent. Now is the time for us to listen, because of that terrifying prophecy, *I will pronounce righteous judgments, when my time comes.* He will "receive the time" for passing righteous judgments, but you have the time now for doing righteous deeds. If he remained silent, you would have no recourse, but through his fortified pillars he shouts to you. What is he shouting? *I said to the wicked, Do not act wickedly.* He is shouting, brothers and sisters—and, to be sure, you are shouting too, because you like what I say; but listen, please listen, to him shouting. Through him I beg you: let that voice of his strike fear into you. It will not do for your voices to give us more pleasure than his voice gives you reason to fear. *I said to the wicked, Do not act wickedly.* But they have acted wickedly already. They are guilty, and already *the earth has melted away, and all its inhabitants.* Those who had crucified Christ were pierced to the heart; they acknowledged their sin, and heard from the apostles why they must not despair of mercy from him who preached to them.[14] Christ had come as a physician, and therefore he was not looking for the healthy: *It is not the healthy who need a doctor, but the sick. I did not come to call the righteous, but sinners to repentance* (Lk 5:31-32), and accordingly, *I said to the wicked, Do not act wickedly.*

But they did not hear. The same thing was said to us at the beginning, and we did not hear; we fell, we became mortal, and inherited mortality. *The earth melted away.* Let them at least listen now; let them listen to the doctor who has come to the sick, that they may get up again. If they refused to listen to him when they were well, when they might have avoided sickness by listening, let them listen now as they lie there in their weakness, that they may rise to their feet once more. *I said to the wicked, Do not act wickedly.* "But we have done so already, so what is left for us?" *And to the delinquent I said, Do not lift up your horn.* What does that mean? If your concupiscence has betrayed you into iniquity, do not defend your sin out of arrogance; confess it, if you have committed it. The

---

14. See Acts 2:37-38. Variant: "...from the apostles why sinners must not despair of mercy."

person who is wicked, but does not confess, is the one who lifts up his horn. *I said to the wicked, Do not act wickedly, and to the delinquent I said, Do not lift up your horn.* Christ's horn will be lifted up in you, if yours is not. Your horn is the symbol of iniquity, Christ's of majesty.

Verses 6-8. Blasphemous speech

8. *Do not be haughty, nor speak sinfully against God.* Listen now to the way many people talk; let each of us listen, and feel compunction. What do you often hear people saying? "Does God really govern human affairs? Is this or that event truly a judgment from God? Does he even care what goes on here on earth? Lots of wicked people are awash with good fortune, while the innocent are weighed down with hardships."

But consider this: when some disaster happens to a person it may well be that God is chastising and warning him or her, and the sufferer's conscience recognizes the fact. If someone knows that he or she may be undergoing well-deserved punishment for sins committed, how can God be blamed for it? Such a person is not in a position to say, "I am just." So what do we find him saying? "There are other wicked people, worse than I am, who don't have to put up with such troubles." And this is precisely how human beings speak sinfully against God. Observe how sinful it is. In wishing to seem just himself, the speaker represents God as unjust. Anyone who says, "It is unjust that I should suffer as I do," is saying that God, by whose judgment he suffers, is unjust, and that he himself is a just person who suffers unjustly. I put it to you, brothers and sisters: is this a fair assessment, that God should be reckoned unjust, and you just? When you say that, you are speaking sinfully against God.

9. What does God say in another psalm? *All this you did.* He enumerates various sins, and then says, *All this you did, and I was silent.* What does he mean by *I was silent*? He is never silent about his commandments, but he is silent for a while about punishment; he holds back from vengeance and from passing sentence on the guilty. But the sinner says, "I did so-and-so ... and so-and so... and God did not punish me. Here I am hale and hearty. Nothing bad happened to me." *All this you did, and I was silent. You were wrong to think that I will be like you.* What does that mean—*that I will be like you*? "Because you are wicked yourself you thought me wicked too; you thought of me as one who would approve your villainy, not as one who would oppose and punish it." And what is the next thing he has to say to you? *I will bring you face to face with yourself* (Ps 49(50):21). And what does that mean? "By your sins you have hidden yourself for the time being behind your back. You do not see yourself, or see into yourself. But I will bring you round in front of your face, and make you into a torment for yourself."

The same lesson is found in the present psalm. *Do not speak sinfully against God.* Pay close attention here. Many people speak in this iniquitous way, but dare not do so openly lest they shock devout persons. They gnaw these thoughts in their hearts, and within themselves feed on this poisonous fare. They enjoy speaking against God, and even if they do not blurt it out, they do not keep silent in their hearts. This is why another psalm says, *The ignorant person has said in his heart, There is no God* (Pss 13(14):1; 52(53):1). The fool said it, but was afraid of what people would think, and unwilling to say it where anyone else would overhear. So he said it where God himself would hear—God, against whom he said it!

God is omnipresent; he sees and hears all

The same is true in the psalm we are studying now—please concentrate, dearly beloved. It urged, *Do not speak sinfully against God*, because it is clear that many do so in their hearts. So now it adds, *Because neither from the east, nor from the west, nor from the deserted mountains; for the judge is God*. The judge of your iniquities is God. If he is God, he is present everywhere. Where are you going to hide yourself from God's eyes? Can you find some place where he will be unable to hear what you say? If God judges from the east, make for the west, and there say whatever you please against him. If he judges from the west, head east, and say it there. If he judges from the deserted mountains, lose yourself among crowds of people: you will be able to mutter it to yourself there. But he judges from no place at all,[15] he who is everywhere secret and everywhere out in the open, he whom no one is allowed to know completely and of whom no one is permitted to be ignorant. Take note of what you are doing. You are speaking sinfully against God, but *the Spirit of the Lord has filled the whole earth, and that which holds all things together knows what is uttered. Therefore no one who speaks sinfully can remain hidden* (Wis 1:7-8). Do not think of God as confined to any place. He is with you in the mode determined by what you are. What does it mean to say that he is as you are? He is good, if you are good; but if you are bad, he will seem bad to you. If you are good, he will be your helper; if you are bad, he will be the avenger.

You have your judge with you in the secret recess of yourself. If you are minded to do some evil thing you withdraw from public places into your own home, where no enemy will see you. Then you withdraw from the parts of your house that are exposed to view and open to the gaze of others. You betake yourself to your bedroom. But even in your bedroom you are afraid that someone else may get to know of your plan, so you withdraw into your own heart, and meditate on it there. But God is more intimately present to you than your own heart.

Wherever you flee, he is there. Whither will you flee from yourself? Will you not be following yourself, wheresoever you flee? But he is within your inmost

---

15. Variant: "There is no place from which he does not judge."

self. There is no place to which you can flee from an angry God—except to a God with whom you are at peace. There is nowhere to flee beyond this. Do you want to flee from him? Then flee to him.

Do not speak sinfully against God, then, not even in that hiding-place where you are speaking. *He plotted iniquity in his bedroom*, says another psalm (Ps 35:5(36:4)). What did that sinner plot in his bedroom? Someone who said, *Offer a sacrifice of justice, and hope in the Lord*, knew that his bedroom meant his heart, for just before this he had said, *Be pierced in your hearts over what you say in your own rooms* (Ps 4:6.5(5.4)). Your pungent crimes are so many goads to compunction and confession. In the very place where you speak sinfully against God, he judges you. It is not the judgment that he postpones, only the penalty. He judges you now; he already knows all about it; he already sees what is done. The punishment remains outstanding, but you will get it when the time comes for sentencing. When there is manifested the countenance of the man who was mocked here, who was judged and crucified, who stood under human jurisdiction, when he appears as judge in his majesty, then you will get your punishment if you have not corrected yourself.

Confession and humility are the only refuge

What are we to do, then? Let us forestall him by hastening into his presence confessing.[16] Forestall him by your confession: he whom you angered will come to you in gentleness.

Nor from the deserted mountains will he come, *for the judge is God*. Not from the east, not from the west, not from the deserted mountains. Why not? Because *the judge is God*. If he were located in some place, he would not be God; but because the judge is God, not a mere human being, do not look for him to come from any locality. You will yourself be his place if you are good, if you confess and call upon him.

10. *He humbles one, and exalts another*. Whom does this judge humble, whom exalt? Think of those two men in the temple, and you will see whom. *They went up to the temple to pray*, says the gospel. *One was a Pharisee, the other a tax collector*. The Pharisee kept saying, *O God, I thank you that I am not like other people: unjust, robbers, adulterers, like that tax collector there. I fast twice a week, and give tithes from everything I own*. He had come to visit the

---

16. See Ps 94(95):2. Augustine puts the phrase in Greek: ἐν ἐξομολογήσοι, "in confession." The word in patristic Greek meant confession of sins, or of praise and thanksgiving to God; it was also the technical term for the arduous public penance undertaken by notable sinners with a view to ecclesial reconciliation. Tertullian (*de poen.* 9) says, "Exomologesis means that we confess our offense to our Lord . . . from confession repentance is born, and by repentance God is propitiated. Therefore exomologesis is the discipline for a man or woman who needs to be humbled."

doctor, yet he was displaying sound limbs and covering his wounds. What about the other man, who knew better where to look for healing? *The tax collector stood a long way off, and beat his breast.* As you see it, he was standing a long way off, but he was really drawing near to the one whom he was invoking. *He beat his breast, saying, Lord, be merciful to me, a sinner. Truly I tell you, that tax collector went down to his house at rights with God, rather than the Pharisee; for anyone who exalts himself will be humbled, but the one who humbles himself will be exalted* (Lk 18:10-14). So the verse in our psalm has been expounded for us. What does the judge do, this judge who is God? *He humbles one, and exalts another*; he humbles the proud and exalts the humble.

Verse 9. Some difficulties arise here

11. *For in the Lord's hand is a cup of pure wine, full of a mixed drink.* Rightly so. *And he tipped it from one to another, yet its dregs were not emptied out. All the sinners on earth will drink it.* Cheer up! This is somewhat obscure; but remember what we were told in a recent gospel reading: *Ask, and you will obtain; seek, and you will find; knock, and the door will be opened to you* (Mt 7:7). You inquire, "Where am I to knock, to have the door opened to me?" *Neither from the east, nor from the west, nor from the deserted mountains, for the judge is God.* If he is present here and present elsewhere, and absent from no place at all, knock where you are standing. Or rather, just stand there, because your standing there is itself a way of knocking. So what is this verse about?

The first difficulty is this: *a cup of pure wine, full of a mixed drink.* How can it be *pure* if it is *mixed*? The second question is prompted by the phrase, *in the Lord's hand is a cup.* But I am addressing you as persons well instructed in the Church of Christ; so when a psalm speaks of the Lord's hand you must not form a picture of God in your hearts as someone circumscribed by a human form. If you do that you will be building idols again in your hearts, just when their temples have been shut down. This cup signifies something, and in a minute we shall try to find out what it is. But the expression, *the Lord's hand*, means "in the Lord's power," for God's power is symbolized by his hand. We often say something similar of human beings: "The matter is in his hands" means that it is in someone's power to deal with when he wants to.

But what about the *cup of pure wine, full of a mixed drink?* This phrase is clarified by what follows: *he tipped it from one to another, yet its dregs were not emptied out.* This is why it is said to be full of mixed wine. Don't be confused by its being called both pure and mixed; in itself it is pure and free from adulteration,[17] but its mixed character lies in its dregs. So what is the wine, and what are the dregs? And what is meant by saying that *he tipped it from one to another*, but in such a way that the dregs were not emptied out?

The obscure points are clarified: revelation to Jews and Gentiles

12. Recall what led us to this point. God *humbles one, and exalts another*. The gospel illustrated this for us with the story of two individuals, a Pharisee and a tax collector; but we can apply the lesson more widely, understanding it of two peoples, the Jews and the Gentiles. The Pharisee stands for the Jews, the tax collector for the Gentiles. The Jewish people flaunted its merits, the Gentiles confessed their sins. Anyone who is familiar with holy scripture, and reads there the letters of Paul and the Acts of the Apostles, can see what I mean. I need not explain at length how the apostles encouraged the Gentiles not to despair over the grievous sins in which they had lain prostrate. Nor need I remind you how the apostles also cautioned the Jews not to be puffed up as though the law had justified them: they were not to think themselves righteous and the Gentiles sinners just because it was they who had been given the law, and the temple, and the priesthood. Very different were all those idol-worshipers and adherents of demons: they were stationed far away, just as the tax collector stood at a distance. But as the Jews moved further off by being proud, so did the Gentiles draw near by confessing.

Now for the full *cup of pure wine in the Lord's hand*. Insofar as the Lord grants me understanding, I think that this symbolizes the law which was given to the Jews, and all those writings we call the Old Testament, full as they are of weighty precepts. (Some other person may produce a better interpretation, for the obscurity of the scriptures is such that a passage scarcely ever yields a single meaning only. But whatever interpretation emerges, it must conform to the rule of faith. Let us not be jealous of those with more powerful minds than our own, nor despair because we are so small. I am expounding to you, beloved ones, whatever seems right to us, but I do not want to close your ears against others, who may perhaps have better things to say.) To resume: in the Old Testament the New lies hidden, as though concealed beneath the dregs of sacred signs still material in character. The circumcision of the flesh, for example, is an ordinance of great mystery,[18] and from it we understand what circumcision of the heart is. The temple at Jerusalem is a great mystery, and from it we understand the body of the Lord.[19] Through the promised land we understand the kingdom of heaven. The sacrifice of cattle and other victims contains a great mystery, but in all these various types of sacrifice we understand the one sacrifice and the unique victim—our Lord on the cross. In place of all those sacrifices we have one only;

---

17. *Propter sinceritatem*, literally, "because of sincerity," but the word "sincere" derives from a practice of adulterating marble with wax; a statute was "sincere" or "without wax" when the cracks had not been disguised with wax by the sculptor. In the present context the "sincerity" Augustine has in mind is the pure wine of God's revelation in Christ, as he goes on to explain.
18. *Magni sacramenti*, here and in the following sentences.
19. See Jn 2:21.

they prefigured our mysteries. The Jewish people received the law; they received just, good commandments. What can be as just as these? *You shall not kill. You shall not commit adultery. You shall not steal. You shall not bear false witness. Honor your father and your mother. You shall not covet your neighbor's property. You shall not covet your neighbor's wife. You shall adore one only God, and serve him alone.*[20] All these are the wine. But the material signs sank to the bottom and remained with the Jews, so that the spiritual meaning could be poured out. The *cup in the Lord's hand*—that is, in the Lord's power—is a cup of *pure wine*, because it is a cup of the truthful, unadulterated law. But the cup is *full of a mixed drink*, because it contains the dregs of those material sacraments. When the psalm says, *He humbles one*, it means the proud Jew; when he *exalts another*, the reference is to the confessing Gentile. *He tipped it from one to another*, from the Jewish people to the Gentile races. What did he tip? The law. Its spiritual meaning flowed out, yet *its dregs were not emptied out*, because all the material observances were perpetuated among the Jews. *All the sinners on earth will drink it.* Who will drink? *All the sinners on earth.* Which are they? The Jews, certainly, were sinners, but proud sinners; the Gentiles too were sinners, but humble ones. *All the sinners will drink*, but notice which ones will quaff the dregs, and which the wine. The former by drinking the dregs have lost their significance; the latter by drinking the wine have been justified. I would go so far as to say that they have been inebriated by it: I do not hesitate to say so; would that all of you might share that intoxication! Remember the cry, *How excellent is your intoxicating chalice!* (Ps 22(23):5).

How can that be said? Well, my brothers and sisters, do you think all those who were willing to die for their confession of Christ were sober? Not at all; so inebriated were they that they could not even recognize members of their own families. The relatives who tried hard to lure them away from their hope of heavenly rewards by means of earthly blandishments went unrecognized, for the martyrs were too drunk to hear. Were they not truly inebriated, these men and women whose hearts had been transformed? Were they not inebriated, whose minds had been estranged from this world? *All the sinners on earth will drink*, says our psalm. But which ones will drink wine? Sinners will drink it, but in order to remain sinners no longer; they will drink to be justified, not as a punishment.

Verses 10-11. The final recompense

13. *But I*—for all drink, but especially I: Christ with his body, that is; *I will rejoice for ever; I will sing psalms to the God of Jacob* over that promise which

---

20. See Ex 20:2-17; Dt 5:6-21.

will be fulfilled at the end, the promise concerning which our psalm besought God, *Do not cancel it.* And I, *I will rejoice for ever.*

14. *I will shatter all the horns of sinners, but the horns of the just one shall be exalted.* This is the same process as that referred to earlier: *he humbles one, and exalts another.* Sinners do not want their horns broken, but they undoubtedly will be at the end. Do you dread that he will break yours for you on that day? Then break it yourself today. You heard his instructions; do not disregard them: *I said to the wicked, Do not act wickedly; and to the delinquent I said, Do not lift up your horn.* But when you heard that admonition, *do not lift up your horn,* you made light of it. You did lift up your horn. So when you arrive at the end, the prophecy will be verified in you: *I will shatter all the horns of sinners, but the horns of the just one shall be exalted.* The horns of sinners are the high status enjoyed by proud persons; the horns of the just one are Christ's gifts; for horns are a symbol of high dignity. May you abhor earthly rank, in order to rank high in heaven. If you are enamored of earthly sublimity he will not admit you to the nobility of heaven. If your horn is broken for you at the end, it will plunge you into confusion, just as it will be to your glory if your horn is exalted on that day. Now is the time for choosing, not then. You will be in no position to say then, "Give me time to make my choice," for the warning, *I said to the wicked...* was issued long since. If I did not say that, prepare your excuses, make ready your defense. But if I did say it, hasten to make your confession in good time, lest you fall under condemnation; for on that day it will be too late for confession, and your defense will be null and void.

Exposition of Psalm 75

A Sermon to the People

Verse 2. Who has the right to the name "Judah"?[1]

1. Our Lord Jesus Christ is known to all, yet the Jews who are his enemies make a point of boasting over the words of the psalm we have just sung. *God is made known in Judah, and great is his name in Israel*, it says; and so they are given to taunting the Gentiles for ignorance of God, and claiming that he is known only by themselves; for since the prophet states that *God is known in Judah* the implication is that he is not known elsewhere. Well now, it is quite true that God is known in Judah, but they must understand what "Judah" means. We may even concede that God is not known anywhere except in Judah. Yes indeed, we too admit this, because God cannot be known to anyone unless that person is in Judah. But what does the apostle say? *A Jew is one who is such inwardly, by circumcision of the heart, not literally but in spirit* (Rom 2:29). Some people, then, are Jews because circumcised in the flesh, and others are Jews by reason of the circumcision of their hearts.[2] Many of our holy fathers carried both bodily circumcision as a seal attesting their faith, and circumcision of heart which was nothing else but faith itself. People who today vaunt an ancestral name, but have abandoned their ancestors' way of life, play false to their pedigree. They have degenerated from those ancestors because, though they have remained Jews in the flesh, they are pagan at heart.

Jews are people descended from Abraham, from whom was born Isaac, and from him Jacob, and from Jacob the twelve patriarchs, and from the twelve patriarchs the whole race of the Jews. But the principal reason for their being called "Jews" is that among Jacob's twelve sons was one named Judah; he was a patriarch among the twelve, and from his stock the kingly rule was established. The people as a whole comprised twelve tribes, which corresponded to the twelve sons of Jacob. "Tribes" are divisions or distinct groups of people. That people

---

1. Augustine does not comment on the title to this psalm, which is "To the end, among the hymns, a psalm of Asaph, a song for the Assyrians."
2. The practice of bodily circumcision, traced back to Abraham (see Gn 17:10 ff), came to be seen as a sign of God's covenant with Israel and hence of membership of the chosen people. The prophets, especially Jeremiah, insisted that the outward rite was of no value unless it stood for an inward attitude of repentance and obedience (see Jer 4:4; Dt 10:16). Paul emphasized that circumcision of heart is the mark of the true Israel (see Rom 2:25-29).

consisted, then, of twelve tribes; one of these was the tribe of Judah, from which sprang the kings, and another was that of Levi, from which came the priests. No territory was apportioned to the priests who served the temple, yet it was imperative that the whole promised land should be shared out among twelve tribes. Since one tribe of higher dignity—that of Levi—was not included in the partition, there would have been only eleven, had not the number twelve been restored through the adoption of Joseph's two sons. Pay attention, now, to the way in which this came about.

One of Jacob's twelve sons was Joseph. This was the same Joseph who was sold into Egypt by his brothers. There he was raised to high office as a reward for his chastity, and God was with him in all his undertakings. When the brothers who had sold him were hard pressed by famine and came down to Egypt in search of bread, Joseph welcomed them, along with their father. Now Joseph had two sons, Ephraim and Manasseh. When Jacob lay dying he adopted these two grandsons of his into the number of his own sons, as a parting bequest. *Any others who may be born shall be yours*, he said to his son Joseph, *but these are to count as mine, and they shall share the land with their brothers* (Gn 48:5.6). The promised land had not yet been given to them, much less apportioned, but he was speaking prophetically in the Spirit. Thus by the inclusion of Joseph's two sons the number of twelve tribes was restored. There were in fact thirteen, for what would have been the single tribe of Joseph now counted as two, but the tribe of Levi was left out. This priestly tribe served the temple, and lived on the tithes of all the others among whom the land was divided, and so the number still stood at twelve.

One of these twelve was the tribe of Judah, whence came the kings. Of course, the first king they were given was Saul, who sprang from a different tribe, but he was rejected as a bad king. In succession to him they were given King David, from the tribe of Judah, and from him were descended the other kings, all members of the tribe of Judah. This had been foretold by Jacob in the blessings he had given to his sons: *Never shall there fail a prince from Judah, nor a leader from his stock, until he comes who is heir to the promise* (Gn 49:10).

From Judah's tribe came our Lord Jesus Christ, for, being born of Mary, he is *of David's lineage* (2 Tm 2:8), as scripture states and as you have just heard. In respect of his divinity our Lord Jesus Christ is equal to the Father; quite evidently then he is not merely prior to the Jews but exists even before Abraham, and not merely before Abraham but before Adam, and not only before Adam but before heaven and earth and before all ages, because *everything was made through him; no part of created being was made without him* (Jn 1:3). Now when the prophetic words were spoken, *never shall there fail a prince from Judah, nor a leader from his stock, until he comes who is heir to the promise*, they referred to the early centuries. We shall find that throughout this time the Jews always had kings from the tribe of Judah, which is why they were called Jews; they had never had a foreigner as king until Herod, who was on the throne when the Lord was born. Only from that time, from Herod, were the kings foreign. Before Herod they were all from the tribe of Judah, but this state of affairs lasted only until the coming of the one *who was heir to the promise.* When the Lord himself came, the Jews' kingdom was overthrown and taken away from them. They have no kingdom now, because they refuse to recognize the true king.

Are they still to be called "Jews" then? Consider that question. No, they are not, and you can see why not. With their own voice they disclaimed their right to the name, and declared themselves unworthy to be called Jews in any but a carnal sense. When did they abdicate that name? When they were speaking against Christ, raging against him and against Judah's race, raging against David's line. Pilate asked them, *Am I to crucify your king?* And they answered, *We have no king but Caesar* (Jn 19:15).

Listen, you who call yourselves Jews, though you have forfeited the reality: if indeed you have no king but Caesar, then there has failed *a prince from Judah*; and that means he must have come *who is heir to the promise.* The more authentic Jews are they who, Jews formerly, became Christians; but the rest of Jewry, who did not believe in Christ, deservedly lost their right even to the name. The real Jewry is Christ's Church, which believes in that king who through the virgin Mary sprang from the tribe of Judah. In him does the Church believe, of whom the apostle was just now speaking in his letter to Timothy: *Remember Jesus Christ, risen from the dead, born of David's lineage, whom my gospel proclaims* (2 Tm 2:8). Since David was descended from Judah, and our Lord Jesus Christ from David, we who believe in Christ belong to Judah; and though we have not seen Christ with our own eyes we truly know him, because we hold fast to him by faith. They have no business to jeer at us, then, those folk who are Jews no longer, for they themselves declared, *We have no king but Caesar.* They would have been better off with Christ as their king, for he was of David's line and of the tribe of Judah.

In our eyes, though, Christ, who is of David's stock according to the flesh, is God, God blessed above all things for ever. And so he is both our king and our God: our king because, being born of the tribe of Judah according to the flesh, he is the Messiah, our Lord and Savior; but our God too, who exists before Judah, and before heaven and earth, for through him all things were made, both spiritual and corporeal. If, then, *everything was made through him* (Jn 1:3), then even Mary, who gave him birth, was made by him. That being the case, how could he possibly have been born in the same way as everyone else, when he had fashioned for himself the mother from whom he would be born? He is the Lord, and we have the apostle's word for it: speaking of the Jews, he said, *The patriarchs belong to them; and from them Christ was born according to the flesh, he who is sovereign over all, God, blessed for ever* (Rom 9:5).

The Jews saw Christ, but failed to see him as God, and crucified him, while the Gentiles, who had not seen him, believed in him and acknowledged him as God. Since God was reconciling the world to himself in Christ,[3] he was indeed made known to them, yet they crucified Christ because they failed to recognize God hidden in the flesh. Accordingly let that Judah back away, the so-called Judah unworthy of the name, and let the rightful Judah approach, the Judah to whom is addressed the invitation, *Draw near to him and receive his light, and then you will not be shamefaced* (Ps 33:6(34:5)). The rightful Judah has no need to blush for shame. They have heard and believed, and the Church has become the true Judah, wherein Christ is acknowledged as a man from David's line, and as God, nobler than David.

The true Israel

2. *God is made known in Judah, and great is his name in Israel.* We must take *Israel* here in the same sense as we took *Judah*. As they are no longer true Jews, so also they are not the true Israel, for to whom is this name *Israel* given? To one who sees God.[4] Did they see God, the people among whom he walked in his humanity, the people who thought he was only a man, and killed him? Rising from the dead he appeared in his godhead to all those to whom he wished to reveal himself. The people fit to be called *Israel* are those counted worthy to recognize Christ as God made present in the flesh, to recognize him and so to worship what they could not see, instead of despising what they saw. Not with their eyes did the Gentiles behold him, but in humility of mind they discerned him whom they did not see, and laid hold on him by faith. In short, the people who laid hands on him killed him, but those who laid hold on him by faith worshiped him.

Great is his name in Israel. Do you aspire to be Israel? Then turn your thoughts to that man of whom the Lord said, *Look, there is a true Israelite, in whom there is no guile* (Jn 1:47). If a person *in whom there is no guile* is a true Israelite, then deceitful and lying persons are no true Israelites. Let not such people claim that God is among them, and that his name is great in Israel; rather let them prove themselves Israelites, and then I will admit that *in Israel his name is great.*

Verses 3-4. Inner peace is compatible with spiritual warfare

3. *His abode is established in peace, and his dwelling in Zion.* Again, Zion represents the Jewish homeland, but the true Zion is the Christian Church.

Now, the meaning of the Hebrew words has been handed down to us as follows: Judah means "confession" and Israel means "one who sees God." Israel comes after Judah, as the order in the text indicates: *God is made known in*

---

3. See 2 Cor 5:19.
4. One of the traditional popular etymologies of the name "Israel."

Judah, and great is his name in Israel. Do you want to see God? Make your confession first. By this means a place for God is prepared within you,[5] because *his abode is established in peace.* As long as you go on refusing to confess your sins, you are in a sense quarrelling with God, for how can you be other than in conflict with him while you commend what displeases him? He punishes a thief, and you commend theft; he punishes a drunkard, and you approve of drinking to excess. You are in conflict with God, and have not prepared a place for him in your heart, for *his abode is in peace.*

How are you to initiate terms of peace with God? Let your approach be through confession. The psalmist's voice invites you, *Attune yourself to the Lord in confession* (Ps 146(147):7). What does this mean, *attune yourself to the Lord in confession*? Make a beginning, make an overture to God. How? In such a way that what displeases him may come to displease you too. Your evil life displeases him; if it gives you pleasure you are out of tune with him, but if it offends you you are in harmony with him through confession. Consider how unlike him you are, because then you will undoubtedly find your unlikeness offensive. You were made in the image of God, human creature, but by your perverted and evil life you have blurred or effaced the image of your creator in you. You have grown unlike him; but look hard at yourself until what you see displeases you, and from this moment you will have begun to recover the likeness, because what displeases God now displeases you as well,

4. But in what sense am I like him, you ask, if I still find myself unpleasant? This is precisely why the psalm said, *Attune yourself.* Make a beginning with the Lord by confession, and you will complete the work in peace. At present you are engaged in war against yourself. War is declared against you, and your warfare is not only against the insinuations of the devil, that tyrant whose power pervades our atmosphere and dominates the children of unbelief; no, not only against him, the devil, with the spirits of wickedness who are his angels.[6] You must wage war against yourself too. What—against *yourself*? Yes, against your bad habits, against your old evil life which drags you towards what is familiar and reins you back from the new. For a new life is being proposed to you, but you are old; tautly expectant with joy in the new, you are weighed down by the old. This means that your war against yourself is already declared. To the extent that you are displeasing to yourself, you are allied with God; and insofar as you are allied with God you will be empowered to win the victory over yourself, because he who conquers all opposition is with you. Take note of what the apostle says: *With my mind I submit to God's law, but with my flesh to the law of sin* (Rom 7:25). In what sense do you obey with your *mind*? Because your evil life is

---

5. Similar ideas in Augustine's Exposition of Psalm 74,2, suggest that this sermon was preached soon after the preceding one.
6. See Eph 6:12.

displeasing to you. And in what sense with your *flesh*? Because sinful thoughts and the pleasure they arouse will not leave you alone. But from the moment that you range yourself on God's side in your mind, you conquer that element in you which is unwilling to comply. With one part of you you have gone ahead, but with another part you are still lagging behind. Drag yourself towards him who lifts you up. You are weighed down by a load of old habits; cry out, then, *"Who will deliver me from this death-ridden body, wretch that I am?* (Rom 7:24). Who will set me free from this crushing load?" The corruptible body does indeed weigh down the soul.[7] Who, then, will set us free? *The grace of God, through Jesus Christ our Lord* (Rom 7:25).

But why does he allow you to be locked in dispute against yourself for so long, until your evil desires are all burnt up? To make you understand that your suffering arises from yourself. The scourge that inwardly afflicts you comes from yourself, so it is with yourself that you must take issue. The punishment inflicted on anyone who rebels against God is this: having refused to be at peace with God, such a person is at war with himself. You must keep your members under control when your evil cravings arise. Suppose anger has surged up; hold your hand, keeping close company with God. Surge up it may, but it will have found no weapons. Anger launched the attack, but the weapons were in your keeping; let the attack remain unarmed, and then anger will learn not to arise in the future, since it has found its upsurge frustrated.

5. Dear friends, I am explaining this to prevent your misunderstanding what was said earlier, *With my flesh I submit to the law of sin*, lest you take it to mean that you ought to submit to your carnal desires. No; even though they can now be nothing more than desires of the flesh, there must be no consenting to them. That is why the apostle did not say, "Let there be no sin in your mortal body"; he knew that as long as the body is mortal there will be sin in it. What did he say? *Do not let sin reign in your mortal body* (Rom 6:12). What does "don't let it reign" signify? He went on to make this clear: *So as to persuade you to yield to its cravings*. Desires there are; they do exist; but you do not obey those cravings by responding with desires of your own. You do not follow them, nor do you give your consent to them. Sin there is in you, but it is dethroned and no longer reigns in you. Later the last enemy, death, will be destroyed,[8] for what is the promise that saying contains for us, *With my mind I submit to God's law, but with my flesh to the law of sin*? Hearken to the promise: unlawful desires will not abide in our flesh for ever. It will rise again and will be changed; and when this mortal flesh has been changed into a spiritual body, it will no longer titillate the soul with worldly ambitions or earthly pleasures, nor turn it away from the contemplation

---

7. See Wis 9:15.
8. See 1 Cor 15:26.

of God. Then will that saying of the apostle come true: *The body indeed is a dead thing by reason of sin, but the spirit is life through righteousness. If he who raised Jesus from the dead lives in you, he who raised Jesus Christ from the dead will bring life to your mortal bodies too, through his Spirit who dwells in you* (Rom 8:10-11).

When your bodies have been brought to life like this, there will be in you that true peace which is God's abode; but confession must be the first step. *God is known in Judah*, so make your confession first. *Great is his name in Israel*: not yet do you see him in vision, but see him in faith, and then the next verse will be verified in you: *his abode is established in peace, and his dwelling in Zion*. Zion means contemplation. We told you yesterday[9] what contemplation is; some of our brethren heard it then, and we see them present again today. Contemplation means that we shall see God face to face. He is promised to us, he whom we do not see at present, but in whom we believe. What will our joy be like when we do see him? If even the promise moves us to such great joy, brothers and sisters, what will its fulfillment do for us? What he has promised will be granted to us, and what has he promised? Himself, so that we may find our joy in his countenance and in contemplation of him. Nothing else will bring us delight, because nothing is better than God, who made all the things that delight us. *His abode is established in peace, and his dwelling in Zion*; this means that his dwelling-place is established in vision, in contemplation, for this is Zion.

6. *There he has crushed the power of the bow, of shield and sword and war.* Where did he crush them? In that eternal peace, in that peace made perfect. So then, my brothers and sisters, people of strong faith perceive that they must not rely on themselves. All their powerful menaces, and whatever is lethally whetted in themselves, they break. Everything they regarded as important for protecting their temporal interests, and the war they were waging against God by defending their sins, all these he shattered there.

Verse 5. Light comes from the mountains, but God is its source. True mountains maintain unity

7. *You send your wondrous light from the eternal mountains.* Who are these eternal mountains? They are the people whom God has made to last for ever; they are the lofty mountains who are preachers of the truth. *You send your light*, your own light, but you send it from the everlasting mountains, because those mighty mountains are the first to receive your light, and afterwards the earth is clothed in that brilliance which the mountains were the first to receive. Those

---

9. Possibly he is referring to his Exposition of Psalm 83, which may have been preached on the day before this one. Compare the note at section 16 below.

great mountains, the apostles, caught it; the apostles intercepted the first glimmers of your rising light. Did they keep for themselves the light they caught? No, for they were afraid you might say to them, *Wicked, lazy servant, you should have handed my money over to the bankers* (Mt 25:26.27). So then, if they did not keep for themselves what they had received, but preached throughout the world, rightly can it be said that *You*, yes you, *send your wondrous light from the eternal mountains*. You made them eternal, and through them you promised eternal life to others: *you send your wondrous light from the eternal mountains*.

You—that is splendidly said, and in a weighty phrase; it should ensure that no one thinks it is the mountains that illumine us. There have been plenty of people who imagined that the mountains themselves were the source of the illumination they received, and so they formed factions and raised up their own mountains; but then the mountains collapsed and they were crushed. Some people set up for themselves Donatus;[10] somebody or other raised up Maximian;[11] some set up this fellow or that. How can they reckon that their salvation is to be found in human beings, not in God?

Listen, everyone: the light comes to you through the mountains, certainly, but it is God who illumines you, not the mountains. *You*, says the psalm, *you send your light*, you, not the mountains. *You send your light*, from the eternal mountains, indeed, but it is *you* who send it. What does another psalm have to tell us? *I have lifted my eyes to the mountains, from where comes help for me* (Ps 120(121):1). What do you mean? Is it in the mountains that you trust? Will aid reach you from them? Are you stuck there in the mountains? See now what is your best course. There is something greater than the mountains, for he before whom the mountains tremble is greater than they. *I have lifted my eyes to the mountains, from where comes help for me*, the psalmist declares; but what follows? *My help is from the Lord, who made heaven and earth* (Ps 120(121):2). To the mountains I have indeed lifted my eyes, because it was through the mountains that the scriptures were shown to me; but I have set my heart on him who sheds light on all mountains.

8. Well now, my brothers and sisters, obviously this declaration was made so that none of you should be minded to pin your hope on any mere human. A human being counts for something only as long as he holds fast to the One by whom all humans were made. Anyone who moves away from him and holds to the mountains instead is nothing at all. Yes, to be sure, you ought to accept guidance that comes through a human agent, but only in such a way that you keep your eyes on him who enlightens all human agents. You can, certainly, draw

---

10. Eponymous leader of the schism that rent the African church during the fourth century and preoccupied Augustine for much of his episcopal career. See note on Exposition of Psalm 10,1.
11. See note at Exposition of Psalm 35,9.

near to God who speaks to you through a human being, for he would not have drawn that man to himself, only to drive you away.

When anyone has come so close to God that God is dwelling within him, it grieves him to see others who do not rely on God. We are given an instance of this in the behavior of those who regarded even the apostles as possessions to which they could lay claim, and were ready to go off into schism, declaring, *I belong to Paul; I belong to Apollos; I belong to Cephas*, that is, Peter. The apostle deplores their attitude and demands, *Is Christ divided?* He looks for someone among them whom he can belittle, and chooses himself: *Was Paul crucified for you? Or were you baptized in the name of Paul?* (1 Cor 1:12-13). In those words you can hear a genuine mountain seeking glory not for himself but for him by whom the mountains are illumined; he did not want people to place their confidence in himself but rather in God, upon whom he, Paul, also relied.

Suppose the case is different, and someone is unwilling to commend himself to the people on those terms; then suppose he happens to be the object of some attack, and he breaks off his followers after him, and splits the Catholic Church in his own cause? Such a person is not one of the mountains illumined by the Most High; so who is he? He is a person darkened by himself, not enlightened by the Lord. How can we tell the genuine mountains? Well, it may come about that some attack is launched against the mountains within the Church, either through vulgar agitation on the part of carnal-minded people or through groundless suspicions others may entertain. An honest mountain shakes off all who want to break away from the unity of the Church on the pretext of supporting him. He will only remain within that unity himself if the unity is not torn apart in his cause. But the other kind were torn away, and when their factions pulled free of the rest of the world, seduced by the leaders' reputation, they were thrilled and elated, but later cast down. If only they had been first humbled, then exalted, as the apostle was humbled when he asked, *Was Paul crucified for you?* and confesses, further on, *I planted, Apollos watered, but God gave the growth. So the planter is nothing, and the one who waters is nothing; only God matters, who grants the increase* (1 Cor 3:6-7). Mountains like this are lowly in their own eyes, but lofty in God's, whereas people who are high and mighty in their own estimation are brought low by God, for *anyone who exalts himself will be humbled, but the one who humbles himself will be exalted* (Lk 14:11). The type of people who are out for their own aggrandizement sow bitterness among peacemakers in the Church. These latter try to consolidate peace, but the others foment dissension. What does another psalm have to say about them? *Let not those who sow bitterness be lifted high in their own esteem* (Ps 65(66):7).

So then, *you send your wondrous light from the eternal mountains*. Notice that the psalm does say, *"You* send."

Verse 6. To be engrossed in temporal goods is to be asleep

9. *All foolish hearts were dismayed.* The truth was preached; the message of eternal life was put about; another life was spoken of, a life not of this earth. So people scorned this present life and fell in love with the life to come, because they were illumined by the mountains that had caught the light first. *Foolish hearts*, though, *were dismayed.* What is this about, why *dismayed*? It was the preaching of the gospel that dismayed them. "What is eternal life? And who is this man who has risen from the dead?" These were the kind of wondering questions put by the Athenians when Paul the apostle spoke to them about the resurrection,[12] for they thought that he was telling them some kind of tall story; but he went on insisting that there is a different life, one that no eye has glimpsed, nor ear caught sound of, nor human heart conceived;[13] and so their *foolish hearts* were perplexed. What happened to them next? *They sank into their native slumber, and no remnant of riches did any of them find in their hands.* They loved the things of this present life, and slept amid them, and found those present things delightful, like someone who dreams that he has discovered treasure, and is a rich man as long as he does not wake up. The dream has made him rich; awakening makes him poor. It may be that sleep claimed him while he was bedded on the ground, lying hard, a poor man, perhaps a beggar; but in his dreams he sees himself reclining on a bed of ivory or gold, relaxing in deep piles of pillows. As long as he slumbers on, his sleep is pleasant, but on awakening he finds himself on the same hard ground where drowsiness overtook him.

The people of whom we were speaking are just like that. They came into this life and through their greed for temporal things they fell asleep here; riches and showy, ephemeral vanities captivated them, and then faded away. They never understood what profit they might have derived from these things. If they had been alert to the future life they would have invested there the wealth that must perish here. Zacchaeus, being a senior tax officer, had an eye to such a profit. On receiving the Lord Jesus as a guest, he declared, *I intend to donate half my property to the poor, and if I have cheated anyone, I will make fourfold restitution* (Lk 19:8). That man was speaking in no dreamer's fantasy, but in the faith of those who are wide awake. Accordingly the Lord, who had entered the house as a doctor visiting a sick man, pronounced Zacchaeus healed: *Salvation has come to this house today, for this man too is a son of Abraham* (Lk 19:9). By this last phrase he showed us how we are Abraham's children by imitating Abraham's faith, whereas the Jews have fallen away from his faith, though they pride themselves on physical descent from him.

Rich men *are sunk in their native slumber, and no remnant of riches do any of them find in their hands.* They have fallen asleep in their greedy desires; this

---

12. See Acts 17:18.32.
13. See 1 Cor 2:9.

slumber is pleasurable, but it passes, as this life also passes away, and they find nothing in their hands because they have entrusted nothing to the hand of Christ.

What about you? Do you hope to find something in your hands hereafter? Then do not disdain the poor man's outstretched hand today. Take heed to empty hands, if you wish to find your own hands full. The Lord said, *I was hungry, and you fed me; I was thirsty, and you gave me a drink; I was a stranger, and you made me welcome*, and so on. And the righteous will reply, *When did we see you hungry, thirsty, or in need of shelter?* His answer is plain, *When you did that for even the least of those who are mine, you did it for me* (Mt 25:35.38.40). He who is rich in heaven has willed to be hungry in the poor. Can you, human as you are, hesitate to give to your fellow-human, when you know that you are making your gift to Christ, from whom you have received all you have to give? But alas, *they sank into their native slumber, and no remnant of riches did any of them find in their hands.*

Verse 7. Pride too is soporific

10. *At your rebuke, O God of Jacob, those who mounted horses fell asleep.* Who are these *who mounted horses*? People who refused to be humble. It is no sin to ride a horse, but to toss one's head proudly against God and think oneself high and mighty—that is sinful. Because you are rich you have mounted your high horse, but God rebukes you and you fall asleep. Fierce must be the anger of him who issues that rebuke, fierce indeed! Consider what a frightening thought this is, beloved: a rebuke is of its nature a noisy thing, and noise generally wakes people up; but God's rebuke falls so heavily that the psalm could say, *At your rebuke, O God of Jacob, those who mounted horses fell asleep!* It was this kind of sleep that overcame Pharaoh when he mobilized his horses; his heart was not wide awake, for the rebukes he had heard had left it hardened, and hardness of heart is like slumber.

Only think, my brothers and sisters, how sleepy are people who still refuse to condemn their old life and awaken to the new, even now, when the gospel resounds throughout the world, with "Amen" and "Alleluia"! The divinely inspired scripture was once found in Judah only, but now it sings through all the earth. In former days that one nation alone proclaimed the one God, maker of all things, as the God to be worshiped and reverenced; but today is there any place where the cry "Christ is risen!" is not heard? He was mocked on the cross, but now he has set that very cross of mockery on the foreheads of kings. And yet people can still sleep? Fierce then must God's anger be, brothers and sisters!

For our part, we heard him to better effect when he invited us, *Arise, sleeper, rise from the dead: Christ will enlighten you.*[14] But who hears him? Those who

---

14. Eph 5:14. Baptism was from an early date called "Enlightenment," and associated with the light of Christ's resurrection.

do not mount horses. And who are they? People who do not flaunt themselves and ride high on their rank and power. *At your rebuke, O God of Jacob, those who mounted horses fell asleep.*

Verse 8. Judgment day will be a rueful awakening

11. *How terrible you are! On that day who will stand against you, who will withstand your anger?* They are asleep now, and unaware of the Lord's anger; but his anger it was that sent them to sleep. What they do not feel now, sunk in slumber, they will feel in the end; for the judge of the living and the dead will appear, and *on that day who will stand against you, who will withstand your anger?* For the time being they say what they like, and argue against God. Tauntingly they ask, "Christians? Who are they? And who is Christ? What fools, to believe in what they cannot see, and give up pleasures they can see, and trust an assurance of things not available to the eyes!"

You are asleep; speak against God in your bleating silliness as far as your strength permits. *How long will sinners gloat, O Lord, how long?* asks the psalmist. *Their answers are no more than bluster* (Ps 93(94):3.4). Will there ever be a time when no one answers like that, no one blusters? Yes, but only when the mocker comes to his senses. When will they turn against themselves those teeth with which they snap at us now, tearing us to pieces as they revile us Christians and sneer at the life of the saints? When the prediction of the Book of Wisdom is verified in their case, then they will come to their senses: *Groaning in anguish of spirit, they will ruefully say to each other*—for when they see the glory of the saints, the cry will be wrung from them—*These are the people we once held in derision!* (Wis 5:3). Yes, you have had a very long sleep, but now you have woken up with a vengeance, and you find yourselves empty-handed. Look at the people you derided as poor, and see how full are their hands with the glory of God. Admit it to yourselves then, when you can no longer resist God's anger, neither by hand nor tongue nor word nor thought; for he whom you took as a butt for your mockery when his coming was announced to you will then appear to you openly. And what will they say? *No doubt of it, we strayed from the path of truth. On us the light of righteousness did not shine, nor did the sun rise for us* (Wis 5:6). How could the sun of righteousness[15] rise for people who were asleep? Yet they sleep now in consequence of his rebuke. Someone may say, "I should not have ridden"; and then they will blame their horses. Listen to them

---

15. See Mal 4:2. The rising sun as a symbol of the risen Christ gathered to itself rich associations. Light had been created on the first day of the week (see Gn 1:3-5), which was also Sun-day and the day of Christ's resurrection. His death was attended by darkness (see Mk 15:33; compare Jn 13:30; Lk 22:53), like a sunset, but was followed by the new dawn of Easter. Ancient peoples outside the Jewish tradition, particularly in Egypt, thought of the sun-god as making a journey below the ocean every night, to reappear as a new, strong sun in the east every morning; the Christian fathers played on this symbolism.

finding fault with the horses on whose backs they fell asleep: *No doubt of it, we strayed from the path of truth. On us the light of righteousness did not shine, nor did the sun rise for us. What good has our pride done us, and what benefit has come to us from our vaunted wealth? All these things have passed away like a shadow* (Wis 5:6.8.9). So you have woken up at last! But it would be better not to mount that horse, and then you would not fall asleep when you ought to stay awake, and you would hear Christ's voice, and Christ would enlighten you. O Lord, *how terrible you are! On that day who will stand against you, who will withstand your anger?* For what will happen then?

Verses 9-10. Earthquake and stillness

12. *When you hurled your judgment from heaven, the earth trembled, and grew still.* Agitated now, talkative now, the earth is destined at the end to be awed and quiet. It would do better to be quiet now, in order to rejoice at the end.

13. *The earth trembled, and grew still.* When was that? *When God arose to judge, to save all the humble of heart.* Who are these humble-hearted? They are people who have not mounted whinnying horses, but have humbly confessed their sins. For them God arose, *to save all the humble of heart.*

Verse 11. Conversion is followed by abiding caution and humility

14. *Human reflection will confess to you, and its abiding traces will keep festival in your presence.* The *reflection* comes first, and after it the *abiding traces* of reflection. Now what is this initial *reflection*? It is the one we begin with, and a very good reflection it is that prompts you to begin your confession; for confession unites us to Christ. But this confession, our first *reflection*, leaves in us its *abiding traces*; and then these *abiding traces will keep festival* in God's presence.

So then, *human reflection will confess to you, and its abiding traces will keep festival in your presence.* What sort of reflection is it that disposes us to confess? It is the frame of mind that condemns one's earlier life, that is dissatisfied with what one has been, in order to become what one was not: that is the first *reflection*. But once this preliminary reflection has brought you to make your confession to God, you must forsake your sins in such a way that you do not forget that you have been a sinner; and it is this very awareness of having been a sinner that leads you to *keep festival in God's presence.*

Let us develop this point more fully. Your initial reflection prompts you to confess, and to abandon your old life; but if you then forget the sins from which you were delivered, you are ungrateful to your deliverer, and so you do not keep festival in his presence.

Take the case of Saul the apostle, the man who became Paul, though he had been Saul at the outset. His preliminary reflection, the one that elicited his confession, came to him when he heard a voice from heaven. He was persecuting Christ, raging against the Christians, and intent on hunting them down wherever they could be found so that he could haul them off to execution. Then he heard the voice from heaven, *Saul, Saul, why are you persecuting me?* (Acts 9:4). Though light shone all round him he was smitten with physical blindness that he might gain interior sight; and he gave effect to his first reflection by obedience, for on hearing the words, *I am Jesus the Nazarene, whom you are persecuting*, he asked, *What do you want me to do, Lord?* (Acts 9:5.6). This is obviously the reflection that prompts him to confess, for already he is addressing as "Lord" the one he has been persecuting.

Now, you have also heard how in Paul's case the *abiding traces* of reflection *will keep festival* in God's presence; you heard it when the apostle's own letter was read, with its injunction, *Remember Jesus Christ, risen from the dead, born of David's lineage, whom my gospel proclaims* (2 Tm 2:8). What does *remember* signify? Do not let that first reflection be blotted out of your memory—the one that led you to confession; rather let the *abiding traces* of that reflection be a lasting memory. With this in mind, observe how the same apostle Paul recalls in another letter the grace that was given to him: *I was originally a persecutor and a blasphemer, and acted unjustly*, he says (1 Tm 1:13). He confesses, *I was originally a blasphemer*, but was he a blasphemer still? Certainly not; his first reflection, determining him to confess, had come to him so that he might be a blasphemer no longer; but the *abiding traces* of his reflection were there to remind him of the grace he had been given, and through those abiding traces he habitually kept solemn festival.

Constant renewal and joy

15. Yes, indeed, my brothers and sisters, think how Christ has made us new. He forgave all our sins, and we turned back to him; but if we forget the grace we have been given, and who gave it, we forget our Savior's gift. But if we do not forget his gift, is not Christ being sacrificed for us every day? It is true that Christ was sacrificed for us once for all, when we first believed, and that was our reflection; but now when we recall what happened to us, and the grace that we were given, these memories are *the abiding traces* of our reflection. Through them, which is to say through our memory, he is sacrificed for us daily in such a way as to renew us every day, as once he made us new by his initial grace. The Lord renewed us in baptism, and we became new men, new women, rejoicing certainly in our hope, that hope that gives us patience under trials;[16] yet the grace

_____

16. See Rom 12:12.

granted to us must never fade from our memory. If your reflection is no longer what once it was (and it hardly could be, for your first thought was to turn away from sin, and you are not in the act of turning away from it now, as you were then), at least maintain the abiding traces of reflection, lest you let slip from your memory who it was that healed you. If you once forget that you had a wound, it means that the abiding traces of reflection are no longer there for you.

What do you make of David's declaration? He was unquestionably speaking for us all. David was a holy man, yet he sinned gravely; the prophet Nathan was sent to him, and rebuked him, and David confessed, *I have sinned* (2 Sm 12:13). This was the first reflection, that of a man confessing his sin, as the psalm has it: *human reflection will confess to you.* Where, then, were the *abiding traces* of his reflection? They were there, surely, when he avowed, *My sin confronts me all the time* (Ps 50:5(51:3)). Now, what was his first reflection? The decision to turn away from sin. But if he has already done that, how comes it that his sin is always confronting him? It can only be because the initial reflection has passed away, but the *abiding traces* of reflection are keeping solemn festival.

Let us keep ourselves mindful, I beg you, dearest brothers and sisters. Everyone who has been freed from sin needs to remember what he or she was formerly; the *abiding traces* of reflection must live on in that person. We are able to carry others towards healing only if we remember that we have been healed ourselves. Each of us must bear in mind what we were, and ask ourselves whether we are still like that; then we shall be in a position to help someone else who is still in that state where we are no longer. If any of us boasts as though he could take the credit for this himself, and spurns sinners as unworthy of his company, and is harsh and merciless toward them, that person is mounting his high horse, and should watch out that sleep does not overtake him, for *those who mounted horses fell asleep.* Such a person gave up his horse some time ago, so he has no business to ride it again: no business, that is, to hoist himself up onto pride. How can he avoid doing so? By letting the *abiding traces* of his reflection keep solemn festival for God.

Verse 12. Different kinds of vows, but all demand constancy

16. *Make your vows to the Lord your God and carry them out.*[17] Each of us should vow what is within our power, and keep the vow. Do not make a vow and then fail to keep it; no, let each make a vow according to his or her capacity and then see it through. Do not hang back from making your vow, for it is not by your own strength that you will fulfill it. If you rely on yourselves you will fail, but if you are relying on him to whom your vow is offered, go ahead and make it, and you need have no anxiety about its fulfillment.

---

17. The whole of this section 16 is found also in Sermon 135, 1-5, by Caesarius of Arles.

Make your vows to the Lord your God and carry them out. Are there any vows that all of us, without distinction, have to make? Yes, we should vow to believe in him, to hope for eternal life as his gift, and to lead the good lives expected of ordinary people; for there is a general pattern of life prescribed for us all. Take the commandment not to steal: this is not an injunction laid upon a nun but irrelevant to a married woman; similarly the commandment not to commit adultery is binding on all; addiction to excessive drinking, which gluts the soul and defiles the temple of God within us, is forbidden to everyone equally; not to be proud is an injunction binding upon all alike; and all of us without distinction are commanded not to kill, not hate our brother or sister, and not to plot another's ruin. All of us have a duty to vow this way of life in its entirety.

There are also vows proper to particular persons. One man vows conjugal chastity to God, promising to have carnal relations with no woman other than his wife; and similarly a woman vows to have no man except her husband. There are others who, although experienced in marital intercourse, vow to be the playthings of passion no more, to desire and continue in such relationships no longer; and these are vowing something greater than the former. Others again vow virginity itself from an early age, promising not even to experience what those others have experienced and then given up; and these have vowed the greatest thing of all. Others make a vow to dedicate their home as a place where any of God's people who pass by may find a welcome, and a generous vow it is that they are making. Another person vows to renounce all his possessions and distribute them to the poor, and enter a company of holy men to live a common life; and he is making a noble vow.

Make your vows to the Lord your God and carry them out. Let each one, then, offer by vow whatever he or she will, only taking care to keep the vow once it is made. If anyone offers something to God by vow and then looks back, that is wrong. Suppose a nun wants to marry: what is it that she desires? Only what any unmarried girl desires. What does she want? Only what her mother wanted. Has she desired anything bad, then? Yes, certainly she has. Why? Because she had already made her vow to the Lord her God. What did the apostle Paul have to say about such cases? Admittedly he says that younger widows may remarry if they wish,[18] yet in one place he says of a widow, *In my opinion, she will be better off if she remains as she is* (1 Cor 7:40). He points out that such a woman will be happier if she keeps her present status; but he does not think she is to be condemned if she wishes to remarry. But what does he say of certain others who made vows and did not keep them? *They are worthy of censure, because they have broken their original pledge* (1 Tm 5:12). In what sense have they *broken their original pledge*? By making a vow but failing to carry it through. No brother who is a member of a monastic community has the right to say, "I'm leaving. After all, it's not only

---

18. See 1 Tm 5:14.

people in monasteries who are heading for the kingdom of heaven, as though God didn't care about all the rest." The right answer to that is, "But they have not taken vows. You have, yet you have looked back."

What was it that the Lord had to say when he was warning us about the day of judgment? *Remember Lot's wife* (Lk 17:32). And this he said to all. Now, what did Lot's wife do? She was rescued from Sodom, but on the way out she looked back, and in that spot where she looked back, she stuck fast.[19] She was turned into a pillar of salt so that other people might be seasoned by her example; they are to have the good sense not to turn insipid, not to look back, lest they remain fixed there themselves, as a bad example that provides seasoning for others. We take the same line today with any of our brethren whom we may happen to notice weakening in their good resolve. "Do you want to be like *him?*" we ask, reminding them of those who have looked back. Insipid in themselves, such persons are seasoning for others when their tale is told, for other people are cautioned against looking back by their example.[20]

Make your vows to the Lord your God and carry them out, for Lot's wife is a lesson to us all. Suppose a married woman has desired to commit adultery: she has looked back from the place she had reached. Or a widow who had vowed to remain in that state desired to marry; what she desired was something legitimate for a bride, but not for her, because she looked back from her own place. Or a virgin has become a nun and is already consecrated to God; let her make sure to have all the other adornments that truly belong to virginity, without which even virginity is a disgrace. What is the point of physical integrity, if her mind is corrupt? What do I mean by saying this? No man has touched her body – but what if she is perhaps a drunkard, or proud, or argumentative, or a chatterbox? God condemns all such habits. If before taking her vow she had married she would not be condemned; but she chose a better course and overleapt what was right, only to do great wrong by overweening pride. What I mean is this: before one takes a vow, marriage is legitimate; but pride is never legitimate. Mark this, virgin dedicated to God: you refused marriage, which is permitted; but now you are haughty, which is not permitted. A humble virgin is better than a humble matron, but a humble matron is better than a proud virgin. If she turns her eyes towards marriage, she is not condemned because she wants to marry, but because she had already gone beyond that, and becomes a Lot's wife by looking back.

You must not hesitate to do what is in your power, you whom God inspires to grasp at some more honorable station, for we are not talking like this to deter you

---

19. See Gn 19:26.
20. The resemblance between this long development on keeping vows, and a similar development in Exposition of Psalm 83,4, may indicate that the two sermons were delivered on successive days. The use of the text, *Remember Lot's wife,* is common to both, and does not occur elsewhere.

from making vows, but only to urge you to keep the vows you make: *make your vows to the Lord your God and carry them out.* Perhaps you were intending to make a vow, but now, after listening to this discussion, you no longer want to? But consider carefully what the psalm has said to you. It did not say, "Do not make vows," but *Make your vows and carry them out.* Does the phrase *carry them out* put you off? Did you, then, intend to make a vow and not keep it? No, you must do both. The first is your promise, the second is achieved by God's help. Keep your eyes on him who is leading you, and you will not look back to that place from which he is leading you out. He who leads you is walking ahead of you; the place he is leading you away from lies behind. Love him who leads you, and he will not condemn you for looking back. *Make your vows to the Lord your God and carry them out.*

Truth is central because it is the common property of all

17. *Let all who are round about him offer him gifts.* Who are these round about him? Where is he, that the psalm can speak of *all who are round about him*? If you think it refers to God the Father, from what place is he absent, he who is present everywhere? If you think of the Son in his godhead, he is present everywhere with his Father, for he is the Wisdom of God, of whom it was said, *Wisdom pervades everything because she is so pure* (Wis 7:24). If, on the other hand, you think it refers to the Son in the humanity he assumed, in which he appeared among us, and was crucified, and rose again—well, we know that he has ascended into heaven. So who are round about him there? The angels. Perhaps, then, it is not for us to offer gifts, because the psalm says, *Let all who are round about him offer him gifts.* If our Lord had been buried here on earth, and his body were lying here like that of some martyr or apostle, we would think the psalm referred to the people nearby, whether they were the local inhabitants or pilgrims who converged upon the place with gifts. But in fact he has ascended; he is up above.

What can it mean, then, *let all who are round about him offer him gifts*? For the present I will tell you what God brings to my mind about this, and expound the interpretation of the phrase which he has deigned to inspire in me. If later on some other meaning seems preferable, that too shall be offered to you as of right, because truth is the common patrimony of us all. There is no mine or yours, no his or hers, where truth is concerned; it belongs to all equally. Perhaps it can be thought of as situated in the middle, so that all who love truth can cluster around it, for whatever belongs to everyone is in the middle of them. But why the middle? So that it is equally far from everyone, and equally near to everyone. Whatever is not centrally placed tends to be cornered as private property. A public thing is placed in the middle so that everyone who comes may see it and be illumined by it. No one has the right to say, "That is mine," for that would be to attempt to draw into one's own corner what is central for all.

If we are on the right lines, then, what do these words mean, *let all who are round about him offer him gifts*? The people who are bidden to offer gifts are all those who understand that truth belongs to everyone, and do not presume to claim it as their own by taking the credit for it, because these are the humble-minded. Other folk, who claim as their own what is centrally placed and thus common to all, are trying to appropriate it for their own faction; and they have no business to offer gifts, because it is *all who are round about him* who are to *offer gifts to him who is terrible*.

Gifts are to be offered to him who is terrible, and therefore all who gather round him must be filled with fear. They have good reason to be afraid, and to praise him with reverent awe, because they are gathered round him for no other purpose than that everyone may have access to him, and he may flow over all of them together, and openly shed his light upon them all. In other words, their reverent awe is shared. But if you try to make him your private property, rather than the common possession of all, you are proudly exalting yourself, for scripture tells us to *serve the Lord in reverence, and rejoice before him with awe* (Ps 2:11). So then, let those who gather round him offer him gifts, for these are the humble folk who know that truth belongs to all without distinction.

Verse 13. Gifts are offered by those who have the Lord's Spirit

18. To whom are they to offer their gifts? *To him who is terrible, and cuts off the breath of princes*. Now the spirit or the breath of princes is the spirit of pride, and therefore no spirit of his. If they have acquired some knowledge, they want to hug it to themselves rather than making it public. He, on the contrary, entrusts himself freely and equally to all, and puts himself in the middle so that all may take as much as they can and whatever they can; and what they take is not something from any man's spirit, but from God's, and therefore from what is their own, since they have become his. Inevitably, then, all such people must be humble: they have lost their own spirit and now possess the Spirit of God. Who took their own spirit from them, their own breath? He who *cuts off the breath of princes*; for indeed the psalmist says to him in another place, *When you withdraw their breath, they die, and return to the dust whence they came. But you will breathe forth your Spirit and they will be created, and you will make the face of the earth new* (Ps 103(104):29-30).

When someone has understood some truth, and wants to keep it for himself, that person still has his own spirit. He would be better off losing his own spirit and receiving the Spirit of God. He is still strutting proudly among the princes; he would do better to return to his native dust and declare, *Remember, O Lord, that we are dust* (Ps 102(103):14). If you confess that you are dust, God makes a human being out of that dust.

All who gather round him offer him their gifts; all the humble-hearted praise and adore him. *To him who is terrible* they make their offerings. But why terrible? *Rejoice before him with awe*, before him who *cuts off the breath of princes*, before him, that is, who strips away the arrogance of the proud.

To him who is terrible among the kings of the earth. The kings of the earth are terrible enough, but he is supreme over all of them, he who strikes terror into earthly kings. You must try to be king of the earth yourself, and then God will be terrible for you. You will ask me, "How can I be king of the earth?" Rule your own earth, then you will be its sovereign. This means that you should not fantasize about exercising dominion over vast countries where you might extend your sway; no, rule the earth that you carry with you. Think how the apostle ruled his portion of earth: *I do not deal blows like someone merely flailing at the air*, he says. *I chastise my body and bring it under control, lest while preaching to others I be disqualified myself* (1 Cor 9:26-27).

Gathered round the truth in humility, we worship the Lord

Make sure, then, my brothers and sisters, that you are gathered around the Lord, so that you do not ascribe truth to its spokesman, whoever he or she may be through whom the truth reaches you. Rather let it be found in the middle and available to all, as it is equally near to everyone. And be humble, taking care that you do not arrogate to yourselves any portion of that good which you may chance to understand. For our part, the best of our understanding belongs to you, and the best of your understanding belongs to us, so that we may all gather round and be humble. In this way we shall lose our own spirit; and then let us offer gifts to him who in his terrible majesty is Lord over all the kings of the earth, that is, over all those who rule their own flesh, but subject themselves to their Creator.

Exposition of Psalm 76

A Sermon to the People

Verse 1. Idithun, the leaper

1. Inscribed over the doorway into this psalm are the words, *To the end, for Idithun, a psalm for Asaph's own use*. Now you know what *to the end* means, for *Christ is the end of the law, bringing justification to everyone who believes* (Rom 10:4). "Idithun" is to be translated "one who leaps across them," and "Asaph" means "a congregation." So the speaker here is a congregation that leaps across something in order to reach the end, which is Christ Jesus. The text of the psalm points out what we must leap over to arrive at that end where we shall no longer find any obstacles to be overleapt.[1] But for the present we certainly must go on leaping over whatever gets in our way, anything that entangles us, anything that clogs us with its sticky toils or makes us too heavy to fly; and we must go on doing this until we arrive at final satisfaction in that reality beyond which there is nothing else. All other things are below this and derive from it. When Philip begged the Lord Jesus Christ, *Show us the Father, and that is enough for us* (Jn 14:8), he was longing to gaze on nothing less. He meant that he wanted to go on leaping over everything else until he reached the Father, but once there he would stand still and untroubled and have no need to seek anything further, as his words, *that is enough*, imply. But Christ, who had claimed in all truthfulness, *I and the Father are one*, chided Philip, and in so doing taught everyone who wished to understand him that they should look for their end in him as well, because he and the Father are one. *Have I been all this time with you, and yet you have not truly seen me?* he asked. *Whoever has seen me, Philip, has seen the Father* (Jn 14:9).

If anyone longs to enter into the spirit of this psalm, to imitate the psalmist and grasp his meaning, such a person must leap over all carnal desires, tread underfoot the ostentation and allurements of this world, and aim at no other place of sure standing than in him who is the source of all else. The psalmist too is laboring at this task until he reaches the end. So what has this swift leaper to tell us?

---

1. Augustine also meditates on Idithun, the leaper, in his Exposition of Psalm 38.

Verse 2. Asking God for God alone

2. *I lifted up my voice and cried to the Lord,* he says. But many people cry to the Lord about riches they hope to gain or losses they want to avoid, or for the safety of their nearest and dearest, or for the security of their household, or temporal happiness, or worldly advancement; or even perhaps just for bodily fitness, which is wealth to a poor man. Many people pray for these and similar things to the Lord, but hardly anyone prays for the Lord himself. Indeed, it seems quite easy for a person to want something from the Lord without wanting the Lord himself, as though anything he gives could be more delightful than the giver. Evidently, then, a person who cries to the Lord for any other thing is not yet leaping over it.

But what does our leaping psalmist say? *I lifted up my voice and cried to the Lord.* But then he wants to guard against your thinking that he raised his voice to ask the Lord for anything other than the Lord himself, and so he adds, *And my voice was directed to God.* We may use our voice as an instrument for crying to God, and yet that voice may be directed to some other thing, not to God; for the voice is directed to whatever object evokes it. How different the psalmist! He loved God without looking for reward, he was accustomed freely to offer sacrifice to God, he had leapt over everything below him and had seen that there was nothing else above him to which he could pour his heart out, nothing except the One by whom and through whom and in whom he had been created. To God had the psalmist lifted up his voice, and he made sure that his voice was for God alone: *My voice was directed to God,* he says.

And for good reason. Look at the next line: *and he hearkened to me.* He does indeed hearken to you when you seek him, but perhaps not when you seek something else through him. Another psalm says of certain people, *They cried to the Lord, but there was no one to save them, they cried but he did not listen to them* (Ps 17:42(18:41)). Why not? Because their voice was not directed to the Lord. Scripture makes the same point in another place, saying of some people that *they have not invoked the Lord.*[2] They cried to him unremittingly, yet *they have not invoked the Lord.* What does that mean, *they have not invoked the Lord?* They have not called the Lord into themselves, have not invited the Lord into their hearts, have not wanted the Lord to dwell within them. So what happened to them? *They quaked with fear where there was nothing to fear* (Ps 13:5(14:4-5)). Obviously they were terrified at the prospect of losing the good things they had, because they were not full of God, never having invoked him. They did not love him disinterestedly in such a way that they would have been able to say of the loss of their temporal possessions, *This has happened as the Lord willed: may*

---

2. Latin *Dominum non invocaverunt.* In the following lines Augustine plays on the strict meaning of *invoco,* to "call into" (oneself). See his Exposition of Psalm 74,2, and note there.

the Lord's name be blessed (Jb 1:21). The psalmist, though, says, *My voice was directed to the Lord, and he hearkened to me.* Now let him teach us how to do it.

Verse 3. Praying with outstretched hands in the night

3. *On my day of trouble I searched for God.* Who are you, who need to do this? Consider now what you may be seeking on your day of trouble. If your trouble consists of being in prison, you seek to get out of prison; if fever is troubling you, you seek recovery; if your trouble is hunger, you seek to be filled; if losses have brought trouble upon you, profit is what you seek; if journeying abroad is a trouble to you, what you seek is your native land. Why need I mention all these—indeed, how could I find time to enumerate all possible troubles? On the day of your own particular trouble, seek God: not some other thing through God, but God himself in the midst of your trouble. Ask God to take away the trouble, so that you may be united with him in peace of mind. *On my day of trouble I searched for God*; God was what I sought, and nothing else, says the psalmist.

And how did you go about it? *With hands outstretched before him I sought him in the night.* Say that again, so that we may see what you mean, and understand you, and imitate you if we can. On your day of trouble what did you seek? *God.* How did you seek him? *With hands outstretched.* When? *In the night.* Where? *Before him.* And what was the outcome of your search? *I was not disappointed.*

Let us examine all these points, my brothers and sisters, let us ponder them and scrutinize them all. We must try to see what this trouble was in which the psalmist sought God, how he could search for God with his hands, what it meant to do so in the night, and what it was to seek in his presence. The phrase that follows everyone can understand: *I was not disappointed*; for what else does that mean except "I found what I was seeking"?

4. We must not think that he is referring merely to this or that particular trouble. I mean, when a person is not yet "leaping over," the only things that seem to be troubles are the sad events that may occur in the course of this life; but for our agile psalmist it is life as a whole that is the trouble. So ardently is he in love with his heavenly homeland that this earthly pilgrimage is for him the greatest trouble of all. I put it to you: how could this life be anything else but trouble? How could it not be, when scripture calls it one long temptation? In the Book of Job you will find it written, *Is not human life on earth all temptation?* (Jb 7:1). Did he say, "subject to temptation"? No. Our life in itself is all temptation, and if it is temptation, it must of necessity be trouble. In this trouble, then, which means in life as a whole, our leaping psalmist searched for God. How did he do it? *With hands outstretched*, he says. What does that mean? With my actions. He was not searching for some material thing, as though trying to lay his

hands on something he had lost, feeling about for a coin, gold, silver, a garment, or some other thing like that which we might grope for with our hands. Our Lord Jesus Christ himself did indeed will to be sought after by exploring hands when he showed his scars to a doubting disciple; but when this man touched the marks of the wounds and cried out, *My Lord and my God*, did he not hear in reply, *Because you have seen, you have believed; blessed are those who have not seen, yet have believed* (Jn 20:28-29)? A disciple who sought Christ with his hands deserved to hear himself rebuked for seeking in that fashion; is it right, then, that we should so seek him with our hands, we who have been pronounced blessed for believing without seeing? Yes, it is. It is our business, as I have said, to seek him by our actions.

And when should this be done? *In the night*. What does *in the night* mean? It means in this world, for here it is still night until daylight floods the skies at the coming of our Lord Jesus Christ in glory. Would you like me to demonstrate that it is still night-time for us? Well, Peter tells us that if we did not have a lantern here, we should be in permanent darkness: *We have the trusty message of the prophets to rely on*, he says, *and you will do well to attend to it, for it is like a lantern burning in a dark place until day breaks and the morning star rises in your hearts* (2 Pt 1:19). Day will dawn, then, after this night; and meanwhile the night is not left without a lamp. Perhaps that is an image of what we are doing at this very moment, for by expounding these scriptures we are bringing in a lamp, so that even amid our night we may find joy. But it must be kept alight always in your own homes, for to people like yourselves Paul addressed his injunction, *Do not quench the Spirit* (1 Thes 5:19); and he makes his meaning clear by adding, *Do not despise prophecy* (1 Thes 5:20), which is to say, "Let the lamp burn within you at all times." Yet the light it affords us is called night by comparison with a day too wonderful to describe, for though the life of the faithful is daylight indeed when contrasted with the life of unbelievers, it can in another sense be called night, and we have shown how this is the case by reference to the apostle Peter. He too mentioned a lamp, advising us to pay attention to the luminous prophetic message *until day breaks and the morning star rises in* our *hearts*. Paul, on the other hand, showed how the life of the faithful is already daylight in contrast to that of the godless, for *Let us cast off the deeds of darkness and don the armor of light*, he bids us. *Let us walk honorably as in daylight* (Rom 13:12). So when we live honorably we are in daylight, which is not true of the godless.

But this daylight in which the faithful pass their lives is not enough for Idithun. He wants to leap over even this day, until he reaches that other day where he need have no fear whatever of the temptation that lurks in the night; for here and now, even though the life of believers is bright with day, still *human life on earth is all temptation*. It is both night and day: day by comparison with that of unbelievers, but night by comparison with that of the angels, who have a daylight we do not yet enjoy. We, the faithful, already have a daylight which unbelievers do not have, but we do not yet have that daylight in which the angels live, though believers will have it when they are made equal to God's angels, as they are promised they will be at the resurrection.[3]

So then, let us seek God with outstretched hands now, when it is already day yet still night: night by contrast with that future day for which we long, but day by contrast with the former night we have left behind. Yes, in this night, I say, let us seek him. Let our works not flag; let us seek God, not yearn ineffectually for him. If we are on the way, let us spend whatever is necessary to bring us to the goal: let us seek God by our actions. Although it is by night that we seek him for whom our hands are groping, we are not disappointed, because our search is conducted *before him*. What does this mean—before him, in his presence? The gospel tells us, *Do not perform your good actions in the presence of other people, in order to be seen by them; otherwise you will have no reward from your Father.* When you give alms those hands of yours are seeking God, so *have no trumpet sounded before you, as do the hypocrites. Rather let your almsgiving be done in secret, and your Father, who sees what is done in secret, will reward you* (Mt 6:1.2.4). To sum up, *with hands outstretched before him in the night* I sought him, *and I was not disappointed*.

5. Now let us listen with keen attention to what great sufferings Idithun had to endure on this earth and throughout this night, and hear how he was almost forced to leap over all of them, as afflictions dashed against him here below and pierced him through, providing the impetus for his leap. *"My soul refused to be comforted.* Such disgust overwhelmed me that my soul closed itself against all consolation," he complains. Why would such a person feel disgust? Could it be because his vineyard had been spoiled by hail, or he had no yield of olive oil, or his vintage was disrupted by rain? No? Then why would this man feel disgusted? Listen to the answer in another psalm, for the same voice speaks there too: *Disgust possessed me at the sinners who abandon your law* (Ps 118(119):53). So great was the disgust that oppressed him in consequence of this wrong, he tells us, that his soul refused all comfort. Disgust had all but engulfed him; grief had swamped him beyond all hope of rescue; he refuses to be comforted. What was left to him?

Verse 4. Disappointed in human support, he finds comfort in God

6. To begin with, consider where he might have expected to find comfort. Had he looked for someone to come and share his sorrow, and found none?[4] Where could he turn to find consolation, when disgust overwhelmed him at the sinners who forsook God's law? Whither could he turn? To some man of God?

---

3. See Mt 22:30.
4. See Ps 68:21(69:20).

But perhaps he had in the past been sadly disappointed in many such people, and all the more so for having expected to find delight in their company. Sometimes righteous people emerge, and we rejoice over them; our joy is natural because charity like this cannot but give rise to joy. But then it may happen that some disgraceful thing is discovered in the people who aroused it, as does indeed happen often, and then our grief is the greater in proportion to the intensity of our earlier delight—so much so that afterward one is afraid to give free rein to joy, and fearful of being unreservedly glad, lest if something goes wrong one's embarrassment may be as acute as one's enjoyment was keen.

The psalmist had been pierced by frequent scandals as by multiple wounds, so he shut his door against human comfort, and his soul refused consolation. Whence could he draw life? Whence any breath of refreshment? *I remembered God, and the memory filled me with delight.* His hands had not worked in vain; they had found a powerful consoler. Not through indolence was he able to say, *I remembered God, and the memory filled me with delight.* It is God who is to be proclaimed as glorious, therefore, since this man remembered him and was delighted with the memory,[5] was consoled in sadness and as though made new after almost despairing of salvation; it is God who is to be extolled.

Then at last, consoled now, the psalmist admits, *I babbled.*[6] "As consolation flooded me, I remembered God, and babbled with delight." What does this signify, *babbled?* "I rejoiced, and chattered exultantly." The people commonly called chatterboxes are properly described as babblers,[7] because when happy they have neither the power nor the wish to be silent. The psalmist came to resemble them. What does he say next? *And my spirit fainted away.*

Verse 5. Never relax your vigilance

7. He had been pining away with disgust, then he had found delight in remembering God; but then he had weakened again in his babbling, for what does he tell us next? *All my enemies outdid me in watchfulness.* All my foes spied on me intently; they were more and more vigilant; so alert were they that they caught me out. Is any place free from the traps they lay? Have my enemies not thwarted all my attempts to be watchful?

Now who are these enemies? Evidently those of whom the apostle warned us: *It is not against flesh and blood that you have to struggle, but against principalities and powers and the rulers of this world of darkness, against wicked spiritual*

---

5. In the background is Augustine's doctrine of *memoria* as more than a repository of knowledge derived from sense-impressions received in the individual's past: *memoria* is the place where the mind is in contact with all the intelligible truth of which it is capable, the place where it knows itself and knows God.

6. *Garrivi.*

7. *Garruli.*

beings in heavenly realms (Eph 6:12). Against the devil and his angels, then, we must do battle. He called them world-rulers because they hold sway over the lovers of this world; they are not world-rulers in the sense of having authority over heaven and earth: for "world" here means sinners. *The world did not know him* (Jn 1:10): this is the kind of world they rule,[8] the world that did not know Christ. Against these we must wage war without end. If you are at odds with human beings it is different, because then you seek a settlement, either by demanding an apology if they have injured you, or by making amends yourself if you have wronged them, or by making concessions on both sides, if the injury was mutual. You strive for some agreement and conciliation. With the devil and his angels no conciliation is possible. They begrudge us the kingdom of heaven. They are utterly incapable of any softening of attitude towards us, all those enemies who *outdid me in watchfulness*. They have been more alert to trick me than I have been to keep myself safe: *all my enemies outdid me in watchfulness.* They have placed stumbling-blocks and laid traps everywhere. What else is this but far-sighted watchfulness? If you weary at heart you should beware that sadness does not overwhelm you; but at times of happiness you must beware lest your spirit be dissipated by chatter. *All my enemies outdid me in watchfulness.* Moreover, when you are talking, and talking very freely, how often amid light-hearted banter there are plenty of things your enemies can pick on and find fault with, things they will eagerly use to misrepresent and discredit you: "This is what he said, that is what he thought, such was his express opinion!"[9]

What is one to do, then? All we can do is take the advice that follows: *I was troubled, and I did not speak.* The psalmist was troubled in case his enemies, alert and vigilant, might seek and find some ground of accusation in his babbling, so he held his tongue; but never would he give up his inward effort to leap over these things. He had to give up babbling, perhaps, because some tendency to seek human approval may have crept into that conversation; but never did he slacken, never did he abandon the effort to transcend this also. So what does he say now?

Verse 6. In silence, he ponders on the mystery of time

8. *I thought about bygone days.* He is like someone who has been thrashed outside, and so has taken refuge indoors, and now transacts his business in the private retreat of his own mind. Let him tell us what this business is. *I thought*

---

8. Scripture and patristic tradition use the word "world" in at least three senses: a) the totality of the material creation; b) this creation as dominated by evil powers and hostile to Christ, or a source of temptation to believers (see 1 Jn 2:15-16); this sense is common in John and is in Augustine's mind here; c) the erring but redeemable creation as loved by God, who sent his Son to save it (see Jn 3:16-17).

9. Perhaps an experience familiar to Augustine himself.

about bygone days. Excellent! Observe the subject of his thoughts, I beg you. He is within, and in his own heart he reflects on bygone days. No one says to him there, "You have said the wrong thing"; no one says to him, "You have talked too much"; no one says to him, "Your opinions are perverse." So let him be content within himself, and may God help him. Let him think about bygone days, and let him tell us what he did in that inner retreat, where his thinking led him, what he leapt over, and where he found a place to abide. *I thought about bygone days, and called to mind the years of eternity.* What are the years of eternity? What a tremendous effort of thought! How can it be achieved without profound silence? Anyone who aspires to think about the years of eternity needs to be at peace, free from all external din and the turmoil of human affairs.

Well now, are the years in which we live eternal, or were those years eternal through which our forebears lived, or will our children's years be eternal? It is unthinkable that any of them should be eternal, for what remains of those years? You know how we commonly say, "This year . . ."; but how much of this year do we have in our grasp, except the current day? The earlier days of this year have passed already, and we cannot hold onto them; while the future days have not yet come. We are living in one day only, yet we say, "This year." You ought to say, "Today," if you want to indicate what is present; for what do you hold as present out of this whole year? The part of it that has passed exists no longer, and the part of it that is still to come does not exist yet. So how can you say, "This year"? Speak more accurately: say, "Today." Yes, you reply, you are right. I will henceforth say, "Today."

But you still need to pay attention to your language, because the early morning hours have already passed, while the later hours have not yet arrived. Correct your mode of speech then; say, "This hour." But how much of this hour is within your grasp? Some of its seconds have already flown by, and those still left have not come yet. Say, "This moment," then. But what moment? It is gone even while I am pronouncing its syllables! Look: two syllables, "mo-ment." The second is not audible until the first has died away. Even if we take a single syllable, a syllable composed of two letters, the second letter cannot make itself heard until the first has faded. What, then, can we hold onto of our years? These years are subject to change.[10] We must focus our thoughts on the years of eternity, the years that are stable, the years that are not a succession of days that arrive and pass away, the years of which scripture says to God in another text, *You are the selfsame, and your years will not fail* (Ps 101:28(102:27)). On these years our leaping psalmist reflected, not in external babbling but within, in silence: *I called to mind the years of eternity.*

---

10. Augustine was fascinated by the mystery of time, the volatile, elusive dimension of creatureliness. He wrestles with it in Book XI of his *Confessions*, showing how the habit of thinking of time as something we can hold onto is a self-delusion and an implicit denial of our slide towards non-being. Only eternity abides.

Verse 7. He searches his spirit

9. *I meditated and communed with my heart.* No one was seeking grounds for accusation against him by ensnaring him in words, so he meditated in his heart. *And I was babbling.* Here is this babbling once more! Take care yet again, in case your spirit faints away. "No," he replies, "this is not the same kind as that earlier, outward babbling; I am babbling quite differently now." So how are you doing it this time? *I babbled, and searched my spirit.* If he were searching the earth to find seams of gold, no one would think him stupid; on the contrary, many would deem him a wise man for wanting to strike gold. Yet what riches does every person have inside, without needing to dig! This man was searching his spirit, conversing with his own spirit, and in that exchange he was babbling. He habitually questioned himself, examined himself, and sat in judgment on himself. So he continues, *I was searching my spirit.* There is a danger, though, that he may remain in his spirit; for when he babbled outside himself, all his enemies outdid him in watchfulness, and so he found only sadness there, and his spirit fainted away. Whereupon this man who had been babbling outwardly took to babbling inwardly instead, where he was safe, where in silence and alone he called to mind the years of eternity. *And I probed my spirit,* he says. There is a danger, therefore, that he may become stuck within his spirit, and be a leaper no more. Still, he is doing better now than he was when preoccupied outside himself. He has left something behind, and from these words we can learn where he is bound for. He is a leaper, and will not rest until he reaches *the end,* as the title of the psalm indicates. *I babbled, and searched my spirit.*

Verse 8. God will not finally reject us

10. And what did you find there? That *God will not reject us for ever.* Weariness was all he had found in this life, and nowhere any solid, reliable consolation. He looked to certain people, but found scandal in them, or at least feared it. Nowhere was he safe. To keep silence was wrong, because that would mean holding back from profitable speech; to talk and babble to other people was a worry to him, for all those enemies who outdid him in vigilance would sift his words for some charge to bring against him. Grievously hampered in this life, he pondered on another life, where there would be no such trial. But when would he reach it? It cannot but be evident that what we are suffering here is the anger of God. Through Isaiah God tells us, *I will not punish you without end, nor be angry with you for ever.* And he explains why not: *From me, who gave life to all, a breath of life will go forth. For a little while I afflicted him on account of his sin, and struck him, and turned my face away from him; and so he went away sad and walked in his own ways* (Is 57:16.17). Will this anger of God be everlasting, then? No, this is not what the psalmist discovered in his silence, for what does he

tell us? *God will not reject us for ever; he will not always be content with that.* He will not go on being content to reject us; and so he will not continue to reject us without end. It is necessary that he call his servants back to him, necessary that he welcome the deserters who return to the Lord, necessary that he hear the pleas of the captives. *God will not reject us for ever; he will not always be content with that.*

Verses 9-10. Assurance of mercy

11. *Will he persist in cutting off his mercy from one generation to the next? Will God forget to be merciful?* You have no source of mercy in yourself; you can show mercy to someone else only because God confers it on you as a gift. Will God himself, then, forget how to be merciful? While the stream flows on, will its very source dry up? *Will God forget to be merciful? Or will he curb his mercies with anger?* In other words, will he be so angry as to exclude pity for us? More easily would he curb his anger than his mercy. This is what God had proclaimed through Isaiah: *I will not punish you without end, nor be angry with you for ever.* And he continued, *Man went away sad and walked in his own ways. But I saw where those ways led him, and I healed him* (Is 57:16-18).

When the psalmist realized this he was so delighted with God that he left even himself behind in order to be with God and babble all the more about God's works, not in his own spirit, nor as the person he was, but in God, by whom he had been created. So he leapt, and left this place behind. Look at this leaper, and see whether he pauses anywhere short of God.

Verses 11-13. The joyful leap; delight in God's natural creation

12. *And I said ...* Yes? What did he say, as he made this leap beyond himself? *Now I have begun!* For I have found my way even out of myself. *Now I have begun!* There is no more danger here; it was remaining in myself that was dangerous. *And I said, Now I have begun! This is a change wrought by the hand of the Most High.* Now the Most High has begun to change me; now I have begun something, here in this place where I can be free from anxiety, now that I have entered a hall of joys where there is no enemy to fear, where none of my foes can outdo me in watchfulness: *Now I have begun! This is a change wrought by the hand of the Most High.*

13. *I was mindful of the works of the Lord.* Watch him now, as he strolls at leisure amid the Lord's works. Babbling away outside himself brought him only sadness, and his spirit pined in consequence, but when he babbled within his own heart, with his own spirit as listener, and when he had probed that spirit, then he called to mind the years of eternity and reflected that the Lord is merciful

and will not reject us for ever. And then, unworried, he began to rejoice in the Lord's works, and to make merry without anxiety.

Let us listen to those same works, and rejoice too, but let us make sure that the impetus of our affections sends us leaping over ourselves, for we must not dally with temporal joys. We too have our inner retreat. Why do we not enter it? Why do we not conduct our business there in silence? Why do we not probe our spirits? Why do we not reflect on the years of eternity, and why are we not gladdened by God's works?

But now at least let us listen in that same readiness, and be gladdened indeed as he speaks to us, so that after we have returned home we may continue to do what we were doing while he spoke. But only if that "beginning" is coming about in us as well, the "beginning" the psalmist made when he exclaimed, *Now I have begun*, shall we be able to do so, for to rejoice in God's works means to forget your very self and find your joy in him alone, if you have the strength for that. For what is better than God? Do you not see that you are turning back to something worse when you turn back to yourself? *I was mindful of the works of the Lord, remembering the wonderful deeds you have wrought from the beginning.*

14. *I will meditate on all your works, and babble about how I enjoy you.* Here he is again, in his third bout of babbling. First he babbled in outward conversation, and pined away; then he babbled inwardly in his own spirit, and made some progress; now he babbles about the works of God, having arrived at this place where his progress took him. *I will babble about how I enjoy you*, not about any enjoyment I find in myself. Does anyone live without enjoyment? And do you suppose, my brothers and sisters, that people who fear God, worship God, love God, get no enjoyment out of it? Do you really think, will you dare to think, that while gaming-board, theatre, hunting, fowling and fishing yield enjoyment, the works of God yield none? Can you doubt that meditation on God affords enjoyment of its own, when people contemplate the natural world, and nature's profusion is displayed before their eyes, and they seek the artist in his work, and find him who is displeasing in no place whatever, but pleasing above all else?

Verse 14. Christ is God's Way

15. *Your way, O God, is in your Holy One.* Now he contemplates the works of God's mercy all around us, and babbles about them, and exults in the enjoyment they give him. He takes as his starting-point *your way in your Holy One*. What "way" is this, a way in one who is holy? He it is who said, *I am the Way, the Truth and the Life* (Jn 14:6). Turn back, then, mortal creatures, from your pleasures. Where are you going? Where would you run? Whither flee, as you shy away not only from God, but even from yourselves? Come back, you rebels, to your heart, probe your own spirit, remember the years of eternity, discover God's mercy

around you, and pay heed to the deeds his mercy has wrought. In the Holy One his way is to be found. *How long will you be heavy-hearted, human creatures? What are you seeking in your pleasures? Why love emptiness and chase falsehood? Be sure of this: the Lord has glorified his Holy One* (Ps 4:3-4(2-3)). *Your way is in your Holy One*. Let us pay close attention to him, then, let us fix our gaze on Christ, because he is God's Way: *Your way is in your Holy One*.

What god is as great as our God? The pagans take affectionate pleasure in their gods, but they worship idols which have eyes but do not see, have ears but no hearing, feet but no power to walk.[11] What is the point of walking towards a god that cannot walk itself? "No," the heathen protests, "I do not pay homage to such things." To what, then? "To the divinity that resides in them." In that case, the object of your worship is mentioned in another psalm: *The gods of the heathen are demons* (Ps 95(96):5). You are offering worship to either idols or demons. "No," he replies, "neither to idols nor to demons." What do you worship, then? "The stars, sun, moon, and all heavenly bodies." But how much better it would be to adore him who made all things, earthly and heavenly! *What god is as great as our God?*

Verse 15. God's power, revealed in wonders physical and spiritual, is proclaimed to the nations

16. *You are God, who work your wonders alone.* You are indeed the great God; you perform wonderful deeds both physical and spiritual, and you perform them alone. The deaf heard, the blind saw, the sick recovered, the dead arose, paralytics were enabled to pull themselves together.[12] All these miracles were wrought in people's bodies; and let us look at what has happened in souls. Sober now are they who lately were drunkards, believers now, who lately worshiped graven images; people who used to steal the goods of others, now give away their wealth to the poor. *What god is as great as our God? You are God, who work your wonders alone.* Moses effected wonders too, but not alone; Elijah worked them, and so did Elisha, and so did the apostles, but none of these achieved them alone. You were with them, empowering them; but when you produced your wonders, they were not with you. When you produced these men themselves, they certainly did not work with you. *You are God, who work your wonders alone.*

But "alone" in what sense? Does it mean that the Father works, but not the Son? Or the Son, but not the Father? By no means: Father, Son and Holy Spirit are at work. Yet *you are God, who work your wonders alone,* for it is not three gods, but one only God who works his wonders alone, including the wonders

---

11. See Ps 113(115):5-7.
12. See Mt 11:5; Lk 7:22.

seen in our leaping psalmist. His very leap to the place he has reached was a miracle of God. When he babbled within, conversing with his own spirit in order to leap even beyond his spirit and find his delight in God's works, he was himself doing wonderful things. But what did God do? *You made your power known among the nations.* So this congregation, this leaping Asaph, only came into existence because God made his power known among the nations.

And what power was that? *We preach Christ crucified, to Jews a stumbling-block and to Gentiles folly; but to those who are called, both Jews and Greeks, a Christ who is the power of God and the wisdom of God* (1 Cor 1:23-24). If, then, Christ is the power of God, it was Christ whom God made known among the nations. Do we not yet recognize this fact? Are we so stupid, so inert, so incapable of leaping over anything, that we cannot see it? Yet *you have made your power known among the nations.*

Verse 16. The two peoples

17. *With your arm you redeemed your people.* "With your arm" means "by your own power." And to whom was the arm of the Lord revealed?[13] *With your arm you redeemed your people, the descendants of Israel and Joseph.* Why does it seem to suggest two peoples, *the descendants of Israel and Joseph*? Did not Joseph's children belong to the race of Israel? Yes, obviously. We know that, we read it, scripture proclaims the fact, and truth demonstrates that Israel, who is the same person as Jacob, had twelve sons, one of whom was Joseph; and all those born to any of Israel's sons belong to the people of Israel. How can the psalm say, then, *the descendants of Israel and Joseph*? It must have been hinting at some distinction. Let us rummage in our minds; perhaps God has put something there which we too need to search for in the night with our groping hands, that we may not be deceived. Perhaps we will even find ourselves foreshadowed in this distinction between *the descendants of Israel, and Joseph.*

By *Joseph* the psalm intended us to understand another people; it meant us to think of the Gentiles. But why should Joseph suggest the Gentiles? Because Joseph was sold into Egypt by his brothers. He was envied by his brothers and sold by them into Egypt; there he underwent hardship and humiliation; but there his worth was recognized, he was exalted, he prospered and he exercised authority.[14] And what did he symbolize by these experiences? What else but Christ, sold by his brethren, and driven out of his own country as though into Egypt, the land of the Gentiles? There he was humiliated at first, while the martyrs suffered persecution, but now he is exalted, as we see, for in him the prophecy is fulfilled, *All the kings of the earth will worship him, and all nations*

---

13. See Is 53:1.
14. See Gn 37-50.

will serve him (Ps 71(72):11). So "Joseph" signifies the people formed from the Gentiles, and "Israel" the Hebrew race. God has redeemed his people, both *the descendants of Israel, and Joseph.* By what means? Through the cornerstone, in whom the two walls are tied together.[15]

Verses 17-18. The roar of waters

18. The psalm continues by telling us how it was done: *The waters saw you, O God.* What is meant by *waters*? The nations. The Book of Revelation answers our question: *waters* represent the nations, for there we find this figurative expression clearly so used.[16] Earlier the psalm said, *You made your power known among the nations*; so with good reason it now says, *The waters saw you, O God, the waters saw you and were afraid.* If they were afraid, they must have undergone some change. *The waters saw you, O God, the waters saw you and were afraid; the depths were stirred.* What are these *depths*? The deepest places in the waters. Is anyone among the nations not stirred, when his conscience is smitten? You may plumb the depths of the sea, but what is deeper than the human conscience? This depth was stirred when with his own arm God redeemed his people. But in what way were the depths stirred? When they all poured out in confession whatever was on their consciences. *The depths were stirred.*

19. *Mighty was the waters' roar.* A great sound there was, a sound of praise offered to God, of sins confessed, of hymns and canticles and prayers: *mighty was the waters' roar.* And this was because *the clouds sent forth their voice.* Yes, this is why there was such a resounding crash of waters, such turbulence in the depths: because *the clouds sent forth their voice.* What clouds are we to understand here? Those of which God spoke when he threatened a certain vineyard that had brought forth thorns instead of grapes: *I will forbid my clouds to send rain upon it* (Is 5:6). Accordingly the apostles forsook the Jews and turned to the Gentiles. Among all nations *the clouds sent forth their voice*, for it was by preaching Christ that the clouds gave utterance.[17]

Verses 18-19. Thunderous preaching

20. *Yes, your arrows found their mark.* Now he has a new name for the voices from the clouds: he calls them arrows. The words of those who preached the gospel were arrows indeed. Both names are metaphorical, for an arrow is not literally rain, nor is rain literally an arrow; but God's word truly is an arrow all

---

15. See Eph 2:14.
16. See Rv 17:15.
17. Augustine frequently uses clouds to represent preachers, sent to shower the earth with the life-giving word. He develops the thought in the following paragraph.

the same, because it pierces, and it is also rain, because it gives moisture. There is no further reason to be surprised, then, by turbulence in the deep, since *your arrows found their mark*. What does it mean by saying, *found their mark*? That they did not stop at the ears, but transfixed people's hearts.

Your thunder echoes as though in a wheel. Whatever does that mean? How are we to understand it? May God help us. *Your thunder echoes as though in a wheel.* When we were children and we heard a roll of thunder in the sky, we imagined that a cart was being driven out of a shed, for thunder causes vibration similar to that made by vehicles. Are we to revert to that childish fancy when we read, *your thunder echoes as though in a wheel*, and understand it to mean that God keeps wagons up there in the clouds, and the clatter we hear is the noise their wheels make? Of course not; that would be puerile, silly and absurd. What does it mean, then, *your thunder echoes as though in a wheel*? That your voice rolls along? But I don't understand that either. What are we to do? Let us question Idithun himself; perhaps he will explain what he meant by it. I do not understand, Idithun, so I will listen to what you have to say.

Your lightning flashed all round the world. Go on; I still do not understand. The world is like a wheel because it lies all round us, so we rightly call it orbicular; similarly even a small wheel is called orbicular or ring-shaped. So *your thunder echoes as though in a wheel, and your lightning flashes all round the world*. Those clouds we heard about rolled around the whole round world; they circled it, thundering and flashing their lightning, and caused turbulence in the deep. They thundered their teaching and coruscated with miracles, for their sound went forth throughout the world, their words to the ends of the earth.[18]

The earth quaked and was left shuddering; that is to say, all who dwelt on earth. But figuratively speaking, the earth itself can be called a "sea." Why is that? Because this name "sea" suggests the totality of nations, and human life is bitter, and subject to squalls and storms. If you watch how people devour each other, as fishes do, the greater swallowing up the smaller, you see why it is like a sea, and into it stepped the preachers of the gospel.

Verse 20. Christ among the Gentiles

21. *Your way is in the sea.* A little while ago we were told, *your way is in your Holy One*; now he says, *your way is in the sea*. Yes, indeed the Holy One himself is present in the sea, and he walked on its waters as of right.[19] *Your way is in the sea* means that your Christ is preached among the Gentiles. Another psalm confirms this: *May God have mercy on us and bless us; may he cause his face to shine on us, that we may know your way on earth.* But then it specifies

---

18. See Ps 18:5(19:4).
19. See Mt 14:25.

whereabout on earth: *and your saving work among all nations* (Ps 66:2-3(67:1-2)). This amounts to the same thing as *your way is in the sea.* He continues, *and your path through deep waters*; that is to say, among many different peoples.

Your footsteps will leave no trace. Yet he must have touched some people, and surely the Jews before anyone else. Christ's mercy is so widely manifested among the Gentiles that scripture can say, *Your way is in the sea, and your path through deep waters*, and yet *your footsteps will leave no trace.* How is that? Who could fail to see those footprints, except people who even today declare, "The Messiah has not come yet"? Why do they say that? Because they do not yet recognize him who walked on the sea.

Verse 21. Most Jews did not recognize him

22. *You led your people like a flock of sheep, under the guidance of Moses and Aaron.* It is rather difficult to ascertain why the psalmist made this statement. Help me now by giving me your close attention, because only a couple of lines remain before the end of both this psalm and our sermon; if you thought there was much more to come you might be so daunted by the effort that you would be less able to concentrate on the matter in hand. After saying, *your way is in the sea*, which we understood to mean "among the Gentiles," and *your path through deep waters*, by which we understood "amid many different peoples," the psalmist added, *and your footsteps will not be recognized.* Then, while we were inquiring who these people were who would not recognize him, the psalm immediately went on to say, *You led your people like a flock of sheep, under the guidance of Moses and Aaron*; so the meaning must be that those footsteps will not be discerned by the very people who were led by Moses and Aaron. Why, then, did the psalm mention that *your way is in the sea*, if not as a reproach and rebuke to them? They drove Christ out. Those sick people would not have him as their healer, but he began to be present among all the Gentiles, and among many different races. A remnant of his own people was saved too. But the ungrateful majority stayed outside, and they are symbolized by the broad part of Jacob's thigh, which was struck, so laming him.[20] This "broad part" of his thigh signifies a large part of his progeny, and indeed it was the majority of the Israelites who were to constitute an empty-headed crowd devoid of wisdom, who would not discern Christ's footprints upon the waters. *You led your people like a flock of sheep*, yet they did not know you. How great were the benefits you had conferred on them! You parted the sea, you brought them through the waters by a dry path, you submerged their pursuing enemies beneath the waves, you rained manna on them in the desert at their time of need, leading them always *under the guidance*

20. See Gn 32:25.31-32.

of Moses and Aaron. Yet they drove you away from them, so that your way would be in the sea, and they should not recognize your footprints.

Exposition of Psalm 77[1]

Verses 1-2. How to approach parables and dark sayings in the hope of understanding

1. Our psalm tells the story of what befell Israel's ancestors long ago. But it does so in order to warn a later Israel, the Israel of the psalmist's own day, to beware of proving ungrateful to God for his merciful dealings, and of provoking to anger the One whose kindness the Israelites ought to receive in obedient faith: *lest they turn out like their forebears,* he says, *a crooked and troublesome set of people, a generation that would not direct its heart aright* (Ps 77(78):8).

Such, then, is the intention of this psalm, such its purpose and extreme usefulness. But although everything that is said and the tale to be told appear plain and simple, the title warns us in advance to keep our eyes open. Not without reason is the psalm headed, *Understanding for Asaph*; for this may suggest that the story demands a reader who will understand not merely the superficial sense, but something conveyed more subtly. Moreover, as he sets out to tell his story and recount these events, which seem to call for a listener rather than an interpreter, the psalmist declares, *I will open my mouth in parables, and give utterance to enigmas hidden from the beginning.* This is a statement calculated to arouse any slumberer. Who would presume to treat parables and ancient, mysterious enigmas as though they could be read straightforwardly, when their very names indicate that we must investigate them more deeply? A parable sets before us the image of some other thing (the word "parable" is Greek, but has been taken over into Latin). What we must notice is that in parables the things directly spoken about are being compared to other things,[2] and these other things are the real matter. Enigmas, which in Greek are called προβλήματα, are dark sayings which set forth some puzzle to be resolved by discussion. In view of these facts, could anyone be content with a cursory reading of parables and obscure enigmas? Would not everyone approach them with mind alert, in order to understand and reap their benefits?

---

1. The prolixity of this Exposition, and its academic tone, suggest that it was not preached. Its atmosphere is markedly different from that of the Expositions immediately preceding it.
2. The word "parable" is derived from the Greek παρά and βάλλω, to throw something alongside something else. An episode or situation familiar in ordinary life is placed alongside some aspect of the kingdom of God to help our understanding.

2. *Hearken to my law, O my people*, he begins. Who is the speaker here? God, surely, for he it was who gave the law to those whom he had freed from Egypt and gathered together as a people. This gathering is properly called a "synagogue," and "Asaph" means "synagogue." Are we, then, to suppose that the title *Understanding for Asaph* means that Asaph himself understood it, or should we take it figuratively, to mean that the synagogue understood it, the people to whom he says, *Hearken to my law, O my people*? It would seem that this can hardly be the case, for God rebukes this same people through a prophet, complaining, *Israel does not know me, nor does my people understand* (Is 1:3). All the same, even among that people there were some who did understand, because they had the faith that was later revealed to be concerned not with the letter of the law but with the grace of the Spirit. Prophets who were able to discern in the law the future revelation of Christ, and announce it in advance, were certainly not devoid of such faith, for those ancient observances were mysterious pointers to what was to come. But was it the prophets alone who had such faith? Did the people not have it too? Surely they did: those who listened to the prophets were assisted by the same grace to understand what they heard.

All that happened to ancient Israel has meaning for us, the Church

Beyond question, the mystery of the kingdom of heaven, which in the fullness of time was to be revealed in the New Testament, was present but veiled in the Old. So the apostle says, *I would not have you ignorant, brothers and sisters, that all our ancestors walked under the cloud, and all crossed the sea, and all were through Moses baptized in cloud and sea; all of them ate the same spiritual food and all drank the same spiritual drink, for they drank from the spiritual rock that followed them, and that rock was Christ* (1 Cor 10:1-4). In a mysterious way their food and drink were the same as ours, but the same only with regard to their meaning, not the same in kind, because the one same Christ who was prefigured to them in the rock has been manifested to us in the flesh. *Yet God was not pleased with all of them*, the apostle continues (1 Cor 10:5). *They all ate the same spiritual food*, to be sure, *and all drank the same spiritual drink* (spiritual, that is, in the sense that it represented something spiritual), yet *God was not pleased with all of them*. Since the text says, *not with all of them*, it implies that there must have been some with whom God was pleased. The sacramental mysteries were available to all alike, but grace, which is the power hidden in the sacraments, was not common to all the people. Today, when the promise then veiled is revealed, this is still true, for the laver of rebirth in the name of Father, Son and Holy Spirit is common to all alike; but grace itself, whereby the members of Christ's body are brought to new life with their head, the grace of which that rite is the sacred sign—that is not common to all. Heretics have the same baptism, and so do false brethren within the Catholic community. Rightly, then, is it said, *God was not pleased with all of them.*

3. Nonetheless, the admonition, *Hearken to my law, O my people,* was not without effect then, nor is it now. In accordance with a practice well known throughout the scriptures, the speaker uses not the singular form of the verb "hearken" as addressing one person, but the plural, as to many; for a people is made up of many individuals, and these numerous listeners are addressed in the words that follow: *Bend your ear to the words I speak.* The command, *bend your ear,* means the same as that other command, *hearken;* and *the words I speak* are equivalent to *my law.* Only a person whose ear is bent down by humility can hearken to God's law devoutly, not one who is stiff-necked with pride; for what is poured in finds plenty of room in the hollow space of humility, but is pushed out by the protuberance of pride. In similar vein another text advises, *Bend your ear, and accept words of wisdom* (Prv 22:17). We too have therefore been told clearly enough to receive this psalm of understanding for Asaph with a bent ear, that is, with humble devotion, for it is "a psalm of understanding," as the use of the genitive in the title indicates. Notice that it refers not to Asaph's own understanding, but to the understanding offered to Asaph, as the article in Greek, found also in some Latin codices, makes plain.

These, then, are words of understanding, words of wisdom, offered to Asaph, which means not to a single person but to the congregation of God's people, from which we must never estrange ourselves. It is true that the term "synagogue" is more properly applied to Jews, and "church" to Christians, because while animals are usually said to be herded together, people are assembled by calling;[3] nevertheless we do find the Church called a congregation, and we have a better right to pray, *Save us, O Lord our God, and gather us from all nations into one flock, that we may praise your holy name* (Ps 105(106):47). We must not think it an affront to our dignity, but rather matter for more fervent thankfulness than words can utter, that we are the sheep he leads by hand, the sheep he foresaw when he said, *Other sheep I have, not counted in this fold; them too I must lead in, that there may be but one flock and one shepherd* (Jn 10:16). He meant to unite the faithful people from the Gentiles to the faithful drawn from the Israelites, of whom he had said earlier, *I was sent only to the lost sheep of the house of Israel* (Mt 15:24); for all nations will be gathered like a single flock before him, and he will sort them out as a shepherd separates sheep from goats.[4] Accordingly we must understand the psalm's admonition, *Hearken to my law, O my people, and bend your ear to the words I speak,* as addressed more to ourselves than to the Jews, or at least to us as well as to them. This is evident from

---

3. The contrast is between *synagoga,* with its Latin equivalent *congregatio,* literally a herding together or gathering together into a flock, and *ecclesia,* a word derived from "calling out."
4. See Mt 25:32.

the apostle's words, for after saying, *God was not pleased with all of them* (and thus implying that there were some among them with whom he was pleased), and adding, *They fell in the desert*, he went on to say, *But there are hints for us in these events: not to desire evil things, as they did; not to pay cult to idols, like some of them, as it is written, "The people sat down to eat and drink, and rose to revel." Neither let us commit fornication, as some of them committed it, and fell to the number of twenty-three thousand in a single day. Nor let us put Christ to the test, as did some of them, only to be killed by snakes. And do not grumble, as some of them grumbled and perished by the hand of the destroyer. All these things happened to them, but with symbolic import, for they are written down as a rebuke to us, upon whom the climax of the ages has come* (1 Cor 10:5-11).

It is for us, then, that these verses are principally sung, as another verse in the same psalm makes clear: *Thus a new generation would be made aware, children yet to be born and rise up.* Now, consider. That death by snakebite, that destruction at the exterminator's hand, that slaying by the sword, were symbols; this is the obvious sense of the apostle's words. Yet all those things quite clearly did happen. He does not say, "They were described metaphorically," or "Scripture meant them to be taken in a purely symbolic sense"; no, he says, *These things* actually *happened to them*, but *with symbolic import*. How much more careful, then, how much more full of holy fear should we be to avoid punishments of which those disasters were but symbols! No one will deny that where good things are concerned, there is far more good in the reality symbolized than in the symbol itself; and similarly where evil is symbolically represented, there must be much deeper evil in the reality, when even the symbols of it are so exceedingly bad. Just as the promised land, toward which the people of Israel were being led, was nothing at all compared with the kingdom of heaven to which the Christian people is being led now, so also those punishments which served as symbols, atrocious though they were, were nothing when compared with the punishments to which they pointed.

Now what the apostle declared to be symbolic events, the psalmist called parables and ancient enigmas, as I see it; for their purpose was to be found not in their mere occurrence, but in those other realities to which we may reasonably compare them. Let us, then, who are God's people, hearken to his law and bend our ears to the words he speaks.

4. *I will open my mouth in parables*, he says, *and give utterance to enigmas hidden from the beginning.* It is evident from the lines that follow which "beginning" he means: not that beginning when heaven and earth were created, nor the beginning when our race took its origin from the first human being, but that beginning when the people who had been brought out of Egypt were formed into a congregation; for his words refer to Asaph, whose name means "congregation." If only he who declared, *I will open my mouth in parables*, would kindly

open our minds to them as well! If he were to open the parables themselves, as well as opening his mouth to utter them, and if he were to give utterance to the explanation of those enigmas in the same way as he gave utterance to the enigmas themselves in the first place, we should not be fretting over it now. But as it is, everything is so closely guarded that even if, with his help, we are able to arrive at some meaning that will provide us with salutary nourishment, we still have to eat our bread in the sweat of our brows and so pay the penalty decreed of old,[5] not only by bodily toil but by the labor of the heart. Let him speak, then, and let us listen to these parables and enigmas.

Verses 3-4. After the opening address by God, we hear a human speaker; but God speaks through him

5. *How great are the wonders we have heard about and experienced, of which our ancestors have told us the tale!* In the verses preceding this one it was the Lord speaking, for how could the words, *Hearken to my law, O my people*, be spoken by anyone else? How is it, then, that we suddenly hear a human speaker? These are unmistakably human expressions: *How great are the wonders we have heard about and experienced, of which our ancestors have told us the tale!* God, of course, is about to speak through a human intermediary, as the apostle indicates is the case when he demands, *Do you presume to interrogate Christ, who speaks through me?* (2 Cor 13:3). God willed the opening words to be spoken in his own person, lest any human who undertook to speak on God's behalf should be despised as human and nothing more. When God addresses us in a message conveyed through our bodily senses, he regularly does so not by allowing his own substance to be changed into anything corporeal or time-conditioned, but in the following way: acting invisibly as Creator he moves the creature subject to him in such a manner that through corporeal and temporal signs perceptible to our eyes and ears he makes his will known to us, insofar as human understanding can grasp it. After all, an angel can make use of sky, air, cloud, fire or any other natural element or bodily shape, and human beings can employ facial expressions, tongue, gestures, pen, writing and any other signs to make their inmost thoughts known. Moreover, human beings can send other humans to carry out their wishes, saying to one, *Go, and he goes, to another, come, and he comes; and to a servant, Do this, and he does it* (Lk 7:8). How much greater and more efficacious, then, must be the power of God, to whom all things are subject as to their Lord, to make use of people and even angels to announce his will!

5. See Gn 3:19.

Accordingly, although it is a man who here exclaims, *How great are the wonders we have heard about and experienced, of which our ancestors have told us the tale!* we must hearken to what he has to say, receiving it as the words of God, not human fabrication. This is why the injunction was put first, *Hearken to my law, O my people, and bend your ear to the words I speak. I will open my mouth in parables, and give utterance to enigmas hidden from the beginning.* Then he continues, *How great are the wonders we have heard about and experienced, of which our ancestors have told us the tale!* The distinction between *heard about* and *experienced* is like that implied in the words of another psalm, *Hearken, my daughter, and see* (Ps 44:11(45:10)). What was heard about in the Old Testament is experienced in the New: heard about when prophesied, experienced when the promises were fulfilled. When the promise comes true, the hearers are not cheated. *Our ancestors*, then, Moses and the prophets, *have told us the tale.*

6. These things *have not been hidden from their descendants in a new generation.* Our own generation is meant, that generation on which regeneration has been conferred.

Proclaiming the praise of the Lord and his might, and the marvelous deeds he has wrought. The proper order of words here is, *of which our ancestors have told us the tale, proclaiming the praise of the Lord.* The Lord is praised that he may be loved, and what other love could so greatly profit us for salvation?

Verse 5. God's testimony was both revelation and law

7. *He raised up a testimony for Jacob, and established a law in Israel.* Here we have the "beginning" which was mentioned earlier when he said, *I will give utterance to enigmas hidden from the beginning.* The beginning is the Old Testament, the end is the New. Fear held sway under the law, and *the fear of the Lord is* only *the beginning of wisdom* (Ps 110(111):10). But *Christ is the end of the law, bringing justification to everyone who believes* (Rom 10:4). Through his bounty *the love of God has been poured out into our hearts through the Holy Spirit who has been given to us* (Rom 5:5); and *charity made perfect casts out fear* (1 Jn 4:18), because *now, independently of law, God's justice has been manifested.* Yet *the testimony of the law and the prophets supports it* (Rom 3:21), which is why the psalm declares: *He raised up a testimony for Jacob, and established a law in Israel.*

That tent of old, the tent set up with workmanship so extraordinary and deeply significant, was called the Tent of the Testimony.[6] Inside it was a veil that screened the ark containing the law, just as a veil also covered the face of each minister of the law, because under that dispensation people had only parables

---

6. See Ex 40:2.

and hidden enigmas. The meaning of both proclamation and event was concealed, their true significance veiled; people did not gaze upon any open manifestation. *But when* you *turn to Christ, the veil is lifted,* says the apostle (2 Cor 3:16); for however many God's promises may have been, in him *they find their "Yes,"* their "Amen" (2 Cor 1:20). Whoever holds fast to Christ, therefore, possesses all that good which we cannot understand in the Old Testament, whereas anyone who is separated from Christ neither understands nor possesses it.

Hence God *raised up a testimony for Jacob, and established a law in Israel.* The psalmist says the same thing twice in different words, as is his custom; for *raised up a testimony* means the same as *established a law,* and *for Jacob* the same as *in Israel.* Just as these two names belong to one man, so also are *law* and *testimony* equivalent.

Someone may object, "But there is a difference between *raised up* and *established.*" I agree. It is like the difference between *Jacob* and *Israel.* These names do not denote two individuals but are given to one person with different connotations: Jacob because he grasped his brother's heel at birth, and so was called a supplanter,[7] and Israel because he wanted to see God.[8] Similarly there is a distinction between *raised up* and *established,* for, as I see it, a *testimony* is said to have been *raised up* because by means of it something was brought to life. The apostle tells us, *In the absence of law, sin lay dead. I lived awhile without the law, but with the coming of the commandment, sin sprang to life* (Rom 7:8-9). So this is what was raised up by that testimony which the law gives, thereby bringing to light what lay hidden, as Paul explains a moment later: *so that sin might be shown up for what it truly is, it used a good thing to deal death to me* (Rom 7:13). God *established a law,* the psalm says, as a yoke upon sinners, for scripture tells us that *law is not imposed on a righteous person* (1 Tm 1:9). It is a testimony inasmuch as it proves something, and a law inasmuch as it issues commands; and both amount to the same thing. Just as Christ, who is called a stone, is the cornerstone for believers, but to unbelievers a stone to trip them up and a rock to stumble over,[9] so too the testimony is the law's witness against those who do not use the law lawfully.[10] The testimony convicts sinners as deserving of punishment, but for those who make right use of the law it is a testimony which shows sinners to whom they must flee for deliverance; for in his grace is found *God's justice,* to which *the law and the prophets bear witness* (Rom 3:21). By that righteousness of God are the ungodly justified, though some *failed to recognize the*

---

7. See Gn 25:25
8. See Gn 32:28.
9. See Ps 117(118):22; Is 8:14; Rom 9:33; 1 Pt 2:7.
10. See 1 Tm 1:8.

righteousness that comes from God and, seeking to set up their own, did not submit to God's righteousness (Rom 10:3).

Verses 5-8. Trust in God and obedience through grace

8. *What marvels he ordered our ancestors to make known to their children! Thus a new generation would be made aware, children yet to be born and rise up, who in turn would instruct their own children to put their trust in God, never to forget his deeds, and to seek after his commandments. Otherwise they might turn out like their forebears, a crooked and troublesome set of people, a generation that would not direct its heart aright, whose spirit did not entrust itself to God.* These words hint at two peoples, one belonging to the Old Testament, the other to the New; for in saying, *What marvels he ordered our ancestors to make known to their children*, the psalmist admits that his forebears did receive God's commands, but only to pass on to their children; they did not acknowledge or carry them out themselves. They received them only that *a new generation* might recognize what their ancestors had failed to recognize. These were the children yet to be born and rise up, for those already born did not rise. Their hearts were not lifted up but dragged down to earth. Only with Christ can anyone arise, which is why scripture says, *If you have risen with Christ, seek what is above* (Col 3:1).

The psalm continues, *who in turn would instruct their own children to put their trust in God.* Accordingly this new generation has no wish to set up its own righteousness; rather it reveals its path to God, and trusts him to act.[11] They are *never to forget his deeds* by glorifying and boasting about their own, as though these were done by their own power; for it is God who is at work in those who accomplish good actions, inspiring both the will and the deed for his own good purpose.[12]

And to seek after his commandments. Since they have learned the commandments already, how can they seek God's commandments? We know they have, because the psalm has mentioned the *marvels he ordered our ancestors to make known to their children, that a new generation might be made aware.* Aware of what? Surely of the commandments enjoined on them. So how can they still seek his commandments? Only by placing their hope in God, and then seeking to fulfill his commandments with his help. *Otherwise they might turn out like their forebears, a crooked and troublesome set of people, a generation that would not direct its heart aright.* The psalmist explains its refusal by adding immediately, *whose spirit did not entrust itself to God*; that is, it lacked the faith that acquires

---

11. See Ps 36(37):5.
12. See Ph 2:13.

what the law requires.[13] When our spirit cooperates with the Spirit of God at work in us, God's commands are fulfilled; but this happens only when we have faith in God who justifies the ungodly.[14] That ignoble and troublesome generation did not have such faith, which is why the psalm says that *their spirit did not entrust itself to God*.

But this expression means something much more positive: it points to the grace of God which not only effects the forgiveness of sins, but also draws the human spirit into cooperation with itself for the performance of good works. It is as though the psalm were saying, "Their spirit had no faith in God." To have a spirit that is faithful to God is to believe that one's own spirit can do nothing right without God, but with God is capable of righteous action. This is believing in God, and it is a great deal more than believing what God says. We may often believe what some human being says, yet know that such a person is not to be believed in. To believe in God is to cling by faith to God who effects the good works in such a way that we collaborate well with him, for, we are told, *Without me you can do nothing* (Jn 15:5). How could the apostle have put the point more strongly than he did, by saying, *Anyone who clings to the Lord is one spirit with him* (1 Cor 6:17)?

Very different is the law, for it is a testimony whereby a guilty person is not absolved, but condemned; for the letter is a threat that convicts transgressors,[15] not a helping spirit that justifies sinners and sets them free. The generation of whose example we are warned to beware was a base and troublesome set of people whose *spirit did not entrust itself to God*. They may have believed some of what God said, but they did not believe in God. They did not cleave to God by faith so as to be healed by him and become effective collaborators with the God who was at work in them.

Verse 9. Ephraim's defection

9. The psalm continues, *The sons of Ephraim, bending their bows and loosing them, turned back on the day of battle*. They keenly pursued the law of righteousness, yet to the law of righteousness they did not attain.[16] Why not? Because they lacked faith. They were the kind of people whose spirit was not entrusted to God, but relied on works. They did not direct their hearts as they stretched and shot their bows (outward actions, these, like the works of the law). No, they did not so direct their hearts. The righteous live in their hearts by that faith which works

---

13. As often, he uses an assonance here to make his point: faith *impetrat quod lex imperat*. The doctrine of faith here assumed and expounded is thoroughly Pauline.
14. See Rom 4:5.
15. See 1 Cor 6:17.
16. See Rom 9:31.

through love,[17] a love which clings to God who is at work in us both to will and to act, according to his good pleasure.[18] What does it mean to bend the bow, and loose it off, and then turn back on the battle day, if not to pay close attention and make promises on the day of hearing the summons, and then desert on the day of testing? It is like engaging in preliminary practice, but refusing to fight when the real clash comes.

When he says, *Bending their bows and loosing them*, though he apparently ought to have said, "Bending their bows and loosing the arrows" (for it is not the bow itself that is shot; rather something is shot from a bow), we may take it as another instance of that idiom we discussed earlier, when the psalm said, *He raised up a testimony*, meaning that he raised up something by means of the testimony; so here likewise, *loosing their bows* means that they loosed something from their bows. Alternatively, this may be an obscure expression which omits a word that we are meant to supply for ourselves: it ought to read, *The sons of Ephraim bending their bows, and shooting* (here we understand "arrows"). So, more fully expressed, it would be "bending their bows and shooting their arrows"; because even if it said, "bending and shooting arrows" we would know that he could not have meant us to understand that the arrows were being bent: we would know he referred "bending" to the bow, even if the bow was not mentioned. In fact Greek codices are said to have the reading, *bending and shooting from their bows*, to make it quite clear that it was the arrows that were shot.

He was figuratively using a part to signify the whole when he made the sons of Ephraim stand for that entire troublesome generation. Perhaps this particular part was chosen to represent the whole because it was from them above all that some good might have been expected. They were the descendants of that grandson of Jacob who, though placed by his father at Jacob's left as the younger, was nonetheless blessed by Jacob's right hand and so given precedence over his elder brother by a mysterious blessing.[19] But since the tribe of Ephraim is censured here, and it is evident that what the blessing promised was not realized in it, we are given to understand that even in the words of the patriarch Jacob something very different was being suggested from what earthbound prudence might expect. Jacob was prophesying that in the future those who were last would be first, and the first would be last,[20] through the coming of our Saviour, of whom it was said, *He who comes after me takes precedence over me* (Jn 1:27). By the same token the righteous Abel was preferred to his elder brother[21] and Isaac to Ishmael[22], and Jacob himself to Esau who, though his twin, was the

17. See Rom 1:17; Gal 5:6.
18. See Ph 2:13.
19. See Gn 48:14.
20. See Mt 20:16.
21. See Gn 4:4-5.
22. See Gn 21:12.

first-born;[23] so too did Perez contrive to be born before his twin who had thrust out a hand and begun to be born first,[24] and David was advanced before his elder brothers.[25] As the reason for all these and similar foreshadowings in both words and actions, the Christian people was given precedence over the people of the Jews. To redeem this Christian people Christ was slain by the Jews, as Abel had been by Cain.[26] The same prophecy was expressed by Jacob's action of stretching his hands out crosswise, so that his right hand rested on Ephraim, who stood at his left, giving him preference over Manasseh who stood to the right, on whom Jacob laid his left hand. For the sons of Ephraim according to the flesh were *bending their bows and loosing them*, but *turned back on the day of battle*.

Verse 10. The human spirit entrusted to God inner obedience and straightness of heart

10. The meaning of the statement *turned back on the day of battle* is made clear by the next verse, where the psalm elaborates it fully: *They did not keep God's covenant, nor were they willing to walk in his law*. So now we know what *turned back on the day of battle* means: they refused to keep God's covenant. While bending and loosing their bows they were perfectly ready to make promises, protesting that *Whatever the Lord our God has said, we will do; we will be obedient* (Ex 19:8). But they are said to have *turned back on the day of battle* because a promise of obedience is proved trustworthy not by mere hearing but by being tested in practice. Those whose spirit is entrusted to God, on the contrary, hold God to be faithful, knowing that he will not allow them to be tested beyond their strength, but will along with the testing ordain the outcome of it, enabling them to stand fast.[27] Then they will not turn back on the day of battle, whereas people who boast of themselves and not of God,[28] even though they parade their promise of courage as though bending and loosing their bows, do turn tail on the battle day. Since their spirit has not been entrusted to God, the Spirit of God is not with them; and, as scripture has it, *Anyone who does not believe in God will not enjoy his protection* (Sir 2:15).

After saying, *They did not keep God's covenant*, the psalmist added *Nor were they willing to walk in his law*. The second phrase is a repetition of the first, with some expansion, for *his law* means the same as *God's covenant*, and *nor were they willing to walk* echoes the thought of *did not keep*. This second thought

---

23. See Gn 25:23.
24. See Gn 38:27-29.
25. See 1 Sm 16:12.
26. See Gn 4:8.
27. See 1 Cor 10:13.
28. See 1 Cor 1:31.

could have been expressed more concisely by saying, "They did not walk in his law"; yet I think the psalmist wanted us to look for a special meaning in his preference for the expression, *nor were they willing to walk,* over "did not walk." It might have been supposed that the law of works is sufficient for justification as long as its injunctions are outwardly complied with by people who all the while wish it did not issue those commands, which they obey indeed, though not from their hearts. They appear to be walking in God's law, but not willingly, since it is not from their hearts that their actions spring. No action that is motivated by fear of punishment, rather than by delight in righteousness, proceeds from the heart. People who are afraid of punishment and those who cherish righteousness equally refrain from stealing. As far as their outward actions are concerned there is no difference: they are on a par with regard to the hand's movement, but in their hearts they are quite different: equal in action but unequal in will.

This is why such people are called *a generation that would not direct its heart aright.* "Heart," the psalm says, not "activity." If the heart is rightly directed, the actions will be too; but if the heart is not directed aright, actions will not be right either, even if they seem to be. Now the reason why that depraved generation did not so direct its heart is plain to see. Their spirit *did not entrust itself to God.* The human heart is crooked in itself, but God is straight. If our heart clings closely to him, as to an unchangeable rule, it too can be straightened. But in order to keep with him, and thus be straight, it must approach God, not by walking towards him but by faith. This is why it is said of the same crooked and troublesome generation in the Letter to the Hebrews that *the message they heard did them no good, because it did not blend with faith in the hearers* (Heb 4:2).

In a person whose heart is straight the will is made ready by God, on the basis of that faith by which the heart has drawn near to the straightness of God in order to be straightened itself. This faith is aroused through obedience as the mercy of God anticipates our human response and calls it forth; so faith begins to attach the heart to God that it may be directed aright. The more it is so directed, the more it sees what it did not see formerly, and the more it is strengthened to achieve what was earlier beyond its powers.

This was not the case with Simon, to whom the apostle Peter said, *You have no share or lot in this faith, for your heart is not straight with God* (Acts 8:21). He thereby showed that it cannot be straight without God; for people must begin to walk, not under the law like slaves driven by fear, but in the law like willing sons and daughters. Those who were not willing to walk in it remained guilty under it. Not fear but charity inspires a will like this, that charity which is poured abroad in the hearts of believers by the Holy Spirit.[29] To them the apostle says, *By grace you have been saved, through faith, and this is not your own doing but the grace of God. It does not come from works, lest anyone boast. We are his own*

---

29. See Rom 5:5.

handiwork, created in Christ Jesus for the good works which God has prepared in advance for us to walk in (Eph 2:8-10). Not so those Israelites who *were not willing to walk,* because they neither believed in him nor revealed their way to him nor trusted in him to act.[30]

Verses 11-12. The leaders of God's people are called "fathers" in a qualified sense. Warning against forgetfulness

11. *They forgot his favors and the wonders he had shown them, the wonderful deeds he wrought in the sight of their fathers.* We must not omit to inquire into the meaning of this verse. A few lines earlier he declared that these same forgetful forebears were a crooked and troublesome generation. His hearers must not *turn out like their forebears,* he said, *a crooked and troublesome set of people, a generation that would not direct its heart aright.* This and similar denunciations were made with reference to that generation whose example a later generation was warned to beware of imitating; rather the later Israelites were to *put their hope in God, never forget his deeds, and seek after his commandments.* We have already discussed that verse sufficiently and interpreted it as seemed best. What can it mean, then, when with reference to that crooked generation, the psalm first asserts that *they forgot God's favors and the wonders he had shown them,* but then adds *and the wonderful deeds he wrought in the sight of their fathers?* What "fathers" can these be, when they were themselves the "fathers" whom the psalmist would not have their posterity imitate? We might take it to mean the ancestors from whom they were descended, such as Abraham, Isaac and Jacob; but these had long since died when God displayed his wonders in Egypt. And these are certainly the wonders alluded to, for it continues, *in the land of Egypt, in the plains of Zoan,* indicating where God had displayed those wonderful deeds in the sight of their fathers. Or were the ancestors perhaps present in spirit, since the Lord says of them in the gospel, *To him they are all alive* (Lk 20:38)? Or should we widen the sense of "fathers" to include Moses and Aaron and the rest of the elders who, as scripture records, also received the spirit which Moses had received, in order to help him in governing and carrying the people?[31] Why should they not be called fathers? Not, of course, in the same sense as God, the sole Father, who by his Spirit brings to new birth sons and daughters for an eternal inheritance, but simply as an honorific title in recognition of their age and kindly solicitude, just as Paul, an elder himself, said, *I do not write so to shame you; I am simply warning you as my most dear children* (1 Cor 4:14.15), although he undoubtedly knew the

---

30. See Ps 36(37):5.
31. See Nb 11:16.17.

Lord's prohibition, *Call no one on earth your father, for you have only one Father—God* (Mt 23:9). This was said not to banish a term of human honor from our customary way of speaking, but to ensure that the grace of God, whereby we are born anew into eternal life, should not be attributed to human nature, or to human capacities, or even to the holiness of some particular person. So then, when Paul claimed, *I have begotten you,* it was only with the qualification *in Christ Jesus* and *through the gospel* (1 Cor 4:14.15), lest what belongs to God should be ascribed to him.

12. So then, that *crooked and troublesome set of people forgot God's favors and the wonders he had shown them, and the wonderful deeds he wrought in the sight of their fathers in the land of Egypt, in the plains of Zoan.* Now he sets about narrating those wonderful deeds. But if they are parables and hidden enigmas, they are certainly meant to be referred to something else by way of comparison. We must not allow our concentration to wander from the point this psalm is trying to make: namely, that the purpose of everything that is said here, and the reason why we are cautioned to listen to it all with the utmost attention, as God enjoins us, *Hearken to my law, O my people; bend your ear to the words I speak,* is that we ourselves should place our hope in God, and not forget his deeds, and seek after his commandments, so that we may not become, like that crooked and troublesome set of people, a generation that has not directed its heart aright and whose spirit has not been entrusted to God. This is the whole purpose of all that is narrated. These events took place as types and symbols, and whatever they signify can be realized spiritually in human beings, either by God's grace, in the case of good things, or by his judgment, in the case of calamities. Just so did good things befall the Israelites, but disasters too were visited upon both them and their enemies.

If we do not forget, but place our hope in God, and are not ungrateful for his grace; if we fear him, not with the servile fear that dreads only corporal pain, but with that chaste awe that abides for ever and ever[32] and esteems it the greatest of punishments to be deprived of the light of goodness, we shall not become like those forebears of old, a crooked and troublesome set.

The land of Egypt is therefore to be understood as a symbol of this world. The plains of Zoan represent the level ground of the commandment on lowliness; for this is what the name Zoan means, "lowly commandment." Let us then take to heart the commandment of humility in this world, that we may deserve to receive in another world the exaltation he promised, who became humble for us.

---

32. See Ps 18:10(19:9).

Verses 13-16. The wonders of the exodus prefigured Christian mysteries

13. Clearly this must be so, for he who *tore the sea apart and led them across, halting the waters as though they were bottled* so that the sea stood still as though confined, can by his grace restrain the unstable, slippery desires of the flesh, when his faithful people forsake the world, see all their sins annihilated like drowned enemies, and are led through the sacrament of baptism.

Similarly, he who *led them by a cloud in daytime, and all night by the luminosity of fire*, is able to direct our spiritual journey, provided that faith cries out to him, *Guide my steps according to your word* (Ps 118(119):133). Another passage speaks in the same way: *He will set you on a straight path, and conduct your journeys in peace* (Prv 4:17), and this through Jesus Christ our Lord. In this world, as by the light of day, the mystery of Christ was made manifest in the flesh, as though in a cloud; but at the judgment he will be manifested in nocturnal terror, like a fire to illumine the righteous but burn the wicked; and great will be the world's distress.

God, who *split open a rock in the desert, gave them water to drink as plentiful as the ocean, drew water from a rock and made it flow in streams*, is certainly able to pour out upon our thirsting faith the gift of the Holy Spirit from the mystical rock that follows, which is Christ.[33] For this is what the episode spiritually signified. Christ it was who stood and cried out, *If anyone is thirsty, let him come to me and drink*, and again, *If anyone drinks of the water I shall give, rivers of living water shall flow from within that person* (Jn 7:37; 4:13; 7:38). And, as the gospel comments, *He said this of the Spirit which those who believed in him were to receive* (Jn 7:39). The wood of his passion struck him like a rod,[34] so that grace might gush forth for believers.

Verses 17-20. Lack of faith during the desert march

14. And yet, like the *crooked and troublesome set of people* they were, that generation *persisted in sinning against him*, that is, persisted in unbelief, for that is the sin with which the Spirit charges the world, according to the Lord's word, *of sin, inasmuch as they have not believed in me* (Jn 16:9).

And they provoked the Most High in the desert, or, as other codices have it, *in that waterless place*, which is a more exact translation of the Greek and means the same as "desert." Was it the desert of the wilderness, or the desert within them? The latter, surely; they had drunk from the rock, but the real aridity was not in their bellies but in their souls, which yielded no green shoots of righteousness. In a drought like that they ought to have prayed to God with yet more

33. See 1 Cor 10:4.
34. See Ex 17:5-6; Nb 20:8-11.

urgent faith, that he who had given them ample nourishment in their mouths would also infuse justice into their conduct. The faithful soul cries out to him, *Let my eyes see justice* (Ps 16(17):2).

15. *And they put God to the test in their hearts by the way they demanded food to live on.* To ask in faith is quite different from asking as a test. The psalm continues, *And they disparaged God, saying, "Will God have the power to provide a meal in the wilderness? He struck the rock, and waters flowed, and torrents gushed out; but will he have the power to give us bread as well, or provide a meal for his people?"* So it was without faith that they demanded food to sustain their life. This is not how the apostle James instructed us to ask for the food of the spirit; he warns us that it must be sought by believers, not by people testing God or disparaging him. *If anyone of you stands in need of wisdom,* he says, *let such a person request it from God, who gives to all in abundance and reproaches no one. The petitioner will receive it, but must ask in faith and with no trace of doubt* (Jas 1:5-6). That generation which had not directed its heart aright, whose spirit was not entrusted to God, lacked this kind of faith.

Verse 21. Why did God delay?

16. *Accordingly the Lord heard, but he held back; fire was kindled in Jacob, and anger broke out against Israel.* The psalmist explains what "fire" means: he calls God's anger "fire," though fire in the literal sense did burn many people. What, then, can be the meaning of *the Lord heard, but he held back*? That he held back from bringing them into the land of promise, to which they were being led? That could have been effected in a few days, had they not deserved by their sins to be ground down in the desert, where indeed such grinding was their fate for forty years. But if this is the meaning, it was the people as a whole that he held back, not the individuals who put God to the test and disparaged him, for all of them perished in the desert, and it was their children who entered the promised land. Or did he perhaps delay the punishment, meaning to satisfy even their faithless desire first, so that no one should believe he was angry with them for asking him (even in an attitude of testing and disrespect) to do something of which he was incapable? *He heard,* therefore, and he deferred his revenge; and after he had done what they thought him unable to do, his *anger broke out against Israel.*

Verses 22-31. Manna, quails, and punishment for infidelity

17. Having made these two points briefly, the psalmist now spells them out. *Because they did not believe in God, or hope in his salvation.* He has given us the reason why fire was kindled in Jacob, and why anger broke out against Israel: namely, *because they did not believe in God, or hope in his salvation*; so now he

immediately lists some of the obvious divine benefits for which they had been ungrateful. *God commanded the clouds above, and flung open the gates of heaven. He rained down manna for them to eat, and gave them bread from heaven. Mortals ate the bread of angels; he sent them lavish nourishment. He swung heaven's wind to a southerly, and drove in the south-westerly by his power. He rained meat down on them like scattered dust, winged birds like the sand on the seashore. Birds fell right into their camp, all around their tents. They ate and were sated; God sent them what they craved for, and their appetite did not go unsatisfied.* So that was why he held back. But now let us listen to what he had been holding back: *The food was yet in their mouths when God's anger broke out against them.* This is what he had held back. For a time he delayed, but then *fire was kindled in Jacob, and anger broke out against Israel.* He had held back, then, to give himself time to do what they had believed him incapable of doing, and then inflict on them what they deserved to suffer.

If only they would put their trust in God, not only would those carnal desires of old be fulfilled, but their spiritual longings too; for he who *commanded the clouds above, and flung open the gates of heaven,* he who *rained down manna for them to eat, and gave them bread from heaven* so that mortals might eat *the bread of angels,* he who *sent them lavish nourishment* to sate even unbelievers, does not lack the power to give believers the true bread from heaven which the manna symbolized. He is the true bread of angels, for as the Word of God he feeds those incorruptible creatures in a way immune to all corruption, but so that mortals may also feed on him, that same Word became flesh and lived among us.[35] As bread from heaven he is rained down on the whole world through the clouds of the gospel. The hearts of his preachers are flung open like heavenly gates, and he is proclaimed not to the grumbling synagogue, ever watchful to put him to the test, but to the Church whose hope is fixed on him.

Moroever he who *swung heaven's wind to a southerly, and drove in the south-westerly by his power,* who *rained meat down on them like scattered dust, winged birds like the sand on the seashore,* who caused birds to fall *right into their camp, all around their tents,* so that *they ate and were sated,* for *God sent them what they craved for, and their appetite did not go unsatisfied*—he is equally able to nourish the puny faith of those who do not put him to the test but believe, to nourish it with meat as he sends forth signs uttered by preachers' voices and winging through the air like birds. But he does not bring them from the north, where cold and mist prevail (that is, the eloquence beloved of this world); he swings heaven's wind around to a southerly. And where else should it blow, but to the earth, so that people who are but children in faith may be nourished by listening to earthly things until they have the capacity for things heav-

---

35. See Jn 1:14. Augustine expounds verses 24-25 in his Exposition 1 of Psalm 33,6.

enly? *If you do not believe when I have spoken to you of earthly things,* said the Lord, *how will you believe if I tell you of things in heaven?* (Jn 3:12).

Paul was in a sense swung round from heaven, where he had been beyond rational thought in God's presence, in order that he might accommodate himself to those whom he addressed: *Not as spiritual persons could I speak to you, but only as carnal* (1 Cor 3:1). In heaven he had heard words beyond all utterance[36] which he was not allowed to speak on earth in audible messages like *winged birds*; but God *drove in the south-westerly by his power*, conveying his truth through the hot south wind, that is, by the glowing, light-bearing spirit of those who preached his word. It was *by his power* though, by God's own power, so that the wind from the south could not claim credit itself for the efficacy it received from God.

Yet it is by their own free cooperation that these winds have blown for the human race to bring us words sent from heaven, so that people may gather up these *winged birds* in their own homes and round about their tents, and every one of us adore the Lord from where we live, even all the islands of the Gentiles.[37]

18. As for unbelievers, a crooked and troublesome set like that earlier generation, *God's anger broke out against them* while the food was still in their mouths, *and slew many among them*, or, as some Greek codices have it, *slew the fat ones among them*. In the Greek codices available to us we have not found that reading, but if it is the more accurate one, what else is to be understood by *the fat ones among them* but people who swagger in pride, of whom another psalm declares, *their iniquity will leak out as though from folds of fat* (Ps 72(73):7)?

And hindered the chosen ones of Israel. So there were some chosen ones there between whose faith and the crooked, troublesome set no blending was possible. But they were hindered, unable to ensure that anything would help their companions, whose welfare they nonetheless desired with the affection of close kin; for what good can human mercy do for people on whom God's anger falls? Or perhaps we are meant to understand rather that the elect were "shackled" along with the rest, so that the chosen ones, distinguished by their attitude and way of life, might serve as an example not merely of right living but of patience as well, by enduring hardships along with their fellows? Indeed, it has been suggested to us that holy people were led captive along with sinners for no other reason, for the Greek codices do not have ἐνεπόδισεν, which means "hindered," but συνεπόδισεν, which rather has the sense of "fettered."

36. See 2 Cor 12:4.
37. See Zep 2:11.

Verses 32-33. Human life is evanescent, and so was their repentance

19. As for that *crooked and troublesome* set of people, *in spite of all this they persisted in sin, and did not believe in his wonderful exploits. And their days dwindled in nothingness*, whereas if they would only believe they could have real days, days without any diminishment in the society of him to whom it was said, *Your years will not fail* (Ps 101:28(102:27)). So *their days dwindled in nothingness, and their years sped away.* Indeed the whole life of mortals speeds away; even a life that seems more extended is but a mist that lasts a little longer.[38]

Verses 34-35. Repentance for the sake of temporal advantage will not do

20. Yet *when he slew them, they sought after him*, not for the sake of eternal life, but because they feared that the mist would be dissipated too quickly. They sought him, therefore—not, of course, those whom he had slain, but others who feared being killed likewise. But scripture speaks as though it were the slain ones who sought after God because they were all one people and can be spoken of as a single body. *They turned back, and came to God early in the morning. And they remembered that God was their helper, God the most high their redeemer.* But this was only because they wanted temporal advantages and sought to escape temporal misfortunes. In seeking after temporal benefits they were certainly not seeking God, but only those benefits; and when this happens God is not worshiped at all, because only what is loved is worshiped. Since God is found to be greater and better than all things, he is to be loved and worshiped above all things.

Verses 36-37. Duplicity

21. Now let us see what follows. *With their lips they protested their love for him, but their tongues were lying, for their hearts were not right with him, nor were they found faithful to his covenant.* He to whom all human secrets are exposed found one thing on their tongues but something different in their hearts, and with penetrating vision he discerned what they really loved. A heart is right with God when it seeks God for God's own sake. It has truly desired only one thing of the Lord, and that it seeks, to live in the Lord's house always and contemplate his joy.[39] To him the heart of the faithful says, "Not with the flesh-pots of the Egyptians will I be sated, nor with melons and pumpkins, nor with garlic and onions" (all of which the crooked and troublesome generation preferred even to bread from heaven[40]), "nor with manna that can be seen nor

---

38. See Jas 4:15.
39. See Ps 26(27):4.
40. See Ex 16:3.

even with those winged birds. I will be satisfied only when your glory is manifested."[41] For this is the inheritance of the New Covenant, and they were not
found faithful to it. Even at that time, when it was veiled, such faith was present
in certain chosen ones; now that it is revealed, faith is not found in all who are
called, *for many are called, few chosen* (Mt 20:16). Such was the attitude of that
crooked and irksome generation when it seemed to be seeking God; it had love
on its lips and lies on its tongue. In its heart it was not right with God, because in
its heart it was loving those things which it sought his help to acquire, rather than
God himself.

Verses 38-39. The patient mercy of God

22. *Yet he is merciful, and will show forbearance towards their sins, and will
not destroy them. He will be yet more generous in turning away his wrath, and
will not unleash all his anger upon them. He remembers that they are mere flesh,
a roving spirit that does not readily return.* On the strength of these words many
people promise themselves that their sins will go unpunished because of God's
mercy, even if they persist in behaving like that generation which is character-
ized as *a crooked and troublesome set of people, a generation that would not
direct its heart aright, whose spirit did not entrust itself to God.* We must not
adopt this attitude. If I were to argue on their terms, I would say, If God, perhaps,
will not destroy even the wicked, obviously he will not destroy the good. Why,
then, should we not choose that course where there can be no risk? People who
lie to him in their verbal protestations, when their heart holds something
different, undeniably think that God is a liar when he threatens such people with
eternal punishment, and they want it to be so. But just as they do not deceive him
by their lies, so he does not deceive when he speaks the truth. Let not a crooked
generation, which flatters itself about these divine utterances, seek to twist them
into crookedness as it twists its own heart, because though its heart is twisted,
God's words remain straight.

The primary way in which we can understand them is indicated in the gospel:
*You must be like your Father in heaven, who causes his sun to rise over the good
and the wicked, and sends rain upon just and unjust alike* (Mt 5:45). How
immensely patient is God's mercy towards the wicked! It is plain to all. But only
on this side of the judgment. So likewise did he spare that people, restraining the
full force of his anger so as not to eradicate them entirely and put an end to them.
This is evident in the words of his servant Moses when he interceded for them on
account of their sins. God says, *Let me destroy them; but I will make of you a
great nation* (Ex 32:10). Moses intercedes, more willing to be destroyed himself
than to see them destroyed, and knowing that he is dealing with a merciful Lord

---

41. See Ps 16(17):15.

who, since he will certainly not destroy Moses, will spare them also for Moses' sake. Indeed, let us see how generously he did spare them, and spares them still. He brought them into the promised land and preserved them as a nation until they took upon themselves the greatest crime of all by slaying Christ. Moreover he did not destroy them even after they were uprooted from their kingdom and he had scattered them throughout all the kingdoms of the Gentiles; they abide as the selfsame people, preserved by successive generations, as though there had been placed upon them the mark of Cain, forbidding anyone to kill them;[42] that is, to destroy them utterly. This is how the psalm-verse is coming true: *he is merciful, and will show forbearance towards their sins, and will not destroy them. He will be yet more generous in turning away his wrath, and will not unleash all his anger upon them*. If he did unleash on them the full weight of his anger—that is, all the anger they deserve—nothing would be left of that nation. The God of whose mercy and judgment we sing[43] *causes his sun to rise over the good and the wicked* (Mt 5:45) in this world, and when this world comes to an end will by his judgment punish the wicked by banishing them from his eternal light into endless darkness.

23. We must not appear to be intensifying the severity of God's words, however, as though when the psalm says, *He will not destroy them*, we were to gloss it by saying, "But he will destroy them later." So let us examine a very common figure of speech in scripture, which occurs also in the present psalm; this will enable us to solve our problem more satisfactorily and accurately. It is quite plain that a little further on, speaking of these same people, and after telling the story of what the Egyptians had suffered on their account, the psalm arrives at the last plague, and continues, *He smote every first-born creature in the land of Egypt, and the first-fruits of everyone's labor in the land of Ham. He drew the people away like sheep, and led them carefully like a flock in the desert. He led them away in hope, and they were not afraid; and he submerged their enemies in the sea. He led them to his holy mountain, the mountain his own right hand had won. He expelled the Gentiles before them, and parcelled out the land to them by lots* (Ps 77(78):51-54). Now suppose someone challenges us on these verses by saying, "How can he list all these as benefits conferred upon them, when the individuals who were freed from Egypt were not admitted into the promised land, but died in the desert?" What can we reply, but that these things were said to have happened to them because the one same people maintained its identity through successive generations of its children? Accordingly, when we hear these verses, and particularly when we notice that the verbs are in the future tense (*he will show forbearance towards their sins, and will not destroy them. He will be yet more generous in turning away his wrath, and will not unleash all his*

---

42. See Gn 4:15.
43. See Ps 100(101):1.

anger upon them), we must understand that the predictions were fulfilled in those of whom the apostle says, *In our own day a remnant has been saved, thanks to election by grace* (Rom 11:5). In the same vein he says, *Surely God has not cast off his people? By no means. For I am myself sprung from the race of Israel, of the tribe of Benjamin, a Hebrew of Hebrew stock* (Rom 11:1; Ph 3:5). These, then, were the individuals scripture had in view, the members of that people destined to believe in Christ and to receive forgiveness for their sins, even to that greatest sin of all in which like madmen they killed the physician himself. This is undoubtedly why it is said, in reference to them, *God is merciful, and will show forbearance towards their sins, and will not destroy them. He will be yet more generous in turning away his wrath*, because he even forgave them for killing his only Son; and he *will not unleash all his anger upon them*. No, truly, for *a remnant has been saved*.

24. *He remembers that they are mere flesh, a roving spirit that does not readily return*. Precisely because they were unable of themselves to come back, he himself called them back by his grace, summoning them and taking pity upon them; for how can a creature of flesh, a spirit that can wander off but not return, borne by the weight of its guilt towards the lowest and farthest places, find its way back, unless through God's gracious election? And this is not given like a reward duly earned; it is granted gratis and unmerited, to the end that an ungodly person may be justified and a lost sheep come home. Nor is this achieved by its own efforts. The sheep is carried home on the shepherd's shoulders.[44] It had the power to ruin itself by wandering where its fancy took it, but it had no power to find itself; and it certainly would not be found if the shepherd did not in his mercy search for it. The son who came to himself and said, *I will rise up and return to my father* (Lk 15:18) was no different from the sheep. He too was sought and brought back to life by hidden calling and inspiration, and only by the One who gives life to all things. By whom was that young man found, if not by him who went forth to save and seek out the lost?[45] *For he was dead, but came back to life; he had perished, but was found* (Lk 15:24).

In the light of this we can solve a perplexing question about a text in Proverbs, where scripture gives a warning about the path of sin: *No one who walks that way will return* (Prv 2:19). This statement refers to the hopeless case of all sinners, but scripture also points to the possibility of grace. Human beings can tread that path of themselves, but cannot find their way back unaided. Yet when called by grace they can return.

---

44. See Lk 15:5.
45. See Lk 19:10.

Verses 40-51. Figurative interpretation of the plagues visited upon Egypt

25. As for that crooked and troublesome lot, *how often they provoked him in the desert, and roused him to anger in that waterless place! They turned away and put God to the test; they provoked the Holy One of Israel.* The psalmist recalls once more that infidelity of theirs which he has related earlier; his reason for repeating it is to set it against the background of the plagues God inflicted on Egypt for Israel's sake. These things needed to be kept in mind, lest the people prove ungrateful. And indeed, what follows? *They did not remember what his hand had wrought on the day he redeemed them from the hand of their harsh master.* Now the psalm begins to list what God did to the Egyptians: *He wrought his wonderful signs in Egypt, his prodigies in the plains of Zoan. He turned their rivers into blood, and made their showers undrinkable,* or better, *their springs,* as some interpret the Greek τὰ ὀβρήματα more correctly; for it means springs of water bubbling from below. The Egyptians dug, but instead of water they found blood. *He sent the dog-fly upon them to bite them, and the frog to bring devastation. He consigned their harvest to mildew, their crops to the locust. He destroyed their vines with hail, their mulberry trees with frost. He exposed their beasts to hailstones, and delivered their possessions to fire. He launched his furious anger against them—fury and anger and tribulation, a visitation by evil angels. He cleared a path for the course of his anger; he did not spare them from death, and he doomed their animals. Then he smote every first-born creature in the land of Egypt, and the first-fruits of everyone's labor amid the tents of Ham.*

26. All these Egyptian plagues can be interpreted allegorically according to the particular way each person chooses to understand them and select terms of comparison. We will attempt to do the same, and the more successfully in proportion to whatever measure of divine help may be available to us. We are compelled to take this approach by the words of this same psalm, *I will open my mouth in parables, and give utterance to enigmas hidden from the beginning.* This in fact is the reason why certain events are related here of which Exodus makes no mention at all among Egypt's misfortunes, even though it enumerates all the plagues in order and with the utmost care. Since we are convinced that there must be some point in the psalm's recounting an episode of which Exodus says nothing, and since we have no option but to interpret it figuratively, we are justified in assuming that the same criterion applies to other episodes which are known to have happened: these things occurred and were recorded on account of their symbolic significance. Scripture commonly proceeds like this in reporting the oracles of the prophets. It makes some assertion for which no ground can be found in the actual event which is apparently being reported; indeed, the facts appear to be at variance with the statement. From this we are meant to conclude that what seems to be said is not the real message; we must be aware of another meaning. Take as an example the prediction that *He will rule from sea to sea,*

from the river to the ends of the earth (Ps 71(72):8). This was manifestly not verified in the reign of Solomon, of which the psalm was ostensibly speaking. It was in fact speaking of Christ the Lord.

The case is similar for Egypt's plagues. In the book of Exodus scripture enumerates all those which afflicted the Egyptians; it relates them with the greatest care and in due order, yet there is no mention of the plague recorded in our psalm, *he consigned their harvest to mildew.* Moreover, after stating that *he exposed their beasts to hailstorms* the psalm adds, *and delivered their possessions to fire*; but although we do read in Exodus of the animals killed by hail,[46] nothing at all is said there of the burning of the Egyptians' property. Noise and fiery flashes may well have accompanied the hail, as thunder and lightning commonly go together, but Exodus does not say that anything was burnt. Furthermore, the soft things which hail could not harm were said not to have been struck or damaged by the hard blows, and in fact the locusts subsequently devoured them. Nor does Exodus relate the destruction of *their mulberry trees with frost*; there is a considerable difference between frost and hail, for it is on still winter nights that the earth turns white with frost.

27. It follows, then, that commentators must do the best they can in deciding what these various things symbolize, and the reader or listener must assess the result. The water changed to blood seems to me a sign of carnal judgment about the causes of things. The dog-fly symbolizes dog-like morals, because at birth puppies do not see even their parents. The frog stands for talkative vanity. Mildew does damage imperceptibly; some take it to be rust, others mold. To which vice can this noxious element more fittingly be compared than that which is detected only with the greatest difficulty, namely excessive self-confidence? Just as a harmful gas brings about this effect in fruit in a hidden way, so too does secret pride in the moral life of those who think they are something, whereas they are nothing. The locust stands for the malice which does its ill work with the mouth, that is, by untruthful testimony. Hail is the sin of taking what belongs to others, and issues in theft, plunder and robbery, though by this vice the one who ruins others is more thoroughly ruined. Frost typifies that vicious process whereby love of our neighbor freezes in the darkness of folly, as though in nocturnal cold. The fire mentioned here cannot be the lightning which accompanied the hail, flashing from thunderclouds, because here we are told that God *delivered their possessions to fire*; this must mean that it burnt their property, which lightning is not said to have done. I take it, then, to represent savage anger, which may even lead on to homicide. The death of the cattle stands for the loss of purity, I think, because we have in common with cattle the sexual desire which gives rise to offspring, and to keep it tamed and regulated is the virtue of purity.

---

46. See Ex 9:25.

The death of the first-born symbolizes the loss of that justice whereby each person lives in right relationships with the rest of the human race.

Whether the figurative meanings of these events are as we have described them, or it is better to take them in some other sense, no one can fail to be struck by the coincidence between the ten plagues that afflicted the Egyptians and the tablets inscribed with the ten commandments for the governance of God's people. Since we have elsewhere drawn comparisons between the plagues and the commandments, however,[47] there is no need to overload the exposition of this psalm with them; we would simply make the point that in this psalm also ten plagues visited upon the Egyptians are enumerated, though not in the same order, for in place of the three mentioned in Exodus that do not appear here—that is, lice, festering sores and darkness[48]—three others are included which are absent from Exodus: mildew, frost and fire; and this fire is not lightning, because it destroyed their property, a fact of which Exodus makes no mention.

God makes good use of bad angels

28. But our psalm has stated clearly enough that by God's judgment such things happen through the agency of bad angels in this wicked world, as they did in Egypt and the plain of Zoan, because here we must be humble until the coming of that other world where we hope to have deserved exaltation by our present humility. The name "Egypt" in Hebrew means darkness or tribulations, and in the same tongue "Zoan" means the lowly commandment of humility, as I have noted already. Now something is inserted about bad angels in our psalm in connection with the plagues, and we should not pass over it without comment: *he launched his furious anger against them—fury and anger and tribulation, a visitation by evil angels.* No one among the faithful is unaware that the devil and his angels are so wicked that eternal fire is prepared for them. But that through their agency a visitation should be sent by the Lord God upon people whom he judges to deserve such a punishment seems harsh to those who have little aptitude for understanding how God's supreme justice makes good use even of bad creatures. As far as their essence is concerned, of course, no one but God made them, but he did not make them bad. Nonetheless, because he is good, he puts them to good use, which is to say he uses them in a fitting and just manner, as, conversely, wicked people use his good creatures in a bad way. God uses bad angels, then, not only to punish bad people, as in the case the psalm speaks of, and in that of King Ahab, who by God's will was misled by a spirit of falsehood

---

47. See his sermon *On the Plagues of Egypt and the Ten Commandments*, Vol. III/1 in this series, pp. 240-247.
48. See Ex 8:17; 9:10; 10:22.

so that he should fall in battle,[49] but also to prove and show up good people, as he did with Job.

As for the physical material of those natural elements, I think that both good and bad angels can make use of it in proportion to the power each of them possesses, just as good and evil men and women also use such things insofar as human frailty allows. We use earth, water, air and fire not only for necessary purposes to support our life, but also for many superfluous and recreational pursuits and for wonderfully intricate operations; for all those innumerable contrivances called μηχανήματα are controlled by these elements, scientifically harnessed. Far greater power over them is enjoyed by the angels, both good and bad, but undoubtedly more by the good, though only insofar as God's will and ordinance either commands or permits. So too with ourselves, for we cannot do anything we like with these elements. In that Book which cannot lie we read that the devil was able even to send fire from the sky to burn up in its amazing, horrifying onslaught most of a holy man's cattle. Perhaps no one among the faithful would dare to attribute so much power to the devil were it not attested by the authority of holy scripture. Yet that man who by God's gift was righteous, and brave, and skilled in holy wisdom, did not say, "The Lord gave, and the devil took them away," but *The Lord gave, and the Lord has taken away* (Jb 1:16.21). He well knew that even what the devil had power to do with those elements he would not have done to a servant of God, except by the will and permission of his Lord. He thus confounded the devil's malice, because he knew who it was who was making use of it to prove him. Among the children of disobedience[50] the devil works as upon his slaves, just as humans have the disposition of their animals, but there too only as far as the just judgment of God allows. But it is one thing when the devil's power to do as he pleases even with his own is restrained by a higher power, and something quite different when power is granted to him even over those who are alien to him. To put it in human terms, a man does as he wishes with his own beast, but not if he is restrained by a higher power, whereas before doing as he will with someone else's beast he must first seek permission from its owner. In the former instance, a power which he held is checked; in the latter, what did not belong to him is granted.

29. This being the case, if God inflicted the plagues on the Egyptians through bad angels, should we presume to say that the water was turned into blood by those same angels, and that the frogs were made by the same angels? After all, Pharaoh's magicians were able to achieve similar feats by their spells, so we would have to say that bad angels were fighting on both sides, on the one hand inflicting plagues and on the other working tricks, and that this occurred by the judgment and dispensation of the most just and almighty God, who was making just use even of the

---

49. See 1 Kgs 22:22.
50. See Eph 2:2.

malice of those wicked creatures. No, I would not dare to say so; for why were Pharaoh's wizards quite unable to produce the lice?[51] Because the wicked angels were not permitted to do so? Perhaps it is preferable to say that the reason is a hidden one which escapes our powers of detection. Suppose we were to conclude that God performed those feats through bad angels because it was a case of punishments being meted out, not benefits conferred, and God never imposes punishments through good angels, but only through those who act as executioners for heaven's army, we should then be forced to believe that Sodom was destroyed by bad angels; and then Abraham and Lot would have entertained bad angels as their guests[52]—all of which must be wrong: God forbid that we should hold an opinion so opposed to the plain sense of the scriptures. It is obvious, therefore, that such misfortunes can be visited upon human beings by either good angels or bad. What these punishments ought to be, and when he should mete them out, is hidden from me, but not from him who acts thus, nor from anyone to whom he chooses to reveal it. Insofar as the divine scripture accommodates itself to our scrutiny, however, we read of penalties imposed on bad people both through good angels, as in the case of the Sodomites, and through bad angels too, as on the Egyptians; but I can think of no instance where righteous people are tested and proved by bodily sufferings through the action of good angels.

30. Now to return to the place we have reached in the present psalm. We dare not attribute to wicked angels the wonderful things wrought in created elements, but there are other effects which we may unhesitatingly ascribe to them, such as the death of cattle, the death of the first-born, and above all that effect on which all the rest are to be blamed, the hardening of the Egyptians' hearts so that they were unwilling to let God's people go. Although it is said that God brings about this most sinful and malicious obstinacy in them,[53] he does so not by instigating or inspiring it, but by abandoning them, so that wicked angels may produce in those children of unbelief[54] what God duly and justly permits. This is how we must interpret that saying of the prophet Isaiah, *Lo, you were angry, Lord, and we sinned; that is why we went astray and have all become unclean* (Is 64:5.6). Something happened initially which provoked God to righteous anger, and so he withdrew his light from them; the consequence was that human blindness in wandering and straying from the path of righteousness stumbled into sins which no subterfuge could make out not to be sinful. When another psalm asserts that God moved the hearts of the Egyptians to hate his people and deal fraudulently with his servants,[55] we are justified in believing that God acted through malevo-

---

51. See Ex 7:20.22; 8:6.7.17.18.
52. See Gn 18 and 19.
53. See Ex 4:21.
54. See Eph 2:2.
55. See Ps 104(105):25.

lent angels, so that the already vicious minds of the children of unbelief might be roused to hatred of God's people through angels who looked favorably on those same vices, and thus prodigies might ensue which would terrify and correct the good people.

Moreover, since our psalm prefixed the words, *I will open my mouth in parables*, we have excellent reason to believe that those immoral dispositions which we saw to be symbolized by the bodily plagues are fomented by bad angels in people who by divine justice are subjected to them. When the apostle's statement is verified, *God has delivered them to their own lusts, so that they behave as they should not* (Rom 1:24), it cannot but be that the evil angels are at home with such conduct and rejoice in it, as in the material with which they can work, for vicious humans (except those whom grace sets free) are most justly subject to them.

Now, *who is equal to the task ahead?* (2 Cor 2:16). After stating that God *launched his furious anger against them—fury and anger and tribulation, a visitation by evil angels*—the psalm adds, *He cleared a path for the course of his anger.* Who can grasp this, whose gaze is penetrating enough to understand the meaning so deeply hidden here? God's anger already had a course it could take to punish the impious Egyptians in accordance with his secret justice; yet he is said to have *cleared a path for* that same *course*, so that by dragging them from concealed sins into open villainy through the agency of malevolent angels he might wreak conspicuous vengeance on those conspicuous evildoers.

Nothing but the grace of God liberates men and women from this dominance by evil angels, as the apostle suggests: *He has plucked us away from the power of darkness and brought us across into the kingdom of his beloved Son* (Col 1:13). The people of Israel experienced this figuratively, for they were plucked away from the power of the Egyptians and brought across into the royal land of promise which flowed with milk and honey, symbol of the sweetness of grace.

Verses 52-54. The good shepherd

31. Accordingly the psalm continues, after enumerating the plagues suffered by the Egyptians, *He drew his people away like sheep, and led them carefully like a flock in the desert. He led them away in hope, and they were not afraid; and he submerged their enemies in the sea.* The more inwardly this happens, the more real it is, because in our own hearts we have been snatched from the power of darkness and brought into God's kingdom. There within we become God's sheep, fed in spiritual pastures, and we walk through this world as through a desert, because our faith is not obvious to anyone. This is why the apostle says, *Your life is hidden with Christ in God* (Col 3:3). But it is in hope that we are being led, for *in hope we have been saved* (Rom 8:24); yet we must not be afraid, for *if*

God is for us, who can stand against us? (Rom 8:31). And he has drowned our enemies in the sea, having wiped them out in baptism by forgiving our sins.

32. The psalm continues, *He led them to his holy mountain.* But how much better to be led into the Church! *The mountain his own right hand had won.* But how much loftier than that mountain is the Church Christ won, Christ, of whom it was said, *To whom has the arm of the Lord been revealed?* (Is 53:1). *He expelled the Gentiles before them*—and before his faithful too, for the malignant spirits of Gentile errors can in a sense be called Gentiles themselves. *And he parcelled out the land to them by lots.* Similarly in us *the one same Spirit is at work in all operations, distributing appropriate gifts to each one as he wills* (1 Cor 12:11).

Verses 55-58. Even in the promised land Israel was still unfaithful

33. *And he made the tribes of Israel dwell in their tents.* Our psalm means that God caused the tribes of Israel to take over the tents of the Gentiles; but I think it makes better sense for us to discuss that spiritually, taking it to mean that through the grace of Christ we are borne up to the glory of heaven, from which the sinful angels were cast out and thrown down. I think so, because that *crooked and troublesome* set did not lay aside the garment of its old ways in response to God's material favors; instead they still *put God the Most High to the test and provoked him to anger, and did not observe his commandments; they turned away and did not keep the covenant, just like their fathers.* By a covenant and a binding promise they had declared, *Whatever the Lord our God has said, we will do; we will be obedient* (Ex 19:8). It is to be noted that the text says, *like their fathers,* although throughout the entire psalm it has apparently been speaking about and to those very people; now it seems to be speaking of those who were already in the promised land, and so it refers to the ones who were troublesome in the desert as "their fathers."

34. *They turned into a crooked bow,* says the psalm, or, as other codices have it, *a warped bow.* What this means is clear from the phrase that follows: *and they stirred him to anger on their hills*: it means that they rushed into idolatry. The bow was so warped that it aimed not at the Lord's name but against it, away from the name of him who had said to this same people, *You shall have no other gods but me* (Ex 20:3). The bow is a symbol of the mind's intention. Finally the psalmist explains the point more clearly by saying, *They provoked him to jealousy with their graven images.*

Verses 59-64. Punishments in the era of the judges

35. *God heard, and rejected them*: that is to say, he noticed what they were doing and asserted his rights. *And he reduced Israel to nothing*. Yes, for if God rejected them, what could be left of these people who had been what they had been only with God's help? There is no doubt that the allusion is to their defeat by foreigners in the time of the priest Eli,[56] when the ark of the Lord was captured and the Israelites were slaughtered in great numbers. This is why the psalm continues, *He forsook his tent at Shiloh, that tent where he dwelt among mortals*. The reason for his forsaking it is made elegantly clear by the phrase, *where he dwelt among mortals*; for since they were unworthy to have him dwelling among them, why should he not forsake his tent, which had been pitched not for its own sake but for theirs, whom he now judged unworthy of his presence among them?

36. *He delivered their strength into captivity, their beauty into the enemy's hands*. The ark, on account of which they thought themselves invincible, and congratulated themselves, is here called *their strength* and *their beauty*. Later on God strikes terror into them for their evil way of life through a prophet who warned, *Look what I did at Shiloh, where once my tent stood* (Jr 7:12).

37. *He consigned his people to the sword, and rejected his inheritance. Fire devoured their young men* (that means his anger did so) *and their young girls did not mourn*. There was no time for lamentation, so afraid were they of their enemies.

38. *Their priests fell by the sword, and for their widows no lamentation was made*. Eli's sons fell by the sword while the wife of one of them, now widowed, was on the point of dying in childbirth; and such was the confusion that no funeral rite could be arranged to mourn her.[57]

Verses 65-66. The Lord arises to save them

39. *The Lord was aroused as though from sleep*. The Lord seems to be asleep when he delivers his people into the hands of those who hate them and taunt them with the question, *Where is your God, then?* (Ps 41:11(42:10)). But now he *was aroused as though from sleep, aroused like a strong man who has slept off his wine*. No one would dare to say such a thing about God except his own Spirit. The meaning is that when God does not come to our help as swiftly as people expect, it seems to ungodly mockers that he is asleep for a long time, like someone overpowered by drink.

40. *And he smote his enemies on their rear*, those enemies who were rejoicing that they had managed to capture the ark. On their back parts the blows fell:[58] this

56. See 1 Sm 4:10,11.
57. See 1 Sm 4:19.20.
58. See 1 Sm 5:6.

seems to me to symbolize the punishment that anyone will suffer who looks back to what has been left behind, to those things which, as the apostle says, are to be rated as dung.[59] People who receive God's testament in such a way that they do not shed the vanities of their old life are like that hostile race who placed the captured ark of the testament alongside their idols. And what happens? Against the worshipers' will those old idols fall down,[60] because *all flesh is but grass, and all* human *splendor like the flower of the field. The grass is dried up and the flower wilted, but the* ark *of the Lord abides for ever* (Is 40:6.7). What *abides* is the secret hidden in the testament: that is, the kingdom of heaven, where lives the eternal Word of God. But people who have set their hearts on the things that lie behind them will be with all justice tormented by those same things; for the psalm declares, *He condemned them to everlasting shame.*

Verses 67-68. The election of Judah foreshadows Christ and the Church

41. He rejected the tent of Joseph, and did not choose the tribe of Ephraim. He chose the tribe of Judah. The psalm does not say, "He rejected the tent of Reuben," who was Jacob's first-born son, nor that he rejected the others who came after Reuben but were born before Judah, in order that the tribe of Judah might be chosen once those had been passed over. It might have been said that they were justly rejected, for even in the blessings which Jacob conferred on his sons[61] he severely condemned their sins as there recorded, even though one of those tribes was that of Levi, which deserved to be the priestly tribe and from which sprang Moses.[62] Nor does the psalm say, "He rejected the tent of Benjamin," from which the kingship took its rise, since Saul was chosen out of Benjamin.[63] It would have seemed fitting that the psalm should mention this since Saul's repudiation and the election of David came so close together in time,[64] yet it does not say so. Rather the psalmist chose to name those who appeared to shine with more obvious merits. Joseph fed his father and brothers in Egypt, and though he had been wickedly sold he was most deservedly exalted in rank on account of his God-fearing faith, chastity and wisdom.[65] Similarly Ephraim was given precedence over his elder brother by his grandfather's blessing;[66] yet God *rejected the tent of Joseph, and did not choose the tribe of Ephraim.*

---

59. See Ph 3:8.
60. See 1 Sm 5:2-4.
61. See Gn 49:1-7.
62. See Ex 2:1.
63. See 1 Sm 9:1.2.
64. See 1 Sm 16:1.13.
65. See Gn 41:39-40.
66. See Gn 48:19.

When persons of such high renown and merit are passed over, what else are we to understand but the rejection and repudiation of that whole people who in their inveterate greed sought earthly rewards from the Lord, and the election of the tribe of Judah, quite independently of any personal merits in Judah himself? Indeed, Joseph's merits far surpassed those of Judah, yet scripture testifies that, because Christ sprang from the tribe of Judah according to the flesh, it was through the tribe of Judah that the new people of Christ was given precedence over that ancient people. Such is our understanding as the Lord opens his mouth in parables.

Moreover in the following words, *Mount Zion, which he loved,* we can discern the Church of Christ still more plainly. This Church does not worship God in the hope of carnal favors for the present age, but with the eyes of faith contemplates from afar the rewards of eternity, for the name "Zion" means "Contemplation."

Verse 69. The temple, sign of the indefectible Church

42. The psalm continues, *And he built his sanctifying place like a place of unicorns,* or, as some interpreters have it, by coining a new word (*sanctificium*), *built his sanctuary.* The best way to take *unicorns* is to refer it to those whose steadfast faith is raised up to that single thing of which another psalm speaks: *One thing have I begged of the Lord, and that will I seek after* (Ps 26(27):4). God's sanctuary has been understood in the light of the apostle Peter's words as the *holy nation, royal priesthood* (1 Pt 2:9).

The next words are *in the land, establishing it for ever.* The Greek codices here have εἰς τὸν αἰῶνα. Latin interpreters can take this to mean either "for ever" or "throughout this age" as they wish, for it means both, and in consequence some Latin codices have the one, some the other. Some others again have the plural, "throughout the ages," but we have not found this reading in the Greek codices we have to hand. Still, can any of the faithful doubt that, although as some depart and others arrive the Church does travel out of this life and is subject to mortality, it is nonetheless established for ever?

Verses 70-72. David, type and ancestor of Christ

43. *He chose his servant David.* So then, God chose the tribe of Judah in view of David, and David in view of Christ, and thus it was in view of Christ that he chose Judah. The blind, who knew that Christ was passing, cried out, *Take pity on us, Son of David* (Mt 20:30), and immediately through that pity of his they did receive their sight,[67] because what they shouted was true. But it was by no means

67. See Mt 20:34.

in passing that the apostle most earnestly admonished Timothy, *Remember Jesus Christ, risen from the dead, born of David's lineage, whom my gospel proclaims. In its service I am laboring even to the point of being fettered like a criminal, but God's word is not bound* (2 Tm 2:8-9). Clearly, then, our Savior, he who according to the flesh was born from David's line, is here typified in our psalm by the name "David," because the Lord is opening his mouth in parables. It should not disconcert us that when saying, *He chose David* (under which name he indicated Christ), the psalmist called him God's *servant* rather than his Son: we should recognize that what is envisaged here is not the substance of the Only-Begotten, coeternal with the Father, but the form of a servant[68] which he received from David's stock.

44. *He called him from the flocks of sheep, from the breeding ewes he took him away, to pasture Jacob his servant, and Israel his own inheritance.* Now the David of old, from whose flesh Christ derived, was seconded from his job of pasturing sheep to that of reigning over human beings; our David, Jesus, passed from humans to other humans, from Jews to Gentiles, yet in terms of the parable he could be said to have been taken away from some sheep and transferred to other sheep. This is so because those churches of Christ in Judea, the churches of the circumcised which were there soon after the passion and resurrection of the Lord, no longer exist in that land. The apostle mentioned them when he declared, *Christ's churches in Judea did not know me by sight; they only heard that "the man who was formerly persecuting us is now spreading the good news of the faith he earlier sought to stamp out"; and they glorified the Lord for me* (Gal 1:22-24). But the churches consisting of circumcised peoples have now passed away from there. In that Judea, the earthly Judea of today, Christ is no longer present; he has been taken away from there and now pastures the flocks of the Gentiles.

With good reason is he said to have been taken from following *the breeding ewes*. Those ancient churches could rightly be called so, for in the Song of Songs churches like this are saluted. One Church is addressed which is composed of many churches, one flock whose members form many flocks. To such as these, then, scripture says, *Your teeth* (this signifies the organs you use to speak with, or those by which you draw others into your own body, as though by eating), *Your teeth are like newly-shorn flocks, coming up from their washing. All of them bear twins; there is never a barren one among them* (Sg 4:2). This is especially true because in those early days believers rid themselves of worldly burdens like fleeces, laying at the feet of the apostles the proceeds from the sale of their property.[69] They were newly come up from the laver about which the apostle Peter

---

68. See Ph 2:7.
69. See Acts 2:45; 4:34.

had exhorted the Jews who were anxious over having shed Christ's blood, urging them, *Repent, and let every one of you be baptized in the name of the Lord Jesus Christ, that your sins may be forgiven* (Acts 2:38). Moreover they did give birth to twins, inasmuch as they brought forth acts of twofold charity—love of God and of their neighbors; and accordingly there was no sterile person among them.

From following these breeding ewes our David was taken, and now he pastures other flocks among the Gentiles. Yet these are truly Jacob and Israel, as our psalm says, *to pasture Jacob his servant, and Israel his own inheritance*, for the fact that these are Gentile sheep does not make them alien to the race of Jacob and Israel. The offspring of Abraham is the offspring by promise, as the Lord told him: *Through Isaac you will have descendants* (Gn 21:12). The apostle explains this by telling us, *Not the children of his flesh, but the children of the promise, are accounted his descendants* (Gal 3:29).

When the psalm says, *Jacob his servant, and Israel his own inheritance*, we simply have a repetition of the thought, as is the custom in scripture. But possibly someone may wish to distinguish between the two phrases, pointing out that Jacob is a servant in this present age, but will be God's eternal inheritance when he sees the Lord face to face, as was implied when Jacob's name was changed to Israel.[70]

45. *He pastured them in the innocence of his heart.* What was more innocent than he who not only was overcome by no sin, but had no sin he needed to overcome?[71] *And he led them by his understanding hands* (or, as some codices have it, *by the understandings of his hands*). Someone else might have thought it made better sense to say, "In the innocence of his hands and the understanding of his heart"; but this author knew better than anyone else what he was saying, and he preferred to link innocence with the heart, and understanding with the hands. As far as I can see, the reason for his choice was that there are many people who commit no evil deeds, and so think themselves innocent; but the reason they commit none is that they are afraid they would suffer for it if they did, and they would have wished to commit them if they could have done so with impunity. Such people may seem to have innocent hands, but have no innocence of heart. And what is innocence like that? What is it worth if it is not found in the heart, where the human person is made in God's image?

When the psalm says, *He led them by his understanding hands*, or *by the intelligence of his hands*, I think it means to refer to that intelligence which he himself creates in believers; that is why it says *his hands*, for hands do creative work. But this implies that the hands are those of God, for Christ is man in such wise that he

---

70. See Gn 32:28.
71. See Jn 8:46.

is God too. The David of old, from whom Christ was descended, certainly could not do this for the people over whom he reigned as a human king; but that King could, to whom the faithful soul may rightly pray, *Make me understand, and I will study your law* (Ps 118(119):34).

So then, let us surrender ourselves by faith into his hands, lest we stray from him by trusting in our own intelligence as though it were something we originated ourselves. May he create it in us, so that he may pluck us from our waywardness and lead us by the understanding of his hands, and bring us home to where we can go astray no longer. This is the reward of God's people, which bends its ear to the words he speaks: in Christ God directs its heart, and its spirit is entrusted to him, and so it is saved from turning into a crooked and troublesome generation. But once it has heard all this teaching, this people must put its hope in God not only with regard to the present life, but for eternal life also, not merely with a view to receiving rewards for good works, but also that it may be empowered to do them.

Exposition of Psalm 78[1]

Introduction: the psalmist prophetically describes future events as though he were contemporary with them

1. I do not think we need spend much time over the title to this psalm, as it is so brief and simple; but we know that the prophecy we read here was unmistakably fulfilled. When these events were sung about in the reign of King David, nothing of the sort had yet happened; there had been no Gentile onslaughts against the city of Jerusalem, or against the temple of God, which was not yet built. Everyone knows that after David's death it was his son Solomon who erected the temple. The psalmist is therefore speaking in the past tense about things that he knew by inspiration would happen in the future: *O God, the Gentiles have invaded your inheritance.* When another psalm prophesies concerning the Lord's passion, *They put poison in my food, and in my thirst gave me vinegar to drink* (Ps 68:22(69:21)), it is adopting the same convention of speech, and this holds for all the other events which, though future, are recounted in that psalm as though they had occurred already.[2]

It should not surprise us that these statements are made to God. He is not being informed about things of which he is ignorant, for it is by his revelation that they are known in advance; rather a soul is conversing with God in a spirit of devotion which God recognizes.[3] When angels make announcements to mortals, these announcements are made to persons who are ignorant, but when they bring tidings to God, they are telling him what he already knows. This is what happens when they offer our prayers to him, or in some way beyond our understanding take counsel about their own actions with his eternal truth, as with an unchangeable law. In a similar way this man of God tells God what he learns from God, as a disciple might give a recital to a master who is not ignorant but judges what he hears, and so will commend the lessons he has himself taught or correct what he has not. This is more especially the case with the psalmist, who in his attitude of prayer puts himself in the place of future generations who will witness the actual

---

1. This Exposition seems to have followed closely on his Exposition of Psalm 77, to which he refers twice.
2. Augustine assumes throughout that the author of the present psalm was a contemporary of King David (10th century B.C.).
3. Variant: "… devotion, for are there any things that God does not see?"

125

events. It is quite usual in prayer for us to relate to God calamities which he has himself visited upon us as punishment, and to add a petition that he will now have mercy and spare us. Here too the psalmist is both telling and foretelling, and recounting the disasters in the persons of those whom they will befall. This lamentation and prayer are a prophecy.

Verses 1-4. In what sense was Israel still "God's inheritance" after Christ's resurrection?

2. *O God, the Gentiles have invaded your inheritance; they have defiled your holy temple, and left Jerusalem no better than a place for storing fruit. They have exposed the corpses of your servants as carrion for the birds of the sky, and the carcasses of your holy ones as prey for the beasts of the earth. They poured out your servants' blood like water round about Jerusalem, and there was no one to bury them.* It is possible that some among us may wish to refer this prophecy to the destruction of Jerusalem by the Roman emperor Titus, at the time when our Lord Jesus Christ, now risen and ascended, was being proclaimed among the Gentiles. But I do not see how the Jewish people could be called God's inheritance at that time, when it had not remained loyal to Christ but had rejected and killed him and was therefore rejected itself, when it had not been willing to believe in him even after his resurrection, and went on to kill the martyrs too. There were some from that Israelite people who believed in Christ; to them Christ was offered and the promise was made good in a way fruitful for their salvation. It is of these that the Lord himself said, *I was not sent except to the lost sheep of the house of Israel* (Mt 15:24). These individuals *are the children of the promise, and are accounted* Abraham's *descendants* (Rom 9:8). They do belong to God's inheritance. From them sprang Joseph, that upright man,[4] and the Virgin Mary who bore Christ; from them was John the Baptist, the bridegroom's friend,[5] and his parents Zechariah and Elizabeth;[6] from them also were the old man Simeon and the widow Anna, who heard Christ though he was not yet speaking to their bodily ears, for their spiritual ears were alert to an infant unable to speak.[7] From them were the blessed apostles, and Nathanael in whom there was no deceit,[8] and another Joseph who was also on the lookout for God's kingdom.[9] From them too was that great crowd who went ahead of Christ's mount and followed it, crying, *Blessed is he who is coming in the name of the Lord* (Mt 21:9); and among these was a group of children, in whom the Lord

---

4. See Mt 1:16.
5. See Jn 3:29.
6. See Lk 1:5.
7. See Lk 2:25.36.
8. See Jn 1:47. On Nathanael see note at Exposition of Psalm 65,4.
9. See Jn 19:38; Lk 23:51.

declared the prophecy fulfilled, *Out of the mouths of infants and nurslings you have perfected praise* (Ps 8:3(2)). From the Jewish people came also that great number who were baptized, three thousand on one day, five thousand on another,[10] who were welded into a single mind and a single heart by the fire of charity, for none among them claimed anything as their own, but everything was held in common for all.[11] From them too came the saintly deacons, including Stephen who was crowned with martyrdom even before the apostles.[12]

From Israel came all those churches of Christ in Judea who did not know Paul by sight;[13] they knew his notorious savagery, but knew the all-merciful grace of Christ even better. From Israel came Paul himself who, according to the prophecy spoken of him long ago, was *a ravening wolf, seizing his prey in the morning, and at evening sharing out food*;[14] this means that after his early career as a ravening persecutor driving people to death he became a preacher who gave them the nourishment of life.

All these were from the Jewish people, and they were God's inheritance. This is why the teacher of the Gentiles, who called himself the least of the apostles,[15] posed the question, *Surely God has not cast off his people?* and replied, *By no means. For I am myself sprung from the stock of Israel, of the tribe of Benjamin. God has not cast off his own people, whom he foreknew* (Rom 11:1-2). The people who came from that nation to unite themselves to the body of Christ are God's inheritance. When the apostle asserts that *God has not cast off his own people, whom he foreknew*, he is undoubtedly corroborating another psalm, which declares, *God will not cast off his people*, and then goes on to clarify this by saying, *Nor will he abandon his inheritance* (Ps 93(94):14). From this it is clear who precisely were the people who were God's inheritance. Before Paul could make that assertion he had cited the witness borne by a prophet to Israel's future unbelief: *All day long I stretched out my hands to an unbelieving people who defied me* (Is 65:2; Rom 10:21). But someone might misunderstand this, and conclude that the entire race had been condemned for the sin of unbelief and defiance, so Paul immediately added, *Surely God has not cast off his people? By no means. For I am myself sprung from the race of Israel, of the tribe of Benjamin*. In these words he shows what "people" he meant: the former people, unquestionably; and if God had cast it off and condemned it in its entirety, Paul, who was of Abraham's stock and of the tribe of Benjamin, would certainly not

---

10. See Acts 2:41; 4:4.
11. See Acts 2:44-45; 4:32.
12. See Acts 7:58. His name in Greek is *Stephanos*, which means "crown."
13. See Gal 1:22.
14. Gn 49:27. In the "Blessings of Jacob" (Gn 49) these words are represented as spoken by Jacob over his youngest son, Benjamin. Paul claimed descent from the tribe of Benjamin; see Phil 3:5.
15. See 1 Cor 15:9.

have been an apostle of Christ. But he adds the further very pertinent testimony, *Are you unaware of what scripture says about Elijah, and how he appealed to God against Israel? "Lord, they have slain your prophets and undermined your altars. I am abandoned and alone, and they are seeking my life." And what is God's reply to him? "I have seven thousand men left to me who have not bent their knees to Baal." Even so in our own day a remnant has been saved, thanks to election by grace.*[16] Now God's inheritance from the nation of Israel is this remnant, not those others of whom Paul goes on to say, *But the rest are blinded,* for, *What are we to think? What Israel was seeking, it failed to win; the elect have won it, but the rest are blinded* (Rom 11:7). So it is these elect, this remnant, this people of God whom God has not rejected, who are called his inheritance. As for the Israel which did not win what it sought, the others who were afflicted with blindness, among them there was no longer any inheritance of God of whom it could be said, after Christ's ascension and in the time of the emperor Titus, *O God, the Gentiles have invaded your inheritance.* Nor could any of the other things be said of them which seem to be foretold in this psalm about the devastation of the nation's temple and its city.

Either the psalm must refer to an earlier time, when the whole of Israel still was God's inheritance, or it refers to the Christian Church

3. We are faced, then, with two possibilities. The first is this: we must understand this psalm to refer to the havoc wrought by other enemies before Christ came in the flesh, since at that time there was no other inheritance of God, and the holy prophets were included in the nation that was terribly ravaged when the deportation to Babylon took place. Then again under Antiochus the Maccabees endured horrible torments and won glorious crowns.[17] Indeed, the slaughter that occurs in war usually results in the kind of experiences our psalm mentions. Alternatively, if we consider that "God's inheritance" here referred to is that of a period later than the Lord's resurrection and ascension, the sufferings must be understood as those which his Church endured in the persons of its great throng

---

16. Rom 11:2-5. "Remnant" was a powerful biblical idea, initiated by the pre-exilic prophets and further refined by the experience of exile in the sixth century B.C. The remnant is the minority that will survive the current disaster and emerge, purified, to be the stock of a renewed and more faithful people. It came to represent an idealized Israel, God's elect, heir to the ancient promises. Paul wrestled with the mystery of the empirical Israel's apparent rejection in Rom 9–11, as Augustine goes on to say. In the end Christ alone is the elect, in whom the promises are fulfilled, and believers are elect in him.

17. He refers to two main periods of suffering and crisis: 1) the destruction of Jerusalem by the armies of Babylon in 587 B.C, which was followed by the deportation of many of the nation to Babylon; see 2 Kgs 25; Jer 39:1-10; and 2) the Hellenizing persecution under Antiochus IV Epiphanes in 167-164 B.C., an attempt by the Seleucid rulers of Judea to stamp out Jewish faith and observance, and impose pagan customs. The resistance was led by the Maccabean family.

of martyrs, at the hands of idolaters and enemies of the name of Christ.[18] It is true that "Asaph" means "synagogue," which in its turn means "congregation" or assembly," and that name is more usually applied to the Jewish people, but our Church too can be called a congregation, just as the earlier people is also called a church. We have dealt clearly and sufficiently with this point while expounding another psalm.[19]

The Church, God's inheritance, is built of Jews and Gentiles

This Church of ours, this inheritance of God, has been assembled from both the circumcised and the uncircumcised, that is, from the people of Israel and from other nations, assembled by *the stone rejected by the builders* which *has become the headstone of the corner* (Ps 117(118):22). They are like two walls, coming from different directions but joined in this cornerstone, for *he is himself our peace, since he united the two, to create from the two of them one new man in himself, so making peace, and to reconcile them to God in one body* (Eph 2:14-16). In this body we are children of God, crying, *Abba, Father!* (Rom 8:15; Gal 4:6). We cry *Abba* because that is their language, and *Father* because it is ours, but *Abba* and *Father* mean the same.

This is why the Lord who said, *I was not sent except for the lost sheep of the house of Israel* (Mt 15:24), thereby showing that God had granted his promised presence to that people in particular, also said in another place, *Other sheep I have, not counted in this fold; them too I must lead in, that there may be but one flock and one shepherd* (Jn 10:16). By these words he indicated the Gentiles whom he would bring in, not indeed by his bodily presence, for his claim that *I was not sent except for the lost sheep of the house of Israel* holds good, but through his gospel, which was to be spread abroad by *the beautiful feet of those who announce peace and bring good news* (Rom 10:15).[20] Truly, *their sound echoed throughout the world, and their words to the ends of the earth* (Ps 18:5(19:4)). The apostle could thus rightly say, *I maintain that Christ Jesus was a servant of the circumcised, to save the faithfulness of God and confirm the promises made to our fathers*, which assertion accords with Christ's words, *I was not sent except for the lost sheep of the house of Israel*; but the apostle immediately added, *to give the Gentiles cause to glorify God for his mercy*, and this in turn echoes Christ's saying, *Other sheep I have, not counted in this fold; them too I must lead in, that there may be but one flock and one shepherd*. Both aspects

---

18. Compare 1 Pt 4:14-16. See also note at Exposition 2 of Psalm 68,4.
19. Compare his Exposition of Psalm 77,3.
20. Compare Is 52:7.

are briefly summed up in a prophetic verse which the apostle quotes: *Rejoice, Gentiles, with his own people* (Rom 15:8-10).[21]

It is this one flock, then, under the one shepherd, which is God's inheritance, and this means not the Father's inheritance only, but the Son's too, for it is the Son's voice that we hear in a psalm, *The measuring-lines have fallen for me in delightful places, indeed my inheritance fills me with delight* (Ps 15(16):6). Through a prophet's voice that same inheritance answers him: *Take possession of us, Lord* (Is 26:13, LXX). The Father did not die to leave his Son this inheritance, but the Son won the right to it himself by his death, and took possession of it by his resurrection.

4. If this is the inheritance of which the psalm prophetically sings, and if we understand the words, *O God, the Gentiles have invaded your inheritance*, to mean that the Gentiles forced their way into the Church not by believing but by persecuting it (that is, they invaded it with the intention of ruining and utterly destroying it, as the example of so many persecutions has demonstrated), we must take the next line, *they have defiled your holy temple*, to refer not to wood and stone, but to human beings, from whom, as from living stones, God's house is being built, as the apostle Peter teaches.[22] The apostle Paul tells us quite plainly, *God's temple is holy, and that temple is yourselves* (1 Cor 3:17). The persecutors certainly did defile that temple in those whom they persuaded by threats or torture to deny Christ, and coerced by insistent pressure to worship idols. But many of these were restored and cleansed from that defilement by repentance. It is a penitent's voice that cries, *Wash me yet more from my offense*, and again, *Create a clean heart in me, O God, and implant a new and right spirit within me* (Ps 50:4.12 (51:2.10)).

The psalm continues, *They have left Jerusalem no better than a place for storing fruit*.[23] Under this description we have good reason to recognize the Church itself, of whom it is said, *The free Jerusalem is our mother. Of her scripture says, "Rejoice, you barren one, you who are childless, leap and cry out for joy, you who have never given birth, for she who has been deserted bears many children, more than the wedded wife"* (Gal 4:26-27).[24] I think the phrase *a place for storing fruit* suggests the deserted scene left by persecution. When people grow fruit the storage-places are left deserted once the fruit has been transferred; and similarly after a persecution the Church has a deserted look, because the souls of the martyrs have been conveyed to the heavenly table, like abundant fruit of delicious sweetness from the Lord's garden.

---

21. Compare Dt 32:43.
22. See 1 Pt 2:5.
23. Compare Is 1:18; Jer 26:18.
24. Compare Is 54:1

Persecution of the saints throughout the world: a lament

5. *They have exposed the corpses of your servants as carrion for the birds of the sky, and the carcasses of your holy ones as prey for the beasts of the earth.* The word *corpses* is echoed in *carcasses*, and the phrase *your servants* recurs as *your holy ones*; the only variation is from *the birds of the sky* to *the beasts of the earth*. Those who used the word "corpses"[25] understood better than other translators who preferred "mortal bodies."[26] The former expression can be used only of the dead, whereas "mortal bodies" can also mean bodies still alive. So, as I have explained, after the souls of the martyrs had been harvested like ripe apples by their farmer, the persecutors exposed their corpses for the birds of the sky and the beasts of the earth. As though any part of them could be lost in the resurrection! He who counts even the hairs on our heads[27] will draw them back from the secret recesses of nature and reintegrate them entirely.

6. *They poured out their blood like water* (that is, recklessly, as though it had no value) *round about Jerusalem*. If we take this to refer to the earthly city of Jerusalem, it means that the enemy shed round about the city the blood of those they caught outside its walls. But if we understand it of that Jerusalem of which scripture says, *She who has been deserted bears many children, more than the wedded wife* (Is 54:1), then "round about her" means all over the world. This is evident from the context of the prophecy, for after stating that *she who has been deserted bears many children, more than the wedded wife*, it says a little further on, *the God of Israel who delivers you will be called the God of all the earth* (Is 54:5). In our psalm, therefore, the district round about Jerusalem must be understood as all those regions to which the Church had spread by that time, growing and bearing fruit throughout the world, while persecution was raging in every part of it, causing the slaughter of martyrs whose blood was being poured out like water, to the great profit of the heavenly treasure-chambers.

The next line, *and there was no one to bury them*, may mean that panic was so intense in some places that there were simply no people available to bury the bodies of the saints; and this would not be hard to believe. Or perhaps it means that in many places their corpses had to lie unburied for a long time, until devout persons managed to steal them away and bury them.

7. Now the psalm declares, *We have become an object of scorn to our neighbors*, for the death of his saints is precious in the sight of the Lord,[28] but not in scornful human eyes. We have become *a butt for mockery and derision*—or, as

---

25. *Morticina*.
26. *Mortalia*.
27. See Mt 10:30.
28. See Ps 115(116):15.

some interpreters have it, "for scoffing"[29]—*to those around us.* The latter phrase repeats the former: where the former said, *object of scorn,* the latter said, *butt for mockery and derision;* and where one had *our neighbors* the other has *those around us.* Obviously if we are thinking of the earthly Jerusalem, her "neighbors," and "those around" that nation must be other nations; but if we think rather of the free Jerusalem who is our mother,[30] her *neighbors* and *those around her* are the enemies amid whom the Church dwells all around the world.

Verse 5. How long, O Lord?

8. The psalmist now pours out an explicit prayer, from which we can infer that the foregoing recital of calamity was meant not as a statement of facts but as a lament. *How long, O Lord?* he asks. *Will you be angry to the very end? Will your jealous wrath blaze like fire?* Clearly he is praying that God will not be angry to the very end, that this dire oppression and tribulation and ruin will not last for ever, but that God will temper his rebuke. In similar vein another psalm says to God, *You will feed us with the bread of tears, and measure out to us our due portion of weeping* (Ps 79:6(80:5)). His words, *How long, O Lord? Will you be angry to the very end?* are a way of saying, "Do not be angry to the very end, Lord." In the phrase that follows, *Will your jealous wrath blaze like fire?* we must supply both *How long?* and *to the very end,* so that this line is equivalently asking, "How long will your anger blaze like fire? Even to the very end?" These insertions must be made here, just as was the case in an earlier verse; for there the first line said, *They have exposed the corpses of your servants as carrion for the birds of the sky,* and the second line lacked the verb *they have exposed,* stating simply *and the carcasses of your holy ones as prey for the beasts of the earth.* Obviously we are to supply the earlier verb *exposed.*

Now clearly God's anger and jealous wrath are not emotional disturbances in God, as some people who do not understand the scriptures accuse them of teaching. We should take "anger" to mean his punishment of sin, and "jealous wrath" the demand of his purity, which will not permit a soul to spurn the law of its Lord and by breaking its troth with him go to ruin. When human beings are in trouble, anger and jealous wrath create turmoil by their very nature; but in God's governance they are tranquil, for to him scripture says, *You judge in tranquillity, O Lord of might* (Wis 12:18). But the text clearly shows that these afflictions are sent on account of people's sins, even those of faithful people, although it is also true that they are the occasion for martyrs to flourish gloriously by the merit of their suffering and their steadfast endurance of the discipline they undergo as the

---

29. Latin *illusio.*
30. See Gal 4:26.

scourge of the Lord. Of this the Maccabees gave proof amid fierce torments,[31] of this the three youths in the midst of flames that did them no harm,[32] of this the holy prophets in captivity; for although they bear God's fatherly correction with the utmost courage and submission, they do not fail to point out that these disasters are the punishment for sin. Their voice is heard also in the psalms: *The Lord chastened me, chastened me severely, but did not deliver me to death* (Ps 117(118):18). He chastises every son whom he accepts; what son is there whose father does not discipline him?[33]

Verses 6-7. Punishment of the ignorant is prophesied

9. The words that follow are not the expression of a wish; they too are a prophecy: *Pour out your anger upon the nations that know you not, and on the kingdoms that do not call upon your name.* These things are not said with malicious intent, but foretold by inspiration, in the same way as the fate that was deservedly to befall the traitor Judas was prophesied as though hoped for.[34] Similarly, although the prophet gives no commands to Christ, he uses the imperative in saying, *Gird on your sword, mighty warrior. Fair and beautiful as you are, set yourself to your task, make your victorious way and reign* (Ps 44:4-5(45:3-4)). Our psalmist is not hoping for such an outcome, but foretelling it, when he says, *Pour out your anger upon the nations that know you not.* As is his custom, he repeats the thought: *and on the kingdoms that do not call upon your name*; for "kingdoms" corresponds to "nations," and "not knowing" is echoed in "not calling upon your name."

How are we to reconcile this with the Lord's words in the gospel, *A servant who is ignorant of his master's will, and behaves in a way that deserves a beating, will be flogged less severely; but a servant who knows his master's will, yet acts in a way that deserves a beating, will be severely flogged* (Lk 12:48.47)? How are we to interpret this, if in the psalm God's sterner anger falls on those who have not known the Lord? And this certainly is the implication, for in saying, *Pour out your anger*, the psalmist indicates what rigorous anger he means; this is confirmed when he says later, *Repay our neighbors sevenfold.*[35] Can it be, perhaps, that there is a wide difference between domestic servants who, though they may be ignorant of their Master's will, yet do call on his name, and strangers outside the household of this great Father who are so ignorant of God that they do not invoke God at all? Instead they call upon graven images, or

---

31. See 2 Mc 7.
31. See Dn 3:21ff.
32. See Heb 12:6-7.
34. See Acts 1:16-20.
35. Verse 12.

demons, or some other creature, but not upon their Creator, who is blessed for ever. In uttering this prophecy the psalmist does not envisage people who, though ignorant of their Lord's will, do still fear the Lord himself; he means people who are so crassly ignorant of the Lord that they do not call upon him, and even set themselves up as enemies of his name. Obviously there is a vast difference between servants who are unaware of their master's will, but live in his household and under his roof, and enemies who are not merely unwilling to know the Lord, but do not call on his name and, moreover, attack his servants.

10. Then the psalm continues, *For they have devoured Jacob, and left his place desolate.* Jacob stands for the Church, as Esau does for the synagogue of old, in accordance with the scriptural prophecy, *The elder shall serve the younger* (Gn 25:23). The name Jacob can be taken to represent the inheritance of God, of which we were speaking just now, into which surged the persecuting pagans after the Lord's resurrection and ascension, invading it and laying it waste. We must consider, though, how "Jacob's place" is to be understood. It might seem preferable to think of it as that city where the temple was sited, the temple to which the Lord had commanded the whole chosen people to come for sacrifice and worship and the celebration of the Passover;[36] we might think this on the ground that if the prophet had meant it to refer to the Christian community hampered and harassed by persecutors, he ought to have said "places," not "place." However, we can take a singular noun to stand for the plural, as with "clothing" for "clothes," or "the soldier" for "soldiers," or "head of cattle" to mean the whole herd. It is customary to speak of many things in this way. Examples occur not only in common parlance but also in the polished diction of very fluent writers. Nor is this idiom absent from the divinely inspired scriptures, for there we read of "the frog" for "frogs," and "the locust" for "locusts."[37] There are innumerable other instances.

The expression *they have devoured Jacob* can therefore plausibly be taken to mean that they have terrified many people into crossing over into their company, as though into their ill-disposed body.

Verses 8-9. Prayer for forgiveness, help, and deliverance

11. The psalmist takes care to record that, although God's anger will wreak just retribution on the persecutors for their evil designs, they would have no power to do anything against God's inheritance if he did not will to chasten it with punishments for its sins. This is why the psalm adds, *Do not remember our age-old sins.* He does not say, "our past sins," which could be quite recent, but

---

36. See Dt 12:2-12; 16:6.
37. See Ps77(78):45-46.

our age-old sins, the sins bequeathed to us by our ancestors; for these merit condemnation, not correction.

Let your mercies come swiftly to meet us. Above all at the time of judgment let them so meet us, for *mercy reigns triumphant at the judgment.* Although *merciless judgment will be passed* then, it will be reserved for *anyone who has not shown mercy* (Jas 2:13). By adding, *for we have become abjectly poor*, the psalmist implies that God's mercies must come swiftly to meet us because we need his compassionate help to enable our poverty (that is, our weakness) to carry out his commands. Thus it will save us from coming to his judgment-seat only to find ourselves condemned.

12. In the same vein he continues, *Help us, O God our salvation.* By saying, *our salvation*, he makes it perfectly clear what kind of poverty he had in mind when he acknowledged, *we have become abjectly poor*: this poverty is the weakness that stands in need of salvation. When he asks that we be helped he is neither belittling grace nor denying free will, for someone who is helped still does the work personally. He adds, *For the glory of your name, O Lord, set us free*, indicating that those who glory must glory not in themselves, but in the Lord.[38] *And deal gently with our sins*, he continues, *for your name's sake*—not for our deserving, for what do our sins merit but just and condign torments? No, *deal gently with our sins for your name's sake.* This is how you set us free, how you pluck us from disaster, when you also help us to act rightly and deal gently with our sins, for free from sins we cannot be in this life. *No living person will be found righteous in your sight* (Ps 142(143):2). Sin is *breaking God's law* (1 Jn 3:4), and *if you take account of our law-breaking, who will stand, O Lord?* (Ps 129(130):3).

Verse 10. A discussion of vengeance, and the sense in which good people can desire it

13. The next verse, *Let it never be said among the Gentiles, "Where is their God?"* is more concerned with these Gentiles themselves. People who have no hope in the living God perish miserably, whether they doubt his existence, or do not believe that he helps his own and is merciful to them. The psalm continues, *May the outpoured blood of your servants be avenged among the nations before our eyes*, and this could be read in either of two ways. It could mean that the vengeance will occur when those who formerly persecuted God's inheritance come to believe in the true God, for it is truly a revenge when their savage iniquity is slain by the sword of God's word, as another psalm implies: *Gird on your*

---

38. See 1 Cor 1:31.

sword (Ps 44:4(45:3)). Alternatively, it could point to the punishment to be meted out at the end to those enemies who remain obdurate; for any bodily sufferings endured in this world are the common lot both of them and of good people.

There is also a different kind of vengeance, and that is the chagrin of sinners, people who refuse to believe and are the Church's enemies, when they see the growth and fecundity of the Church in this world, after so many persecutions which they thought would destroy it entirely. On seeing this they are enraged; they gnash their teeth and pine away.[39] Who can doubt that this is a very severe punishment? I am not sure, though, whether punishment of this kind, which is endured in the hidden places of the heart, and torments even some whose outward attitude to us is one of smiling flattery, can be meant here; such an interpretation does not fit well with the phrase, *before our eyes*, for we cannot see the pains anyone suffers inwardly.

We may conclude without any shadow of doubt, however, that the petition, "Wreak vengeance among the nations before our eyes," can safely be interpreted either of the destruction of their iniquity when they embrace the faith, or of the final retribution suffered by those who persist in evil.

14. As we remarked earlier, this is a prophecy, not a wish. All the same, we cannot avoid considering how we are to take the passage in the Book of Revelation, where beneath God's altar the martyrs cry out to God, *How long, O Lord? Will you not avenge our blood?* (Rv 6:10). If we neglect to discuss this passage, some might think that the saints long for revenge to satisfy their hatred, but such an attitude would be quite incompatible with their perfection. Nevertheless, scripture does say, *The righteous will rejoice to see vengeance done on the godless; they will wash their hands in the blood of sinners* (Ps 57:11(58:10)); and though the apostle warns, *Do not seek revenge yourselves, dearly beloved, but leave space for God's wrath, for it is written, "Revenge is for me; I will see justice done," says the Lord* (Rom 12:19), he is not forbidding them to want vengeance; he is only telling them that they must not seek it themselves, but must *leave space* for the wrath of God, who said, *Revenge is for me; I will see justice done.* Moreover, in the gospel the Lord sets before us the parable of the widow who in her desire to see her wrongs avenged appealed to the unjust judge. He eventually listened to her, not because justice impelled him, but because he was overcome by weariness.[40] The Lord told us this story to show that God is far more willing to see justice done for his chosen ones who cry to him day and night. And that is why the martyrs cry out beneath God's altar, longing to be vindicated by the judgment of God.

---

39. See Ps 111(112):10.
40. See Lk 18:3-7.

What, then, has become of the Lord's injunction, *Love your enemies, do good to people who hate you, and pray for those who persecute you* (Mt 5:44)? And what are we to make of *Do not return evil for evil, or curse for curse* (1 Pt 3:9)? And what of *Repay no one evil for evil* (Rom 12:17)? If we are forbidden to pay anyone back with evil for evil, that rules out not only repaying an evil deed with another evil deed, but even retaliating for a malevolent act with a malevolent wish. Yet someone who refrains from seeking vengeance personally, but expects and hopes that God will punish his enemy, is paying that enemy back with a malevolent wish. Since, then, both a righteous person and a bad person desire to be avenged on their enemies by the Lord, how are we to distinguish between them? Surely in that the righteous want to see their enemies corrected rather than punished. When they see the Lord executing vengeance upon their enemies, the just do not gloat over the punishment, because they do not hate their enemies, but they delight in divine justice, because they love God. If such vindication occurs in this world the righteous are happy, either because their enemies are corrected, or for the sake of others who will thereby be deterred from imitating them. Thus the righteous are improved themselves, not by feeding their hatred on the pain of others, but by seeing wrongs put right. It is out of kindness, then, not out of malice, that a just person rejoices to see revenge, and washes his hands (that is, cleanses his conduct) in the blood, or rather, in the ruin, of a sinner, deriving from it not pleasure in another's misfortune but a lesson in divine chastisement. If, however, the just are avenged only in the world to come, at God's last judgment, they are content, because that is what God wills: namely that the wicked should not flourish, nor the ungodly enjoy the rewards kept for the godfearing. That would obviously be unjust, and would diverge from the rule of truth which the just love.

Are we to suppose that when the Lord urged us to love our enemies, and pointed to the example of our Father in heaven, *who causes his sun to rise over the good and the wicked, and sends rain upon just and unjust alike* (Mt 5:45), he meant that God does not chasten us with temporal reproofs, or that he does not finally condemn those who persist in their defiance? Our enemy is to be loved in such a way that we are not dissatisfied with the divine justice that punishes him; yet our satisfaction in that punitive justice must derive not from the bad consequences for the offender but from the goodness of the judge.

A person of malicious disposition, on the contrary, may be upset at seeing an enemy accept correction and so escape punishment. Or again, if such a one sees an enemy being punished he is glad about his own vindication, but his pleasure is not in the justice of God, whom he does not love, but in the misery of the person he hates. If people like this leave judgment to God, it is in the hope that God will do more hurt than they could do themselves; and when they feed a hungry enemy or give a thirsty enemy a drink, they misunderstand the scriptural advice that *in so doing you will heap burning coals upon his head* (Rom 12:20). They do it to make matters worse, and to arouse against their enemy the anger of God, which they think the burning coals represent. They fail to understand that this fire is the pain of repentance, which goes on burning until the head which was held high in pride is bowed in salutary humility by the kindness of an enemy, so that the evil disposition of the one is conquered by the goodness of the other. The apostle was well aware of this when he immediately added, *Do not be conquered by evil; rather conquer evil with good* (Rom 12:21). But how can someone who is good only on the surface, but bad in the depths, conquer evil with good? Or anyone who behaves in a forgiving way, but is furious at heart? Or who acts gently but harbors cruel desires?

To sum up, then, the vengeance that will be wreaked on the godless in the future is predicted in this psalm, and the prediction is expressed as a plea, but in such a way that we must understand that God's holy ones loved their enemies, and willed to everyone nothing but good, which means reverence for God in this world and eternity in the next. When they took pleasure in the punishment of the wicked, it was not the evils they suffered but the good judgments of God that pleased his saints. Wherever in the sacred scriptures we read of their hating human beings, the hatred is directed not at persons but at their vices; and every single one of us must hate these vices in ourselves, if we love ourselves.

Verses 11-13. The groaning of the imprisoned will be succeeded by unending praise offered to God by his people

15. Let us look now at the next verse. *May the groans of fettered captives come before you* (or, as some codices have it, *come into your presence*).[41] It is not easy to find instances of God's holy ones being shackled by persecutors; and if, among the great variety of sufferings they endured, even this did sometimes happen, at any rate it happened so rarely that we can hardly think the prophet singled it out for mention in this verse. But in fact the body's shackles are its weakness and vulnerability, and these weigh heavily upon the soul; and so the body's fragility was like the material ready to the persecutor's hand for causing pains and distress, which he could use to drive the saints to betrayal of God. The apostle longed to be released from these shackles and to be with Christ, though it was necessary for those to whom he was preaching the gospel that he should remain in the flesh.[42] Clearly, until this imperishable nature has been clothed in imperishability, and this mortal nature in immortality,[43] the weak flesh will hamper the willing spirit.[44] The only people who feel these shackles are the ones

---

41. Respectively *ante conspectum tuum* and *in conspectu tuo*.
42. See Phil 1:23-24.
43. See 1 Cor 15:53.
44. See Mk 14:38.

who habitually groan within themselves under the weight, earnestly desiring to have that new dwelling-place that comes from heaven put on over it,[45] for death is horrifying to us, yet mortal life a grievous burden. For these groaners the prophet prays, that their groaning may find its way into God's presence.

We may also understand these shackled ones to be people who are bound fast to wisdom's disciplines, which when patiently borne turn into adornments. So scripture invites us, *Thrust your foot into her fetters* (Sir 6:25).

By the might of your arm, the psalm resumes, *take for your own the children of those done to death* or, according to other codices, *make them your possession.*[46]

16. *Repay our neighbors sevenfold; pour back disgrace into their laps.* He is not hoping that evil will befall them, but he is foretelling what will be just and proclaiming what will happen. "Sevenfold" means a retribution seven times more severe, and by this the psalmist indicates a perfect punishment, because seven is usually a number that stands for completion. This is why it is said with reference to good things, "Such a person will receive sevenfold in this world,"[47] which means everything, as we can see from another text, *We are like people who have nothing, yet possess all things* (2 Cor 6:10). He speaks of *our neighbors,* because until the day of discernment the Church dwells among its enemies; there is no physical separation as yet. His expression, *into their laps,* must mean covertly now, so that the vengeance which is wrought in a secret way in this life may hereafter *be made known among the nations before our eyes.* When persons are abandoned to their own degraded minds, they are receiving now, in their inmost being, the punishments they will have earned in the future.

Pour back disgrace into the laps of those who have dishonored you, O Lord. Pour back that disgrace sevenfold into their own laps, he prays; that is, rebuke them with the utmost severity in their inmost being for that disgraceful behavior, for they have dishonored your name by supposing that they could blot you out, in the persons of your servants, from the earth.

---

45. See 2 Cor 5:4.
46. Respectively *recipe in adoptionem* and *posside*. It seems obvious to me that scripture is here identifying that groaning which came from the shackled prisoners, who for Christ's sake suffered the fierce persecutions plainly referred to in our psalm. Amid their varied torments they customarily prayed for the Church, begging that their blood might not be sterile for posterity, and that the Lord's crop might grow more abundantly through the very persecution which its enemies thought would spell its ruin. The psalm speaks of *the children of those done to death,* who were not merely undaunted by the sufferings of those who had gone before, but came in droves to believe in him for whose name they knew their predecessors had suffered, and under the inspiration of such glory were fired to imitate them. This is why the psalm says, *By the might of your arm:* so great an effect followed among the Christian people that those who thought to gain their ends by persecuting the Church would never have believed it could happen.
47. See Mk 10:30.

17. *But we, your people* — this is to be taken in a general sense, embracing all kinds of devout and true Christians. We, then, we whom they thought they could destroy, *we, your people, the sheep of your flock* (this is said to ensure that anyone minded to boast will boast only in the Lord[48]), *will confess to you throughout this age.* Other codices have *will confess to you for ever.* The discrepancy arises from an ambiguity in the Greek: when the Greek has εἰς τὸν αἰῶνα it can be rendered either "for ever" or "throughout the present age,"[49] but the context must determine which is preferable. The context here inclines me to think we should translate it *throughout this age,* that is, until the world ends. My reasons are these: the line that follows is a repetition of the preceding line, but with the order inverted, as is common practice in scripture and particularly in the psalms. So it puts first what came second in the previous line, and second what there was first. Where the previous line said, *We will confess to you,* the following line substitutes, *We will declare your praise.* Where the previous line had *throughout this age,* this one has *through generation after generation.* Now these successive generations represent perpetuity, unless, with some inter-preters, we take it to mean that there are two generations—the old and the new. But in either case the reference is to what happens in this world, because no one will enter the kingdom of heaven unless born again of water and the Spirit.[50] Moreover it is in this world that God's praise is declared; in the world to come we shall see him as he is,[51] and thereafter there will be no one to whom it will need to be declared.

We, then, your people, the sheep of your flock, whom they believed they could destroy, *will confess to you throughout this age,* for the Church they tried to stamp out abides to the end. *Through generation after generation we will declare your praise,* though they tried to silence it by making an end of us. We have already pointed out with reference to many texts of holy scripture that "confession" can also mean "praise";[52] it is written, for example, *This is how you must confess to him: "All the Lord's works are exceedingly good"* (Sir 39:15-16(20-21)). It is true above all of the words of our Savior himself, who had no sin whatever to repent of or confess: *I confess to you, Father, Lord of heaven and earth, because you have hidden these matters from the wise and knowing, and have revealed them to little ones* (Mt 11:25).

I have pointed this out to make it clear that when the psalm says, *We will declare your praise,* it is repeating what was said previously, *We will confess to you.*

---

48. See 1 Cor 1:31.
49. Either *in aeternum* or *in saeculum.*
50. See Jn 3:5.
51. See 1 Jn 3:2.
52. He made the point extremely clear in his greatest work, *The Confessions.*

Exposition of Psalm 79

A Sermon

Verses 1-2. A simple psalm about Christ and his vine

1. There are not too many things in this psalm that need make our sermon a laborious undertaking, or pose any obstacles to comprehension for an attentive audience. Like proficient scholars in the school of Christ, then, we must with the Lord's help run through the simple elements of it, intent on hearing and seeing what was prophesied about him, so that even if any obscure passages need the services of an interpreter, at any rate the straightforward parts will demand of me no more than the role of a reader.

The psalm sings of the coming of our Lord and Savior Jesus Christ, and of his vine; but the singer is that Asaph who, it would seem, has been enlightened and corrected, the man whose name means "synagogue." Now the title of the psalm is *To the end, for those who are to be changed*, and changed for the better, evidently, because Christ came as the end of the law[1] in order to transform us into something better. The title adds, *a testimony for Asaph himself*, and a good, truthful testimony it is. What we have here is a testimony that confesses both Christ and his vine, which is to say the head and the body, the King and his people, Shepherd and flock: in short, Christ and his Church, that total mystery with which all the scriptures are concerned. The title concludes, though, with the words, *for the Assyrians*, and "Assyrians" means "directors." The generation it addresses must therefore not be a generation unwilling to direct its heart aright,[2] but one that is already so directing it. Now let us listen to what the psalm has to say by way of testimony.

2. *Give ear, Shepherd of Israel.* What does this mean, *Give ear, Shepherd of Israel, you who lead Joseph like a flock of sheep*? God is called upon to come, his coming is looked for and longed for. May he find well-directed people. *You who lead Joseph like a flock of sheep*, it says, so it is Joseph himself who is being led. Joseph is a flock of sheep, but also an individual sheep. So now Joseph's name has been mentioned;[3] and the interpretation of the name is a considerable help,

---

1. See Rom 10:4.
2. See Ps 77(78):8.
3. From this early introduction of the name "Joseph" Augustine takes a double indication of the mystery of Christ and the Church. The meaning "increase" and the story of Joseph, shamefully treated by his own people but honored by foreigners, are both pointers to the paschal mystery of Christ, as he goes on to explain.

for it means "increase." Christ came, as we know, so that the grain of wheat which died[4] might fructify many times over, that is, so that God's people might increase. But that is not all. When you hear that name you should be reminded of what you already know about Joseph and all that happened to him. You should recall that he was sold by his brothers, and recall too how he was dishonored by his own people but exalted by foreigners, and then you will understand whose flock we ought to belong to, in fellowship with those who are already directing their hearts aright, so that the stone rejected by the builders may become the cornerstone,[5] tying together two walls which come from different quarters but meet at the corner.

You who are seated above the cherubim. The cherubim are the throne of God's glory, and their name means "fullness of knowledge." Upon them, in fullness of knowledge, God is enthroned. We know that the cherubim are the sublime authorities and potentates of the heavens, and yet, if you will, you can be one of them, for though the cherubs are God's throne, listen to what scripture says elsewhere: "The soul of a just person is the throne of Wisdom."[6]

"But how can I be the fullness of knowledge?" you ask. "Who could aspire to fullness like that?" Such plenitude is within your reach, for *the fullness of the law is love* (Rom 13:10). Do not think you must overextend yourself toward many achievements. You may find wide-spreading branches a daunting prospect, but hold onto the root, and do not think about the vast size of the tree. Only let charity be in you, and fullness of knowledge will inevitably follow, for of what can a person who knows charity be ignorant, when it is written, *God is charity* (1 Jn 4:8)?

Verses 3-4. Though throned above the cherubim, God was manifested in weakness

3. *You who are seated above the cherubim, show yourself.* That is why we went astray, because you were not showing yourself. *Show yourself before Ephraim, Benjamin and Manasseh.* Show yourself, it is asking, in the presence of the Jewish nation, in the presence of the people of Israel, for among them were Ephraim, Benjamin and Manasseh. But there is more, for let us look to the interpretation of these names. Ephraim means "bearing fruit," Benjamin "son of my right hand," and Manasseh "forgetful." Show yourself, then, before the fruitful one, and before the son of your right hand; but especially show yourself before the forgetful one, that he may be forgetful no longer, but mindful of his deliverer. If the Gentiles are to remember, and all the ends of the earth to be converted to

4. See Jn 12:25.
5. See Ps 117(118):22; Mt 21:42; Eph 2:20.
6. See Is 57:15; Wis 7:28.

the Lord,[7] can it be that the very people descended from Abraham can produce no wall of its own to gladden the corner, when scripture says, *A remnant shall be saved* (Rom 9:27)?

Stir up your power. You were weak at that time when they said, "If he is the Son of God, let him come down from the cross."[8] You seemed then to have no strength; the persecutor had overpowered you. Long ago you had given us another hint of the same mystery, for Jacob had shown himself the stronger in a wrestling bout, a man overpowering an angel.[9] But when could such a thing happen, except when the angel allowed it? So a man proved the stronger, and an angel was overcome. The human champion holds the angel fast and declares, *I will not let you go until you bless me* (Gn 32:26). What a deep mystery is here! The wrestler stands conquered, and blesses his conqueror, conquered because he willed to be, weak in his flesh, powerful in his majesty.[10] And he blessed Jacob with the words, "You will be called Israel." All the same, he touched the broad part of Jacob's thigh, and it withered, so he left the one same man both blessed and lame. Look at the Jewish people: it has walked lame ever since, but how blessed it is in that it produced the apostles! *Stir up your power*, then, Lord; how long will you go on seeming weak? You were crucified in weakness; rise, then, in strength.[11] *Stir up your power, and come to save us.*

4. *Convert us, O God*, for we are turned away from you, and unless you turn us round, we shall not be converted. *Let your face shine forth, and we shall be saved.* Is God's face darkened? No, indeed not, but he has hidden it behind the cloud of his flesh, as though behind a veil of weakness. And so he who hung upon the cross was not thought to be the One whom they would be compelled to acknowledge when he reigned in heaven. But this was indeed what happened. Asaph did not recognize Christ while he was present on earth working miracles; but once he had died, and then risen and ascended into heaven, Asaph acknowledged him and was pierced with sorrow, and spoke this whole testimony concerning him that we now read in this psalm. *Let your face shine forth, and we shall be saved.* You covered your face, and we fell ill; let it shine forth unclouded, and we shall be well again.

---

7. See Ps 21:28(22:27).
8. See Mt 27:40; Mk 15:32.
9. See Gn 32:24-32.
10. As often in the Old Testament, the "angel" is a manifestation of God himself. Augustine here understands him to be a kind of pre-incarnation of the divine Son.
11. See 2 Cor 13:4.

Verses 5-7. Chastisement and tears

5. *Lord God of hosts, how long will you be angry with the prayer of your servant?* Notice that he is God's "servant" now. You were angry with your enemy's prayer, but are you still angry with the prayer of your servant? You have converted us, we have acknowledged you; can you still be angry with your servant's prayer? You can be angry, indeed, but only now as a father who corrects us, not as a judge who condemns. Your anger can be only that which scripture suggests: *My son, when you enter God's service, stand fast in righteousness and reverence, and prepare your soul for trials* (Sir 2:1). Do not suppose that God's anger has passed now that you are converted; passed it has, but only insofar as he will not condemn you for eternity. He chastises still and does not spare the rod, because he chastens every child whom he acknowledges as his.[12] If you refuse chastisement, why look to be accepted? He chastises every child he acknowledges as his; every one without exception he chastises, for he did not spare even his only Son.[13] Yet *how long will you be angry with the prayer of your servant*—not your enemy now, but *your servant*? How long?

6. *You will feed us with the bread of tears, and measure out to us our due portion of weeping to drink.* What does *our due portion* mean? The apostle gives us the explanation: *God is faithful, and he does not allow you to be tempted more fiercely than you can bear* (1 Cor 10:13). The due measure is the measure of your strength to bear it. The due measure is what will serve to educate you, but not crush you.

7. *You have set us in opposition to our neighbors.* Undeniably that did happen, for some members of Asaph were chosen to go and preach Christ among the Gentiles, and so earned the taunt, *Who is this, peddling new deities?* (Acts 17:18). Yes, *you set us in opposition to our neighbors*, for your envoys were preaching him against whom the opposition pitted itself. Whom were they preaching? Christ. Christ who, once dead, was risen. Who would be prepared to listen to that? Would anyone want to know? It was something new and unheard of. But signs followed the preaching, and miracles attested this incredible thing. It was opposed, but the opponent was defeated and changed into a believer. A great fire was kindled. There the martyrs were fed with the bread of tears, and given their portion of weeping to drink, but in due measure, not more than they could bear, so that after their measure of tears a crown of joys should await them.

And our enemies derided us. Yes, but where are they now, those derisive enemies? For a long time indeed it may have been said, "Who are these people, worshippers of a dead man, adorers of someone who was crucified?" But for a long time now something different has been said: "Where now is the scorn of

---

12. See Heb 12:6.
13. See Rom 8:32.

those who mocked us? Our critics are looking for hiding-holes to flee to, to avoid being seen!" *And our enemies derided us.*

Verses 8-12. The transplanting of the vine; it grows tall and strong

8. Now you see what follows: *Convert us, Lord God of hosts, show us your face and we shall be saved. You brought a vine out of Egypt, you drove out the Gentiles and planted it.* Yes, we know that was what happened. What a crowd of Gentiles was cast out! Once the Amorites, Hittites, Jebusites, Girgashites, and Hivites had been expelled and routed, the people of Israel who had been freed from Egypt were brought into the promised land. We have heard where the vine had been uprooted from, and where it was now planted. Let us see what happened to it next; how it came to believe, how luxuriantly it grew, how much ground it occupied. *You brought a vine out of Egypt, you drove out the Gentiles and planted it.*[14]

9. *You cleared the way for it, you spread its roots, and it filled the earth.* Could it have filled the earth if there had been no way before it? And what "way" is this, opening up? *I am the Way, the Truth and the Life* (Jn 14:6). With good reason, then, has it filled the earth. This is said of the vine which by the end of time has grown perfect, but what about before that?

Its shade covered the mountains, its boughs overtopped the cedars of God.[15] *You stretched out its branches as far as the sea, its shoots even to the river.* This verse calls for the services of an expositor, for merely to read and admire the text is not enough. Help me by concentrating hard now, for the figure of the vine in this psalm is often obscure to the less attentive. The prodigious size of it we have suggested already; where it originated and how it grew so large we have explained. *You cleared the way for it, you spread its roots, and it filled the earth*; this is a statement about its final perfect state, but the original vine was the Jewish people. This race, the Jews, held sovereignty as far as the sea, and to the river. As far as the sea, because it is clear from scripture that the sea closely

---

14. The vine, choicest of crops, yielding the wine which "gives joy to gods and men" (Jg 9:13), was tended with the utmost care; a farmer's fondest hopes focused on it. Hence the vine or vineyard became a symbol of the chosen people, object of the Lord's hopes and cherished by him (Is 5:1-7), but yielding him only bitter disappointment. In this psalm Israel, though conscious of failure, articulates a faith in God's abiding love; but in the parable of the wicked vine-dressers (Mt 21:33-43) Jesus sounds a sterner warning. Ultimately the beloved Son will come not merely to collect the profits but to be himself the vine which gives joy to God and all Christ's members (Jn 15). The Latin *vinea* can mean either vine or vineyard, and Augustine oscillates between the two in the present Exposition. He also associates them with Paul's metaphor of the olive tree in Rom 11:16-24.

15. The phrase "cedars of God" simply means "the tallest cedars," as in "mountains of God" (Ps 35:7(36:6)), though Augustine gets a holy meaning out of it. Ronald Knox's translation of this psalm neatly captures the spirit of the original: "How the cedars, divinely tall, were overtopped by its branches!"

bordered them, and to the river, that is, the Jordan,[16] for although some part of
Jewry was settled beyond the Jordan, the nation as a whole was on the near side.
The kingdom of the Jews, the kingdom of Israel, extended therefore *as far as the
sea* and *even to the river*, but not *from sea to sea, from the river to the ends of the
earth* (Ps 71(72):8), for that is the perfected range of the vine which is here
prophetically described in the words, *You cleared the way for it, you spread its
roots, and it filled the earth.*

So after foretelling the vine's perfected stage, the psalm went back to the
beginning, to tell you about the initial stage from which that perfection sprang.
Would you like to hear about its beginning? It extended *as far as the sea, and
even to the river.* Now would you like to be reminded of its final stage? *He will
rule from sea to sea, from the river to the ends of the earth*; that is to say, *it filled
the earth.*

Let us examine Asaph's testimony, and learn what became of the first vine,
and what is to be expected of the second—though both are one vine, for the
second is not a different vine but the selfsame. From it sprang Christ, for salvation comes from the Jews;[17] from it came the apostles, and from it the first
believers, who laid the proceeds from the sale of their property at the apostles'
feet.[18] All these were shoots of the first vine. And if some part of the branches
*were broken off, they were broken off because of their unbelief. You, for your
part,* Gentile race, *stand in faith; be not high-minded, but wary. If God did not
spare the natural branches, he will not spare you either. And if you are tempted
to be high-minded, remember that it is not you who support the root, but the root
you* (Rom 11:19-21.18). Now, where was it at first, this vine for which the way
was cleared, so that it could fill the earth? *Its shade covered the mountains.* What
mountains? The prophets. Why is its shade said to have covered them? Because
they spoke obscurely about the future events they announced. From the prophets
you hear such instructions as, "Observe the Sabbath, circumcise your child on
the eighth day, offer a ram, or a calf, or a goat in sacrifice." Do not be perplexed;
the vine's shade is covering God's mountains, but clear daylight will follow. *Its
boughs overtopped the cedars of God.* They are exceedingly tall, these cedars,
but they are God's cedars, unlike some other cedars which symbolize proud
persons due for cutting down. This vine grew so tall that it towered above both
the cedars of Lebanon, which are the high and mighty of this world, and God's
mountains, the holy prophets and patriarchs.

---

16. More probably the psalmist was thinking of the ideal limits of the empire of David and
    Solomon, the large territory bounded on the northeast by "the Great River," the Euphrates. See
    Gn 15:18; Ex 25:31; 2 Kgs 24:7.
17. See Jn 4:22.
18. See Acts 2:45; 4:35.

Verses 13-14. The ruination of the vineyard

10. How far did you *stretch out its branches? As far as the sea, and its shoots even to the river.* Then what? *Why*, asks the psalmist, *why have you broken down its wall?* Here you can see that ravaging of the Jewish people of which you have heard already in another psalm: *They felled it with pick and battering-ram* (Ps 73(74):6). When could such a thing happen? Only when its boundary wall was destroyed. What is this wall, if not its defense? The vine reared up in pride against its planter. The tenants of the vineyard whipped the servants sent to them to demand the revenue, beat them, killed them. Then came the Son, even the only Son, and they said, *"This is the heir. Come on, let's kill him, and the inheritance will be for us." So they killed him, and threw him out of the vineyard* (Mt 21:38-39). But after his rejection he only gained more surely the inheritance from which he had been cast out. This is what he threatened as he spoke to it through Isaiah: *I will break down its wall.* Why? Because *I looked for it to produce grapes, and all it bore was thorns.*[19] I expected fruit from it, and I found sin. How then can you ask, Asaph, *Why have you broken down its wall?* Do you really not know? *I looked for it to work righteousness, and its work was only iniquity* (Is 5:7). Did its wall not deserve to be destroyed?

So, with the wall demolished, in came the Gentiles. The vineyard was overrun, and the kingdom of the Jews ruined. At first the psalm laments it, but not without hope, for it speaks now of the right direction of the heart; this is a psalm "for the Assyrians," which means for those who direct their hearts aright. *Why have you broken down its wall, so that all who pass by may pluck its grapes?* Who are these passers-by? People who exercise temporal power.[20]

11. *The boar from the forest has ravaged it.* What are we to understand by the boar? To the Jews pigs are abhorrent, and typical of the uncleanness of the Gentiles. The Jewish nation was defeated by Gentiles, and the king who defeated it was not merely an unclean pig, but a boar; for what is a boar but a savage pig, a proud pig? *The boar from the forest has ravaged it.* "From the forest" means from the Gentiles. The Jews were a vineyard, the Gentiles a forest. But when the Gentiles came to believe, what does scripture say about that? *All the trees of the forest will shout for joy* (Ps 95(96):12). So *the boar from the forest has ravaged* the vineyard, and *the solitary beast has fed on it.* The boar who wrecked it is a solitary beast, solitary in the sense of proud, for every proud person talks like this: "Me, me. No one else matters."

19. See Is 5:5.2.
20. Or perhaps "exercise power, but only for a time."

Verses 15-16. The prospect of its ultimate perfection in the Son of Man

12. But what was the purpose of all this? He continues, *O God of hosts, turn again.* Even though these things have happened, *turn again. Look down from heaven and see, tend your vineyard. Bring to perfection what your right hand planted.* Do not plant another; perfect this one. This is Abraham's offspring, the seed in which all nations are blessed.[21] This is the root that carries the engrafted wild olive.[22] *Bring to perfection what your right hand planted.* But where? *Upon the son of man, to whom you have given your strength.* What could be clearer than that? Do you still expect us to interpret the psalm to you by arguing it out? Should we not rather, all of us together, cry out in wonder, *Bring to perfection what your right hand has planted,* and perfect it *upon the Son of Man?* What Son of Man is this? He *to whom you have given your strength.* A sound foundation, that! Build on it as high as you can, for *no one can lay any other foundation than that which is laid, which is Christ Jesus* (1 Cor 3:11).

Verse 17. Love and fear are the springs of human conduct

13. *Burnt up by fire and dug out, they will perish at your frowning rebuke.* What are these things, burnt up and dug out by his frowning face? Let us ponder it and try to understand. What did Christ rebuke? Sins, of course, and at his rebuking frown sins withered away. But why are sins said to be burnt with fire, and dug out?

There are two things in human beings from which all sins spring: desire and fear. Think about it now, discuss it, question your own hearts, scrutinize your consciences, and see whether any sins can be committed except when prompted by either desire or fear. Suppose a reward is offered to you to induce you to sin, something that you find very attractive; you commit the sin for the sake of what you desire. Or perhaps you are not seduced by bribes, but are intimidated by threats; then you do it because of something you fear. Someone wants to corrupt you by persuading you to bear lying witness, for example (there are instances without number, but I am suggesting simple ones, from which you can infer the rest). You have put the matter before God, and said to yourself in your own mind, *"What advantage is it to anyone to gain even the whole world, and suffer the ruin of his own soul?* (Mt 16:26). I am not so tempted by the profit as to lose my soul in order to gain money." Then the other person changes his tactics and tries to strike fear into you; having failed to corrupt you by the prospect of gain he begins to threaten loss, expulsion, a beating, perhaps even your death. If greed did not overcome you, perhaps fear will be enough to make you sin. But just as you

---

21. See Gn 22:18.
22. See Rom 11:17-18.

remembered scripture's warning against greed, *What advantage is it to anyone to gain even the whole world, and suffer the ruin of his own soul?* now let another text come to your mind to fortify you against fear: *Do not be afraid of those who kill the body, but cannot kill the soul* (Mt 10:28). Whoever wants to kill you has license only as far as your body is concerned, and no license to touch your soul. Your soul will not die unless you want to kill it yourself. Let the iniquity of another slay your flesh, provided that truth safeguards your soul. But if you shrink from the truth, what more harm will an enemy do to you than you are doing to yourself? A savage enemy can only kill your flesh, but by giving false testimony you are killing your soul. Listen to scripture's warning: *A lie in the mouth kills the soul* (Wis 1:11).

So then, my brothers and sisters, love and fear lead us to every right action, and love and fear lead us to every sin. In order to do good, you love God and you fear God; but to do evil you love the world and you fear the world. Let these last two be turned round towards good: you loved this earth, so love eternal life; you feared death, so fear hell. Whatever it was that the world promised you for your iniquity, can it give as much as God will give you for your righteousness? Whatever the world threatened to do to you for your just conduct, can it do what God does to the wicked? Would you like to see what God will give you, if you have lived honorably? *Come, you whom my Father has blessed; take possession of the kingdom prepared for you since the world was made* (Mt 25:34). And would you like to see what he will do to the wicked? *Depart into the eternal fire which was prepared for the devil and his angels* (Mt 25:41). You are right to want nothing but your own well-being. In what you love, you want your well-being, and in what you fear, you do not want things to go badly for you; but you are not looking in the right place, not looking where you ought to. You are in a hurry, for you want to be free from both need and harassment. Your desire is good; but put up with what you do not want in order to obtain what you do want.

What will the Lord's face do, then, that frowning countenance that blots out sins? What are the sins burnt up by fire and dug out? Well, what had the wrong kind of love effected? It had lighted a fire. And what had the wrong kind of fear achieved? It had dug a pit. Love inflames us, fear brings us down; and so the sins of evil love have been burnt up, and the sins of evil fear dug out. The right kind of fear also brings us low, and the right kind of love enkindles us, but quite differently, in both cases. A tenant-farmer, pleading that an unfruitful tree should not be cut down, promised, *I will dig round it, and give it a dressing of manure* (Lk 13:8). The trench he digs represents the loving humility of one who fears God, the bucket of manure the squalid mourning garb of a penitent. The Lord refers to the fire of holy love in his claim, *I have come to set fire to the earth* (Lk 12:49). May this fire enkindle all those of fervent spirit, all who are aglow with charity toward God and their neighbor.

We see, then, that as all righteous actions are carried through by the good kind of love and good fear, so too are all sins committed out of evil love and evil fear. Therefore all sins will be *burnt up and dug out; they will perish at* the Lord's *frowning rebuke*.

Verses 18-20. Loving God above all created things

14. *Let your hand be on the man you rely on, the son of man to whom you have given your strength. And we will not forsake you.* How long will they be *a crooked and troublesome set of people, a generation that would not direct its heart aright?* (Ps 77(78):8). Asaph will tell us: Let your mercy show itself; deal kindly with your vine and bring it to perfection, for *blindness has fallen upon part of Israel, until the full tally of the Gentiles comes in, and so all Israel may be saved* (Rom 11:25-26). Once you have let the light of your face shine over the man on whom you rely, the man to whom you have given your strength, we will not forsake you. How long will you continue to rebuke us? How long will you chide us? Only do that, and *we will not forsake you; you will give us life, and we will call upon your name.* In you we will find sweetness, and then *you will give us life.* Time was when we were in love with this earth, not you; but you condemned our earthly desires[23] to death. The Old Testament contained earthly promises, and so it seemed to invite people to serve God for what they could gain thereby: he is to be loved for providing good things in this world. But what do you love, that holds you back from loving God? Tell me. Love anything he did not make, if you can. Look about you at all creation. Name anything that holds you fast in the sticky toils of greed and hinders you from loving the Creator, that he whom you are disregarding did not himself create. In any case, why do you love those things? Because they are beautiful? But can they be as beautiful as he who made them? You are bewitched by them because you do not see him. Through the things that enchant you, then, love him whom you do not see. Question the creation: if it exists of itself, stay with it. If it derives from him, it cannot be harmful to anyone who loves it, unless it is loved more than its Creator.

Why am I saying this? It is prompted by the verse in our psalm, brothers and sisters. Those people who worshiped God for the sake of temporal benefits were dead, for it is death to judge by the standards of the flesh,[24] and they too are dead who do not worship God disinterestedly, which means because he himself is good, and not merely because he gives us such goods as he gives also to people who are not good. Do you hope God will give you money? The robber has it too. A wife, then, a brood of children, bodily health, worldly advancement? But look

---

23. Literally "earthly members," an allusion to Col 3:5.
24. See Rom 8:6.

how many evildoers have all these. Is this your only motive for worshipping him? Then your feet will stumble,[25] and when you see people who do not worship him enjoying these things, you will think you worship him to no purpose. He gives them all to bad people, but for the good he reserves himself alone.

You will give us life, for we were dead while we clung to earthly things; we were dead as long as we bore the image of the earthly man.[26] *You will give us life*, you will renew us, you will give us that inner life proper to the human spirit. *And we will call upon your name*; that is, we will set our hearts on you.[27] We will know your sweetness when you forgive our sins, and when you have justified us you will be our whole reward. *Convert us, Lord God of hosts; show us your face, and we shall be saved.*

---

25. See Ps 72(73):2.
26. See 1 Cor 15:49.
27. Latin *te diligemus*, the love of choice, rational and graced, as opposed to the more earthy type of which he has been speaking.

Exposition of Psalm 80

A Sermon[1]

Verse 1. The title: olive presses separate valuable oil from rubbish

1. Since I have undertaken to speak to you about this psalm you must help me by keeping quiet, because my voice is rather hoarse. But it will be given strength by the attention of my hearers, and by the assistance of him who commands me to speak.[2]

This psalm is entitled, *To the end, for the olive presses, on the fifth day of the week. A psalm for Asaph himself.* Many mysteries are packed into this one title, yet the doorway into the psalm gives a fair indication of what is to be found inside it. We are to speak, then, about olive presses; but none of you must expect us to say anything about the trough, or the press-beam, or the baskets, for the psalm has nothing to say about these, and this very fact hints more clearly at the mystery. If the text of the psalm did contain terms of this kind there might be some people who would think that "olive presses" were meant literally, so that we would not need to look for anything else, or suppose that there is any mystical meaning intended, or find any sacred significance in it. Such a person would say, "The psalm is simply talking about olive presses, yet you regale me with your surmises about something quite different." But you heard none of these terms when the psalm was being read, so take it for granted that it is concerned with the mystery of the Church, symbolized by olive presses.

When we think of olive presses we notice three things. First, there is the process of pressing out the fruit, and then from that flow two others: the collection of some of the extract for storage, and the discarding of the rest. In the press trampling, squeezing and crushing take place. As these occur the oil is strained out into a vessel, but invisibly, while the dregs run out onto the pavement for everyone to see. This is a wonderful spectacle: focus your attention on it. God never fails to provide us with sights which fill us with joy. Could any of the crazy things displayed in the circus compare with a show like this?[3] Circus shows are like the dregs, but this one is like the precious oil.

---

1. Possibly delivered in September 411. Other scholars propose December 403.
2. Augustine had begun to experience problems with his lungs while he was teaching rhetoric, some time before becoming a Christian, as he relates in his *Confessions* IX,2,4.
3. In their pre-conversion days theatrical shows had been Augustine's particular weakness, as the circus had been Alypius' passion; see *The Confessions*, III,2,2-4; VI,8,13. Augustine came to regard *spectacula* as dangerous because of the mawkish sentiments they aroused. He returns to the thought in the closing remarks of the present sermon.

So when you hear blasphemers chattering in their pigheaded way and saying that pressures have increased in Christian times, you can think, "Well, they would say that." A popular saying has come down to us; it is quite an old one, but it arose in the Christian era: "God is sending no rain; put that down to the Christians." Although people said that in earlier generations, the blasphemers of today go further: "God is pouring rain on us; blame the Christians. If God does not send rain we can't sow; but when he does, we can't thresh."[4] And they turn what ought to have driven them to more urgent supplication into an occasion for arrogance, choosing to blaspheme instead of praying. So when they echo those clichés, when they brag like that, when they say this and stubbornly go on saying it not with respect but in a spirit of arrogance, do not be put out by them. If there are pressures aplenty, you be the oil.[5] The dregs are black with the darkness of ignorance; let them jeer. They will have space to parade their mockery when they are thrown out onto the pavement in full view of all. You, for your part, must flow down quietly into the collecting vessel, and this you must do secretly in your own heart, where he who sees in secret will reward you.[6] While the olive is still on the tree it is shaken by any storms that come, but it is not yet being ground by the pressing process; and so for the time being both sorts of material are hanging there together—what will in the end be thrown away, and what is to be stored. But when it is taken to the olive press for the process to begin, the two constituents are distinguished and separated, and while one is valued the other is disregarded as useless.

Would you like to see a demonstration of the power of these olive presses? Well, I will mention one effect only, taking my cue from the complaints of people who themselves are guilty of the abuses they complain about. "Look at the scale of violent crime in our day," they say, "the widespread victimization of innocent people, the wholesale plundering of the property of others!" Yes, but when you concentrate on the seizure of other people's goods you are looking only at the dregs; you fail to notice the oil, which is the giving away of even one's own goods to the poor. Bygone days were not troubled by such robbers of the property of others, but bygone days did not have such donors of their own prop-

---

4. There is a variety of readings in the manuscripts here, but the general sense is evident. The enemies of Christianity will blame any natural inconvenience on the faithful. Tertullian had quoted a similar saying: "If the Tiber rises in flood to the city walls, if the Nile fails to flood the fields, if the heavens halt or the earth moves, if there is famine, if there is pestilence, at once the cry goes up, Throw the Christians to the lions!" (See *Apol. adv. gentes pro Christianis*, XL,2.) Tertullian argues that before Christianity arose there were worse calamities, and that since its rise they have been milder because the prayers of Christians avert the just punishments God would inflict, though the idolaters ascribe the amelioration to their own gods. Augustine also refers to these allegations in *The City of God* II,3,3: "A vulgar saying became current, There is no rain, and it is the Christians' fault."
5. He makes a similar point in Sermon 113A; see Vol. III/4 in this series.
6. See Mt 6:6.

erty either. Investigate the olive-press a little more closely. Do not stop at what flows out in full view, because there is something else which you will find only if you look for it. Examine the facts, listen, and observe how many there are who respond to that word from the Lord which a certain rich man heard, though he went away sadly. Many there are who hear the gospel call, *Go and sell all you possess and give the money to the poor: you will have treasure in heaven. Then come, follow me* (Mt 19:21). Do you not see how many are doing that? "No, only a few," they say. All the same, those few are the oil, and those who make good use of their property belong to the oil too. Add them all together, and you will see your Father's storerooms full. You see a more outrageous robber than you have ever seen before, do you? Look then at people who make light of their own belongings as you have never seen any do before. Give the olive presses credit, as that prophecy in the Book of Revelation is fulfilled, *Let the righteous become more righteous yet, and the filthy still wallow in their filth* (Rv 22:11). In that saying you can recognize the olive-press: *let the righteous become more righteous yet, and the filthy still wallow in their filth.*

The title, continued: the significance of the fifth day

2. But why *on the fifth day of the week*? What does that mean? Let us go back to the original works of God; we may find something there which we can understand in a mystical sense. The Sabbath is that seventh day on which God rested from all his works,[7] and it symbolizes for us the mystery of our own future rest from all our works.[8] The name "first of the Sabbath" is given to the first day of the week, the day we also call the Lord's day; the "second of the Sabbath" is the second day; the "third of the Sabbath" the third day; the "fourth of the Sabbath" the fourth day; and so *the fifth of the Sabbath* is the fifth from the Lord's day. After that comes the "sixth of the Sabbath," the sixth day of the week; and finally the Sabbath itself, the seventh day. Consider, then, to whom this psalm is speaking. It seems to me that it is addressing the baptized. On the fifth day God created living creatures from the waters, for on the fifth day of the week (that is, on *the fifth of the Sabbath*) God said, *Let the waters bring forth living things that crawl* (Gn 1:20).

Take heed to yourselves, then, you in whom the waters have already brought forth these living, crawling creatures. You belong to the olive presses, and among you whom the waters have brought forth there is both trickling oil and discarded dregs. There are many who do not lead lives consistent with the baptism they received: look how many have today chosen to crowd into the

---

7. See Gn 2:2.
8. A yearning for ultimate rest in God, for the eternal Sabbath, is typical of Augustine, and is a theme of his *Confessions*.

circus rather than this basilica! And how many of the baptized are either setting up shop in the streets, or else complaining that there are no shops there!

This is a psalm sung *for the olive presses* and also *on the fifth day of the week*; it is sung about the pressing process which distinguishes the elements, about the sacrament of baptism, and *for Asaph himself*. "Asaph" refers to a man called by that name, like "Idithun" or "Korah" or others whose names occur in the titles of the psalms. But the interpretation of his name points us towards a mysterious, secret truth. "Asaph" means in our language "a congregation"; therefore this psalm, which is sung *for the olive presses on the fifth day of the week*, is sung *for Asaph himself*. This means it is a psalm sung for the pressing-out process that separates the elements, sung for the baptized who have been reborn from the waters, and sung for the Lord's congregation.

So now we have read the title over the lintel, and have understood what is meant by these press-beams. We can now take a look at the workshop itself, that is, the inner parts of the olive-press. Let us enter, and look round, and rejoice, and feel awe, and learn what we must long for and what we must flee from. You will find all this in the interior of the house, which is to say, in the text of this psalm, once we begin to read it and, with the Lord's help, to speak about it as he gives us grace.

Verse 2. A joyful noise to celebrate the ineffable

3. Now then, Asaph, congregation of the Lord, *shout with joy to God, our helper*. You are congregated here today, and you today are the Lord's Asaph, so the psalm is sung for you, the real Asaph. *Shout for joy*, then, *to God, our helper*. Other people shout for joy at the circus, but you, you do it for God. Others shout for their deceiver; you must shout for your helper. Some ring out their joy to the god they have made of their bellies,[9] but for your part, ring out your joy to God, your helper. *Make a joyful noise for the God of Jacob*, because you too belong to Jacob's family; or rather, more than that: you are Jacob, the younger people whom the elder serves.[10] *Make a joyful noise for the God of Jacob.* There may be something you cannot express in words, but do not stop exulting for all that. What you can express, cry aloud, and what you cannot, put into *a joyful noise*. Anyone who finds words insufficient to do justice to overflowing joys often bursts out into noisy happiness, so *make a joyful noise for the God of Jacob*.[11]

---

9. See Phil 3:19.
10. See Gn 25:23.
11. Compare his remarks on Psalm 99,4.

Verses 3-5. Psalm and drum, psaltery and lyre; the new life

4. *Take up a psalm, and bring a drum.* "Take" and "bring," it says. What are
you to take, and what bring? *Take up a psalm, and bring a drum.* The apostle
Paul says somewhere, in a sad and reproachful tone, that no one has been in
touch with him *in the business of disbursements and receipts* (Phil 4:15). What
does that mean, *disbursements and receipts*, if not what he pointed out explicitly
in another place, *If we have sown spiritual seeds for your benefit, is it too much to
ask that we reap a carnal harvest from you?* (1 Cor 9:11). It is obvious that a
drum, which is made from hide, is a fleshly thing. Therefore, people of God,
God's congregation, take a psalm, and give a drum. Receive spiritual benefits
and give carnal ones in exchange.

At the blessed martyr's table[12] too we urged you to receive spiritual blessings
and contribute carnal ones. Buildings erected in this present age are necessary to
house the bodies either of the living or of the dead, but only in this passing era.
After God's judgment, shall we be raising these structures up to heaven? No, but
in the present age we cannot do without them if we are to achieve what will win
us heaven. If you are avid to receive spiritual blessings, then, be assiduous about
material contributions. *Take up a psalm, and bring a drum*: receive our voice,
and give us in return what your hands produce.

5. *The tuneful psaltery with the lyre.* I remember explaining to you the difference between a psaltery and a lyre on another occasion, beloved.[13] Let any of you
who paid close attention and remember it recognize the difference now, and let
any who did not hear or do not remember take this opportunity to learn. The
difference between these two musical instruments, psaltery and lyre, is this. In a
psaltery the hollow wooden piece from which the melodious notes resound is at
the top; the strings are plucked lower down, but yield their sound higher up. In a
lyre the hollow wooden sounding-board is below. It is as though the former
gives its melody from heaven, the latter from the earth. The preaching of God's
word is a heavenly melody; but if we look for heavenly things, let us not be slug-
gish in working at those on earth, because we must have *the tuneful psaltery*, but
with the lyre. This is an alternative expression for what was said above: *take up a
psalm, and bring a drum.* Here we have a psaltery instead of a psalm, and a lyre
instead of a drum. But the admonition we are given is the same: we must respond
to the preaching of God's word by bodily efforts.

---

12. That is, the table or altar of Saint Cyprian, mentioned again at the end of this Exposition. In his
    Sermon 310,2, Augustine says that where Cyprian was martyred at Carthage "a table was
    erected to God in the same place; and yet it's called Cyprian's table, not because Cyprian ever
    dined there, but because he was sacrificed there, and because by this very sacrifice of himself
    he prepared this table, not as one on which to feed or be fed, but as one on which sacrifice might
    be offered to God, to whom he offered his very self." See Vol. III/9 in this series.
13. In his Exposition 2 of Psalm 35,5; Exposition of Psalm 42,5; see also Exposition 2 of Psalm
    70,11.

6. *Blow the trumpet—that is, preach more loudly, more confidently; do not be fearful but, as the prophet says somewhere, Shout aloud unceasingly, raise your voice like a trumpet* (Is 58:1). *Blow the trumpet at the beginning of the trumpet month.* There was an ordinance that a trumpet should be sounded at the beginning of the month,[14] and the Jews still obey it literally, though they do not understand its spiritual significance. The opening of a month is a new moon, and a new moon represents new life. What is a new moon? *If anyone is in Christ, there is a new creation* (2 Cor 5:17). What then does it mean — *blow the trumpet at the beginning of the trumpet month?* Preach the new life with complete confidence, and do not be intimidated by the din of the old life.

7. *For this is a command laid on Israel, and a matter for the God of Jacob to judge.* Where a precept is given, there will judgment be, for those who have sinned under the law will be judged by the law.[15] The giver of the precept, the Lord Christ himself, the Word made flesh, confirms it: *I came into this world for judgment, so that they who do not see may see, and those who see may become blind* (Jn 9:39). What can that mean, *so that they who do not see may see, and those who see may become blind,* except that the humble are to be exalted, and the proud cast down? It cannot mean that they who truly see are to be struck blind, but that those who think they can see are to be convicted of blindness. This is what the mystery of the olive-press brings about, *that they who do not see may see, and those who see may become blind.*

Verses 6-7. Exodus to freedom

8. *He imposed it on Joseph as a testimony.* Well now, my brothers and sisters, what is this about? "Joseph" means "increase." You remember? You know how Joseph was sold into Egypt,[16] and this stands for Christ passing over to the Gentiles. There Joseph was raised high after his troubles, and Christ was glorified after the sufferings of his martyrs. Joseph therefore has special relevance for the Gentiles, and so is justly called "increase," because the woman who was deserted bears many children, more than the wedded wife.[17] *He imposed it on Joseph as a testimony when he escaped from Egypt.* Look now, and see how the fifth day of the week is here hinted at again. When Joseph, or rather the people multiplied through Joseph, left the land of Egypt, it was conducted through the Red Sea.[18] And that was when the waters brought forth living things that crawl. The passage of the Israelites through the sea prefigured and symbolized one thing only: the passage of believers through baptism. The apostle bears witness

---

14. See Nb 10:10.
15. See Rom 2:12.
16. See Gn 37ff.
17. See Is 54:1; Gal 4:27.
18. See Ex 14.

to it: *I would not have you ignorant, brothers and sisters, that all our ancestors walked under the cloud, and all crossed the sea, and all were through Moses baptized in cloud and sea* (1 Cor 10:1-2). The journey through the sea was a type of the sacrament received by the baptized, and of nothing else but this; the pursuing Egyptians represent our hordes of past sins, and nothing else. The mysteries are plain for you to see. The Egyptians are pressing hard, harrying us, just as sins are hot on our heels, but only as far as the water's brink. Why then are you afraid to approach Christ's baptism, you who have not come yet, why fear to cross the Red Sea? Why is it red? Because the Lord's blood has hallowed it. Why are you afraid? Perhaps the consciousness of some heinous sins pierces you and tortures your soul within you, telling you that the sin you have committed is so great that you must despair of being forgiven. In that case, fear indeed that some remnant of your sins may linger, but fear it only if even one of the Egyptians survived!

Once you have crossed the Red Sea, and been led out of your sins by a mighty hand and a strong arm,[19] you will behold mysteries hitherto unknown to you, for Joseph too, *when he escaped from Egypt, heard an unfamiliar utterance.* You too will hear an utterance strange to you, one which the initiated know already and recognize, bearing witness to something of which they have experience. You will hear where you must fix your heart. When I remarked on that just now, many people understood and shouted their agreement, but the rest stood there dumb, because what they heard was speech unfamiliar to them. Let these latter hurry up, let them cross the sea and learn it. *Joseph heard an unfamiliar utterance.*

9. *God eased their backs of burdens.* Who was this who *eased their backs of burdens*? No other than he who cried out, *Come to me, all you who labor and are heavily burdened* (Mt 11:28). The same thing is suggested in another way as well. The pursuit by the Egyptians had a similar effect to the load of our sins. *He eased their backs of burdens.* Then the psalm forestalls your question, "What burdens?" by explaining, *Their hands had slaved with baskets.* Baskets symbolize servile labor. Laundry work, dung-spreading, carting soil—all these are done with baskets. Now anyone who commits sin is enslaved to sin, but if the Son sets you free, you will be free indeed.[20] With good reason are the things this world disregards as contemptible thought no better than baskets; but God filled baskets with scraps, twelve baskets full of crumbs,[21] by choosing things the world held contemptible to shame the strong.[22] But when Joseph was slaving with baskets it was to carry earth for the making of bricks. *Their hands had slaved with baskets.*

---

19. See Ps 135(136):12.
20. See Jn 8:34.36.
21. See Mt 14:20.
22. See 1 Cor 1:27.

Verse 8. The waters of contradiction

10. *In your affliction you called upon me, and I rescued you.* Every Christian conscience must recognize this if it has devoutly crossed the Red Sea, if on its commitment to believe and obey it has heard a language previously unknown. It must recognize that its prayer was heard in time of affliction. A great affliction it was indeed, to be weighed down by the load of one's sins, and how glad our conscience is when it is lifted! Yes, you have been baptized, and the conscience that yesterday was weighed down is today making merry. You were heard in your affliction, but remember what your affliction was like. Before you approached the water, what anxieties were you carrying? What fasts did you observe? How afflicted was your heart with inward prayers, fervent, heartfelt prayers? And your enemies were slain; all your sins were blotted out: *in your affliction you called upon me, and I rescued you.*

11. *I heard you in the eye of the storm*, not a storm at sea, but a storm in the heart. *I heard you in the eye of the storm, and I proved you in the water of contradiction.* Yes, my brothers and sisters, very true it is that a person who has been heard in the eye of the storm must also be proved in the water of contradiction, for when anyone has come to the faith, has been baptized, has begun to lay hold on the way to God, has determined to trickle down into the collecting vessel, and has struggled free from the dregs that are spilt abroad, such a person will find plenty of others bent on disturbing, mocking, defaming, discouraging and even threatening if they can, many to discourage and cut him down to size. All this is the water of contradiction. I think it is true of us here today, for I suspect that there are some of you here whose friends wanted to drag you off to the circus or to some trashy festival that is being kept. Perhaps these people brought their friends with them to church instead. But whether they brought their friends along, or whether they simply resisted those friends' attempts to lure them to the circus, they have been proved in the water of contradiction.

So do not be shy about preaching what you know, and defending what you believe, even among blasphemers, for if you are heard in the eye of the storm, then there is faith in your heart that will justify you, and if you are proved in the water of contradiction, there is confession on your lips that will bring you to salvation.[23] After all, what does this water of contradiction amount to? It has all but dried up by now. Our ancestors were well aware of it, when the heathen fiercely resisted the word of God and the mystery of Christ. The water was turbulent then. The Book of Revelation plainly shows that "waters" are sometimes to be understood as representing "peoples"; for when a vision of many waters was granted, and the seer wondered what they were, the answer came, *They are the peoples* (Rv 17:15). Our forebears endured the water of contradiction when the

---

23. See Rom 10:10.

Gentiles raged, and the peoples devised futile schemes, when earth's kings formed alliances and princes presented a common front against the Lord and against his Christ.[24] Amid this raging of the Gentiles a ravening lion waylaid the strong man, Samson, as he came to seek a wife from among foreigners;[25] he stands for Christ, who came down to win himself a Church from the Gentiles. But what did he do? He seized and gripped the lion, smashed it and tore it apart, and in his hands it became like a nanny-goat's kid. For what became of that raging people? It was reduced to a weary sinner. But now that its savagery has been quelled, royal power rages no longer, and the Gentiles waylay Christ with ravening fury no more. On the contrary, even among Gentile sovereignties we find laws in favor of the Church, like a honeycomb in the mouth of a lion. What have I now to fear from the water of contradiction, almost dried up as it is? It is all but silent now, provided the dregs do not set themselves to contradict us. Let wicked outsiders be as savage as they like, as long as wicked people from among ourselves do not help them. *I heard you in the eye of the storm, and I proved you in the water of contradiction.*

You recall what was said of Christ, that he was born for the downfall of many and the raising up of many more, and as a sign that would be contradicted.[26] We know that, and we see the prophecy fulfilled: the sign of the cross is raised up, and people speak against it. The glory of the cross is denied, but there was an inscription over the cross which was not altered. There is a title over a psalm[27] too; it runs, *Title inscribed, not to be altered.* There was a sign that was contradicted, for the Jews said, *Do not put, "The King of the Jews"; put "He said he was the King of the Jews."* But the contradiction was overruled, and the answer given them was, *What I have written, I have written* (Jn 19:21-22). *I heard you in the eye of the storm, and I proved you in the water of contradiction.*

Verses 9-10. After the oil, God turns to the dregs: idolaters and heretics

12. All that we have heard, from the beginning of the psalm to this verse, concerns the oil from the press. What follows is matter for grief and meant to warn us, for all the rest is about the dregs. Perhaps it is significant that a musical pause occurs at this point. Yet even this next part can be profitably listened to, so that those who see themselves already in the oil may be glad about it, while anyone in danger of running out in the dregs may be cautioned. Listen to both, then, and set your hearts on the one, but fear the other. *Listen, my people, and I*

---

24. See Ps 2:1-2.
25. See Jg 14:5-8.
26. See Lk 2:34.
27. See Ps 56(57), and Augustine's commentaries on the inviolable title in his Expositions of Psalms 55,2; 56,3; 57,3.

will speak, and bring my charge against you. He is not speaking, then, to some alien people, to some race that has nothing to do with the oil-press. *Give judgment between me and my vineyard*, he says (Is 5:3). *Listen, my people, and I will speak, and bring my charge against you*.

13. *If you hearken to me, Israel, there will be no newfangled god in your midst*. A newfangled god is a short-term construction. Our God is not a latecomer, but exists from eternity to eternity. True, our Christ is as man new-made, but as God he is eternal, for what can be earlier than "the beginning?" And beyond question the Word was in the beginning and the Word was with God, and the Word was God.[28] And our Christ is the Word who was made flesh in order to live among us.[29]

Let no one, then, harbor a newfangled god, for a newfangled god is either a thing of stone or a fantasy.[30] "No," the worshipper retorts, "not stone; I have silver and gold ones." The psalmist was right then when he mentioned those precious metals: *The idols of the Gentiles are fashioned of silver and gold* (Ps 113B(115):4). These gold and silver idols are immense, and precious, and glittering, but though they have eyes, they cannot see. They are newfangled gods. What is more newly-made than a god raw from the workshop? Even if they are old and festooned with cobwebs, they are still newfangled because they are not eternal. So much for the pagans.

Now someone else, misusing the name of the Lord his God,[31] fashioned a Christ for himself who is no more than a creature, a Christ who is unlike and unequal to the One who begot him. Such persons[32] call him the Son of God, yet deny the Son of God; for if he is truly the Son of God he is whatever the Father is, and is this from eternity. But you have dreamed up some notion in your own mind, and in so doing have set up a newfangled god.

Another man again[33] fashioned for himself a god at war with the race of darkness, a god always fearful of being invaded, at pains to avoid being damaged, a god who had been partly damaged in his efforts to remain uncorrupted and safe, though safe he clearly was not, because partly damaged. This is what the Manichees say; and they too construct a newfangled god in their hearts. Our God is not like that; your portion, Jacob, is not like that. The God who made heaven and earth, he is your God, he who neither needs benefits nor fears misfortune.

14. So then, there have been plenty of heretics who, along with the pagans, have made a variety of gods for themselves, inventing a whole range of them.

---

28. See Jn 1:1.
29. See Jn 1:14.
30. In this paragraph he envisages pagans.
31. See Ex 20:7.
32. The Arians; see note at Exposition of Psalm 54, 22.
33. Mani, founder of a theosophy in the third century A.D. in Persia. See notes at Augustine's Expositions of Psalms 10,3; 67,39.

Perhaps they have not always set up their gods in temples, but they have done something worse by enthroning them in their own hearts, and so they themselves have become the temples for false and ridiculous images. To break these idols within oneself, and cleanse a fit place for the living God who is no latecomer, is a mighty achievement.[34] All these people with their different views, all making different gods for themselves and distorting the one faith with their falsehood, appear to be disagreeing, but they have this in common, that none of them break free from earthbound thoughts; in fact they all agree to think in this earthy way. Their outlook varies, but the same emptiness is common to them all. Another psalm says of them, *In emptiness they are as one* (Ps 61:10(62:9)); for although their opinions are variegated and discordant, they are united by a similar emptiness. Now you know that it is what lies behind us that is empty, the things that we have left and passed beyond. Anyone, therefore, who has forgotten what lies behind—has forgotten empty things, that is—and has stretched forward to what lies ahead, which is the truth, is racing for the prize. And that prize is God's heavenly call to us in Christ Jesus.[35] We can see, then, that though all these folk appear to diverge from one another, they are in woeful agreement.

This is why Samson tied the foxes' tails together.[36] Foxes represent cunning people, especially heretics, deceitful, sly people who hide in winding lairs and delude others, giving off a foul stench. The apostle indicates the opposite when he claims, *We are the fragrance of Christ in every place* (2 Cor 2:15). The Song of Songs refers to these foxes when it pleads, *Catch the little foxes for us, the ones that ruin the vineyards and live in twisting lairs* (Sg 2:15). *Catch them for us* means convict them, to our profit; for when you convict people of falsehood it is as though you were catching them. When certain little foxes were arguing with our Lord, demanding, *By what authority are you doing these things?* he replied, *You, too, answer me one question: John's baptism—where did it come from? Heaven or earth?* Now foxes are usually trapped in the following way: the animals enter by one opening and leave by another, but the trapper will have placed his nets over both. "Tell me, *where did it come from? Heaven or earth?*" They sense that he has stretched his nets to catch them either way, and they say to each other, *If we say, "From heaven," he will retort, "Then why did you not believe him?"*, and John bore witness to Christ. *But if we say, "From earth," the people will stone us, for they regard John as a prophet.* Realizing that they are caught either way, they answer, *We do not know.* And the Lord replies, *"Neither am I going to tell you by what authority I am doing these things.*[37] You are

34. Augustine had struggled to achieve it himself, and in his *Confessions* prayed for the grace to do it still; see *The Confessions* I,6,6.
35. See Phil 3:13-14.
36. See Jg 15:4.
37. See Mt 21:23-27.

pretending ignorance of what you really know. I am not going to give you the answer you want, and because you have not dared to emerge by either exit, you remain in your darkness."

Let us then do our best to obey the Lord's command, *Catch the little foxes for us, the ones that ruin the vineyards.* Let us see if we can trap a few fox-cubs; let us place our snares at each exit, so that whichever way a fox chooses to come out, it will be caught. Take the Manichee, for example, who makes a newfangled god for himself and sets up in his heart something that has no existence: let us put to him the question, Is the substance of God corruptible or incorruptible? Make your choice, leave by whichever exit you prefer; you will not escape. If you say, "Corruptible," you will be stoned, not by the populace, but by yourself. But if you maintain that God is incorruptible, you will have to explain why something immune to corruption and injury should fear the race of darkness.[38] So what is left to you but to say, *We do not know?*

However, if someone gives this reply with no deceitful intent but from genuine ignorance, such a person need not remain in darkness, but should change from a fox to a sheep, and believe in the invisible, incorruptible, unique God[39] who is no latecomer, and believe in him alone because he is the sole God, not because he is some solar deity; for if we admitted that, we might be guilty of offering the fleeing fox an alternative bolt-hole. Not that we need to shy away from calling God after the sun, for we find our own scriptures referring to *the Sun of Righteousness, with healing in his wings.*[40] Perhaps we long for shade from the heat of this sun, yet it is under his pinions that we are sheltered from the heat, for in his wings there is healing. He is that sun of whom the wicked will repine one day, *No doubt of it, we strayed from the path of truth. On us the light of righteousness did not shine, nor did the sun rise for us* (Wis 5:6). Sun-worshippers will confess, *The sun did not rise for us*, because while they adore the sun which God causes to rise over both good and bad people,[41] that Sun which illumines the good alone has not risen for them. They make for themselves newfangled gods according to their several tastes, for what is to hinder the workshop of a beguiled heart from fashioning fantasies as it chooses? But all such people concur in looking to what lies behind, for they are all held back by the same kind of nonsense.

---

38. This demonstration of the self-contradiction involved in Manichean theory had been offered to Augustine by his friend Nebridius before the conversion of either of them to Christianity, as Augustine relates in his *Confessions* VII,2,3. He clearly felt its force even before he abandoned the Manichees.

39. *Soli Deo.* In the following lines Augustine engages in largely untranslatable puns on *solus*, "sole, only, unique," and *sol*, "the sun." For the Manichees sun and moon were in some sense divine.

40. See Mal 4:2 and note at Exposition of Psalm 75,11.

41. See Mt 5:45.

Now to return to Samson. His name can mean that he is "a sun to some," that is, for those on whom he shines—not to everybody, like that sun which rises over both the good and the evildoers—the sun for certain people only, a sun of righteousness. And in this respect he was a type of Christ. Now, as I began to point out, he tied the foxes' tails together and fastened burning torches to them, so that the fire would spread, but only among the harvests of the foreigners. Similarly the people we were speaking of, those who look towards what lies behind, are as though tied together by their tails, and they drag the damaging fire along with them; but they do not burn the crops of our faithful, for *the Lord knows his own, and everyone who calls on the name of the Lord keeps clear of iniquity. In a great house there are not only gold and silver vessels, but also others of wood and earthenware; some are designed for honorable purposes and others for common use. But those who have cleansed themselves from sin will be vessels fit for honorable service, useful to the Lord and ready for every good purpose* (2 Tm 2:19-21). Such persons will have nothing to fear from either the foxes' tails or their firebrands.

But let us consider God's warning to Israel: *If you hearken to me, there will be no newfangled god in your midst.* He says, "in your midst," which could also be translated, "within you," and this I find moving. He does not say "of your own making," as of a statue they might set up outside themselves, but "within you." In your heart, in your fanciful imagination, in the erroneous notion that has beguiled you, you will be carrying around with you your newfangled god—newfangled, yet antiquated. But *if you hearken to me*—to me, notice, for I AM WHO AM[42]—*there will be no newfangled god in your midst, nor will you worship any foreign god.* If there is nothing of the kind within you, you will not worship it. If your thoughts do not dwell on any false god, you will not worship any god of your own making, for *there will be no newfangled god in your midst.*

Verses 11-15. God's gifts at the exodus; Israel refuses to listen

15. *For I am....* Why worship what has no being? *For I am the Lord your God*, because I AM WHO AM. Indeed, he says, I am he, the Lord over all creation; yet in the course of time, think what benefits I have conferred on you. *I am he who led you out of the land of Egypt.* Not to that people only are these words addressed, for all of us have been led out of the land of Egypt, and all of us have passed through the Red Sea, and seen our pursuing enemies perish in its waves. Let us not be ungrateful to our God; let us not forget the God who abides, and construct some newfangled god within ourselves. *I led you out of the land of Egypt*; it is God who is speaking. *Open your mouth, and I will fill it.* You have a

---

42. See Ex 3:14.

problem of overcrowding inside yourself on account of the newfangled god you have set up in your heart; break your worthless image, rid your conscience of the home-made idol. *Open your mouth* in confession and love, *and I will fill it*, for in me is the fountain of life.[43]

16. These are the Lord's words, but what comes next? *Yet my people did not listen to my voice.* Only to his own people could he say this, because we know that whatever the law enjoins, it is addressing those who stand within the law.[44] *Yet my people did not listen to my voice, and Israel paid no heed to me.* Who paid no heed to whom? *Israel*, and *to me*. Think how ungrateful a soul this is! A soul created by me and called by me, washed of its sins by me, led back to hope by me. Yet *Israel paid no heed to me*.[45] They are baptized and they cross the Red Sea, but on the journey they grumble, quarrel and complain; they are rent by rebellions and ungrateful to him who freed them from their pursuant enemies, who leads them through a waterless desert yet provides them with food and drink, with light by night and with shade by day, *yet Israel paid no heed to me*.

17. *And I let them go, in accordance with the desires of their own hearts.* Remember the oil-press. The vents are open, and the dregs are running out. *And I let them go*, but not to follow my wholesome commandments; I handed them over to themselves *in accordance with the desires of their own hearts*. The apostle speaks similarly, *God has delivered them to their own lusts* (Rom 1:24). *I let them go, in accordance with the desires of their own hearts, and they will go off after their passions.* This is what you dread, as long as you are trickling into the hidden collecting vessels of the Lord. If you have set your heart on his storehouses, this is what you dread. Some urge the claims of the circus, others those of the amphitheater; some support the shops in the streets, others the theater, others this or that ... and finally others again their newfangled god. *They will go off after their passions.*

18. *If only my people had hearkened to me, if Israel had walked in my ways.* Israel may perhaps counter this with, "Yes, I do sin, that is obvious; I do go after the desires of my heart. But how much of that is my fault? The devil it is who does it. The demons do it." What is the devil? And who are the demons? Your enemies, undoubtedly. But *if Israel had walked in my ways, I would have reduced their enemies to nothing*. So, if *my* people had hearkened to me—but how can they be called mine, if they do not listen to me? *If my people had hearkened to me.* What does *my people* mean? Israel. And what does he mean by *had hearkened to me*? It means, *If Israel had walked in my ways*. Israel moans and

---

43. See Ps 35:10(36:9).
44. See Rom 3:19.
45. Throughout this paragraph his thought is moving freely between Israel and a baptized Christian, both seen within the one mystery of salvation.

groans, oppressed by its enemies, but *I would have reduced their enemies to nothing, and laid a heavy hand on any who troubled them.*

Verse 16. There are enemies of God among his own people. Stern warnings

19. What do they mean by complaining about their enemies? They have become worse enemies themselves. How so? Well, look at the next line. If you are minded to complain about your enemies, think what you are yourselves. *The Lord's enemies have lied to him.* Do you renounce your sins? "I do renounce them," someone asserts.[46] And back he goes to what he has renounced. What are these things you renounce? Theft, robbery, perjury, homicide, adultery, sacrilege, impious rites, the seductions of the eyes.[47] You renounce all these, but then you crane your head round again, and are overcome by them. The things you turn back to now are worse than before. The dog returns to his vomit, and the sow newly washed rolls in the mud once more.[48]

The Lord's enemies have lied to him. How enormously patient the Lord is! Why are they not struck down? Why not slaughtered? Why does the earth not crack open and swallow them up? Because the Lord is enormously patient. They will go unpunished, then? By no means. Let them not so delude themselves about God's mercy as to promise themselves that he will be unjust. Do you not realize that God's patience is meant to lead you to repentance? In your obstinacy and impenitence of heart you are storing up anger against yourself for that day when God's wrath and his just judgment will be revealed, and he will render to each of us in accordance with our deeds.[49] If he does not settle the account now, he will on that day. If he does settle it now, his reckoning is provisional, but for those who do not change and correct their ways, the reckoning will be for eternity.

If you want further evidence that they will not go unpunished, look at the next lines. *The Lord's enemies have lied to him.* "Yes," you will say, "and what has he done to them? They are still alive, aren't they? Fortune favors them, doesn't it? They rejoice in the light, drink from earth's fountains and eat of its fruits, don't they?" But *for them the reckoning will last for ever.*

20. Let none of us flatter ourselves on merely belonging to the oil-press; we are safe only if we belong to the oil. Anyone who is guilty of those wicked deeds

---

46. Probably an echo of the baptismal interrogation.
47. *Curiositatibus*, literally "curiosities," but for Augustine the word had a more sinister ring than "curiosity" has in English. He was aware of having been seduced in his pre-Christian days by desire for superficial and titillating knowledge, which he came to understand, in the light of 1 Jn 2:16, as a perversion of the quest for truth. Compare Exposition of Psalm 39,8, and note there.
48. See 2 Pt 2:20-22; Prv 26:11.
49. See Rom 2:4-6.

which debar us from possessing the kingdom of God must put no trust in such self-delusory promises as "I have Christ's sign and Christ's sacraments, so I shall not perish for ever. If I need purification, I shall be saved through fire." They go on to argue, "After all, what does the apostle say about those who have the foundation in them? *No one can lay any other foundation than that which is laid, which is Christ Jesus.* And what has the rest of the passage to say? *Let everyone look to what he builds on the foundation; for one person builds in gold, silver and precious stones, another in wood, hay and straw. The day of the Lord will disclose the work of each one, for it will be revealed by fire. If the work anyone has put into building survives, that builder will be rewarded,* rewarded, that is, for building up good works on the foundation—*gold, silver and precious stones.* But if someone has superimposed sins instead—*wood, hay and straw*—such a person will be saved indeed, though it be through fire" (1 Cor 3:10-15).

I want to be extremely cautious here, my brothers and sisters, for it is better not to lull you into false security. I will give you no assurance that I do not have myself. If I frighten you it is because I am afraid; I would reassure you only if I were reassured. I am fearful of everlasting fire. When the psalm says, *For them the reckoning will last for ever,* I take it to refer to the eternal fire of which another passage says, *The fire that consumes them will never be extinguished, nor will the worm that devours them ever die* (Is 66:24). "That may be," someone will reply, "but the threat is addressed to the godless, not to me. Sinner I may be, an adulterer, a swindler, a robber,[50] or a perjurer; but I have Christ as my foundation. I am a Christian; I am baptized. I shall be purged through fire, therefore, but I shall not perish. I rely on the foundation."

Just tell me that again: what are you? "A Christian," you say. Carry on: what else? A robber, an adulterer, and all those other things of which the apostle says, *Those who commit these sins will not possess the kingdom of God* (Gal 5:21). If you have not amended your life or repented of these sins, do you really hope to gain the kingdom of heaven? I do not think you will, for *those who commit these sins will not possess the kingdom of God.* Do you not realize that God's patience is meant to lead you to repentance? You may make delusory promises to yourself, but in your obstinacy and impenitence of heart you are storing up anger against yourself for that day when God's wrath and his just judgment will be revealed, and he will render to each of us in accordance with our deeds.

Look now to the judge who is coming. And it is a good thing for us that we can. Thanks be to him who has not hidden from us what the definitive sentence will be; he does not will to cast the guilty outside and then draw a veil over their fate. He willed to make known to us in advance what he has decided to do. *All*

---

50. *Raptor* could also mean a rapist.

nations will assemble before him. And what will he do with them? He will sort them out, and will place some at his right hand, others at his left. There will be no middle ground, will there? And what will he say to those on his right? *Come, you whom my Father has blessed; take possession of the kingdom.* And to those at his left? *Depart from me, you accursed, into the eternal fire which was prepared for the devil and his angels* (Mt 25:32.34.41). If your destination does not terrify you, at least think who your companions will be.

If, then, all those deeds will not possess the kingdom of God (or, rather, the perpetrators of them, for the sins themselves are not likely to be committed in the fire; people burning in it are not going to be stealing or committing adultery); if, as I was saying, *those who commit these sins will not possess the kingdom of God,* they will have no place at the Lord's right hand beside the people to whom the invitation will be addressed, *Come, you whom my Father has blessed; take possession of the kingdom.* Obviously not, because *those who commit these sins will not possess the kingdom of God.* So if they are not on his right, there is nowhere for them to be but on his left; and what will he say to those at his left? *Depart into the eternal fire,* because *for them the reckoning will last for ever.*

Sound building

21. "Very well, then," someone may say, "but explain to us how it is that people who build upon the foundation with wood, hay, and straw do not perish, but are saved, even though it is through fire."[51]

This is a difficult question, but I will speak on it briefly, as best I can. My brothers and sisters, there are certain people who are completely disdainful of this world. The things that pass away with time mean nothing to them; they are not affectionately attached to mundane affairs; they are holy, chaste, continent and just. Perhaps they sell all their goods and distribute the proceeds to the poor; or else they own property as though they owned nothing, and make use of this world, but never to the full.[52] But there are other people who cling with some affection to the things permitted to our human weakness. A man does not seize another's estate, but he so loves his own that if he loses it he is deeply distressed. He does not covet someone else's wife, but he is so possessive of his own, and so passionate in his conjugal relations with her, that he fails to observe the law prescribed in these matters, that the procreation of children must be the intention. He does not steal anyone's property, but he does seek the return of his own.[53] He goes to law in dispute with a brother, despite the apostle's words to such people, *This is very wrong of you, to have any lawsuits between you at all* (1

---

51. Sections 21 and 22 are found also in Eugippius CXLI, 157.
52. See 1 Cor 7:30.
53. See Lk 6:30.

Cor 6:7). It is true that Paul orders such differences to be settled within the Church, not dragged to a court of law, but even that he condemns as sinful, for it means that a Christian is battling for earthly goods more vehemently than is becoming for someone to whom the kingdom of heaven has been promised. The heart of such a person is not entirely lifted up,[54] but partly dragging along the ground.

Now there comes a time of testing that is likely to lead to martyrdom. How will they respond, who have Christ as their foundation, and build upon it in gold, silver and precious stones? What will they say when the opportunity arises? "It is good for me to perish and to be with Christ."[55] They run ahead eagerly, dismayed not at all, or very little, by the fragility of their mortal state. The others, by contrast, those in love with their own goods and their own houses, are thoroughly upset; and the hay, straw and wood of their workmanship go up in flames. They have used wood, hay and straw for their materials and laid them on the foundation, but these are things permitted, not unlawful.

Well then, brothers and sisters, this is what I have to say to every one of you who have Christ as your foundation: set your heart on heaven and tread the earth underfoot. If you do this you are building in gold, silver and precious stones, and in nothing else. But when you say, "I love this property of mine, and I am going to take good care that it is not destroyed," then, when the loss threatens, you are distressed. You do not value it more highly than Christ; no, your affection for it is such that if someone asked you, "Which will you have—this property or Christ?" then even though you would be sorry to give it up, you would prefer to embrace Christ, whom you have chosen as your foundation. You will be saved, but as though through fire. Think of another case: you cannot hold on to this property except by bearing false witness. To refuse the falsehood is to make Christ your foundation, for Truth itself declares, *A lie in the mouth kills the soul* (Wis 1:11).

If, then, you love your possessions, but refuse to commit robbery on their account, or to bear false witness, commit murder or swear a false oath, you are refusing to deny Christ for their sake and, by so refusing, you are showing that you have Christ as your foundation. All the same, because you are attached to your property, and are saddened at losing it, you have built up on that foundation not gold, silver or precious stones, but wood, hay and straw. You will be saved indeed when what you have built goes up in flames, but you will be saved through fire.

But people who build adultery, blasphemy, sacrilege, idolatry or perjury upon the foundation must not suppose that they too will be saved through fire, as though these sins were wood, hay and straw. No; but if someone raises a super-

54. Possibly an allusion to the liturgical invitation "Lift up your hearts"; see note on Exposition of Psalm 10, 3.
55. See Phil 1:23.

structure of attachment to temporal goods upon the foundation of the kingdom of heaven—that is, upon Christ—then the attachment to temporal goods will burn away, but that person will be saved through having the right foundation.

Verse 17. Some of those fed on the sacraments are the Lord's enemies

22. *The Lord's enemies have lied to him* by saying, "I am going to the vineyard," but not going.[56] *For them the reckoning will last* not for a time, but *for ever.* And who are they? *He fed them on the richest wheat.* You know this richest wheat. Many of his enemies are fed on it, people who have lied to him. *He fed them on the richest wheat,* for he has united them bodily with his sacraments. He fed even Judas with the richest wheat when he handed him the morsel,[57] and then his enemy lied to him; for such a one the reckoning will last for ever. *He fed them on the richest wheat, and gave them their fill of honey from the rock.* How ungrateful they were! *He fed them on the richest wheat, and gave them their fill of honey from the rock.* In the wilderness what he brought out of the rock was water, not honey. Honey represents wisdom, which holds prime place for sweetness to the palate of the heart.[58] Think how many of the Lord's enemies, how many who lie to the Lord, are fed not only on the richest wheat, but also on honey from the rock, on the wisdom of Christ! How many there are who relish his word and prize their initiation into his sacraments, who enjoy unravelling his parables! How many shout their delight! And this is not honey from any ordinary person, but from the rock, *and that rock is Christ* (1 Cor 10:4). How many people are gorged on this honey, and cry out, "This is sweet! We can't think of anything better or sweeter, or begin to describe it!" And yet they are the Lord's enemies and have lied to him.

Concluding exhortations

I do not want to spend any more time on such gloomy considerations. Of set purpose does this psalm close on a terrifying note, but let us, please, turn away from its ending to its opening verse, *Shout with joy to God, our helper.* We shall have turned back to God.[59]

23. God has put on for you in Christ's name entertainments[60] that have gripped your imagination and held you spellbound, not only kindling your desire for certain things but warning you to avoid others. Shows like this are useful,

---

56. See Mt 21:30.
57. See Jn 13:26.
58. See Sir 11:3.
59. The last three words, *Conversi ad Deum,* may be an invitation to the congregation to turn to God in prayer by reciting the whole psalm. But Augustine adds a few further remarks.
60. *Spectacula,* "shows." See note at the opening section of this Exposition.

salutary, and designed to build up, not destroy; or, rather, they both destroy and build up, for they destroy newfangled gods and build up your faith in the true and eternal God.

We invite you to come along tomorrow as well, dearly beloved. Tomorrow at the theatre they are putting on a show about the sea, we understand; so let us have a harbor in Christ. We cannot convene at Cyprian's table[61] on the day after tomorrow, Wednesday, because that is the feast-day of the holy martyrs; so let us meet at Cyprian's table tomorrow.

---

61. See note at section 4 of this Exposition.

Exposition of Psalm 81

Verse 1. Among whom did God "take his stand," and what was the mode of his presence?

1. The title is *A psalm for Asaph himself.* As in the case of other psalms where we find a similar prefix, this psalm may have been given its title either because this was the name of the man who wrote it, or because of the interpretation of his name. In the latter case, this title was intended to suggest that the psalm is to be understood as dealing with the synagogue, since this is what "Asaph" means; and this is the more likely in that the first verse of the psalm also refers to the synagogue: *God has taken his stand in the synagogue of the gods.*[1] We should certainly not understand this to be a reference to the gods of the Gentiles or their idols, or to any creature in heaven or on earth other than human beings, because a little further on our psalm declares more plainly what kind of assembly of gods it is in which God has taken his stand. *This is my sentence: you are gods, sons of the Most High, all of you; yet you shall die as mortals die, and fall as any lordly ruler falls* (verses 6-7).

God has taken his stand, then, in the synagogue of those sons of the Most High of whom he, God Most High himself, complains through Isaiah, *I have brought children to birth and ennobled them, but they have despised me* (Is 1:2). The word *synagogue* indicates the people of Israel: their assembly is ordinarily called so, though it may occasionally be called "church." But of our assembly the apostles never used the word "synagogue,"[2] but always "church."[3] They may have done so simply to distinguish the one from the other, or because there is some difference between a "congregation" (this is the same term as "synagogue"), and a "convocation," which is what "church" means. Animals too are "congregated" or "herded," and the term is appropriate for them, which is why we speak of them in "herds," whereas human beings, rational creatures, are more properly said to be "convoked." Accordingly another psalm sings, in the person of this same Asaph, *I have become like a beast in your presence, yet I am always with you* (Ps 72:23(73:22)), for although to all appearances he was surrendered

---

1. This verse is considered again by Augustine in his Exposition of Psalm 94,6.
2. *Synagoga.*
3. *Ecclesia.*

to the one true God, what God was being asked for was carnal, earthly and temporal favors, as though these were the supreme and highest goods.

We often find the Israelites being called God's children, not in virtue of the grace of the New Testament, but of that which belongs to the Old. It was by this Old Testament grace that God chose Abraham and propagated so numerous a race from his flesh; by the same grace he loved Jacob but hated Esau even before they were born;[4] by the same grace he freed Israel from Egypt and led them into the land of promise, ousting the Gentiles. This was truly grace; were it not, the evangelist could not have said of us, to whom has been given power to become children of God and to lay hold on no earthly kingdom but the kingdom of heaven, that we have received grace for grace.[5] We have received the promises of the New Testament in exchange for the promises of the Old. From all this it is plain, I think, what this "synagogue" is, in which God has taken his stand.

2. The next thing we need to establish is whether God the Father is meant, or the Son, or the Holy Spirit, or the whole Trinity, when God is said to stand *in the synagogue of the gods, to make a distinction among them*; for each of the Persons is God, and the Trinity is one God. It is not easy to sift this matter, because it is undeniable that God is present to created things not in any corporeal way but by a spiritual presence that accords with his own substance; and this presence is something wonderful, understood by very few. In response to it a psalmist cries to God, *If I mount to heaven, you are there; if I sink down to hell, even there you are present* (Ps 138(139):8). There is good reason, then, to state that God stands invisibly in an assembly of human beings, just as he fills heaven and earth, as he says of himself through a prophet.[6] But we can do more than merely make this statement about him: the human mind must be in some degree capable of knowing his presence as he stands in the things he has created, if a mere man could stand and hear him, and be filled with joy at his quiet voice.[7]

In my view, however, this psalm is trying to hint that it was only from a certain point in time that God took his stand in the synagogue of the gods, for the kind of stance whereby he fills heaven and earth is not proper to the synagogue, nor does it vary with time. So *God took his stand in the synagogue of the gods*—he, that is, who said of himself, *I was not sent except to the lost sheep of the house of Israel* (Mt 15:24). His reason for doing so is indicated: he took his stand *to make a distinction among them*. I infer that God took his stand in the midst of those "gods" of whom it was said, *The patriarchs belong to them; and from them Christ was born according to the flesh* (Rom 9:5). It was precisely in order to stand in this synagogue of gods that God took from them his descent

---

4. See Ml 1:2.3; Rom 9:13.
5. See Jn 1:12.16.
6. See Jr 23:24.
7. See Jn 3:29.

according to the flesh. But what is God? He is not like them among whom he stood, but, as the apostle continues in the same text, he is *sovereign over all, God, blessed for ever.* I know that he stood among them, and I know that God stood there as their bridegroom, for the bridegroom's friend said of him, *Someone is standing among you whom you do not recognize* (Jn 1:26). Our psalm says of them a little further on, *They have neither known nor understood, they walk in darkness* (verse 5); and the apostle bears witness in the same sense: *Blindness has fallen upon part of Israel, until the full tally of the Gentiles comes in* (Rom 11:25). They saw him well enough as he stood among them, but they did not see him as God, which was how he willed to be seen, as he told us by saying, *Whoever has seen me has seen the Father* (Jn 14:9).

Now the distinction he makes among the gods is based not on their merits but on his own grace, since he fashions from the same clay some vessels for honorable purposes and others for common use.[8] What gives you any distinction? What have you, that you have not received as gift, and if it is a gift to you, why boast as though it were not?[9]

Verses 2-3. The psalm's denunciation of unjust judges is referred to those who condemned Christ

3. Listen to God's voice as he makes the distinction, listen as the voice of the Lord strikes fiery flame:[10] *How long will you judge unjustly, favoring the wicked?* He asks a similar question elsewhere: *How long will you be heavy-hearted?* (Ps 4:3(2)). Even until he comes who is the light of human hearts? I gave you the law, but you resisted it stubbornly; I sent prophets to you, but you ill-treated them or killed them, or at least connived at the actions of those who did. But if the people who killed the servants whom God sent to them are not worthy even to be addressed, what about you, who were silent when these deeds were done, you, that is, who are now willing to imitate those who were silent then, as though they were innocent? *How long will you judge unjustly, favoring the wicked?* Now the heir himself is coming. Is he to be killed too?[11] Did he not will to be fatherless, like an orphan, for your sake? Did he not hunger and thirst like a poor and needy man, and for you? Did he not cry out to you, *Learn of me, for I am meek and humble of heart* (Mt 11:29)? Did not he, who was rich, make himself poor, to enrich you by his poverty?[12] *Give just judgment,* then, *for the orphan and the needy person, vindicate the humble and the poor.* Account him

---

8. See Rom 9:21.
9. See 1 Cor 4:7.
10. See Ps 28(29):7.
11. See Mt 21:38.
12. See 2 Cor 8:9.

just, proclaim him just, who for your sake was lowly and poor. Do not call them just who are proud and rich for their own advantage.[13]

Verse 4. *The people were as guilty as their leaders*

4. But they will regard him with jealous hatred, and show him no mercy at all. *This is the heir*, they will say. *Come on, let's kill him, and the inheritance will be for us* (Mt 21:38). *Deliver the weak man*, then, *and save the poor man from the sinner's clutches*. This is said to warn the people among whom Christ was born and died that they are by no means guiltless of that heinous crime. So large was the populace that the Jews were afraid, as the gospel tells us,[14] and therefore did not dare to lay hands on Christ. Yet later the people connived at the crime, allowing him to be slain by their malevolent and spiteful leaders. Had the onlookers but willed it, they could have been just as much an object of fear to their leaders even then, so that the hands of those criminals would have been powerless against Christ. Another text says of the people, *Dumb dogs they are, who do not know how to bark* (Is 56:10), and again, *See how the righteous man perished, and no one cares* (Is 57:1).

He perished, but only insofar as they were able to ensure that he perished, for how could death be the end of him who was by his death seeking what had perished?[15] Those who pretended not to be involved, and thereby made so great a crime possible, are justly rebuked and with good reason held guilty; what kind of rebuke, then—or not even rebuke, but how severe a condemnation—do they deserve who by their plotting and wickedness committed it?

Verse 5. *Earthly and heavenly foundations*

5. The verse that follows applies equally to both groups. *They have neither known nor understood, they walk in darkness*. If the leaders had recognized him, they would never have crucified the Lord of glory;[16] if the crowd had recognized him, they would not have demanded that Barabbas be released and Christ crucified.[17] But we have been reminded already that *blindness has fallen upon part of Israel, until the full tally of the Gentiles comes in* (Rom 11:25). Christ was crucified through that blindness, and the psalm predicts that *all the foundations of the world will be moved*. Moved they were, and so they will continue to be, until the

---

13. The original psalm is a denunciation of corrupt authorities who oppress the poor—any poor. Augustine sees in it the archetypal "poor man," Christ.
14. See Lk 22:2.
15. See Mt 18:11.
16. See 1 Cor 2:8.
17. See Mt 27:21-23.

predestined multitude of the Gentiles shall come in. At the moment of the Lord's death the earth quaked and the rocks were split;[18] and if we take the foundations of the earth to represent persons who are reckoned fortunate in the abundance of their earthly goods, then the prediction that they would be moved has been proved correct. Either they are moved to wonder that the humility, poverty and death of Christ, which seem to them to be his abject misery, are so greatly loved and venerated; or else they are moved to love and imitate it themselves, scorning the worthless happiness the world offers. Thus all the foundations of the earth are moved, as some wonder and others are transformed.

There is a parallel which can clarify this point. We speak quite reasonably of the foundations of heaven. On them the kingdom of heaven is being built up in the saints and the faithful, whom scripture calls living stones.[19] Their foundation is first of all Christ himself, born of a virgin, of whom the apostle says, *No one can lay any other foundation than that which is laid, which is Christ Jesus* (1 Cor 3:11). Next come the apostles and prophets, on whose authority our choice of that heavenly place is made, so that in obedience to them we may be built up together, as the Letter to the Ephesians testifies: *You are pilgrims and sojourners no longer; rather are you fellow citizens with the saints and members of God's household, built up on the foundation of the apostles and prophets, Christ Jesus himself being the chief cornerstone. In him the whole edifice is bound together and grows into a holy temple for the Lord* (Eph 2:19-22). In an analogous way the "foundations of the earth" can be taken to represent those whose earthly fortune is so pre-eminent and powerful as to make them the envy of other people, who are irresistibly drawn by their authority to covet the same kind of wealth. Then on gaining it they are built in with those they envied, like earth upon earth, as in the heavenly building heaven is upon heaven.[20] This is why the sinner is admonished, *Earth you are, and back to earth you shall go* (Gn 3:19), whereas *the heavens proclaim God's glory*, since *their sound echoed throughout the world, and their words to the ends of the earth* (Ps 18:2.5(19:1.4)).

Verses 6-7. The proud earthly kingdom

6. The kingdom of earthly happiness is pride. Against it was pitted the humility of Christ, who reproaches those whom he wishes to make children of God Most High through humility. He rebukes them, saying, *This is my sentence: you are gods, sons of the Most High, all of you; yet you shall die as mortals die,*

---

18. See Mt 27:51.
19. See 1 Pt 2:5.
20. This contrast between the heavenly temple built on Christ and the apostles, and the earthly building founded on human wealth and pride, is reminiscent of his much greater development of the theme of the two cities in *The City of God*.

and fall as any lordly ruler falls. One way to understand this is to take *this is my sentence: you are gods, sons of the Most High, all of you* as addressed to those who have been predestined to eternal life, and his words, *yet you shall die as mortals die, and fall as any lordly ruler falls* as spoken to the rest; in this way he is making a distinction among the gods. Alternatively, it can be interpreted as a rebuke to all of them alike, so that he may distinguish those who obey and accept correction. *This is my sentence: you are gods, sons of the Most High, all of you,* he says. "I have promised heavenly bliss to you all, but because of your fleshly weakness *you shall die as mortals die*; and because of your haughty self-importance you will not be exalted, but will *fall as any lordly ruler falls.*" That is, like the devil.

He is telling them, "Though your life is so short that very soon you must die as mortals do, it still profits you little as a time for correction. The devil has many days in this world, since he is not made of flesh and so does not die; yet you, like him, exalt yourselves, and you will fall." It was indeed through diabolical pride that the perverse and blind rulers of the Jews looked with envious hatred at Christ's glory; and through this vice it happened then, and still happens now, that the humility of Christ, that humility which took him even to death by crucifixion,[21] is a thing to be despised in the eyes of those who set their hearts on this world's honors.

Verse 8. Christ's ultimate act of judgment

7. Hoping for the cure of this vice, the psalm continues, *Arise, O God, judge the earth.* It is the prophet's own voice that we hear now. "The earth was swollen with pride when it crucified you; rise from the dead, then, and judge the earth." *Because you will destroy it among all nations.* Destroy what? The earth, of course; that is, those who relish earthly things. This could refer either to believers, in whom he extinguishes the desire for earthly enrichment along with their pride, or to unbelievers, whom he marks out from the rest as earth which deserves to be trampled on and thrown away. Thus he judges the earth through his members, whose way of life is in heaven,[22] and destroys it throughout all nations.

We must not omit to notice that some codices have *Because you will claim your inheritance among all nations.* This also makes good sense, and there is nothing to stop us understanding the passage both ways. His inheritance comes into being through charity, for in cultivating charity by his commandments and his grace he destroys earthly greed.

---

21. See Ph 2:8.
22. See Ph 3:20.

Exposition of Psalm 82

Verse 1. The title: Asaph again

1. The title of this psalm is *A psalm sung for Asaph*. We have already pointed out several times that the name "Asaph" means a congregation. This is why the man called Asaph represents the congregation of God's people in the titles of many psalms. But our word "congregation" is "synagogue" in Greek, and the name "synagogue" has been appropriated by the Jewish people, just as the Christian people is more usually called "Church," although it too is congregated.[1]

Verse 2. A question is put to Christ, who will one day come in glory

2. The people of God says in this psalm, *Who will be like you, O God?* This question can be more suitably understood as addressed to Christ, I think. Fashioned in human form[2] he was reckoned by the Jews as deserving of contempt and no different from other human beings; in fact he was even relegated to the company of criminals,[3] but only so that he might submit to judgment. When he comes to judge, then it is that the question, *Who will be like you, O God?* will take on its true sense. It is not uncommon for the psalms to address Christ our Lord; so we find another psalm using words which every believer must recognize as spoken to him: *Your throne, O God, stands for ever and ever, and your royal scepter is the scepter of righteous rule. You have loved justice and hated iniquity; therefore God, your God, has anointed you with the oil of joy, more abundantly than your companions* (Ps 44:7-8(45:6-7)). Just so the present psalm says to him, "*Who will be like you, O God?* In the days of your lowliness you willed to be like many others, even like the robbers who were crucified with you; but when you come in glory, *who will be like you* then?" There would be little point in asking God, *Who will be like you?* unless the question were put to him who once willed to be like human beings, taking on him the nature of a slave, being made in human likeness and revealed in human form.[4] This is why the psalm

---

1. See note at Exposition of Psalm 77,3.
2. See Phil 2:7.
3. See Is 53:12.
4. See Phil 2:7-8.

does not ask, "Who *is* like you?" Such a question would be correctly formulated if it referred to his godhead only. But since it envisages his servile nature, it is only when he appears in glory that his unlikeness to the rest of humankind will be seen.

Now the psalm continues, *Do not be silent, do not hold back, O God*. The reason for this petition is that he did once keep silence in order to submit to judgment, when he held back his power, and like a lamb before its shearer was voiceless, not opening his mouth.[5] He proved that he was voluntarily restraining himself by that utterance, *I am*, at which the men who were trying to arrest him recoiled and fell down.[6] How else could he have been seized, how else could he have suffered, unless he was holding back and restraining himself, almost taming himself, so to say? Some interpreters, though, have understood these words of the psalm, *Do not hold back, O God*, to mean, *Do not grow gentler, O God*. He says of himself elsewhere, *I have long been silent and patient, but shall I be silent for ever?* (Is 42:14). The plea is made to him here, *Do not be silent*, and of him it is said in another psalm, *God will come openly; our God will not keep silence* (Ps 49(50):3). So here the psalm begs him, *Do not be silent*, for he was indeed silent in order to undergo their judgment when he came in hidden wise; but at his manifest coming he will not keep silence, for then he will come to judge.

Verses 3-4. The din raised by Christ's enemies

3. *Listen to the din your enemies have made. Those who hate you have reared their head.* This verse seems to point to the final days when the forces which at present are held in check by fear will burst out in full voice, but in a voice so obviously irrational that it is more aptly termed a din than speech or words. That day will not see the beginning of their hatred; rather will those who hate already then rear their head. And it does say *head*, not "heads," for they will reach the point where they have as their head that enemy who exalts himself against anything claiming to be God, everything that people worship.[7] But in him the prediction will be most fully verified, that *anyone who exalts himself will be humbled* (Lk 14:11). Then God, to whom the psalm prays, *Do not be silent, do not grow gentler*, will slay this enemy with the breath of his mouth, and do away with him by his own radiant presence.[8]

---

5. See Is 53:7.
6. See Jn 18:5-6. As often in John's gospel, Jesus' words are true at different levels. The superficial sense is an assertion of his identity as "Jesus of Nazareth" whom they are seeking; the more profound sense suggests the divine name revealed in Ex 3:14; compare Jn 8:58. Augustine has this latter sense in mind here.
7. See 2 Th 2:4.
8. See 2 Th 2:8.

4. *They have hatched malevolent plots against your people*, or, as other codices have it, *they have devised cunning plans, plans against your holy ones*. This statement is made in a mocking spirit; since when have they had any power to harm God's people, or hurt his holy ones who have the wit to say, *If God is for us, who can stand against us?* (Rom 8:31).

Verses 5-6. They plot against God's people

5. *Come, they said, let us destroy them from the nation*. It says *nation* in the singular to suggest the plural, as when we say "head of cattle" to mean the whole herd. Other codices, however, do have the plural, *from the nations*, because interpreters have there followed the sense rather than the words. *Come, let us destroy them from the nation*: this is the din they raised; we cannot call it speaking because with their empty minds they made empty noises. *And let no memory of Israel's name remain.*[9] The name *Israel* is undoubtedly to be understood here as embracing those descendants of Abraham to whom the apostle says, *You are the descendants of Abraham, his heirs according to the promise* (Gal 3:29), not those who are his carnal posterity, of whom Paul says, *Consider Israel according to the flesh* (1 Cor 10:18).

6. *They are of one mind in their scheming, and with common accord they have made a pact against you.*[10] As though they could ever prove stronger! The word *testamentum* is used in scripture to signify a will which comes into force only on the death of the testator, but also any pact or treaty. Laban and Jacob, for instance, made a treaty[11] which was certainly valid during their own lifetime; and many similar examples are recorded in holy scripture.

---

9. *Et non memoretur nominis Israel ultra*. Augustine goes on to say that this is an unusual construction in Latin, being an over-literal translation of the Greek from which his Latin psalter is derived, and that some copyists have therefore amended it to *Et non sit memoria nominis Israel adhuc*. These two sentences are omitted in the English translation.

10. *Adversum te testamentum disposuerunt*. Augustine's following remarks depend on the polyvalence of the Greek word διαθήκη. The basic idea is that of a "dispositio" or decree setting forth a person's intentions. Hence it was used by the LXX to represent the Hebrew *berîth*, a covenant between God and his people which was not a covenant as between equals, because the terms were dictated by God. An extension of the idea of disposition led to the use of διαθήκη for "last will and testament," a meaning that predominated in Hellenistic literature. These two meanings, covenant and testament, lie behind the elaborate argument in Heb 9:15-22. Augustine in the present context refers to another common (secular) usage, διαθήκη as a pact or agreement between contracting parties.

11. See Gn 31:44.

Verses 7-8. A list of traditional enemies, whose names reveal their characters

7. The psalm now begins to enumerate Christ's enemies under the names of various Gentile races. The interpretation of these names is sufficient indication of the meaning we are meant to gather, for the enemies of the truth are very aptly described by them. "Edomites" means persons stained with blood or earth; "Ishmaelites" those who are obedient to themselves, and if to themselves, obviously not to God. The pejorative sense of "Moab," which means "from the father," can best be understood by recalling the story of how Moab's father Lot had intercourse with his own daughter, who unlawfully seduced him, so that Lot begot Moab;[12] this was the origin of his name. The father was a good man, just as the law is good, but only for one who makes legitimate use of it,[13] not when used incestuously and illicitly. "Hagar's people" means "converts," that is, strangers. Among the enemies of God's people they represent not those who become citizens, but those who persist in their foreign and outlandish attitude, and emerge whenever an occasion arises for doing harm. "Gebal" means "a false valley," and so anyone whose humility is a sham; "Ammon" a people "in confusion or sadness." "Amalek" means "a race that licks," which is why another text prophesies, *His enemies will lick the dust* (Ps 71(72):9). Then, where our text has "foreigners," the meaning of which term is self-evident and suggests enemies, the Hebrew has "Philistines," a name which means "falling over through drink," hinting that they are intoxicated by worldly luxury. "Tyre" is *Zôr* in Hebrew, which could be interpreted as "distress" or "tribulation," and we must see in these enemies of God's people the fulfillment of the apostle's words, *Tribulation and distress upon every human soul whose deeds are evil* (Rom 2:9).

All these races are listed in our psalm as follows: *The tents of the Edomites and Ishmaelites, Moab and Hagar's people, Gebal and Ammon and Amalek, foreigners and dwellers in Tyre.*

Verse 9. They all serve the prince of darkness

8. The psalm now proceeds to indicate the reason why all these are enemies of God's people. *Assyria too comes with them*, it says. "Assyria" or "Asshur" is usually understood as a figurative expression for the devil himself, who is at work in the children of disobedience,[14] using them as his instruments and prevailing upon them to attack God's people. *They allied themselves with the sons of Lot*, says our psalm, because all those enemies, under their leader the devil who was doing his work within them, *allied themselves with the sons of*

---

12. See Gn 19:36-37, and note at Exposition of Psalm 59,10.
13. See 1 Tm 1:8.
14. See Eph 2:2.

Lot, whose name means "turning away." Now the apostate angels can be very aptly called "sons who turned away"; they did indeed turn away from the truth, and swerved into the devil's cohorts. Of them the apostle says, *It is not against flesh and blood that you have to struggle, but against principalities and powers and the rulers of this world of darkness, against wicked spiritual beings in heavenly realms* (Eph 6:12). Thus it happens that these invisible enemies are aided by unbelieving humans, in whom they are at work in assailing the people of God.

Verses 10-13. Historical victories as exemplars of future triumph

9. Let us see now what kind of fate the prophetic spirit prays will overtake them, though it is forecasting rather than cursing. *Deal with them as with Midian and Sisera*, it says, *and as with Jabin at the Wadi of Kishon, as with all those who perished at Endor, and became like dung on the ground*. History relates that Israel, which was at that time God's people, fought against all these and defeated them,[15] as they also defeated others whom the psalm goes on to enumerate. *Make their chieftains like Oreb and Zeeb, like Zebah and Zalmunna.*[16]

The interpretation of their names goes like this: Midian means "crooked judgment"; Sisera "joy excluded"; Jabin "wise person," though the only "wise" person to be recognized in these enemies overcome by the people of God is the kind of whom the apostle demands, *Where is the wise man? Where the scholar? Where is this world's savant?* (1 Cor 1:20). Oreb means "dryness," Zeeb "a wolf," Zebah "victim" (clearly the wolf's victim, for he too has his prey), Zalmunna "shadow of commotion." All these characteristics correspond to the evils which God's people conquers by good. Furthermore the Wadi of Kishon, where they were routed, is interpreted as "their stubbornness." Endor, where they perished, means "fount of generation," but the reference is certainly to carnal generation; being preoccupied solely with that, they perished, giving no thought to the regeneration that leads to the life where there is no marrying or taking of wives, because no one tends towards death.[17] They are deservedly said to have *become like dung on the ground*, for no increase comes from them except in the soil's fertility.

So then, just as all those tribes were figuratively vanquished by God's people, the psalm prays that these present enemies may likewise be overpowered by truth.

10. *All their leaders who have said, "Let us take possession of God's holy place."* This is a senseless noise, the *din your enemies raise*, as we heard earlier. What are we to understand by God's holy place, or sanctuary, but that temple of

---

15. See Jgs 4–5.
16. See Jgs 7–8.
17. See Lk 20:35-36.

God of which the apostle says, *God's temple is holy, and that temple is your-selves* (1 Cor 3:17)? What else are those enemies striving to possess, and so enslave, except God's people, in order to force them to consent to their own impious designs?

Verses 14-16. God's punishment of them foretold

11. Now what follows? *Whirl them round like dust, O my God.* This can very well be taken to mean that they are not stable in anything they think; but I believe another acceptable interpretation would be this: *Make them like a wheel,* because a wheel rises up from what is behind it and is brought down by what lies ahead, and this is true of all enemies of God's people. This is not a wish, but a prophecy. The psalmist adds, *Like straw in the face of the wind. Face* obviously means "presence," for what kind of face could the wind have? It has no bodily shape, for it is only a movement, a kind of flowing of the air. But it is a symbol of temptation, because lightweights, empty hearts, are snatched away by it.

12. Lighthearted, easy consent to evildoing is followed, however, by heavy anguish, and so the psalm goes on, *Like fire that burns down a forest, like flames devouring the mountains, even so will you pursue them with your tempest, and harass them in your anger.* It mentions a forest to signify sterility, and mountains for their loftiness, for this is what the enemies of God's people are like—barren of righteousness but full of pride. When it speaks of both fire and flames it means the same reality under different names, wishing to indicate that God both judges and punishes. The words *your tempest* are clarified by his subsequent expression, *your anger*; and *you will pursue them* is illuminated by *harass them.* We must, of course, remember to eliminate any idea of emotional disturbance from our concept of God's anger. To say that he is angry is to assert that he has just cause to punish; it is like saying that the law is angry, when its servants are roused to punish someone in accord with it.

Verses 17-19. Some individuals among them will be shamed with salutary effect. God's universal sovereignty

13. *Cover their faces with shame; then they will seek your name, O Lord*, the psalmist continues. In these words it is certainly a benefit and something desir-able that is being prophetically spoken about in their regard; and no such prophetic wish could be expressed unless within the ranks of the enemies of God's people there were also certain individuals to whom this grace is to be granted before the final judgment. For the present these latter are identified with the rest, and form part of the host of enemies in their ill-will and envy towards the people of God. All these make their din and hold their heads high at the present

time wherever they can; but they do so severally, not all together as they will do at the end of the world when the last judgment is at hand. Yet this host consists both of those who will later believe, and pass over into a different company (for their faces will be shamed to good effect, causing them to seek the name of the Lord), and also of those others who persist in unchanging malice to the end. They are made like *straw in the face of the wind*, and like forest or barren mountains they are burnt up. He returns to them yet again, begging God, *May they blush with shame and be thrown into confusion for ever*. But those among them who seek the name of the Lord are not thrown into confusion for ever; they recognize the disgrace of their sins and are so confused that they seek the name of the Lord, to be saved by it from their confusion.

14. Accordingly he looks once more to those in the enemies' ranks whose destiny it is to be embarrassed in such a way that they will not be embarrassed for ever, those destined to be destroyed insofar as they are evil, in order to be made good and found alive for all eternity. That this is his intention is evident, because after praying, *May they be embarrassed and ruined*, he immediately adds, *Let them know that your name is the Lord, and that you alone are the Most High throughout the earth*. When they come to that realization, may they be so embarrassed as to become acceptable to you; may they be so ruined as to survive for ever. *Let them know*, he says, *that your name is the Lord*. He implies that any other beings who are called lords have no right to be called so, nor does that name belong to them. They are like slaves pretending to be despots; they are no lords, nor are they to be compared with the true Lord, who declares, *I AM WHO AM* (Ex 3:14), for things that are made have no being when compared with him by whom they were made.

When the psalmist adds, *You alone are the Most High throughout the earth* (or, as other codices have it, *over all the earth*), he obviously means throughout heaven as well, or over all heaven; but he preferred to put it this way to indicate the means by which *earth* would be suppressed. Earth stands for human pride, for on proud humans was the sentence passed, *Earth you are* (Gn 3:19); and of them scripture asks, *What business have earth and ashes to be proud?* (Sir 10:9). But earth ceases to be proud when it acknowledges the Lord to be the Most High over all the earth: acknowledges, that is to say, that no human scheming can prevail against those who are called according to God's purpose;[18] for of them it is written, *If God is for us, who can stand against us?* (Rom 8:31).

---

18. See Rom 8:28.

Exposition of Psalm 83

A Sermon to the People

Verse 1. The wine presses and the children of Korah

1. Over this psalm stands the title, *For the wine presses*. Beloved, we saw you listening with the utmost attention, yet in the text of the psalm neither you nor we heard any mention of a press-beam, or baskets, or a trough, or the utensils needed in a wine press, or the building in which the work is done. We heard nothing whatever of this sort of thing, so it is not easy to say what the title, *for the wine presses,* can mean. If some of the things I have enumerated did occur after the title, carnal-minded hearers would assuredly think that the psalm intended to sing about visible wine presses; but since although it was given the title, *for the wine presses*, nothing is said thereafter in any of its verses about the kind of wine presses with which our eyes are familiar, we can be in no doubt that the Spirit of God willed us to seek and discern in it some other wine presses. Accordingly let us call to mind what goes on in visible wine presses, and then consider how the same thing takes place spiritually in the Church.

Now it is for grapes and olives that presses are built. The cluster of grapes hangs on the vine and the olive on the tree, and as long as they hang there on their stalks they are free to enjoy the breeze; the grapes are not yet wine, nor the olives yet oil, before the pressing. So it is with men and women whom God predestined before time began to be conformed to the image of his only-begotten Son,[1] who was in an unparalleled way the mighty grape, pressed out in his passion. Before such people enlist in God's service they enjoy delightful freedom in the world, like grapes or olives hanging there. But scripture warns us, *My son, when you enter God's service, stand fast in righteousness and reverence, and prepare your soul for trials* (Sir 2:1); and so any who approach God's service must know that they have come to the wine presses. They will be bruised, trampled and squeezed, not so that they may perish in this world but to ensure that they trickle down into God's storage vats. They are stripped of their vesture of fleshly desires as the fruit is denuded of its skin. The process of which the apostle speaks has taken effect in them as far as carnal desires are concerned: *Strip yourselves of the old self, and be clothed in the new* (Col 3:9-10). This happens only as a result of the pressing, which is why the churches of God today are called wine presses.

---

1. See Rom 8:29.

2. But who are we, who find ourselves in the wine presses? Children of Korah. This phrase is added to the title, which reads in full, *For the wine presses, for the sons of Korah*. As far as those who know the original language have been able to interpret it for us, in the course of the service they owed to God, we understand this to mean, "sons of a bald man." I am not going to shirk the effort of looking for a great mystery here, and finding it with you, as the Lord may enable us. Not all baldness is to be mocked, as it once was by a certain pestilential brood, and any who make fun of a baldness that is a sign of consecration may find themselves scattered by demons. Elisha was on his way when some silly boys yelled after him, *Baldy! Baldy!* (2 Kgs 2:23-24), and in order to enact a holy sign with full effect, Elisha turned to the Lord and begged that bears might break from the woods and devour them. Admittedly they were snatched away in their infancy, dispatched from life and from this world, and they died as children who would otherwise not have died until they were old men; yes, but a terrifying sign was given to warn the rest of us. This was because Elisha stood as a type of someone else of whom we are sons and daughters, for we are children of Korah, which means of Jesus Christ our Lord. You will already have understood from the gospel, beloved, why a bald man was a figure of Christ. You remember that Christ was crucified at a place called Calvary.[2]

So then, whether *sons of Korah* means what we have said, following early commentators, or something different which is perhaps hidden from us, you can see that what has already come to our notice is full of holy mystery. The sons of Korah are children of Christ, for he is the bridegroom who claims us as his children, saying, *The bridegroom's children cannot fast as long as the bridegroom is with them* (Mt 9:15). In short, these wine presses belong to Christians.

3. We are under pressure, and are being crushed for a purpose. Our love carried us away towards earthly, worldly, temporal goods, things that were fleeting and perishable, and we suffered the torments and troubles of the pressures they brought to bear on us in this life, and the overwhelming temptations; so now let us begin to seek that rest which is not afforded by this life or this earth. Then, as scripture says, the Lord becomes *a refuge for the poor* (Ps 9:10(9)). What does the psalm mean here by *the poor*? It means that God is a refuge for anyone who is destitute, helpless, without resources, without anything to rely on in this world. To those who are poor in this sense God is near, for such people look to what the apostle said, even while others wallow in this world's wealth: *Instruct the rich of this world not to be high-minded, nor to put their trust in unreliable wealth*, Paul told Timothy (1 Tm 6:17). These poor reflect how very uncertain was the life they enjoyed before they entered the service of God; before, that is, they stepped into the wine presses. They see that either those very

---

2. The Latin for "bald" is *calvus*, and *Calvaria* means "a skull"; hence "the place of a/the skull" in Mt 27:33. Compare the Exposition of Psalm 41, 2, and note there.

riches gave rise to thoughts that pressed hard upon them as to how their wealth was to be administered, and how kept safe; or else, if they were even a little swayed towards greedy love of it, they were filled with fear rather than with enjoyment. What is as unreliable as something that rolls? And it is with good reason that money itself is coined in a rounded shape, because it will not stand still. Such people are poor, then, even if they have possessions. On the other hand, those who have none of these things, yet desire to have them, are reckoned with the rich who deserve to be rejected, for God looks not to our means, but to our will.

Augustine sounds the note of holy desire

As for those poor who are bereft of all secular resources, because even though wealth flows all around them they are aware how unreliable it is, those poor people who sigh to God and have nothing in this world that gives them pleasure or holds them captive—yes, as for all these who because of the overwhelming pressures and trials they endure are as though trapped in wine presses, let them flow down as wine, or flow down as oil. For what are wine and oil? Good desires. Only God now remains to them as the object of their desires, for they no longer love the earth. They love him who made heaven and earth; they love him, and they are not yet with him. Their desire is kept waiting so that it may grow, and it grows that it may lay hold on its object. It is no paltry thing that God will give to one who longs, but himself, who made all that exists; and no small effort must a lover make to be capable of receiving so great a good. Train yourself until you have a capacity for God; long and long for what you will possess for ever.

On not looking back

Among the Israelites those who were in too much of a hurry were condemned. Indeed, the attitude of people in a hurry is repeatedly censured in scripture. Who are they? They are people who have turned to God, but on not finding here the rest they were seeking, or the joys they were constantly being promised, grow weary on the way. They suppose that there is still a long stretch in front of them, until the end of the world or the end of their lives. They seek some kind of rest here, which, even if obtainable, is illusory, so they look back, and fall away from their purpose. They do not reflect on that fearful admonition, *Remember Lot's wife* (Lk 17:32). Why was she turned into a pillar of salt,[3] if not because her function is to season people, and impart to them the savor of wisdom? The example of her misfortune redounds to your advantage, if you are careful. Remember Lot's wife, says scripture; she looked back at Sodom, from which she had been set free, and there she remained,

---

3. See Gn 19:26.

in that place whence she had cast her backward glance. She was to stay there, to season others who would pass by.

We have been freed from the Sodom of our past lives, so let us not look behind us; for this is what being in a hurry means—paying no heed to what God has promised, because it is a long way off, and looking back at what is very close, from which you have just been delivered. What has the apostle Peter to say about such people? *The proverb is proved true by what happens to them: the dog has returned to its vomit* (2 Pt 2:22). It was like a load on your chest, that former consciousness of your sins. When you received forgiveness it was as though you vomited and got it off your chest; your bad conscience became a good conscience. So why go back again to your vomit? If the sight of a dog doing that is loathsome to you, what are you in God's sight?

4. Beloved brothers and sisters, each one of us looks back if we forsake the place on our journey which we have reached, the place to which we have progressed, the place where we have vowed to God that we will be. For example, someone has resolved to maintain conjugal fidelity (this is the beginning of righteous living); he has given up fornication and unlawful lust. If he returns to fornication once more, he has looked back. Another person has by God's gift vowed something greater, in deciding not to marry at all. He would not have been condemned if he had taken a wife, but if he does so after making that vow to God, he will be condemned, though he is only acting in the same way as someone else who has not made the vow. Yet the latter is not condemned, the former is. Why? Because he looked behind him. He was already further on than that, whereas the other man had not yet reached that point. Similarly a virgin would commit no sin if she married,[4] but if a nun marries she is held to have committed adultery against Christ. She has looked back from the place she had reached. Then again others have chosen to leave behind all secular ambitions and worldly conduct, and betake themselves to a community of holy people, to that life in common where no one claims anything as private property but all goods are common to all, and there is among them but one mind, one heart directed to God.[5] But anyone who decides to abandon that community is not on a par with someone else who never entered it; the latter had not reached that point, but the former had, and looked back.

Well then, dearly beloved, in proportion to the ability of each one, make your vows to the Lord your God, and carry them out[6] as the strength of each permits.

---

4. See 1 Cor 7:28.
5. See Acts 2:44; 4:32. This ideal picture of life in the post-Easter Church was a powerful and creative force in the mind of Augustine, as in those of Basil, Benedict, and many another. On returning to Africa from Italy in A.D. 388 he attempted to realize it in common with his companions, as his followers have continued to do.
6. See Ps 75:12(76:11). Augustine's Exposition of Psalm 75,16, contains reflections very similar to those found in the present sermon.

Let none of us look back, none of us take pleasure in our former interests. Let none of us turn away from what lies ahead, to look back to what lies behind us. Let every one of us run until we arrive, for we run not with our feet but with our desire. And let no one claim to have reached the goal while still in this life. Who could be as perfect as Paul was? Yet he says, *I do not suppose, brethren, that I have attained it; one thing only I do: forgetting what lies behind and straining to what lies ahead, I bend my whole effort to follow after the prize of God's heavenly call in Christ Jesus* (Phil 3:13-14). When you see Paul still running, do you imagine you have already arrived?

Verse 2. During this life we are all in the wine press

5. If you are conscious of the pressures of this world, even when you are enjoying prosperity, you have understood that you are in the wine press. Do you suppose that misfortune in this world is something to be feared, and prosperity is not, my brothers and sisters? By no means: no misfortune can break a person whom no prosperity corrupts. How distrustful, how wary you must be of prosperity, that corrupting jade, lest she seduce you by flattery! Do not lean on a reed for support, for scripture warns us that some did so.[7] Do not trust yourself to it. What you are leaning on is fragile; it will break and stab you.

If this world smiles on you with its favors, reckon yourself to be in the wine press, and say, *I have found anguish and sorrow, and I called on the name of the Lord* (Ps 114(116):3-4). He would not have said, *I have found* it, unless the anguish were something hidden. There is a certain anguish which is hidden from those in this world who assume that, even while they are on pilgrimage and away from the Lord, all is nonetheless well with them. *As long as we are in the body we are on pilgrimage and away from the Lord*, says scripture (2 Cor 5:6). If you were on a journey and far from your human father, you would be unhappy; can you be a pilgrim, away from the Lord, and feel pleased about it? But some there are who do imagine that all is well with them.

But there are others who, though wealth and pleasures flow all round them in abundance, though everything obeys their least whim, though no nuisance sneaks in and no adversity arouses fear, still understand that they are in evil case as long as they are on pilgrimage away from the Lord. Their penetrating gaze has found the anguish and the sorrow, and they have called on the name of the Lord. The singer in this psalm is one of them. Who is the singer? The body of Christ. And who is that? You, if you are willing to be; all of us, if we are willing, all the children of Korah; and they are all one person, because all are the one body of Christ. How could it not be a single person, when it has but one head? Christ is the head of us all, and we are all the body that belongs to that head.

---

7. See 2 Kgs 18:21.

And all of us are in the wine press during this life. If we have the wisdom to know it, we have already arrived at the wine presses. Caught under the pressures of temptation, let us call out in these words, and send our desire ahead of us: *How delightful are your tabernacles, O Lord of hosts!* The singer was in tabernacles[8] of a kind, namely in the wine presses, but was longing for different tabernacles, where there is no pressing out. In the tabernacles of this life he was yearning for those other tabernacles, and from here he was flowing towards them through the channel of desire.

Verse 3. Faint with longing

6. Now what follows? *My soul faints with longing for the courts of the Lord.* To say only that it *faints with longing* would be to say little. For what is it fainting? For *the courts of the Lord.* A grape pressed out is fainting, certainly, but to what is it aspiring? To the wine, to the trough, to the restful storage-vat, where it will be kept safe in great peace. Here we desire, there we receive; here we sigh with longing, there we rejoice; here we pray, there praise; here we groan, there exult. No one must avoid the process I have described, dismissing it as harsh; no one must avoid it out of reluctance to suffer. A grape that escapes the press must fear being gobbled up by birds or wild animals.

The singer might seem to be in great sadness when he declares, *My soul faints with longing for the courts of the Lord.* Clearly he does not possess what he longs for; but he is not therefore denied joy, is he? What joy, then? The joy of which the apostle spoke: *Rejoicing in hope* (Rom 12:12). Hereafter he will rejoice in the substance, here still in hope. These people who rejoice in hope endure all pressures in the wine press, because they are certain that they will receive what they long for. This is why the apostle, after saying, *Rejoicing in hope*, immediately added, *Patient in anguish*, as though he were addressing those already under the press. *In anguish*, then, we are to be patient. Anything else? Yes, *enduring in prayer*. Why *enduring*? Because you are kept waiting. You pray and you are kept waiting, but go on enduring as you wait. It is worth enduring the waiting for what is withheld, because when it comes it will never be withdrawn.

Verse 4. Heart and flesh; the sparrow and the turtledove

7. You have heard the groan that goes up from the wine press, *My soul faints with longing for the courts of the Lord*; hear now whence the singer draws strength as he rejoices in hope: *My heart and my flesh leap for joy to the living*

---

8. Or tents, throughout this paragraph. In the background is the memory of the tent where God kept his people company during the desert march; hence the later temple in Jerusalem was sometimes called so.

God. They leap for joy here, towards that other place. What else impels them to leap, but hope? Where does their leaping tend? *To the living God.* What is it in you that leaps for joy? *My heart and my flesh.* And why? Because *the sparrow has found himself a home,* he replies, *and the turtledove a nest where she may place her squabs.* What is this about?

First he mentioned two things, then he substituted two others by way of comparison: he spoke of his heart and his flesh, and then replaced these two with a sparrow and a turtledove; the heart is represented by a sparrow, the flesh by a turtledove. The sparrow has found himself a home; my heart has found itself a home. It plies its wings in the virtues proper to this present life, in faith and hope and charity, using them to fly to its home. When it arrives there it will stay for good, and the puling voice of the sparrow will be heard no more. This is the plaintive sparrow of which another psalm speaks: *Like a lonely sparrow on a roof* (Ps 101:8(102:7)). From the roof he flies to his home. Let him take his stand on the roof already, treading his carnal home underfoot, for he will have a heavenly perch, an everlasting home; then this sparrow will have done with his complaints.

To the turtledove the psalm also assigns squabs; that is to say, it indicates that these are produced by the flesh. *The turtledove has found herself a nest where she may place her squabs.* The sparrow a home, the turtledove a nest, and a nest, moreover, for her young. We choose a home to last for ever, but a nest is built only for a time; in our heart we think about God, like the sparrow winging his way home, but with the body we perform good works. You can see the impressive good works performed bodily by holy people, for through the body we carry out the works enjoined on us to meet our needs in this life. *Break your bread for the hungry, and take the person with no shelter into your home. If you see anyone naked, clothe him* (Is 58:7). These and similar commands laid on us cannot be obeyed except through our bodies. That sparrow whose thoughts turn homewards does not hold aloof from the turtledove seeking a nest in which to place her squabs (for she does not toss them about at random; she finds a nest to put them in).

What I am saying, my brothers and sisters, is something you know already. How many appear to be engaged in good works outside the Church? How many even among the pagans feed the hungry, clothe the naked, welcome guests, visit the sick, console prisoners? How many are there who do all this? It looks as though the turtledove is hatching chicks, but she has not found herself a nest. How many good works are carried out by great numbers of heretics, but not in the Church—carried out by heretics who do not put their squabs in the nest? Their little ones will be trodden on and crushed; they will not survive or be kept safe.

A certain woman was presented to us by the apostle Paul as a type of these bodily works, when he said, *Adam was not seduced, but the woman was seduced* (1 Tm 2:14). But afterwards Adam consented to the wishes of the woman who had been seduced by the serpent.[9] It is the same today: the only evil persuasion that can initially arouse your desire is the prompting of your flesh, and if you subsequently consent to it in your mind, the sparrow has fallen; but if you conquer your carnal desires your members are disciplined to perform good works, and concupiscence is robbed of its weapons. Then the turtledove begins to hatch her squabs. That is why the apostle comments, *She will be saved through childbearing* (1 Tm 2:15). But what about a childless widow? If she perseveres in her state, will she not be more blessed? Is she to be debarred from salvation because she bears no children? Will a virgin dedicated to God not be better off as she is? Surely she will not be denied salvation because she has no children? Does she not belong to God?

Yes, of course she does; so the woman who will be saved through childbearing—saved, that is, if she performs good works—obviously represents the flesh. But the turtledove must not find herself a nest for her chicks haphazardly; she must bring forth her good works within the true faith, in communion with the unity of the Church. This is why when the apostle was speaking on the subject of this woman, he added, *She will be saved through childbearing, provided she perseveres in faith and charity, and a holy, sober way of life* (1 Tm 2:15). When you persevere in faith, it is faith itself that forms the nest for the chicks you will hatch; for our gracious Lord, knowing how weak your turtledove's squabs are, has provided you with your nest-building material. He put on the grass that is your flesh[10] in order to come to you. Place your chicks in this faith; perform your good works in this nest.

What the nests are—or, rather, what nest is meant—the psalm immediately tells us: *your altars, O Lord of hosts*. It is as though after hearing, *The turtledove has found herself a nest where she may place her squabs*, you had asked, "But what is this nest?" *Your altars, O Lord of hosts, my King and my God*. And what does that mean, *my King and my God*? You who rule me and created me.

Verse 5. Longing for eternal joy; but what shall we find to occupy us in heaven? Praising God will never tire or bore us

8. Here we have the nest, here our pilgrimage, here our longings, here the friction and here the pressing-out, because this is the wine press. But what does the psalmist desire, what does he yearn for, where is he going? Where does our desire tend, whither is it pulling us? The psalmist is here in body, but far ahead in

---

9. See Gn 3.
10. See Is 40:6.

thought; he is set amid temptations, amid pressures; he is in the wine press, but longing for the heavenly rewards promised him. In anticipation he ponders those future joys, as though meditating already on what he will be doing when he reaches them. *Blessed are they who dwell in your house*, he says. Blessed—but from what will their beatitude spring? What will they have, what will they do? All those who are judged blessed on earth either possess something or are engaged in some activity. "He is a lucky man," we say, because he has so much land, so numerous a household, so much gold and silver. So he is called blessed because of what he has. Or another is pronounced blessed for attaining certain honors, a proconsulate perhaps, or a prefecture. He is said to be blessed because of what he does. So it is either the having or the doing that renders them blessed.

But what of those who will be blessed hereafter? What will they have, what will they be doing? What they will possess I have indicated already: *blessed are they who dwell in your house.* If you possess your own house you are poor, but if you possess God's house you are rich. In your own house you will have burglars to fear; in God's house God himself is the defensive wall. This is why they are *blessed who dwell in your house.* They possess the heavenly Jerusalem without overcrowding, without pressure, without divisions or exclusive boundaries, for all possess it, and each owns the whole. That is wealth indeed. No one cramps his neighbor, and no one is in need.

In that case, what will they find to do? Necessity is the mother of all human activities. I have stated that briefly before, my brothers and sisters: cast your minds over all types of activity, and see if there is any motive for them other than necessity. Take those celebrated arts which are highly valued because they help people by pleading their case or providing medical care: these are excellent activities in this world, but if you get rid of all litigants, who will need the services of an advocate? Eliminate injuries and disease, and what will there be for a doctor to cure? The same is true of all the activities which are carried out in response to the demands of our daily life; they too proceed from necessity. Plowing, sowing, raising young plants, maritime trading—what is it that prompts all such work, if not necessity and our wants? Get rid of hunger, thirst and nakedness, and what will be the point of them all? The same holds also for the good works enjoined upon us—for the activities I have mentioned are honorable, but common to all humankind (I am not speaking, of course, of wicked and detestable deeds like shameful or criminal acts, homicides, housebreaking, adulteries, for I do not count these as human activities). The former are honorable, as I say, and spring from one cause only: necessity, the necessity of our fragile, fleshly condition. The same holds for those charitable works which, as I said, are enjoined upon us. *Break your bread for the hungry*—but for whom will you break it, where no one is hungry? *Take the person with no shelter into your home*—but whom will you welcome as a guest, where all are at home, living in their own country? What sick person can you visit, where all enjoy perpetual health? How will you appease a litigant, where peace reigns eternally? What dead body will you bury, where all live for ever?

It seems, then, that you will engage in none of those honorable activities common to all humankind, but neither will you perform any of the aforementioned charitable works, because these turtledove chicks will have flown from the nest. What will you do? I have already told you what we shall have: *blessed are they who dwell in your house.* But tell me what they are to do, because I cannot see any kind of necessity there which could impel me to action. Even what I am doing now as I talk and discuss with you is the child of necessity. Will there be any such discussion then, in which someone instructs the ignorant or reminds the forgetful? Or will the gospel be proclaimed there in our homeland, where we shall contemplate the very Word of God?

The psalmist has given voice to our desire and our longings, telling us what we are to have in that homeland for which we long, by his words, *blessed are they who dwell in your house*; let him also tell us what we are to do. *They will praise you for ever and ever.* This will be the work that occupies us totally, an "Alleluia" that never fades away.

Brothers and sisters, do not imagine that there will be weariness in that. If you go on saying it for a long time now, you flag, but only because your needs distract you from the joy. What we do not see delights us less, and so if even amid the pressure and the weakness of our flesh we praise with such eagerness what we believe in, how shall we hereafter praise what we see? When death is swallowed up by victory, when our mortal flesh is clothed with immortality and this corruptible body apparelled with incorruption,[11] no one will say, "I have been standing for a long time," no one will say, "I have kept a long fast, and a long vigil." We shall be empowered for unshakable standing, and our bodily immortality will itself be sustained by contemplating God. If the word we preach to you now keeps our weak bodies standing for so long, what will that joy do? How will it change us? *We shall be like him, because we shall see him as he is* (1 Jn 3:2). Already we are like him, but then? Shall we weaken? To what shall we turn aside?

Let us have no anxiety, then, brothers and sisters. Praising God, loving God, will not be boring. If you weary of love, you will weary of praise; but if love is everlasting, because that beauty can never cloy, have no fear that you will find yourself unable to praise for ever him whom you will have strength to love for ever. *Blessed*, then, *are they who dwell in your house; they will praise you for ever and ever.* Let us yearn for that life.

---

11. See 1 Cor 15:53.54.

Verse 6. How to get there? The need for grace

9. But how are we going to get there? *Blessed is anyone whom you take by the hand, Lord.*[12] The psalmist understood his position, and knew that the weakness of his flesh made it impossible for him to fly to that beatitude. He looked at what weighed him down on every side,[13] for, as scripture says elsewhere, *The corruptible body weighs down the soul, and this earthly dwelling oppresses a mind that considers many things* (Wis 9:15). The spirit calls him upwards, but the weight of the flesh calls him down again; the tension between these two—the upward pull and the dragging weight—is a struggle, and struggle is characteristic of the pressing-out process. Listen to the apostle describing this contest from his position in the wine press, for he too was trampled and crushed there: *I take great delight in God's law as far as my inner self is concerned*, he says, *but I am aware of a different law in my members that opposes the law of my mind, and imprisons me under the law of sin inherent in my members* (Rom 7:22-23). This is a mighty conflict, and mighty would be his despair of surviving it, if help did not come to him from the quarter he goes on to indicate: *Who will deliver me from this death-ridden body, wretch that I am? Only the grace of God, through Jesus Christ our Lord* (Rom 7:24-25).

Our psalmist likewise saw those future joys, and in his mind reflected, *Blessed are they who dwell in your house, O Lord; they will praise you for ever and ever.* But who will ascend to that place? What am I to do about this heavy flesh? *Blessed are they who dwell in your house; they will praise you for ever and ever. For I take great delight in God's law as far as my inner self is concerned.* But what am I to do? How shall I fly there? How reach it? *I am aware of a different law in my members that opposes the law of my mind.* He confessed himself to be a wretch, and asked, *Who will deliver me from this death-ridden body*, that I may dwell in the Lord's house, and praise him for ever and ever? *Who will deliver me? Only the grace of God, through Jesus Christ our Lord.*

In the apostle's case what brought him succor in that difficulty, or, rather, that almost unwinnable conflict, was the power he spoke of as *the grace of God, through Jesus Christ our Lord*; so too as the psalmist yearned with burning desire for God's house and a life spent in praising him, yet considered the weight of his own body and the burden of his flesh, and felt despair beginning to sweep

---

12. *Cuius susceptio eius abs te.* The noun *susceptio* and its cognate verb *suscipio* are rich in meaning: to receive, undertake, take upon oneself, catch from below to save someone from falling, support, accept, and (where the father of a newborn child is the subject) to recognize as one's own and accept into the family. In the following lines Augustine probably has all these nuances in mind, but the translation "pick up" or "carry" will not do, as the pilgrim has to climb steps. The present translation offers "take by the hand" as an approximation. Compare the note at Exposition of Psalm 45,11.
13. The idea of "carrying around" the weight of the mortal body occurs also in *The Confessions* I,1,1.

over him, he aroused his mind once more to hope, saying, *Blessed is anyone whom you take by the hand, Lord.*

Verses 6-7. God places steps in our hearts, in the valley of weeping

10. What does God provide by this grace of his for the person whom he has taken by the hand? The next line tells us. God *arranges ascents in his heart.* God sets up steps for him to climb. Where? In the person's heart. It follows, then, that the more you love, the higher you will climb. God *arranges ascents in his heart.* Who put them there? The One who took him by the hand, for *blessed is anyone whom you take by the hand, Lord.* He can make no progress by himself, so your grace is needed to take him by the hand. And what does your grace effect? It arranges ascents in his heart. Where are they established? *In his heart, in the valley of weeping enclosed on all sides.* So now, you see, the wine press is called a *valley of weeping,* for the tender tears of the contrite are themselves the grape juice that will be the wine of lovers. God *arranges ascents in his heart.* Where, then? *In the valley of weeping.* Here is the place where he has set the steps, *in the valley of weeping,* for here there are tears at the sowing, as another psalm says, *They went on their way weeping, as they scattered their seed* (Ps 125(126):6). Let there be these steps in your heart, then, these steps set up by God through his grace. Climb them by loving. While you are climbing, the song of ascents rings out.[14] And where has he set up these steps for you? *In* your *heart, in the valley of weeping.*

So the psalm has told us where he put the steps, and where they lead to. What has he set up? Steps. Where? Within you, *in* your *heart.* And in what country-side, what place of sojourning? *In the valley of weeping.* And where will they enable you to climb? *To the place he has appointed.* What does that mean, my brothers and sisters, *to the place he has appointed*? He would tell us what place that is, the place God has appointed, if it could be put into words. You have been told that God *arranges ascents in his heart, in the valley of weeping*; do you now ask where they lead? What answer can he give you? They lead to *what eye has not seen, nor ear heard, nor human heart conceived* (1 Cor 2:9). A mountain, a country, a meadow—all these names have been used for that place. But who can describe it for us as it truly is, without recourse to any imagery? Who can describe it for us, who see now only tantalizing reflections of what that place is, and only hereafter will see face to face?[15] When you hear *to the place he has appointed,* do not ask whither the steps are leading. He knows whither; he knows, for he has placed his steps in your heart to lead you there. Are you afraid to mount them, as though he who leads you might miss the way?

---

14. The "gradual psalms" or "songs of ascent" were the psalms traditionally sung by pilgrims going up to Jerusalem, Pss 119-133(120-134).

15. See 1 Cor 13:12.

In the valley of weeping, this is where he has set the steps that lead to *the place he has appointed*. We are in tears now, and where are we, as we weep? In the place where are set the steps we must climb. Why do we weep, if not for that same condition the apostle lamented, seeing a different law in his members, at odds with the law of his mind? And why do we suffer this? As a penalty for sin. We presumed that we could easily be righteous by our own efforts before we received the commandment; but when the commandment was issued sin sprang to life again, and I died; so says the apostle.[16] The law was given to humankind not to bring them immediate salvation, but to reveal to them the sickness in which they lay. Listen to the apostle's words: *If a law capable of giving life had been granted to us, then of course righteousness would have been obtainable through the law; but scripture has included all things under sin, so that through faith in Jesus Christ the promise may be given to believers* (Gal 3:21-22), and so that grace, coming after law, may find us not merely lying sick but also confessing and lamenting, *Who will deliver me from this death-ridden body, wretch that I am?* The physician was to come to the valley of weeping when he was most sorely needed, and to say to us, "You are fully convinced now that you have fallen; listen to me that you may get up again, since you fell by despising me." The purpose of the law was to persuade the patient of his disease when he deluded himself that he was in good health; its purpose was to show up our sins for what they were, not to remove them. But once the law had been given, and sin shown up thereby for what it was, sin increased, because now it was both sin and transgression of the law: *Taking advantage of the commandment, sin caused every kind of concupiscence to arise in me*, says scripture (Rom 7:8). What does *taking advantage of the commandment* mean? People attempted to keep by their own strength the commandment they had been given; but when they were over-powered by concupiscence they became all the more guilty through their patent disobedience to the commandment.

But what else has the apostle to say? *Where sin abounded, grace abounded all the more* (Rom 5:20); that is to say, as the disease grew graver, the remedy was supplied. This is why we are told about those five porticoes of Solomon, my brothers and sisters. There was a pool in the center of them, but were the sick cured? *The sick were accustomed to lie in the five porticoes*, we read in the gospel (Jn 5:3). The five porticoes represent the law recorded in the five books of Moses. The sick were brought from their homes to lie in the porticoes; and the law likewise exposed sick persons without healing them. But the water was disturbed from time to time as though by the descent of an angel, and when this was observed one person, whoever could manage it, would go down into it and be cured. Now that pool ringed by five porticoes represents the Jewish people confined by the law. The Lord disturbed them very gravely by his presence, to the end that he might be

---

16. See Rom 7:7-10.

killed. Would the Lord have been crucified if he had not disturbed the Jews by his descent? No, and therefore the troubled water represents the Lord's passion, which took place when the Jewish nation was disturbed. Any ailing person who believes in Christ's passion goes down, as it were, into the turbulent water, and is restored to health. Having found no healing in the law (that is, in the porticoes), such a one is healed by grace, through faith in the passion of our Lord Jesus Christ. And he is one, not many. Indeed, he is unity itself.

What, then, has our psalm to say? *God arranges ascents in his heart, in the valley of weeping enclosed on all sides, leading to the place he has appointed.* Already we have the prospect of joy in that place.

Verses 8-10. Progress from the many virtues of action to the one virtue of contemplation

11. But why *in the valley of weeping*? What is this valley of weeping from which we are to travel to that place of joy? *For he who gave the law will give a blessing too*, says the psalm. He has cast us down with the law, oppressed us under the law, and shown us the wine press. We in turn have witnessed the pressing-out, recognized the pressure exerted by our flesh, and groaned as sin rebelled against our minds. We have cried out, *Wretch that I am!* and we have moaned under the law's domination. What is left for us now, except for the lawgiver to give us his blessing instead? Grace will come after the law, and grace is itself the blessing. And what does this grace, this blessing, do for us? *They will walk from many powers to one single power.*[17] Here below many powers are conferred through grace: *to one is given wise utterance through the Spirit, to another knowledgeable speech according to the same Spirit, to another faith, to another gifts of healing, to another various tongues, to another powers of interpretation, and to another prophecy* (1 Cor 12:8-10). There is a multiplicity of powers because here they are all necessary, but we shall proceed from these many powers to one alone. What is this unique power? Christ, the power of God and the wisdom of God.[18] He it is who grants these varied powers in our present circumstances, powers which are necessary or useful in the valley of weeping; but in their place he will give us one single power—himself.

---

17. In these paragraphs Augustine is using the word *virtus*, which means primarily a quality proper to a true man (*vir*) such as courage, strength, resolution; then more generally any quality of excellence or merit; and finally the moral quality of virtue or goodness. In the light of 1 Corinthians 12 he has applied it to the various gifts or "powers" conferred by the Spirit, but only because he has in mind Paul's affirmation in 1 Cor 1:24 that Christ is "the power of God," the sole answer to both the Jews' demand for "signs" (that is, powerful demonstrations) and the Greeks' search for wisdom.

18. See 1 Cor 1:24.

Indeed, the powers or virtues we need to practice in our lives are four in number; they are described by many writers, and found also in scripture.[19] One is called prudence, and by it we differentiate between good and evil. Another is called justice; by it we render to every person what is due, being in debt to no one, but loving them all.[20] Temperance comes next, the virtue by which we control our bodily impulses. Finally there is fortitude, which enables us to bear all vexations. These virtues are granted to us now in the valley of weeping, but from them we progress to a single virtue. And what will that be? The virtue of contemplating God alone. Our prudence will not be necessary there, because we shall encounter no evils we need to avoid. And what of the rest, my brothers and sisters? There will be no need for justice, where no one will be in poverty and in need of our assistance. Nor will there be any occasion for temperance, because no unruly passions will be there to require control. Fortitude will have no place either, where no distress exists to be endured. We shall pass, then, from these many virtues of action to that one virtue of contemplation, by which we are empowered to contemplate God, according to the scriptural word, *In the morning I will stand before you, and contemplate you* (Ps 5:5(3)).

Listen now to further evidence that we shall proceed from these virtues of action to contemplation. The psalm prophesies, *They will walk from many virtues to one single virtue.* What virtue is that? The virtue of contemplating. And what does "contemplating" imply? *The God of gods will be seen in Zion.* By *the God of gods* we should understand the Christ of Christians. Perhaps you are wondering how that can be? Remember, *I have spoken, and you are gods, sons of the Most High, all of you* (Ps 81(82):6), for he gave them power to become children of God,[21] he in whom we have believed, the beautiful bridegroom who on account of our deformity was seen here himself deformed, for *we saw him*, says the prophet, *and he had no beauty to attract us* (Is 53:2). But when all the neediness of our mortality is over and done with, he who is God with God, the Word with the Father, the Word through whom all things were made,[22] will show himself to the pure-hearted. *Blessed are the clean of heart, for they shall see God* (Mt 5:8). *The God of gods will be seen in Zion.*

12. Back he turns now from the thought of those joys, back to his sighing. He takes stock of what he has anticipated in hope, and of where he still is in fact. *The God of gods will* hereafter *be seen in Zion*, and that is the spring of our joy; we

---

19. Prudence, justice, temperance, and fortitude, the four traditional moral virtues of ancient philosophy. Found in Plato and Aristotle, they reappear in the Book of Wisdom 8:7, and were adopted by Ambrose, Augustine, and Thomas Aquinas as the "cardinal virtues," that is, the essential moral virtues which bear upon created realities as their object, as opposed to the "theological virtues" of faith, hope, and charity, which relate directly to God.

20. See Rom 13:8.

21. See Jn 1:12.

22. See Jn 1:1-3.

shall praise him for ever and ever. But now it is still the season for prayer and petition, and if for some rejoicing, then only in hope. We are on pilgrimage, still in the valley of weeping. The psalmist resumes the groaning proper to this place as he says, *Lord, God of hosts, hear my prayer; hearken to me, O God of Jacob*, because you made Jacob into Israel. God appeared to Jacob, and in consequence he was called Israel,[23] which means "one who sees God." Hear me, then, O God of Jacob, and make me Israel. When shall I become Israel? When the God of gods shows himself in Zion.

13. *Turn your gaze upon us, God our protector.* It is written that under the shadow of your wings they will hope[24] for protection, so *turn your gaze upon us, God our protector, and look into the face of your anointed.*[25] When does God ever cease to look into the face of his Christ, his anointed one? What can it mean, then, to pray to him, *Look into the face of your anointed*? It is by our faces that we are known to others, so what is the force of *look into the face of your anointed*? It means, "Let your Christ be known to everyone," so that we may pass from manifold virtues to the one virtue, and grace overflow yet more copiously where sin overflowed.

Verse 11. To be in the courts, the house, of the Lord is all that matters

14. *One day within your courts is better than thousands elsewhere.* Those courts are the place for which he was sighing and fainting. My soul is longing and fainting for the courts of the Lord, for one day there is better than thousands of days. Thousands of days—this is what many people aspire to, for they want a long life here. Let them make light of thousands of days and desire one day, the day that has no sunrise, no sunset, the one day that is an eternal day, the day that does not displace yesterday or find itself hard pressed by tomorrow. That one day is what we should desire. What use are thousands of days to us? We are traveling from thousands of days towards one day, just as we are proceeding from many virtues to one alone.

15. *I would rather be degraded in the Lord's house than dwell in the tents of sinners.* The speaker has experienced the valley of weeping, he has found that humility from which he may make his way upward, he knows that if he tries to exalt himself he will fall, but that if he humbles himself he will be lifted up; so he has chosen to be cast down in order to be uplifted. How many there are outside this tent that houses the Lord's wine press, that is, outside the Catholic Church, who are so keen to be exalted, so enamored of their rank, that they are unwilling

23. See Gn 32:28.
24. See Ps 35:8(36:7).
25. *In faciem Christi tui.*

to acknowledge the truth![26] If they only took this verse to heart, *I would rather be degraded in the Lord's house than dwell in the tents of sinners*, would they not throw away the trappings of rank and come running to the valley of weeping, to find the steps in their hearts that lead up from here, and progress from many virtues to the one virtue, placing their hope in Christ, rather than in any mere human? A good saying it is, a saying to rejoice over and make our own: *I would rather be degraded in the Lord's house than dwell in the tents of sinners*. The speaker has chosen to be degraded in the Lord's house, but he who has invited us to the banquet calls the guest who chose a lower place to a more honorable one, commanding him, *Move up higher* (Lk 14:10). For his own part all he wanted was to be in the Lord's house: whereabouts did not matter, as long as he was not outside.

Verse 12. How the Lord combines mercy with justice

16. Why did he choose to be degraded in the Lord's house, rather than dwell in the tents of sinners? *Because God loves mercy and justice.* The Lord loves that mercy which prompted him to come to my aid in the first instance; but he also loves justice because he wills to give to the believer what he promised. Look at the mercy and justice shown to the apostle Paul, who was at first Saul the persecutor. He needed mercy, and testified that it had been shown to him: *I was originally a persecutor and a blasphemer, and harmed people. But I received mercy that Christ Jesus might give proof in me of his long forbearance toward those who will believe in him unto eternal life* (1 Tm 1:13.16). He meant to ensure that none of us shall despair of our sins being forgiven, whatever they may be, seeing that Paul received pardon for such great offenses. There you have divine mercy. God was not willing to exercise his justice at that time by punishing a sinner. If he had, would that not have been justice? Would anyone who was in no position to claim, "I have not sinned," have the audacity to say, "I should not be punished"? And if such a person were to say, "I have not sinned," to whom would such a claim be made? Who would be deceived by it? No, the Lord granted mercy to Paul as a privilege in advance, and then after the mercy came the justice. Listen now to Paul demanding justice: *I was originally a persecutor and a blasphemer, and harmed people; but by God's grace I am what I am* (1 Tm 1:13; 1 Cor 15:10). Later, as he approached his suffering, he declared, *I have fought the good fight, I have run the whole course, I have kept the faith; all that remains for me now is the crown of righteousness.* He who granted mercy to me reserves justice now. On what grounds? With *the crown of righteousness*, Paul

---

26. Probably an allusion to high-ranking Donatist clerics. A canon of the Council of Carthage in A.D. 411 decreed, however, that on conversion they should be received with their honors intact.

says, *the just judge will recompense me on that day* (2 Tm 4:7-8). He granted forgiveness as a free gift, but he will give the crown as just recompense; he is a donor of forgiveness, but a debtor when it comes to the crown. How can he be a debtor? Has he received any favor? Does God owe anything to anyone? Yet we see Paul holding God to his debts, for having received mercy, he now demands justice. *The Lord will recompense me on that day*, he says. What is given you as a recompense? Something that is owed to you, obviously. But how does God owe it to you? What did you give him? Who took any initiative in giving to God, so as to earn a recompense?[27] The Lord has made himself a debtor, not by receiving anything but by making promises. We cannot say to him, "Give back what you received," but we can say, "Give what you promised." Paul testifies, "He expended mercy for me, to make me innocent. Until then I had been a blasphemer and I harmed people, but by his grace I became innocent." Could the one who granted mercy as a privilege in advance now renege on his debt? He *loves mercy and justice; he will grant grace and glory*. And what grace is that? Surely what Paul spoke of: *By God's grace I am what I am*. And what glory, if not that of which he said, *All that remains for me now is the crown of righteousness*?

Verse 13. The ultimate good, God himself

17. Accordingly the psalm continues, *The Lord will not deprive those who walk in innocence of any good things*. Now why, mortal creatures, are you reluctant to preserve your innocence? Because you hope to possess good things? Suppose someone is unwilling to hold on to his innocence by giving back something entrusted to him: that person wants to have gold, and loses innocence. Where is the gain? And what is the loss? He gains the gold, but suffers the loss of innocence. Is anything more precious than innocence? "But if I keep my innocence I shall be poor," he objects. Is not innocence itself considerable wealth? If you have a chest full of gold, you will be rich; if you have a heart full of innocence, will you be poor? While you long for good things now, in your penury, in distress, in the valley of weeping, under pressure, amid trials, preserve your innocence. Afterwards there will be that good time you hanker for. Rest, eternity, immortality, freedom from suffering—the time for these will come later, for these are the good things God is keeping for the righteous ones who belong to him.

As for those good things by which you set such store now, for the sake of which you are prepared to be not innocent but noxious,[28] consider the people who have them, and have them in plenty. You see wealth in the hands of robbers, godless folk, criminals and base characters; you see the vicious and the villainous in possession of riches. God allows them these things because out of

---

27. See Rom 11:35.
28. *Nocens, et non innocens.*

his overflowing, boundless goodness he treats us all as members of one human community; and so he causes his sun to rise over the good and the wicked, and sends his rain upon righteous and unrighteous alike.[29] If he gives so much even to bad people, does he keep nothing in reserve for you? Is his promise to you not to be trusted? He keeps it; do not worry. Will he who took pity on you when you were strangers desert you now that you are his loyal friends? If he forgave a sinner through the death of his Son, what is he reserving for one who has been saved through the death of his Son? Have no anxiety, .hen. Hold him to his debt, because you believed him when he made the promise. *The Lord will not deprive those who walk in innocence of any good things.* What is being kept for us, then, for us in the wine press, in vexation, in hardship, in our present, perilous life? What is kept for us, that we may make our way to it? *Lord, God of hosts, blessed is everyone who hopes in you.*[30]

29. See Mt 5:45.
30. Three codices add the following comment: "Once you are converted to the Lord, what will you lack in your innocence, you innocent person, provided you are innocent for the sake of the Lord? You will possess the Lord himself, the author of all powers/virtues, the Lord who grants virtues to those who persevere in their innocence. Blessed, therefore, is the person who hopes in you, O God."

Exposition of Psalm 84

A Sermon to the People, preached at Carthage

Introduction: We need to be healed by the Lord in order to see what he reveals

1. We begged the Lord our God to show us his mercy, and to grant us his salvation.[1] When the psalms were originally spoken and written this petition was made with prophetic import, but if we consider it from the standpoint of our own times, it is clear that the Lord has now shown his mercy to the Gentiles, and granted them his salvation. Yes, he has shown it, but there are many who are unwilling to be healed so that they can see what he has shown. The Lord himself, however, heals the eyes of our hearts to enable us to see what he shows us. This is why the psalmist first prays, *Show us your mercy*, but then adds, *and grant us your salvation*, because he has in mind the many blind people who will object, "How are we going to see it, when he does begin to reveal it?" By granting us his salvation the Lord heals the sickness in us and so makes us able to see what he reveals. His healing work is not like that of an ordinary physician who enables the patients he has cured to see the light, because in this latter case the light which the doctor's work enables the patient to see is one thing, and the doctor who heals the eyes is another; the doctor himself is not the light. It is quite otherwise with the Lord our God, for he is the physician who cures us so that we may be able to see, and he is the light which we are enabled to see.

All the same, we must try to concentrate now, and run through this whole psalm as quickly as we can, as the Lord will allow us, because we are short of time.

Verse 1. The children of Korah. A story about Elisha prefigures Christ

2. The title is *Unto the end, a psalm for the sons of Korah*. The only "end" we should think of is that of which the apostle said, *Christ is the end of the law, bringing justification to everyone who believes* (Rom 10:4). When the psalmist put those words *unto the end* in the title of the psalm, he directed our hearts to Christ. If we keep our gaze fixed on him we shall not go astray, because he is the

---

1. That is, when the psalm was read or sung before he began to comment on it. See verse 8 below.

Truth to which we are hastening, and he is the Way by which we are running there.[2] Now, what does *for the sons of Korah* mean? The Hebrew name *Korah* is interpreted as "bald," so *for the sons of Korah* means "for the sons of the bald man." Who is this bald man? This is not said to provoke us to derision but to lead us to weep before him.[3] There were some who did deride a bald man, and they were destroyed by demons. The Book of the Kingdoms relates how some boys mocked the bald Elisha, shouting after him, *Baldy! Baldy!* Bears broke from the wood and devoured those boys; they had no business to mock, but they were mourned by their parents.[4] This event was a prophetic sign of the coming of our Lord Jesus Christ. He was derided like a bald man[5] by the jeering Jews, inasmuch as he was crucified at a place called Calvary.

But if we have believed in him, we are his children; and therefore this psalm, entitled *for the sons of Korah*, is sung for us, for we are the bridegroom's children.[6] Truly he is the bridegroom, for he endowed his bride with his own blood and his Holy Spirit as a token of his love to enrich us for the present time while we are on pilgrimage, though he is keeping secret treasures in reserve for us. If he has given us here a pledge like this, what must he be keeping for us there?

Verse 2. The reversal of the true Jacob's captivity to sin

3. The prophet sings of Christ who is to come, but he expresses himself in the past tense. He speaks of future events as though they were already past, because with God what to us is future is already accomplished. In seeing things that would happen for us in days to come, the prophet saw them as having happened already in God's providence and absolute predestination. The case is similar in another psalm where everyone acknowledges that Christ is the subject, for to listen to the psalm being recited is just like listening to the reading of the gospel: *They dug holes in my hands and my feet, and numbered all my bones. They looked on and watched me, they shared out my clothing among them, and cast lots for my tunic* (Ps 21:17-19(22:16-18)). When the reader recites that psalm, could anyone fail to recognize the gospel story? And yet in the psalm's account of events, we do not hear, "They will dig holes in my hands and my feet," but *they dug holes in my hands and my feet.* Nor does it say, "They will share out my clothing," but *they shared out my clothing among them.* The prophet described as past events all these things that he foresaw in the future. And the same is true in our present psalm when he says, *You once blessed your land, O Lord.*

---

2. See Jn 14:6.
3. See Ps 94(95):6.
4. See 2 Kgs 2:23.24, and Augustine's comments on the episode in his Exposition of Psalm 83,2.
5. *Calvus.*
6. See Mt 9:15

4. *You reversed Jacob's captivity*. God's people of old was Jacob, the race of Israel descended from Abraham, and according to the promise it was to be God's heir. Israel was that people, and to it the Old Testament was given; but in the Old Testament the New was foreshadowed, the one being a type, and the other the revelation of the truth. In that type and foreshadowing a land of promise was given to the people as a proclamation in advance of what was to come. The land was the region where the Jewish people lived, in which was sited the city of Jerusalem, a name familiar to us all. Now after the people had received their land they were the object of constant molestation from hostile neighbors who made war on them from all sides. Whenever Israel sinned against its God it was delivered into captivity, but for the sake of discipline, not destruction, as though by a father who beats his son but does not disown him. The land was occupied, and then set free again, several times, and the people too was taken captive a number of times and freed again. It is in captivity still today, and this for the great sin it committed when it crucified its Lord. If the verse, *you reversed Jacob's captivity*, is applied to them, therefore, what meaning can we assign to it?

Perhaps we should do better to understand the verse as referring to a different captivity, from which we all desire to be set free. And such an interpretation is justified, because we all belong to Jacob if we are Abraham's descendants. The apostle testifies that Abraham was promised, *It is through Isaac that posterity will be yours; and this means that not the children of his flesh, but the children of the promise, are accounted his descendants* (Rom 9:7-8). But if it is the children of the promise who are accounted Abraham's descendants, it follows that the Jews have played false to their ancestry by offending God, whereas we who have proved worthy of God have been made members of Abraham's race, not by carnal descent but through kinship with him in faith. By imitating his faith we have become his children, while the Jews by falling away from that faith have been deservedly disinherited. You know how they lost their prerogative of descent from Abraham when they boasted arrogantly in the presence of our Lord Jesus Christ, *We have Abraham for our father*, to which the Lord replied, pointing out their degeneracy, *If you are Abraham's children, act as Abraham did* (Jn 8:39). From this we infer that if they forfeited the right to be Abraham's children because they did not imitate his conduct, we are his children because we do. Which of Abraham's actions do we imitate? Abraham believed God, and it was reckoned to him as righteousness.[7] By this token we all belong to Jacob by imitating the faith of Abraham, who believed God, and had it reckoned to him as righteousness.

What, then, is the captivity from which we desire to be freed? I do not think that any of us are held by barbarians, or that any armed nation has invaded our

---

7. See Gn 15:6; Rom 4:3; Gal 3:6. Faith in the biblical sense is wider than belief, though it includes it. It implies trust, obedience to God, and self-surrender to his promise and his will.

territory and carried us off as prisoners.[8] But I will point out to you what that captivity is under which we are groaning, the captivity from which we long to be delivered. Let the apostle Paul speak first and give it a name; let him speak, and be the mirror in which we may see ourselves; none of us will fail to recognize ourselves in it. The blessed apostle avers, *I take great delight in God's law as far as my inner self is concerned—God's law is a delight to me inwardly—but I am aware of a different law in my members that opposes the law of my mind.* You heard him mention a law, and you heard him speak of a fight; but you have not yet heard about a captivity. Listen further: *a different law in my members opposes the law of my mind,* he says, *and it imprisons me under the law of sin inherent in my members* (Rom 7:22-25). Now we know what captivity is in question. Is there anyone among us who does not want to be freed from it?

Where will liberation come from? When the psalmist sang of future events, *You reversed Jacob's captivity,* to whom was he speaking? To Christ, as the title, *Unto the end,* and the dedication to the children of Korah, made clear; it is Christ who has reversed Jacob's captivity. Listen to Paul making the same declaration. Feeling himself being dragged away captive by the law inherent in his members that warred against the law of his mind, feeling himself caught, he cried out, *Who will deliver me from this death-ridden body, wretch that I am?* He asked "Who?" and immediately the answer came to him: *Only the grace of God, through Jesus Christ our Lord* (Rom 7:25).

It is with the grace of God in mind that the prophet says to this same Jesus Christ, our Lord, *You reversed Jacob's captivity.* Think what Jacob's captivity was, and then understand that this is what is meant: you have reversed our captivity, not by rescuing us from barbarians, with whom we are not at war, but by setting us free from our evildoing, from our sins, through which Satan tyrannized over us. No one who has been freed from sins affords any foothold to the tyranny of the prince of sinners.

Verses 3-5. Our sins are covered

5. How did he reverse Jacob's captivity? You must observe that a spiritual liberation is in question, one that is effected within us. *You forgave your people's iniquity and covered all their sins.* Here you have the means by which our captivity was reversed: it was through the forgiveness of our iniquity. Iniquity was holding you captive, but when your iniquity is forgiven you are freed. Confess that you are in captivity, then, so that you may deserve to be set free, for how can those who do not know their enemy call upon their deliverer?

---

8. This sentence, together with the phrase later in the section, "barbarians, with whom we are not at war," would seem to indicate that the sermon was preached earlier than the sack of Rome by Alaric in 410. Augustine could hardly have spoken so when refugees from Italy were pouring into Africa.

You covered all their sins. What does *covered* mean?[9] You arranged not to see them. In what sense, arranged not to see them? You willed not to, so that you would not have to punish them. You do not see our sins because you have willed not to see them; you have chosen not to. *You covered all their sins. You calmed all your anger, and turned away from your fierce displeasure.*

6. Remember now, the psalmist is talking about future events, even though he uses the past tense. Only because he looks to the future can he pray for something to happen, something that he was just now relating as though it was already accomplished. That he can do so shows us that he wanted his previous statements to be understood prophetically. He proves that what he stated as already done was in fact not done yet, by praying now that it may happen: *Convert us, O God our constant healer, and turn your wrath away from us.* But were you not saying, not long since, *You reversed Jacob's captivity; you covered all their sins; you calmed all your anger; you turned away from your angry displeasure*? How, then, can you pray in this next verse, *Turn away your wrath from us*? The prophet replies, "I describe those things as having taken place already because I see that they will take place. But because in fact they have not happened yet, I pray that what I have already seen will happen." *Turn away your wrath from us.*

Verse 6. Our inheritance from Adam

7. *Do not be angry with us for ever.* As a consequence of God's anger we are mortal, and in consequence of his anger we eat our bread on this earth in poverty and the laborious sweat of our faces.[10] This is the sentence Adam heard when he sinned, and we are all Adam, for in Adam all die.[11] What he heard concerns us equally. In our own persons we did not yet exist, but we were present in Adam, and therefore whatever befell Adam was our fate too. We too therefore had to die, inasmuch as we were in him. The sins of parents do not affect their children if committed after the children are born, for once born the children are responsible for their own actions, as the parents are for theirs. If the children after birth keep to their parents' evil way of life, they will inevitably bear their parents' guilt; but if they change their lives and do not imitate their bad parents, they begin to deserve well on their own account, not badly like their parents. Your father's sin ceases to be a liability to you, if you have reformed your life, but this is true only to the same degree that it is no longer a liability to your father himself, if he has changed his. However, what our nature inherited in the way of proneness to mortality, it derived from Adam. What did it derive? The fragility

---

9. Originally the idea may have been the covering of spilt blood, which otherwise would cry out for vengeance to God from the earth, like Abel's; see Gn 4:10.
10. See Gn 3:19.
11. See 1 Cor 15:22.

of our flesh, the agonizing pain we experience, the poverty of our earthly dwelling, our bondage to death, the snares of temptation. All these we carry in this flesh of ours, and all of them are signs of God's anger, because they are the punishment he has laid upon us.

But the prophet foresaw that one day we would be born anew and become new creatures through faith, and that all this mortality would be taken up into resurrection, and our whole selves be restored and made new, for as in Adam all die, so in Christ will all be brought to life.[12] And because he saw all this, he prayed, *Do not be angry with us for ever, nor prolong your ire from generation to generation.* The first generation was mortal because of your anger; but another generation will be immortal through your mercy.

Verse 7. Our conversion to God, and our joy in him, are his gift

8. But wait: was this something you did for yourself, poor creature? Was it your own doing that you were converted to God, and now deserve his mercy? And what of those who have not been converted, and have not received mercy: have they found God's wrath? What could you have done towards your own conversion, if you had not been called? Did not he who called you, when you were turned away from him, himself grant you the power to turn towards him? Claim no credit, then. No, not even for your conversion itself, because if he had not called you when you were in flight from him, you could not have turned back.

This is why the prophet attributes even the grace of conversion to God, and prays, *O God, in converting us you will give us life.* It is not as though we were converted to you of our own accord, with your mercy playing no part, and then you give us life; no, *in converting us you will give us life*, so that it is not only our rising to life that is your gift, but even the conversion that makes our rising to life possible.

O God, in converting us you will give us life, and your people will rejoice in you. Over its misdeeds it will rejoice in itself, but over its good, in you; for when it tried to enjoy itself, it found only matter for mourning in itself, but now, since God is our whole joy, anyone who wants to rejoice without any worry at all should seek joy in him who cannot perish. Why look for joy in money, my brothers and sisters? Either the money fades away or you do, and no one knows which will fail first. The only certain thing is that both will perish, but which one first is uncertain. No human being can stay here for ever, but money cannot either; and the same applies to your gold, clothing, house, property, large estates, and finally this light of day itself. Make no attempt, then, to find your joy in these things, but rejoice in that light which knows no setting, rejoice in that light which

---

12. See 1 Cor 15:22.

is neither ushered in by yesterday nor followed by tomorrow. And what light is that? *I am the light of the world*, he says (Jn 8:12). He who assures you, *I am the light of the world*, calls you to himself. As he calls you, he converts you; as he converts you, he heals you; when he has healed you, you will see him who converted you; and he it is to whom the psalm says, *Your people will rejoice in you.*

Verse 8. *"Grant us your Christ"*

9. *Show us, Lord, your mercy.* That is what we sang, and hence we have already considered it. *Show us, Lord, your mercy, and grant us your salvation.* "Your salvation"[13] means your Christ. Happy the person to whom God shows his mercy. Such a one cannot be proud, for in showing us mercy God convinces us that whatever good we humans have, we have only from him who is our total good. When we see that whatever good we have, we hold not from ourselves but from our God, we also see that whatever is praiseworthy in us comes from God's mercy, not from our own merits. When we see that, we cannot be proud, and if we are not proud we do not exalt ourselves, and if we do not exalt ourselves we do not fall over, and if we do not fall we stand, and if we stand we cling to God, and if we cling we abide, and when we abide in him we enjoy him to the full, and make merry in the Lord our God. Our delight will be the God who made us, and delights like that no one spoils; no one challenges us for them, nor does anyone take them away. Where is the powerful person who might threaten to take them from us? What malicious neighbor, what brigand, what plotter, can steal your God from you? He may take away from you all your bodily possessions, but he cannot steal away the one you possess in your heart.

This is the mercy which we pray that God will show us. *Show us, Lord, your mercy, and grant us your salvation.* "Grant us your Christ," prays the psalm, "for in him your mercy dwells." Let us echo it: Grant us your Christ. Yes, it is true that he has given his Christ to us already, yet let us go on saying to him, Grant us your Christ. After all, we are accustomed to beg him, *Give us this day our daily bread* (Lk 11:3), and who is "our bread," if not he who claimed, *I am the living bread which has come down from heaven* (Jn 6:41)? Let us appeal to God, then, "Grant us your Christ." He has given us Christ, but Christ the man; this very Christ, whom he gave us as man, he will one day give as God. He gave him as human to human beings because he gave him to us in a form we humans could humanly accept. No human being has the capacity to receive God. He became man for men and women, but he is saving himself as God for gods. Does that seem to you an arrogant statement? Arrogant it certainly would be, had not he himself said, *I have spoken, and you are gods, sons of the Most High, all of you* (Ps 81(82):6).

---

13. *Salutare*, salvation in the holistic sense, with overtones of healing, deliverance, new life.

To fit us for this adoption we are being made new, for we are to be children of God. Such indeed we are already, but only in faith; we are children of God in hope, but not yet in plain fact. *In hope we have been saved,* as the apostle testifies. *But if hope is seen, it is hope no longer, for when someone sees what he hopes for, why should he hope for it? But if we hope for what we do not see, we wait for it in patience* (Rom 8:24-25). What is it that we *wait for in patience*? We wait to see that in which we now believe. At present we believe in what we do not see; by abiding in him whom we believe in without seeing, we shall deserve to see him in whom we believe. What has John to say in his Letter about this? *Dearly beloved, we are children of God already, but what we shall be has not yet appeared* (1 Jn 3:2). Can you imagine how a person would leap for joy if, while traveling abroad and ignorant of his parentage, suffering want and habituated to hardship and toil, he received the message, "You are the son of a senator. Your father enjoys an ample fortune on your family estate, and I have come to summon you home to him." What a transport of joy that would be, assuming that the one who made the promise was not lying! Well then, an apostle of Christ who was no liar has come to say to us, "What do you mean by despairing about your prospects? Why grovel and make yourselves miserable? What are you about, obedient to your appetites and pursuing only wretchedness in the emptiness of those very pleasures? You have a father, you have a homeland, you have an inheritance." Who is your father? *Dearly beloved, we are children of God.* Why then can we not yet see our Father? Because *what we shall be has not yet appeared.* Children already, we are so in hope, for *what we shall be has not yet appeared* And what shall we be? *We know that when he appears, we shall be like him, because we shall see him as he is.*

But it was of the Father that scripture made that promise. Has it nothing to say of the Son, our Lord Jesus Christ? Shall we, perhaps, find our beatitude in seeing the Father but not the Son? Listen to Christ's own words: *Whoever sees me sees the Father* (Jn 14:9). When the one God offers himself to our sight, the Trinity is seen—Father, Son and Holy Spirit. There is an even more explicit promise that seeing the Son himself will be our happiness, and that there is no difference between seeing him and seeing the Father, for he says himself in the gospel, *Whoever loves me keeps my commandments; and I will love him, and will show myself to him* (Jn 14:21). He was there talking with him, yet he said, "I will show myself to anyone who loves me." Why did he say that? Was he not there in person, conversing with them? But they were flesh, and saw him in the flesh; their hearts did not see his godhead. Yet flesh saw flesh to the end that hearts might be cleansed by faith, and readied for the vision of God. Scripture says of the Lord that he was *cleansing hearts by faith* (Acts 15:9); and the Lord himself declared, *Blessed are the pure of heart, for they shall see God* (Mt 5:8).

So he has promised to show himself to us. Think, my brothers and sisters, think what his beauty is like! All these beautiful things that you see and love—he made them. If they are beautiful, what of him? If they are great, how great is he? Let us rise up from the things we love here to desire him even more; let us hold them cheap and choose him for our love, and by this love so cleanse our hearts through faith that the vision of God may find our hearts already purified. The light that will be revealed to us must find us with healthy eyes, and this is the work of faith now. That is why we have prayed here, *Grant us your salvation.* Grant us your Christ, let us know your Christ, let us see your Christ, not in the way the Jews saw him, and crucified him, but as the angels see him, and rejoice.

Verse 9. The peace of God

10. *I will listen to what the Lord God speaks within me.* This is the prophet speaking. God was speaking to him within, in a hidden way, and the world was raising its din for him outside. Withdrawing a little from the world's racket, turning himself away from it to himself, and then from himself to the One whose voice he was hearing within, he tried to block his ears against the tumultuous restlessness of this life, against his own soul weighed down by the corruptible body, and against the teeming mind oppressed by its earthly habitation.[14] *I will listen to what the Lord God speaks within me,* he said. And what did he hear? *He will speak peace to his people.* The voice of Christ, the voice of God, is peace, and it calls us to peace. Come, he says, love peace, all you who are not yet at peace, for what greater benefit to yourselves can you find in me than peace?

What is peace? The absence of war. A state of affairs where there is no strife, no resistance, no adversity. Consider now: are we in that state yet, have we left behind all conflict with the devil, are all holy and faithful people free from struggle with the prince of demons? No, but how can they struggle with someone they cannot see? They struggle with their unruly desires, through which he suggests sinful acts to them; but even if they do not consent to his suggestions, even if they are not vanquished, still they have to fight. Where there is continued fighting, there is not yet peace.

Show me a person who suffers no carnal temptation, and can therefore tell me that peace is established. It may be true that such persons succumb to no temptation by enjoying forbidden pleasures, but they do at least have to put up with the suggestions. Either a suggestion is made which they must reject, or a pleasure beckons from which they must hold back. Or suppose no unlawful pleasure arouses them any longer: they still have to fight daily against hunger and thirst, for what right-living person is a stranger to these? Hunger and thirst fight against us, bodily weariness fights against us, the lure of sleep fights against us, and the burden of the body. We want to keep watch and we fall asleep; we want to fast but feel hungry and thirsty; we want to remain standing but are tired out and have

---

14. See Wis 9:15.

to sit down; if we go on sitting for a long time, that too debilitates us. Whatever we have provided for ourselves as a pick-me-up pulls us down again.[15] "Are you hungry?" someone asks. "Yes, I am," you reply. He places food before you to build you up, so continue with what he served to you. Your intention was certainly to sustain yourself, so keep going. But as you do so you get tired of what you took to refresh yourself. Again, you were fatigued by sitting for a long time, so you get up and walk about, and find relief; persist in what relieves you and you grow weary with too much walking, and want to sit down again. Tell me anything that you use as a pick-me-up which does not pull you down again if you persist in it.

What kind of peace is this, then, which we experience in the teeth of such fierce resistance from vexations, cravings, wants and weariness? This is no true peace, no perfect peace. When will peace be perfect? *This corruptible body must put on incorruption, and this mortal body be clothed in immortality; then the saying will come true: Death is swallowed up into victory. Where, O death, is your sting? Where is your strife, O death?* (1 Cor 15:53-55). For where mortality[16] still dominates, how can there be complete peace? From death comes that lassitude we experience in everything that sustains us. From death it flows, because we carry a mortal body, a body which the apostle even calls a dead body, and that even before the soul has left it: *the body indeed is a dead thing, by reason of sin,* he says (Rom 8:10). So true is this that if you go too far with the commodity you are using to refresh yourself, you will even die. Eat to excess, and the food itself will kill you; prolong your fasting, and you will die of it; stay sitting all the time until you no longer want to get up, and that will be the death of you; walk about uninterruptedly without consenting to rest, and you will drop dead; stay awake all the time, denying the claims of sleep, and that will be fatal; sleep on and on, refusing to wake up, and you will die of it. When death is swallowed up into victory, things will be different; then there will be total, everlasting peace. We shall be in a city ... my brothers and sisters, when I begin to speak about that city I do not want to stop, especially when offenses grow rank all around us. We cannot help desiring that city, whence no friend departs, where no enemy gains entrance, where there is no tempter, no disturber of the peace, no one to cause divisions within God's people, none to collude with the devil in harassing the Church, when the prince of demons is flung into eternal fire, along with all those who support him and refuse to abandon his service. A peace made pure will reign among[17] God's children: they will all love themselves as they see themselves full of God, and God will be all in all.[18] For all of us God will be the

15. *Quidquid nobis providerimus ad refectionem, illic rursus invenimus defectionem.*
16. Variant: "death."
17. Or "within."
18. See 1 Cor 15:28.

object of our contemplation; he will be our common possession, he our common peace. Whatever he gives us now, he himself will be for us then in place of what he gives. He himself will be our peace, perfect and total.

This peace is what he speaks to his people, and this is what the psalmist longed to hear as he said, *I will listen to what the Lord God speaks within me, for he will speak peace to his people, to his holy ones, and to those who turn their hearts to him.* Well then, brothers and sisters, do you want that peace which God speaks to be your portion too? Turn your hearts to him, then, not to me, or to him or her, or to anyone else. Anybody who tries to attract human hearts toward himself falls along with them. Which is better, to fall with someone to whom you are converted, or to stand alongside someone with whom you are converted? God alone is our joy, our rest, our final freedom from all distress. Blessed are they who *turn their hearts to him.*

Verse 10. The glory dwells in Israel

11. *Yet his salvation is near to those who fear him.* There were some who already feared him, among the Jewish people. Everywhere else, throughout other nations, idols were worshiped and demons were feared, not God; but among that one people God was feared. But why? In the Old Testament he was feared lest he should consign them to captivity, or take their land away from them, or smash their vines with hail, or make their wives sterile, or take away their children. These were the material benefits promised by God, and they enthralled minds still childish. On account of them God was feared. Yet he was near those who feared him, even though they feared him for such reasons. The pagan would beg for land from the devil, the Jew would beg for land from God. Both were asking for the same thing, but not from the same power. The Jew was making the same plea as the pagan, but in making it he differed from the pagan because he made his plea to the One who had created all things.

God was near to them, and far away from the Gentiles, yet his eyes were upon both those who were far off and those who were near, as the apostle tells us: *He came to bring the good news of peace to you who were far away, and peace to those who were near* (Eph 2:17). Whom did he mean by those who were near? The Jews, who worshiped the one God. And whom by those who were far off? The Gentiles, because they had abandoned him by whom they were made, and were worshipping things they had made themselves. No one is far away from God geographically, only by disposition. If you love God, you are near him; if you hate him, you are distant. You can stand in the one same place, and be either near or far away.

The prophet had all this in mind, my brothers and sisters, and though he was aware of the universal mercy of God over all peoples, he saw something special, something proper to the race in Judea, and that is why he said, *Yet his salvation is near to those who fear him.*

Just before this he had declared, *I will listen to what the Lord God speaks within me, for he will speak peace to his people.* God's people will not consist of Judah alone, but will be gathered from all nations, because he will speak peace *to his holy ones, and to those who turn their hearts to him*, to all who will turn their hearts to him from anywhere throughout the world. Nonetheless, *his salvation is near to those who fear him, so that glory may dwell in our land.* The prophet prays that in the very land where he himself was born a still greater glory may dwell, because from there Christ began to be preached. The apostles sprang from that land, and to it they were initially sent.[19] From that land sprang the prophets, there stood the temple, there was sacrifice offered to God, there lived the patriarchs, there too was he born of Abraham's line who was manifested as the Messiah. There did Christ appear, because thence sprang Mary, who gave birth to Christ. That land was trodden by his feet, and there he worked his miracles. In the end he treated that nation with such honor that when a Canaanite woman accosted him, seeking a cure for her daughter, he replied, *I was not sent except for the lost sheep of the house of Israel* (Mt 15:24). With this in view the prophet said, *Yet his salvation is near to those who fear him, so that glory may dwell in our land.*

Verse 11. Justice and peace are inseparable friends

12. *Mercy and truth have run to meet each other.* Truth is in our land, the land personified by the Jewish nation. Mercy is in the lands of the Gentiles. For where was truth? Where God's revelation was. And where mercy? Among those who had abandoned their God, and turned to demons. But did God disdain even those? No, how could that be, if he said, "Call them too, who have fled afar, the people who have wholly forsaken me; call them; let them find me seeking them, since they were unwilling to seek me"? So, the psalm declares, *Mercy and truth have run to meet each other; justice and peace have kissed.* Act justly and you will have peace, so that justice and peace may kiss. If you do not love justice you will not have peace, for these two, justice and peace, love each other, and they embrace, so that anyone who does justice finds peace kissing justice. They are friends, these two; you may perhaps want one without practicing the other, for there is no one who does not want peace, though not everyone wants to act justly. Put the question to all: "Do you want peace?" The entire human race will answer you with a single voice, "I hope for it, I long for it, I want it, I love it." Love justice as well, then, for justice and peace are two friends, kissing each other, and if you do not love peace's friend, peace will not love you or come to you. After

---

19. See Mt 10:5-6.

all, what is so special about the desire for peace? Every bad person desires peace, for peace is a good thing. But deal justly, because justice and peace kiss each other; there is no quarrel between them. Why do you quarrel with justice? You know that justice tells you, "You must not steal," and you turn a deaf ear; she says, "You must not commit adultery," but you do not want to hear that. Do not do to another what you would not wish to endure yourself, nor say to another what you would not wish to have said to you. "You are an enemy to my friend," says peace, "so why seek me? I am the friend of justice, and I do not approach anyone I find to be hostile to my friend." You want to attain peace, then? Practice justice. Another psalm tells you, *Turn away from evil and do good* (that is, love justice), and when you have done that, *seek peace and pursue it* (Ps 33:15(34:14)). You will not need to seek her for long, for she will run to meet you, so that she may kiss justice.

Verse 12. Truth has sprung up from the earth: the incarnation

13. *Truth has sprung up from the earth, and righteousness has looked down from heaven.* Yes, *truth has sprung up from the earth*, because Christ was born from a woman. *Truth has sprung up from the earth*, because the Son of God has come forth from the flesh. What is Truth? The Son of God. What is the earth? Our flesh. Inquire whence Christ was born, and you will see that *truth has sprung up from the earth.* Yet this Truth that has sprung up from the earth existed before the earth, for heaven and earth were made through him; but in order that righteousness might look down from heaven, that is, that human beings might be made righteous through divine grace, Truth was born from the virgin Mary, that he might be in a position to offer sacrifice for those who needed justification, the sacrifice of his passion, the sacrifice of the cross. How could he offer his sacrifice for our sins, except by dying? But how could he die, unless he took from us what could die? Had he not taken mortal flesh from us, Christ could not have died, for the Word does not die, the Godhead does not die, the Power and Wisdom of God[20] does not die. How could he offer himself as a saving victim, if he did not die? But how die, without clothing himself in flesh? And how put on flesh, unless Truth sprang up from the earth? But *truth has sprung up from the earth, and righteousness has looked down from heaven.*

Truth has sprung up from the earth: confession

14. We can take it in another sense. *Truth has sprung up from the earth* means that confession has come from us humans. You, human creature, were a sinner. You were "earth" when you sinned, for then you heard God say, *Earth you are,*

---

20. See 1 Cor 1:24.

and back to earth you shall go (Gn 3:19); but let truth spring up from you who are earth, so that righteousness may look down from heaven. How can truth spring up from you, sinner that you are, unjust as you are? Confess your sins, and truth will spring up from you. If you claim to be just when you are unjust, how can truth spring up from you? But if when you are unjust you admit to being unjust, *truth has sprung up from the earth.* Study the tax collector who prayed in the temple far removed from the Pharisee. He did not even presume to raise his eyes to heaven; he simply beat his breast, saying, *Lord, be merciful to me, a sinner* (Lk 18:13). There you have truth springing up from the earth, because confession of sins was made by a human creature. And what followed it? *Truly I tell you, that tax collector went down to his house at rights with God, for anyone who exalts himself will be humbled, but the one who humbles himself will be exalted* (Lk 18:14). So *truth sprang up from the earth* in his confession of sins, and *righteousness looked down from heaven* to send the tax collector away justified, rather than the Pharisee. To assure you that truth implies the confession of sins, John the evangelist teaches, *If we say we have no sin, we deceive ourselves, and the truth is not in us* (1 Jn 1:8). But listen to what comes next, as he tells us how truth springs up from the earth so that righteousness may look down from heaven: *If we confess our sins, he is so faithful and just that he forgives us our sins, and cleanses us from all iniquity* (1 Jn 1:9). Then *truth has sprung up from the earth, and righteousness has looked down from heaven.* What righteousness is this, that *has looked down from heaven?* The righteousness of God, who says, "Let us pardon this person, because he has not pardoned himself; let us overlook his sin because he has looked honestly at it himself.[21] He has turned back to punish his own sin, so I too will turn to him to set him free from it." *Truth has sprung up from the earth, and righteousness has looked down from heaven.*

Verse 13. The sweet fruit of justification

15. *For truly the Lord will give sweetness, and then our earth will yield its fruit.* Only one verse left. I pray that what I have to say will not weary you. Concentrate on the essential point, my brothers and sisters; concentrate, grasp it and take it away with you, so that God's seed sown in your hearts may not remain sterile. *Truth has sprung up from the earth,* the psalm tells us: that is, the confession made by the sinner. *Righteousness has looked down from heaven:* this means that justification has been conferred by the Lord God on the one who confesses. Estranged from God as he is, he cannot become God's loyal friend unless God makes him so, and the sinner must recognize this. In confessing to God, he is putting his faith in him who justifies the ungodly.

---

21. *Ignoscamus, quia ipse agnoscit.*

You can claim ownership of your sins, but you will bear no fruit unless he grants it, he to whom you confess your sins. After the psalmist has said, *Truth has sprung up from the earth, and righteousness has looked down from heaven*, someone may perhaps ask, "What does that mean—*righteousness has looked down from heaven*?" He therefore spells it out: *Truly the Lord will give sweetness, and then our earth will yield its fruit*. Let us examine ourselves, then, and if we find in ourselves nothing but sins, let us hate the sins and desire righteousness. When we begin to hate our sins that very hatred is already beginning to make us like God, because what God hates, we hate too. So when you begin to hate your sins and confess them to God, and then unlawful pleasures ensnare you and lead you to things that do you no good, send up your groans to God. As you confess your sins to him you will deserve to receive delight from him in return; and he will accord to you sweetness in acting righteously. In consequence, you who formerly took pleasure in sin will now begin to delight in righteousness: you used to enjoy getting drunk, but now you enjoy sobriety; you took pleasure in theft, in taking away from someone else something you did not possess, but now you seek to give what you do possess to someone who does not have it. You found gratification in shows, but now in prayer; worthless and bawdy songs used to afford you pleasure, but now you enjoy singing a hymn to God; you were wont to run to the theatre, but now you hasten to church. Where does this sweetness come from? Only from God, who *will give sweetness, and then our earth will yield its fruit*.

Do you see what I am getting at? We have preached God's word to you, we have scattered the seed in your faithful hearts, finding them well furrowed by the plow of confession. With ready minds and devout intention you have welcomed the seed. Think about the word you have heard, as though you were breaking up the clods of earth, so that instead of the birds carrying it off, the newly-sown seed may germinate. But unless God sends rain, what is the use of sowing? This is why the psalm acknowledges that it is God who *will give sweetness, and then our earth will yield its fruit*. May he visit you when you are at leisure, when you are busy, at home, in bed, at a feast, during a conversation, as you are out walking; may he visit your hearts then, when we are not there. May God's shower fall and bring fruit from what has been sown. While we are not with you, while we are taking a rest, or doing something else, may God grant increase to the seeds we have scattered, so that when later on we notice your good conduct we may rejoice in the fruit you bear, *for truly the Lord will give sweetness, and then our earth will yield its fruit*.

Verse 14. Preparing a way for the Lord

16. *Justice will walk before him, and he will direct his steps in the way.* The justice mentioned here is that exercised in the confession of our sins, for that is truthfulness. You must mete out justice to yourself by punishing yourself; justice for human beings begins with your punishing your bad self, and God making you good. And since this is the initiation of human justice, it becomes a pathway for God, a way along which God may come to you. Make a pathway for him, then, by confessing your sins. When John was baptizing in the water of repentance, and wanted his penitents to turn away from their former deeds and come to themselves, he always said, *Prepare a way for the Lord, straighten his paths* (Mt 3:3). You were pleasing in your own eyes, poor mortal, when you were in your sins; let what you were be displeasing to you now, so that you may become what you were not. *Prepare a way for the Lord:* let that justice that consists in the confession of your sins go on ahead; then he will come and visit you, *he will direct his steps in the way,* for now he will have somewhere to tread, a way by which he can come to you. Before you confessed your sins you had blocked God's road; he had no way to reach you. Confess the Way[22] and you open the way; then Christ will come and *direct his steps in the way,* to refashion you as you follow in his footsteps.[23]

---

22. Evidently an allusion to Christ, the Way; see Jn 14:6. The Exposition ends as it began; see section 2 above.

23. *Ut te informet vestigiis suis.* A pregnant phrase to end the sermon in a hurry; given more time he might have developed the idea. Augustine's thought is habitually trinitarian, and he dwells frequently on the triadic pattern stamped upon creation, especially on human nature in creation and grace. In this pattern *forma,* the principle of differentiation which gives to each thing its identity, usually corresponds to the Second Person of the Trinity. Created in the Word, the human person is recreated in grace as the "form" of Christ is given to us in baptism. It would be possible to give a weaker translation here, however: "... to guide you in his footsteps."

Exposition of Psalm 85

A Sermon[1]

Introduction: the prayer of head and body

1. God could have granted no greater gift to human beings than to cause his Word, through whom he created all things, to be their head, and to fit them to him as his members. He was thus to be both Son of God and Son of Man, one God with the Father, one human being with us. The consequence is that when we speak to God in prayer we do not separate the Son from God, and when the body of the Son prays it does not separate its head from itself. The one sole savior of his body is our Lord Jesus Christ, the Son of God, who prays for us, prays in us, and is prayed to by us. He prays for us as our priest, he prays in us as our head, and he is prayed to by us as our God. Accordingly we must recognize our voices in him, and his accents in ourselves. When something is said about the Lord Jesus Christ, particularly in prophecy, which seems to imply some lowly condition unworthy of God, we must not shrink from ascribing it to him, who did not shrink from uniting himself to us. In fact the entire creation is at his service, because the entire creation was made by him, but if we do not keep his unity with us in mind, we may be very disconcerted. We consider his sublime godhead, we hear the text, *in the beginning was the Word, and the Word was with God; he was God. He was with God in the beginning. Everything was made through him; no part of created being was made without him* (Jn 1:1-3); we contemplate the super-eminent divinity of God's Son, which transcends every nobility found among creatures. Yet then we hear him in some scriptural text apparently groaning, praying, and confessing. We shrink from ascribing these words to him, because our minds, so recently engaged in contemplation of his divinity, balk at descending to his humility. We think that it would be an affront to him if we were to admit that words spoken by a man could be his words—his, to whom words were addressed when we prayed to God. Our minds often come to a standstill, and attempt to alter the meaning. The only scriptural passages we can think of are those which bring us back to him and keep us firmly with him.

---

1. Preached on the eve of the festival of Saint Cyprian, 13 September, possibly in 401 or 416, at Mappalia, thought to have been a site outside the walls of Carthage, where Saint Cyprian's body was buried. The year 412 is also proposed.

When this happens our meditation needs to wake up and be more alert in faith, remembering that he whom we were just now contemplating in the form of God took upon himself the form of a servant, and that bearing the human likeness, sharing the human lot, he humbled himself and became obedient to the point of death;[2] and that as he hung on the cross he willed to make the words of a psalm his own, crying, *My God, my God, why have you forsaken me?* (Ps 21:2(22:1)). In the form of God, therefore, he is prayed to, but in the form of a servant he prays, in the former case as Creator, in the latter as created. Without any change in himself he takes upon himself the creature who needs to be changed, making of us one single man with himself, head and body.

We pray, then, to him, through him and in him; we speak with him and he speaks with us. We utter in him, and he utters in us, the plea made in this psalm, which is entitled, *A Prayer of David*. According to the flesh our Lord is the son of David; but in his godhead he is David's Lord and David's Creator. He exists not only before David came to be, but before Abraham, from whom David was descended, and before Adam, from whom all our race derives, and even before heaven and earth, in which all creation is comprised. Let no one, then, on hearing these words, maintain, "This is not said by Christ," or, on the other hand, "I am not speaking in this text." Rather let each of us who know ourselves to be within Christ's body acknowledge both truths, that "Christ speaks here," and that "I speak here." Say nothing apart from him, as he says nothing apart from you.

Does the gospel not make this plain to us? We read there, certainly, *In the beginning was the Word, and the Word was with God; he was God. He was with God in the beginning. Everything was made through him;* but with equal certainty we read there that Jesus was overcome by sadness,[3] that Jesus was tired,[4] that he slept,[5] that he was hungry and thirsty,[6] that Jesus prayed—indeed, that he persevered in prayer all night. He prolonged his prayer throughout the night, the gospel tells us,[7] and at a later time, as he continued in prayer, drops of blood ran down his body.[8] What did that suggest, when drops of blood oozed from his body as he prayed? Surely that the Church, which is his body, was already dripping with the blood of its martyrs.

---

2. See Phil 2:5-8.
3. See Mk 14:34.
4. See Jn 4:6.
5. See Mt 8:24.
6. See Mt 4:2; Jn 4:7; 19:28.
7. See Lk 6:12.
8. See Lk 22:43.44.

Verse 1. God inclines his ear to the truly poor and humble

2. *Bend down your ear and hear me, Lord.* He is speaking in the person of a servant, and you, who are a servant, are speaking in the person of your Lord. *Bend down your ear.* He does bend down his ear as long as you do not stiffen your neck, for he draws near to anyone who has been humbled, but distances himself from exalted people, unless they are the humbled ones whom he has himself exalted. God does bend down his ear to us, for he is above, and we are below, he in the heights, we in lowliness—but not therefore abandoned. *God displays his love for us in that while we were still sinners Christ died for us. Scarcely would anyone die for a righteous person,* says scripture, *though perhaps for a good person some might dare to die. But our Lord died for the wicked* (Rom 5:8.9.7.6). No merits on our part had been in place beforehand to induce the Son of God to die; no, rather because merits there were none, great was his mercy. How certain, then, how unshakable is his promise to keep his life for the just, when he gave away his death for the unjust?

Bend down your ear and hear me, Lord, for I am needy and destitute. Not to the rich does he bend down his ear, but to the destitute and the needy; that is, to the humble, to the one who confesses to him, to the one who needs mercy, not to the person who is sated and self-important and boastful as though in need of nothing, the kind who says, *I thank you that I am not like that tax collector there* (Lk 18:11). The rich Pharisee was flaunting his merits; the poor tax collector was confessing his sins.

3. But now, my brothers and sisters, you must not take what I have said, "He does not bend his ear down to the rich," to mean that God does not hear those who have gold and silver, a large household and country estates. Such persons may have been born in those circumstances, or may hold that rank in human society, only they should keep the apostle's warning in mind: *Instruct the rich of this world not to be high-minded* (1 Tm 6:17). Those who are not high-minded are poor in God, and to the poor and destitute and needy he bows down his ear. Such people know that their hope does not lie in gold or silver, nor in any of those things with which they seem to be surrounded for a time. Let them count themselves lucky if their riches do not ruin them; it is gain enough if their wealth is no hindrance, for it cannot be any profit to them. What does profit rich and poor alike is a work of mercy, which a rich person can perform in both will and deed, but a poor person in will only. When people in comfortable circumstances despise whatever there is in them that ordinarily blows up human pride, they are God's poor. God bows down his ear to them, for he knows that their hearts are bruised.[9]

---

9. See Ps 33:19 (34:18).

We are left in no doubt about the poor man who lay, covered with ulcers, at the rich man's gate, my brothers and sisters; he was carried away by angels to Abraham's embrace: so we read in the gospel, and so we believe.[10] The rich man, who went clad in purple and fine linen, and was accustomed to lavish banquets every day, was carried off to torments in the underworld. Are we really to think that the poor man was escorted by angels simply on account of his destitution, and the rich man sent to torments for the sin of being rich? No: in the poor man we must see humility honored, in the rich man pride condemned.

Here is a concise proof that what earned the rich man agony was not wealth, but pride: we know for certain that the poor man was carried away into Abraham's embrace, but scripture says that Abraham himself had plenty of gold and silver here below, and was a rich man while on earth.[11] If everyone who is rich is snatched away into hell, how did it happen that Abraham had gone ahead of the poor man, ready to welcome him into his embrace when he arrived? But Abraham amid all his riches was poor and humble, in awe of the Lord's every command, and obedient. How little store he set by those riches of his is evident from the way he was ready to immolate his son to the Lord when ordered to, though it was for that son that he was saving his wealth.[12]

Learn to be destitute and poor, whether you have possessions in this world or not, for you may find a proud beggar, or again a man of property confessing to God. God thwarts the proud,[13] whether they are clothed from head to foot in silk or in rags, but he grants grace to the humble, whether they own this world's wealth or nothing at all. God's scrutiny is conducted within: there he weighs, there he examines. You do not see God's balance, but your thoughts are lifted onto it. Notice where the psalmist based his claim to be heard, what he pointed to as justification for his plea for a hearing: *because I am needy and destitute.* Be careful lest you fail to be needy and destitute, for if you are not, you will not be heard. Whatever there is around you or inside you that could be a ground for presumption, throw it away from you. Let God be your whole presumption; let your neediness be for him, that you may be filled with him; for whatever else you may have without him will leave you still more profoundly empty.

Verse 2. The Church can claim to be holy

4. *Keep guard over my soul, for I am holy.* I do not know if anyone has the right to say, *I am holy,* except the One who was sinless in this world, he who committed no sin but forgives them all.[14] We recognize whose voice it is that

---

10. See Lk 16:19-31.
11. See Gn 13:2.6.
12. See Gn 22.
13. See Jas 4:6; 1 Pt 5:5.
14. *Peccatorum omnium non commissor, sed dimissor.*

prays, *I am holy, keep guard over my soul*, and, of course, he says it in that form
of a servant which he had assumed. For where his flesh was present, so too was
his soul. It was not the case, as some alleged,[15] that he was simply flesh plus the
Word; he was flesh, and soul, and the Word; and this whole Christ was Son of
God, one Christ, one Savior, in the form of God equal to the Father, and in the
form of a servant head of his Church. It is his voice, then, that I recognize when I
hear the words, *I am holy*, but must I exclude mine from his? No; I can be certain
that when he speaks, he speaks inseparably from his body. Shall even I then dare
to say, *I am holy*? If I meant "holy" in the sense of making others holy and
standing in no need of anyone to sanctify me, I should be arrogant to claim it, and
a liar; but if it means "holy" in the sense of "made holy," as scripture uses the
phrase, *Be holy, because I am holy* (Lv 19:2), then yes, let Christ's body dare to
say it, let this one single person who cries from the ends of the earth[16] dare to say
with his head and in subordination to his head, *I am holy*, for he has received the
grace of holiness, the grace of baptism and the forgiveness of sins. *This is what
you were*, says the apostle, listing many sins both slight and grave, common and
horrifying. *This is what you were, but you have been through the waters, and
made holy* (1 Cor 6:11). If he says they have been made holy, each one of the
faithful can claim, *I am holy*. This is not the pride of a conceited person, but the
confession of one who is not ungrateful. If you say you are holy by your own
efforts, you are proud; on the other hand, if you, faithful in Christ, a member of
Christ, deny that you are holy, you are ungrateful. When the apostle was
rebuking the proud, he did not say, "You have nothing," but, *What have you that
you did not receive?* (1 Cor 4:7). You were not being chided for pretending to
have something you did not have, but because you were trying to make out that
something you have came to you from yourself. Recognize, rather, that you do
possess it, and that you have nothing as from yourself; in that way you will be
neither proud nor ungrateful. Say to your God, "I am holy, because you have
sanctified me, because I have received holiness, not because I had it already;
because you endowed me with it, not because I earned it."

   You could be in danger of dishonoring our Lord Jesus Christ himself if you
fail to do this. If all Christians, all believers, and all who have been baptized in
him have put on Christ like a garment, as the apostle declares, *As many of you as*

---

15. The Apollinarians. Apollinarius, who became Bishop of Laodicea c. A.D.360, was a friend of
    Athanasius and, like the latter, concerned to assert the full divinity of Christ, and the unity of
    godhead and humanity in him. Despite confusion over the meaning of such terms as "person"
    and "nature," it appears that Apollinarius denied the existence of a human spirit in Christ, this
    being rendered unnecessary by the presence of the Logos. The Christ of Apollinarius' system
    was therefore fully and perfectly God, but not fully man. Apollinarius seceded from the
    Church, and his teaching was condemned at the Council of Constantinople in 381. The
    orthodox Fathers loved to repeat the axiom, "What was not assumed [by God the Son] was not
    healed."
16. See Ps 60:3(61:2).

have been baptized in Christ, have clothed yourselves in Christ (Gal 3:27), if they have become members of his body and then say that they are not holy, they are insulting the head himself by casting doubt on the holiness of his members. Take stock of your position, and claim your dignity, the dignity that flows from your head. You were indeed formerly in darkness, *but now you are light in the Lord* (Eph 5:8). Yes, says scripture, *you were darkness once*, but did you remain darkness? Was it for this that the Enlightener came, to leave you in darkness still, and not rather that in him you might become light?

Let each individual Christian say, then, or, rather, let the entire body of Christ say, let it cry out as it endures troubles, manifold temptations, and scandals beyond counting all over the world—let it say, *Keep guard over my soul, for I am holy; save your servant who hopes in you, O my God.* This holy person is not proud, you see, because he hopes in the Lord.

Verse 3. The whole Christ perpetually cries to God

5. *Have mercy on me, Lord, for I have cried to you all day long.* Not just on one day; *all day long* must be understood as throughout time. From the day when Christ's body began to groan in the wine press, until the end of the world when the pressures have passed away, this one person groans and cries out to God, and we, each of us in our measure, add our own contribution to the clamor of the whole body. You have cried out during your days, and your days have expired; someone else took your place and cried out in his days; you here, he there, she somewhere else. The body of Christ cries out all day long, as its members give place to each other and succeed each other. One single person spans the ages to the end of time, and it is still the members of Christ who go on crying out, though some of them are already at rest in him, others are raising their cry now, others will cry out when we have gone to rest, and others again after them. God hears the voice of Christ's entire body saying, *I have cried to you all day long.* But our head is at the Father's right hand to intercede for us;[17] some of his members he welcomes, others he chastises, others he is cleansing, others he consoles, others he is creating, others calling, others recalling, others correcting, others reinstating.

Verses 4-5. Longing for the sweetness of God amid earth's bitterness

6. *Give delight to the soul of your servant; to you have I lifted my soul, O Lord.* Give it delight, because I have lifted it to you. It was on earth, and felt earth's bitterness. Fearing that it would wither away in bitterness and lose all the sweetness of your grace, I lifted it up to you. Give it delight in your presence; you alone

---

17. See Rom 8:34.

are delight, and the world is full of bitterness. Christ certainly has good reason to warn his members to raise their hearts on high. Let them hearken to him and do so, let them lift up to him what is unhappy on earth. Our hearts will not go moldy, if raised up to him. If you had grain down in the basement, you would move it higher up, lest it rot. You find a better place for your grain: will you allow your heart to molder on earth? If you think it right to take your grain upstairs, lift your heart to heaven.

"How can I?" you ask. "What kind of ropes, pulleys, ladders, would be needed?" The steps are your dispositions, the way there, your will. You rise up by loving, and sink down by neglecting to love. You may be standing on earth, but you are in heaven if you choose God as your love. The heart is not lifted up after the manner of the body: the body has to change its place if it is to be raised up, but for the heart to be lifted up, it is the will that must be changed. *To you have I lifted up my soul, O Lord.*

God's patience: a realistic description of prayer

7. *For you, O Lord, are kind and patient,* and so I ask you to give delight to my soul. The psalmist was disgusted by the bitterness of earthly things and longed to taste sweetness; he sought a fountain of sweetness, but did not find it on earth. Whichever way he turned, he always found scandals, terrors, troubles and temptations. In what human being was security to be found? To whom could one look for joy, with any confidence? Clearly not to oneself, so how much less to anyone else? Other people are either bad, in which case we must put up with them and hope they can be changed, or good, and then we may set our love upon them, but a love mixed with apprehension that, since they are prone to change, they may deteriorate. With the former, their malice causes us bitterness of soul; with the latter, anxiety and fear produce a like effect, for one who is walking well may slip. Whichever way we turn, we find bitterness in earthly things, and nothing to sweeten us unless we raise ourselves up to God, for *you, O Lord, are kind and patient.*

What does *patient* call to mind? You go on carrying me, Lord, until your work in me is finished. Truly, my brothers and sisters, in my human condition and from my own human experience I will speak to yours; let each of us bring our own heart under scrutiny and examine ourselves without flattery or blandishment, for nothing is more foolish than to cajole and deceive oneself. Let each one closely observe what goes on in the human heart, and see how our very prayers are for the most part so hindered by idle thoughts that the heart can scarcely stand before its God. It wants to take hold of itself so that it may stand, but somehow it runs away from itself, and can find no fence to shut itself in, nor barricades to constrain its flightiness and tendency to wander, so that it may stand still and be delighted with its God. Scarcely one such prayer comes its way amid a great deal of praying. Each of us might say that this is what happens to me, but surely not to anyone else, but for the fact that in the divine scriptures we find David praying in a certain place, and saying to God, *I have found my heart, Lord, so that I can make this prayer to you* (2 Sm 7:27). He said he had found his heart: it looks as though he was accustomed to seeing it escape from him, and having to pursue it as it fled, and finding himself unable to catch it, and crying out to God, *My heart forsook me* (Ps 39:13(40:12)).

When I consider the psalmist's words, *you are kind and patient*, in the light of this experience, my brothers and sisters, I think I can see what is meant here by "patient." *Give delight to the soul of your servant; to you have I lifted up my soul, for you are kind and patient*. I think I can see that he described God as patient because he puts up with all this from us, and still waits hopefully for a prayer from us so that he may make us perfect. When we give him one he accepts it gratefully, and hearkens to it; he does not remember all the others that we may have poured out confusedly, but accepts that one which we ourselves could hardly detect.

Imagine a man whose friend has begun a conversation with him. He wants to reply to his friend's remarks, but then he sees his friend turning away from him and saying something to someone else. Who would tolerate such behavior? Or suppose you appeal to a judge, and arrange with him to hear you in a certain place, and then as you are addressing him you suddenly brush him aside and begin to chatter to your friend, will he put up with you? Yet God puts up with the hearts of all those people who say their prayers while thinking about all sorts of things. I will not even mention evil thoughts; I am leaving out of consideration thoughts that sometimes run on perverse lines, abhorrent to God. Simply to think about irrelevant matters is to dishonor him with whom you have begun to converse. Your prayer is a conversation with God: when you read, God is speaking to you; when you pray, you are speaking to God.

What are we to conclude, then? That there is no hope for the human race, and that if any thought sneaks into the mind of someone praying, and interrupts the prayer, that person is already fit for damnation? If we say that, brothers and sisters, I do not see what hope is left for us. Yet because there is hope for us in turning to God, because his mercy is great, let us say to him, *Give delight to your servant; to you have I lifted up my soul, O Lord*. How did I lift it up? As best I could, insofar as you gave me strength, insofar as I managed to catch my fugitive soul. And then imagine God replying, "It eluded you because every time you stood before me you let your mind run on so many idle and inappropriate subjects, and scarcely offered me any firm, stable prayer." *You are kind, Lord, and patient*; patient, because you go on tolerating me. I collapse, because I am sick; cure me and I will stand; steady me, and I will stand steady. But until you have done that you bear with me, *for you are kind, Lord, and patient*.

Pray to God to give you himself

8. *And exceedingly merciful.* Not just merciful, but *exceedingly merciful,* for abundant as is our iniquity, even so is your mercy abundant. *Exceedingly merciful to all who call upon you*: how can it be, then, that scripture often tells us, *They will call, but I will not listen to them* (Prv 1:28), when it is certain that you are *merciful to all who call upon you*? How can it be—unless some people who call do not call upon God? Of them scripture says, *They have not called upon God* (Ps 52:6(53:4)); they call indeed, but not on God. You invoke[18] whatever you love; you invoke whatever you "call into" yourself, you invoke what you want to come to you. Now, if your motive in calling upon God is that money may come to you, or an inheritance come to you, or worldly rank come to you, you are invoking, or calling into yourself, the things you want to come to you, but you are making God the accomplice of your greed, not the hearer of your desires. God for you is good only if he gives you what you want. But think: if you wish for something bad, will he not be more merciful in withholding it? No, you go further, and think God is nothing to you if he does not give it. "How earnestly I have begged him, how often I have begged him, and I have not been heard!"

So what were you asking? For the death of your enemy, perhaps? And suppose he was asking God for yours! The God who created you created him too; you are human, and so is your enemy. But God is the judge; he hears both of you, but answers neither. You are downcast because your petition against him was not granted; you should be glad that his petition against you was not.

"But that was not what I was asking," you object. "I did not request my enemy's death, but my son's life. What was wrong with praying for that?" Nothing, to your way of thinking. But what if he was snatched away so that malice might not corrupt his mind?[19] "No," you say, "he was a sinner. That was why I wanted him to live, so that he could be corrected." You were hoping that he would live, in order to improve; what if God knew that if he lived, he would only get worse? How do you know which was better for him, to die or to survive? And if you do not know, go back to you own heart, and leave the decision to God.

"But then what am I to do?" you ask. "What shall I pray for?" What are you to pray for? Pray for what the Lord taught you to pray for; pray as your heavenly teacher instructed you, Call upon God as God, love God as God; nothing is better than he is, so desire God himself, hunger for God. Listen to someone invoking God in another psalm: *One thing have I asked of the Lord, and that will I seek after.* And what is he asking? *To live in the Lord's house all the days of my life.* What for? *That I may find delight in contemplating the Lord* (Ps 26(27):4). If you want to be a lover of God, then, choose him from the bottom of your heart and

---

18. Latin *invoco*, call into, call upon, invoke, throughout these lines.
19. See Wis 4:11.

with the utmost sincerity, love him with chaste longing, burn for him, thirst for him. You will find nothing better, nothing more joyful, nothing more lasting, than God. What could be more lasting than what lasts for ever? You need not fear that he will one day vanish away from you, for he it is who ensures that you do not vanish. If you call upon God as God, have no anxiety: you are heard, and to you this verse applies, *You, Lord, are exceedingly merciful to all who call upon you.*

9. Do not object, then, "He did not give me this or that." Return to your conscience, weigh it in a balance, question it, do not let it off lightly. If you did truly call upon God, you may be certain that if he perhaps withheld from you some temporal good that you wanted, he did so because it would not have profited you. Let your heart, your Christian heart, your faithful heart, be built up by this experience, my brothers and sisters; do not grow angry with God in your disappointment, as though you had been cheated of your longings, for it does you no good to kick against the goad.[20] Hurry back to the scriptures. The devil's prayer is heard, and the apostle's is not: what do you think of that? What do I mean—demons are heard? Yes, they begged to enter the pigs, and they were allowed to.[21] The devil himself heard? Yes, he sought to have Job delivered to him to be tempted, and this was granted.[22] But when was the apostle not heard? *To make sure that I would not grow conceited over these great revelations*, he says, *a sting of the flesh was sent to me, a messenger of Satan to buffet me. Three times I begged the Lord to take it away from me, but he said to me, "My grace is sufficient for you, for my power finds complete scope in weakness"* (2 Cor 12:7-9). So God heard the plea of one whom he willed to be lost, and did not hear that of the man he willed to heal. A sick person likewise begs many things from the physician which the physician does not grant; he will not accede to the patient's whims, because he means to satisfy the real will to health.

Take God as your physician. Beg him to give you health and salvation,[23] and he himself will be your salvation. Do not pray for external health merely, but for that health, that salvation, which is himself; pray that you may never again be attracted to any kind of health apart from him, but make the prayer of another psalm your own: *Say to my soul, "I am your salvation"* (Ps 34(35):3). What does it ultimately matter to you how he answers, as long as he gives himself to you? Do you want him to give himself to you? What if his reason for not wanting you to have the thing you want is that he intends to give you himself? He is shifting obstacles out of the way, so that he may come into your home.

---

20. See Acts 9:5.
21. See Mk 5:12-13.
22. See Jb 1:11-12; 2:5-6.
23. *Salus.*

Think, my brothers and sisters, reflect on the good things God gives to sinners, and infer from them what he is keeping in reserve for his servants. He gives the sky and the earth to sinners who blaspheme him every day; he gives
) them fountains, crops, good health, children, wealth and plenitude. God alone is the giver of all these good things. If he gives such gifts to sinners, what do you think he is keeping for his faithful? Could you think him so niggardly as to hold nothing in reserve for the good, when he gives such gifts to the wicked? Far from it: he is reserving for them not earth, but heaven. Or perhaps I am understating it when I say, "heaven," for he is reserving himself, who made heaven. Heaven is beautiful, yet he who fashioned it is more beautiful still. "But I can see the heavens, and I do not see him," you complain. You have eyes capable of seeing heaven; you do not yet have a heart that can see the Creator of heaven. But that is why he came from heaven to earth, to cleanse our hearts, so that he who made both heaven and earth could be seen.

Obviously, though, you must await your healing with patience. What remedies he will apply to cure you, he knows; what surgery, what cauterizations, he knows. You brought your sickness on yourself by sinning; he has come not merely to coddle you, but to cut and burn. Do you not see what dire treatment people submit to at the hands of doctors, all at the promise of a mere man who offers uncertain prospects? "You will get better," says the doctor, "you will get better if I cut this." A human doctor says it to a human patient. Neither the one who makes the claim nor the one who listens has any certainty, for the doctor who speaks to a human patient did not make human beings, nor does he perfectly understand what goes on in the human body. Yet the patient believes in the words of this man who is even more ignorant that he is himself of what is going on in him; he submits his limbs, allows himself to be tied down, or in many cases is cut or cauterized without even being tied. Perhaps he gets a few days' health, but after being healed he does not know when he may die. Or perhaps he dies while undergoing treatment; or again the treatment may fail to cure him. But when has God ever promised anything, and let us down?

Verses 6-7. Praying amid ever-present trouble. Even immortality would not satisfy us, without the vision of God

10. *Fix my prayer in your ears, O Lord*. How very earnest is this man's entreaty! *Fix my prayer in your ears, O Lord*; do not let it drop out of your hearing, but fix it there in your ears. How did he travail, to fix his prayer in God's ears? Let God reply and tell us: "Do you want to fix your prayer in my ears? Then fix my law in your heart." *Fix my prayer in your ears, O Lord, and listen to my voice as I pray.*

11. *On my day of trouble I called to you, because you have heard me*. Yet the reason why you would be disposed to hear me is that *on my day of trouble I*

called to you. A few verses earlier he had said, *I have cried to you all day long*, for all day long I have been in trouble. Let Christians not claim that there is any day when they have not been in trouble. We understand "all day long" to mean "all the time," and all day we are troubled. Does this mean that we have trouble even when things are going well with us? Yes, trouble indeed. Why is that? Because as long as we are in the body, we are on pilgrimage, away from the Lord.[24] However well off we are here, we are not yet in that homeland whither we are hurrying to return. Anyone who enjoys being on pilgrimage is no lover of home; if our homeland is sweet to us, pilgrimage is bitter; and if pilgrimage is bitter, we are in trouble all day and every day. When shall we be free of it? When we are delighted to be at home. *Your right hand will be full of delights for ever. You will fill me with joy in beholding your face, that I may find delight in contemplating the Lord* (Pss 15(16):11; 26(27):4). There labor and groaning will pass away; there will be supplication no longer, but only praise; there we shall sing "Alleluia," there "Amen,"[25] our voices harmonizing with the angels; there will vision be unclouded, love without satiety. As long as you are not there, you see that you are not in a good state. But you have plenty of everything, you say? Plenty of everything you may well have, but ask yourself whether you can be sure it will not all be lost. "But I have now what I did not have earlier. Money has come my way that I did not have before." And perhaps anxiety that you did not have before has come your way too; it may be that the poorer you were, the more carefree. But suppose, after all, ample means are at your disposal, the wealth of this world flows around you, and assurance is given you that these things will not be lost; and then God says to you from on high, "You will live for ever amid these things, they will always abide with you, but you will not see my face."

Think about that, not in terms of the body's cravings but in the spirit;[26] let your heart tell you what to make of it; let the hope, faith and charity already born in you tell you the answer. Well now, if we received the assurance that we would live for ever in a profusion of worldly goods, and God were to say to us, "You will not see my face," would we rejoice in those good things? Perhaps there might be someone who would choose to find joy in them, and declare, "I have plenty of these things, this is fine for me; I am not looking for anything else." Such a person has not yet begun to be a lover of God, nor yet begun to heave a pilgrim's sighs. No, no, far be that from us! Let all these seductions be put to flight, all delusive blandishments be routed; let all those daily taunts, *Where is your God?* (Ps 41:11(42:10)), be far from us. Let us pour out our souls within us, and confess with tears, groaning as we confess to him and sighing in our wretchedness. Whatever is available to us apart from our God has no sweetness in it; we

---

24. See 2 Cor 5:6.
25. See Rv 19:4.
26. Or perhaps "... look not to the body's cravings but to the Spirit."

do not want any of his gifts if he who gave them all does not give us himself. *Fix my prayer in your ears, O Lord, and listen to my voice as I pray. On my day of trouble I called to you, because you heard me.*

Verse 8. God is incomparable, and only he is to be worshiped

12. *There is no one like you among the gods, O Lord.* What is he saying? *There is no one like you among the gods, O Lord.* Let the pagans fashion for themselves all the gods they want; let them employ silversmiths, goldsmiths, burnishers and sculptors, and let them make gods. But what kind of gods? Gods that have eyes but cannot see, and all the other defects the psalm lists.[27] "But," objects the pagan, "we do not worship them. No, of course we do not worship them; they serve as signs." So what do you worship? Something even worse. *The gods of the heathen are demons* (Ps 95(96):5). What about that? "No, we do not worship demons either," they reply. But you have nothing else in your temples! Nothing but a demon inspires your soothsayers. What else can you allege? "We worship the angels; we regard the angels as divine." Then it is obvious that you do not understand angels. Angels worship the one God, and they do not look favorably on mortals who try to worship them rather than God; we find examples of angels, when honored, forbidding[28] humans to do so, and directing them to worship God instead.[29]

But whether it is angels that they claim to worship, or humans (because, after all, scripture says, *I have spoken, and you are gods, sons of the Most High, all of you* (Ps 81(82):6)), it remains true that *there is no one like you among the gods, O Lord.* Whatever else the human mind may think of, nothing that is made is like the Maker. Everything in the universe, except God himself, was made by God. Who could conceive an adequate idea of the difference between him who made it, and what was made? This is why the psalmist said, *There is no one like you among the gods, O Lord*, but did not attempt to state how different God is, because that cannot be expressed. Try to understand, beloved: God is beyond all utterance; we can more easily state what he is not than what he is.[30] You think of the earth: God is not that; you think of the sea: God is not that; of all things on earth, humans and animals: God is not that; of all the creatures in the sea or flying through the air: God is not that; of everything that shines in the heavens—stars, sun and moon: God is not that; of heaven itself: God is not that. Think of angels,

---

27. See Ps 113B(115):5-7.
28. Or "angels of high rank forbidding ...."
29. See Rv 19:10.
30. The tradition of apophatic theology (that is, denying that various human concepts of perfection can be applied to God) was already represented in Augustine's older contemporary, Saint Gregory of Nyssa, and was to be powerfully developed in the writings of Pseudo-Dionysius in the late fifth century. God ultimately transcends all negation and affirmation.

virtues, powers, archangels, thrones, principalities and dominations: God is none of these. What is he? I have not been able to say; all I could say is what he is not. Do you ask what he is? He is what *eye has not seen, nor ear heard, nor human heart conceived* (1 Cor 2:9). Do you suppose the tongue could utter it, when not even the heart can conceive it? *There is no one like you among the gods, O Lord, nor any work to compare with yours.*

Verses 9-10. The Church is one and universal

13. *All the nations you have created will come and worship before you, O Lord.* This verse proclaimed the Church-to-be: *all the nations you have created.* If there is any nation God has not created, it will not worship him; but there is no nation he did not make, because he created Adam and Eve as the fountainhead of all peoples, and from them all nations are descended. So God made all nations. *All the nations you have created will come and worship before you, O Lord.* When was that said? When no one was worshipping before him except a few holy people in the one race of the Hebrews; then it was prophesied, and now we see the prophecy fulfilled: *all the nations you have created will come and worship before you, O Lord.* When those events were foretold, they were not seen but only believed in; why should we contest them now, when they are plain to see? *All the nations you have created will come and worship before you, O Lord, and they will give glory to your name.*

14. *For you are great and you do wondrous things; you alone are great, O God.* No one else has the right to call himself great. In the future there were to be some who would claim to be great, and to refute them the psalm says, *You alone are great, O God.* Are we saying anything significant to God, when we say that God alone is great? Is there anyone who does not know this? But there would be some people later who would call themselves great, and make God out to be small, and it is against them that the psalm declares, *You alone are great, O God.* And indeed, it is what you say that is proved true, not the claims of those who call themselves great. What did God say through his Spirit? *All the nations you have created will come and worship before you, O Lord.* Now, what does some fellow who calls himself great have to say to that? "Nonsense," he says. "God is not worshiped among all nations. All other nations have fallen away, and only Africa is left." So you say, you who call yourself great, but he who alone is great, our God, says something different. What does this sole great God tell us? *All the nations you have created will come and worship before you, O Lord.* And I can see the fulfillment of his prediction, the prediction of the only God, of him who is great; so let that man fall silent who is falsely called great. His scornful refusal to be small shows how false is his claim to be great. Who disdains to be small? The one who made such a claim. But the Lord said, *Whoever wishes to be greater among you will be your servant* (Mt 20:26-27). If that man were prepared to be a

servant to his brethren, he would not separate them from their mother,[31] but since he wants to be great, and is unwilling to be little for the sake of salvation, God (who thwarts the proud but gives grace to the humble,[32] because he alone is great) fulfills all his predictions and confounds those who blaspheme him. They who proclaim that the Church has disappeared from all the world, and remains only in Africa,[33] do indeed blaspheme Christ. If you were to say to such an opponent, "You are about to lose your country house," you might feel the weight of his fist, yet he alleges that Christ has lost the inheritance he redeemed with his own blood! Look at the dishonor he thereby does to Christ, my brothers and sisters. Scripture testifies that *a populous realm is a king's glory, but a shrinking nation is sadness to its leader* (Prv 14:28). You are insulting Christ, therefore, when you say that his people has been reduced to such tiny proportions. Were you born for this, do you call yourself a Christian for this, to begrudge Christ his glory? You flaunt his sign on your forehead, but you have lost him from your heart. *A populous realm is a king's glory*: acknowledge your king, give him glory, allow him his populous realm. "What populous realm shall I give him?" you ask. Well, do not give it from your own heart, at any rate, if you want to give it aright. "From where, then?" you will ask. Give it from the psalmist's words: *All the nations you have created will come and worship before you, O Lord.* Say that, confess that, and you have assigned to him his populous realm, for in him who is one, all nations are one nation, and that is unity indeed. There is one Church and many churches, but those many churches are the one Church; so too those many nations form one nation: formerly they were nations, many in number, but now they are one nation. Why? Because there is in them one faith, one hope, one charity, one expectation. In any case, how could it not be a single nation, if it has but one homeland? Its homeland is in heaven, its homeland is Jerusalem; anyone who is not a citizen of Jerusalem does not belong to the nation, but anyone who is a citizen is found within the people of God. And this nation stretches from east to west, from the north and the sea, throughout the four quarters of the wide world. This is what the Lord says: from east and west, from the north and the sea, give glory to God.[34] This he foretold, and this he has brought about, for he alone is great. Let the man who has refused to be small stop insulting the sole Great One, for there cannot be two greats—God and Donatus.

---

31. That is, their mother the Church. Donatus, eponymous leader of the schism, is the object of Augustine's polemic in these lines, and is named at the end of the paragraph. See note on Donatus, in Exposition of Psalm 10,1.
32. See Jas 4:6; 1 Pt 5:5.
33. The Donatist church of the pure.
34. See Is 24:14-15.

Verse 11. Lead us in Christ, the Way, the Truth, and the Life, in fear and gladness

15. *Lead me in your way, Lord, and I will walk in your truth.* Your way and your truth are your life, which is Christ. The Body is on its way to him, but also draws its life from him: *I am the Way, the Truth, and the Life* (Jn 14:6). *Lead me in your way, Lord.* In what way? *I will walk in your truth.* It is one thing for him to bring you to the way, and another for him to lead you along it. Look at human-kind—everywhere poor, everywhere in need of help. Those who are adrift from the way are not Christians, or are not yet Catholics; they must be led to the way. But once they have been guided to the way, and have become Catholics in Christ, they must be led along by him in the way itself, to make sure they do not fall. They are now walking in the way; there is no doubt of that. *Lead me in your way, Lord.* I am certainly on the way, Lord, your way, but lead me in it. *And I will walk in your truth*: with you to lead me I shall not go astray, but I will if you let go of me.

Pray, then, that he will not let you go, but will lead you to the very end. How does he lead? By constantly admonishing, constantly giving you his hand. *To whom has the arm of the Lord been revealed?* (Is 53:1). By giving us his Christ, he gives us his hand; in giving his hand, he gives his Christ. He leads us to his way by leading us to his Christ; he leads us in his way by leading us in his Christ. But Christ is the truth. *Lead me in your way*, then, *Lord, and I will walk in your truth*, in him who said, *I am the Way, the Truth, and the Life*. If you lead us along the way and in the truth, where else but to life will you bring us? You lead us in him, and to him. *Lead me in your way, Lord, and I will walk in your truth.*

16. *Let my heart be so gladdened as to fear your name.* There is room for fear in gladness, then. But how can there be gladness, if fear is present? Is not fear usually a painful experience? One day we shall have gladness free from all fear, but our gladness is tempered by fear at the present time; we do not yet enjoy full security, and therefore we are not perfectly gladdened either. If we have no glad-ness at all, we pine away; if we are completely secure, we exult in the wrong way. May God then both sprinkle gladness upon us, and strike fear into us, so that he may lead us from this sweet gladness to the resting-place where we shall be secure, but by inspiring fear may save us from exulting to our harm and aban-doning the way. Accordingly another psalm prays, *Serve the Lord in reverence, and rejoice before him with awe* (Ps 2:11), and Paul the apostle likewise warns, *Work out your own salvation in fear and trembling; for it is God who is at work in you* (Phil 2:12-13).

Whenever our undertakings prosper, my brothers and sisters, we should be the more fearful; what you deem prosperous is the more fraught with tempta-tions. An inheritance falls to you, an ample fortune comes your way, or you are awash with some kind of happiness: these things are temptations; take care that they do not corrupt you. The same is true even when things prosper for us in the affairs of Christ and true Christian charity. Perhaps you have won over your wife, who belonged to the Donatist sect; perhaps your children, who were pagans, have come to believe; perhaps you have won over a friend of yours who tried to lure you to the theatre with him, and you persuaded him to church instead; perhaps some opponent, who was hostile to you and savage in his fury, has given up that fury, grown gentle and acknowledged God, and no longer rails at you but joins you in denouncing evil—all such happenings make us glad. What else would we rejoice about, if not over things like these? What other joys have we? Yet there are plentiful troubles too, and trials, and quarrels, and schisms, and other evils. This world cannot be without them, *until iniquity shall pass away* (Ps 56:2(57:1)). Our rejoicing must not make us careless; our hearts must be so gladdened as to fear the name of the Lord, lest they look for gladness elsewhere, and be stricken from elsewhere. Let us not expect security while we are on pilgrimage. When we do find ourselves wanting it, what we are looking for is bodily sluggishness rather than personal security. *Let my heart be so glad-dened as to fear your name.*

Verses 12-13. Tentative speculation on the regions of hell

17. *I will praise you, Lord my God, with all my heart, and glorify your name for ever, for great is your mercy upon me, and you have rescued my soul from a deeper hell.* You must not resent it, my brothers and sisters, if I do not expound to you with any certainty these words I have just spoken. I am only a man. I dare to say only as much as is granted to me from the holy scriptures, and nothing from myself. I have not yet experienced hell,[35] neither have you. Perhaps there is another route, one that does not pass through hell. These matters are obscure. But since scripture, which cannot be contradicted, says, *You have delivered my soul from a deeper hell*, we infer that there must be two hells, an upper and a lower, for how could a hell be called "deeper" unless there is another one higher up? The former would not be called deeper, except by comparison with the upper region.

It seems, then, brothers and sisters, that there is a heavenly region where the angels dwell. There life is full of joys beyond telling, there is immortality, there incorruption, and there, thanks to the gift and grace of God, all things abide for ever. This region is the upper part of the universe. Now, if that is the heavenly part, our region is the earthly part, the home of flesh and blood, of corruptibility, birth and mortality, departures and new beginnings, mutability and inconstancy, fears, cravings, horrors, precarious joys, frail hope and fleeting fortunes. I think that this whole region is unworthy of comparison with that heaven of which I

---

35. Or "the underworld," corresponding to the Hebrew *she'ol*, the place of the dead.

was speaking just now; and if our region cannot be compared with that other, we may call that other region the upper, and ours the lower. Where shall we go when, after death, we depart from this place? Surely to a yet deeper region, below this lower part where we live in the flesh in the time of our mortality. The apostle tells us that *the body is a dead thing by reason of sin* (Rom 8:10). So if people are dead even here, small wonder that our world, overflowing with dead people, is called a hell, for the apostle does not say, "the body is about to die," but *the body is a dead thing.* Our bodies do still have some life, admittedly, but in comparison with the bodies we shall have one day, which will be like angelic bodies, human bodies now seem like corpses, though still animated.

Lower again than this underworld of ours there is another, and to it travel the dead. From that hell God has willed to deliver our souls, even by sending his Son there. Yes, brethren, it is true: the Son of God was sent to save both these underworlds, to bring freedom in every place that exists. At his birth he was sent to our underworld, by his death to that other. This is why we can be certain of hearing his voice in a psalm, saying, *You will not leave my soul in hell* (Ps 15(16):10); this is no ignorant conjecture, but an interpretation authorized by the apostle.[36] We may therefore take the verse, *you have delivered my soul from a deeper hell,* either as spoken by Christ himself, or as spoken by our own voices through Christ our Lord, because he penetrated even into hell in order that we should not remain there.

18. I have another opinion to put before you. Possibly within hell itself there is another still deeper region, into which wicked people who have sinned most gravely are pushed, for we cannot say with any certainty whether there may not have been some places in hell where Abraham had not been. The Lord had not yet visited hell to rescue the souls of all the holy people of old, yet Abraham was at rest there, and when a rich man was being tormented in hell, he lifted his eyes and saw Abraham. He could not have seen him by gazing upwards unless Abraham was higher up and he below. And when he put his request to Abraham, *Father Abraham, send Lazarus to dip his finger in water and drip it onto my tongue, for I am in agony in this flame,* what did Abraham reply? *My son,* he said, *remember that you received good things in your lifetime, but only bad things fell to Lazarus. Now he is at rest here, while you are tormented. Furthermore, there is a great, immovable abyss between us and you, so that we cannot cross over to you, nor can anyone come from there to us* (Lk 16:24-26).

It may be, then, that the psalmist who is praying here found himself poised between these two hells, in one of which the souls of the just have found peace,

---

36. By "the apostle" he usually means Paul, so he may be thinking of Paul's sermon at Pisidian Antioch, where reference is made to the same psalm-verse, though these words are not quoted; see Acts 13:35. They are explicitly quoted in Peter's Pentecost sermon, Acts 2:27.31. In both cases they are interpreted of Christ's resurrection from the abode of the dead.

while in the other the souls of the godless are tormented. He was already a member of the body of Christ, and so he prayed with Christ's voice, and when he declared that God had delivered his soul from the pit of hell, he did so because he knew he had freed himself from the kind of sins that could have brought him to it. It is as though a doctor saw that you were in imminent danger of falling ill, perhaps in consequence of some work, and said to you, "Take it easy, follow my instructions, rest, eat these foods. If you do not, you will be ill." Now if you do as he advises and keep your good health, you have reason to say to the doctor, "You saved me from that illness," not because you already had it, but because you would have had it. Or suppose someone is facing serious charges and is to be committed to prison; then another person comes along and pleads in his defense. What does he say, when he thanks his defense counsel? "You rescued me from prison." Again, a debtor was due to be hanged; someone paid his debts, and he is said to have been saved from hanging. The persons concerned had not yet been overtaken by calamity, but because their predicament was such that they inevitably would have been, if help had not been available, they rightly assert that they have been freed from a fate which, thanks to their deliverers, was not allowed to befall them.

Well then, brothers and sisters, whichever interpretation may be the right one, you must regard me in this instance as a careful student of God's word, not as someone who asserts his own opinion with undue confidence.[37]

Verses 14-15. The Church is persecuted, as Christ was

19. *O God, those who disobey your law have risen up against me.* Who are these people who disobey the law? Not the pagans, for they never received it. No one disobeys what he has not received; the apostle says quite clearly, *Where there is no law, there is no violation of it* (Rom 4:15). So by those who disobey the law the psalm means those who violate it. And whom shall we understand them to be, my brothers and sisters? If we take these words as spoken by our Lord, those who disobeyed were the Jews. *Those who disobey your law have risen up against me*; they did not keep the law themselves, but accused Christ of not keeping it. They have risen up against me, those who disobey your law: what the Lord endured we know. Do you think his body endures nothing of the sort today? How could that be? *If they have called the master of the household Beelzebub, how much more his servants? A disciple is not above his teacher, nor a servant above his master* (Mt 10:25.24). The body too suffers from those who disobey the law, and they rise up against Christ's body just as much as against him. Who, then, are these people, who disobey the law? Surely the Jews do not

---

37. Sections 17 and 18 are found also in Eugippius LXXXVI, 101.

dare now to rise against Christ? No; nor do they give us much trouble, though they have not yet come to believe, nor yet recognized their salvation.

It is bad Christians who rise up against the body of Christ, and his body has to suffer daily harassment from them. All those schisms, all the heresies, and all those who live disgracefully within the Church, who foist their evil conduct on those who lead good lives, drawing them into their own company and corrupting good morals by bad society[38] — all these are the people who *disobey the law* and *have risen up against me*. Let every devout soul, every Christian soul, say this. Anyone who does not endure it will not say so. But if a soul is Christian, it knows that it suffers; if it recognizes the suffering in itself, let it recognize its own voice here; if it is a stranger to such suffering, it must disclaim this voice. But in order not to remain a stranger to the suffering, let it walk in the narrow way[39] and begin to live a God-fearing life in Christ; then it will inevitably suffer persecution, for the apostle teaches that *all who want to live devoted to God in Christ suffer persecution* (2 Tm 3:12).

O God, those who disobey your law have risen up against me, and the synagogue of the powerful sought my life. The synagogue of the powerful means the congregation of the proud. The synagogue of the powerful rose up against our head, the Lord Jesus Christ, shouting with one voice, *Crucify him, crucify him!* (Jn 19:6). Of them another psalm says, *The teeth of human beings are weapons and arrows, their tongue a sharp sword* (Ps 56:5(57:4)). They did not strike him, but they shouted; by shouting they scourged him, by shouting they crucified him. The shouting crowd got what it wanted when the Lord was crucified. *The synagogue of the powerful sought my life.*

They did not set you before their eyes. How did they not? They did not see that he was God. Even so, they should have shown him mercy as a man; they should have conducted themselves in accordance with what they did see. Even supposing he had not been God, he was still a man, and did he deserve to die? Spare the man, and recognize God in him.

20. *You, Lord God, are compassionate and merciful, long-suffering and very merciful and true.* Why is he said to be *long-suffering and very merciful* and *compassionate*? Because while hanging on the cross he prayed, *Father, forgive them, for they do not know what they are doing* (Lk 23:34). With whom did he plead? For whom did he plead? Who made the plea, and in what circumstances? The Son pleaded with the Father; the crucified pleaded on behalf of the godless; he pleaded not merely under verbal abuse but as mortal injuries were inflicted on him, as he hung on a cross. It seems as though his arms were stretched out for this very purpose, that he might pray for them by that gesture, that his prayer might

---

38. See 1 Cor 15:33.
39. See Mt 7:14.

be directed like incense in the Father's presence, and the lifting up of his hands be an evening sacrifice.[40] He is *long-suffering and very merciful and true.*

Verse 16. *After Christ's patience, his power will be revealed*

21. If you are true, then, *look upon me and have mercy on me; and give authority to your child.*[41] Because you are true, it says, *give authority to your child.* Let the time for patience pass away, and the time for judgment come. In what sense does God *give authority to* his *child?* He does so inasmuch as *the Father judges no one, but has entrusted all judgment to the Son* (Jn 5:22). Risen from the dead, he will come back to earth to judge it himself; he will appear in terrible guise, who seemed once contemptible. He will give proof of his power, who once gave proof of his patience: on the cross patience, at the judgment power. He will be seen as man when he sits as judge, but a man in glory, for as the angels foretold, *he will come again, even as you have seen him go* (Acts 1:11). In that same form he will come to judge, and therefore the wicked too will see him. No vision of the form of God will be granted them, for the gospel testifies, *Blessed are the pure of heart, for they shall see God* (Mt 5:8). Appearing thus in human form, he will say, *Depart into the eternal fire* (Mt 25:41), in accordance with Isaiah's words, *Let the wicked be expelled, and not see the glory of God* (Is 26:13, LXX): let him be expelled, and the vision of God's form be denied him. The wicked will see Christ's human form only, and be debarred from the vision of him who *being in the form of God* is God's equal.[42] Nor will they see that of which scripture also speaks: *In the beginning was the Word, and the Word was with God; he was God* (Jn 1:1), for it follows that, if the Word is God, and the pure of heart are *blessed, because they will see God*, the wicked will obviously not see him, for they are impure of heart. And what are we to infer from the text, *they will gaze on him whom they pierced* (Jn 19:37), except that they will apparently behold Christ's human form so that they may undergo judgment, while only those who are at his right hand will see his divine form? When these latter have been allotted their place at his right, they will hear the invitation, *Come, you who are blessed by my Father, take possession of the kingdom prepared for you since the creation of the world.* But what will be said to the wicked at his left? *Depart from me into the eternal fire which was prepared by my Father for the devil and his angels.* And when the judgment is finished, how does the story end? *Thus the wicked will go into eternal burning, but the righteous into eternal life* (Mt 25:34.41.46), for these will now progress from seeing Christ's human form to the vision of him in the form of God. He testifies that *this is eternal life,*

---

40. See Ps 140(141):2.
41. Or "servant" (*puero tuo*).
42. See Phil 2:6.

that they know you, the one true God, and Jesus Christ, whom you sent (Jn 17:3): you must understand, "who is also himself the one true God," because Father and Son are both the one true God. The sense is "that they may know both you, and Jesus Christ whom you sent, as the one true God." The righteous will not pass to a vision of the Father in which the Son is not to be seen. If the Son were not also to be seen in our vision of his Father, the Son would not have told his disciples that the Son is in the Father, and the Father in the Son. The disciples say to him, *Show us the Father, and that is enough for us*, and he replies, *Have I been all this time with you, and yet you have not known me? Whoever has seen me, Philip, has seen the Father* (Jn 14:8-9). In the vision of the Father the vision of the Son is included, and in the vision of the Son, the vision of the Father also. This is why he went on to say, *Do you not know that I am in the Father, and that the Father is in me?* In other words, when you see me, the Father too is seen; when you see the Father, the Son is seen also. The vision of the Father cannot be separated from that of the Son, for where there is no separation of nature and substance, there can be no separate vision either.

To help you understand that our hearts must be made ready to contemplate the divinity of the Father, Son and Holy Spirit, in which we believe, and by believing cleanse our hearts to make that contemplation possible, the Lord himself says in another passage, *Anyone who cherishes my commandments and keeps them, that is the one who loves me; and whoever loves me will be loved by my Father, and I will love him, and will show myself to him* (Jn 14:21). But were not those to whom he spoke seeing him already? Yes and no: they saw something, but believed something further; they saw a man, but believed him to be God. At the judgment they, along with the wicked, will see our Lord Jesus Christ as man, but after the judgment they will see him as God, without the wicked. *Give authority to your child.*

Children of the handmaiden

22. *And save the son of your handmaiden.* The Lord is the handmaiden's son. What handmaiden is in question here? She who, on being told that he was to be born of her, replied, *Behold the Lord's handmaiden* (Lk 1:38). God did save the son of the handmaiden, who was his own Son too: his Son in the form of God, the handmaiden's son in the form of a servant. From God's handmaiden the Lord was born in the form of a servant, and he prayed, *Save the son of your handmaiden.* Saved he was, from death, by the resurrection of that flesh which had died, as you well know. But to make it clear to you that he is God, and was not raised up by the Father in such a way that he was not raised up by his own power, but that he did also raise his own flesh, he says in the gospel, *Destroy this temple, and in three days I will raise it up again* (Jn 2:19); and lest we misunderstand the

reference, the evangelist adds, *He was speaking of the temple of his body* (Jn 2:21). That was how the handmaiden's son was saved.

Every Christian engrafted into the body of Christ can also say, *Save your handmaiden's son*. Perhaps it is not for us to plead, *Give authority to your child*, because Christ is the Son who received that power. But why should we not ask even that? Were not Christ's servants promised, *You will sit upon twelve thrones, judging the twelve tribes of Israel* (Mt 19:28)? And the servants ask, *Do you not realize that we shall judge angels?* (1 Cor 6:3). Every one of the saints is given authority, and every one of the saints is the child of God's handmaiden. What if someone was born of a pagan mother, and then became a Christian? How can the son or daughter of a pagan mother be called a child of his handmaiden? Because although such a person is born of a pagan according to the flesh, he or she is spiritually a child of the Church. *Save the son of your handmaiden*.

Verse 17. The sign of the resurrection

23. *Give me a promising sign*. What sign, if not the sign of resurrection? The Lord says, *This depraved, provocative generation is seeking a sign, but no sign will be given it except the sign of the prophet Jonah; for as Jonah was in the belly of the whale for three days and three nights, so also will the Son of Man be in the heart of the earth* (Mt 12:39-40). The promising sign has already been given to our head, then, and each one of us must now pray, *Give me a promising sign*; for to us it will be given when the last trumpet sounds at the coming of the Lord, when the dead will arise incorrupt, and we shall be changed.[43] This will be the promising sign for us.

Give me a promising sign, so that those who hate me may see it and be shamed. At the judgment they will be shamed to their harm, if they are unwilling to be shamed now for their salvation. Let them consent to be shamed now, let them repudiate their sinful ways and hold to a good way, for none of us can live without being shamed, unless we have first been shamed and then risen to a new life. God allows them access now to the shame that heals them, provided they do not disdain the medicine of confession; but if they refuse to be shamed now, they will be shamed one day, when their iniquities confront them openly.[44] How will that shaming be brought about? They will say, *These are the people we once held in derision, as a byword and a butt for our mockery! Fools that we were, we thought their life madness and their end a disgrace, but now they are reckoned among the children of God! What good has our pride done us?* (Wis 5:3-5.8). That is what they will say then; let them say it now, for their healing. Let each one turn humbly to God, and ask now, "What good has my pride done me?" and

---

43. See 1 Cor 15:52.
44. See Wis 4:20.

hear the apostle demanding, *What fruit have you reaped from those things of which you are now ashamed?* (Rom 6:21). So you see, there is the possibility of salutary shame now, in this place of repentance, but hereafter it will be a shame that is useless, sterile and too late. *What good has our pride done us, or what benefit has come to us from our vaunted wealth? All these things have passed away like a shadow* (Wis 5:8-9). What? Did you not realize during your lifetime that all these things were passing away like a shadow? You could have abandoned the shadow and lived in the light, and then you would not have had to say later, *All these things have passed away like a shadow*, as you wend your way from shadow into darkness. *Give me a promising sign, so that those who hate me may see it and be shamed.*

Present mourning, eternal consolation

For you, O Lord, have helped me and consoled me. You have helped me in the battle, and consoled me in sadness. No one looks for consolation except those who are sad. You do not need any consolation? Declare yourselves happy then. But you hear in scripture, *O my people...* (Ah, you are responding already! I can hear the murmuring from those who know their scriptures well. May God, who has written his word in your hearts, make it effective in your actions. You know, brothers and sisters, that those who tell you you are happy are deceiving you.) *O my people, those who call you happy are leading you into error and confusing your steps* (Is 3:12). You hear the same message from the Letter of the apostle James: *Be wretched and mourn, let your laughter be turned into lamentation* (Jas 4:9). Well now, think over what you have heard: would this advice have been given us in a land of security? No, this is a land of scandals and temptations and all kinds of woes; we must groan here, and earn the right to be joyful in another land; we have to be afflicted here, and consoled in that other land where we shall say, *You have freed my eyes from tears, and my feet from slippery places; I will find favor with the Lord in the land of the living* (Ps 114(116):8-9). This is the land of the dead. The land of the dead passes away, but the land of the living will come. In the land of the dead there is labor, pain, fear, distress, temptation, groaning and sighs; here are people falsely happy but truly unhappy, because false happiness is real misery. To recognize truthfully that one is in real misery is to ensure real happiness later; yet because you are at present miserable, listen to the Lord's words, *Blessed are those who mourn* (Mt 5:5). Yes, that is what he says, *Blessed are those who mourn!* Nothing is so akin to misery as mourning; nothing so distant from misery, so opposed to misery, as blessedness, yet you speak of mourners, Lord, and call them blessed. "Understand what I am saying," he replies. "I call mourners blessed; why blessed? Blessed in hope. Why mourners? Mourners in actual fact. They mourn in earnest in this deathly existence, amid these troubles, on their pilgrimage; and because they recognize that they are in this misery, and groan over it, they are blessed." Why do they mourn? Blessed Cyprian was sorrowful in his passion, but consoled now in his crown. Yet even in his consolation there is for him a certain sadness, for our Lord Jesus Christ still intercedes for us,[45] and all the martyrs in his company intercede for us too. Their intercession will not cease until this groaning of ours has passed away; but once it is done away with we shall all be consoled in our common homeland, as one people, singing with one voice, thousands upon thousands of us, joined with angels playing harps, united with choirs of heavenly powers in the one city of the living. Who groans in that city? Who sighs there? Who labors? Who is in need, who dies? Who provides charitable relief there? Who breaks bread for the hungry, where all are full-fed on the bread of righteousness? No one there bids you, "Take this person in as a guest," for no one is a traveler there; all are at home in their own land. No one tells you, "Reconcile those friends of yours who are arguing in court," for they enjoy the contemplation of God's face in everlasting peace. No one urges you, "Visit that sick person," where health and immortality abide. No one tells you, "Bury the dead," because everyone will share in eternal life. The works of mercy have no place, because no misery is to be found there.

What shall we do there, then? Sleep, perhaps? No: in this life we struggle against ourselves, for we carry a dormitory in this flesh of ours; yet in spite of that we keep lighted vigil on the eve of feastdays, and this solemnity gives us an incentive to stay awake. What kind of vigils will that day arouse us to keep? We shall be wakeful then, not asleep. So what shall we find to do? The works of mercy we perform here will be superseded there, where no misery will exist. Perhaps, though, the activities which here are driven by necessity will continue there—works such as sowing, plowing, cooking, grinding, weaving? No, none of these; there will be no need for them. Just as there will be no works of mercy, because misery has passed away, so where there is neither necessity nor misery, there will be no works driven by either necessity or misery.

What will there be? What will be our occupation? Our activity? Or will there be no activity at all, but simply rest? Shall we sit about lazily, doing nothing? Well, if our love grows cold, then indeed our activity will cool down too.[46] But if we long for God even now, sigh for him even now, with what a fire will quiet love in God's presence consume us when we reach him? If we yearn for him like this when we have not yet seen him, how will he illumine us when we come to him? How will he change us? What will he make of us?

So, brothers and sisters, what shall we be doing there? Let a psalm tell us: *Blessed are they who dwell in your house.* Why blessed? *They will praise you for ever and ever* (Ps 83:5(84:4)). This will be our activity: praising God. If you love

---

45. See Rom 8:34.
46. These ideas on activity in heaven occur several times in Augustine's *Expositions of the Psalms*; compare, for example, his similar development in the Exposition of Psalm 83,8.

him, you also praise him. You will break off your praise only if you stop loving. But you will not stop loving because it is characteristic of the One you see that he cannot cause the slightest weariness in you: he satisfies you, yet he leaves you unsatisfied. This is an odd thing to say. But if I say that he satisfies you, I am afraid you may wish to get up and go, because you have had enough, as you might from a dinner or a supper. How shall I put it, then? Am I to say that he does not satisfy you? But then I have the opposite anxiety, that if I tell you he does not satisfy you, you may imagine you will suffer want, or feel somewhat empty, and there will be a void in you that should be filled. What am I to say, then, except something that can be stated, but scarcely thought? He both satisfies you and leaves you unsatisfied; I find both these stated in scripture. Though the Lord said, *Blessed are the hungry, for they will be satisfied* (Mt 5:6), it was also said of Wisdom, *Those who eat you will be hungry again; those who drink you will thirst again* (Sir 24:29). But no, it does not mean "again," but "still"; for "will thirst again" would imply that someone has drunk sufficiently, goes away and digests it, and then comes back to drink some more. The real meaning is, *Those who eat you will still be hungry*; in other words, even as they eat they will still feel hunger, and those who drink of you will be made thirsty even by drinking. What does it mean, to be made thirsty by the very act of drinking? It means never to experience satiety.

If then this inexpressible and everlasting sweetness is waiting for us, my brothers and sisters, what does it demand of us now, except sincere faith, firm hope, and pure charity, and that we should walk in the way our Lord has given us, bear trials and receive his consolations.

Exposition of Psalm 86

A Sermon[1]

Introduction: a song of the beloved city

1. The psalm which has just been sung is a short one as far as the number of its verses goes, but a great one with regard to the importance of its content. Although the whole psalm was read, you see how quickly we reached the end. It has been suggested by our very blessed father, who is here with us,[2] that we should study the psalm together with you, beloved, insofar as the Lord graciously enables us. This unexpected suggestion would be burdensome to us, were not the prayer of the one who made it ready to support me. Let me have your attention, then, beloved.

In this psalm a city is sung about and celebrated, a city of which we are citizens by virtue of being Christians, a city from which we are absent abroad as long as we are mortal, and towards which we are traveling. The approach to it would scarcely be discoverable, blocked as it is by thornbushes and briars, but the King of the city has made himself the way through,[3] so that we may reach it. As we walk along in Christ, pilgrims still until we arrive, sighing with desire for the unutterable peace that abides in that city—a peace concerning which we are promised *what eye has not seen, nor ear heard, nor human heart conceived* (1 Cor 2:9)—as we walk, I say, let us so sing as to enkindle our longing. All who long for it are singing in their hearts, even if their tongues are silent, whereas anyone who has no longing is dumb in God's presence, however great a din such a person makes in human ears. See what fervent lovers of that city they were, those people by whom this song was sung and through whom the message reached us: how great was the ardor with which they sang of it! Such ardor was aroused in them by love for the city, and it was the Spirit of God who infused that love, for, as scripture says, *the love of God has been poured out into our hearts through the Holy Spirit who has been given to us* (Rom 5:5). Fired by the same Spirit, let us listen now to what is said about this city.

---

1. Possibly preached at Carthage on the day after the preceding sermon, 14 September, the feast of Saint Cyprian; see section 9. The year could be 401, 416, or 412.
2. Presumably Aurelius, bishop of Carthage.
3. *Se fecit viam* recalls Jn 14:6, a beloved text for Augustine.

Verses 2-3. The foundations of the city; Christ the cornerstone

2. *Her foundations are on the holy mountains.* The psalm has not mentioned her yet; it only begins here. Yet it says, *Her foundations are on the holy mountains.* Whose foundations? We can scarcely doubt that if something is said to have foundations, and especially if they are on mountains, some city must be meant. The citizen who speaks was filled with the Holy Spirit and was turning over in his mind many thoughts relating to his love and longing for the city; then he suddenly blurted out the teeming fruit of his meditation in the words, *her foundations are on the holy mountains,* as though he had mentioned her already. Was it possible that he had said nothing on the subject, when he had never been silent about it in his heart? But how can one say "her," when she has not been spoken of? No; as I have explained, he was silently travailing with abundant thoughts in his mind concerning the city, and uttering them to God, but now he burst out with them in human hearing as well: *her foundations are on the holy mountains.* But since his hearers might retort, "Whose foundations?" he says, *The Lord loves the gates of Zion.*

Now we know whose foundations are on the holy mountains: the foundations of a city called Zion, whose gates are beloved of the Lord *more than all the tents of Jacob,* as the psalmist goes on to say. But what does he mean by saying, *Her foundations are on the holy mountains?* Which holy mountains are these, upon which the city is founded? Another of her citizens told us more plainly, the apostle Paul. The prophet was a citizen of that city, and so was the apostle, and both of them spoke in order to encourage their fellow-citizens. But in what sense are the prophets and apostles citizens? Perhaps in such a way that they are the mountains too, mountains on which are laid the foundations of this city whose gates the Lord loves. Let the other citizen make the point clearly, lest anyone think we are romancing. Paul was speaking to the Gentiles, and admonishing them to come back and be built into the holy fabric, built up, he says, *on the foundation of the apostles and prophets.* Then, in order to emphasize that not even the apostles and prophets, foundations of the city though they were, could hold up of themselves, he went on to say, *Christ Jesus himself being the chief cornerstone* (Eph 2:20). The Gentiles might suppose, though, that they had no place in Zion, for there was an earthly city of Zion which foreshadowed the Zion of which we are now speaking, the heavenly Jerusalem which, as the apostle says, *is the mother of us all* (Gal 4:26). So in case the Gentiles might be deemed to have no place in Zion, not being Jews, he said to them, *You are pilgrims and lodgers no more; rather are you fellow-citizens with the saints and members of God's household, built up on the foundation of the apostles and prophets* (Eph 2:19-20). There you have the essential building components of the great city. But on what does the structure rest, what bears its weight and ensures that it does not collapse? *Christ Jesus himself is the chief cornerstone.*

3. Possibly someone may raise an objection here. If Christ Jesus is the chief cornerstone, then yes, indeed, the two walls are joined together in him, for you can only have a corner if two walls come from different directions and meet; and in this way two peoples—from the circumcised and from the uncircumcised—come together into Christian peace, bound to one another by one faith, one hope and one charity. But if Christ Jesus is the supreme cornerstone, it looks as though the foundations were laid first, and the cornerstone later. It might be said, then, that Christ rests upon the prophets and apostles, rather than they upon him, if they are in the foundations and he at the corner.

Anyone who raises this objection should reflect that there is also a cornerstone in the foundations. The corner is not only present in the part we can see, where it rises towards the highest point, but begins in the foundation. As you know, Christ is the first and greatest foundation; as the apostle says, *No one can lay any other foundation than that which is laid, which is Christ Jesus* (1 Cor 3:11). How then can both be true—that the prophets and apostles are the foundations, and that Christ Jesus is the foundation, beside whom there can be no other?

How are we to think of it, except that as he is properly said to be the Holy One of all holy ones, so he is figuratively called the foundation of foundations? If you think of sacred realities, Christ is the Holy One of all holy ones; if you envisage the flock subject to him, Christ is the Shepherd of shepherds; if you consider the edifice, Christ is the foundation of foundations. In the buildings we know, the same stone cannot be at the base and the summit; if it is at the base, it will not be at the top; if at the top, it will not be at the base. Almost all bodily creatures suffer from limitations: they cannot be everywhere, nor abide always. But since the Godhead is immediately present everywhere, symbols of it may be drawn from everywhere, and it can be entirely present in the symbols because it is properly speaking none of these things. Is Christ a door like the doors we see made by a carpenter? Of course not; yet he said, *I am the door* (Jn 10:9). Or is he a shepherd like the ones we see in charge of animals? No; yet he said *I am the shepherd* (Jn 10:11). Moreover he made both statements in the same context. He said in the gospel that the shepherd goes in by the door. In the same passage he said, *I am the door.* So the shepherd enters through the door; and who is this shepherd who enters through the door? He who said, *I am the good shepherd.* And what door is this through which you enter, good shepherd? *I am the door.* How can you be everything? "In the same way that everything exists through me," he replies. For instance, when Paul enters through the door, does not Christ enter through the door? Yes, and why? Not because Christ is Paul, but because Christ is in Paul, and Paul exists through Christ. Paul himself demanded, *Do you presume to interrogate Christ, who speaks through me?* (2 Cor 13:3). When Christ's saints, Christ's faithful, enter through the door, is it not Christ entering through the door? How can we prove that? Because when Saul (who was not yet Paul) was persecuting those very saints, Christ cried to him from heaven, *Saul, Saul, why are you persecuting me?* (Acts 9:4).

Christ is both the foundation and the cornerstone, rising up from the lowest point—if we can speak of the lowest, for this foundation springs from the uttermost heights. The foundation of a material edifice is at the base, but the foundation of a spiritual edifice is in the heights. If we were being built into a structure for this earth, we would need to lay its foundations at the base; but because the construction is a heavenly one, our foundation has gone ahead of us to heaven. Christ the cornerstone, and the foundations which are the apostles and the great prophets, bear the weight of the city, and form a kind of living edifice.

Is this edifice clamoring now, from your hearts? Then God's skillful hand, using even our tongue as his tool, is producing this effect in you, squaring you ready for the fabric of the building. It is no accident that Noah's ark too was built with squared beams,[4] for it was a type of the Church. What does "squared" mean? Consider the properties of a squared stone, which a Christian ought to resemble. A Christian does not topple over, whatever temptation strikes. Even if pushed, and nearly overturned, a Christian does not fall over, just as a squared stone stands steady whichever way you turn it. The martyrs appeared to fall when they were being beaten, but what does a singer's voice have to say of them? *When the just falls he will suffer no harm, for the Lord strengthens his hand* (Ps 36(37):24). Be squared like that and ready for all temptations; then, whatever pushes against you, it will not tip you over. Let every crisis find you still standing. You will be built up into this structure by your loyal dispositions and sincere reverence for God, by faith, hope and charity; and being built like this is nothing else but to journey onward. In the cities familiar to us the fabric of the buildings is one thing, the citizens who live within them another; but that city is constructed of the citizens themselves, for they are living stones. So scripture says, *Allow yourselves to be built, like living stones, into a spiritual house* (1 Pt 2:5). That injunction is addressed to us. Let us pursue our contemplation of this city.

The foundations and the gates of the city: the twelve apostles

4. *Her foundations are on the holy mountains; the Lord loves the gates of Zion.* I have given you the foregoing explanation to make sure you do not think foundations and gates are two different things. Why are the apostles and prophets foundations? Because their authority bears up our weakness. And why are they gates? Because we enter God's kingdom through them, for they preach to us. And when we enter through them, we enter through Christ, for he is the door.

Now Jerusalem is said to have twelve gates.[5] Christ is at once one single gate, and all twelve gates, because Christ is in those twelve gates. This is why there are twelve apostles. There is a profound mystery in this number twelve. *You will sit*

---

4. See Gn 6:14, LXX.
5. See Rv 21:12.

upon twelve thrones, judging the twelve tribes of Israel, Christ promised (Mt 19:28). But if there are to be twelve thrones, there is nowhere for the thirteenth apostle, Paul, to sit. That means he will not be in a position to exercise judgment; yet he claimed that he would judge not human beings only, but even angels. Which angels would that be? The apostate angels, surely. *Do you not realize that we shall judge angels?* he asks (1 Cor 6:3). The populace might have retorted, "Why boast that you will exercise judgment? Where will you sit? The Lord promised twelve seats to the twelve apostles; one of them, Judas, fell away, and Matthias was co-opted in his place. So the twelve seats were filled. Find yourself a place to sit first, and then threaten that you will judge!"

We had better look into the significance of these twelve seats. Twelve is a mystical sign of universality, because the Church was destined to spread throughout the entire world, and would be summoned from every quarter to be joined to Christ in the building. Because it is brought from all sides to exercise judgment there are twelve seats, just as there are twelve gates because they enter the city from every part of the world. It is not just those twelve plus the apostle Paul, but all those who will be empowered to judge, who have the right to the twelve thrones which signify universality, just as all those who will enter are typified by the twelve gates. Now there are four quarters to the world—east, west, north and south. These four quarters are frequently referred to in the scriptures. From them come the four winds, and so the Lord says in the gospel that he will gather his elect from the four winds.[6] The Church is therefore called from the four winds. How? It is called in the Trinity from every place; only through baptism in the name of the Father, and of the Son, and of the Holy Spirit is it called. And three times four makes twelve.

5. Knock at these doors with the hand of devotion, and let Christ cry out in you, *Open the gates of righteousness to me* (Ps 117(118):19); for he has gone before us as our head, but he follows himself in his body. Look at what the apostle says about Christ suffering in him: *That I may fill up what is lacking to the sufferings of Christ in my own flesh.*[7] What is he going to *fill up*? That which *is lacking.* Lacking to what? *To the sufferings of Christ.* And where are they deficient? *In my own flesh.* Could any kind of pain be lacking in that man himself, the man that the Word of God became, the man who was born of the virgin Mary? He suffered whatever it was appointed to him to suffer, and he did so of his own volition, not under any necessity flowing from sin. It seems that he endured everything possible, because when, hanging on the cross, he accepted the final sip of vinegar, he said, *"It is accomplished"; and bowing his head he breathed forth his spirit* (Jn 19:30). What does that mean—*It is accomplished*? "Nothing is missing now from the measure of

---

6. See Mk 13:27.
7. Col 1:24. The more probable meaning is "fill up in my own flesh what is lacking to the sufferings of Christ," but Augustine takes it in the sense given in the translation adopted here.

suffering allotted to me; all that was prophesied of me has been fulfilled." It was as though he was waiting for everything to be completed. Who is this, who departs from life in the way that Christ went forth from his body? Who ever could? He alone who had first said, *I have the power to lay down my life, and I have the power to take it up again. No one takes it away from me; but I lay it down of my own accord, and I take it up again* (Jn 10:18.17). He laid it down when he willed, and took it up when he willed; no one took it away, no one wrested it from him. All forms of suffering were fully endured, then, but in the head. There still remained sufferings for Christ to undergo in his body.

You are Christ's body, Christ's members. Because the apostle was among his members, he said, *That I may fill up what is lacking to the sufferings of Christ in my own flesh.* We are traveling to the place whither Christ has gone before, but it is equally true to say that Christ is making his way to the place where he has already gone in advance, for though Christ has gone before us as head, he follows in his body. And Christ still labors here, and Christ was suffering here from Saul, when Saul heard the words, *Saul, Saul, why are you persecuting me?* (Acts 9:4). It is the same when your tongue instinctively protests, "You are treading on me," when it is your foot that has been trodden on. No one has touched your tongue; it cries out in sympathy, not because it has itself been crushed. Even so Christ is in want here, Christ is a stranger here, Christ is ill here, Christ is confined to prison here. We would be insulting him by saying so, had he not said himself, *I was hungry, and you fed me; I was thirsty, and you gave me a drink; I was a stranger, and you made me welcome; I was naked and you clothed me, sick, and you visited me. And the just will reply, "When did we see you suffering all this, and minister to you?" He will say, "When you did that for even the least of those who are mine, you did it for me"* (Mt 25:35-37.40).

Let us, then, be built up into Christ upon the foundation of the apostles and prophets, with Christ himself as the chief cornerstone, for *the Lord loves the gates of Zion more than all the tents of Jacob.* This sounds as though Zion is not among the tents of Jacob. But where else would Zion be, if not amid the people of Jacob? Jacob was the grandson of Abraham, from whom the Jews were descended, and they were called the people of Israel because Jacob himself was given the name Israel.[8] You know this well, holy brethren.[9] But there were various tents used only for a time that served as images of the real one; and the psalmist is speaking of a city which is to be understood spiritually, one of which the earthly city was but a shadow and a type. He says, therefore, *The Lord loves the gates of Zion more than all the tents of Jacob.* He loves the spiritual city more than all those that prefigured it, more than those earthly ones which hinted at the city that abides for ever, the eternal, heavenly city of peace.

---

8. See Gn 32:28.
9. *Sanctitas vestra*, a variant on his more usual *Caritas vestra*.

Verses 4-5. The holy city of the Gentiles

6. *Glorious things are spoken of you, city of God.* He seems to be contemplating the city of Jerusalem on earth; but consider what city this was, of which
glorious prophecies were uttered: a city destroyed on earth, a city that was razed
to the ground by enemy attacks, and is no longer what it once was. It served as a
type, but like a shadow it passed away. Why, then, does the psalm declare that
glorious things are spoken of you, city of God?
	Listen to the reason why. *I will be mindful of Rahab and of Babylon, with
those who know me.* From within that city he speaks in God's name, "I will
remember Rahab, and I will remember Babylon." Rahab does not belong to the
Jewish people; Babylon does not belong to the Jewish people. This is why the
psalm continues, *Indeed, foreigners—Tyre, and the Ethiopian race—all these
have been here.*[10] God's city deserved to have *glorious things spoken* about it,
for not only the Jews, who were Abraham's descendants according to the flesh,
but all nations were there, a few of whom were named to stand for all the rest. *I
will be mindful of Rahab,* he says, and she was a prostitute, that prostitute in
Jericho who sheltered the messengers and dispatched them by a different route.[11]
She anticipated the promise because she feared God, and she was told to hang a
scarlet token from her window, that is, to bear the sign of Christ's blood on her
forehead. She was saved there, and so she represented the Church of the
Gentiles. This is why the Lord said to the proud Pharisees, *Truly I tell you, the tax
collectors and prostitutes are going ahead of you into the kingdom of heaven* (Mt
21:31). They are thrusting in ahead because they are doing violence to it; they are
attacking it by believing, and it yields to their faith. No one can halt them, for
these people who do it violence are grabbing it like plunder. In the same gospel it
is said, *The kingdom of heaven is subjected to violence, and the violent snatch it
away* (Mt 11:12). The thief did just this,[12] the thief who was more powerful on
the cross than at the throat.[13] *I will be mindful of Rahab and of Babylon.* By
Babylon the city of this world is meant.[14] Just as there is one holy city, Jerusalem,
so also there is one wicked city, Babylon; all the wicked belong to Babylon, as all
the saints to Jerusalem. But Babylon gradually changes into Jerusalem, and how

---

10. The foreigners (*alienigenae*) were probably the Philistines in the original reference of the
	psalm. The term carries the connotation "heathens."
11. See Jos 2. The original psalm more probably used "Rahab" as a (disparaging) name for Egypt,
	as elsewhere in the Old Testament. But the point remains the same: the psalm envisages the
	gathering of the Gentiles to Mother Zion.
12. See Lk 23:40-43.
13. *Fortior in cruce quam in fauce.* An assonance, clearly, but the meaning is less clear. The
	translation assumes that *fauce* means the throat of his victims, but it can also mean a narrow pass
	or defile, and so a place of ambush, which would also make good sense.
14. An idea with a great future in Augustine's mind. Compare Exposition of Psalm 61,6,
	Exposition of Psalm 64,2, and note at the latter place.

could it do that, unless through him who justifies the godless?[15] Jerusalem is the city of those loyal to God, Babylon the city of the godless; but he who justifies the godless came; and so it says, *I will be mindful* not only of Rahab, but even *of Babylon*. But of whom will he be mindful in Rahab and Babylon? Of *those who know me*. With this in mind scripture says somewhere, *Pour out your anger upon the nations that know you not* (Ps 78(79):6). So in the one place we read, *Pour out your anger upon the nations that know you not*, and elsewhere, *Extend your mercy to those who know you* (Ps 35:11(36:10)).

In order to put it beyond doubt that the Gentiles are symbolized by Rahab and Babylon, the psalmist replies to the question he seems to hear us asking: "What do you mean by *I will be mindful of Rahab and of Babylon, with those who know me*? Why did you say that?" He answers, "Indeed, I say, foreigners—that is, people who belong to Rahab and to Babylon—and Tyrians too: all will be there." From how far distant will those foreigners come? Even from the ends of the earth, for he chose to name a people from the most remote region: *and the Ethiopian race, all these have been there*. If the people there include Rahab, some from Babylon, foreigners, people from Tyre, and the Ethiopians, it is with good reason that *glorious things are spoken of you, city of God*.

Mother Zion

7. Now turn your minds to a great mystery. Through Christ Rahab came to be there, and through Christ Babylon also came to be there. But we should speak of her as one who is losing her identity as Babylon and being transformed into Jerusalem; for she is a daughter estranged from her mother[16] and finding her place among the members of the queen who is bidden, *Forget your own people and your father's house; the King has desired your beauty* (Ps 44:11-12(45:10-11)). How could Babylon aspire to Jerusalem? And how could Rahab attain to those foundations? How could any foreigners, or Tyrians, or the Ethiopian race?

Listen now to the answer: *"Zion, my mother," a man will say*. So it is a man who says, *"Zion, my mother,"* and through him all these peoples gain entry. But who is this man? The psalm tells us, if we listen and have the wit to hear: *"Zion, my mother," a man will say*. Then, as though you were inquiring through whom all these arrived here—Rahab, Babylon, foreigners, Tyre, Ethiopians—the psalm goes on to tell you: *"Zion, my mother," a man will say, he who was made man in her, and the Most High himself established her*. What could be plainer, my brothers and sisters? True it is that *glorious things are spoken of you, city of God*. Think about it: *"Zion, my mother," a man will say*. What man? He who *was made man in her*. He was made man in her, and he himself founded her. How

---

15. See Rom 4:5.
16. See Mt 10:35.

could he have both been made in her, and founded her himself? She must have been founded already for him to be made man in her. Understand it in this way, if you can: *"Zion, my mother,"* he will say, but it is a man who says this; he was *made man in her*, but *he himself established her* not as man but as *the Most High*. He founded the city in which he was to be born, just as he created the mother from whom he was to be born. What does this mean for us, my brothers and sisters? What promises are ours, what hope we hold! On our account he who as the Most High founded the city calls the city "Mother." *He was made man in her, and the Most High himself established her.*

Verse 6. The ennoblement of the lowly apostles

8. It might be asked, "How do you know all this?" We have all sung the psalm, and in all of us sings the one man, Christ, who is man for our sake but is God before we came to be. But are we saying much thereby? "Before we came to be"? He exists before the earth, before heaven, before the ages. He it is who became man in her for our sake, and himself as the Most High founded her. How do we know all this? Because *the Lord will record it in his list of the peoples and the princes*: this is how the psalm goes on. *"Zion, my mother,"* a man will say, he who was made man in her, and the Most High himself established her. The Lord will record it in his list of the peoples and the princes. What princes are these? Those who became so in her. Those who became princes within her were made princes there, and only there, because before appointing them princes God had chosen what the world despised, to shame the powerful.[17] Was a fisherman a prince? Was a tax collector a prince? Princes they certainly were, but only because they were made princes in her. What kind of princes were they? Later princes came from Babylon, believing monarchs from this world came to the city of Rome, acknowledging it as Babylon's overlord; and they went not to the emperor's precinct but to the memorial of the fisherman. Why then were the original princes ennobled? Because God has chosen the weak things of this world to shame the strong, and has chosen the contemptible, those who seemed to be nothing as well as those with status, so that those with status may be emptied of significance.[18] He does it, he who lifts up the needy person from the ground, and raises the poor from the dungheap. To what purpose? In order to range the needy with princes, with the princes of his people.[19] This is a mighty achievement, and for us a mighty joy and a mighty triumph. Later there came to the city orators as well, but they would not have come if the fisherman had not

17. See 1 Cor 1:27-28.
18. See 1 Cor 1:27-28.
19. See Ps 112(113):7-8.

come first. These are great events; and where do they take place? In this city of God, of which glorious things are spoken.

Verse 7. A different joy, the true joy

9. The singer now gathers all these joys together and blends them into one. How does he conclude the psalm? *As though the dwelling of all who are made glad were in you.* It is as though the home of all happy people—all those who have been gladdened—were in this city. During our pilgrimage we are worn out, but our home will be pure gladness. Toil and groaning will disappear; supplications will fade and songs of praise take their place. There will be the dwelling of those made glad; no groans of longing will be heard, but only the rejoicing of those who possess their whole desire, because he for whom we sigh now will be present to us, and *we shall be like him, because we shall see him as he is* (1 Jn 3:2). We shall have no other occupation than to praise God, to enjoy God. What else should we seek, where he through whom all things were made is our entire sufficiency? Dwelling there, we shall be his dwelling; all things will be subjected to him, that God may be all in all.[20]

Blessed, then, *are they who dwell in your house.* Why blessed? Blessed in the possession of gold, silver, a large household, a fine brood of children? No. Why blessed? *Blessed are they who dwell in your house; they will praise you for ever and ever* (Ps 83:5(84:4)). This busy idleness[21] alone will be our beatitude. So then, my brothers and sisters, let what will be our occupation when we arrive there be our sole desire now; let us prepare ourselves to rejoice in God and praise God. The good works that further us along our way now will have no place there. We spoke about this yesterday[22] insofar as we could, pointing out that there will be no works of mercy where no misery exists. You will find there no one in need, no one who lacks clothing; no thirsty person will accost you, no pilgrim will pass by; there will be no sick person for you to visit, no dead for you to bury, no disputants whom you must try to reconcile. What will you find to do, then? Perhaps bodily necessities will oblige us to raise young plants, plow the earth, engage in business, or travel abroad? No, there will be profound peace; all the work dictated by necessity will be obsolete, for when necessity is dead, the works driven by necessity will perish likewise.

What will happen, then? A human tongue attempted to express it: it will be *as though the dwelling of all who are made glad were in you.* What is the force of *as though*? Why did he put in *as though*? Because such gladness will be there as we have never experienced. I observe many forms of gladness here; many people

---

20. See 1 Cor 15:28.
21. *Otioso negotio*, an Augustinian oxymoron.
22. See Exposition of Psalm 85,23.

rejoice in this world, some over one thing, some over another, and nowhere do I find anything to be compared with our future joy. Yet it will be *like* gladness. If I say "gladness" without qualification, the sort of gladness will spring to mind that a person ordinarily finds in wine, in feasting, in avarice, or in worldly honors. People are carried away by these things and go mad with joy, but *there is no joy for the wicked* (Is 48:22, LXX), says the Lord. There is a gladness that no eye has seen, nor ear heard, nor human heart conceived,[23] *as though the dwelling of all who are made glad were in you.* Let us prepare ourselves for a different joy, because here we find only a semblance of it, not the real thing. We must beware of preparing ourselves to enjoy there the kind of pleasures we rejoice in here, for if we do that, our self-restraint will be mere greed. Think of people who are invited to a sumptuous banquet where abundant, choice foods are to be served: they miss a meal beforehand, and if you ask them why they do not take it, they reply, "We are fasting." Now that is a great undertaking, the Christian custom of fasting. But do not be in too much of a hurry to commend them. Look for the motive. It is the belly's interests that are being served, not those of religion. Why do they fast? In order not to stuff their bellies with cheap food, and have no room for the delicacies. So they are looking to the profit of their gullets when they fast. Fasting is a valuable exercise, to be sure; it fights against the demands of belly and gullet; but sometimes it fights for them instead.

My brothers and sisters, if you imagine that in our heavenly country, to which the trumpet call from heaven invites us, we shall have the same sort of things over again, and you restrain yourselves from present pleasures with the object of enjoying them more plentifully there, you are like people who fast with an eye to more lavish banquets, and restrain themselves only for greater excesses. Beware of that. Prepare yourselves for something beyond the power of speech to utter, cleanse your hearts from all your earthly and worldly attachments. We are destined for vision, a vision that will be our beatitude, and that reality alone will be enough for us. What! Shall we not eat, then? Yes, indeed we shall eat, and he himself will be our food who can re-create us, and who never fails. It is *as though the dwelling of all who have been made glad were in you.* We have already been told the source of our happiness: *Blessed are they who dwell in your house; they will praise you for ever and ever.*

Let us then praise the Lord now, as best we can, amid our present groaning, because by praising him we long for him whom we do not yet possess. When we possess him all groaning will be done away with, and there will remain only pure, eternal praise.

Now let us turn to the Lord.[24]

---

23. See 1 Cor 2:9.
24. See the note on this phrase at the end of his Exposition of Psalm 80,22.

Exposition of Psalm 87

Verse 1: The title. Christ in his passion is the precentor, his choir responds

1. The title of this eighty-seventh psalm contains an element which may give a commentator some unaccustomed trouble, for nowhere else in the psalms do we find a phrase which occurs here: *for melech, to be responded to*. We have said something elsewhere[1] on the phrases, *a psalm of a canticle* and *a canticle of a psalm*. We have very often discussed the heading, *for the children of Korah*, which is common in the psalms; and we have also explained the meaning of *unto the end*. But the next phrase in the present title, *for melech, to be responded to*, is unusual. *For melech* may signify in our language, "for the choir," since that seems to be the meaning of the Hebrew word. What else can it mean, then, to say, "For the choir, to be responded to," but that the choir is to sing in unison, responding to its cantor?[2]

It is likely, however, that this was not the only psalm that was sung; others probably were too, even though they bore different titles. The variation was intended to guard against monotony, I think. It is unlikely that this would have been the only psalm thought worthy of choral response, since it is certainly not the only one that relates to the Lord's passion. If any other reason can be demonstrated for so wide a variety of titles, one that could prove, for instance, that the psalms were given different superscriptions in order that no psalm should bear a title that suits any other, I must confess that I have not managed to discover it, in spite of repeated efforts. Furthermore, nothing I have read on the subject in the works of my predecessors has satisfied my hope—or, perhaps, my slow understanding. I will therefore set forth what I believe to be the significance of the saying, *for the choir, to be responded to*, which is an instruction to the choir to make its response to the cantor.

---

1. See Exposition of Psalm 67,1.
2. The title in Hebrew means something like "A canticle, a psalm for the sons of Korah. For the choirmaster, in sickness, in suffering" (or, if the last two phrases are read as proper names, "according to Mahalath Leannoth"). "A poem for Heman the Ezrahite." The Greek of the Septuagint turns this into "A canticle of a psalm for the sons of Korah, unto the end for Maheleth" (or perhaps "the Maheleth"), "to be responded to, of understanding for Heman the Israelite." In Augustine's Latin version the unusual element, "for the choirmaster," becomes *pro melech*, which he takes to mean "the choir," but the connection with the Hebrew meaning survives.

257

The passion of our Lord is prophesied here. But the apostle Peter reminds us, *Christ suffered for us, leaving us an example, so that we may follow in his footsteps* (1 Pt 2:21); and that is what responding to the cantor means. The apostle John speaks similarly: *Christ laid down his life for us, and so we too must lay down our lives for our brethren* (1 Jn 3:16); that also is what responding to the cantor means. Now "choir" suggests "concord," and concord is established by charity. It follows that any who pretend to imitate our Lord's passion, even to handing over their bodies for burning, yet lack charity, are not making the proper choral response, and so their efforts profit them not at all.[3]

Another way of putting it is this: in musical parlance officials are called precentor and succentor; the Latin language lends itself to this terminology used by the experts. The precentor, obviously, is the one who takes the lead in raising his voice in song, and the succentor the one who follows him. So too in the song of suffering, Christ takes the lead, and the choir of martyrs sings after him, aspiring to heavenly laurels. Now the present song is sung *for the children of Korah*, which is to say, for those who imitate Christ's sufferings, because Christ was crucified at a place called Calvary, which is said to be an interpretation of the Hebrew name, Korah.

The last element in the title speaks of *understanding for Heman the Israelite. The name Heman is said to mean "his brother."*[4] Christ has deigned to make all those his brothers and sisters who understand the mystery of his cross so well that they are not merely unashamed of it, but even boast about it in faith, all those who do not pride themselves on their own merits but are grateful for his grace. Of each of them it can accordingly be said, *Look, there is a true Israelite, in whom there is no guile* (Jn 1:47), for scripture declares concerning Israel himself that he was without guile.[5] Let us now listen to the voice of Christ the Precentor in this prophecy, and let his choir respond to him, either by imitation or by thanksgiving.

---

3. See 1 Cor 13:3.
4. According to 1 Chr 2:6, Heman and Ethan were the sons of Zerah. Their names appear in the title of this psalm and the following, respectively. 1 Kgs 4:31 claims that Solomon was wiser than "Ethan the Ezrahite, and Heman...." In the Hebrew title to the present psalm Heman is called "Heman the Ezrahite," which means "one of the family of Zerah." But a different reading of the same Hebrew word can take it as not "Ezrahite," but "a native, one arising from the soil, a native-born Israelite." The LXX adopted this latter meaning, and it passed into Augustine's Latin.
5. It is not easy to see which scriptural passage Augustine has in mind, though the CCL editors point to Gn 25:27, where Jacob, in contrast to Esau, is said to be "complete" or "sound" or "wholesome." The overwhelming impression of Jacob in Genesis is hardly one of guilelessness.

Verses 2-4. The agony in Christ's soul

2. *O Lord, God of my salvation, by day and by night I have cried before you. Let my prayer enter your presence; bend your ear to my entreaty.* The Lord himself prayed, not in his form as God, but in the form of the servant, and in that form he also suffered. He prayed when engaged in things that brought him joy, which are symbolized by "day," and also in adversity, which is what I think is meant by praying at night. The entry of prayer into God's presence means his acceptance of it. The bending of God's ear is an expression meaning that he mercifully hears our prayer, for God does not have bodily members as we have. The repetition is in accord with scripture's usual idiom: *let my prayer enter your presence* is synonymous with *bend your ear to my entreaty.*

3. *For my soul is filled with evils, and my life has drawn near to the underworld.* Can we dare to say that Christ's soul was filled with evils, when it was surely in his flesh that his agony exerted whatever force it had? We might appeal to the assurance he himself gave to his followers when he fired them to the endurance of suffering, as though encouraging his choir to respond to him: *Do not be afraid of those who kill the body, but cannot kill the soul* (Mt 10:28). Is it possible that, while the soul cannot be killed by persecutors, it can nonetheless be filled with evils? If the answer is yes, we must inquire what evils these are. We cannot say that Christ's soul was filled with vices, through which iniquity holds sway over others. So perhaps it was filled with pains, since his soul suffered along with his flesh in the passion. What we call bodily pain cannot leave the soul unaffected, for when bodily pain looms it is invariably preceded by sadness, which is the pain of the soul alone. The soul can be in pain even when there is no pain in the body, but the body cannot be in pain without there being pain in the soul.

What is to prevent us, then, from saying that Christ's soul was filled, not with human sins, but with human evils? Another prophet testifies that he bore our sorrows;[6] and the evangelist records that *he took with him Peter and the two sons of Zebedee, and he began to grow sad and sorrowful* (Mt 26:37). The Lord declared the same of himself when he said to them, *My soul is sorrowful to the point of death* (Mt 26:38). The prophet who was the author of our present psalm foresaw these events, and he represents Christ as lamenting, *My soul is filled with evils, and my life has drawn near to the underworld.* This is certain, because Christ himself expressed exactly the same thing in different words when he said, *My soul is sorrowful to the point of death.* His phrase, *my soul is sorrowful,* corresponds to *my soul is filled with evils*; and his next words, *to the point of death,* echo the psalmist's *my life has drawn near to the underworld.*

---

6. See Is 53:4.

The Lord Jesus took upon himself these feelings of human weakness, just as he also took on weak human flesh with its liability to death, not from any necessity in his own nature but by his merciful will. He did so in order to pattern upon himself his body, the Church.[7] He is its head, and its members are his saints and faithful followers. It might happen to any one of them to be saddened and feel pain amid human trials, and Christ wanted to make sure that anyone in that state would not think himself or herself distant from his grace. The body would learn from its head that these experiences are not sins, but only signs of human infirmity, and so the choir would be chiming in with Christ's leading voice.

Indeed, an outstanding member of this body, the apostle Paul, confesses that his soul too was filled with evils of this sort, as we read and hear. He testifies that his distress is profound, and the pain in his heart continuous, for his brethren according to the flesh, who are Israelites.[8] I think we shall not be far wrong if we surmise that the Lord also was bitterly distressed on their account on the approach of his passion, in which they were to involve themselves in the most heinous of crimes.

Verses 5-6. Christ alone was free among the dead, and was never without help

4. On the cross Christ prayed, *Father, forgive them, for they do not know what they are doing* (Lk 23:34), and the next line in the psalm corresponds with that prayer. *I am reckoned with those who go down to the pit*, he says, but reckoned so by those who did not know what they were doing, who thought he was dying as other mortals did, inescapably subject to the human condition and in the end defeated by it. He speaks of *the pit* to suggest either the depth of misery, or the depth of the underworld.

5. *I have become like a man bereft of help, free among the dead.* In these words the person of the Lord appears most plainly; for who else is free among the dead, if not he who, though living in the likeness of sinful flesh, was alone sinless among sinners?[9] Some there were who foolishly believed themselves free, but to them he said, *Whoever commits sin is the slave of sin.* They needed to be set free from their sins by him who had no sin, as he went on to tell them: *If the Son sets you free, you will be free indeed* (Jn 8:34-35).

He was *free among the dead*, he who had it in his power to lay down his life and to take it up again,[10] he from whom no one snatched it away, because he laid it down freely. He was free among the dead, he who when he willed could raise his flesh up again, a temple rebuilt after they had destroyed it.[11] He became, but

---

7. *Ut transfiguraret in se corpus suum, quod est ecclesia*, a key idea in Augustine's ecclesiology.
8. See Rom 9:2-4.
9. See Rom 8:3.
10. See Jn 10:18.
11. See Jn 2:19.

only in the sense that he was reckoned to be, *like a man bereft of help*. So thought the enemies who did not know what they were doing, but for whom he prayed. *He saved others, but he can't save himself*, they jeered. *If he is the Son of God, let him come down from the cross, and we will believe him. Let God deliver him now, if he wants him* (Mt 27:42-43). All others had abandoned him when he was about to suffer, yet never was he left alone, because the Father did not abandon him, as he testified.[12]

Like the wounded sleeping in the grave, he continues, but he qualifies it with *whom you do not yet remember*,[13] and in this addition the difference between Christ our Lord and the rest of the dead is to be noted. He, like others, was mortally wounded and laid in a grave; and those who did not know what they were doing, or who he was, assumed that he was like all others who have been wounded and slain, and now sleep in their graves. These are not yet remembered by God; that is to say, the time for their resurrection has not yet come. Scripture customarily speaks of the dead as "those who have fallen asleep" because it wishes us to understand that they will awaken one day; they are destined to rise again. But when Christ was wounded and slept in his tomb, he awakened on the third day. He became like a sparrow sitting alone on a roof,[14] that is, at the right hand of the Father in heaven. He will never die anymore, nor will death ever have dominion over him again.[15] This is what differentiates him from those whom God does not yet remember in such a way as to raise them up, for it was necessary that the resurrection which first took place in the head should be reserved for the body at the end of time. God is said to "remember" something when he does it, and to "forget" when he does not do it. This does not mean that God succumbs to forgetfulness. He is subject to no change whatever; and he cannot remember what he never forgets.

So, then, *I became like a man bereft of help* in the estimation of those who did not know what they were doing, although in fact I was *free among the dead*. By men who were ignorant of what they were doing I was reckoned to be *like the wounded sleeping in the grave*.

They were thrust away from your hand. That is to say, after I had been reduced to that state by them, they were themselves *thrust away from your hand*. These people who deemed me bereft of help were themselves deprived of the help of your hand. As he says in another psalm, *they dug a pit in front of me, but fell into it themselves* (Ps 56:7(57:6)). I think it is better to understand it in this way than to refer the statement, *they were thrust away from your hand*, to the dead asleep in their graves, whom the Lord does not yet remember. The trouble

---

12. See Jn 8:29; 16:32.
13. The sense of the original is more likely to be "whom you remember no longer," but Augustine takes it differently.
14. See Ps 101:8(102:7).
15. See Rom 6:9.

with this latter interpretation is that there are righteous people among the sleeping dead, and although God does not yet remember them in the sense of allowing them to rise immediately, scripture nonetheless says of them, *The souls of the just are in the hand of God* (Wis 3:1), which implies that they dwell within the help of the Most High, and abide under the protection of the God of heaven.[16] But the others, the ones who believed that Christ the Lord had been thrust away from God's hand, since they had succeeded in getting him condemned with criminals—these were themselves thrust away from God's hand.

Verses 7-8. Darkness and overwhelming waters

6. *They consigned me to the lower pit*, he says; or, rather, as the Greek has it, *to the lowest pit*. But what is the lowest pit? The most profound wretchedness, deeper than any other misery. This is the place of which it is said elsewhere, *You led me out of a pit of misery* (Ps 39:3(40:2)).

In dark places and the shadow of death. That was where they put him, his foes who thought so misguidedly and knew not what they did, ignorant of him whom not a single one of this world's rulers recognized.[17] As for the shadow of death, I do not know whether we should take this to mean bodily death, or rather that of which scripture says, *On those who sat in darkness and the shadow of death a light has dawned* (Is 9:2), because by believing in light and life[18] they were led out of the darkness and death of unbelief. Christ's enemies who did not know what they were doing thought the Lord's plight was the same as that of those dwellers in the dark, and in their ignorance they thrust him there; yet it was he who came to the aid of such benighted folk, that they might be such no longer.

7. *Your displeasure has been confirmed upon me*, or *your anger*, as some codices have it, or with others again, *your fury*. The Greek has θυμός, and our translators have chosen various equivalents. Where a Greek codex reads ὀργή scarcely any Latin translator hesitated to use "anger";[19] but where the Greek is θυμός, many translators did not think that this too should be rendered "anger,"[20] even though great writers of stylish Latin did so translate this word when they found it in the books of Greek philosophers. We need not spend much time arguing about this. All the same, if we are to suggest any other name for it, I would think "displeasure"[21] more acceptable than "fury,"[22] for "fury," at any rate in Latin usage, is not an attribute of the sane.

---

16. See Ps 90(91):1.
17. See 1 Cor 2:8.
18. Or "in the Light and the Life," two titles used by Christ of himself in Jn 8:12; 14:6.
19. *Ira.*
20. *Ira.*
21. *Indignatio.*
22. *Furor.*

But what is the meaning of the cry, *Your anger has been confirmed upon me*? It must imply that this was the view taken by those who did not recognize the Lord of glory.[23] According to their way of thinking the anger of God was not merely stirred up, but even *confirmed* upon the man whom they succeeded in bringing to his death—and not any common death, either, but that which they held to be most execrable of all, death on a cross. This is why the apostle says, *Christ redeemed us from the curse of the law, becoming a curse for us; for scripture says, accursed is anyone who is hanged upon a tree* (Gal 3:13; Dt 21:23). And when he wished to make it clear that Christ's obedience impelled him to the uttermost humility, Paul said, *He humbled himself and was made obedient to the point of death*; and then, as though even that were not enough, he added, *even death on a cross* (Phil 2:8).

As I see it, this explains why we have as the next verse in our psalm *You have brought all your breakers to bear upon me*; or, as other translators have rendered it, *all your waves*; or, with others again, *all your towering waters*.[24] In another psalm it is written, *All your waves and your breakers have invaded me* (Ps 41:8(42:7)), or, as some have translated it better, *have coursed over me*, for the Greek is διῆλθον, not εἰσῆλθον. When the two terms, *fluctus* and *suspensiones*, occurred together, translators obviously could not treat them as equivalents. While expounding that other psalm we said that "breakers" could represent threatening disasters, but "waves" actual sufferings;[25] and both of these proceed from the judgment of God. But while the earlier psalm said, *They all coursed over me*, this one says, *You have brought them all to bear upon me*. Whereas on that former occasion, even though some calamities befell him, the speaker declared that all the evils he mentioned *coursed over* him, this time he says, *You have brought them all to bear upon me*. Disasters are said to course over us either when they do not actually occur but only threaten, like the breakers, or when they do afflict us, but pass on, like the waves. But now he does not say that all the breakers have coursed over him; he says, *You have brought all your breakers to bear upon me*, indicating that all the evils which menaced him have come to pass. Everything that was foretold about Christ's passion was only a threat, as long as it loomed in prophecy.

Verses 9-10. Loneliness, failing eyes, outstretched hands

8. *You have driven my acquaintances far away from me*, he complains. If by *acquaintances* he means those known to him, this must include everybody, for is there anyone whom he did not know? More probably he calls *acquaintances*

---

23. See 1 Cor 2:8.
24. Respectively *suspensiones, fluctus, elationes*.
25. See Exposition of Psalm 41,15.

those who also knew him insofar as they were able, at least to the degree that they knew he was innocent, even though they thought of him as simply a man and not God. It is to be remembered, though, that he may have meant good people when he spoke of them as known to him, for he implied that bad people are unrecognized when he predicted that at the end he will say to them, *I never knew you* (Mt 7:23). He adds, *They deemed me an abomination.* We could take this to refer to those whom he called his acquaintances, because they too loathed this sort of death. But it is better to take it as a reference to the ones he was speaking about earlier as his persecutors.

I was handed over to them, and I kept on refusing to go forth, he continues. Does this simply mean that his disciples were outside while he was being tried inside the building? Possibly; but perhaps we should take *I kept on refusing to go forth* in a deeper sense. He may mean, "I was continuously hidden within my own being; I never showed who I was; at no point was I made public or manifest." This would connect well with the following statement, *My eyes were weakened from deprivation.* To whom is he alluding when he speaks of his *eyes*? He could mean the eyes in his head, the eyes that belonged to the flesh in which he was suffering. But we read nothing about his eyes being dimmed through deprivation during his passion, or languishing from hunger, which would be the usual cause. On the contrary: he was committed for trial after supper, and crucified on the same day. Yet if he meant his interior eyes, how could they weaken through privation, when they enjoyed indefectible light?

No, he undoubtedly called his "eyes" certain members of that body of which he is the head, those especially clear-sighted and noble and important members for whom he had a predilection. When the apostle spoke about the body of Christ, using our bodies as a comparison, he said, *If the body were all eye, how would it hear? If it were all hearing, how would it smell? If all the parts formed one single organ, what would become of the body? But as it is, there are many members, yet one body. The eye cannot say to the hands, "I do not need you." And if the* ear *says, "Since I am not an eye, I do not belong to the body," would that mean it was not part of the body?* (1 Cor 12:17.19.20.21.16). He drives home what he means us to understand by saying even more plainly, *You are Christ's body, and his limbs* (1 Cor 12:27). In line with this we can see why the "eyes" of the body—that is, the holy apostles—were *weakened from deprivation* when their light was withdrawn from them; it was as though their food had been withdrawn. Not flesh and blood, but Christ's Father in heaven, had revealed to them the truth which Peter articulated: *You are the Christ, the Son of the living God* (Mt 16:16). Yet when they saw him arrested, and enduring such terrible ill-treatment, they could not see him in the form they wished, for he kept refusing to go forth; he was not revealing himself in his mighty power, but remaining concealed within his own being. He was undergoing it all like a man defeated and helpless. And so, denied the light which was like food for them, these *eyes were weakened from deprivation*.

9. *And I cried to you, O Lord*. He did so most clearly of all when hanging on the cross. But we have reason to inquire how best to understand the next clause: *all day long I stretched out my hands to you*. If we take *I stretched out my hands* as a reference to his being hanged on the cross, what are we to make of the words, *all day long*? Since a whole day comprises both day and night, he cannot be said to have been there for a whole day, can he? We could, of course, assume that he meant "day" as opposed to night; but even then the early part of the day had passed before he was crucified, and no small part. Suppose, then, we take "day" to be used simply as an expression for "time." (This is especially plausible because the feminine has been used, which generally indicates a lapse of time in Latin, although the same cannot be said for Greek, since "day" is always feminine in that language, which I suspect is why our translators used the feminine.) In that case the problem becomes still more knotty. How can he say, "all the time," if he did not stretch out his hands on the cross for even a whole day? We could, no doubt, say that a part represents the whole, because that is a customary idiom in scripture; but I cannot think of any instance where, when a part is meant to stand for the whole, the actual word "whole" or "all" is added. The Lord did indeed say in the gospel, *So will the Son of Man be in the heart of the earth for three days and three nights* (Mt 12:40). But he did not say, "For three entire days and three entire nights," so his words can reasonably be understood as an example of the part representing the whole; for the middle day was a complete day, and there was also the later part of the first day and the first part of the third.

Another approach is to assume that in these words the prophetic psalm is not referring to his cross, but rather to the prayer which in his status as servant he poured out to God, his Father. The gospel testifies that he did so long before his passion, and on the day of his passion, and on the cross itself. We have learned about this and we remember that he prayed at these times, but nowhere do we read of his praying all day long.

The best way to understand the statement that his hands were stretched out all day long is to refer it to his unflagging continuance in good works. He never slackened in his concentration on these.

Verse 11. *Only the grace of God can raise up the spiritually dead*

10. His good works, however, were of benefit only to people predestined to eternal salvation, not to all and sundry, and not even to all those among whom they were performed. This is why he goes on to ask, *You will surely not work your wonders for the dead?* If we take this to mean the people whose flesh and blood had fallen lifeless, we must say that great wonders were indeed worked for the dead, since some of them were even restored to life. Moreover, when the

Lord invaded the underworld, and rose from it as conqueror of death, a great
wonder certainly was wrought for the dead. In asking, *You will surely not work
your wonders for the dead?* he must therefore refer to people who were so dead
in their hearts that even his great and wonderful works did not quicken them to
the life of faith. By questioning whether wonders could be worked for them he
did not mean that such persons see none, but that the wonders they do see do
them no good. He says, *All day long I spread out my hands to you,*[26] because he
refers all his actions to the will of the Father, declaring solemnly and very often
that he had come to carry out the Father's will. But since those actions were seen
by an unbelieving people, another prophet says, *All day long I spread out my
hands to an unbelieving people who defied me* (Is 65:2). These are the truly dead,
these are the people for whom his wonders were not worked—not in the sense
that they did not see them, but because they did not come back to life in consequence.

The next line asks, *Or will doctors raise the dead to confess to you?* No, dead
people will not be resuscitated by doctors in order to confess to you. Some assert
that the meaning is different in the Hebrew, where not doctors[27] but giants[28] are
mentioned. But the authority of the seventy Greek translators is so great that they
are reliably believed, in view of their amazing unanimity, to have been inspired
by the Spirit of God;[29] and they wished to signify to us how "giants" are to be
understood here. They were not making a mistake, but taking advantage of the
similarity of the words for "giants" and "doctors" in Hebrew, where the distinction between them is minimal. Now, if we take it that the term "giants" hints at
proud persons, the kind the apostle had in mind when he demanded, *Where is the
wise man? Where the scholar? Where is this world's savant?* (1 Cor 1:20), such
proud persons could quite fittingly be dubbed "doctors" inasmuch as they
pretended to save souls by their wise arts. Scripture contradicted them by
asserting, *Salvation is from the Lord.*[30]

---

26. When commenting on verse 10 Augustine read it as *extendi manus meas*; here it is *expandi
manus meas*, as also in the quotation from Isaiah which follows.
27. *Repha'im*, the participle from the verb *rapha'*, to heal, hence "healers."
28. Again *repha'im*, but probably derived from a different verb, *raphah*, to sink down. The
repha'im were legendary aboriginal inhabitants of parts of Canaan before the Israelite invasion
under Joshua; see Gn 14:4; Dt 2:11; 3:11; Jos 12:4. Og, the king of Bashan (see Ps
135(136):20), was reputed to be one of the last of them. Popular tradition held that they were of
huge stature, being the offspring of marriages between humans and angelic beings. The
connection with the verb *raphah* is obscure; possibly the idea was that they had sunk into
extinction and become powerless.
29. According to Jewish tradition, Ptolomy Philadelphus (third century B.C.) wanted a Greek
translation of the Hebrew law for his library at Alexandria, and set seventy (or seventy-two)
translators to work. They were strictly secluded from each other, yet all the versions turned out
to be exactly the same, suggesting divine assistance. Although there is no evidence for the truth
of the story, the Septuagint influenced the New Testament and was widely regarded as inspired
in the early centuries of the Church. See also note at Exposition of Psalm 67,16.
30. Ps 3:9(8). *Salus* can mean either salvation or health/healing. See Exposition of Psalm 70,18.

We could, however, take "giants" in a favorable sense. Of the Lord himself it was said, *He leaps up like a giant to run his course with joy* (Ps 18:6(19:5)). This suggests that he is the Giant of giants—that is to say, the most gigantic among those great, strong people who are the spiritual champions in his Church. The same idiom is used when he is called the Mountain of mountains, as in the text, *in the last days the mountain of the Lord shall be manifested, established above all other mountains* (Is 2:2; Mic 4:1), or the Holy One of all holy ones. Nor is there any reason why those same strong athletes should not also be called doctors. The apostle Paul says, *I try by every means in my power to provoke my kindred to emulation, so as to save some of them* (Rom 11:14).

Yet these spiritual physicians, even though it is not by their own power that they heal (as, for that matter, doctors of the body do not heal by their own power, either), and even though they help mightily towards our salvation by their faithful ministry, can heal only the living. They cannot bring to life those dead people concerning whom the question was asked, *You will surely not work your wonders for the dead?* The grace of God is something secret. As it works in human souls they somehow come back to life, so that they are capable of hearing instructions conducive to health from some one or other of his ministers. Christ draws our attention to this grace in the gospel when he says, *No one can come to me unless drawn to me by the Father who sent me*; and a little further on he repeats the same truth still more clearly: *the words I have spoken to you are spirit and life, but there are some among you who do not believe.* Then the evangelist comments, *For Jesus knew from the outset who the believers were, and who was going to betray him.*[31] He goes on to reinforce it with the Lord's own words: *that is why I told you that no one can come to me, except by the Father's gift* (Jn 6:44.64-66). Just before this he had said, *There are some among you who do not believe*; and now he seems to be explaining why not: *that is why I told you that no one can come to me, except by the Father's gift.* He was showing us that even the faith by which a person believes, the faith whereby our soul revives after the death of our heart, is given us by God.

However excellent, then, are the preachers of your word, however effectively they, like skilled doctors, treat human beings, persuading them of the truth even by miracles, the same questions must still be asked: If men and women are dead, and are not revived by your grace, *you will surely not work your wonders for the dead? Or will doctors raise the dead?* Will there be any raised up by them *to confess to you*? No, because such confession is the work of those who are alive. Scripture testifies elsewhere that *no confession can be made by a dead person: he is as though non-existent* (Sir 17:26).

---

31. The Greek in this verse reads, "…who the unbelievers were…." Both here and in his *Homilies on the Gospel of John* 27,7 Augustine read it without the negative in his Latin version.

Verses 12-13. Darkness and death cannot hear the message

11. *Will anyone recount your mercy in the grave, or your faithfulness in the land of the lost?* The introductory words are, of course, to be understood as repeated in the second half of the line, as though this read, "Will anyone recount your faithfulness in the land of the lost?" Scripture loves to link mercy with faithfulness, especially in the psalms. By saying, *In the land of the lost*, the psalm repeats the idea contained in *the grave*. But the grave means people who are in the grave, those same people described earlier as dead: *you will surely not work your wonders for the dead?* Well may it speak of a grave, for if the soul is dead, the body is no more than a tomb. This is why the Lord says to such people in the gospel, *You are like whitewashed tombs; outwardly they appear beautiful to onlookers, but inwardly they are full of dead men's bones and all kinds of filth. So too do you appear righteous to those who regard you from the outside, but within you are full of hypocrisy and iniquity* (Mt 23:27-28).

12. *Will your wondrous deeds be known in the darkness, or your righteousness in the land of oblivion?* Again there is repetition: *darkness* means the same thing as *the land of oblivion*. This is evident, because darkness is the symbol of unbelievers; as the apostle says, *You were darkness once* (Eph 5:8). Likewise a land of oblivion is nothing else but a man or woman who is unmindful of God. Unbelieving souls can reach such a depth of darkness that they say like fools in their hearts, *There is no God* (Ps 13(14):1).

The sense of all that has been said is carried coherently forward as follows: *I cried to you, O Lord*, amid my suffering; *all day long I spread out my hands to you*, ceaselessly extending my activities to glorify you. Why, then, do the impious rage against me? It can only be because you will not work your wonders for the dead. Those wondrous deeds will not arouse them to faith, nor will doctors raise them up to confess to you, for in such people your secret grace is not at work to draw them to belief. As I have testified, no one comes to me, except one whom you have attracted. *Will anyone recount your mercy in the grave*, tell the tale of it to a dead soul, crushed and lifeless under the weight of its body? Will anyone relate *your faithfulness in the land of the lost*, relate it to those so dead that they can neither credit nor perceive anything of the kind? *Will your wondrous deeds or your righteousness be known* in the darkness of a death like that, in a person who by forgetting you has lost the light of life?

Verse 14. The Church's confession

13. I have sometimes wondered what purpose such dead people serve, and how God uses them for the benefit of Christ's body, the Church. It must be to give proof of the power of his grace in those who are predestined, in those whom

he has called according to his purpose.[32] This is why the body proclaims in another psalm, *He is my God, because his mercy will forestall me. My God will give me proof of it, by his dealings with my enemies* (Ps 58:11-12(59:10)). The body speaks similarly here: *Yet even I have called to you, O Lord.* In these words we must hear Christ the Lord speaking in the voice of his body, the Church; for what else could *yet even I* mean? It can only be an acknowledgment that in our natural condition we too deserved God's wrath like all the rest.[33] Nonetheless, *even I have called to you, O Lord,* in order to be saved. When I hear the apostle delivering his terrible rebuke to others who lie under God's just anger, can I think that I shall be accounted different from the rest? *Who distinguishes you?* he demands. *What have you that you did not receive? And if you did receive it, why boast as though you had not?* (1 Cor 4:7). *Salvation is from the Lord* (Ps 3:9(8)): not even a giant will be saved by his immense prowess.[34] As scripture teaches, *Whoever calls upon the name of the Lord will be saved. But how will they call upon one in whom they have not yet believed? And how will they believe in him of whom they have not heard? And how will they hear without anyone to preach to them? And how will any preach, if they are not sent? As it is written, How beautiful are the feet of those who announce peace and bring good news!* (Rom 10:13-15; Is 52:7). They are the physicians who care for the man wounded by robbers, but it is the Lord who took him to the inn.[35] They are laborers in the Lord's field; yet the planter is nothing, and the irrigator is nothing; only God gives the increase.[36] Even I called upon the Lord, cried to him that I might be saved; but how could I have invoked him unless I had believed in him? And how could I have come to believe in him, unless I had heard about him first? Yet he attracted me inwardly, empowering me to believe what I heard, because it was no doctor who awakened me from the deadness of my heart, but the Lord himself, working in secret. Many there were who heard the preachers' message, for their sound went forth through all the earth, and their words to the uttermost parts of the world;[37] but faith is not given to all, and the Lord knows who belongs to him.[38] I could not even have believed had God's mercy not forestalled me, had he not led me out of darkness into the light of faith by secretly calling me, and raising me to life, and drawing me on; for he raises the dead and calls things that have no being as though they already were.[39]

---

32. See Rom 8:28.
33. See Eph 2:3.
34. See Ps 32(33):16.
35. See Lk 10:34.
36. See 1 Cor 3:7.
37. See Ps 18:5(19:4).
38. See 2 Th 3:2; 2 Tm 2:19.
39. See Rom 4:17.

Accordingly the Church continues, *In the morning my prayer will rise before you.* Already morning has broken, for the darkness of unbelief has dispersed. Your mercy forestalled me, so that I might see this morning light; but another dawn awaits me, when all the hidden things of darkness will be bathed in light, and the thoughts of all hearts made manifest, and each of us receive our commendation from you.[40] While I am in this life, still on this my journey, I walk in the light of faith. In comparison with the darkness of unbelievers this is already daylight for me, though compared with that day when we shall see you face to face it is night still. Yet all the while *my prayer will rise before you.*

Verse 15. Why our prayer seems to be rejected

14. Meanwhile the good things we shall enjoy for eternity are delayed, and the evils that will pass are thickening, but only so that our prayer may grow more fervent and persevering, for the benefit we derive from such prayer is, I think, beyond description. The psalm therefore continues, *Why have you rejected my prayer, Lord?* This is the same question that was asked in those other words, *O God, my God, look upon me, why have you forsaken me?* (Ps 21:2(22:1)). The suppliant was there begging to know why, not presuming to find fault with the wisdom of God, as though he were acting without a reason; and the same is true here: *why have you rejected my prayer, Lord?* But if we examine the matter carefully we shall see that the reason has been suggested already. The prayer of the saints seems to be rejected as the great gifts they hope for are deferred and tribulations beset them; but this is only to kindle their prayer into a hotter flame, like a fire fanned by a gust of air.

Verses 16-19. The Church suffers and endures, until its hope is fulfilled

15. The psalm therefore enumerates the troubles that Christ's body too must undergo, for these do not afflict the head alone, as was made clear by Christ's question to Saul: *Why are you persecuting me?* (Acts 9:4). This same man, now transformed into Paul and functioning as a chosen member in the body, declared his desire: to *fill up what is lacking to the sufferings of Christ in my own flesh* (Col 1:24). So the psalm begs, *Why have you rejected my prayer, Lord? Why do you turn your face away from me? I am poor and afflicted from my very youth; I was exalted but then humbled and confused.*[41] *The waves of your anger have swept over me, and your terrors have left me badly shaken. They surround me like flood-water all day long, all of them encircling me together. You have sent*

---

40. See 1 Cor 4:5.
41. Variant: "gravely disturbed."

my friend far away from me, distanced my familiar companions from my wretch-edness. All these woes have befallen the members of Christ's body, and befall them still. God does turn his face away from those who pray, by not hearing and granting their requests when they fail to understand that what they ask for is not for their good. And the Church truly is poor, since it hungers and thirsts on pilgrimage for what will satisfy it when it reaches home. The Church is afflicted from its very youth, for this same body laments in another psalm, *Very often have they attacked me, ever since I was young* (Ps 128(129):1). Some of its members are exalted even in this world, to the end that in them there may be the greater lowliness. Over this body, composed of the unity of holy people and believers with Christ their head, pass the waves of God's anger. But they pass, they do not abide; not of a believer but of an unbeliever was it said, *The anger of God remains upon him* (Jn 3:36). And God's terrors do badly shake the faithful in their weakness, because they prudently fear any disaster that may happen, even if in fact it does not. At times these terrors cause great disquiet in a soul that thinks of them as breakers towering all around it; they seem like encircling waters, trapping the fearful soul on every side. These tribulations are never lacking to the Church while it makes its pilgrim way through this world; now they afflict some members, now others, for the calamities strike from every direction. This is why the Church says, *All day long*, suggesting the long stretch of time until the world ends. And often enough friends and acquaintances who see their worldly interests at risk forsake the saints out of fear;[42] of friends like that the apostle complains, *One and all, they left me in the lurch: may it not be held against them* (2 Tm 4:16).

To what purpose do all these things happen? Surely so that the prayer of this holy body may rise before God in the morning, that is, in the light of faith that succeeds the night of unbelief. Rise before him it must until the definitive coming of our salvation; for we are saved already, but in hope, not in full realiza-tion, and so we wait for the reality patiently and in faith.[43] When it comes at last God will not reject our prayer, because there will be nothing that we need to ask of him; we shall simply look to receive whatever we rightly asked of him in the past. Nor will he turn his face away from us, for we shall see him as he is.[44] No longer shall we be poor, because God himself will be our wealth, all things in all of us.[45] No more shall we be afflicted, because no infirmity will be left in us; nor shall we be exalted only to be humbled and badly shaken, because no adversity

---

42. *Amici et noti periclitantes secundum saeculum, sanctos formidine deserunt.* The translation offered above assumes the insertion of the comma after *saeculum*. If it is omitted, we could understand the sentence to mean "Friends and acquaintances forsake the saints out of fear when they [the saints] are in danger as the world sees it."
43. See Rom 8:24-25.
44. See 1 Jn 3:2.
45. See 1 Cor 15:28.

will come near us. We shall never again endure even the passing waves of God's anger, for we shall abide in his abiding kindness. His terrors will not shake us, because the fulfillment of his promises will bring us joy. No acquaintance, no friend, will be driven far from us by fear, for there will be no enemy to dread.

Exposition 1 of Psalm 88

First Sermon[1]

Verse 1. Understanding for the weak made strong

1. By our Lord's grace we have undertaken to speak to you about this psalm, beloved,[2] and you should be aware that it deals with the hope we hold in him, Christ Jesus our Lord. Keep your expectation high, because he who has promised will fulfill all that remains still to be realized, as he has already fulfilled so much. It is not any merit on our part that gives us such confidence in him, but only his mercy. This, I think, is the insight attained by the man mentioned in the title, for the psalm is headed *Understanding for Ethan the Israelite*.[3] I think this must be right, for look who this man Ethan was. His name means "strong," or "solid and firm,"[4] and no one in this world is strong or firm except through hope in God's promise. As far as our own resources are concerned we are weak and infirm, but through his mercy we are strong. So this is how he begins his psalm, the speaker who is so weak in himself, but strong in the mercy of God:

Verses 2-3. The mercy and the faithfulness of God

2. *O Lord, I will sing of your mercies for ever; I will proclaim your faithfulness from generation to generation with my own mouth.* "Let my bodily organs obey my Lord," he says. "I speak, but what I say is about you: *I will proclaim your faithfulness with my own mouth.* If I am not obedient, I am not your servant; but if I speak of myself, I am a liar. If I am to speak as you inspire me, and yet truly speak myself, two things are necessary; one is yours, the other mine. Your faithfulness is needed, and my mouth." So now let us hear what this faithfulness is that he proclaims, and what are the mercies he sings.

3. *You have said, For ages unending mercy will be built up.* This is what I am singing about; this is your faithfulness, and my mouth is doing its duty in proclaiming that *you have said, For ages unending mercy will be built up.* "I so build," you tell us, "as never to dismantle." There are instances where you

---

1. Possibly preached at Carthage, in some year between 399 and 411, on the morning of 13 September.
2. *Caritati vestrae.*
3. See Exposition of Psalm 87,1, and note there.
4. *Robustus.*

destroy certain peoples with no intention of rebuilding, whereas others you destroy only to rebuild. If this were not so, if none were ever due for demolition only to be built up again, Jeremiah would not have been told, *See, I have given you authority to overthrow, and then to build up* (Jer 1:10); and certainly none of those peoples who used to serve idols and worship gods of stone would have been built up in Christ unless they had been dismantled with respect to their original errors. On the other hand, some there have been who were destroyed without prospect of rebuilding; this we can infer from the passage which says, *You will overthrow them, and not build them up* (Ps 27(28):5).

Now the speaker considers the case of those who are broken down in order to be built up again. Such people might have thought that since their devastation was only a temporary stage, their rebuilding would likewise be temporary. But this man, whose mouth was at the service of God's faithfulness, held tight to the same faithfulness in correcting them. I proclaim, I speak, he said, only because *you have said* it. As a human speaker I am confident, because you have said it, and you are my God. Though in any utterance of my own I well might waver, in your word I will be firmly established.

You have said .... What have you said? *You have said that for ages unending mercy will be built up. In the heavens your faithfulness will be held ready.* Here again we find these two being linked—mercy and faithfulness—as in the preceding verse. There it said, *O Lord, I will sing of your mercies for ever; I will proclaim your faithfulness from generation to generation with my own mouth.* And now the psalm links them again: *You have said that for ages unending mercy will be built up. In the heavens your faithfulness will be held ready.* Mercy and faithfulness are reiterated together, because *all the Lord's ways are mercy and faithfulness* (Ps 24(25):10); there would be no question of faithfulness in the fulfillment of the promises unless there had first been mercy in the forgiveness of sins.

Another point is this. Many things were promised through prophecy to the people of Israel who according to the flesh are of Abraham's stock. Indeed, the reason for that people's increase was that God's promises might be fulfilled in it. But God did not seal up the fountain of his goodness against other nations, whom he had put under the authority of the angels,[5] while reserving Israel as his own special people. The apostle apportioned the mercy and faithfulness of the Lord between Jews and Gentiles, but each in its own way. *I maintain that Christ Jesus was a servant of the circumcised, to save the faithfulness of God and confirm the promises made to our fathers*, he says (Rom 15:8). So you see, God did not let them down; you see that he did not reject his own, the people he had known as his before they came to be. Even when the apostle was discussing the falling away of the Jews, he took care that no one should suppose them to have been so totally

---

5. Or perhaps "whom he had created below the angels," referring to Ps 8:6(5).

repudiated that no grain of wheat found its way into the barn after the sifting. So he says, *God has not cast off his own people, whom he foreknew; for I am myself sprung from the race of Israel* (Rom 11:2.1). If the whole harvest was nothing but thorns, how could I be speaking as a grain? Clearly, God's faithfulness was maintained toward those Israelites who believed, and so there emerged from the circumcised one wall to fit itself into the cornerstone.[6] But this stone would not form a corner if there were no other wall to join it from the direction of the Gentiles. The former wall has a special claim on God's faithfulness, the latter on his mercy, for, as the apostle puts it, *I maintain that Christ Jesus was a servant of the circumcised, to save the faithfulness of God and confirm the promises made to our fathers, but to give the Gentiles cause to glorify God for his mercy* (Rom 15:8-9).

It is particularly fitting, then, to say, *In the heavens your faithfulness will be held ready*, for all those Israelites who were called to be apostles were turned into heavens, apt to proclaim the glory of God. Of them it was said, *The heavens proclaim God's glory, and the firmament tells of his handiwork*. From that verse in isolation you might not be sure that the "heavens" are the apostles, but the next one leaves us in no doubt: *there is no speech, no language, in which their voices are not heard*. If you ask, "Whose voices?" you will find that no one has been mentioned except the heavens. If, then, it is the apostles whose voice has been heard in all these languages, it is equally of the apostles that the psalm goes on to say, *Their sound went forth throughout the world, their words to the ends of the earth* (Ps 18:2.4.5(19:1.3.4)). They were drawn from Israel before the Church had come to fill the whole world, but their words reached the very ends of the earth; and we may see fulfilled in them the psalm's declaration, *in the heavens your faithfulness will be held ready*.

Verses 4-5. The promises to Abraham's seed. Confidence in preaching is based on God's word

4. *I have established a covenant with my chosen ones*. Understand that this is part of what the Lord has said: *You have said, I have established a covenant with my chosen ones*. What covenant can this be, if not the New Covenant? What covenant—if not that by which we ourselves are made new and fit for our new inheritance? What covenant? Surely that which entitles us to the inheritance we long for and love so passionately that we sing a new song. *I have established a covenant with my chosen ones*, he says. *I have sworn to my servant David*. How confidently the psalmist speaks, knowing for whose faithfulness his mouth is performing its service! "Because you have said it, I speak with confidence. If by simply saying it you give me such assurance, how much more confident do you

---

6. See Eph 2:20.

make me now that you have sworn?" When God swears an oath, it is to confirm his promise. Men and women are with good reason forbidden to swear, because if they get into the habit of doing so they may slip into perjury, given the fallibility of human beings. God alone swears safely, for he cannot be wrong.

5. Let us see what God has sworn. *I have sworn to my servant David: even to eternity I will provide for your seed.* But David's seed is Abraham's seed, surely? And what is Abraham's seed? The apostle tells us: scripture says, *And to your seed, which is Christ* (Gal 3:16). So yes, Christ who is the head of the Church and the savior of his body[7] is the seed of Abraham, and also of David; but are not we too Abraham's seed? Certainly we are; the apostle directly asserts this: *if you belong to Christ, you are the descendants of Abraham, his heirs according to the promise* (Gal 3:29).

In the light of this we should take the promise, *even to eternity I will provide for your seed,* to refer not only to that flesh of Christ which was born from the virgin Mary, but also to all of us who believe in Christ, my brothers and sisters; for we are the limbs of the body which has Christ as its head. Now the body cannot be decapitated; if the head is to be glorified for eternity, the members must be as well, so that Christ may be whole and entire for ever. *Even to eternity I will provide for your seed, and I will build you a throne to last from generation to generation.* We think that the words, *from generation to generation,* mean the same thing as *even to eternity,* for a little earlier the psalmist had said, *I will proclaim your faithfulness from generation to generation with my own mouth.* What does *from generation to generation* signify? Probably "to every generation." It is not as though the word needed to be repeated every time a generation comes and goes. The doubling in the phrase—from generation to generation—suggests and emphasizes the great number of generations there will be.

Another approach, though, would be to understand the phrase as a reference to two different "generations." You know about these, dearly beloved,[8] because we have pointed it out before,[9] and you remember, don't you? There is the generation of flesh and blood at the present time; but there will be a different generation at the resurrection of the dead. Christ is preached here, and he will be preached there too; but here he is preached in order that people may believe in him, there he will be preached that they may see him.

I will build you a throne to last from generation to generation. Even now Christ is enthroned in us, for his throne has been built up in us. If he were not enthroned within us he would not be ruling and guiding us, and if we were not guided by him, we would blunder and fall under our own guidance. He is enthroned in us and reigns over us; but he is enthroned also in that other genera-

7. See Eph 5:23.
8. *Vestrae Caritati.*
9. See his Exposition of Psalm 71,8.

tion, the one that shall be when the dead rise again. Christ will reign for all eternity in his saints. God has promised this, God has said it; and as though that were not enough, God has sworn it. Since, then, the promise is confirmed not in proportion to what we deserve but in accordance with his own mercy, no one should have any timidity about preaching it, for there is no room for doubt. Let there be in our hearts that solid strength from which Ethan took his name, "Strong of heart." Let us preach God's faithfulness, God's utterance, God's promises, God's oath. Fortified on all sides, let us preach him. And let us too become "heavens" by carrying God.

Verse 6. The newly-made "heavens" proclaim the Lord's wonders

6. *The heavens will confess your wonderful works, O Lord.* What the heavens will confess is not their own merits, but *your wonderful works, O Lord.* In every mercy shown to those who were lost, in the justification of the godless, what else do we praise but the wondrous works of God? You praise him because the dead have risen to life; praise him all the more because the lost have been redeemed. What a grace is this, what a mercy on God's part! You observe how someone who yesterday was a sink for liquor has today become a shining example of sobriety. Someone else was yesterday a cesspit of debauchery, but today is honored for temperance. Another was a blasphemer yesterday, but today a praiser of God. Another whom you saw serving created things yesterday is today a worshipper of their creator. People are converted from all these desperate states. Let them not look to any merits of their own, but become "heavens," and let the heavens confess the wonderful exploits of him by whom they were made into heavens. *I shall see the heavens, the work of your fingers*, says another psalm (Ps 8:4(3)).

The heavens will confess your wonderful works, O Lord. To make sure you are aware who these heavens are who will be confessing, look what they confess. The next words tell you: *and your faithfulness in the church of the saints.* In view of this there can be no doubt that those who preach the word of truth are to be understood as "heavens." And where will the heavens confess your wonderful works and your faithfulness? *In the church of the saints.* Let the Church accept the dew from the heavens. Let the heavens send their rain upon the thirsty earth, and let the earth that receives the rain sprout the healthy growth of good actions, lest its only response to the good grain be thorns, and it be doomed to expect the fire rather than the barn.

The heavens will confess your wonderful works, O Lord, and your faithfulness in the church of the saints. What the heavens are to confess, then, are your wondrous deeds and your reliable truthfulness. Whatever the heavens preach is from you and about you. That is why they preach without misgivings, for they know to whom they are preaching, and they know that over him whom they preach they will never have occasion to blush.

Verse 7. Preachers of truth are rain-bearing clouds, but none equal the Lord. We are children of God, but the only-begotten is unique

7. What do the heavens proclaim? What do they confess in the church of the saints? *Who among the clouds shall be reckoned equal to the Lord?* So this is what the heavens will confess, is it, this is what the skies rain down? What do they say? *Who among the clouds shall be reckoned equal to the Lord?* Preachers can ask that question in all confidence, because no one among the clouds will be found the Lord's equal. Does that seem like high praise offered to the Lord, brothers and sisters, to say that the clouds are not equal to their Creator? If we take it literally, without any spiritual meaning, it is no great praise of the Lord to say that the clouds are not his equals. How could they be? The stars are above them, and are the stars equal to the Lord? No? Well then, what about the sun, the moon, the angels, the highest sky: can any of them be even compared with the Lord? Are we saying anything much, then, in asking, *Who among the clouds shall be reckoned equal to the Lord?*

But we understand these "clouds" to represent the preachers of the truth, brothers and sisters, just as the "heavens" do; they symbolize the prophets and apostles, and all who proclaim the word of God. We gather that all these types of preachers are called "clouds" from the prophecy where God, angry with his vineyard, said, *I will forbid my clouds to send rain upon it*, for this same passage explains clearly and unambiguously what vineyard is in question by continuing, *The vineyard of the Lord of Hosts is the house of Israel* (Is 5:6.7). You might have ignored the human participants and searched for the vineyard as a plot of ground; so the prophecy excludes this mistake by telling you, *the vineyard of the Lord of Hosts is the house of Israel.* "The house of Israel is not to understand the prophecy in any other way," the Lord is saying; "it is to recognize itself as my vineyard. It is to understand that it has yielded me not grapes but thorns; it is to perceive how ungrateful it has shown itself to its planter and cultivator, how ungrateful to the giver of its rain." If, then, *the vineyard of the Lord of Hosts is the house of Israel,* what does its angry owner have to say? *I will forbid my clouds to send rain upon it.* And this is indeed how he dealt with it. The apostles, like clouds, were sent to pour rain upon the Jews. But the Jews, who had been yielding thorns instead of grapes, rejected God's word. The apostles therefore told them, *We were sent to you, but because you have rejected the word of God, we are turning now to the Gentiles* (Acts 13:46). And from that time the clouds ceased to shower rain on the vineyard.

Clearly, then, clouds represent preachers of the truth, but we must first inquire, Why clouds? The same people are called both "heavens" and "clouds":

heavens because of the blazing glory of truth, but clouds because of the obscurity of the flesh, for all these clouds have something foggy about them in consequence of their mortality. They come, and then pass over. With this obscurity of their carnal nature in mind, this mistiness of the clouds, the apostle warned, *Pass no judgment prematurely, before the coming of the Lord, for he will light up the dark, hidden places* (1 Cor 4:5). You are aware in the present of what a person says, but you do not see what is hidden in the heart; you see what is squeezed out from the cloud, but what is retained inside the cloud you do not see. Can anyone's eyes penetrate a cloud? We are justified, therefore, in taking clouds as preachers of the truth in their fleshly condition.

The Creator of all things came himself in the flesh. But *who among the clouds shall be reckoned equal to the Lord? Or who will be like the Lord among the sons of God?* No one: this is what is implied. No one among God's children will be like the Son of God. True, he is called the Son of God, as we too are called sons and daughters of God; but for all that, *who will be like the Lord among the sons of God?* He is the unique Son, and we are many; he is one, and we are one in him; he was born Son, but we are adopted; he is the Son begotten of God by nature from eternity, but we have been made children of God within time and through grace; he is without sin, but we have been freed from sin through him. *Who among the clouds shall be reckoned equal to the Lord? Or who will be like the Lord among the sons of God?* We are called "clouds" on account of our flesh, and because as clouds we shower down rain we are known as preachers of the truth; but our flesh and his flesh arise differently. We are called children of God, but he is Son of God in a different sense. The cloud of his flesh came from a virgin, and he is Son from eternity, equal to the Father. Who, then, *among the clouds shall be reckoned equal to the Lord? Or who will be like the Lord among the sons of God?*

Let the Lord himself tell us whether he found his like. *Who do people say I am, I, the Son of Man?* Tell me. I am seen, I am closely observed, I walk about among you, and perhaps I am deemed unimportant because you are so used to me. Tell me, then, *Who do people say I am, I, the Son of Man?* They see a son of man, and therefore they see a cloud. Let them tell me—or, rather, you tell me— *who people say I am.* They relayed popular opinions to him: *Some say Jeremiah, others say Elijah, others John the Baptist, or one of the prophets.* Many clouds, many sons of God, were nominated; for certainly those just and holy men were also sons of God. Jeremiah, Elijah and John were undoubtedly sons of God, and clouds too, because they were God's preachers. So, says the Lord, you have told me about the clouds with whom people identify me, and about the sons of God with whom they rank me; but now tell me *who you say I am.* Peter replied on behalf of them all, the one speaker expressing their unity, *You are the Christ, the Son of the living God.*[10] For who among the clouds shall be deemed the Lord's

---

10. See Mt 16:13-16.

equal? Or who among all those sons of God shall be thought like the Lord? *You are the Christ, the Son of the living God*, but differently from those sons of God who are not your equals. You have come in the flesh, but not like those other clouds: they cannot be held equal to you.

Verses 8-9. The diffusion of God's truth and mercy

8. Who are you, then, you to whom the answer was given, *You are the Christ, the Son of the living God*, you whom other men and women, themselves neither holy nor just, believed to be one of the prophets, Elijah, Jeremiah, or John the Baptist—who are you?

Listen to the next verse: *God, to be glorified in the assembly of the just. Who among the clouds shall be reckoned equal to the Lord, or who will be like the Lord among the sons of God*, if he is *God, to be glorified in the assembly of the just?* Since they cannot pretend to be his equal, they will be well advised to believe in him. Neither clouds nor children of God can be his equals, so the best advice for weak human beings is this: if any are minded to glory, let them glory in the Lord.[11]

God, to be glorified in the assembly of the just, great and terrible to all who surround him. God is everywhere, so how can any be round about him? If he has other beings surrounding him, it seems that he must be limited on every side. But if what another psalm confesses to God and about God is true, that *there is no limit to his greatness* (Ps 144(145):3), are there any left of whom we can say that they are round about him? We must understand it in this way: he who is present everywhere willed to be born according to the flesh in a particular place, to pass his life in one nation, to be crucified in a unique place, to rise from one special location, to ascend to heaven from one particular place. And the place where he did all these things was surrounded by the Gentiles. If he had remained in that one place where he did it all he would not have become *great and terrible to all who surround him.* But he preached in that place in such a way as to send the preachers of his name throughout the Gentiles all over the wide world, and by performing miracles through his servants he has become *great and terrible to all who surround him.*

9. *O Lord, God of hosts, who is like you? You are mighty, O Lord, and encompassed by your faithfulness.* Very great is your might, for you made heaven and earth, and everything that is in them. But greater still is your mercy, which has made your faithfulness known to all around you. If you had been preached only in that one place where you willed to be born, to suffer, and to rise again, in that one place whence you willed to ascend, then God's faithfulness would have been safeguarded, *to confirm the promises made to the fathers.* But if the apostle

---

11. See 1 Cor 1:31.

were to be proved right in the rest of what he said, and the Gentiles given cause *to glorify God for his mercy*, truth and faithfulness had to spread outward, to be diffused all around from that center where you willed to appear. In that one place you did indeed thunder from your own cloud, but then you sent other clouds to pour out their moisture all round the Gentile world. In your great might you fulfilled the prophecy you had spoken: *Hereafter you shall see the Son of Man coming in the clouds* (Mt 26:64). *You are mighty, O Lord, and encompassed by your faithfulness.*

Verses 10-11. The sea is tamed and the sea-monster wounded

10. Once your truth had begun to be preached all around, then indeed the nations raged and the peoples devised futile schemes. The kings of the earth arose and the rulers made common cause against the Lord and against his Anointed.[12] When your truth and faithfulness began to be proclaimed all round you it was as though you had come to choose a bride from among foreigners, and so a ravening lion barred your way; but you strangled it.[13] These events were foreshadowed in the story of Samson. (Before I had mentioned his name you had responded enthusiastically to my words, brothers and sisters; you would not have done that if you had not picked up the reference. But you did, because you have been listening like people accustomed to being rained on from God's clouds.) So, as I was saying, your faithfulness, Lord, was to spread far and wide. But how was this ever likely to happen without persecutions, or without evoking contradiction, when it had been prophesied that the Lord himself was born to be a sign that would be contradicted?[14]

That nation in which you willed to be born, Lord, in which you willed to lead your earthly life, was like a piece of dry land separated from the teeming sea of the Gentiles, destined to be arid ground thirsting for your rain. The other nations were like the sea, salty, harsh and sterile. What are your preachers to do, then, as they try to sprinkle your truth all around you? What is to be done, if the waves of the sea are so rough? *You subdue the power of the sea.* What did the tempestuous sea produce? The festival we celebrate today! It killed the martyrs and scattered their blood like seeds, and the crop of the Church sprang up.[15] Let the clouds float along serenely, let them diffuse your truth all around you and not fear the furious waves, for *you subdue the power of the sea.* The sea heaves, the sea contradicts him, the sea raises its din; but God is faithful and does not allow you, his followers, to be tried beyond your strength.[16] And because he is faithful, and

---

12. See Ps 2:1-2.
13. See Jgs 14:5-6.
14. See Lk 2:34.
15. Compare Tertullian, *Apol.* 50.
16. See 1 Cor 10:13.

does not allow you to be overwhelmed by trials you cannot bear, the psalm testifies, *You calm the surging of its waves.*

11. Since you willed that the sea should be rendered tranquil, or, rather, that
the sea's savagery should be tamed, what did you do within it? *You humbled the
proud one, leaving him as though wounded.* There is a proud dragon in the sea,
you know. Another passage in scripture says of it, *I will order the dragon that
lives there to bite him;*[17] this is the same sea-monster which was referred to as *the
dragon you made to play with* (Ps 103(104):26), the one whose head God pounds
upon the waters.[18] *You humbled the proud one, leaving him as though wounded,*
says the psalm. You humbled yourself, and the proud one was thereby humbled.
He was proud, and kept control over proud humans by means of their pride. The
great one was humbled, and everyone who believes in him has become little.
While the little one is sustained by the example of the great one who made
himself small, the devil loses his grip, for that proud captor could keep hold only
of the proud. In the face of so mighty an example of humility, men and women
learned to repudiate their pride and imitate the humility of God. The devil, for his
part, was humiliated by losing his captives—not corrected, but laid low. *You
humbled the proud one, leaving him as though wounded.* You were humbled,
and so humbled him; you were wounded, and so wounded him. Your blood
could not do otherwise than wound him, for it was poured out to efface the
written record of sins.[19] What had he to be proud about, except that he held a
legal title to us? But by your blood you blotted out that title-deed, that written
record; and by robbing him of so many prisoners you left him wounded. When
you hear of the devil being wounded, brothers and sisters, you must not take it to
mean that his flesh was pierced, for he had none. But he has been struck in his
heart, where lurks his pride. *And with your strong arm you have scattered your
enemies.*

Verses 12-14. Creation and redemption: all is God's gift

12. *Yours are the heavens, yours the earth.* The heavens receive the rain from
you, and pour it down on the earth that belongs to you. *Yours are the heavens,*
through whom your faithfulness has been preached all around you; *yours the
earth,* which all around you has welcomed it.

Then the psalm speaks of the effect of the rain. What is it? *You have created
the round world in all its fullness; the north and the seas are of your making.* The

---

17. Am 9:3. The prophet, speaking in God's name, was pointing out that sinful Israelites would
    find no place of refuge from divine retribution, even if they were to hide in the sea.
18. An echo of Babylonian mythology. As adapted and played with in Israelite imagination the
    myth became a defeat by the Lord of the monster who represented watery chaos. Compare Jb
    7:12; Ps 73(74):13-14; 76:17(77:16).
19. See Col 2:14.

world has no power to do anything against you, its creator. It can behave very savagely out of its own malice and through the perversity of its own will; but can it trespass beyond the boundary set by its creator, who made all things? Why, then, should I be afraid of the north? Why fear the seas? It is true that the north is the abode of the devil, who said, *I will set my throne in the north, I shall be like the Most High*,[20] but you humbled that proud upstart and left him as though wounded. Your dealings with these creatures are more effective in establishing your dominance than is their striving to gain their malicious ends. *The north and the seas are of your making.*

13. *Tabor and Hermon will exult in your name.* These two are known to be actual mountains, but they also represent something. *Tabor and Hermon will exult in your name.* Tabor means "the light that comes." But if Christ's disciples are told, *You are the light of the world* (Mt 5:14), whence do they derive their light? Undoubtedly from him of whom it was said, *He was the true Light, which illumines every human person who comes into this world* (Jn 1:9). The light which is the light of the world comes from that primal Light which is kindled from no other, and so there is no fear of its being extinguished. The light which derives from him is the lamp which is not placed under a tub, but on a candle-stick, the "coming light" which Tabor represents.

Hermon is interpreted "anathema to him." The light came, and became anathema to him. To whom? To the devil—who else? To the wounded, proud one. By your gift we have been illuminated; by your gift it is that he who once held us prisoners in his error and pride has become anathema to us. That is why *Tabor and Hermon will exult in your name*: not in their own merits, but *in your name*. These must pray, *Not to us, Lord, not to us, but to your name give the glory*. They must pray thus because of the raging sea, *lest perhaps the pagans ask, Where is their God?* (Ps 113B(115):1.2).

14. *Mighty is your arm.* Let none of us arrogantly claim anything. *Mighty is your arm*: we were made by you, and we are defended by you. *Mighty is your arm; may your hand be strengthened, your right hand glorified.*

Verse 15. God's mercy and truth forestall the future judgment

15. *Righteousness and judgment are the foundation of your throne.* Your righteousness will be revealed at the end, along with your judgment; but for the present they are hidden. Another psalm alludes to your judgment in the words, *for the hidden things of the son*.[21] But there will be a manifestation of these hidden things—your judgment and your righteousness. Some people will be

---

20. Is 14:13-14. On the mythology behind this poetic passage, see note at Exposition of Psalm 59,10.
21. See the title of Psalm 9.

placed at your right hand, others at your left. Unbelievers will be terrified when they see what now they laugh at and refuse to believe in, while the just rejoice on seeing what they believe in now without seeing. *Righteousness and judgment are the foundation of your throne*; this will be the case on judgment day; so much is certain. What about now? *Mercy and faithfulness run ahead of you.* The foundation of your throne would fill me with fear, and the prospect of your righteousness and judgment would terrify me, had not your mercy and faithfulness preceded you. Why should I fear your judgments at the end, when your mercy has raced ahead of you to blot out my sins, and you are demonstrating your faithfulness by keeping your promises? *Mercy and faithfulness run ahead of you*, for all the Lord's ways are mercy and faithfulness.[22]

Verses 16-17. Delighting in grace, God's people walks in the light of his countenance

16. All this must surely delight us; but shall we be able to grasp how delighted we are?[23] Or will words suffice to express our gladness? Will any tongue be apt to articulate our joy? If no words can do it justice, then *blessed the people that knows how to shout with joy.* O blessed people, do you think you apprehend what shouting for joy[24] is? You cannot be blessed unless you do understand it. Oh, that you may know how to rejoice in something that you cannot put into words, for your joy does not spring from yourself; rather let anyone who would glory, glory in the Lord.[25] Take no joy in your pride, but only in the grace of God. So great is his grace that no tongue is fit to express it. Grasp this, and you have understood about shouting for joy.

17. Well then, if you have understood that grace is something to make you shout for joy, listen now as the psalm speaks of grace more explicitly. *Blessed the people that knows how to shout with joy*, yes, to be sure; but what kind of joy is this? See if it is not delight in grace, delight in God, and no delight whatever in yourself. *They will walk in the light of your countenance, O Lord.* Tabor is "a light that comes," but if it does not walk in the light of your countenance its lamp is blown out by the wind of pride. *They will walk in the light of your countenance, O Lord, and exult in your name all day long.* Tabor and Hermon will *exult in your name*; if they hope to exult *all day long* it can be only in your name. If they try to exult in their own, their exultation will not last all day. If they seek joy in themselves their joy will be short-lived, and they will fall through pride. To exult all day long, let them *exult in your name, and they will be exalted in your*

---

22. See Ps 24(25):10.
23. *Aut quod exsultamus capiemus?* Possibly we could take this as *"Shall we be able to contain our delight?"* but this would strain the Latin somewhat.
24. *Iubilatio.*
25. See 1 Cor 1:31.

righteousness. Not in their own righteousness, but in yours; otherwise they would risk having a zeal for God that is not informed by knowledge. Certain people are mentioned by the apostle as having fallen into this trap: *they failed to recognize the righteousness that comes from God,* refusing to exult in your light. The result was that *they did not submit to God's righteousness.* How did it happen? Because *they had zeal for God, indeed, but it was not informed by knowledge* (Rom 10:3.2). Devoid of understanding they were, unlike the blessed people that knows how to shout with joy. Where should this blessed people find its delight, in what should it exult? In your name, of course, as it walks in the light of your countenance. It will deserve to be exalted, but in your righteousness alone. Let it cast aside its own righteousness and be humbled; then it will be open to God's righteousness, and will be exalted. *They will be exalted in your righteousness.*

Verses 18-19. Exalted and upheld in God

18. *For you are the glory of their strength, and by your good pleasure our horn shall be exalted.* Exalted it will be, because that has pleased you, not because we have deserved it.

19. *For it is the Lord who takes us up.*[26] I was pushed like a heap of sand, and all but knocked over; I would have collapsed had the Lord not upheld me.[27] *For it is the Lord who takes us up, the holy one of Israel, our king.* He is himself your taking-up. He illuminates you. In his light you are safe, in his light you walk, in his righteousness you are exalted. He has taken you up and he himself guards you, weak as you are. He makes you firm and strong, but in his strength, not yours.

Verses 20-24. God's promise to David, and to Christ, the son of David

20. *Then you spoke to your children through a vision, and you said....* This phrase, *you spoke through a vision,* means "you revealed it to your prophets." He spoke through a vision in the sense that he revealed things to them; this is why the prophets were called seers.[28] They saw within themselves what they were to say outwardly, as they also heard in secret what they preached openly. *Then you spoke to your children through a vision, and you said, I have given my aid to a powerful man.* You know who this powerful man is. *I have raised up my chosen one from among my people.* You know this chosen one, the one whose exaltation gives you such joy.

---

26. *Domini est susceptio.* On the nuances of the verb *suscipere* see the Expositions of Psalm 45,11; 83,9, and notes at both places.
27. Or "taken me up."
28. See 1 Sm 9:9.

21. *I have found David, my servant*: this is the "David" who sprang from the first David's line. *With my holy oil I have anointed him.* Elsewhere it is written of him, *God, your God, has anointed you with the oil of joy, more abundantly than your companions* (Ps 44:8(45:7)).

22. *For my hand will help him, and my arm will strengthen him.* This refers to the taking up of humanity that was wrought in Christ, to the flesh that he assumed in the womb of the Virgin. This promise was fulfilled when he who in the form of God is equal to the Father took on himself the form of a slave and became obedient to the point of death, even death on a cross.[29]

23. *The enemy shall not gain the mastery over him.* The enemy rampages, but will never win against him; accustomed to do harm, the enemy will do none this time. What does it matter if he troubles us? He will put us to the test, but do us no harm; in fact his savage attacks will be good for us, because those against whom he launches them will be crowned for their victories. Where would our victory come from, if he never attacked us? How can God prove himself our helper, if we never have to fight? The foe will act in his characteristic way, but *the enemy shall not gain the mastery over him, nor shall the son of iniquity come near to hurting him.*

24. *And I will cut his enemies to pieces before him.* They are cut down in their plotting, but they are cut to pieces in a different sense if they come to faith. Little by little they begin to believe, and are mixed into a drink for the people of God, as the calf's head was pulverized. Moses ground the head of the golden calf to powder, and gave it to the Israelites to drink.[30] In a similar fashion all unbelievers are ground down as they gradually come to faith; they are drunk by God's people and sucked into the body of Christ. *I will cut his enemies to pieces before him, and put to flight those who hate him*, that they may do him no harm. But perhaps some of those who have been routed may say, *Whither shall I go from your spirit, and whither flee from your face?* (Ps 138(139):7). And seeing that there is nowhere to flee from the Almighty, they turn round and flee to the Almighty. *I will put to flight those who hate him.*

Verses 25-28. Our response to God's mercy and faithfulness

25. *My faithfulness and my mercy shall be with him.* All the Lord's ways are mercy and faithfulness.[31] Try to remember how often these two qualities are

---

29. See Phil 2:6-8.
30. See Ex 32:20.
31. See Ps 24(25):10. The Latin versions read *veritas*, which Augustine usually interprets in the biblical sense of truth: namely being true to what one is, a moral rather than a speculative quality, hence faithfulness, authenticity, reliability. It retains this meaning when he speaks of God's fulfillment of his promises; but when later in this section he speaks of human judgment, the word "truth" moves nearer to the Western concept: a conformity between mind and reality.

brought to our attention, to teach us that we in our turn must render them to God. As he showed mercy to us in blotting out our sins, and true fidelity in keeping his promises, so we too, if we are walking in his way, must offer mercy and truth back to him. We must show mercy by dealing mercifully with the miserable, and truth in keeping clear of unjust judgment. Do not allow truth to hinder you from acting with mercy, or mercy to stand in the way of truth; for if mercy induces you to act against truth, or rigid adherence to truth causes you to forget mercy, you will not be walking in the way of God, where mercy and truth have met.[32] *And in my name his horn shall be exalted.* Need we linger over that phrase? You are Christians: recognize Christ here.

26. *I will stretch his hand over the sea*; that is, he will be sovereign over the Gentiles. *And his right hand over the rivers.* Rivers run into the sea, and greedy men and women slide down into the salty harshness of this world. But all these kinds of people will be subjected to Christ.

27. *He will call to me, "You are my Father; you, my God, take me up and save me." And I will make him my first-born, highest among the kings of the earth.* The martyrs whose birthday we are celebrating shed their blood in testimony to their faith in these things, but they had not seen them. How much greater should our fortitude be, when we see what they believed in? The martyrs had not seen Christ raised to highest dignity above all earth's kings, for in their day princes were still conspiring against the Lord and against his Christ. A later verse in that other psalm had not yet been heeded: *And now, kings, understand; be instructed, all you who judge the earth* (Ps 2:10). But in our day Christ has indeed become most high king among the kings of the earth.

Verses 29-30. The new covenant and our inheritance

28. *I will maintain my mercy to him for ever, and for him my covenant shall be trustworthy.* Because of Christ the covenant is trustworthy; in him is the covenant established; he is the mediator of the covenant,[33] he is the one who puts his seal to it, who guarantees it and witnesses it. He is the inheritance that God's testament pledges to us, and he is our co-heir.[34]

29. *And I will extend his progeny to the age beyond this age.* Not just in the present age, but *to the age beyond this age,*[35] to that eternity into which his progeny will cross over; for the progeny is the promised inheritance, Abraham's seed, which is Christ. But if you belong to Christ you are Abraham's progeny;[36]

---

32. See Ps 84:11(85:10).
33. See Heb 9:15.
34. In this last sentence Augustine, following the Letter to the Hebrews, plays on the double meaning of "testament": covenant and will.
35. *In saeculum saeculi.*
36. See Gal 3:16.29.

and if you are destined to receive an inheritance that will last for ever, it is true that God will extend that progeny *to the age beyond this age.*

And his throne will be like the days of heaven. The thrones of earthly kings are like earthly days, for heavenly days and earthly days are different. Heavenly days are those years of which it is said, *You are the selfsame, and your years will not fail* (Ps 101:28(102:27)). Days on earth are hard pressed by those that follow them, and once they have gone they are beyond our reach. Nor do the succeeding days abide; they come only to pass away, and pass away when they have scarcely come. This is the manner of earthly days. But heavenly days, and those years that do not fail, have neither beginning nor ending. There no day is squeezed between yesterday and tomorrow; no one there looks forward to the future, nor does anyone lose the past, for in heaven, where God is enthroned for ever, the days are always present.

Let us postpone the rest of the psalm, please. It is a long psalm and we still have a good deal to study with you, in Christ's name. Go and recruit your strength—not your mental strength, I mean, for I see that your minds are tireless. No, I mean, have consideration for the servants of your souls, and give some refreshment to your bodies, so that they may bear up in their service. Then come back refreshed to your nourishment.[37]

Now let us turn to the Lord.[38]

---

37. Variant: "from your nourishment."
38. For this closing formula see the note at Exposition of Psalm 80,22. Some codices omit it.

Exposition 2 of Psalm 88

Second Sermon[1]

A link with the preceding sermon

1. Focus your minds now on what is left of the psalm about which we spoke this morning. Demand from our loving service what is still owing to you; then he who created both us and you will himself discharge the debt. The earlier verses of the psalm proclaimed Christ our Lord through the promises made by God, and he is still proclaimed in the part we are to deal with. Among other things said about him in the earlier verses we read, *I will make him my first-born, highest among the kings of the earth. I will maintain my mercy to him for ever, and for him my covenant shall be trustworthy. I will extend his progeny to the age beyond this age, and his throne will be like the days of heaven.* Of these promises, and all the others that occur from the opening of the psalm, we have spoken to the best of our ability.

Verses 31-35. Sin, punishment, the far-reaching promise of mercy, and the abiding covenant

2. It continues like this: *If his children forsake my law, and do not walk according to my ordinances, if they violate my righteous decrees and break my commandments, I will punish their iniquities with the rod, and their offenses with whips. Yet I will not dispel my mercy from him,*[2] *nor in my justice*[3] *do any injury, nor will I violate my covenant; what proceeds from my lips I will not annul.* God's promise is given a mighty confirmation. The "children" of this David are the children of the bridegroom, so we are the ones called David's children here, all of us who are Christians. But God is making a far-reaching promise. *If* Christians, who are *his children, forsake my law, and do not walk according to my ordinances, if they violate my righteous decrees and break my commandments,* I will not spurn them or send them to perdition. What will I do? *I*

---

1. Probably preached at the vigil of Saint Cyprian's feast, 14 September, in some year between 399 and 411.
2. The singular "him" seems to be right. Augustine discusses it in section 3 below, concluding that the codices which read "them" are less reliable, and makes a powerful theological point out of the singular. The verb rendered "dispel" is the somewhat unexpected *dispergam*.
3. Here *veritas* again, but now with the overtone of vindictive justice.

289

will punish their iniquities with the rod, and their offenses with whips. Mercy is the policy not only of him who calls us, but equally of him who strikes and whips us. Allow your Father's hand to fall upon you, and if you are a good son or daughter, do not fend off his chastisement. Is there any son who is not disciplined by his father? Let him lay on the correction, provided he does not cut off his mercy; let him beat his rebellious children, as long as he does not disinherit them. If you have understood your Father's promises aright, what you should be afraid of is being disinherited, not being whipped, for the Lord corrects every child whom he loves, and whips every son or daughter whom he acknowledges as his.[4] Can a sinful son think a whipping beneath his dignity, when he sees the only-begotten Son being whipped? *I will punish their iniquities with the rod*, God says. The apostle issues a similar threat when he demands, *What do you want? Shall I come to you with a rod?* (1 Cor 4:21). Let us hope none of those dutiful children replied, "If you mean to come with a rod, don't come at all," for it is better to be corrected by a father's rod than to perish through the smooth talk of a robber.

3. *I will punish their iniquities with the rod*, he says, *and their offenses with whips. Yet I will not dispel my mercy from him*. From whom? From the "David" to whom I have made these magnificent promises, whom I have anointed with my holy oil more abundantly than his companions.[5] Do you understand who it is, from whom God will not dispel his mercy? I do not want any anxious person to say, "Well, all right, God firmly promises that he will not dispel his mercy from Christ. But what about sinners? He didn't say, 'I will not dispel my mercy from *them*,' did he? What he did say is, *I will punish their iniquities with the rod, and their offenses with whips*." So you were hoping to be reassured by hearing him say, "I will not dispel my mercy from them," were you? It is true that some codices do have that reading, but not the ones that are better emended. All the same, those which do have the plural reading contain nothing out of place. Ask yourselves this: in what sense does God not dispel his mercy from Christ? Did he who is the Savior of the body ever sin, either on earth or in heaven—he who there sits at the Father's right hand and intercedes for us?[6] Certainly not. But do you not see that it makes sense to say that God never withdraws his mercy from Christ in his members, never withdraws it from Christ's body, which is the Church? We must, as it were, turn our minds away from the only-begotten Son clasped in the Father's embrace,[7] where he does not count as man simply, but is acknowledged as God and man in his one person; then we shall see how important it is that God is said never to withdraw his mercy from Christ. Mercy is

---

4. See Heb 12:6-7.
5. See Ps 44:8(45:7).
6. See Rom 8:34.
7. See Jn 1:18.

rightly said not to be withheld from him when it is not withheld from his members, from his body. In that body he continued to suffer persecution on earth, even while in his own person he was already seated in heaven. From heaven he cried out, *Saul! Saul!* But not, "Why are you persecuting my servants?" nor, "Why are you persecuting my saints?" nor "Why are you persecuting my disciples?" but *Why are you persecuting me?* (Acts 9:4). He was seated in heaven, and no one was persecuting him personally, yet he cried, *Why are you persecuting me?* because the head acknowledged his members, and charity could not allow the head to be divorced from the organic unity of the body. It is just as true today: if God does not dispel his mercy from Christ, he certainly does not dispel it from us, who are his limbs and his body.

This does not mean that we can sin recklessly, making wrongheaded promises to ourselves that whatever we have done, we shall get away with it. Not at all. It is beyond my power to discuss and define different kinds of sins and iniquity, and even if I could, it would take too long. Suffice it to say that no one can claim to be without sin. Anyone who makes such a claim will be lying, for scripture warns us, *If we say that we have no sin, we deceive ourselves, and the truth is not in us* (1 Jn 1:8). Each one must necessarily be chastised for his or her own sins; but if we are Christians, God's mercy is not dispelled from us. But obviously if you go off into such serious iniquities that you thrust away the rod of him who beats you, and push his hand away when he applies the whip, and disdain God's discipline, and flee from the Father who strikes you, and refuse to have him as your Father because he does not condone your sin—well, then, you have cut yourself off from your inheritance. He has not cast you off, because if you had stayed to take your whipping, you would have stayed on as his heir. *I will not dispel my mercy from him, nor in my justice do any injury.* He sets us free and does not dispel his mercy, because it is not his will that his avenging justice should hurt us.

4. *Nor will I violate my covenant; what proceeds from my lips I will not annul.* "His children may sin, but that will not make me a liar. What I have promised, I will do." Suppose those children decide to sin beyond all hope, to sink so thoroughly into their sins that they are offensive in their Father's eyes and deserve to be disinherited; even so, is he not the God of whom it was said, *God will raise up children to Abraham even from these stones* (Mt 3:9)? I tell you, brothers and sisters, many Christians sin in less desperate fashion, many are corrected from their sinful ways by the whip and are brought to a better mind and healed. But many others turn away entirely; they obstinately resist their Father's discipline and altogether refuse to have God for their Father. Even though they bear the sign of Christ they plunge so far into their grievous iniquities that the only thing that can be said of them is, *Those who commit these sins will not possess the kingdom of God* (Gal 5:21). Yet Christ will not be despoiled of his inheritance on

their account. Not all the grains will be lost because there is so much straw.[8] Bad fishes may abound, but that does not mean that nothing will be unloaded from the seine and put into containers.[9] The Lord knows his own.[10] Since he predestined us before we existed, his promise is unshakeable. *Those whom he predestined, he also called; those whom he called, he also justified; and those whom he justified, he glorified as well* (Rom 8:30). Let those desperate people sin as they will, but let Christ's members respond, *If God is for us, who can stand against us?* (Rom 8:31). God in his justice will do them no injury, nor will he violate his covenant. His covenant, his testament, stands unshakeable, because in his foreknowledge he has predestined heirs for himself, and what proceeds from his lips he will not annul.

Verses 36-38. *Eternal life for the body as well as the soul*

5. Now, if you know yourself to be among Christ's members, listen to something else, something that will further strengthen you and make you more secure. *Once have I sworn in my holiness,*[11] *and I will not lie to David.* Do you expect God to swear again? If he is false to the oath once sworn, how many times will he need to swear? In sending his only Son to death he has sworn once only, to ensure that we may live. *Once have I sworn in my holiness, and I will not lie to David: his seed shall abide for ever.* His seed abides for ever, because the Lord knows those who are his own.[12]

His throne is like the sun in my sight, like the moon perfect for ever, a faithful witness in the sky. His throne is the people over whom he exercises his sovereignty, in whom he is enthroned, over whom he reigns. And if they are his throne, they are also his members, for in our own bodies too our various members are a throne for the head. Think how our head is supported by all our other members; the head itself carries nothing on top of it, but is carried by the others as though the whole body were a throne for the head. Similarly all the people over whom God reigns are his throne. They will be like the sun in my sight, Christ promises, for the just will shine like the sun in the kingdom of my Father.[13]

But we must take "sun" in a spiritual sense; it is not the material sun that is meant, the sun God causes to rise over good and bad alike.[14] Clearly this cannot

---

8. See Mt 3:12.
8. See Mt 13:47-48.
9. See 2 Tm 2:19.
11. *In sancto meo,* which could mean "in my holy one" (David, as a type of Christ) or "in my prophet" or "in my holy place." But from a comment at the end of section 6 it seems that Augustine thought of it as within God himself.
12. See 2 Tm 2:19.
13. See Mt 13:43.
14. See Mt 5:45.

be in question, for the material sun is perceptible to the eyes not of human beings only, but also to those of cattle and the tiniest flies; for which of the most insignificant living creatures is incapable of seeing this material sun? But what does God say of a different kind of sun? David's throne will be *like the sun in my sight*. Not in the sight of human beings, not in fleshly sight, not in the sight of any mortal creatures, but *in my sight*.

And like the moon perfect for ever. Like the moon, but what sort of moon? One that is *perfect for ever*. The moon with which we are familiar is not like that; on the very day after it has reached perfection it begins to wane. But the psalm speaks of a moon that is *perfect for ever*; David's throne will be made perfect like the moon, but like a moon for ever perfect. We have heard it compared to the sun, but why the moon? The scriptures generally use the moon as a symbol of the mortality of our flesh. It is an apt symbol because it waxes and wanes; its appearance is inconstant. Furthermore, Jericho means "moon," and a certain man who went down from Jerusalem to Jericho fell among robbers,[15] for he was descending from immortality to mortality. Our flesh, then, is like the moon which all the time, every month, undergoes growth and diminishment; but this same flesh of ours will be perfect at the resurrection. And then there will be *a faithful witness in the sky*.

If it were in our souls alone that we were to be made perfect, the psalm would have compared us only to the sun. Again, if we were to be perfected only in our bodies, it would have compared us to the moon only. But God will make us perfect in both soul and body; and therefore with reference to our souls the psalm says that Christ's throne will be *like the sun in my sight*, because God alone sees the soul. But at the resurrection of the dead our flesh too will be made perfect, *like the moon perfect for ever*. And thus it will be *a faithful witness in the sky*, because everything prophesied about the resurrection of the dead will have come true.

I beg you to listen to this again, more plainly stated, and be sure to remember it, for I know that while some of you have understood, there are others still puzzling over what I have said. On no other point is the Christian faith so vehemently contradicted as it is on this teaching about the resurrection of the body. However, he who was born as a sign destined to be contradicted[16] raised up his own flesh in order to meet those disputants head-on. He could have healed his own limbs so perfectly that no trace of wounds appeared in them, but he kept the scars in his body in order to heal the wound of doubt in our hearts. Yet on no other point is the Christian faith contradicted so passionately, so persistently, so strenuously and obstinately, as on the resurrection of the flesh. Many philosophers, even among the pagans, have argued at length about the immortality of

15. See Lk 10:30.
16. See Lk 2:34.

the soul, and in their numerous and various books have left it on record that the human soul is indeed immortal.[17] But when it comes to the resurrection of the flesh they never falter, but openly and plainly deny it. So flatly do they contradict us on this that they declare it impossible for earthly flesh to ascend to heaven. This is why the moon made perfect for ever will stand as a faithful witness in the sky against all who contradict.

Verses 39-46. Disappointment and calamities instead of the fulfillment of the promises

6. How certain, how firm, how plain, how unambiguous are all these promises concerning Christ! True, some elements within them seem shrouded in mystery, but since others are so clear, they can very easily elucidate the dark sayings. Keep this in mind as we look at the next passage. *Yet you, you yourself, have rejected him, reduced him to nothing and put off your Anointed. You have overturned your covenant with your servant, and violated his holy place in the land. You have destroyed all his walls, and turned his fortifications into a fearful warning. All who pass along the way have plundered him, and he has become an object of reproach to his neighbors. You have exalted the right hand of his enemies, and given all his foes cause to rejoice. You have withdrawn your aid from his sword, and not helped him in war. You have turned him loose with no prospect of purification, and dashed his throne to the ground. You have short-ened the days of his reign, and covered him with confusion.*

What does this mean? You promised all these things, yet you have done the opposite. What has become of the promises over which we so lately rejoiced, the pledges we used to applaud so eagerly, secure and happy as we were on their account? We might almost think that he who promised is someone other than he who overthrew us; but the dismaying truth is that he is no other. *You, you your-self,* you who made the promises, you who reaffirmed them, you who even gave your oath to exclude human doubting, you promised these things and you have brought to pass something so different. Can I get any secure grip on your oath? Can I find your promise anywhere? Whatever does it mean? That God really made insincere promises, or swore falsely? Why did he promise one thing and do something else?

This is wrong. I maintain that he brought all this about precisely to establish his promises. But who am I to say so? Let us see whether truth itself says so, and then what I say will not be negligible. David was set up for a purpose: he was to

---

17. Notably the Neo-Platonists, especially Plotinus, whom Augustine knew through Porphyry. In *The City of God* VIII,12, he mentions Plotinus, Porphyry, Iamblichus and Apuleius Afer as "very noble." The Neo-Platonic doctrine of God, and of the human soul as it mounts toward union with the One, was a major factor in Augustine's search for the truth, as he recounts in *The Confessions* VII,9,13-15.

receive certain promises that were to be fulfilled in his seed, namely Christ. But because the promises were made to David, people thought that they would be realized in David. Now, if they had been, a Christian might have said, "But he was speaking about Christ"; and someone else might have replied, "Not at all; he was speaking about David." And the latter would have been wrong, misled by seeing that in David they had indeed been fulfilled. To make sure that we would not be so misled God cancelled them as far as David personally was concerned, so that when you see promises which must of necessity find fulfillment somewhere not finding it in David, you are forced to look for someone else in whom they have demonstrably been fulfilled.

A parallel case is that of Esau and Jacob. We find the elder being reverenced by the younger,[18] even though it was written that *the elder shall serve the younger* (Gn 25:33). This was to help you understand that when you see the prophecy unfulfilled in the two brothers, you must look for two peoples, in whom the promise made by God, who cannot lie, may be verified. Similarly he said to David, *See, I will put upon your throne one from your own line* (Ps 131(132):11). He promised that something everlasting would spring from David's seed. Then Solomon was born, and he became a man of such profound wisdom that everyone supposed God's promise concerning David's offspring had been fulfilled in him. But no, Solomon fell, and so made room for people to stretch their hope toward Christ. God can neither be deceived nor deceive us, so we can be certain that he did not ground his promise in Solomon, for he knew Solomon would fall. The divine purpose was that after Solomon's fall you would look to God, and earnestly press him for what he had promised.

Did you lie, then, Lord? Do you go back on your promises? Do you fail to deliver what you swore to give? Perhaps God will counter you by saying, "I did swear and I did promise, but that man did not persevere." But how can that be the answer? Did you not foresee, O Lord God, that he would not persevere? Of course you foresaw it. Why, then, did you promise me something that would last for ever, and attach that promise to someone who would not persevere? You said to me, "*If his children forsake my law, and do not walk according to my ordinances, if they break my commandments and violate my covenant*, nevertheless my promise shall endure, and my oath shall be fulfilled. *Once have I sworn in my holiness*, within myself." In that most secret place you swore it, in the fountain whence the prophets drank, those prophets who belched out for us the words, *Once have I sworn in my holiness, and I will not lie to David*. Make good your oath, then, and deliver what you promised. It was stripped away from David of old, lest in that David we should hope for its fulfillment, and so that you can say to us, "Keep hoping for what I promised."

---

18. See Gn 33:3.

The coming of the Anointed One is only deferred

7. Even David himself was aware of this. Look what he says: *Yet you, you yourself, have rejected him, reduced him to nothing*. So what has become of your promise? *You have put off your Anointed*. The speaker has doleful things to relate, but by these very words he cheers us, because he is implying, "What you promised stands absolutely firm, O God, for you have not taken your Anointed right away from us, but only put him off."[19] The ill-informed were hoping that God was about to carry out what he had promised in King David; but consider what happened to that man, in order that the good things of the promise might be hoped for yet more eagerly in someone else, and in that other be realized. *You have put off your Anointed; you have overturned your covenant with your servant*. Where is the old covenant, made with the Jews? Where is their promised land, the land in which they sinned, and from which they were exiled after its devastation? You look for the Jewish kingdom; it is not there. You look for the Jewish altar; it is not there. You seek the Jewish priesthood, and you do not find it. *You have overturned your covenant with your servant, and violated his holy place in the land*.[20] You have proved that the holy things he cherished were no more than earthly. *You have destroyed all his walls*, the walls you had given him as a defense; for how could he have been plundered if they had not been broken down? *You have turned his fortifications into a fearful warning*. Fearful? Why? Because then sinners could be warned, *If God did not spare the natural branches, he may not spare you either* (Rom 11:21).

All who pass along the way have plundered him. This refers to all those Gentiles who, as they *pass along the way* of this life, have plundered Israel, plundered David. Consider especially how fragments of Israel have been scattered among all nations, for of them it was prophesied, *They shall become the prey of foxes* (Ps 62:11(63:10)). Scripture called pagan kings "foxes" because they are crafty and cowardly, terrified by the strength of others. That is why the Lord himself said of Herod, who was threatening him, *Tell that fox* (Lk 13:32). But our King, who is afraid of no mortal man, is himself no fox; he is the lion from the tribe of Judah, to whom it was said, *You lay down and slept like a lion, but now you have arisen* (Gn 49:9). You arose in your power, as you had also slept by your power; you slept because you willed it. Another psalm says in this connection, "I, of myself, *I rested*." Would the sense not have been perfectly clear if it had said, *I rested, and fell asleep, and I arose because the Lord upheld me* (Ps 3:6(5))?[21] Why, then, add the "I"? It is to be uttered with all solemnity,

---

19. *Non abstulisti, sed distulisti.*
20. Or "on earth."
21. Augustine is making a point that cannot be conveyed well in English: that his Latin version of Psalm 3 inserted the pronoun *ego*, for emphasis.

this "I." I, of my own accord, I rested and fell asleep. They raged, and persecuted me, but I would not have slept if I had not willed it. I, of myself, I rested and slept.

So then, as of the Jews it was said, *They shall become the prey of foxes*, so now of them it is also said, *All who pass along the way have plundered him, and he has become an object of reproach to his neighbors. You have exalted the right hand of his enemies, and given all his foes cause to rejoice.* Look at the Jews, and observe how fully all these predictions have been verified. *You have withdrawn your aid from his sword.* How accustomed they were to put a few fighters into the field, and cut down so many! But now *you have withdrawn your aid from his sword, and not helped him in war.* They deserved to be beaten, deserved to be overrun, deserved to be driven out of their kingdom, for the land they lost was the land for the sake of which they slew the Lord.[22]

You have withdrawn your aid from his sword, and not helped him in war. You have turned him loose with no prospect of purification. What does that mean? Amid the catalogue of disasters this is a particular horror, for however much God strikes us, however angry he is, however severely he beats and whips us, he still holds the whipped child bound fast to himself. He is purifying the sinner, and does not turn us loose from that cleansing. If he were to turn us loose from the cleansing process he would no longer be holding someone in need of purification; there would be only someone fit to be thrown away. From what process of purification is the Jew turned loose? From faith. We live on faith,[23] and scripture says that God is *cleansing hearts by faith* (Acts 15:9). Since nothing but faith in Christ cleanses us, the Jews by refusing to believe in him have been cut loose from the process of cleansing. *You have turned him loose without prospect of purification, and dashed his throne to the ground.* Yes, and smashed it, with good reason. *You have shortened the days of his reign*, though the Jews supposed they would be sovereign for ever. *You have covered him with confusion.* All these calamities befell the Jews; yet the Anointed was not taken right away, only put off.

Verses 47-49. The fulfillment in Christ is already suggested in the psalm

8. So now let us see whether God does keep his promises. The psalm has recounted all the disasters that fell upon that people and that kingdom, all the harsh things that were allowed to happen to them. They happened for a reason: no one was to be misled into thinking that God had already fulfilled in them what he had promised, and did not intend to set up in Christ a kingdom that would have no end.[24] After this recital the prophet speaks again to God: *How long, O*

---

22. See Jn 11:48.
23. See Gal 3:11.
24. See Lk 1:33.

Lord? Will you turn away for ever? No, perhaps not for ever even from them, because blindness has fallen upon part of Israel, but only until the full tally of the Gentiles comes in, so that in the end all Israel may be saved.[25] But meanwhile, *How long will your anger blaze like fire?*

9. *Remember what my substance is.* This plea is made by David, who was rooted by carnal descent in the Jews, but rooted by hope in Christ. *Remember what my substance is.* My substance has not perished with the defection of the Jews. From that people sprang the virgin Mary, and from the virgin Mary came the flesh of Christ. That flesh was not sinful flesh, but the means of cleansing us from sin, and in it, says David, is my substance. *Remember what my substance is.* The root has not perished entirely, for from it will come that seed to whom the promise was made, ministered by angels through the hands of a mediator.[26] *Remember what my substance is, for you have not created all human beings in vain.* To be sure, all human beings have gone their own way in pursuit of emptiness, but for no empty purpose did you create them. But if all of them have gone to chase emptiness, these people you did not create in vain, have you kept nothing for yourself to use in purifying them from their empty vanity? Indeed you have; for what you reserved to yourself as your means of cleansing them is your holy one, made from my substance. All those human beings whom you did not create without a purpose, whom you did not form from their native emptiness, all those of whom a psalm asks, *How long will you be heavy-hearted, human creatures? Why love emptiness and chase falsehood?* (Ps 4:3(2))—all these are cleansed by him. If they begin to be anxious they may, perhaps, be turned back from their empty pursuits; they may find themselves defiled by their vanities and look for a means of cleansing. Help them, relieve their fears. *Be sure of this: the Lord has glorified his holy one* (Ps 4:4(3)). He has made his holy one marvellous, and through him he has cleansed us all of the defilement of our emptiness. And there, in him, says David, is my substance: remember him. *You have not created all human beings in vain,* and therefore you kept something through which they might be purified.

Whom did you keep? *What human being is there who will live but not see death?* The man who will live, and will never see death, is he who cleanses them from their empty defilement. God has not created all human beings in vain, nor can their creator so despise them as not to convert them and purify them.

---

25. See Rom 11:25-26.
26. See Gal 3:19; but Augustine has considerably altered the bearing of the text, where Paul is contrasting the law, ministered by angels according to a Jewish tradition, through the mediation of Moses, with the primal, direct promise of God, which is fulfilled in Christ for those who believe in him.

Christ's resurrection foreshadowed

10. *What human being is there who will live but never see death?* Rising from the dead, this man can never die, nor will death ever again have dominion over him.[27] That this is the right interpretation is confirmed by some verses in another psalm, which were taken up by the apostles in their teaching: *You will not leave my soul in hell, nor allow your holy one to suffer corruption* (Ps 15(16):10). In the Acts of the Apostles we find this text used in disputation with unbelievers: *Men, brethren, we know that the patriarch David is dead, and that his flesh did see corruption*; it cannot therefore be of him that the psalm says, *You will not allow your holy one to suffer corruption* (Acts 2:29.27). But if not to David, to whom does the text apply, *What human being is there who will live but never see death?* To no one, perhaps?

That cannot be right. The question, *What human being is there…?* is posed to make you seek an answer, not to leave you in despair. But, you may wonder, even if there is someone at whom the question hints, someone *who will live but never see death*, it cannot refer to Christ, can it, because he did die?

To this I will say that there is absolutely no human being *who will live but never see death*, except the one who has already died for mortals. If you are still unsure that it refers to him, look at the next words. *What human being is there who will live but never see death?* So Christ was never dead? On the contrary, he was. How, then, can it be said that he *will live but never see death*? Because, as the psalm continues, *he will pluck his soul from the grasp of hell*. He is the only one, absolutely the only one, who *will live but never see death*, because *he will pluck his soul from the grasp of hell*. All the rest, all believers, will rise from the dead, and they too will live for ever without seeing death; but they will not deliver their own souls from the grasp of the underworld. He alone, who delivered his own soul, will deliver the souls of his faithful, for they are impotent to deliver themselves. "Prove to me," you say, "that he delivered his own soul." By his words I prove it: *I have the power to lay down my life, and I have the power to take it up again. No one takes it away from me. I, I myself, fell asleep, but I lay down my life of my own accord, and I take it up again.*[28] Therefore he it is who delivers his soul from the grasp of hell.

Verses 50-52. Believers have still had to suffer hardship and insult

11. Even for those who believed in Christ, however, there were still hard days ahead. For a long time the angry pagans asked, *When will he die, and his name disappear?* (Ps 40:6(41:5)). Speaking on behalf of those who already believe in

---

27. See Rom 6:9.
28. See Jn 10:18.17; Ps 3:6(5).

Christ but must struggle for some time longer, the psalm continues, *Where are your ancient mercies, O Lord?* Already we have acknowledged Christ as the one who cleanses us, already we hold fast to him as the one in whom you fulfill all your promises. Reveal in him, then, what you have promised. He is the one who will live and not see death; he it is who has delivered his soul from the grip of the underworld; yet we are still struggling. Thus spoke the martyrs whose birthday we celebrate today. Christ will live on and never see death; he has delivered his soul from the power of the underworld. Yet we are done to death all day long, reckoned as sheep for the slaughter.[29] *Where are your ancient mercies, O Lord, the mercies you swore to David in your faithfulness?*

12. *Remember the reproach your servants bear, O Lord.* Even though Christ was alive, even though he was already enthroned at the Father's right hand, Christians were for a long time open to accusations on his account. That widow who was giving birth, bearing more children than the woman who had a husband,[30] was forced to listen to scurrilous insults and mockery. But now that the Church has grown and spread abroad to right and to left she remembers no more the disgrace of her widowhood.

Remember, O Lord, for in you is an abundance of sweet memory;[31] *remember*, do not forget. Remember what? *Remember the reproach your servants bear, the reproach of many pagans which I have held within me.* I went out to preach, he says, and always I heard insults. I contained it all within me, for I knew that in me the scripture was being fulfilled: *we are cursed, but we appeal to them; we are treated like the refuse of this world, the common offscouring* (1 Cor 4:13). For a long time Christians contained the insults within them, in their own hearts, and did not dare offer their accusers any resistance. In those early days it was considered an offense to answer back to a pagan, whereas now it is an offense to remain a pagan. Thanks be to the Lord, for he has remembered the reproaches we endured; he has exalted the horn of his Christ and made him wonderful in the eyes of earthly kings. No one insults Christians nowadays, or at any rate not publicly. If anyone does insult us, he does so in such a way as to seem more frightened of being overheard than anxious to be believed. *The reproach of many pagans I held within me.*

13. *O Lord, your enemies have insulted*—enemies both Jewish and pagan—*they have insulted...*what have they insulted? *The transformation in your Christ.* That is what they have insulted, *the transformation in your Christ,* because their objection is that Christ died, that he was crucified. But why focus your objections on that, you stupid people? Well, perhaps there are no more such objectors today; but supposing that there are a few of you left: why taunt us that

---

29. See Ps 43(44):22.
30. See Is 54:1; Gal 4:27.
31. See Ps 144(145):7.

Christ died? He did not perish; he was transformed. He is rightly said to have been dead during those three days; but the event his enemies jeer at was not sheer loss, not a ceasing to be, but the *transformation in your Christ*. He was transformed by passing from temporal life to life eternal; he was transformed by moving from the Jews to the Gentiles; he was transformed by departing from earth to heaven. Let your enemies pursue their empty objection now, and mock this *transformation in your Christ*. May they be transformed themselves, then they will not jibe at the transformation of Christ. But the change in Christ offends them because they are unwilling to be changed themselves; so no transformation has been wrought in them, and they have not come to fear God.[32] *Your enemies have insulted the transformation in your Christ.*

Verse 53. The unfailing blessing of the Lord. Concluding exhortations

14. So they have railed at the transformation; but what have you to say? *The blessing of the Lord lasts for ever. So be it, so be it.* Thanks be to his mercy, thanks be to his grace.[33] He has saved us gratis, taking no account of our unfilial behavior. He sought us when we were not seeking him. He found us, redeemed us, and freed us from the domination of the devil and the power of demons. He bound us to himself to be cleansed by faith, but left unbound those enemies who refuse to believe and therefore cannot be cleansed. Let any of these unbelievers who still linger on say whatever they wish; let them keep on saying it daily if they like; they will dwindle with every day that passes. Let them object, and mock, and fling their insults, for what they are reviling is *the transformation in your Christ*, not his demise. Can they not see that even as they talk like that they are fading away, either by coming to believe or by dying out? Their cursing is a temporary affair, but *the blessing of the Lord lasts for ever*. And now this blessing is confirmed by the words, *So be it, so be it*, in case anyone is still afraid. That coda is God's warranty.

Certain of his promises, let us believe in what has been done already, and rejoice in what is being fulfilled in the present, and hope for what is still to come. Let no enemy divert us from the true way. May he who gathers us like chicks under his wings cherish us, and may no hawkish raptor from the sky[34] seize the squabs before they have even grown their feathers. Christians must never rely on themselves; anyone who wants to grow strong needs to be fostered by a mother's

---

32. See Ps 54:20(55:19).

33. A sentence is omitted here, because not reproducible in English. Augustine comments on the Latin expression, *gratias agere*, literally "to do thanks," and says that we can only "do our thanks" verbally. There is no return or repayment that we can make to God, but we must mean what we say. There is a crop of variants for the sentence, indicating that copyists found it difficult.

34. An allusion perhaps to Eph 2:2.

warmth. This hen who gathers her chicks is the one whom the Lord used as a symbol of himself when reproaching the unfaithful city, Jerusalem: *How often I wanted to gather your children to myself, as a hen gathers her chicks under her wings, but you would have none of it! See then, your house will be left to you derelict* (Mt 23:37-38). This is why it is said of the city, *You have turned its fortifications into a fearful warning.* They refused to be protected under the hen's wings, and gave us a terrible example. From them we must learn to be wary of unclean flying spirits, ever hunting for prey to snatch. Let us seek shelter under the wings of divine Wisdom, who for the sake of her children became weakened even to death.[35]

Let us love the Lord our God, and let us love his Church: him as our Father, her as our Mother; him as Lord and her as his handmaiden, for we are his handmaiden's children.[36] But this marriage is cemented by intense charity. Nobody can offend the one and curry favor with the other. Let nobody say, "Yes, I frequent the idols, to be sure; I consult the possessed[37] and soothsayers, but I do not forsake God's Church. I am a Catholic." Then you have held fast to your Mother, but offended your Father. Another person says, "Far be that from me. I do not consult any soothsayer or raver, nor do I seek sacrilegious fortune-telling. I do not go worshipping demons, or serve stone idols. But I belong to the Donatist party." Then how does it benefit you to avoid offending your Father, when he is bound to punish the insult you are offering to your Mother? What is the use of confessing the Lord, honoring him, preaching him, acknowledging his Son and confessing that the Son is at the Father's right hand, if you blaspheme against his Church? The example set by human couples puts you right, surely? Suppose you have some patron, and you hang around him every day with flattering attentions, wearing out his doorstep in your anxiety to be of service to him. Not content with saluting him, you almost worship him, and pour out your obsequious devotion. But then you make some accusation against his wife—just one. Do you think you will be admitted to his house?

Dearly beloved, hold fast to both. Be united, all of you, in this. Hold fast to God, your Father, and to the Church, your Mother. Celebrate the birthdays of the saints in sober fashion, so that we may imitate those who have gone before us, and that they who pray for you may also find joy in you. Thus may *the blessing of the Lord* remain upon you *for ever. So be it, so be it.*

---

35. Augustine remarks elsewhere that no bird is so weakened over its young as the hen seems to be. In Christ's passion love expressed itself as weakness, which is why he chose this simile. Compare Exposition 1 of Psalm 58,10; Exposition 1 of Psalm 90,5. The thought here seems to be the same.

36. See Ps 85(86):16.

37. *Arreptitios*, from *arripio*, to seize. It could mean any kind of inspired or delirious persons. In *The City of God* II,4, Augustine says that as a young man he sometimes attended sacrilegious entertainments where pagan priests "raved in religious excitement."

Exposition of Psalm 89

Verse 1. The role of Moses

1. Over this psalm we find written, *A prayer of the man of God, Moses.* Through his man Moses God gave the law to his people; and through this same man of his he freed his people from the regime of slavery, and led them through the wilderness for forty years. Moses was a servant of the Old Covenant, and a prophet of the New. Now the apostle tells us that *all these things happened to them, but with symbolic import, for they are written down as a rebuke to us, upon whom the climax of the ages has come* (1 Cor 10:11), and so we need to examine this psalm with reference to the dispensation established through Moses. From his prayer the psalm derived its title.

2. *O Lord, you have become a refuge for us, in one generation and another.* This could simply mean "in every generation." Alternatively, we could take it to mean two different generations, an old and a new, because, as I said, Moses was a servant of the covenant that was given to the older generation, and a prophet of the covenant to be given to another generation, the new. Jesus was the guarantor of the covenant, as he was also the bridegroom in the marriage appointed for him with that generation; as he said himself, *If you believed Moses, you would believe in me as well; for he wrote about me.*[1] It is by no means to be supposed that this psalm was written by Moses personally, for it is not marked by any of the literary characteristics which are found in the songs he wrote; but the name of so deserving a servant of God was attached to it as an indication of its significance: this name was to direct the intention of reader or hearer aright. So the psalm begins, *O Lord, you have become a refuge for us, in one generation and another.*

Verse 2. The eternity of God is our refuge

3. It certainly cannot be thought that God did not exist before we came into existence; yet he is said to have become for us something that he was not before: namely, our refuge. We need to find out, therefore, what kind of refuge is meant.

---

1. Jn 5:46. The ideas sketched in these first two sections of the Exposition are taken up again in the conclusion; see section 17.

So the psalm continues, *Before the mountains were made, or the earth and the round world were formed, from age unto age, you are*. You exist eternally, before we came to be, and before the world came to be; but from the time when we turned back to you, you have become for us a refuge.

I cannot see how we are meant to understand the phrase, *before the mountains were made, or the earth was formed* (or, as other codices have it, *the earth was molded*; these are alternative translations of the same Greek word). Mountains are the higher regions of the earth, to be sure; but if God, who formed the earth, exists before the earth was formed at all, what is the point of singling out mountains or any other parts of it? God exists not merely before the earth, but also before heaven and earth, before all bodily and spiritual creatures. Most probably, though, the universe of rational creatures is being distinguished here, with the heavenly nature of the angels being suggested by the mountains, and the lowliness of human beings by the earth. If this interpretation is correct, we can see why different verbs are used. It is quite appropriate to say of any creature whatsoever that it "was made" or that it "was formed." Either expression is acceptable. But if they are being used with precision, we may note that the angels are said to have been "made" in another psalm. After enumerating God's heavenly works, that psalm sums them up thus: *He spoke, and they were made; he gave the command, and they were created* (Ps 148:5). But the earth, from which the human body was formed, is said to have been "formed" itself; and so scripture used this word in the text, *God molded* (or *God formed*) *man from the mud of the earth* (Gn 2:7).

From age unto age, you are, before the highest and noblest of your creatures were made—for what is greater than a heavenly, intelligent creature? Before the earth was molded, you are, the earth that was formed in order that even on earth there would be someone to know you and praise you. But to say this is little indeed, because all these things had a beginning, either within time or when time itself began,[2] whereas *from age unto age, you are*. More fittingly should we say, "From everlasting unto everlasting," for God does not exist from any age, but before the ages; nor does he live unto any age which reaches its end, for he is without end. Owing to an ambiguity in the Greek word used in the scriptures, a Latin translator may often use "age" and "eternity" as interchangeable. Nonetheless the psalm very properly avoided saying, "From age you were and unto age you will be." It used the present tense of the verb, hinting that God's substance is in every respect unchangeable. There is no "was" or "will be" in

---

2. Time is itself a creature of God, not a pre-existing container into which God's creative acts are inserted. Augustine occasionally wonders whether the angels may be/have been created outside time (see his *Unfinished Literal Commentary on Genesis* III,7 and *The City of God* XII,16); but even if the answer is yes, no creature is co-eternal with God. Augustine wrestles with the mystery of time as the condition of created, contingent beings, so near to non-existence, in Book XI of *The Confessions*.

God, but only "is." This is why God said, *I AM WHO I AM. Thus shall you say to the children of Israel, HE WHO IS has sent me to you*, and why it was said to him in a psalm, *You will discard them, and so they will be changed, but you are the selfsame, and your years will not fail* (Ex 3:14; Ps 101:27-28(102:26-27)). Such is the eternity which has become for us a refuge, so that we may flee to it from our changeable, time-bound condition, knowing that there we shall abide.[3]

Verses 3-6. The transience of human life, contrasted with God's eternal, immutable being

4. But for the present we live here, beset by many severe temptations that threaten to lure us away from our refuge. Let us see, then, what the prayer of the man of God goes on to ask. *Do not turn men and women away toward base things*: that is, do not let them be turned aside from your eternal, sublime realities, to covet temporal goods and lose all sensitivity save for the things of earth. In making this petition he is asking only for what God himself commanded. In a similar way we pray, *Do not bring us into temptation*. Moreover, here too in the psalm the next phrase is, *You have said, Be converted, human creatures*. It is as though the psalm were saying, "I am asking you to grant the very thing you have enjoined on us"; and this is to glorify God's grace, so that anyone minded to boast may boast only in the Lord.[4] We cannot conquer the temptations of this life without his help, by the exercise of our wills alone. *Do not turn men and women away toward base things*, it prays, and yet *you have said, Be converted, human creatures*. But give us what you have commanded us;[5] give it by hearing the prayer of everyone who begs, and aiding the faith of everyone who tries.

5. *For to your eyes a thousand years are like yesterday, which has passed by*, and so we must be turned around, away from these things which pass by and slip away, to our refuge in you, where you exist unchanging; for however long a life we may hope to live here, *to your eyes a thousand years are like yesterday, which has passed by*. They are not even compared with tomorrow, which at least is still to come. All those things which are to be closed down at the end of time are to be regarded as business already finished. This is why the apostle willed to put them all behind him, forgetting what was behind his back, which we can take to mean temporal matters, and stretching out toward those ahead in his eagerness for what is eternal.[6]

---

3. Compare *The Confessions* XI,29,39.
4. See 1 Cor 1:31.
5. *Da quod iussisti*. It echoes the famous phrase in *The Confessions* X,29,40, "Give what you command, and then command whatever you will." The Pelagians took exception to this uncompromising stand on grace, as Augustine relates in *The Gift of Perseverance* 20,53.
6. See Phil 3:13.

The psalm added, *And like a watch in the night,* in case anyone might take the comparison of a thousand years to one day in God's sight to mean that God has long, leisurely days. No; the passage is intended in the opposite sense, as a denial that time is long. Hence the further comparison to a night watch, which lasts no more than three hours. In spite of this people have presumptuously claimed to know all about times, as the disciples also wished to know, only to receive the Lord's rebuke, *It is not for you to know the times which the Father has appointed by his own authority* (Acts 1:7). People have taken it upon themselves to define the limits of this age: it can be finished in six thousand years, they say, as though in six days. They failed to notice that the psalm said, *Like one day, which has passed by,* and that when that was said, more than a thousand years had already elapsed. Furthermore, they should have been warned against being deluded over the uncertainty of time by the comparison, *like a watch in the night;* for even if they do seem to have held a fairly plausible view about the six days (since it was also in six days that God completed his creative work), the same is not true of six night watches. These would total a mere eighteen hours, which cannot be accommodated to such an opinion.

6. In the next verses this man of God—or, rather, the spirit of prophecy in him—seems almost to promulgate a law of God, one written in his secret wisdom: the law whereby he has determined the limits to which the sinful life of mortals shall be prolonged, and the bitterness of their mortal state. *Like things esteemed as nothing shall their years be,* he says. *Let them pass away like morning grass: let them flourish in the morning but then fade away; in the evening let them fall, stiffen, and shrivel.* The heirs of the Old Covenant longed for happiness, and entreated God for it as a great boon, but the law appointed for it by God's hidden providence seems to be promulgated here by Moses: *like things esteemed as nothing shall their years be.* Things that already are not, even before they come, are indeed esteemed as nothing. When they have come, they are already slipping into non-existence, for they do not arrive to remain present with us, but only to cease to be. *Let them pass away like morning grass.* In the morning, that is, before they come, *let them flourish, but then fade away;* in the evening, after they have come, *let them fall, stiffen, and shrivel.* Their falling is into death, obviously; their stiffening is corpse-like; they shrivel as they crumble to dust. Of what is this said? Undoubtedly of the flesh, wherein lodges the condemned lust for carnal things. All flesh is grass, and human grandeur is the bloom of grass. The grass wilts and the flower droops, but the word of the Lord abides for ever.[7]

---

7. See Is 40:6-8.

Verses 7-10. Death is the punishment for sin, but an abbreviated life is not necessarily a sign of God's anger

7. The psalm does not conceal the origin of this punishment. It is the consequence of sin, and so the psalmist immediately adds, *We fainted at your anger, and under your wrath we were dismayed.* We fainted in our weakness, and our dismay sprang from our fear of death; for though we have become so weak we tremble at the prospect of an end to our weakness. *Someone else will fasten your belt for you, and take you where you do not want to go* (Jn 21:18), said the Lord, even though your martyrdom will be no punishment but the means of winning you your crown.[8] Even the Lord's own soul was sorrowful to the point of death, and in this he patterned us upon himself;[9] even for the Lord there was no way out except through death.[10]

8. *You have placed our iniquities where you can see them*; or, in other words, you have not turned a blind eye to them. *Our age in the light that streams from your face* (we must supply the verb, "you have placed"). In saying, *The light that streams from your face*, he is repeating the thought of *where you can see them*, just as *our age* echoes *our iniquities* in the first clause.

9. *For all our days have failed, and we too have failed under your anger.* These words plainly demonstrate that our mortality is our punishment. Our days are said to have failed either because people who live in them fail through being enamored of transient things, or because the days themselves have dwindled. This point is made clear by what follows: *Our years toiled around[11] like a spider. The days of our years are seventy years in themselves, though in the strong they may reach eighty. Any more than these are labor and sorrow.* These words certainly seem to describe the brevity and wretchedness of this life, for nowadays even people who have survived to seventy are deemed long-lived. They may seem to retain some vigor even to eighty years, but if they live longer than that, they struggle under the burden of manifold ailments.

But while some who have not yet attained seventy endure an old age full of extreme weakness and distress, other elderly folk have been found in amazingly good health even beyond eighty. In view of these differences it is better to search for some spiritual meaning in the numbers. It will not do to say that our life-span, so drastically reduced in comparison with that of the ancients, is a sign of greater anger on God's part toward the children of Adam. It is true that through one man

---

8. Variant: "Though this was said to a martyr who was destined not for punishment but for a crown."

9. *Nos in se transfigurans*, another of the pithy phrases that reveal Augustine's conviction of Christ's power to identify us with himself in every mystery of his life. This identification is the key to Christian use of the psalms. See the *Introduction* in Volume 1.

10. *Domini exitus nonnisi mortis*... The words echo Ps 67:21(68:20). See Augustine's Exposition of Psalm 67,29, and note there.

11. *Meditabantur.*

sin entered the world, and through sin, death, and that death has thereby spread through the whole human race.[12] But the very length of life ascribed to the patriarchs[13] has itself been held up to derision in the verse where a thousand years were compared to a vanished yesterday or a three-hour watch. In any case, that era when people lived so long was the one in which they provoked God's anger to the point where he sent the flood, and they perished.

Spiritual interpretations are offered for the seventy and eighty years

10. Now, seventy years plus eighty make a hundred and fifty, and that is a sacred number, as we gather from the Book of 150 Psalms. The significance of 150 is, moreover, the same as that of 15, which is the sum of 7 and 8. Of these two, the former suggests the Old Testament, because it recalls the observance of the Sabbath; the latter represents the New Testament because it recalls the resurrection of the Lord.[14] Accordingly there are fifteen steps in the temple, and fifteen psalms called "The Songs of Ascents,"[15] and the waters of the flood submerged the summits of the mountains by fifteen cubits.[16] In various other places too this number is given special prominence and regarded as sacred. The psalm therefore laments that *our years toiled around like a spider.* We were for ever toiling at enterprises that would have no durability, ever weaving perishable products which, as the prophet Isaiah warned, were useless for covering us.[17]

The days of our years are seventy years in themselves, though in the strong they may reach eighty. A distinction is noted between *in themselves* and *in the strong.* The former, *in themselves,* are simply the years or days, and consequently they signify temporal matters; they number seventy because temporal benefits are promised in the Old Testament. But if we consider the years not in themselves, but *in the strong,* in relation not to temporal affairs but to eternity, they attain to *eighty,* because the New Testament confirms our hope of renewal and resurrection for eternity.

Yet the psalm cautions us that *any more than these are labor and sorrow;* in other words, a person who tries to overstep this faith and find anything beyond it will find only labors and pains. But there is another way of understanding this clause. Although we have been given our place under the New Covenant, which is symbolized by the number eighty, this life of ours is subject all the more to labor and sorrow, as we groan within ourselves, awaiting our full adoption in the

12. See Rom 5:12.
13. See Gn 5:4–6:3.
14. On the reasons for this, see Augustine's Exposition of Psalm 6,1-2, and note there.
15. Psalms 119(120)–133(134).
16. See Gn 7:20.
17. See Is 59:6.

redemption of our bodies. We are saved, but as yet only in hope, and we wait patiently for what we do not yet see.[18] This too is part of God's merciful dealing with us, and the psalm therefore goes on to say, *For gentleness has overtaken us, and we shall be corrected.* The Lord corrects the one he chooses and loves; he scourges every child he acknowledges as his.[19] Even to certain of the mighty he gives a sting in the flesh to belabor them and prevent them from being pretentious over the great revelations granted them, so that strength may find its full scope in their weakness.[20] Some codices have "we shall be instructed" instead of *we shall be corrected*, but this evokes the same gentleness, for no one can be instructed without labor and sorrow. Strength finds its full scope in weakness.

Verses 11-12. What it means to attain true understanding of God's anger, and knowledge of his right hand

11. *Who knows the power of your anger? Who takes account of your wrath in fear of you?* To very few is it given to know the power of your anger, says the psalm. With most people you are in fact the more angry when you deal leniently; this is to make sure that we understand the labor and sorrow we endure to be part of your gentle dealing, not a manifestation of your displeasure. By these sufferings you correct and instruct those you love, that they may not be condemned to eternal torments, whereas in another psalm we read, *The sinner has provoked the Lord, but the Lord is too angry to demand an account* (Ps 9B(10):4). But few realize this. *Who*, then, *knows the power of your anger? Who takes account of your wrath in fear of you?* Who knows how to take due account of it? How difficult it is to find anyone to whom fear of you has given such insight that he can take due account of your wrath, and go even further, to perceive it as still part of that wrath when you seem indulgent toward those with whom you are really more angry. Such a person will understand that through your seeming indulgence sinners prosper in their course, but only to receive more severe punishment at the end. When human beings are angry they may kill an enemy's body, but afterwards there is no more that they can do. God has the power both to punish here, and to send sinners to hell after their bodily death.[21] The few people who are well instructed rate the empty, delusory happiness of the wicked as a manifestation of God's more severe anger. A psalmist had at first failed to understand this, he whose feet had all but slipped because he envied sinners, seeing the peace they enjoyed. But he learned the truth when he entered God's holy place and perceived what the final outcome must be.[22] Few they are who

---

18. See Rom 8:23-25.
19. See Heb 12:6.
20. See 2 Cor 12:7.9.
21. See Mt 10:28.
22. See Ps 72(73):2-3.17.

enter there to take account of God's wrath in fear of him, and to reckon the prosperity of wicked persons an element in their punishment.

12. *Make your right hand so known....* The Greek codices favor this reading, as against certain of the Latin, which have "Make your right hand known to me." What does it mean to say, *Make your right hand so known?* Surely it is a way of saying, "Make known your Christ, him of whom scripture asked, *To whom has the arm of the Lord been revealed?* (Is 53:1). Make him so well known that in him your faithful ones may learn to pray and hope for the rewards of faith which do not appear in the Old Testament, but are revealed in the New." Unless you make him so well known, they may deem the prosperity that flows from earthly, temporal goods a thing to be valued, desired, and ardently loved. Then their feet may slip, as they see it enjoyed even by people who do not worship you. Their steps may slide away out of control for lack of knowing how to take account of your wrath.

But what happened? This prayer of the man of God was answered, and God made his Christ known indeed. Through his passion Christ showed that we should not crave the rewards which seem to be trumpeted in the Old Testament, where only shadows are to be found of what was to come. Eternal rewards alone are worth our desires.

God's right hand can also be interpreted in another way. His right hand is where he will station the just, segregated from the wicked.[23] His right hand becomes very well known when he whips every child he acknowledges as his own,[24] allowing none of them to proceed successfully in their own ways. He chastises them and shows them more drastic anger; but this is a mark of kindness, for he whips an erring child with his left hand in order to place the corrected child at his right.

The alternative reading, found in most codices, *Make your right hand known to me,* can fit both interpretations mentioned, referring either to Christ, or to eternal blessedness; for God does not have a right hand in the sense of a bodily member, any more than he is angry in the sense of being disturbed.

13. Another thought is now added. Make them know, it says, make *those who are fettered in their hearts to wisdom* know.[25] Other codices have *instructed in their hearts* instead of *fettered,* for the two words sound very similar in Greek differing by only a syllable.[26] Those who *thrust their foot into her fetters,* as scripture has it (Sir 6:25), are instructed by wisdom. It does not mean the foot of the body, of course, but the foot of the heart. They are as if bound by wisdom's golden chains, and never deviate from the way of God, or seek to escape him. It

---

23. See Mt 25:32-33.
24. See Heb 12:6.
25. The meaning of *notos* in section 13 appears to shift from the passive "known" to the active "knowing."
26. πεπεδημένους, fettered, and πεπαιδευμένους, instructed.

does not matter which reading we accept, since the meaning is preserved either way.

Under the New Covenant God made those who were *fettered* (or instructed) *in their hearts to wisdom* so knowledgeable that for the sake of a faith detested by Jewish and Gentile impiety alike they made light of all temporal things. They willingly allowed themselves to be stripped of the goods promised by the Old Testament, the goods considered important by persons of carnal outlook.

Verse 13. Long-suffering

14. So it happened that certain disciples became so knowledgeable that they spurned earthly things and by their sufferings bore witness to the desirability of the good things that are eternal. They are therefore called martyrs, a Greek word which means witnesses. Cruel, fierce treatment of all kinds was often inflicted on them, and the man of God who speaks in our psalm was aware of this. The prophetic spirit to which Moses gave utterance prayed, *Turn back, O Lord; how long? Be open to your servants' entreaty.* This is the voice of people who under the world's persecution are suffering much ill-treatment, or, at least, the words are uttered on their behalf. Being fettered to wisdom in their hearts they become so knowledgeable that not even under such duress are they driven to flee from the Lord and take refuge in the good things of this world.

Elsewhere a question is asked of the Lord, *How long will you turn your face away from me?* (Ps 12(13):1), and in the same mood the prayer is offered here: *Turn back, O Lord; how long?* But some people are so carnal-minded that they attribute to God a form like that of the human body, and so they might think that God turns away his face or turns back to us by some movement like that of our own bodies. To exclude such a mistake, let them recall earlier lines in the psalm: *you have placed our iniquities where you can see them, our age in the light that streams from your face.* How can we reconcile these sayings? In the verse we have reached, the psalm begs God, *Turn back, O Lord*, evidently asking him to turn back to us in readiness to forgive, as though he had turned his face away in anger. But the earlier verse showed him so angry that he would not avert his face from the iniquities and the age of those who provoked his anger, but rather kept them in sight, placing them where the light from his face would show them up.[27]

When the psalm asks, *How long?* what we are hearing is prayerful righteousness, not indignant impatience. The next phrase is, *Be open to your servants' entreaty*,[28] but other translators have rendered it *Be entreated*.[29] The former

---

27. Augustine leaves unanswered here the question of how to reconcile the two sayings. In other contexts he suggests that we should ask God to avert his gaze from our sins, but not from ourselves. See, for example, Exposition 2 of Psalm 26,16; Exposition of Psalm 50,14.
28. *Deprecabilis esto.*
29. *Deprecare.*

avoids ambiguity, for the verb *deprecare* can bear either active or passive meaning; it may be used of the one who entreats or of the one who is entreated. We could take it to mean either "I entreat you" or "I am entreated by you."

Verses 14-15. The promise of morning

15. Now at last the speaker thinks of the good things of the future, and because he anticipates them in hope, he regards them as already achieved. *In the morning we have been filled with your mercy*, he declares. We are like people laboring and grieving in the night, but prophecy has been kindled for us like a lamp in a dark place, until dawn breaks and the day-star arises in our hearts.[30] Blessed are the pure of heart, for they will see God. Then will the righteous be filled with that good for which they now hunger and thirst,[31] as they walk in faith, pilgrims still, and away from the Lord.[32] Another psalm speaks in the same way: *You will fill me with joy in beholding your face* (Ps 15(16):11). In the morning they will stand in your presence and contemplate you,[33] satisfied at last. Other translators of our present psalm use this word here: *In the morning we have been fully satisfied by your mercy*; and another psalm again anticipates that *I shall be satisfied when your glory is revealed* (Ps 16(17):15). This same hope prompted the request, *Show us the Father, and that is enough for us*, to which corresponds the Lord's promise, *I will show myself to him* (Jn 14:8.21). Until that happens, no good thing is enough for us, nor should it be, lest our longing linger in the way, that longing which must be at full stretch until it reaches home.

In the morning we have been filled with your mercy; we have exulted and been made joyful all our days. The day that is coming is a day without end. All those days we know now will be present together, and that is why they will satisfy us. Where there is nothing of which it could be said that this does not exist because it has not come yet, and nothing that has ceased to exist because it has come already, the days do not yield place to other days that follow. All days are present at once, because there is but a single day that stands, and does not slip away; and that is eternity. These are the days concerning which a psalm asks, *Is there anyone who wants life, and loves to see good days?* (Ps 33:13(34:12)). The same days are called years in another place, where a psalm says to God, *You are the selfsame, and your years will not fail* (Ps 101:28(102:27)); for they are not the kind of years to be reckoned as nothing, or days which have shrunk like a shadow.[34] These are days which truly *are*, the days of which a psalmist prayed to know the number when he said, *Make known to me my end, O Lord* (for once I

30. See 2 Pt 1:19.
31. See Mt 5:8.6.
32. See 2 Cor 5:6-7.
33. See Ps 5:5(3).
34. See Ps 101:12(102:11).

reach it I shall abide, and seek nothing further), *and the number of my days, the number that is.* This is the point: *that is*, as opposed to that which is not. The days we know here are those of which he goes on to say, *Lo, you have given me a short measure of days* (Ps 38:5-6(39:4-5)), and they do not truly exist because they do not stand still; they do not stay, but speed past, always unstable. Not a single hour can we find within them where no part has slipped away, and no other part is still awaited. No moment is so stable that we might say of it, "This is."

How different are those years, those days, that fail not, where we shall not fail either, yet shall be unfailingly refreshed! May our souls burn with desire for those days, may we thirst for them ardently and passionately, and there be filled, there satisfied. And then may we say in realization what now we say by anticipation, *In the morning we have been filled with your mercy; we have exulted and been made joyful all our days. We rejoice over the days when you humbled us, the years when we saw misfortune.*

Verses 16-17. Works and the one work

16. But now, in these still unfruitful[35] days, let us make the next line our prayer: *Look upon your servants and upon your works.* Your servants are themselves your works, for you not only created us human but also made us your servants, obedient to your commands. We are of God's fashioning, not only in Adam, but also as created in Christ Jesus for the good works which God prepared in advance for us to walk in;[36] for it is God who is at work in us, effecting both the will and the execution, according to his good purpose.[37]

And guide their children aright, so that they may be right of heart, the kind of people to whom God is good; for God is indeed good to Israel, but to those whose hearts are straightforward. Let them not be like that psalmist whose steps had all but slipped, because as he considered the peace enjoyed by sinners he began to be discontented with God. It almost seemed to him that God was unaware of the injustice, or at any rate God took no heed, and appeared not to be guiding human destinies.[38]

17. *And may the splendor of the Lord our God be upon us.* The prayer is like that of another psalm, where it is said, *The light of your countenance is stamped upon us, O Lord* (Ps 4:7(6)). *And keep straight the works of our hands above us,* so that we do not perform them for a material, earthly reward; for then they would be bent, not straight.

---

35. Or perhaps simply "bad." *Diebus adhuc malignis* may be contrasted with the "good days" we hope to see (as in Ps 33(34) just quoted), or with the fruitfulness in good works which the present section evokes.
36. See Eph 2:10.
37. See Phil 2:13.
38. See Ps 72(73):1-14.

Many codices terminate the psalm here, but in some others a further line occurs: *And keep straight the work of our hands.* Careful scholars prefix a star to this line. Such stars they call asterisks. They are used to indicate words which are found in the Hebrew or in certain Greek translations, but not in the Septuagint. Now if we try to expound this line, it seems to me to convey the idea that all our good works are reducible to one work only: the work of charity; for charity is the perfect fulfillment of the law.[39] This is why I think so: in the previous line it had said, *Keep straight the works of our hands above us,* but in this last line it said not *works* but *work.* It says, *Keep straight the work of our hands.* It seems as though in this last line the psalm tried to show that all works are one work; that is to say, they are all directed to this one. Works are right and straight when directed to this end. The end of the commandment is charity welling from a pure heart, and from a good conscience, and from genuine faith.[40] Thus the sole work, in which all others are comprised, is faith working through love,[41] which is why the Lord says in the gospel, *This is the work God wants, that you believe in the one he has sent* (Jn 6:29).

Conclusion: the psalm goes under the name of Moses for a special reason

In this psalm clear distinctions have been drawn between the old life and the new, between a life doomed to death and a life that is life indeed, between years that are counted as nothing and days that contain the fullness of mercy and true joy. In short, the distinction has been clearly drawn between the punishment of the first man and the reign of the second. In view of these contrasts I believe that the name of the man of God, Moses, was attached to this psalm so that people who devoutly and with a right intention search the scriptures[42] may discern by means of the contrasts that the law of God given through the ministry of Moses undoubtedly contained, though in a veiled form, something of what this psalm sets forth. This is true even though under the law God seems to promise as a reward for good works earthly benefits and nothing else—or almost nothing else. But for any who make the passover to Christ the veil will be lifted.[43] The blindfold will be removed, so that they may consider the wondrous things in God's law. This is granted by him to whom we pray, *Take the veil from my eyes, and I will contemplate the wonders of your law* (Ps 118(119):18).

---

39. See Rom 13:10.
40. See 1 Tm 1:5.
41. See Gal 5:6.
42. See Jn 5:39.
43. See 2 Cor 3:16.

Exposition 1 of Psalm 90

What it means to imitate Christ, particularly when we are tempted

1. This psalm is the one which the devil quoted when he dared to tempt our Lord Jesus Christ. Let us listen to it and so be armed against the tempter. We must put no trust in ourselves, but only in him who was first tempted to ensure that in our temptations we may not be defeated. Temptation was not necessary to Christ, but his temptation is a lesson for us. If we hearken to the replies he gave to the devil, and learn from them how to reply likewise when the devil tempts us, we shall be entering by the door. What does that mean, to enter by the door? To enter through Christ, for he said himself, *I am the door* (Jn 10:9). But what does entering through Christ imply? It means following in Christ's ways. But how are we to follow in Christ's ways? Are we expected to imitate the glory of God incarnate? Does he exhort us, or require us, to perform miracles like those he wrought? Does not our Lord Jesus Christ, together with the Father, govern the whole world, now and always? Surely he does not call men and women to imitate him in that respect, governing heaven and earth and all they contain, in collaboration with him? Surely we are not called to be creators too, creators of all that comes to be, as all things were indeed made through Christ?

No. Our Lord Jesus Christ, our God and Savior, does not invite you to attempt the same works that he wrought from the beginning, the works of which scripture says, *Everything was made through him* (Jn 1:3); nor are you required to emulate the works he performed on earth. He does not say to you, "You cannot be my disciple unless you walk on the sea, unless you raise up someone dead for four days, unless you open the eyes of someone born blind." No, he does not say that. What does it mean, then, to go in by the door? *Learn from me, for I am gentle and humble of heart* (Mt 11:29). You must concentrate on what he became for your sake; that is what you are to imitate in him.

Even before he was born from Mary he worked miracles; for who was it who ever worked any, except the one of whom it was said, *He alone works wonders* (Ps 71(72):18)? Even those who achieved prodigies before Christ's coming were able to do so only by Christ's power. It was by the power of Christ that Elijah raised a dead child to life.[1] And are we to think that Peter was greater than

---

1. See 1 Kgs 17:22.

Christ, because sick persons were brought out when Peter passed by so that his mere shadow might fall upon them,[2] whereas Christ cured the sick by using his voice? Does that make Peter more powerful than Christ? Anyone who would say so must be quite crazy. Why was there so much power in Peter? Because Christ was in Peter. To clear up any doubts, he said, *All who have come are thieves and robbers* (Jn 10:8); all who have come of their own accord, he meant, all those who have come without any mandate from me and without me, all those in whom I have not been present and whom I did not bring in. However many miracles were wrought, whether by people who lived before Christ's day or by those who came later, it was the Lord himself who performed them, just as he also performed those he worked in his own lifetime. Neither does he exhort you to imitate the mighty works he wrought even before human beings were created.

So in what respect are you invited to imitate him? Your business is to imitate what he could not have done had he not been made man. Could he ever have endured suffering, if he had never become human? Could he have died, been crucified, been humiliated, except in virtue of his human estate? You too, then, must be strong and endure patiently when you encounter vexations in this life contrived by the devil, whether they come in open attack through other people, or by a hidden route, as in the case of Job. Then you will dwell within the help of the Most High, as the psalm says.[3] If you distance yourself from the help of the Most High you will fall, for you are far too weak to help yourself.

2. Many people are valiant when they endure persecution from human beings who are raging against them openly. They are aware that they are imitating Christ's sufferings when people persecute them outright; but if they are buffeted by hidden persecution from the devil, they think they are unworthy to be crowned by Christ.[4] But you must not be afraid to be like Christ in this matter. When the devil tempted the Lord in the desert no one else was present. The devil tempted him in secret, and was defeated, just as he was defeated when he raged openly. It is the same for you, if you want to enter by the door, the same when the enemy tempts in secret, when he begs leave to get his hands on someone he can hurt with bodily afflictions, fevers, diseases, and all sorts of physical distress, like those visited upon Job. In none of these did Job see the devil; all he could discern was the power of God. He knew that the devil could not touch him except by permission from the one who held supreme power, so he ascribed all glory to God, and no rights at all to the devil. Even when the tempter took everything away, Job said, *The Lord gave, and the Lord has taken away* (Jb 1:21). He did not say, "The Lord gave, and the devil has taken away," for the devil could not have

---

2. See Acts 5:15.
3. Variant: "You too, then, must be strong and endure patiently, dwelling within the help of the Most High, as the psalm says, when you encounter. . . ."
4. In other words, we cannot always disentangle sin and suffering.

taken anything if the Lord had not allowed it. But the Lord did allow it so that a human being might be tested, and the devil vanquished. Even when the devil wounded Job, the Lord still allowed it; and Job knew this, for although he was dripping from head to foot with corruption and maggots, he attributed nothing whatever to the devil's power. His wife suggested something of the kind to him. She was all the devil had left to Job—left, though, as an ally for the devil himself, not as a consoler for her husband—and she urged him, *Curse God, and die.* He replied, *You have spoken like the silly woman you are. If we have received good things from the Lord's hands, should we not endure the bad too?* (Jb 2:9-10).

Verses 1-3. Dwelling safely and humbly within the help of the Most High

3. When anyone imitates Christ in such a way as to bear all the vexations of this world, hoping in God, and being neither entrapped by a bait nor broken down by fear, that person *dwells within the help of the Most High*, and will *abide under the protection of the God of heaven*, as you heard and sang in the psalm. These are its opening words; we shall come later to the part the devil quoted to tempt Christ, and you will recognize them as familiar. This person *will say to the Lord, You are my support and my refuge, O my God.* Who addresses the Lord like this? The one *who dwells within the help of the Most High.* But who *dwells within the help of the Most High*? People who do not set up home within their own help. Who *dwells within the help of the Most High*? A person who is not proud, like those two who ate in the hope of becoming like gods, and thereby lost that endowment of being immortal humans with which they had been created. They aspired to dwell within their own help, not within that of the Most High, and so they listened to the snake's insinuation, spurning God's command. They discovered that the outcome was what God had threatened, not what the devil had promised.

4. You too must say, therefore, *In him will I trust, for he will deliver me*; I shall not deliver myself. What else are we being taught, but that we must place no hope at all in ourselves, or in any human helper? From what will God deliver you? *From the hunters' trap and from the harsh word.* It is important, certainly, to be delivered *from the hunters' trap*, but is it any great matter to be delivered *from the harsh word*? It could be: remember that a harsh word has landed many people in the hunters' trap. What do I mean by saying that? The devil, with his angels to aid him, sets traps just as hunters set them. People who walk in Christ walk well clear of those traps, for the devil dare not set them in Christ; he lays them on the verge of the way, but not in the way. Let Christ be your way, and you will not fall into the devil's trap. If anyone wanders off the way, the trap is there, ready. The devil sets his snares on this side and that, to right and to left of us he positions them. You are walking between snares. Do you want to walk safely?

Then do not deviate either to right or to left; let him be your way who for you became the way,[5] so that he may lead you through himself to himself, and you need not fear the hunters' snares.

But what does it mean to be delivered *from the harsh word*? The devil has caught many a victim in his trap by means of a word. Those who try to live as Christians among pagans, for example, have to put up with mockery from their pagan neighbors. They are embarrassed by the taunts, and a harsh word can be enough to drive them off the way. Then they fall into the hunters' snares. What harm is a harsh word going to do you? None at all. But does it follow that you will come to no harm in the snare, into which the enemy pushes you by a harsh word? When nets are spread to catch birds, they are usually stretched across the top[6] of a hedge. Then people throw stones into the hedge. The stones do no harm to the birds—well, I ask you, did you ever hit a bird by shying a stone into a hedge? But a bird is startled by the harmless noise, and gets caught in the net. It is the same with people who take fright at the futile, harmless insults of the mockers. In their embarrassment at the silly noise they fall into the huntsmen's snares, and are captured by the devil.

But now, brothers and sisters, why should I hold back from saying something that ought not to be passed over in silence, something God is compelling me to say? However you may take this, God is driving me to say it, and if I keep quiet I am falling into the hunters' snares myself. If I am so fearful of human criticism that I shrink from saying it, I am being pushed by a harsh word into the huntsmen's traps—I who warn you not to be afraid of the words of other people. Well then, what is it that I have to say?

Just as someone who has been a Christian but is living among pagans may be shamed by the harsh words he hears from them, and fall into the hunters' trap, so too will those who live among Christians, but desire to live better, more dedicated lives, hear themselves vilified even by their Christian neighbors. Will it help you, my brother or sister, to find a town in which no one is a pagan? I don't think so. In a place like that no one derides a Christian simply for being a Christian, of course, since no pagans are to be found there; but many Christians living disreputable lives there surely will be. Among these there may be someone who wants to live a good life: he or she wants to be sober among drunkards, perhaps, and to be chaste among the debauched. Among people who consult astrologers[7] such a person tries to worship God sincerely and have nothing to do with superstitious practices; and though all around are fans of theatrical fripperies, he or she will go only to church. A Christian of this stamp is exposed to insults from fellow-Christians, and has to endure harsh words. "How important you are, how

---

5. See Jn 14:6.
6. Or "at the end."
7. *Mathematicorum*; see note at Exposition 2 of Psalm 33,25.

righteous!" they say. "Elijah, are you? Or Peter, perhaps? Did you drop down from heaven?" From every side, turn where they will, fervent Christians hear the harsh word. If they are frightened into forsaking the way of Christ, they fall into the hunters' snares.

But how can they bear not to forsake the way, when these words are flung at them? What does it mean, not to forsake the way? When they hear harsh words, where are they to look for such powerful comfort that they will care nothing for what is said, and keep to the way, and enter through the door? Let them say to themselves, "What sort of words do I have to listen to, I who am only a servant, and a sinful one at that? My Lord heard people say to him, *You have a demon*" (Jn 8:48). What you heard then is a harsh word spoken against the Lord. He did not deserve to hear it himself, but he heard it in order to forewarn you against harsh words, and so save you from falling into the snares of huntsmen.

Verse 4. Sheltered under the wings of incarnate Wisdom

5. *He will overshadow you between his shoulders, and you will find security beneath his wings.* This he says to warn you against trying to be your own protection, to disabuse you of the idea that you are powerful enough to protect yourself. He will protect you in order to deliver you; he will deliver you from the hunters' trap and the harsh word.

He will overshadow you between his shoulders: the phrase could mean either at his back or against his breast, since the shoulders are close to the head. But when the next phrase is added, *you will find security beneath his wings*, it is clear that God's way of sheltering you is to place you under his outstretched wings. The wings of God are open on either side of you, and you are in the middle. There you need not fear that anyone will hurt you. All you have to do is take care not to leave that place where no enemy dare approach. If a hen protects her chicks under her wings, how much safer will you be under the wings of God, safe against the devil and his angels, those powers of the air[8] which hover like hawks, all ready to snatch the feeble hatchlings! The comparison of a hen with God's Wisdom is apposite, for Christ, our Lord and Savior, used the same comparison himself. He likened himself to a hen in his lament, *Jerusalem, Jerusalem, how often I wanted to gather your children to myself, as a hen gathers her chicks under her wings, but you would have none of it!* (Mt 23:37). Jerusalem would have none of it, but as for us, that is what we want. Jerusalem fled from the hen's wings, trusting in its own resources, though in truth so weak; and it was snatched by the raptors of the air. Let us confess our weakness and flee under God's wings; then God will be for us like a mothering hen protecting her squabs. You

---

8. See Eph 2:2.

must not think it irreverent to use the hen as a symbol of God, brothers and sisters. Observe the other birds, all those many species that raise their young and keep them warm as we watch. Not one of them is so much weakened over its chicks as is the hen. Think about it, beloved. When we watch the swallows, sparrows,[9] and storks away from their nests we do not even know whether they have young; but we certainly do know it in the hen's case. Her voice becomes hoarse, her feathers droop and her whole demeanor changes when she has chicks; because they are weak, she makes herself weak with them. So too did the Wisdom of God become weak, for the Word was made flesh, and dwelt among us,[10] so that we may find security beneath his wings.[11]

Verses 5-6. God's shield in our warfare; the dangers from different weapons

6. *His truth will throw a shield around you.* This shield is the same thing as the wings just mentioned, because the reality is neither wings nor shield. If the terms were being used literally, could wings be a shield, or a shield wings? No; but since everything is being couched in figurative language and imagery, the same realities can be called both wings and shield. Think of the imagery used for Christ: if he were really a stone, he could not also be a lion; if he were a lion, he could not be a lamb. But he can be called a lion,[12] and a lamb,[13] and a stone,[14] and a bull-calf, and all sorts of similar things because he is neither stone nor lion nor lamb nor bull, but the Savior of us all, Jesus Christ. All these expressions are metaphorical, not literally exact.

His truth will throw a shield around you. His truth acts like a shield in not allowing those who hope in themselves to be confused with those who hope in God. There are sinners and sinners. Find me the kind of sinner who presumes on his own merits, who is scornful and unwilling to confess his sins, and that kind will say, "If my sins really displeased God, he would not allow me to go on living." But the other sort would not even lift his eyes to heaven, but only beat his breast, saying, *Lord, be merciful to me, a sinner* (Lk 18:14). Both of them were sinners, but the one mocked while the other mourned; the one made light of his sins but the other made confession of his. The truth of God takes no account of human self-importance. Truth distinguished the penitent from the blusterer, the humble from the proud, those who presume on themselves from those who presume on God. *His truth,* therefore, will be like *a shield* thrown about you.

---

9. A few codices read "geese" instead of "sparrows."
10. See Jn 1:14.
11. For the simile of the mother-hen, compare Exposition 1 of Psalm 58,10, and Exposition 2 of Psalm 88,14.
12. See Rv 5:5.
13. See Rv 5:6; Jn 1:29.
14. See Acts 4:11; Ps 117(118):22.

7. *You will not fear the terror of the night, or the arrow that flies by day, the prowler in darkness or the daylight defeat and the noontide demon.* Two pairs are mentioned, the second pair corresponding to the first. The psalm says, *You will not fear the terror of the night, or the arrow that flies by day*; and then the terrors of the night are echoed by *the prowler in darkness*, while the *arrow that flies by day* has its counterpart in *the daylight defeat and the noontide demon.* What should we fear at night, and what by day?

When a person sins in ignorance, it is like sinning in the night; when one sins knowingly, it is like sinning by day. So the first item in each pair is less serious, and the second members indicate graver sins. Concentrate now, so that I may explain this to you carefully, if the Lord allows; for this is an obscure subject, and it will be very profitable for you to understand it.

The psalm called a temptation which is mild and happens to the ignorant "night-time terror"; it called a temptation which is mild and happens to people who have more awareness "an arrow flying by day." What are "mild" temptations? Temptations that are not so insistent, not so pressing, as to overwhelm us, and may quickly pass us by if we refuse them. But now suppose they are more serious. Imagine that a persecutor is threatening. People who lack awareness are absolutely terrified—those people, I mean, who are not yet firm in their faith, and have not understood that the very reason for their being Christians is that they must hope for a future life. As terror grips them in the face of temporal dangers they think that Christ has deserted them, and that they gain nothing by being Christians; for, as I said, they do not know that they are Christians in order to overcome present threats and hope for future rewards. The prowler in darkness finds such people and captures them. But there are others who know full well that they have been called to hope in the future, because what God has promised us is not to be found on this earth or in this life. These better-informed people know that all such trials are to be borne so that we may receive and gain what God has promised us for eternity. They are well aware of this, yet when the persecutor begins to take a more ferocious stance, and to make use of threats, penalties and tortures, they sometimes yield. And because these people know what they are doing, they are falling in daylight.

8. But now, why does the psalm speak of noontide? Because persecution can grow very hot, and this fiercer heat the psalm compares to noon. Listen, beloved,[15] as I prove this to you from the scriptures. The Lord spoke about a sower, describing him as he went out to scatter his seed. Some fell along the path, some on stony ground, some among thorns. Later the Lord graciously expounded the parable, and when he came to the stony ground, he said, *These are the ones who hear the word, and rejoice over the word for a while; but when*

---

15. *Caritas vestra.*

tribulation arises over the word they are swiftly brought down. What had he said earlier about the seedlings which sprang up in stony ground? *As soon as the sun came up they withered away, because they lacked deep roots* (Mt 13:20-21.6). These shallow-rooted seedlings are the people who rejoice over the word for a while, but dry up when persecution arises over the word. Why do they dry up? *Because they lacked deep roots.* And what is the root? Charity. The apostle exhorted his people to be *rooted in charity and built up on charity* (Eph 3:17). Just as greed is the root of all evils,[16] so is charity the root of all that is good.

You know all this, and it has been repeated often, so why am I reminding you of it? So that you may understand the psalm, which used the expression, "noontide demon," to suggest the heat of fierce persecution. The Lord says, "The sun rose and the shoot withered because it had no root"; and to make it clear to us why the new growth is withered by the sun—why, that is, such persons do not withstand mounting persecution—he explains, *They lacked deep roots.* In view of this parable we are justified in taking the noontide demon to be a symbol of fierce persecution.

Let me remind you, brothers and sisters, what persecution was like in the old days. Pay attention, please, beloved, while I recall what it was from which the Lord delivered his Church. Emperors and earthly rulers thought at first that by persecution they could obliterate the name of Christ and the name of Christian from the earth, so they ordered that anyone who confessed to being a Christian should be executed.[17] Under that regime anyone who was not prepared to face execution denied being a Christian. If he or she understood the gravity of such a denial, that person was shot by the day-flying arrow. But others, who cared little for the present life, confidently hoping for the life to come, dodged the daytime arrow by confessing themselves Christians. They were struck in the flesh, certainly, but set free in spirit; they found their home with God in peace, and could begin to look forward to the redemption of their bodies as well, at the resurrection of the dead. They escaped the temptation represented by the day-flying arrow. So the decree, "Anyone who confesses to being a Christian shall be executed," was in a sense like an arrow shot in full daylight.

Not yet was there a noontide demon, afire with cruelty and whipping up fierce heat for the valiant. But listen to what happened next. Christ's enemies observed that many people were hastening to martyrdom; the more who suffered, the more there were who believed in him. So they said to themselves, "At this rate we shall be killing the whole human race, so many thousands are there who believe in this name. If we kill them all, scarcely anyone will be left on earth."

---

16. See 1 Tm 6:10.
17. This was substantially the position of Trajan (A.D. 98-117) as revealed by his reply to the famous letter from Pliny (c. 112), though he forbade the governor to initiate inquiries or to accept anonymous accusations. Compare Exposition 2 of Psalm 68,4, and note there.

The sun was waxing hot, you see, the temperature was beginning to soar. So a new decree was promulgated. Listen to what it was. Earlier they had ordered, "Anyone who confesses to being a Christian shall be executed"; but now they changed it to "Anyone who confesses to being a Christian shall be tortured. The torture shall be prolonged until the prisoner denies being a Christian."[18] Now contrast the daytime arrow with the noontide demon. What was the daytime arrow? "Anyone who confesses to being a Christian shall be executed." Would any believer hesitate to dodge the arrow, seeing how swift death was likely to be? But the later decree provided that any who confessed themselves Christians should not be executed, but tortured until they denied it, and released when they did so; and that was the noontide demon. There were many people who did not deny their Christianity,[19] yet gave way under torture, for the torture was prolonged until they recanted. Under the former policy, what was the sword able to do against those who persevered in their refusal to deny Christ? Dispatch them with one blow, killing their bodies but sending their souls to God. Prolonged agonies might achieve the same result; but how many people would be found to endure such intense and long-drawn anguish? Many apostatized; and I believe that those who did so were the ones who trusted in themselves, who did not dwell within the help of the Most High, under the protection of the God of heaven. They were the ones who did not say to the Lord, You are my support, who did not look for security under the shade of his wings, but expected too much of their own strength. They were knocked away from God, so that he might show them that it is he who protects us, he who modulates the temptations, he who allows only so much to come upon us as the person on trial can bear.

Verse 7. No one can afford to be complacent. Christ identifies himself with his hard-pressed members

9. In this way many fell prey to the noontide demon. How many, are you wondering? The psalm continues, A thousand shall fall from your side, and ten thousand from your right hand; but it shall not come near you. To whom is this promise addressed? To the Lord Jesus Christ, brothers and sisters: who else?

18. Tertullian commented eloquently on the discrepancy between this policy and the usual procedure in the Roman Empire for dealing with those suspected of crimes. Whereas the use of torture in ordinary cases was directed to eliciting from the suspect a confession of guilt, Christians were tortured to elicit a denial of what was viewed by the authorities as their crime, namely their Christianity. If apostates were to be pardoned, it was tantamount to saying that an adequate defense against a criminal charge was that one had ceased to commit the crime. "You are acting with extreme perversity when you hold us to be proved guilty by our confession of the name of Christ, yet attempt by torture to dislodge us from our confession.... 'I am a Christian,' the tortured person cries out. He tells you truly what he is, but you want to hear from him what he is not" (Apol. 2).
19. Or, perhaps, "had not denied it" under the previous regime.

The Lord Jesus is present not only in himself, but in us too. Remember his words, *Saul, Saul, why are you persecuting me?* (Acts 9:4). When he demanded, *Why are you persecuting me?* at a time when no one was touching him, was he not ranging himself with us? And when he said, *What a person did for even the least of those who are mine was done to me,*[20] was he not ranging himself with us? Head and body are parts of a whole, and cannot be divided from each other. What are these—head and body? The Savior and the Church. What does it mean, then, to say, *A thousand shall fall from your side, and ten thousand from your right hand?* They will fall, you remember, under the onslaught from the noontide demon. It is a terrifying prospect, brothers and sisters, this possibility of falling away from Christ's side, or from his right hand.[21] How will they fall from his side? And why do some fall from his side, and others from his right? Why a thousand from his side, and ten thousand from his right hand? What can it mean, "a thousand from your side"? Evidently this crowd of a thousand is smaller than the ten thousand who will fall away from his right; but who are they? All will shortly be made plain; everything will be clear in Christ's name in a minute.

Christ promised certain people that they will share in his judicial function; these were the apostles who left everything to follow him. Peter said to Jesus, *Look, we have left everything, and followed you*; and he responded with the promise, *You will sit upon twelve thrones, judging the twelve tribes of Israel* (Mt 19:27.28). But you must not think the promise was meant for them alone. If it were, where would the apostle Paul find his seat? He worked harder than all of them,[22] and are there to be seats for no more than twelve? Paul is the thirteenth, because one of the twelve, Judas, fell away, and in the place of the traitor Matthias was elected. We read about this in the Acts of the Apostles.[23] This meant that the twelve seats were all taken. So will there be no room for the apostle who worked harder than any of them? That cannot be the case; probably we should take the twelve judicial seats to represent the perfect character of that tribunal, for thousands will sit on those twelve seats.

But I hear someone challenging me: "How can you prove that Paul too will be among the judges?" I suggest that you listen to his own claim: *Do you not realize that we shall judge angels?* (1 Cor 6:3). He stated, *We shall judge.* With the assurance inspired by his faith, he did not hesitate to include himself among those who will judge alongside Christ.

It seems certain, then, that those who will judge beside Christ are the principal members of the Church, the ones who are perfect. To such as these the invi-

---

20. See Mt 25:40.
21. The more natural meaning would be "at your side…at your right hand," but Augustine takes it to mean "from," as is clear from the following reflections.
22. See 1 Cor 15:10.
23. See Acts 1:15-26.

tation was addressed, *If you want to be perfect, go and sell all you possess and give the money to the poor* (Mt 19:21). What did Christ imply by "Do you want to be perfect"? He meant, "Do you want to judge, along with me, rather than be judged?" The one to whom he put the question went sadly away;[24] but many others accepted the invitation, and many still do. All these will exercise the judicial function together with Christ. However, there are many others who promise themselves that, having left everything and followed Christ, they will join him as judges, and yet rest all their confidence on themselves. They are motivated by a conceit and pride that only God can know, and so they cannot escape the noontide demon, if the blazing heat of relentless persecution happens to scorch them. This was what frequently occurred in the early days. Many people of that type had distributed all their possessions among the poor, promising themselves that they would take their seats beside Christ to judge the nations; but the heat of persecution increased and they apostatized under the pain of it, and forswore Christ. These are the folk who fell from his side, because although they seemed destined to sit with him and judge the world, they fell away.

10. Now I will tell you who the others are, the ones who fall from his right hand. You know what will happen when that tribunal is set up, for the Lord has told us, *All nations will assemble before him. He will separate them from one another, as a shepherd divides sheep from goats; and he will station the sheep at his right hand, and the goats at his left* (Mt 25:32-33). Then they will be judged. Some people will be his fellow-judges in the tribunal, those who have chosen to be perfect and have truly become perfect, being so deeply rooted and grounded in charity that they could not be withered by the sun or the noontide demon. There will be many to exercise this judicial office, but they will be far outnumbered by those who will stand before the court; this is why the former are like a thousand, but the latter like ten thousand. What will Christ say to those on his right? *I was hungry, and you fed me; I was a stranger and you made me welcome* (Mt 25:35). He will say this, obviously, to those who owned property in this world, and so had the resources to do such human kindnesses. These people will indeed reign along with the perfect, for while the perfect are the professional soldiers, the charitable donors are like civilians who pay the soldiers their subsistence allowance;[25] and both soldier and civilian will be subjects of the same emperor in his kingdom. The soldier is brave, the civilian dutiful; the

---

24. See Mt 19:22.
25. Augustine refers to this custom in his *Homilies on the Gospel of John* CXXII,3, where he speaks of Paul's decision to support himself by manual work in order not to burden his converts, although as a soldier of Christ he would have had the right to this contribution from the *provinciales* or civilians. Augustine also refers to the custom more briefly in *Homilies on the Gospel of John* XIII,17, in connection with the Donatists: the faithful must be on their guard when subsistence demands are made by those who appear to be part of Christ's professional militia, but are not.

soldier, fortified by prayer, fights against the devil, the dutiful civilian pays the regular stipend to the troops. You must understand this, beloved ones.[26] So those who at the end find themselves at Christ's right hand will hear him say, *Come, you who are blessed by my Father, take possession of the kingdom prepared for you since the creation of the world* (Mt 25:34).

Now in the early days many were promising themselves that they would judge with Christ; but when the sun of persecution and the noontide demon stepped up the heat, they could not bear the fiery persecution and fell away from his side. At the same time there were others who did not expect to sit as judges, but were promising themselves places at Christ's right hand on the strength of their almsgiving; they hoped to hear him say, *Come, you who are blessed by my Father, take possession of the kingdom prepared for you since the creation of the world.* And just as many fell short of the dignity as judges to which they aspired, so too did many—in fact, many more—fall short of their hoped-for place at Christ's right hand. This is why the psalm says to Christ, *A thousand shall fall from your side, and ten thousand from your right hand.*

All the same, there will be many with him who did not concern themselves with these prospects, people with whom Christ unites himself and whom he makes his members, and so the psalm continued, *But it shall not come near you.* Did this promise, *it shall not come near you,* apply to the head alone? Certainly not; it does not come near to Peter, or to Paul, or to any of the apostles, or to any of the martyrs who held out under torture. But how can it be said of them that *it shall not come near you*? Why were they put through such agony? The pain did come very near to their flesh, but did not reach the place of their faith. Their faith was far removed from any fear of their tormentors. Let the persecutors do their worst, but terror will not come near; let them torture as they will, but the martyrs will laugh at the anguish, for they put their trust in him who conquered first so that the rest of us might conquer. And who are the conquerors? Those who have not relied on themselves.

It is important to concentrate here, beloved,[27] because this is what all the earlier verses have been driving at. Remember what they said: *He will say to the Lord, You are my support and my refuge*; and again, *In him will I trust, for he will deliver me from the hunters' trap.* Notice that it is *he* who will *deliver me*; I shall not deliver myself. *He will overshadow you between his shoulders* — but when? Only when you look to *find security beneath his wings.* Then *his truth will throw a shield around you.* You have trusted in the Lord, then, and put your entire hope in him; so how does the psalm continue? *You will not fear the terror of the night, or the arrow that flies by day, the prowler in darkness or the daylight defeat and*

---

26. *Caritas vestra.*
27. *Caritas vestra.*

the noontide demon. Who will be delivered from fear? The one who relies not on self, but on Christ. It is otherwise with those who trust in themselves, even if they were hoping for a place at Christ's side and the honor of judging with him, or even if they were hoping to find themselves at his right hand, listening to the words, *Come, you who are blessed by my Father, take possession of the kingdom prepared for you since the creation of the world.* Upon such persons came the attack of the noontide demon, the searing heat of persecution. They were exceedingly terrified, and many fell away from the judicial bench to which they had aspired. Of these the psalm said, *A thousand shall fall from your side.* Many others likewise fell away from the reward they expected for their devoted services, and of them it said, *And ten thousand from your right hand.* But as for you—you, head and body—daytime defeat and the noontide demon *shall not come near you,* for the Lord knows those who are his own.[28]

Verse 8. The insight that comes from faith

11. *Nevertheless you will use your eyes and consider, and you will see the punishment of sinners.* What does this mean? Why does it say, *Nevertheless*? Because, Lord, the godless have been given leave to domineer over your servants, even to persecute them. You have allowed it. Will they go unpunished on that account? They will not, even though you have allowed it, and your faithful ones have been the more gloriously crowned as a result of their persecution. *Nevertheless you will use your eyes and consider, and you will see the punishment of sinners,* for the retribution in store for them will be in proportion to the evil they intended, not the good that they brought about unwittingly. What we need now are the eyes of faith; we need to see how the persecutors are exalted for a time, but will mourn for eternity. Those who have been granted power over God's servants in the present age will be commanded, *Depart from me into the eternal fire which was prepared for the devil and his angels* (Mt 25:41). But we need eyes to see this now, the insight implied by the psalm when it said, *You will use your eyes and consider.* It is not easy to see the godless person prospering in this world, and to regard them with such penetrating insight that you can consider in faith what they will suffer at the end, if they do not mend their ways; for those who want to thunder now will be struck by lightning later. *Nevertheless you will use your eyes and consider, and you will see the punishment of sinners.*

---

28. See 2 Tm 2:19.

Verses 9-12. Hasty conclusion: we must leave the rest for tomorrow

12. *Because you, O Lord, are my hope.* Now at last the psalm has come to the reason why the one he addresses does not fall in daytime defeat and is not worsted by the noontide demon: it is *because you, O Lord, are my hope; very high have you set your refuge.* What is this lofty refuge? Many people claim God's refuge for themselves, as a place to which they can flee from the heat of this temporal life. God's refuge is on high, and very well hidden, and you may shelter there from the wrath to come. Within us, *very high, you have set your refuge. Evils shall not come near you, nor the scourge approach your tent, for he has given his angels orders concerning you, to guard you in all your ways. They shall bear you up with their hands, so that you may never stub your foot on a stone.* These are the words the devil quoted to our Lord Jesus Christ while tempting him. But they need more careful consideration, so let us defer them until tomorrow, for we do not want to tire you out. A sermon is owing to you tomorrow as well,[29] so we can begin then from this place in the psalm. We must take your weariness into account. We don't want to rush over obscure matters in an effort to finish the psalm today, and risk your being unable to take them in.

---

29. Variant: "If the Lord wills, there shall be a sermon on them tomorrow."

Exposition 2 of Psalm 90

Second Sermon[1]

Augustine reiterates his teaching on the whole Christ, head and members; this is the key to understanding in all the psalms

1. No doubt you remember, beloved—those of you at any rate who were present to hear yesterday's sermon—that we ran out of time and were unable to finish the psalm we had begun to expound. Part of it was held over until today. So if you were here yesterday, recall what we said, and if you were not, set yourselves to learn. We deliberately arranged for that passage of the gospel to be proclaimed where the Lord was tempted with the very words of the psalm which you have heard now. Christ was tempted so that no Christian need be overcome by the tempter. He is our teacher, and he willed to be tempted in all respects, because we are tempted,[2] just as he willed to die, because we die, and willed to rise again, because we shall rise again. He became man for our sake, although he was the God through whom we were made, and whatever he demonstrated in his humanity, he demonstrated for us.

Dearly beloved,[3] we have reminded you of these truths very often, but we are never tired of repeating them, because there may be many among you who cannot read, either because they lack the time or because they have never learned, but at least by listening assiduously they will not forget the faith that can save them. Better that we bore some, provided we edify others. We are aware that many of you have very retentive memories and are accustomed to sacred reading; these are already well versed in what we are going to say, and perhaps wish we would tell them something they do not know. But if they have quicker minds, they ought to look about them and observe that they are walking along a road with slower companions. When two people walk together on the same way, and one is fleet of foot, the other tardy, the quicker one is perfectly capable of walking more slowly to match his pace with the other's, but the slower one does not have the same power to adjust his. If the nimbler one walks as fast as he possibly can, the slower one cannot keep up. The fast walker must reduce his speed, and not leave his slower companion behind.

---

1. Preached on the day after the preceding sermon.
2. See Heb 4:15. But it would be possible to translate, "He is our teacher in all things, and he willed to be tempted, because we are tempted."
3. *Caritati vestrae.*

Well now, this is what I have told you frequently, and now tell you once more (for, as the apostle said, *To keep writing the same things to you causes me no weariness, and makes for your safety* (Phil 3:1)): our Lord Jesus Christ consists of head and body, as a perfect man. We recognize the head in the man who was born of the Virgin Mary, suffered under Pontius Pilate, was buried, rose again, ascended into heaven, and is seated at the Father's right hand, from where we expect him to come again as judge of the living and the dead. He is the head of the Church. The Church is the body that belongs to this head. By this we do not mean just the church present in this place, but the Church both here and throughout the whole world; and not the Church of our own day alone, but that which began with Abel and extends to all who will be born and will believe in Christ to the very end, the whole people of the saints who belong to the one city. That city is the body of Christ, and Christ is its head. There the angels are our fellow citizens; but while we are still toiling along on our pilgrimage, they, at home in the city, look forward to our arrival.

From that city whence we are still exiles letters have reached us; these letters are the scriptures which exhort us to live good lives.[4] But why speak merely of letters? There is more than that: the king himself came down and made himself the way[5] for us on our pilgrimage, so that by walking in him we may not go astray, or faint on the journey, or fall in with robbers, or stumble into the traps that are set alongside the path.

We know him thus as the whole Christ, which means Christ in this universal sense, Christ with his Church. But he alone was born of the Virgin, and he alone is the Church's head, he who is the mediator between God and humankind, Christ Jesus.[6] A mediator he had to be, in order to reconcile through himself those who had gone far away from God; for mediation implies two parties. We had gone far away from God's majesty and offended him by our sin; so God's Son was sent as mediator to destroy by his blood the sins which had estranged us from God. He placed himself in between, to restore us and reconcile us to God, for by turning away from him we had become prisoners of our sins and trespasses. He is our head, he who is God, equal to the Father, the Word through whom all things were made;[7] but though as God he is our creator, he became man to re-create us. He is God to make us, but man to make us anew.

Let us keep him before our eyes as we listen to the psalm. Pay close attention, beloved, for it is the discipline and teaching of our school, and it will empower you to understand not this psalm only but many others, if you hold onto this rule. Sometimes a psalm—and indeed not only a psalm but any prophecy—speaks of

---

4. On the scriptures as a letter from God, see note at Exposition of Psalm 73,5.
5. See Jn 14:6.
6. See 1 Tm 2:5.
7. See Jn 1:3.

Christ in such a way that it clearly refers to the head alone; but sometimes it passes from the head to the body, by which I mean the Church, apparently without any change of person. This happens because the head is not separated from the body, so scripture speaks of them as one sole person. I will give you an example of what I am talking about, dearly beloved. There is a psalm where Christ's passion is described in a manner plain to everyone: *They dug holes in my hands and my feet; they numbered all my bones. They shared out my garments among them, and cast lots for my tunic* (Ps 21:17-19(22:16-18)). Even the Jews are embarrassed when they hear these verses, so very obvious is it that the prophecy refers to the passion of our Lord Jesus Christ. Yet though our Lord Jesus Christ was free from sin, at the opening of that same psalm he says, *O God, my God, why have you forsaken me? The tale of my sins leaves me far from salvation* (Ps 21:2(22:1)). You can distinguish between what is said in the person of the head, and what in the person of the body. The sins belong to us; the suffering undergone for our sake belongs to the head. But in virtue of the passion he endured for us, the sins that belong to us are blotted out. The same principle holds for our present psalm.

Verses 1-8. Recapitulation of yesterday's explanation of the early verses. God will protect us even in the heat of persecution if we trust in him, not in ourselves

2. Let us now briefly recall the verses we dealt with yesterday. *The one who dwells within the help of the Most High will abide under the protection of the God of heaven.* The point we made in connection with these lines, dearly beloved,[8] is that no one should trust in self. We must rest all our hope in God, for in him all our strength is to be found. We conquer through his help, not through any self-reliance. The God of heaven protects us if we pray to him as the psalm goes on to indicate: such a person *will say to the Lord, You are my support and my refuge, O my God. In him will I trust, for he will deliver me from the hunters' trap and from the harsh word.* We explained how it happens that many people fall into the hunters' trap by fearing that harsh word. A person may be vilified for being a Christian, so he or she regrets having become a Christian, and is precipitated by harsh words into the devil's trap. Or again, someone who lives among other Christians is mocked for living a more fervent life than others; if that good Christian is intimidated by the harsh words of the mockers, he or she falls into the devil's snare, and instead of being wheat on the threshing floor is disposed of with the chaff. Anyone who hopes in God, however, is delivered from the hunters' trap and the harsh word.

---

8. *Caritati vestrae.*

Now how does God protect you? *He will overshadow you between his shoulders*, which means that he will clasp you against his breast and keep you safe beneath his wings, if only you acknowledge your weakness, and like a feeble chick run beneath your mother's wings, where no kite can seize you. The kites are the powers of the air,[9] the devil and his angels, who try to grab us, knowing how weak we are. Let us run for cover under the wings of Wisdom, our mother, because Wisdom herself became weak for us when the Word was made flesh. As a mother hen becomes weak with her squabs in order to protect them under her wings, so did our Lord Jesus Christ with us. He was in the form of God, and deemed it no robbery to be God's equal, yet he emptied himself and took on the form of a slave, bearing the human likeness and sharing the human lot[10] in order to be weak along with us, and protect us beneath his wings. *Under his wings you will find security.*

His truth will throw a shield around you. You will not fear the terror of the night. Nocturnal terror stands for the temptations of the ignorant, but the arrow that flies by day is a figure of sins committed in full awareness; for night is a symbol of unwitting behavior, day of what is plainly obvious. Some people sin in ignorance, others knowingly. Those who sin in ignorance are tripped up by the terror of the night; those who sin in full awareness are pierced by the arrow that flies in daylight. But when temptations occur in times of fierce persecution, when the temperature is rising as though toward noon, whoever succumbs to that heat will be slain by the noontide demon. Many indeed did fall during that heat, as we explained yesterday, dearly beloved, because when the persecution grew hotter the edict went out, "Christians are to be tortured until they deny that they are Christians." In earlier days the usual thing was that people who confessed their faith were summarily executed, but later they were tortured to make them deny it. An accused person is customarily tortured only as long as he persists in denying his crime, whereas Christians were tortured for confessing, and denial merited pardon.[11] That age of persecutions subjected Christians to intense heat, and those who succumbed to persecution were as though felled by the noontide demon. And how many there were who did succumb! Many people who hoped to sit beside the Lord as fellow judges fell away from his side. Many others fell away too, those who counted on taking their place at his right hand, as civilians who belonged to the holy people, like taxpayers who supported the army. They expected to hear at the end, *I was hungry, and you fed me*; and certainly there will be many there to hear it. Yet some fell away, and in still greater numbers than those from the former group, inasmuch as the company at the Lord's right hand will be so large. The ones destined to exercise judgment with the Lord will be

---

9. See Eph 2:2.
10. See Phil 2:6-7.
11. For Tertullian's comments on this anomaly compare the note at Exposition 1 of Psalm 90,8.

fewer, while those who stand before him to be judged will be a vast multitude, but of diverse conditions. Some will be placed at his left, some at his right; some called to reign, others marked for punishment; some to hear, *Come, you who are blessed by my Father, take possession of the kingdom*, others to hear, *Depart from me, you accursed, into the eternal fire which was prepared for the devil and his angels* (Mt 25:35.34.41). This is why the psalm says that through the daylight defeat and the noontide demon *a thousand shall fall from your side, and ten thousand from your right hand.*

But *it shall not come near you*. What will not? The noontide demon will not throw you down. Small wonder that he does not defeat the head, but neither does he overthrow those who hold fast to the head in the way suggested by the apostle's words: *the Lord knows his own* (2 Tm 2:19); for some are predestined, and therefore known to the Lord as belonging to his own body. Since that temptation will not come near enough to these people to overthrow them, they can be recognized as the ones mentioned in the psalm's promise, *it shall not come near you.*

There could be a danger, though, that certain weak persons might look at the persecutors who were given leave to inflict great suffering on the Christians, and wonder, "How can God have allowed it? How can such wicked, criminal folk be permitted to torment God's servants so cruelly?" And the answer comes: use your eyes, the eyes of faith, even a little, and you will see the final retribution in store for those sinners. They are given such license now so that you may be tested. Accordingly the psalm continues, *Nevertheless you will use your eyes and consider, and you will see the punishment of sinners.*

Verses 9-12. Our lofty refuge: Christ was tempted to empower us when we are tempted

3. *Because you, O Lord, are my hope; very high have you set your refuge. Evils shall not come near you.* It is to the Lord that he says this: *Because you, O Lord, are my hope; very high have you set your refuge. Evils shall not come near you, nor the scourge approach your tent.* But now we are getting to the words spoken by the devil: *For he has given his angels orders concerning you, to guard you in all your ways. They shall bear you up with their hands, so that you may never stub your foot on a stone.* To whom are these words addressed? To the same person to whom it was said, *You, O Lord, are my hope.* I do not think it necessary to explain to Christians who *the Lord* is in this instance. If God the Father were meant, how could the angels be said to bear him up on their hands, to save him from stumbling on a stone? Clearly Christ too is called *the Lord*, and though the psalm had been speaking about the body, it has suddenly begun to speak about the head. He was addressed as our head when the psalm said, *You, O Lord, are my hope; very high have you set your refuge.* The reason why you have

set it so high is that *you, O Lord, are my hope*. What does this mean? Let me have your attention, beloved. The psalm has said, *You, O Lord, are my hope; very high have you set your refuge*. There is nothing strange about that, in view of the lines, *Evils shall not come near you*, because *very high have you set your refuge*. Nor will *the scourge approach your tent*, because *very high have you set your refuge*.

We do not read in the gospel that angels carried our Lord anywhere to save him from stumbling; and yet we do understand. These things did happen, and they were prophesied only because they truly were going to happen. It will not do to say, "Well, Christ will come again," as though that will be the occasion for him to be saved from stumbling; because then he will come as judge. Where, then, was the prophecy fulfilled? Be very alert now, beloved.

4. Listen first of all to these lines: *You, O Lord, are my refuge; very high have you set your refuge*. The human race well knew that people die, but did not know that anyone could rise again. This meant that our race had something to fear, but nothing to hope for. God imposed the fear of death upon us as a discipline, but he wanted us to have a reward too; he wanted to give us hope of eternal life, and therefore our Lord Jesus Christ rose again, and rose as the first. He died after many others had died; he rose before all others. In dying he endured what many had endured, but in rising he did what no one before him had ever done. When will the Church experience it? Not until the end. But the members can now hope for what has already happened in their head. You know how they talk of this among themselves, dearly beloved.

Let the Church say to its Lord, Jesus Christ, let the body say to its head, "*You, O Lord, are my hope; very high have you set your refuge*. You have risen from the dead, and ascended into heaven in order to set your lofty refuge there, and so become my hope. On earth I was hopeless, not believing that I would rise from death; but now I do believe it, because my head has ascended into heaven, and where the head has gone first, the members will follow." Already, I think, the truth of the psalm's profession is manifest: *You, O Lord, are my hope; very high have you set your refuge*. Let me put it still more plainly: "You rose first so that I might have a hope of resurrection that I did not have before. You rose that I might hope to follow where you led the way." We hear the Church saying this to its Lord, the voice of the body speaking to its head.

5. In view of this there is nothing surprising about the promise, *evils shall not come near you, nor the scourge approach your tent*. God's tent is the flesh. The Word dwelt in flesh, and flesh served as a tent for God. In that tent the Commander-in-Chief fought for us; in that tent he was tempted by the enemy so that no common soldier need be defeated. He revealed this flesh to our eyes, to these eyes of ours which enjoy the light and find pleasure in seeing the radiance of day; and because he manifested his flesh so that all could see it, another psalm says, *He has pitched his tent in the sun*. Why does it say, *In the sun*? It means

openly, plainly, in a manner discernible by earthly light. In the light which he pours out from heaven over all lands, he pitched his tent. But how could he have pitched his tent there, if he had not first come forth like a bridegroom from his wedding chamber? *He has pitched his tent in the sun*, it states; and then, as though someone had asked, "But how?" it continues, *And he is like a bride-groom coming forth from his tent; he leaps up like a giant to run his course with joy* (Ps 18:6(19:4-5)).

Now his tent is the same thing as his bride. The Word is the bridegroom, flesh is the bride, and their wedding chamber is a virgin's womb. What does the apostle have to say about their marriage? *They will be two in one flesh. This is a great mystery, but I am referring it to Christ and the Church* (Eph 5:31-32). And what does the Lord himself say in the gospel? *So they are two no longer, but one flesh* (Mt 19:6). Out of two is made one only; from the Word and flesh there is one man, one God.

His tent certainly felt scourges on earth; we know well that our Lord was scourged. Does he feel scourges in heaven? Absolutely not. Why not? Because he has established his refuge very high up in order to be our hope, and therefore no evils will come near him, nor the scourge approach his tent. He is far beyond the highest heavens, but he has his feet on earth; the head is in heaven, the feet on the ground. When those feet were being scourged and trodden on by Saul, the head cried out, *Saul, Saul, why are you persecuting me?* (Acts 9:4). No one is persecuting the head, obviously, for the head is in heaven. Christ, having risen from the dead, can die no more, nor will death ever have dominion over him again.[12] So he is promised, *Evils shall not come near you, nor the scourge approach your tent.* Yet we are warned that there is no separation between head and body. They are divided as to place, but joined in love; and it was this union of love that shouted from heaven, *Saul, Saul, why are you persecuting me?* Christ laid Saul low with a word of rebuke, but lifted him up with a compassionate right hand. The man who had been wont to persecute Christ's body became a member of Christ, so as to share within the body the suffering he had formerly inflicted on it.

6. What conclusion should we draw, brothers and sisters? What has been said about our head? *You, O Lord, are my hope; very high have you set your refuge. Evils shall not come near you, nor the scourge approach your tent.* After this the psalm continues, *For he has given his angels orders concerning you, to guard you in all your ways.* You heard those words just now, when the gospel was proclaimed; keep them carefully in mind. The Lord fasted after his baptism. Why was he baptized? So that we should not be too proud to seek baptism, for when John protested to the Lord, *Do you come to me for baptism? I ought to be*

---

12. See Rom 6:9.

baptized by you, the Lord replied, *Let it be so for the present, for it is fitting that we should in this way meet all the demands of righteousness* (Mt 3:14-15). He wanted to go the whole way in humility, by seeking to be washed though he had no stain. Why? Because there would be proud people later. Now and then some catechumen emerges who is perhaps superior to many of the faithful in knowledge of the faith and personal conduct. He observes that many of the baptized are poorly instructed, and that many of them do not live as he does himself, with impressive self-control and chastity. He does not so much as seek a wife, yet he sees a believer, if not actually committing fornication, at least intemperate in relations with his wife. Such a catechumen may proudly toss his head and say, "Why do I need baptism? Why should I try to get what that fellow has, when I am already more advanced than he is in my way of life and learning?" To such a person the Lord says, "Ahead of him, are you? By how far? By as much as I am ahead of you? *A servant is not above his master, nor a disciple above his teacher. It is enough for a servant to be like his master, and a disciple like his teacher* (Mt 10:24-25). Do not be too high and mighty to seek baptism. You will be asking baptism from your Lord; I sought it from a servant."

Hunger: the temptation to conjure bread out of stones

So the Lord was baptized, and after his baptism he was tempted. He fasted for forty days because this was a mystical period, as I have often pointed out to you. (We can't say everything on every occasion, because that would use up the time required for necessary instruction.) After the forty days he was hungry. It would have been within his power never to feel hunger, but then how would he have been tempted? And if he had not routed the tempter, how would you learn to fight the tempter when your turn comes? He was hungry, and now the tempter suggested, *Say to these stones, Become loaves of bread, if you are the Son of God* (Mt 4:3). If our Lord Jesus Christ satisfied so many thousands with five loaves, would it have taken any great effort on his part to make bread out of stones? He made bread out of nothing; for where did it come from, that abundance of food which fed the thousands? Fountains of bread were in the Lord's hands. And even that is not so strange when we remember that he who from five loaves made enough bread to satisfy many thousands is not other than he who every day makes huge harvests from a few grains in the soil.[13] These too are the Lord's miracles, but we take them for granted because we are so used to them. What do you think, then, brothers and sisters: was it beyond the Lord's power to make bread out of stones? He made human beings out of stones, according to John the Baptist: *God is able to raise up children to Abraham even from these stones* (Mt 3:9). So why did he not make bread? Because he wanted to teach you how to

---

13. Or "… makes huge harvests on earth from a few grains."

answer the tempter. You may find yourself in a tight place, and hear the tempter hinting, "If you really were a Christian, if you really belonged to Christ, would he be deserting you now? Wouldn't he have sent you help?" But perhaps the doctor is still plying the knife, and that is why he is deserting you. It is not real desertion. Paul seemed to be refused a hearing, but that was because God was hearing him in reality. Paul tells us that he was not heard when he prayed about the sting of the flesh, the messenger of Satan that punched him: *Three times I begged the Lord to take it away from me, but he said to me, My grace is sufficient for you, for my power finds complete scope in weakness* (2 Cor 12:7-9). Suppose a physician applied a poultice, and you were to protest, "I can't bear having this plaster on me. Take it off, I beg you." And the doctor replied, "No, it must stay on for quite a long time. You cannot be healed otherwise." The doctor would be turning a deaf ear to the patient's entreaty, because he would be hearing his will to get better.

Be brave then, brothers and sisters. In some circumstances you may suffer want because God is chastening and educating you as his children, the children for whom he is preparing and reserving an eternal inheritance. Do not let the devil whisper to you, "If you really were a righteous person, wouldn't God send a raven to bring you bread, as he did to Elijah?[14] What has become of that text you read, *Never have I seen a just person destitute, or a child of righteous parents begging for bread* (Ps 36(37):25)?" You must then reply, "Scripture spoke truly when it said, "Never have I seen a just person destitute, or a child of righteous parents begging for bread, for I have bread of my own, of which you know nothing." What bread is that? Listen to the Lord's answer: *A human being does not live on bread alone, but on every word of God* (Dt 8:3; Lk 4:4). Do you not realize that God's word is bread? If the Word of God, he through whom all things were made, were not truly bread, he would not have told us, *I am the living bread which has come down from heaven* (Jn 6:51). So now you have learned how to reply to the tempter under pressure of hunger.

Another temptation: the lust for power

7. But now, suppose he tempts you from another angle, saying to you, "If you were a real Christian you would work miracles, as many Christians have done." And suppose you were taken in by that wicked suggestion, and said to the Lord our God, "If I am a Christian, if I really am standing in your sight and you count me among those who belong to you, let me work one, like the miracles many of your saints worked." You have put God to the test by assuming that you are not a Christian unless you work miracles. Many people have come to grief by hankering after such power. Simon the Magician was trying to get something of

---

14. See 1 Kgs 17:6.

the sort from the apostles when he tried to buy the Holy Spirit with money.[15] His ambition was to emulate their miracles, but not to imitate their humility. There was another disciple—or, rather, someone in the crowd who aspired to follow the Lord when he saw the miracles he worked; but the Lord saw that this man was seeking not the way of humility but the power that leads to pride. To him the Lord said, *Foxes have holes, and the birds of the sky have nests; but the Son of Man has nowhere to rest his head* (Mt 8:20; Lk 9:58). Foxes have holes in you; birds of the sky have nests in you. Deceit is like foxes, and pride is like birds; for as birds seek the heights, so too do proud people, and as foxes skulk in deceitful lairs, so do all lurkers. What answer did the Lord give to this man? "Pride and deceit can find homes in you, but Christ can find in you no home where he can rest his head." The resting of the head is a figure of Christ's humility; if he had not rested his head, you would not have been justified.

Even the disciples coveted this kind of distinction. They tried to put in a claim for thrones in the kingdom before they had taken the way of humility; hence the request made to the Lord by the mother of two disciples: *Say that one of them may sit at your right hand, and the other at your left.* They were seeking power. But power in the kingdom is attained through suffering and humility.[16] The Lord answered, "*Are you able to drink the cup I am to drink?* (Mt 20:21.22). Can you think about high rank in the kingdom without imitating my lowliness?"

If the devil puts you to the test with the suggestion, "Go on, work miracles!" how should you reply, in order not to put God to the test? In the same way as the Lord himself replied. The devil said to him, "*Throw yourself down, for scripture says, He has given his angels orders to take care of you, and they will carry you in their hands, so that you will not even stub your foot on a stone* (Mt 4:6). If you throw yourself over, the angels will catch you." And indeed, brothers and sisters, it is quite possible that ministering angels would have upheld the Lord's flesh if he had thrown himself over. But what did he say? "*It is also written, You shall not put the Lord your God to the test* (Dt 6:16; Mt 4:7). You think me to be no more than a man." Indeed it was in order to find out if Christ was the Son of God that the devil had approached him. Christ's flesh was unmistakable, yet his majesty showed through in his actions. Angels had borne witness to him.[17] The devil saw a mortal man whom he could tempt, so that through Christ's temptation every Christian might be instructed. What does scripture say? *You shall not put the Lord your God to the test.* Let us, then, beware of tempting the Lord by saying, "If we belong to you, allow us to work miracles."

---

15. See Acts 8:18-19.
16. Variant: "through patient humility."
17. See Lk 2:9-14.

How did the angels bear up the Lord? Stumbling on the stone means falling foul of the law

8. Now let us get back closer to the words of the psalm. *He has given his angels orders concerning you, to guard you in all your ways*, it says. *They shall bear you up with their hands, so that you may never stub your foot on a stone.* Christ was borne up on the hands of angels when he was taken up into heaven, not because he was in danger of falling if they did not carry him, but because they were paying homage to their king. Do not object, "But those who carried him were superior to the one who was carried." Do you think horses and donkeys better than their human riders, simply because they carry us humans because we are weak? But this analogy will not fit the present case, because if the beasts slip away from under them, the riders fall. How should we speak about the angels carrying Christ, then? Remember that even of God it was written, *Heaven is my throne* (Is 66:1; Acts 7:49). Does this mean that since God is seated there, and heaven carries him, heaven is more honorable? Of course it doesn't; and we may understand the service rendered by the angels in the same way. The psalm speaks of it as a sign not of weakness on the Lord's part, but of their desire to honor and serve him.

But why did our Lord Jesus Christ rise from the dead? Listen to the apostle's statement: *He died for our transgressions, and rose for our justification* (Rom 4:25). And with reference to the Holy Spirit, the gospel says, *The Spirit had not yet been given, because Jesus was not yet glorified* (Jn 7:39). Now what is this glorification of Jesus? It means his resurrection and ascension into heaven. When he had been glorified by God through his ascension into heaven, he sent his Holy Spirit on the day of Pentecost. According to the law, as set forth in Moses' book, Exodus, fifty days are counted from the day on which the lamb was slain and eaten;[18] and this feast commemorates the giving of the law, which was written on stone tablets by the finger of God.[19] The gospel explains to us what the finger of God is: it is God's Holy Spirit. How can we demonstrate this? When the Jews accused our Lord of casting out demons in the name of Beelzebub, he replied, *If I cast out demons by the Spirit of God...* (Mt 12:28); but another evangelist when describing the same event reports his words thus: *If I cast out demons by the finger of God...* (Lk 11:20). What was stated clearly in one gospel was stated obscurely in the other. You would not have known what the finger of God might be, if the other evangelist had not explained that it was the Spirit of God. So, then, the law written by the finger of God was given on the fiftieth day after the slaying of the lamb, and the Holy Spirit came on the fiftieth

---

18. See Ex 23:16; and for the reckoning of the date, Lv 23:16; Dt 16:9.
19. The "Feast of Weeks" was agricultural in origin, marking the end of the wheat harvest, but Jewish tradition associated it with the giving of the law to Moses on Sinai.

day after the passion of our Lord Jesus Christ. Long ago the lamb was slain and the Passover observed; then, when fifty days had elapsed, the law was given. But that law provoked fear, not love. In order that fear might be transformed into love, the righteous one was slain in actual fact, that righteous one typified by the lamb which the Jews were accustomed to slaughter. He rose again, and fifty days are counted from our Lord's Passover, just as fifty days were counted from the slaying of the lamb. Then comes the Holy Spirit in the fullness of love, not threatening punishment or striking fear.

Now why have I recalled all this? Because the Lord rose from the dead and was lifted up in glory in order to send the Holy Spirit. And I have been telling you for a long time that while our head is in heaven, his feet are on earth. If the head is in heaven and the feet on earth, what are these feet of the Lord? His saints on earth, obviously. Who are the Lord's feet? The apostles, who were sent out all over the world. Who are the Lord's feet? All preachers of the gospel, for through them the Lord travels among all peoples. But there was some risk that these evangelists might stumble against a stone, for though the head was in heaven, a stone might easily trip the feet working hard on earth. What stone would that be? The law, given on stone tablets.

Stumbling means being held guilty under the law. It was necessary that they should not incur guilt in the law's terms, or be held accountable according to its precepts as though they had not received grace. The Lord therefore set free those whom the law had imprisoned under guilt, so that they would stumble against the law no longer. To ensure that the feet who belonged to the head would not incur legal guilt, the Holy Spirit was sent to establish love and free us from fear. Fear had not fulfilled the law, but love fulfilled it. People had been afraid, and unable to keep the law, but when they began to love they kept it. In what sense is this true—that they did not keep it when they were afraid, but kept it when they loved? When men and women were ruled by fear, they stole the property of others; but once they had begun to love, they gave away their own.

Small wonder, then, that the Lord was carried to heaven on the hands of angels, so that his foot need never be stubbed against a stone. To ensure that the members of his body who toiled on earth and tramped all over the world should not incur guilt under the law, he took away their fear and filled them with love. Peter denied him three times out of fear, for he had not then received the Holy Spirit. Later he did receive the Holy Spirit, and began to preach boldly. The man who had denied Christ three times at the word of a servant girl confessed him under the scourges of rulers once he had received the Holy Spirit—confessed the Christ he had denied. That should not surprise us, for the Lord dissolved the triple fear in triple love. Rising from the dead he asked Peter, *Peter, do you love me?* He did not ask, "Do you fear me?" If he had still been afraid, he would have stubbed his foot against the stone. He asked, *Do you love me?* and Peter answered, *I love you.* One affirmation would have been enough. It would have been enough even for me, who cannot see another's heart; how much more should it have sufficed for the Lord, who saw from what intimate depths Peter had declared, *I love you*? Yet the Lord was not satisfied with a single reply. He put the question a second time, and again Peter said, *I love you*. He asked a third time, and now Peter was distressed, thinking that perhaps the Lord doubted his love, so he answered, *Lord, you know everything; you know I love you* (Jn 21:15-17). But in prolonging it like this the Lord was seeming to say to Peter, "You denied me three times out of fear. Now confess three times out of love." With this love, this charity, he filled his disciples. Why? Because he set his refuge very high; because being now glorified he sent the Holy Spirit and released his faithful ones from the guilt of the law, so that the feet of Christ should never be stubbed against a stone.

Verse 13. The devil, whether savage or insidious, will be defeated

9. The remaining verses pose no difficulties for us, brothers and sisters, because they have often been expounded. *You will walk on asp and basilisk; on both lion and snake you will trample*.[20] You know who the snake is, and how the Church tramples on him, undefeated because on guard against his wiles. But I think you also know, beloved,[21] how he can be both a lion and a snake. A lion rampages openly, while a snake lies hidden, awaiting its prey; and the devil has power and skill to do both. When the martyrs were being killed, he was a rampant lion; when heretics are sneaking in, he is a slithering snake. You have overcome the lion, so overcome the snake as well. Let the lion not crush you,[22] nor the snake deceive you. We can prove that the devil was a lion in the days when he used to rampage openly. Peter encouraged martyrs by asking them, *Do you not know that your enemy the devil stalks about like a roaring lion, seeking whom he may devour?* (1 Pt 5:8). So the lion was raging openly then, looking for people to savage; but how does the snake lie in ambush? Through heretics. Paul was afraid of these, because he knew that through them the Church might lose the virginity of faith which it keeps in its heart; so he warned, *I have betrothed you to your one husband, Christ, as a chaste virgin; but I am afraid that, just as the serpent seduced Eve by his cunning, so too your minds may be led astray, and fall away from that chastity which you have in Christ* (2 Cor 11:2-3). Few women in the Church preserve virginity of body, but all the faithful have virginity of heart. Paul feared that this virginity of heart which is the essence of faith might be corrupted by the devil. If anyone loses that, virginity of body is meaningless. Once the heart is corrupted, what does such a person preserve in

---

20. Compare Augustine's explanation of this verse in his Exposition of Psalm 39,1.

21. *Caritatem vestram.*

22. The CCL editors propose an indicative: "the lion has not crushed you."

body? A Catholic married woman is much better than a virginal heretic. The former is not a virgin in body, but the latter has lost virginity of heart, and this not through marriage to God but through violation by the snake. But what of the Church? *You will walk on asp and basilisk*, it is promised. The basilisk is the king of snakes,[23] as the devil is the king of demons. *On both lion and snake you will trample.*

Verses 14-16. Deliverance and eternal life

10. Now we hear God's promises to his Church. *Because he hoped in me, I will deliver him.* The promise concerns not the head alone. It is not just for him who is now enthroned in heaven because he has set his refuge very high, where no evils shall come near him, nor scourge approach his tent. We too, who struggle here on earth and still live among temptations, we whose steps must be ever wary lest they slip into snares—we must listen to the voice of the Lord our God consoling us, and promising, *Because he hoped in me, I will deliver him; I will protect him because he knows my name.*

11. *He will call upon me*[24] *and I will hear him; in tribulation I am with him.* Do not be afraid when you are thrust into tribulation, or think it means that God is not with you. Let your faith stay with you, and then God is with you in your trouble. The sea is rough and you are tossed about in your boat because Christ is asleep. There was an occasion when Christ slept in a fishing vessel and his companions were nearly shipwrecked.[25] If your faith is dormant in your heart, it is as though Christ were sleeping in your boat, because it is through faith that Christ dwells in you.[26] When the sea begins to get choppy, awaken the sleeping Christ; arouse your faith, and you will know that he is not abandoning you. The only reason why you may think you are abandoned is that he does not pluck you from danger at the moment you want him to.[27] He plucked the three young men out of the fire.[28] Did he who delivered the three young men abandon the Maccabees? By no means. He snatched both sets of people from danger: the former through bodily release, so that unbelievers might be shamed, the latter spiritually, that believers might imitate them.[29] *In tribulation I am with him; I will both rescue him and glorify him.*

---

23. The basilisk, a mythical reptile, was reputed to kill with its breath.
24. Variant: "he called upon me."
25. See Mk 4:36-40.
26. See Eph 3:17.
27. Variant: "as you want him to." The manuscript that has this reading also has a marginal note: "That is, he does not pluck you from danger in bodily fashion."
28. See Dn 3:49-50.
29. See 2 Mac 7.

12. *I will fill him completely with length of days.* What does length of days
mean? Eternal life. Do not suppose, brothers and sisters, that the psalm speaks of
lengthy days in the sense that our winter days are shorter, and our summer days
longer. Are they the sort of days God is storing up for us? No; the length of days
he speaks of is eternal life, life without end; this is what he is promising us, and
this is what will wholly satisfy us, which is why he says, *I will fill him
completely.* No stretch of time, however lengthy, can satisfy us if it has an end,
and therefore it does not even deserve to be called long. If we are greedy, we
should be greedy for eternal life. Yearn for the life that has no end. That is where
our greed should stretch. Do you covet endless money? Then desire eternal,
endless life. Do you hope that your possessions will be unlimited? Seek eternal
life. *I will fill him completely with length of days.*

13. *And I will show him my salvation.* We must not pass over this too quickly,
brothers and sisters. When he promises, *I will show him my salvation,* he is
saying, "I will show him Christ." Why does he say that? Was Christ not seen on
earth? Is it anything special that he has to show us?

But Christ was not seen then in the way that we shall see him. He was seen in
such a way that it was possible for those who saw him to crucify him. Think of it:
those who saw him crucified him, whereas we did not see him but have believed
in him. Those others had eyes, and have we none? Far from it; we have the eyes
of the heart, but for the present we still live[30] by faith, not by sight.[31] When will be
the time for our seeing? When we behold him *face to face* (1 Cor 13:12), as the
apostle says. Or, rather, this is what God himself promises as the mighty reward
for all our labors. Whatever your labors may be, labor for this end, that you may
see. We are destined to see something great beyond telling on that day when
vision will be our total recompense; and this great sight will be our Lord Jesus
Christ. He was seen once in his lowly state, but then he will be seen in his greatness and will fill us with joy. He will be seen as he is seen now by the angels. *In
the beginning was the Word, and the Word was with God; he was God* (Jn 1:1).
Listen to the Lord promising us this in the gospel: *Whoever loves me will be
loved by my Father, and I will love him.* Then, as though responding to an
unspoken question, "What will you give to anyone who loves you?" he
continued, *I will show myself to him* (Jn 14:21).

Let us long for him and love him, if we are his bride. The bridegroom is
absent, but let us hold out patiently, for he whom we long for will come. So great
is the pledge he has given that the bride need not fear he will desert her; he will
not leave his pledge unclaimed. What pledge has he given? He has poured out his
blood. What pledge has he left us? He has sent the Holy Spirit. Will the bride-

30. Variant: "see."
31. See 2 Cor 5:7.

groom let slip such pledges as these? If he did not love us, he would not have given us such guarantees.

But he does love us. If only we could repay him with a like love! *No one can have greater love than this, to lay down one's life for one's friends* (Jn 15:13); but how can we lay down our lives for him? What use would that be to him, who has already set his refuge very high, where no scourge will approach his tent? Ah, but what does John tell us? As Christ *laid down his life for us, so we too must lay down our lives for our brothers and sisters* (1 Jn 3:16). Everyone who lays down his or her life for one of the brethren lays it down for Christ, just as we feed Christ whenever we feed a brother or sister. *When you did that for even the least of those who are mine, you did it for me* (Mt 25:40).

Let us love him and imitate him; let us run after his sweetly scented ointments, as the Song of Songs suggests: *We shall run toward the fragrance of your ointments* (Sg 1:3). He came, he spread his sweet fragrance, and his scent has filled the whole world. Where did such scent originate? In heaven. Follow him to heaven, then, if you are not lying when you make your response to the invitation, "Lift up your hearts."[32] Lift up your thoughts, lift up your love, and lift up your hope, lest it go bad on earth. You do not risk storing your grain in damp earth, in case it goes moldy after all your hard work and harvest and threshing and winnowing. You seek a safe place for your grain, and will you not seek a safe place for your heart? Will you not look for a secure place to lodge your treasure? Do as much as you can with it on earth: give it away. You will not lose it, you will only bank it securely. Who keeps it safe for you? Christ, who keeps you safe as well. Can he who knows how to look after you not look after your treasure too? Why does he want you to shift your treasure? Because he wants you to shift your heart. Everyone's preoccupation is for the safety of his precious possessions. Out of all the crowd that is listening to me at this moment, are there any whose hearts are not on their money bags? You are stuck on earth, because what you love is on earth. Send it to heaven, and then your heart will be there too. Wherever your treasure has been laid up, there too your heart will be.[33]

---

32. On the antiquity of this liturgical phrase, see note at Exposition of Psalm 10,3.
33. See Mt 6:21.

Exposition of Psalm 91

A Sermon[1]

Faith, hope, and charity in our time of endurance

1. Give your attention to this psalm, I beg you; and may the Lord enable us to open the mysteries hidden within it, because the same subjects are dealt with here in various different ways, with an eye to the spiritual weariness that can afflict us. God has no other song to teach us than the song of faith, hope, and charity. Our faith must be firm in him as long as we do not see him; we believe in him whom we do not see, so that we may rejoice when we do see him, and so that our faith may one day be replaced by the beauty of his light. On that day we shall not be instructed, "Believe in what you do not see," but rather, "Rejoice, because you see." Let our hope also be steadfast. Let it be fixed in him, never sagging or wavering or shaken, just as God himself, the fixed point in whom our hope is fastened, can never be shaken either. In this life it is called hope, but in the life beyond it will be realization.[2] It is named hope only as long as its object is not seen, as the apostle teaches, *If hope is seen, it is hope no longer, for when someone sees what he hopes for, why should he hope for it? But if we hope for what we do not see, we wait for it in patience* (Rom 8:24-25). This is why we need patience in the present life, until the coming of what has been promised. But no one need practice patience in times of good fortune. It is of a person beset by ill fortune that patience is demanded, one to whom it is said, "Be patient, put up with it, stand fast. This trouble has come upon you, but God wants you to be brave under it, forbearing, long-suffering, and patient." God made the promise, and he does not deceive us, does he? A surgeon unsheathes the knife to operate on the wound, and says to the sick person, "Be patient now, bear up, you must endure this." He requires patience under the pain, but promises health when the painful time is past. The sick person who submits to the agony under the doctor's knife could not face it, if it were not for the prospect of the health he does not yet enjoy. There are many evils in this world, both within us and without. They never seem to diminish at all. Scandals increase, and the only people who are conscious of them are the ones who walk in the way of God. On every page of scripture these people are exhorted to endure present conditions and hope for the

---

1. Preached on a Saturday.
2. The contrast is between *spes* and *res*, as often.

future, and to love him whom they do not see, so that when they do see him they may clasp him to their hearts.

Over and above faith and hope there is a third virtue: charity. It is nobler than faith and hope. Faith is directed to things not seen as yet, and once they are seen it will be succeeded by vision. Hope is focused on things not yet possessed, and once the realization comes, hope will exist no more, because we shall not hope for the reality, but embrace it. But charity can only go on increasing. If we already love him whom we see not, how shall we love him when we have seen him? Let our desire grow; we are Christians only in view of the world to come. Let no one hope for good things in this present life, and let us not promise ourselves worldly happiness on the strength of our Christianity. Rather let Christians make use of present felicity as occasion offers, in any way they can, whenever they can, insofar as they can. When it is available, let them give thanks for God's consolation; when it is absent, let them give thanks for God's justice. Christians should be grateful in all circumstances, and ungrateful in none whatever. They must be grateful to their Father when he consoles and caresses, and grateful to their Father when he corrects and whips and imposes discipline; for he loves them all the time, whether he is caressing or threatening. Let Christians make their own the words you heard in the psalm: *It is good to confess to the Lord, and play psalms to your name, O Most High.*

Verse 1. The title: the Sabbath of the heart

2. The title of the psalm is, *A psalm to be sung on the Sabbath day.* Well now, today is the Sabbath, and the Jews are even now celebrating it by bodily rest, but with a lazy, lax, and dissolute sort of rest. They refrain from work only to give themselves to frivolous pursuits, and although God commanded the observance of the Sabbath,[3] they spend it in ways God forbids. We rest from wrongdoing; they rest from good works. It is better to plow than to dance. They take a rest from good behavior, but give themselves no respite from worthless occupations.

God formally appoints the Sabbath for us; but what kind of Sabbath? Consider above all where it is to be kept. Our Sabbath is within, in our hearts. Many people there are who take repose for their bodies, but their consciences are in tumult. Nobody with a bad conscience can keep the Sabbath. Such a person's conscience cannot be at peace anywhere, so of necessity he or she lives amid a hullabaloo. But a person with a good conscience is tranquil, and this tranquillity is itself the Sabbath of the heart. Such tranquil persons keep their eyes on God's

---

3. See Ex 20:8-11, where the reason given is that God's people are to imitate his rest after creation; and Dt 5:12-15, where the Sabbath rest recalls the liberation of God's people from slavery in Egypt. Creation and exodus: two poles of Israel's faith and equally valid in Christianity, though the manner of Sabbath observance has undergone a change, as Augustine points out.

promise; even if they have to struggle at present, they stretch out in hope toward the future. For them all clouds of sadness clear away, for, as the apostle says, they are forever *rejoicing in hope* (Rom 12:12).

This tranquil joy, born of our hope, is our Sabbath. What this psalm has to enjoin upon us, what it has to sing about, is how Christians are to conduct themselves in the Sabbath of their hearts, in that freedom and tranquillity and serenity of conscience where no disturbance touches them. The psalm speaks about situations which may often trouble people seriously, and it teaches you how, in spite of all, you are to celebrate the Sabbath in your heart.

Verse 2. Confess to the Lord that your sins are your work,
your good deeds his

3. The most important thing is this. If you have made some progress, you must confess to the Lord about your progress, because it is the result of his gifts, not your merits. Begin your Sabbath from this point, not attributing any good to yourself, as though you had not received what you know very well you did receive,[4] nor making excuses for yourself over your misdeeds, for they truly do belong to you. Twisted, disturbed persons who are not keeping the Sabbath attribute their bad actions to God, and their good ones to themselves. If they have done something laudable they say, "I did that!" If they have done wrong they look for someone to blame, in order to avoid confessing to God.

Now how do they go about it in their attempt to find someone to blame? If the wrongdoer is not entirely godless, he has someone ready to hand whom he can accuse: Satan. "Satan did it," he claims. "He persuaded me." Anyone would think Satan had the power to force us. Persuasive cunning he certainly does have, and if Satan were speaking and God altogether silent, you would have some excuse. But as it is, your ears are midway between God who warns you, and the snake with his suggestions. Why lean toward the latter, and turn a deaf ear to God? Satan never tires of luring you to evil, but neither does God cease to urge you to good. Moreover, Satan cannot coerce an unwilling victim; it is within your power to consent or refuse. And if at Satan's persuasion you have done wrong, forget about Satan. Accuse yourself, so that by your self-accusation you may deserve God's mercy. Are you trying to bring a case against someone who is beyond pardon? Accuse yourself, rather, and you will receive forgiveness.

Many people, however, blame not Satan, but fate. "My fate led me astray," someone will say. If you say to him, "Why did you do it? Why did you commit that sin?" he answers, "It was due to my unfavorable destiny." He wants to avoid saying, "I did it," and so he points the finger at God, and blasphemes[5] with his

---

4. See 1 Cor 4:7.
5. Or possibly, "...and so, even as he lifts his hands to God [in worship] he is blaspheming."

tongue. True, he is not yet saying it openly, but look carefully and see how he truly is saying it. Ask him what fate is, and he replies, "Malignant stars." Ask him who made the stars, and set them in order, and he can give you no answer except "God." He has left himself no option but to catch God in his accusations, whether with a net, or by poking at him with a long stick, or outright. And although God punishes sins, this person makes God the author of his sins. It is impossible for God to punish what he has done himself. He punishes what you do, in order to set his own handiwork free.

Sometimes it happens that when people are in the wrong they ignore all such excuses and refer directly to God. When they sin they say, "God willed this to happen. If God had not willed it, I would not have sinned."[6] Is this God's intention in admonishing you, that you not only refuse to hear him when he warns you not to sin, but even blame him for the fact that you do?

What does this psalm teach us? *It is good to confess to the Lord.* What does confessing to the Lord imply? Confess to him in both situations: in your sin, because you did it, and in your good achievement, because he did it. Then you will be singing psalms to the name of God Most High, seeking God's glory, not your own, praising his name, not yours. If you seek the honor of God's name, he seeks the honor of your name too; but if you are careless about God's name, he erases yours. What do I mean by that: he seeks the honor of your name? I am thinking of the time when the disciples came back to the Lord, after he had sent them out to preach. They had worked many miracles, and cast out demons in Christ's name, so on their return they exulted, *Lord, even demons submitted to us!* They did add, *in your name*, admittedly. But the Lord saw through them. He knew that they were enjoying the prestige it brought them, that they were self-important, and that they were falling into pride because they had been empowered to expel demons. He saw that they were seeking their own glory, but he was looking after that himself. Indeed, he had their names safe in his own keeping, so he said to them, *Do not rejoice over that; rejoice because your names have been written in heaven* (Lk 10:17.20). That is where your name will be honored, if you do not neglect God's name. Play psalms to God's name, so that your name may be immovably preserved with God. What does it mean to play psalms, brothers and sisters? The psaltery is a kind of musical instrument with strings. Our psaltery is a symbol of the work we do, so all those who employ their hands in good works are playing psalms to God, while all those who confess with their lips are singing to God. Sing with your mouth, and play psalms with your works. To what purpose?

---

6. Or "if God did not will it, I would not sin." This is the more exact translation, since the verbs are imperfect subjunctive; but Augustine often uses this tense for unfulfilled conditions in past time, where we would have expected the pluperfect subjunctive.

Verses 3-4. Praise in light and darkness, with deeds and words

4. *To proclaim your mercy in the morning, and your truth throughout the night.* What does this suggest? Why is God's mercy to be proclaimed in the morning, but his truth through the night? "Morning" means the times when things go well with us; "night" signifies the times when we are sad and troubled. So what has the psalm said in this short verse? When your affairs are going well, rejoice to God, because this is due to his mercy. But perhaps you might have been inclined to say, "Well, then, if I rejoice to God when all is well with me, because this is due to his mercy, what am I to do when I am sad or in trouble? If my well-being is the effect of his mercy, is it a sign of his cruelty when things go badly for me? If I praise his mercy when everything is going well, should I grumble at his cruelty when things are bad?" No. When things are going well, praise his mercy; when badly, praise his truth, because he is not acting unjustly when he punishes sins. Daniel used to pray during what for him was night, for Jerusalem was a captured city, lying under the power of its enemies. In those days the holy people were suffering grave hardships; Daniel himself was thrown into the lions' pit, and the other three young men into the fire.[7] The Israelites were subjected to all this in their captivity, so for them it was night. Throughout the night Daniel kept on confessing God's truth. He prayed constantly, *We have sinned, we have acted wickedly, we have committed iniquity. To you be glory, O Lord, but to us confusion of face* (Dn 9:5.7). He was proclaiming God's truth throughout the night. What does it mean, then, to proclaim God's truth through the night? It means not accusing God when you are having a bad time, but attributing your woes to your own sins and his corrective discipline, *to proclaim* his *mercy in the morning, and* his *truth throughout the night.* When you proclaim his mercy in the morning and his truth at night you are praising God all the time, confessing to God always, and playing psalms to his name.

5. *On the ten-stringed psaltery, with a song and on the lyre.* This is not the first time you have heard about the ten-stringed psaltery.[8] A psaltery with its ten strings represents the ten precepts of the law. But we must sing to our psaltery, not just carry it about. The Jews too have the law, but they merely carry it without playing psalms on it. Who are the psalm-players? The people who act on those precepts. But that is not enough, because people who act on them, but in a mood of sadness, are not yet playing the psalms. Who are the psalm-players, then? The people who do the right thing cheerfully, for playing psalms is a cheerful activity. What does the apostle say? *God loves a cheerful giver* (2 Cor 9:7). Whatever your work, do it cheerfully; then both the deed and the manner of it

---

7. See Dn 6:10-24; 3:19-27.
8. Augustine mentions it frequently. See Exposition 2 of Psalm 32,5-6, and note there on other passages in the *Expositions* where he contrasts the psaltery with the lyre.

will be good. If you act sadly you are not really acting at all, but being acted upon; and you are carrying your psaltery rather than singing to it.

On the ten-stringed psaltery, with a song and on the lyre: this means that both words and deeds are required. *With a song* implies words; *on the lyre* indicates actions. If you speak words only, it is as though you were singing unaccompanied, without using your lyre; if you act but do not say anything, it is like making use of the lyre alone. Speak rightly and act rightly if you want to sing to the accompaniment of the lyre.

Verse 5. Any good we do is of God's making; the evil is from ourselves. The temptation to be scandalized at the prosperity of the wicked

6. *Because you have gladdened me with what you made, O Lord, and I will exult over the works of your hands*. Mark what he says: "You have made me a good-living person, you have formed me into what I am. If I perhaps do something good, therefore, I will exult in what your hands have made, as the apostle says, *We are his own handiwork, created for good works*" (Eph 2:10). If God had not shaped you for good actions, you would not have been capable of anything except your own bad deeds. It would have been as the gospel says, *One who tells lies speaks from what is his own* (Jn 8:44). Every sin is a lie, because anything that contravenes the law and opposes the truth is rightly called a lie. So what does scripture say? *One who tells lies speaks from what is his own*. Or, in other words, those who sin, sin from what is truly theirs.

Now consider the opposite proposition. If the liar speaks from what is his own, we conclude that those who speak the truth speak from what is God's. Accordingly scripture says elsewhere, *God alone is true; every human being is a liar* (Rom 3:4; Ps 115(116):11). Do not imagine, though, that this is tantamount to the permission, "Off you go, then, and lie as much as you like, since you are only human after all." No, you will do better to recognize that you are human from the very fact that you are such a liar, and then drink from the truth, so that you may be true, and belch forth from what you have received from God, and so be truthful yourself. You cannot possess[9] truth from your own store, so it only remains for you to drink from its source. If you move away from the light, you will be in darkness. Similarly a stone does not get hot by itself, but only by drawing heat from the sun or from a fire, and if you move it away from the heat,[10] it gets cold again. From this fact you can see that it did not derive its heat from its own resources; it was heated by the sun or by a fire. It is the same with you. If you come close to God, you grow warm; as the apostle says, you will be *ardent in the Spirit* (Rom 12:11). And what does scripture have to say about light? If you

---

9. Variant: "drink."
10. Variant: "the heat away from it."

approach God, you will be in the light, and so a psalm invites us, *Draw near to him and receive his light, and then you shall not be put out of countenance* (Ps 33:6(34:5)).

You can perform no good action unless you are illumined by God's light and set on fire by God's Spirit; so when you find yourself acting well, confess to God and tell yourself not to be conceited about it. Remind yourself of the apostle's words, *What have you that you did not receive? And if you did receive it, why boast as though you had not?* (1 Cor 4:7). This present psalm confesses to God, and teaches us likewise to make a good confession, by saying, *You have gladdened me with what you made, O Lord, and I will exult over the works of your hands.*

7. What are we to think of people who live sinfully, yet flourish all the same? Anyone who loses his or her Sabbath peace will be troubled in mind over this question. Such a person is conscious[11] of being daily exercised in good works, and struggling under difficult conditions, perhaps from lack of money, perhaps in hunger and thirst and lack of clothing. One may be in prison in spite of one's good conduct, and see the person by whom one was sent there behaving badly and crowing about it. And then a wicked thought against God may slink into one's heart. "O God, why should I serve you? Why should I be obedient to your words? I have not seized the property of others, I have not stolen, I have killed no one, I have not coveted what belongs to another, I have borne no false witness against anyone, I have not wronged my father or mother, I have not bowed before idols, I have not taken the name of the Lord God in vain. I have kept myself entirely from sin." Each of the ten strings that represent the ten commandments of the law is touched. The aggrieved speaker questions himself about each one in turn, and sees that he has not offended, not even against a single one. And so he is very downcast about having to suffer such great hardships.

Then there are others, people who do nothing good and frequent idols. It is not enough to say of them that they play on few of the strings, for they do not even touch the psaltery. They may appear to be Christians as long as their household is not suffering any misfortune, but as soon as trouble comes their way, off they run to a soothsayer,[12] or a fortune-teller or an astrologer. If someone of this type is reminded of the name of Christ he mocks and grimaces. If you say to him, "You are a believer; how can you have recourse to an astrologer?" he replies, "Get away from me! He recovered my property for me. Without him I should have

---

11. Variant: "These people have troubled minds and lose their Sabbath peace. And anyone who loses Sabbath peace is conscious...."

12. *Ad pythonem.* The name was originally associated with Delphi and the snake which, according to legend, was killed near there by Apollo; but it came to be used of a familiar spirit which possessed a soothsayer. In the Vulgate it is used in this sense in the prohibition in Dt 18:11, and of the demon-possessed girl in Acts 16:16.

lost it, and faced ruin." My good man, do you not sign yourself with the cross of Christ? The law forbids all those practices. Can you rejoice over finding your lost property, and not mourn because you yourself are lost? Would it not have been far better to lose your tunic than to lose your soul? But he mocks, in spite of all you say. He is unkind to his parents, he hates his enemy and hounds him to death, he steals when opportunity offers, constantly bears false witness, undermines another's marriage, and covets his neighbor's property. All this he does, yet he prospers amid wealth and honors, and is highly regarded by this world.

The other person—the one who for all his good works endures hardships—observes him and is deeply troubled. "O God, I think bad people must be your favorites," he says. "You hate the good, and love those who commit iniquity." If he is shaken in his faith and consents to that thought, he will lose the Sabbath of his heart. He is beginning to forget about the psaltery and turn away from it. If he sings, *It is good to confess to the Lord, and play psalms to your name, O Most High*, it is devoid of meaning for him. Once he has lost the Sabbath from his inmost being, and shut out peace from his heart, and rejected his good thoughts, he begins to imitate the person he has observed to flourish amid evil deeds, and so turns aside to do the same bad things himself. But God is patient, because he is eternal. He knows when his judgment day will come, the day when he will conduct an examination into everything.

Verse 6. The deep, high wisdom of God

8. This is the lesson the psalm is trying to teach us, so what else does it say? *How glorious are your works, O Lord! Exceedingly deep are your designs.* How true that is, brothers and sisters, for no sea is as deep as this design of God, whereby he allows the wicked to flourish while good people labor under hardships. Nothing is so deep, nothing so high; and every unbeliever is shipwrecked in this high, deep wisdom.[13] Do you hope to make your passage across this deep sea? Then do not recoil from Christ's wooden cross. You will not sink; hold tight to Christ.

What do I mean by telling you to hold tight to Christ? I mean that this precisely was his object in bearing hardships himself while on earth. In the reading from the prophet you heard how he did not shield his shoulders from scourges, or turn his face from men's spittle, or protect his cheek from their hands.[14] Why should he want to suffer all this, if not to comfort others who suffer? Moreover, he could have waited until the end of time to raise up his own

---

13. He uses two adjectives, *altus* and *profundus*, both of which can be translated "deep," and the image of the sea and shipwreck might demand this. But *altus* can also mean "high," and it is likely that he intends the double meaning.
14. See Is 50:6.

flesh; but then you would not have seen him rise, and so you would have had nothing to hope for. And so he did not defer his resurrection, to ensure that you would not remain in doubt. Bear the troubles you encounter in this world, then, endure them with the same outcome in view that you have witnessed in Christ, and do not be thrown off course by people who do bad things yet enjoy worldly prosperity. God's *designs are exceedingly deep.*

Where do we find this plan of God? He holds the reins loosely at present, but he will tighten them later. Do not congratulate the fish that is enjoying its tasty bait. The fisherman has not yet drawn in the line,[15] but the hook is already in the fish's jaw. What feels like a long time to you is brief really, for all things pass away very quickly. Even if a human being has a long life, what is that to the eternity of God? Do you aspire to be forbearing? Contemplate the eternity of God. You are focusing on your few days, and in those few days you expect all the promises to be fulfilled. What are they? That all the godless will be condemned, and all the good people crowned. Do you hope to see all that happening in your day? God brings it about in his own time. Why are you so weary, why keep telling yourself it is so irksome to wait? God is eternal. He delays because he is long-suffering. But you say, "I can't be long-suffering, because I am a creature of time." All the same, it is within your power. Fasten your heart to God's eternity, and then you will be eternal with him. What was said of temporal beings? *All flesh is but grass, and human glory like the flower of grass. The grass is dried up and the flower is fallen.* All things are drying up and falling, but not the Word, for *the Word of the Lord abides for ever* (Is 40:6-8). The grass fades away and the beauty of the grass is fleeting; but you have something on which to stay yourself: *the Word of the Lord abides for ever.*

Say to him, then, *Exceedingly deep are your designs.* Then you will have grasped the wood, and you can navigate safely across the deep sea. Do you espy anything on your voyage? Do you understand anything there? "Yes, I understand," you say. If you are a Christian, and well instructed, this is what you will say: "God keeps everything subject to his own judgment. Good people undergo hardships, but this is because they are being whipped as God's children;[16] bad people make merry, but only because they are condemned as outsiders." Suppose someone has two sons. He chastises one, and allows the other to go his own way. The latter behaves badly, but is not corrected by his father, while the other is beaten and whipped as soon as he steps out of line. Why is the one given his head, while the other is beaten? Only because an inheritance is being kept for the one who is beaten, whereas the other has been disinherited. The father knows this one will come to nothing, so he lets him do as he likes. As for the other son, the one who gets the whippings, if he has an unfeeling heart, if he lacks discern-

---

15. Variant: "his hand."
16. See Heb 12:6.

ment and is stupid, he congratulates his brother on escaping the thrashing, and groans over his own fate. He says in his heart, "My brother does so many bad things, and disobeys my father's orders as much as he pleases, and no one says an angry word to him. Yet as soon as I put a foot wrong, I get a beating." The boy is crass and thoughtless. All he can see is his present pain; he has no eyes for what is being kept for him.

Verses 7-8. If you covet temporal glory, you may perish eternally

9. This is why, after exclaiming, *Exceedingly deep are your designs*, the psalm immediately continues, *The thoughtless man will not recognize these things, nor the fool understand.* What are the things which the fool will not understand, nor the thoughtless person recognize? *When sinners spring up like grass....* Why *like grass*? Because they are verdant enough in winter, but when summer comes they wilt. Look at the bloom on the grass. Does anything fall more quickly? Yet what is more lustrous, what greener? Do not be dazzled by its greenness; beware of its withering.

You have heard about the sinners who are like grass, so hear now about the righteous. *For see* — oh, wait a minute, we haven't finished with the sinners.[17] They bloom like grass, that is clear. But who are the ones who do not recognize the true situation? Fools and thoughtless people. *When sinners spring up like grass, all those who commit iniquity have regard for them.* All those who do not think rightly about God in their hearts keep an eye on sinners as they spring up like grass, to flourish for a brief spell. Why do they look out for those sinners? Only because they themselves are to *perish for ever*. They are beguiled by the ephemeral flowering of sinners into imitating them, and through their desire to flourish likewise in time, they perish for eternity. They act thus *that they may perish for ever*.

Verses 9-10. Who are God's hidden enemies?

10. *But you, O Lord, are the Most High for ever*, and from on high, from your eternity, you look forth on the passing away of the time of the wicked, and the coming of the time of the just. *For see....* Pay close attention here, brothers and sisters, for the speaker has already united himself to God's eternity, and he is praying in our name, in the name of Christ's body. Indeed, this is Christ himself speaking in his body, the Church. As I was telling you a few minutes ago, God is long-suffering and patient; he bears with us even as he sees all the bad deeds of bad people. Why does he put up with it? Because he is eternal, and knows what

---

17. *For see* is an anticipation of verse 10, but Augustine suddenly remembered that he had a few more points to make on verse 8 before proceeding.

he is holding in reserve for them. Do you want to be long-suffering and patient, like God? Join yourself to God's eternity, and in union with him look forth on what passes below you; for when your heart is clinging closely to the Most High all mortal things will be beneath you. Say to him, in the next words of the psalm, *For see, your enemies will perish.* They are flourishing now, but they will perish later.

Who are God's enemies? You might suppose, brothers and sisters, that only people who blaspheme are enemies of God. Well, they certainly are; they are violent enemies who never cease to insult God with tongue or thought. But what do they effect against God, the Most High, the eternal? If you strike a pillar with your fist it is you who will be hurt; and do you imagine that you can hit out at God with your blasphemy and not shatter yourself? You will not hurt God in the least. However, blasphemers are openly God's enemies; but every day secret enemies come to light. You must watch out for this kind of hostility toward God. Scripture shows up some of God's hidden enemies, so that if you cannot recognize them by your own insight you will at least know them from scripture, and take care that you are not to be found among them. James plainly tells us in his letter, *Do you not know that any friend of this world is a proven enemy of God?* (Jas 4:4). Yes, you heard! You don't want to be God's enemy? Do not be a friend of this world, then; for if you make yourself the world's friend you will be God's enemy. It is like the case of an adulterous wife: she can become an adulteress only by becoming an enemy to her husband; similarly a soul that commits adultery by falling in love with secular things must necessarily be an enemy to God. Such a soul fears him, but does not love him; it dreads punishment but takes no pleasure in righteousness. You see, then, that all those who are enamored of the world are God's enemies, all who pursue frivolities, and all who consult fortune-tellers, astrologers, and soothsayers. They may or may not come to church, but they are God's enemies either way. They may flourish like grass for a time, but they will perish when he begins his inspection and passes judgment on all flesh. Hold fast to God's scripture, and say to him with the psalm, *See, your enemies will perish.* May you not be found among them when they do. *And all who act sinfully will be routed.*

Verse 11. The Church's ever-green youth

11. Now what about you who are struggling still, though all God's enemies are doomed to perish, and all the perpetrators of iniquity are to be scattered? What of you, who amid all these difficulties and human sinfulness are groaning now, you who are troubled in the flesh but joyful in heart? What is your hope, O body of Christ? O Christ, you are enthroned in heaven at the Father's right hand, but you still labor in your feet and other members on earth, and still you cry out, *Saul, Saul, why are you persecuting me?* (Acts 9:4); so what hope is yours, if

God's enemies will perish, and all who commit iniquity will be routed?[18] What do you look to have? *My horn shall be raised up like a unicorn's.* Why this comparison, *like a unicorn's*? Sometimes the unicorn represents pride, but in other contexts the unicorn stands for the triumph of unity. Because unity is raised up, all heresies will perish along with the rest of God's enemies. *My horn shall be raised up like a unicorn's.*

When will that be? *Mercy will render my old age fertile.* What does *my old age* signify? My last, newest times.[19] In our own lives the period of old age is the latest, the newest. So too for the Church: everything that the body of Christ is enduring now—struggles, bitter pain, vigils, hunger, thirst, scandals, sins, constricting circumstances—all this is part of the Church's youth. Its old age, which will be its last, newest period, will be all joy. You must understand, beloved, that though the psalm spoke of old age, you are not to think of it as the approach to death. An individual grows old in body and tends toward death; but the Church's old age will be hoary with the shining whiteness of good deeds; it will not crumble into death. Our actions correspond to an elderly person's head. You are familiar with the way the head turns hoary and white with advancing age. When someone well on in years is in typical condition you may look for a dark hair on his head and fail to find a single one; and so it is with us, once our life has reached the stage where the blackness of sins can no longer be found. That old age is youthfulness, that old age is fresh and vigorous, and it will be freshly green for ever.[20] You heard earlier about sinners being like grass, but now listen to what the old age of the just is like. *Mercy will render my old age fertile.*

Verses 12-13. The prospect of judgment. Palm trees and cedars

12. *My eye looked down and probed my enemies.* Whom does he regard as his enemies? All who act sinfully. Do not try to observe whether your friend is a sinner;[21] let some difficulty arise and you will probe his character. When you begin to take a stand against his iniquity, you will see that when he was accustomed to speak pleasantly to you he was all the while your enemy. You had not knocked at his door then. Not that your knocking set up anything in his heart that was not there: it only brought what was already there bursting out.

My eye looked down and probed my enemies, and my ear will hear what is said to the malevolent who attack me. When will that happen? In old age. What does that mean—in old age? At the last. And what will our ear hear then? When

---

18. Augustine often addresses the Church as "Body of Christ," but in this sentence he goes further and addresses it simply as "Christ."
19. *Novissima mea.*
20. He is speaking of the Church, but the same was surely true of Augustine personally in his zestful pursuit of ever-green wisdom.
21. Variant: "Take no notice if a wicked person is friendly to you."

we stand at Christ's right hand we shall hear what is said to those who stand at his left: *Depart from me into the eternal fire which was prepared for the devil and his angels* (Mt 25:41). A just person will have no fear at hearing those dire words. You know that in another psalm we hear the assurance, *The just will be held in eternal remembrance; what they are to hear holds no terrors for them* (Ps 111:7(112:6-7)). What fearful saying is in mind there? The command, *Depart from me into the eternal fire which was prepared for the devil and his angels*; this is the fearful saying. But *my ear will hear what is said to the malevolent who attack me*.

13. The grass fades away, the bloom of sinners fades away; but what of the righteous? *The just person will flourish like a palm tree.* Sinners spring up like grass, but *the just person will flourish like a palm tree*. The psalm chose a palm tree to suggest height, but perhaps for another reason too: because it is beautiful in the latest stages of its growth. If you consider it from its beginning in the earth to the highest point it attains, you see where its full beauty is to be found. Its root in the earth has a rough appearance, but its foliage is lovely against the sky. Your beauty too will be apparent at the end. Let your root be firmly fixed; only in our case the root stretches upwards, for Christ is our root, Christ who has ascended into heaven. The person who has been humbled will be lifted up.

Like a cedar on Lebanon shall the righteous one be multiplied. Look at the choice of trees: *the just person will flourish like a palm tree, like a cedar on Lebanon shall the righteous one be multiplied.* Does a palm tree dry up when the sun comes out? Does a cedar dry up? No, of course not; but sometimes when the sun burns hot the grass does. Judgment will come, and sinners shall be shrivelled, but the faithful will only grow greener. *Like a cedar on Lebanon shall the righteous one be multiplied.*

Verses 14-16. Be tranquil, and proclaim God's just dealing

14. *Planted in the house of the Lord, they will flourish in the courts of our God. They will grow more and more in their fruitful old age; they will be tranquil, that they may proclaim….* This is the Sabbath of which I reminded you not long since, from which the psalm took its title. *They will be tranquil, that they may proclaim….* Why do they need to be tranquil to make their proclamation? The verdure of sinners leaves them unmoved; cedar and palm are not bent even in storms. Let them be tranquil so as to make their proclamation; indeed they must be, since they are to make it even to ill-disposed hearers. You wretched folk, lovers of this world, to you is the message proclaimed by preachers planted in the Lord's house. Those who confess to the Lord with a song and on the lyre, in word and work, are proclaiming it; and what they are telling you is this: do not be misled by the good fortune of wicked people, have no regard for the bloom on the grass. Do not be impressed by those who are happy for a time, but will be

miserable for eternity. That outward show of present happiness is not even real, for they are not happy in their hearts, but tormented by their bad consciences.

For your part, be tranquil, and hope in the promises of the Lord your God. What will you proclaim in your tranquillity? *That the Lord God is upright, and there is no injustice in him.* Consider this carefully, brothers and sisters, if you are planted in the house of the Lord, if you want to flourish like a palm tree and grow tall like a cedar on Lebanon. Consider it carefully if you have no wish to be scorched when the sun waxes hot, like those who seem to flower so confidently as long as the sun is not on them. If you want to be not grass but palm and cedar, what will you proclaim? *That the Lord God is upright, and there is no injustice in him.* "But how can that be?" someone will ask. "How can it be true that in God there is no injustice? That fellow does very wicked things, yet he stays healthy, he has children and a well-provided household. His reputation stands high, he is given exalted rank and he avenges himself on his enemies. Yet he commits every kind of villainy. There is another man who deals fairly in his business,[22] never seizes the property of others, and does no harm to anyone. Yet he endures ill-treatment, bondage and imprisonment; he sweats and sighs in poverty. How can it be said that in God *there is no injustice?*"

Be tranquil, and you will understand. So far you have been in turmoil, and in your private, inner place you are obscuring the light for yourself. The eternal God wants to send his beams upon you, so do not becloud yourself with your agitation. Be tranquil inside yourself, and then listen to what I will tell you. *There is no injustice in him,* because God is eternal. He spares bad people now in order to lead them to repentance, and he whips the good to educate them for the kingdom of heaven. So there is no need to be afraid.

Still you object, "Yes, I certainly have had a whipping, no mistake about that. And I confess that I have sinned. I do not call myself a righteous person." Many people talk in this vein. Someone may be in distress, or in pain, and you go in to console him or her. The sufferer complains, "Yes, I have sinned, I admit it. The sins are mine, and I acknowledge them. But have I sinned as gravely as So-and-So? I know how heinous his sins are, I know what he is guilty of. My sins are real enough, and I confess them to God, but they are slight compared with his. Yet look at him: nothing bad happens to him!"

Do not be upset. Be tranquil, and then you will know *that the Lord is upright, and there is no injustice in him.* Is it not possible that he is whipping you now precisely because he is not saving up eternal fire for you? Is it not possible that he is letting the other person off because that one is destined to hear, *Depart into eternal fire?* And when will he hear it? When you have been placed at Christ's right hand, he will say to those at his left, *Depart from me into the eternal fire which was prepared for the devil and his angels.* So do not let these events

---

22. Variant: "who is guilty of no double-dealing."

disturb you. Be tranquil, celebrate your Sabbath, and proclaim *that the Lord God is upright, and there is no injustice in him.*

Exposition of Psalm 92

A Sermon to the People

Verse 1. The sixth day and the sixth age

1. When the title of this psalm was announced, we all heard it. There is no difficulty about understanding what it means, if we refer to God's scriptures, and to the Book of Genesis in particular. The title is like a notice over a threshold, which indicates what we are to look for inside. This inscription reads, *A song of praise, for David himself, for the day before the Sabbath, on which the earth was established.* These words recall the six days during which God created all things and set them in order, from the first day to the sixth; because he sanctified the seventh, and rested on that day from all the exceedingly good work he had been doing.[1] Now if we remember the sequence of his six days' work we find that on the sixth (that is, on *the day before the Sabbath*, as the title has it) he made all the land animals, and finally, still on that same day, human beings in his own image and likeness.

There was a good reason for this arrangement of the days, for the ages were destined to roll past one by one in the same way, until we find rest in God. But we rest only if we have first performed good works; and so a pattern was held before us when scripture wrote of God, *God rested on the seventh day* (Gn 2:2), when he had completed all his exceedingly good works. He did not rest because he was tired, nor does scripture imply that he is working no longer; on the contrary. Christ our Lord plainly declared, *My Father has been at work from the beginning* (Jn 5:17). This he said to the Jews, who entertained carnal notions about God, and failed to understand that God acts in quiet stillness. He works all the time, and all the time he is at rest.

God willed to model us on himself, and so we too shall have rest after all our good works. But in our case the good works which occupy us in this world, before the time comes for our rest, demand effort on our part, and we enjoy our rest only in hope, not yet as a reality.[2] If we did not hope for it we would faint under our labors, yet all these good works which require so much effort are transient. Is any action as good as doling out bread to the starving? And what is as good as the liberality which was recommended to all of us alike in the gospel

---

1. See Gn 1:1–2:4.
2. *In spe ... in re.*

passage we heard just now? *Anyone who has two tunics should give to someone who has none, and anyone who has food must feed the hungry* (Lk 3:11). To clothe a naked person is a good thing to do; but will there always be scope for that good deed? It requires some little hard work on your part, but it brings you consolation too, because you hope for peaceful rest in the future. But after all, how much labor does it cost you, this clothing of a naked person? A good deed is not such a laborious business, at any rate not as laborious as a bad action. Anyone who clothes the naked does not have to try very hard, assuming that he or she has the wherewithal to do so; and if not, then *Glory to God in the highest, and peace on earth to men of good will* (Lk 2:14).[3] But think of the opposite case: how hard a person has to work in order to strip someone else of a garment! Unconscionably hard work, that could be. Yet all these good actions will be superseded when we reach that rest where there is no hungry person needing to be fed, no naked person to be clothed. And because all such good works are to pass away, the sixth day, which sees their completion, is said to have an evening. But the Sabbath has no evening, because "evening" signifies the end of something, and our rest will never end.

As we find that God made men and women in his own image on the sixth day, so too do we find that our Lord Jesus Christ came in the sixth age, so that human beings might be reshaped in God's image. The first period of time, which corresponds to the first day, lasted from Adam until Noah; the second period, corresponding to the second day, was from Noah to Abraham; the third age, or third day, was from Abraham to David; the fourth age, or fourth day, was from David to the Babylonian exile; the fifth age, or fifth day, lasted from the Babylonian exile until the preaching of John. The sixth day is still going on: it stretches from the time of John until after this sixth day we reach our rest.

But if this sixth day is still running its course, notice the implication of the psalm's title: *for the day before the Sabbath, on which the earth was established.* So let us listen now to this psalm, and find out from it how the earth was established, and whether it was in fact established on that day—although we do not read in Genesis that it was.

When is the earth established? Remember what we heard not long since in the passage from the apostle. If you stand in the faith, he said, *Be stable and immovable* (1 Cor 15:58). When throughout the whole world all believers are immovable in their faith, then the earth is established, then human beings are refashioned in the image of God. This is what the sixth day in Genesis symbolizes. But how did God achieve it? How was the earth established? By the coming of Christ, for he came to establish the earth's foundations. *No one can lay any*

---

3. Augustine likes to stress that works of charity require the will to give, whether the material means are available or not; hence this rather unexpected quotation which mentions "good will."

other foundation than that which is laid, which is Christ Jesus (1 Cor 3:11). Accordingly the psalm sings of him, *The Lord reigns; he has arrayed himself in beauty. He has put on strength and girded himself.*

Beauty and strength are the Lord's apparel, and both are required by an apostle

2. *The Lord reigns; he has arrayed himself in beauty. He has put on strength and girded himself.* His raiment, as we see, is twofold: beauty and strength. Why is that? Because he was equipped to found the earth; and so the psalm continues, *For indeed he has made the round earth so firm that it will not be shaken.* How did he make it firm? By arraying himself in beauty. But if he had put on beauty alone that would not have sufficed to make it firm; he needed strength as well. Why beauty? Why strength? The psalm mentions both: *the Lord reigns; he has arrayed himself in beauty. He has put on strength and girded himself.*

Well, brothers and sisters, you know that when our Lord had come in the flesh, and was preaching the gospel of the kingdom, he was given a favorable hearing by some, but aroused hostility in others. The Jews argued among themselves. *Some were saying, He is a good man; but others said, No, he is misleading the people* (Jn 7:12). Words of admiration were on the lips of some, but others were abusing him, tearing his reputation to pieces, snapping at him and reviling him. For those who received him in a positive spirit *he arrayed himself in beauty*, but to confront those who rejected him *he put on strength*.

You in your turn must imitate your Lord, so that you may become his apparel. With people who approve of your good works, adorn yourself with beauty; but don strength in the face of those who revile you. Listen to the way in which the apostle Paul imitated his Lord, displaying both gracious beauty and fortitude. *We are the fragrance of Christ in every place*, he says, *both for those who are on the way to salvation, and for those who are perishing.* Those who approve what is good are on the way to salvation; those who disparage the good are perishing. Paul gave off good fragrance, or rather he was himself this fragrance; but it was lethal to the wretched folk who can die even of a sweet scent. Notice that he did not say, "To some we are a good fragrance, to others a bad smell"; but *We are the fragrance of Christ in every place*, and then he immediately added, *For some this is the scent of life, leading to life, but for others the stench of death unto death* (2 Cor 2:14-16). He had clothed himself in beauteous grace for those who received him as a fragrance redolent of life and life-giving, but to others who perceived him as the smell of death, and death-dealing, he appeared clad in strength.

If you are happy when people praise you and approve your good actions, but then when you are censured you slacken, and think your good works futile merely because you have encountered criticism, you have not stood immovably firm. You do not belong to *the round earth* that *will not be moved.*

The Lord has put on strength and girded himself. There is another passage in Paul's writings where he suggests both beauty and strength. *With the weapons of righteousness in right hand and left,* he says; but look where the beauty is found and where the strength is needed: *in high renown and ignominy.* He is splendid when his reputation stands high, but brave and strong when his lot is ignominy. In some circles he was lauded as glorious, in others scorned as disreputable. He displayed beauty to those who welcomed him, but faced down hostile critics in his strength. He runs through a catalogue of vicissitudes, until at the end he claims, *Seeming like people who have nothing, we possess all things* (2 Cor 6:7.8.10). When all things are his, he is dignified and beautiful; when he has nothing, he is brave and strong.

Little wonder, then, that the psalm continues, *Indeed the Lord has made the round earth so firm that it will not be shaken.* How can this round earth not be shaken? By all the faithful believing in Christ and being prepared to face whichever comes: prepared to rejoice with those who praise them and stand in strength against those who find fault, prepared not to let praising tongues make them soft, or fault-finding tongues wear them down.

A meditation on the Lord's girdle: the incarnation and humility

3. It may be a good thing for us to examine the expression, *He has girded himself.* A girdle suggests work, because when people want to tackle some work they hitch up their garments.[4] In another psalm he is urged, *Gird your sword upon your thigh, mighty warrior; peoples will fall under your assault* (Ps 44:4(45:3)). In that place it said neither *cingere* nor *praecingere* but *accingere.* You gird something on[5] when you attach it to your side, or buckle it onto you, and so that other psalm says, *Gird on your sword.* The Lord's sword, with which he conquered the round world by slaying wickedness, is the Spirit of God, active through the truth of God's word.[6] Why is he said to gird his sword onto his thigh? We said something about this girding in a different connection while discussing another psalm,[7] but since it has been mentioned here, we should not pass over it. What does it mean to gird a sword onto one's thigh? The thigh symbolizes the flesh. The Lord could have conquered the round world in no other way; the sword of truth had to be united with flesh. So why was he girded with these? A

---

4. A sentence is omitted here: Augustine enquires why his Latin version uses the compound verb *praecingere* instead of the simple *cingere.*

5. *Accingeris.*

6. Variant: "...by slaying wicked spirits in the truth of God's word." The codices vary considerably in this sentence.

7. See Exposition of Psalm 44,13.

person who girds[8] himself puts something in front of him, something he wants to fasten onto his front. This is why the gospel says, *He girded himself with a towel, and washed the feet of his disciples.* In his humility, signified by his linen apron, he washed the disciples' feet. Whatever is strong finds its home in humility, for all pride is fragile. This is why, after speaking of the Lord's strength, the psalm added, *He has girded himself,* to remind you of how humble God was when he washed the feet of the disciples. Peter was horrified to see his Lord, his teacher (but what is it to call him merely "teacher," when I have just called him "Lord"?), bending down at his feet, and washing them. He was appalled, and protested, *Lord, you won't wash my feet!* And the Lord replied, *You do not know at present what I am doing, but you will know later.* Peter insisted, *You will not wash my feet, not ever!* Jesus answered, *If I do not wash you, you will have no fellowship with me.* Peter had been appalled first of all at the idea of the Lord washing his feet, but now he was more appalled still by the warning, *you will have no fellowship with me.* He believed that the Lord had good reason for what he did, and that it was perhaps some mystery of grace,[9] so he said, *Lord, not just my feet, then, but my head too, and all of me.* The Lord assured him, *When a person has been washed once, there is no need to be washed again. That person is wholly clean.* So the Lord's action in washing their feet was not like a sacrament of cleansing,[10] but an example of humility, as he made clear when he told them, *You do not know at present what I am doing, but you will know later.* Let us see whether they did know later, let us see whether he let them into the secret of what he was doing, so that we may contemplate the Lord girded with strength, a strength that, as always, expresses itself in humility. After he had washed their feet he sat down again, and said to them, *You call me Teacher, and you are right, for so I am. You call me Lord, and you speak truly, for so I am. If then I, your Teacher and Lord, have washed your feet, is it not incumbent on you to do the same for each other?* (Jn 13:4-10.13-14).

If strength expresses itself in humility, do not be intimidated by the proud. Humble people are like rock. Rock is something you look down on, but it is solid. What about the proud? They are like smoke: they may be rising high, but they vanish as they rise. When the psalm speaks of the Lord as girding himself, we should associate it with his humility, because the gospel makes this connection when it tells us that he girded himself in order to wash the feet of his disciples.

4. We may understand something further from this statement. We remarked just now that to gird oneself implies placing something in front of oneself which one intends to bind on. Now people who want to disparage us sometimes do so in

---

8. *Praecingit*: the compound verb here seems to carry the nuance of "gird in front."
9. *Sacramentum.*
10. Variant: "was not only a sacrament of cleansing."

our absence, behind our backs, as it were; but sometimes they do it to our face, as they did to the Lord when he was hanging on the cross, and they taunted him, *If he is the Son of God, let him come down from the cross* (Mt 27:40.42). When someone vilifies you in your absence, you do not need strength or fortitude, because you do not hear and do not feel it. But if someone speaks like that to your face, you need to be strong. Why do you need strength in that case? In order to bear it. You must not think that when you hear an insult you prove yourself strong by swinging a punch at the speaker; all that proves is that you have been overcome by the derogatory remark. It is no fortitude to hit out when you are belittled; it is proof that you have been conquered by anger. And it is very stupid to call someone who has been conquered "strong." Scripture declares, *Better is the one who overcomes anger than the one who captures a city* (Prv 16:32, LXX). The conqueror of anger is ranked above the captor of a city! That means you have a mighty adversary inside yourself. When you hear yourself insulted and anger begins to surge up, remember the words of the apostle: *Do not return evil for evil, or curse for curse* (1 Pt 3:9). If you recall these words you stem the force of your anger and hold fast to your strength. When the other person has spoken spitefully to your face, rather than behind your back, you have girded yourself in front[11] with strength.

There is a movable world, and a stable, immovable world

5. Now let us listen to the rest. This psalm is only a short one. *Indeed, the Lord has made the round earth so firm that it will not be shaken.* You observe, brothers and sisters, that a great many people believe in Christ. They form a vast crowd. And yet, as you heard when the gospel was read just now, the Lord will come among this vast crowd, bearing his winnowing-shovel in his hand, and he will cleanse his threshing-floor.[12] He will store the grain in a barn, but the chaff he will burn in a fire that can never be put out. When the sledge is brought into the threshing-floor it chops the straw but cleanses the grain.

So what is this round earth *that will not be shaken*? The assertion would not have been made if there were not also a round earth that will be shaken. We must infer that a distinction is intended: there is a round earth that will not be shaken, and another round earth that will be. What I mean is that good people, who are steadfast in faith, are called a "round earth," so that no one can pretend that they are to be found in one region only.[13] On the other hand there are bad folk who when aware of any trouble do not stand fast in faith; and they too are found throughout the round earth. This is why we can say that there is a movable round

---

11. *Praecinctus es.*
12. See Mt 3:12.
13. Aimed at the Donatists, evidently.

earth, and an immovable round earth, and the apostle mentions both. Consider the movable earth first. Of whom did the apostle utter this condemnation? *Of their number are Hymenaeus and Philetus, who have strayed away from the truth, asserting that the resurrection has already taken place; and they are upsetting the faith of some.* Did people of this type belong to the round earth that will not be shaken? Hardly. They were part of the chaff. Moreover, scripture states that they were *upsetting the faith of some.* Note that it says, *Some,* not all. If it had said, "The faith of all," we should have been obliged to take it as a reference to all who belong to the city of Babylon,[14] which is destined to be doomed with the devil. But no, it said, *Some.* Then perhaps the apostle expected someone to ask, "Who can resist such people?" So he immediately added, *But God's foundation stands firm,* and there you have the round earth that will not be shaken. This firm foundation is described as bearing a seal. What seal is this? *The Lord knows his own.* This is the round earth that will not be shaken: *the Lord knows his own.* And what is stamped on this unshakeable earth? *Everyone who calls on the name of the Lord keeps clear of iniquity* (2 Tm 2:17-19). It must keep clear of sin here and now; but it cannot keep clear of sinners, because straw and grain are mixed together until the winnowing. What are we saying, brothers and sisters? This is the amazing thing about the grain, that it is separated from the chaff as it is hulled, but it does not leave the threshing-floor while the threshing is still in progress. When will grain and chaff be entirely separated? When the winnower arrives. For the present, the threshing-floor extends throughout the round world, and if you want to make progress you have no option but to live among the wicked. You cannot keep clear of sinners, but keep clear of sin. *Everyone who calls on the name of the Lord keeps clear of iniquity,* and then he or she will be within the round earth that will not be shaken.

Verse 2. God's throne in humble souls. Christ's eternal birth

6. *Your throne has been prepared, O God, from then.* What does *from then* mean? From of old. It seems to prompt the question, "What is God's throne? Where does God sit?" His throne is in his saints. Do you want to be God's throne? Then prepare a place in your heart where he may sit. And what is God's throne, if not the place where God dwells? Where does he dwell? Surely in his temple. What is his temple? Is it built with walls? No, of course not. Perhaps we should say, then, that this world is his temple; after all, it is very big, and so it could be a worthy container for God? By no means: it cannot contain him by whom it was made. So where is he contained? In a soul at peace, in a righteous soul; such a soul carries him. This is a mighty truth, brothers and sisters, for although God is undoubtedly mighty, and a heavy weight to the strong, he bears

---

14. See note at Exposition of Psalm 44,25.

lightly on the weak. Whom do I mean by "the strong"? I mean proud people, who presume on their own powers; for a much greater strength is the weakness of humility. Listen to the apostle's declaration: *When I am weak, then I am strong* (2 Cor 12:10). This is what I reminded you[15] about: the Lord was girded with strength when he was teaching us humility. This is where God sets his throne. In another passage a prophet makes the point clearly. *Upon whom shall my Spirit rest?* Where else should God's Spirit rest, if not on God's throne? Now listen to the prophet's description of that throne. You expected, perhaps, to hear about a marble dwelling with spacious halls and lofty, glittering ceilings? Listen to what God prepares for himself: *Upon whom shall my Spirit rest, but upon the humble, peaceable person, the one who trembles at my words?* (Is 66:2). You see, then, that if you are humble and peaceable God dwells in you too. God is very high, but if you aspire to be lifted high, he does not dwell in you. You want that, don't you—to be high up—because you think that then he will dwell in you? Be humble, rather, and tremble at his words, and then he will. He is not nervous about a shaky home, because he himself establishes it firmly.

Your throne has been prepared, O God, from then. The words "from then" seem to imply some definite time. From then? From when? Possibly from *the day before the Sabbath*, because the title of the psalm gave us a hint of that. On the sixth day, or in the sixth age of this world, the Lord came in the flesh. From then, yes, from then obviously, if we are speaking of his humanity, from that time he was born from the womb. What does another psalm say on this? *In the splendor of the saints, from the womb.* The first phrase, *in the splendor of the saints*, means that he came in order that the saints may be illumined, and see God in the flesh; thus their hearts are purified so that they may behold him in his divinity. *In the splendor of the saints, from the womb.*

But how does that other psalm continue? If it had said nothing further you might have thought that Christ's existence began only in the womb; so it added, *Before the daystar I begot you.* Had this phrase not been immediately added to the preceding one, *in the splendor of the saints, from the womb*, you might have supposed that Christ began to exist from the time of his birth, as Adam began, as did Abraham, as did David. So the psalm clarified it: *before the daystar I begot you*: that is, before anything that could be illumined.[16] There are two ways to interpret this allusion to the daystar. It may represent all the stars, and through the stars the passage of time, since God made the stars to demarcate temporal periods.[17] So the phrase would mean that Christ was born before all times; and if he was born before all times, he cannot be thought to have been born from any point in time, because all times themselves are creatures of God. If all things were made through

---

15. Variants: "It [the psalm] reminded you"; "the gospel reminded you."
16. Variant: "before all things that give light."
17. See Gn 1:14.

him,[18] time too was made through him. The other way to interpret *before the daystar I begot you* is to take it as a reference to Wisdom's having been begotten before the creation of every spirit that receives illumination.

Give me your close attention now, beloved. We have seen how, after saying, *From the womb*, the psalm alerted our faith by immediately adding, *Before the daystar I begot you*. This was to make sure that we should not suppose Christ to have begun to exist only from the time he was born from the Virgin's womb. And now, in the same way, after saying, *From then*, which means from a particular time, from the day before the Sabbath, from that sixth age of the world when Christ our Lord was born in the flesh, it added, *Your throne has been prepared, O God*, to make sure that when you contemplate the day of the Lord's nativity, you do not mistakenly think he began to exist only on that day. He did indeed graciously become man for our sake, but he is God, not only before Abraham, but before the creation of heaven and earth. He claimed, *Before Abraham came to be, I AM* (Jn 8:58); but in fact he existed not only before Abraham, but before Adam; and not only before Adam, but before all the angels, and before heaven and earth, because all things were made through him. Who is this God? *From eternity, you are*. From eternity, it says, ἀπὸ αἰῶνος, as the Greek has it; for though in Greek αἰών can mean an age, it is often used to signify eternity. You seem, O Lord, to have been born only "from that time"; but from all eternity, you are. Let us not make the mistake of thinking that the psalm refers to his human birth, but raise our minds to his eternal generation.

From the time of his human birth he began to grow, as you heard in the gospel.[19] He chose his disciples, and filled them, and they began to preach. Perhaps this is what the next verses of our psalm reflect.

Verses 3-4. The loud voice of the rivers

7. *The rivers have lifted up their voices.*[20] What are these rivers that lift up their voices? We have not heard about them before. We are not told that at the time of the Lord's birth any rivers spoke. Nor do we hear of rivers having spoken when he was baptized, or when he suffered. Read the gospel: you will not find anything about rivers speaking. Yet to say, "speaking," is an understatement, for *they lifted up their voices*; they did not just speak, they shouted loudly, at the top of their voices. So what are these eloquent rivers? We have said that we read nothing of it in the gospel; all the same, it is there that we must search, for if we do not find anything there, where else shall we find it? I could be telling you tall stories! Then all at once I am a trustworthy steward no longer, but only an imper-

18. See Jn 1:3.
19. See Lk 2:52.
20. Variant: "their voice," as in the comments later in this section.

tinent spinner of fables.[21] Let us seek the answer in the gospel; let us seek together, and find out what these rivers were that lifted up their voices.

Jesus stood up and shouted, the gospel tells us. What was he shouting? Listen, the fountain-head of all rivers is crying out, he who is the font of life, the source from which the rivers will spring; he was the first to raise his voice. And what was Jesus crying out? *If anyone believes in me, as scripture says, rivers of living water shall flow from within that person.* The evangelist promptly explains, *He said this of the Spirit which those who believed in him were to receive; for the Spirit had not yet been given, because Jesus was not yet glorified* (Jn 7:37-39). As you know, brothers and sisters, after Jesus had been glorified by his resurrection and ascension into heaven, and after he had allowed ten days to elapse because of the mystical significance of that period, he sent his Holy Spirit and filled his disciples. The Spirit himself is the mighty river whence many other rivers derive. Concerning that river another psalm says, *The vehement impulses of a river give joy to God's city* (Ps 45:5(46:4)). Clearly, then, rivers flowing from within the disciples were created when they received the Holy Spirit; indeed, once they had received the Spirit they became rivers themselves.

How can it be said that they lifted up their voices? Why did they lift them? Because initially they had been afraid. Peter was not yet a river when he three times denied Christ at the question of a servant girl: *I do not know the man* (Mk 14:71). He is afraid, so he lies. He is not yet lifting up his voice, he is not yet a river. But after the apostles had been filled with the Holy Spirit the Jews arraigned them and ordered them not to speak at all or to teach in the name of Jesus. Peter and John replied, *If it is right in God's sight for us to obey you rather than God, judge for yourselves. We cannot refrain from speaking of what we have seen and heard* (Acts 4:19-20). This was an occasion when *the rivers lifted up their voice, from the voices of many waters.* Another text illustrates this uplifting of their voices: *Peter stood up with the Eleven, and lifting up his voice he addressed them: Men of Judea...* (Acts 2:14). You know the rest, you remember how he proclaimed Jesus fearlessly and with high confidence. *The rivers have lifted up their voice, from the voices of many waters.* This too was realized when, after being dismissed from the council of the Jews, the apostles went back to their own people and related how seriously they had been admonished by the priests and elders. When the other disciples heard it they unanimously raised their voice to the Lord, saying, *You, O Lord, made heaven and earth, and the sea, and all things in them* (Acts 4:24), and so on. This was an example of the rivers being empowered to raise their voice.

Wonderful were the breakers in the sea, for when those disciples had lifted their voices many people came to believe, and many received the Holy Spirit; so the clamor began to rise from many rivers that had flowed from the first few.

---

21. Variant: "disputant."

This is why the psalm continues, *From the voices of many waters, wonderful were the breakers in the sea,* for the sea represents this world. As Christ began to be preached by many strong voices the sea began to surge fiercely, and persecutions intensified. Therefore it could be said that when *the rivers lifted up their voices,* then *from the voices of many waters, wonderful were the breakers in the sea.* Breakers[22] are waves that mount high; when the sea is rough the waves swell and hang overhead, as though suspended. Let the waves surge as high as they wish, let the sea rage as it will, wonderful be the threats, wonderful the persecutions; but mark what follows: *wonderful is the Lord on high.* The sea had best restrain itself, then, and grow tranquil at last; let peace be granted to Christians. The sea was turbulent, and the little ship was tossed about: this little ship is the Church, and the sea is the world. The Lord came and walked on the sea, treading down its waves.[23] How did the Lord walk on the sea? He trod on the crests of those mighty, foaming waves, for powerful people believed—kings, even—and were subjected to Christ. Let us not be afraid, then, for *wonderful were the breakers in the sea,* but *wonderful is the Lord on high.*

Verse 5. Christ has conquered the world

8. *Your testimonies have been very surely believed.* More wonderful than were the breakers in the sea, is the Lord wonderful on high. *Your testimonies have been very surely believed.* The psalm speaks of *your testimonies* because Christ said to us in advance, *I tell you these things so that in me you may have peace, though in the world you will have distress* (Jn 16:33). "I tell you, the world will heap distress upon you," he warned them. Then, when they began to suffer, they verified the Lord's prophecy in their own experience, and that gave them all the more strength, because when they saw his prediction of suffering coming true in themselves, they hoped that his promises concerning their crowns would as well. Rightly, then, does the psalm say, *Wonderful were the breakers in the sea,* because *wonderful is the Lord on high.* "I have told you in advance," he said, *so that in me you may have peace, though in the world you will have distress.*

What are we to do, then? The sea rages, the waves surge and rage and roar; we suffer distress. Are we not in danger of going under? Not at all. *Wonderful is the Lord on high,* so wonderful that when he had foretold these things to them, *so that in me you may have peace, though in the world you will have distress,* and their implied response was, "Don't you think the world will overwhelm us, and drown us?" he immediately bade them, *Be glad, for I have overcome the world.* Since Christ claimed, *I have overcome the world,* cling closely to him who has

---

22. *Suspensurae.*
23. See Mt 14:25.

vanquished it and subdued the sea. Sing joyfully to him that the Lord is wonderful on high, and tell him, *Your testimonies are very sure indeed.*

And what is the result of all this? *Holiness befits your house, O Lord.* It befits your house, your whole house; not here alone, not there alone, but your entire house throughout the whole round world. Why throughout the world? Because he has set this round earth to rights, and it will not be shaken.[24] The Lord's house will stand strong, and it will spread throughout the world. Many people will fall, but that house shall stand; many will be agitated, but that house shall not be shaken. *Holiness befits your house, O Lord.* For a short time only, perhaps? By no means, but *unto length of days.*

---

24. See Ps 95(96):10.

Exposition of Psalm 93

A Sermon[1]

The scope of this psalm: a corrective to people who believe God's dispositions to be unjust

1. When this psalm was being read out we listened with keen attention, so now let us listen just as keenly while the Lord unveils the mysteries he has graciously hidden within it. Certain holy mysteries[2] are kept behind closed doors in the scriptures, not to be withheld from us, but to be opened when we knock.[3] If you knock with devout mind and sincere charity in your heart, he who sees what moves you to knock will open the door to you.

Now we all know very well that there are many people (and let us hope that we are not ourselves of their number) who resent God's forbearance, and begrudge the way he allows the godless to live on earth and even wield extensive power. What is worse, bad people commonly enjoy such power to the disadvantage of the good; the wicked often oppress the good, and make merry while the good struggle along, and behave arrogantly while the good are humiliated. Weak-minded and impatient persons observe such tendencies in human affairs—and there are plenty of examples, certainly—and are swayed from their purpose, as though their own laudable practice were useless. God ignores the good deeds of devout and faithful folk, they think, or at any rate he seems to ignore them, while heaping upon evildoers the things they covet. The weak therefore conclude that their own good lives are a waste of time, and they are tempted to imitate the villainy of those who seem to be flourishing. In some cases these observers may be deterred by their own physical or mental feebleness from actually doing wrong, fearful perhaps of falling foul of the secular law. Their restraint does not spring from any love of justice, but—to put it bluntly—simply from the fear of incurring human retribution; and so they refrain from unlawful actions, but not from evil thoughts. Among the wicked ideas that may occur to them there is one of extreme impiety, a very fountain-head of sin. This is the opinion that God is uninvolved and takes no interest in human affairs, or that he reckons good and bad people as equal, or even that he

---

1. Possibly preached at the insistence of fellow-bishops; see section 30.
2. *Sacramenta.*
3. See Mt 7:7. Augustine loved this promise of Christ; compare his *Confessions* XII,1,1; XIII,38,53.

harasses the good and favors the wicked, which is the most pernicious view of all. When people think like that they do grave harm to themselves, even though they do none to others. They are undutiful toward themselves, and self-destructive, but their iniquity does not hurt God. Those who entertain such notions are too timid to injure other people, but God sees the murders, the adulteries, the fraud and violence they commit in their thoughts, and he punishes them; for he takes cognizance of their desires, and his gaze is not so blocked by the flesh as to be unable to reach the will. If people of this stamp get their chance, they do not suddenly become bad, but are shown up for what they are. You must not look on what has come to light as something newly born; regard it as something hitherto bottled up and concealed.

Only a few years ago, almost yesterday as it seems, we were given so plain an instance of such developments that even the slowest minds can take the point. A certain family was extremely powerful for a time. God had made it into a scourge with which he whipped the human race, in the hope that they would recognize in this a Father's chastisement and respect a Judge's sentence. While this house was dominant here many people groaned under it; they grumbled and found fault and cursed and blasphemed. How people box themselves in, so that many are handed over by divine judgment to the lusts of their own hearts![4] Those who had been accustomed to grouse about the powerful household suddenly began to join it, so that other people suffered at their hands the very ill-treatment they had themselves habitually complained about not long before.

The good person is one who does not act wrongly even when the opportunity is there. Scripture speaks of *one who could have transgressed, and did not, could have done wrong, and would not. Who is this, to deserve our praise? Marvelous is the life of such a person* (Sir 31:10.9). It was referring to those who did no harm even though they were powerful. A wolf attempts to wreak as much havoc as a lion; the damage done by the two animals is dissimilar, but their instincts are not. A lion not only scorns a barking dog; he puts him to flight, and approaches the sheepfold, and seizes all he can while the dogs are silenced. The wolf, on the contrary, dare not attempt it while the dogs are barking. So because the wolf was scared off by the dogs, and unable to get away with his prey, would we judge him more innocent[5] than the lion? Hardly. God teaches us innocence, but it is the kind of innocence that springs not from fear of punishment, but from love of righteousness. Only then is the innocent person both free and truly innocent, whereas someone who out of fear refrains from harming others is not innocent, even if he cannot give effect to his desire to do harm. He does not hurt another person by

---

4. See Rom 1:24.
5. Where Augustine speaks of innocence in the rest of this section he is using it in its exact meaning of "non-harmful" or "not-harming," as contrasted with the actions of one who harms others. The point is more obvious in Latin.

any malicious action, but he does great harm to himself by his evil desire. Listen to the scriptural warning about how we can harm ourselves: *Whoever loves iniquity hates his own soul* (Ps 10:6(11:5)). Indeed, people who think that their unjust conduct harms others but not themselves are very wide of the mark. Unjust dealing attacks others inasmuch as it wounds our neighbor's body, harms him financially, invades his house, kidnaps his slave, and steals his gold, or silver, or other property.[6] To that extent, the iniquity does strike at another person. But do you suppose your iniquity can injure someone else's body, and leave your own soul unharmed?

2. This is truthful and straightforward teaching. Good people are instructed to love righteousness for its own sake, to please God by practicing it, and under his schooling to grasp that their souls are flooded by a kind of intelligible light which enables them to act justly. They are admonished to value this light of wisdom above every other lovable thing in this world. A simple, truthful doctrine it is, yet people murmur their objections to it, and even if the words are not uttered, those who grumble in thought are being eaten away in their hearts. What do they say? "Am I really going to please God by living righteously? Can the righteous be pleasing to a God under whose dominion malefactors prosper? They commit grave sins, yet nothing bad happens to them." But then suppose something bad does befall one of them, and you begin to reason with the objector: "Look at him! Think what wicked things he did, and how retribution overtook him. What kind of death did he have?" But they have their answer ready. They point to just persons on whom calamities fell, and they argue against us: "If misfortune befell him because he was wicked, why did it also fall upon that other fellow who lived such a righteous life? He gave away a great deal in alms, and did many good deeds in the Church, so why did he meet such a fate? Why was his death as hard as that of the one who committed many sins?"

These objections betray the speakers as people who refrain from acting wrongly because they are either unable to do wrong, or do not dare. The tongue is bearing witness to the desires of the heart; and if the tongue itself were to be restrained by fear and keep silence, God would still see what the person was thinking inwardly, even if it were hidden from other men and women. Our psalm offers a remedy for such silent human thoughts, and even for those that burst out into words or deeds, provided only these people consent to be cured. Let them pay attention, then, and find healing.[7]

It is our dearest hope that among the whole crowd within these walls, among all of you who are listening to the word of the Lord through us, there are no wounds of this kind that need healing. Yes, I certainly hope that there are none. But even if no such wounds are to be found here, what we are saying is not super-

---

6. Variant: "or silver, or does anything else in its power."
7. On Augustine's idea of the psalms as therapeutic, see the *Introduction* in Volume 1.

fluous. When faithful hearts begin to listen to this instruction they may be trained to heal others. Suppose a Christian hears someone talking in the vein we have described. Provided he or she is a good and faithful Christian, one who firmly believes in God and hopes in the world to come rather than in this earth and this life, one who hears to good purpose the exhortation, "Lift up your hearts!"[8] then, I say, this Christian derides and pities those who complain about God's justice, and reflects, "God knows what he is doing. We cannot understand his dispensation, or why he spares bad people for a time, or why the good have it so hard for the present. It is enough for me to know that the struggles of a good person will be only temporary, and the prosperity of a bad one equally short-lived."

People who take this line are free from worry. They bear up patiently when evildoers get all the luck, and they bear patiently, tolerantly, the hardships that fall to good people until this world comes to an end, until iniquity shall pass away.[9] They are blessed already, for God has instructed them in his law, and made them gentle through days of misery, until a pit is dug for the sinner.[10] Any of you who are not yet so blessed should listen now to whatever the Lord wants them to hear through us. But may the Lord himself instruct them much more fully in their hearts, for he sees more clearly the wound he means to heal.

Verse 1. The title points us to the stars

3. The psalm bears the following title, attached to it as an inscription: *A psalm for David himself, on the fourth day of the week.* The intention of the psalm is to teach patience to the just amid their tribulations. Patience is what teaches us in the face of the good fortune enjoyed by the godless; patience is what builds us up. This is the message of the whole psalm, from beginning to end. Why, then, does it have this title, *On the fourth day of the week?* The first day of the week is the Lord's day; the second is the day worldly people call Monday, the Moon's day; the third day they call the day of Mars.[11] So the fourth day of the week is the day named after Mercury[12] by pagans, and by many Christians too, alas. We do not like this practice, and we wish Christians would amend their custom and not employ the pagan name. They have a language of their own that they can use. After all, this name is not current among all nations. Many other peoples have their own customs, and all of them call it something different. The Church's mode of speech comes more fittingly from the mouth of a Christian.

---

8. See the note at Exposition of Psalm 10,3.
9. See Ps 56:2(57:1).
10. An anticipation of verses 12-13 below.
11. Still discernible, for instance, in French, *mardi.*
12. As in French, *mercredi.*

However, habit is powerful, and the old name may slip out, so that Christians find on their lips a name of which their hearts disapprove; and in that case they should be aware that all those legendary people after whom the heavenly bodies were named were no more than human. The stars in the sky did not come into existence at the time those heroes were born; they were there long before. Certain human beings, powerful and eminent in the world of their own day, were held in high esteem by their contemporaries on account of mortal benefits conferred on fellow-mortals. They were reckoned important, not in the perspective of eternal life, but only because they were so useful in temporal matters; and so divine honors were accorded to them. The ancients of this world,[13] deceived themselves and bent on deceiving others, wished to flatter the eminent persons who had granted them some favors or advanced their worldly fortunes, and so they pointed to the sky, declaring that this star was So-and-So's star, and that one somebody else's. Ordinary people had not looked carefully before, and had not observed that those particular stars had been in the sky before the great men were born. They were therefore hoodwinked, and believed the story. Thus was the stupid idea conceived. The devil bolstered the erroneous opinion, but Christ overturned it.

In our idiom, when we speak of "the fourth day of the week," we mean the fourth from the Lord's day, and from this usage we can gather what the title is indicating. There is a great mystery here, something truly hidden, so pay close attention, beloved.[14] Many elements in the psalm sound quite plain, and just as plainly affect us; but this title, it must be admitted, holds no little obscurity. However the Lord will stand by us, and turn the cloudy conditions into fair weather. Then you will see the psalm clearly, and know it from its frontage; for this psalm carries on its façade *A psalm for David himself, on the fourth day of the week*. We encounter this title at the threshold, affixed to the doorpost. People need to read the title before entering the house.

Let us turn our mind to the holy scripture, and recall what Genesis describes as being made on the first day. We find that it was light. What was made on the second day? The firmament, which God called "sky." If we ask what was done on the third day, we find the beauty of the earth and the sea, and the separation of them from each other, so that the whole gathering of waters was named "sea," and the dry land, "earth." On the fourth day God made the luminaries in the sky: the sun to rule the day, and the moon and stars to rule the night. This was the work of the fourth day. What is being hinted, then, if the psalm took its title from the fourth day, this psalm in which we are taught to be patient when we observe the prosperity of the wicked and the struggles of the good? You find the apostle Paul telling his holy, faithful people, who have been strengthened in Christ, *Do*

---

13. Variant: "the ancient seers."
14. *Caritas vestra.*

everything without grumbling or dispute, that you may be irreproachable and sincere, as stainless children of God amid a crooked and perverse race. To them you appear like luminaries in this world, holding fast the word of life (Phil 2:14-16). The radiant heavenly bodies are presented to the saints as an image of what they should be: never grumbling though surrounded by a crooked, perverse race.

4. There is a danger, though, that because the luminaries in the sky were used as a metaphor for the saints, someone may think that they are therefore to be reverenced and worshiped. We must therefore begin by explaining in Christ's name that because the sun, or moon, or stars, or sky provides an image to represent the saints, it does not follow that you should regard these things as objects of worship. There are many things from which metaphors can be drawn to signify the saints, but they are not to be adored. If you think that anything used metaphorically in this way is a fit object of adoration, go ahead and worship mountains and hills, for scripture says, *The mountains skipped like rams, and the hills like newborn lambs* (Ps 113(114):4). But you are talking only about saints; I will go further and make the same point about Christ. Worship a lion, because scripture says, *The lion from the tribe of Judah has conquered* (Rv 5:5). Worship a rock, because it says, *The rock was Christ* (1 Cor 10:4). But you don't worship these earthly things as Christ, do you, even though they provided a metaphor? In the same way, then, whenever a metaphor is drawn from any created thing to represent the saints, understand that it is an image, and worship the God who created it. Our Lord Jesus Christ is called the sun,[15] but is he the sun which all the tiniest living things see, along with us? No; he it is of whom scripture says, *He was the true light, which illumines every human person who comes into this world* (Jn 1:9). The sun in the sky gives light not only to human beings, but to the beasts and the cattle and all living creatures, whereas the true light which illumines every human person sheds light in the heart, where alone understanding resides.

The serenity of the high stars, reflected in the forbearance of the saints

5. You must understand, dearly beloved,[16] that when the apostle said to the saints, *Amid a crooked and perverse race*, by which he means sinners, *you appear like luminaries in this world, holding fast the word of life*, he was in a sense giving us advice. He was helping us to understand this psalm, and to get our minds clear at the outset about its title. The kind of holy people in whom dwells the word of life disregard all the wicked things that are done on earth, because their citizenship is in heaven.[17] They are in this respect like the lumi-

---

15. See Wis 5:6; Mal 4:2; Lk 1:78.
16. *Caritas vestra.*
17. See Ph 3:20. *Conversatio*, here translated "citizenship," connotes also a particular way of life or conduct.

naries in the sky, which carry on through day and night, keeping to their pathways and observing their appointed courses, however great the evils perpetrated
on earth. The stars in the sky above us never deviate, but track their heavenly
ways as their creator has determined and appointed for them; and the saints must
do likewise if their hearts are fixed in heaven, if they hear to good purpose the
invitation, "Lift up your hearts!" and act on it, if they imitate him who testified,
Our citizenship is in heaven (Phil 3:20). They live in heavenly realities, and keep
their minds on heavenly realities, according to the gospel saying, *Where your
treasure is, your heart will be too* (Mt 6:21), and in the strength of this meditation on the things of heaven they grow in patience. Persevering in their own journeys, they are unconcerned about bad deeds committed on earth, just as the
luminaries in the sky are concerned with nothing but regulating the orderly
succession of days and nights, even though great scandals on earth may be
evident to them.

Someone may object that it is easy enough for holy people to endure the
unjust actions of bad people as long as such actions do not impinge upon themselves. That is true; but they do bear injuries against themselves as patiently as
those committed against others. They are under an obligation to bear and tolerate
such attacks, but not only when other people are the targets; they are equally
obliged not to lose the spirit of tolerance if they are targeted themselves. Anyone
who has lost that forbearance has fallen out of heaven, but the saints have their
hearts fixed in heaven even while their earthly nature labors on earth. Think
what fables people spin about the luminaries themselves, and how patiently they
bear it! Just so must the righteous bear all accusations, even false ones.
Remember what I said a few minutes ago: that people say this star belongs to
Mercury, this one to Saturn, that other one to Jupiter. Now these attributions are
outrageous insults to the very stars. Yet when they hear such a violent outcry, are
they thrown off course? Do they waver in their journeys? Not in the least. A
person who dwells amid a crooked and perverse race, yet holds onto God's
word, is like that too; he or she is like a luminous body radiant in the sky. How
many people there are who imagine that they are honoring the sun by telling lies
about it! Those who say, "The sun is Christ," are lying about the sun. The sun
knows that Christ is its Lord and its creator; and if it is capable of feeling indignation, it is more annoyed with someone who pays it spurious honor than with
someone who speaks of it slightingly, for any good servant is especially grieved
by an insult to his master. How many false assertions do people make about the
luminaries in the sky? Yet they bear it, they put up with it, they do not wobble.
Why not? Because they are in heaven. But what is heaven? (Oh, I forgot something that should be mentioned: what shameless lies people tell when they see
the moon darkened, and say, "Sorcerers are pulling her down," when the moon
has her appointed times for waning, according to God's dispensation. Yet the
moon, being in heaven, takes no notice of what people say.) But, as I was asking

just now, what is it to be in heaven? It means to be in the firmament. And so too anyone whose heart is in the firmament of God's book takes no notice of such things.

The unrolled book of the sky symbolizes scripture, which we must read now, and fix our hearts in now, but not for eternity

6. The sky, or more properly the firmament, is to be understood figuratively as the book of the law. Somewhere it is said, *He stretched out the sky like a skin.*[18] It is stretched out as a book is unrolled, so that it can be read. But when the proper time has passed, it is read no longer. The law[19] is read now because we have not yet reached that Wisdom who fills the hearts and minds of those who contemplate her; when we come into that presence there will be no need for anything to be read to us. What is read to us now consists of syllables that become audible and then die away, but the light of truth does not fade. It abides steadfastly and intoxicates the hearts of those who gaze on it; as scripture says, *They will be inebriated by the rich abundance of your house, and you will give them the full torrent of your delights to drink, for with you, Lord, is the fountain of life.* And now contemplate the fountain itself: *in your light we will see light* (Ps 35:9-10(36:8-9)). Reading is necessary at present, as long as we *know only in part, and utter partial prophecies*, as the apostle says, *but when perfection comes, what is partial will be superseded* (1 Cor 13:9-10). Jerusalem is that city[20] where the angels live, the city from which we are absent like travelers abroad, groaning in our exile. But we groan only in the measure that we know ourselves to be exiles, for anyone who thinks himself well off while still on pilgrimage must hate his homeland. And in that city where the angels dwell, is the gospel read, or the apostle's letters? No, for they are directly nourished by the Word of God. Yet that very Word was made flesh and lived among us so that it might sound in our ears for a time.

All the same, the written law is a firmament for us, and if our hearts are set fast in it, they will not be wrenched loose[21] by the iniquities of men and women. It is written, *He stretched out the sky like a skin.* But when the era has passed in which books are necessary, what does scripture say will happen? *The sky will be rolled up like a scroll* (Is 34:4). When we keep our hearts lifted high, our very hearts are lamps; they shine in heaven and are not quenched by the darkness below them. The darkness is iniquity, and is by no means unchangeable. We spoke about this

---

18. Ps 103(104):2. *Pellis* meant primarily the skin or hide of an animal, and by extension an object made from this. So in Ps 103(104) it is more likely to mean a tent; but in the present context Augustine is thinking of a scroll made from parchment.
19. He means, of course, scripture as a whole.
20. Variant: "In that city, Jerusalem, no book will be necessary, nor shall we read, where ..."
21. Variant: "constrained."

yesterday.[22] Those who today are darkness will be light tomorrow if only they consent to be, and those who were darkness when they walked into this church can be light this minute if they want to. The apostle makes it quite plain, lest anyone should think that sins are our natural condition and cannot be changed: *You were darkness once*, he says, *but now you are light in the Lord; walk as children of the light* (Eph 5:8). Notice that he says, *Light in the Lord*, not in yourselves.

Let our hearts be in the book, then, for if our hearts are in God's book, they are in the firmament of heaven. If your heart is there, let it shine from there, and then it will not be shaken by iniquities below it. I do not mean, of course, that anyone's heart is in heaven in the physical sense, but it is there by its way of life and sense of homeland, in accordance with scripture's assertion that *our citizenship is in heaven* (Phil 3:20). You cannot think directly about that city, because you do not see it yet. Do you want to think about heaven? Think about God's book, then. Hearken to a psalm: *On his law will the just person reflect day and night.* The same psalm declares that person blessed *who has not gone astray in the council of the ungodly, nor stood in the way of sinners, nor sat in the seat of pestilence, but whose will has been in the law of the Lord* (Ps 1:1-2). Observe the shining light in heaven: *On his law will the just person reflect day and night.* Does someone want to bear up under all trials? Then let him or her not come down from heaven, but meditate on the law of the Lord day and night. Such a person has a heart in heaven; and to one whose heart is in heaven, to one who meditates on God's law day and night, all the sins that are committed on earth in this present time, all the good luck that comes the way of bad people, and all the hardships of the righteous, are as nothing. This kind of person not only puts up with all of it, but will be blessed, because taught by God. How can he or she be in the firmament of heaven? Because the law is a firmament. So our psalm says, further on,[23] *Blessed is the person whom you train, O Lord; from your law you will have instructed him, to make him gentle through days of misery until a pit is dug for the sinner.* Watch the luminous bodies in the sky: see how they circle, and decline, and return, and pursue their courses, and distinguish day from night, and revolve through years and eons of time. Heinous deeds are done on earth, but they keep their peace in the sky. What is God teaching us? Let us study the psalm to find out.

---

22. This seems to be the meaning of the sentence: *Iam et hesterno die commemoravimus*; but possibly we could take it as "We have spoken of how things were yesterday, but...."
23. See verses 12-13 below.

The universal fairness of God's punitive judgments

7. *The Lord is a God of vengeance, and this avenging God has dealt faithfully.* Do you think he does not vindicate his rights? The *God of vengeance* certainly does. What does *God of vengeance* mean? The God who punishes.

At that you certainly begin to object that he does not assert his rights against evildoers. Do not grumble, or you may find yourself among those against whom he does vindicate his rights. That other fellow steals, and stays alive, so you grumble against God because the man who stole from you does not die. But check whether you steal yourself; and if you do not steal now, check whether you ever did before. If it is daytime for you now, remember your night; if you are set firmly in heaven now, recall your earthly days. You discover that you were a thief once, and perhaps you will find someone else who was peeved because, although you stole, you went on living and were not struck dead. You used to steal, but you were allowed to live so that later you would give up stealing; so do not hack down the bridge of God's mercy after you have crossed it. Do you not realize that many others will make the same crossing that you made? Would you be around today to grumble, if the person who complained about you earlier had been heard?

And yet here are you today hoping that God's vengeance will fall upon wrongdoers, so that a thief may die; and you murmur against God because the thief does not die. Weigh theft against blasphemy in the scales of equity. You say that you are not a thief now, but by grumbling against God you have become a blasphemer. The other fellow watches for his chance while his victim is asleep, so that he can seize something, and you say that God must be asleep because he does not see the thief. If you want the thief to restrain his hand, you must first restrain your tongue; if you want him to set his heart to rights with regard to his human neighbor, you set yours to rights with regard to God. Otherwise, while you are hoping to witness God's revenge, he may come and visit you first. For come he will. He will come and judge those who persist in their wickedness, those who were ungrateful for the mercy he held out to them without any prior deserving on their side, and those who are ungrateful for his patience, stirring up anger for themselves against the day of wrath when God's just judgment will be revealed. He will render to all as their deeds deserve,[24] because *the Lord is a God of vengeance, and this avenging God has dealt faithfully.*

When the Lord spoke, he excused no one. Our Lord himself was weak as to his flesh, but powerful in his words. He was no respecter of persons where the Jewish leaders were concerned. How harshly he denounced them! And yet, as the psalm says, he dealt faithfully; as another psalm passage says of him, *Now I will arise, because the needy are in wretched straits and the poor are groaning,*

---

24. See Rom 2:5-6.

says the Lord (Ps 11:6(12:5)). Who are the poor? Who are the needy? Those who have no hope, save in him alone who never lets us down. You must be quite clear who the poor and needy are, brothers and sisters. When scripture commends the poor, it is definitely not talking about people who have no possessions. How do we know this? Because you may find a poor man who suffers some injustice, and has no thought but to appeal to his patron. Perhaps he dwells in the powerful man's house, perhaps he is his lodger, his tenant-farmer, his client; and so he protests that he should not have to endure the injury, because he belongs to that important person. His heart trusts in a human being, his hope is in a human being, ashes in ashes. But there are others who are wealthy, and sustained for a time by the high esteem in which their fellows hold them; yet they rest their hope not on their riches, nor on their estates, nor on their well-established household, nor on the splendor of rank, which anyway does not last. They put all their hope in him who is never succeeded by anyone else because he cannot die, who cannot be deceived, and cannot deceive us. People of this stamp may have ample property as the world reckons, but they administer it well for the relief of the needy, and so they are themselves numbered among the Lord's poor. They see how precarious their life is, and recognize that they are pilgrims; they regard their wealth as no more than a temporary lodging to be used as a wayfarer uses a stable, intent on going further and with no thought of settling down there. What does the Lord declare? *Now I will arise, because the needy are in wretched straits and the poor are groaning, says the Lord. I will place their hope in salvation.*[25] Our salvation is our Savior, and in him God willed the hope of all destitute and needy people to be placed.

How about the next words? *In him I will deal confidently.* What does *I will deal confidently* suggest?[26] That Christ will not be timorous, nor will he be indulgent toward the vices and lusts of men and women. He was indeed a conscientious doctor who came equipped with the surgeon's knife of preaching to operate on all wounds. As such he had been prophesied and proclaimed of old, and precisely such did he prove himself to be. While speaking on the mountain he said, *Blessed are the poor in spirit, for the kingdom of heaven is theirs.* But there, in that same sermon, he also declared, *Blessed are those who suffer persecution in the cause of right, for the kingdom of heaven is theirs.* He willed to make them into shining heavenly bodies, able to bear patiently all such unjust but transient treatment, and so he assured them, *Blessed will you be when people persecute you, and speak all kinds of evil against you. Rejoice and dance for joy, because*

---

25. Literally "I will place in salvation." No object of the verb "place" is expressed, as Augustine remarked when commenting on Psalm 11(12); but in the present context he understands the object to be the hope of the unworldly rich. In both contexts he takes "salvation" to be a name for Christ.

26. The adverbs *fidenter* and *fiducialiter* which recur through this section and the next include the ideas of boldness and confidence in speech, truthfulness, and faithful dealing.

your reward is great in heaven (Mt 5:3.10-12). After this he continued with his inaugural sermon, and although there were people crowding round him, he said things to his disciples that would be like a slap in the face to the Pharisees and the Jews who were supposed to have the prerogative in expounding the scriptures. They considered themselves righteous, and were confident that they were reputed so, and the obedience of the people seemed to be an acknowledgement of their superior status. Yet Christ did not spare them. *When you pray, you must not be like the hypocrites who love to stand praying in synagogues and at street corners, to make sure of being seen* (Mt 6:5), he said, and other things like this. He touched every one of them and was afraid of none.

When he had finished this sermon, the gospel narrative says of him by way of summary, *It came about that when Jesus had completed all these sayings, the crowds were astonished at his teaching; for he was teaching them like someone who had authority, not like the scribes and Pharisees* (Mt 7:28-29). Think how fiercely he spoke, this man of whom it could be said, *He was teaching them like someone who had authority*! How boldly he castigated them: *Woe to you, scribes and Pharisees, hypocrites!* (Mt 23:13-15). How confidently he said it to their faces! He was afraid of no one. Why not? Because he is the God of vengeance. He spared them nothing in his words, because he wanted to find them later the kind of people he could spare at his judgment, whereas if they refused to accept the medicine of the word they would incur the sentence of the judge and certainly fall under it.[27] Why so? Because, as the psalm says, *the Lord is a God of vengeance, and this avenging God has dealt faithfully*; so his denunciations spared no one. If he spared no one in his words when he was himself destined to suffer, will he spare them in his sentence when he comes to judge? If in his humble estate he was afraid of no one, will he be afraid of anyone in his glory? From his faithful dealings at that first coming, infer how he will act at the end of the world.

For your part, then, do not grumble against God when he appears to let bad people down lightly. Rather be good yourself, so that even if his chastisements do not spare you in this present time, he may spare you at the judgment. *The Lord is a God of vengeance, and this avenging God has dealt faithfully.*

Verse 2. Retribution will fall only on the proud

8. He dealt confidently, and they could not endure his truthfulness. He had come in humility, he had clothed himself in mortal flesh and had come to die; he had come not to do what sinners do but to suffer what sinners suffer. Because he had come for this purpose, and because he had dealt faithfully and they could not endure the truthful condemnations he had uttered, what did they do? They seized

---

27. Variant: "…would incur the sentence of the judge who is to come."

him, scourged him, mocked him, punched him, spat at him, crowned him with thorns, hoisted him onto a cross, and finally killed him. But what follows upon his faithful dealing? *Be exalted, you who judge the earth.* Do you think that because they laid hands on a humble man, they will lay their hands on him in his high glory? Do you not think that, having passed judgment on a mortal, they will be judged by the immortal? What does the psalm say? *Be exalted,* you who dealt so faithfully. The iniquitous could not endure your bold, faithful speech, and they thought they had dealt with you by taking hold of you and crucifying you. It should have been by faith that they took hold of you; but no, they grasped you with persecuting hands. Because you dealt confidently among the wicked, and never cringed to any of them, and because you suffered, *be exalted* now, rise again, and depart for heaven. And let it be the Church's part also to suffer patiently, because the Church's head suffered patiently.

Be exalted, you who judge the earth; give the proud their just deserts. He will, brothers and sisters, he will. What does it mean, this plea, *Be exalted, you who judge the earth; give the proud their just deserts*? It is a prophecy uttered by one who foretells events, not a peremptory order; for we cannot think that because the prophet said, *Be exalted, you who judge the earth,* Christ obeyed the prophet's orders by rising again and ascending to heaven. It is the other way round: the prophet foretold it because that was what Christ was going to do. Christ did not do it because the prophet had foretold it; rather the prophet had foretold it because he would later do it. The prophet sees in the Spirit[28] the humble Christ. He sees him humble, afraid of no one, sparing no one in his words, and says of him, *He has dealt faithfully.* Then he sees this man who has dealt so boldly and faithfully being arrested; he sees him crucified, he sees him humiliated, he sees him rising again and ascending into heaven, and coming again to judge those at whose hands he suffered all this ill-treatment. So the prophet cries, *Be exalted, you who judge the earth; give the proud their just deserts.*

It is to the proud that he will mete out punishment, not the humble. Who are the proud? Those who think little of doing bad things, and then want to defend their sins. This is an important distinction, for among those who crucified Christ wonderful things happened later. Many of the Jews themselves believed, and the blood of Christ came to them as a gift. Their hands were impious and stained with Christ's blood, but he whose blood they had spilt washed them. These people, who had looked upon his mortal body and hounded him, were now joined to his body, the Church. They spilt their own ransom so that they might drink their own ransom, for many of them were afterward converted. Seeing many miracles worked by the apostles, several thousand people believed in a single day,[29] and they proved to be such close kin to the disciples that they sold

---

28. Or "in his spirit."
29. See Acts 4:4.

all their possessions and laid the price of their property at the apostles' feet, so that provision could be made for everyone according to need.[30] There was but one mind and one heart among them,[31] among these very people who had crucified the Lord. Why was no punishment meted out to them? Because of the principle, *give the proud their just deserts*, and these people had no mind to be proud. When they watched many miracles being wrought through the name of Christ, whom they thought they had killed, they were very disconcerted, and heard Peter declaring in whose name the miracles were worked. (You see, the servants had no wish to arrogate to themselves the power of their Lord by claiming that what had been done by him, using them as agents, was their own work. As servants they gave credit to their Lord, stating that the deeds which evoked the Jews' wonder were performed in the name of him whom the Jews had crucified.) The hearers were humbled, and pierced to the heart. In distress, they confessed their sin and sought advice. *What shall we do, then?* they asked. They were not despairing of salvation, but seeking a remedy. Then Peter answered, *Repent, and let every one of you be baptized in the name of our Lord Jesus Christ* (Acts 2:37.38). Those who repented were humble, and were therefore not punished, for look what our psalm says: *Be exalted, you who judge the earth; give the proud their just deserts.* These penitents were excluded from the number of the proud; and for them the Lord's prayer, offered on the cross, had its full effect: *Father, forgive them, for they do not know what they are doing* (Lk 23:34). *Be exalted, you who judge the earth; give the proud their just deserts.* Will he mete out punishment? Yes, but only to the proud.

Verses 3-4. The psalm is therapeutic. Why is God so patient?

9. But when? When will he requite them? Meanwhile the wicked triumph, the wicked exult, the wicked blaspheme and commit all manner of crimes. Does this upset you? Seek the reason in a spirit of devotion, not of carping pride. Does it upset you? The psalm grieves with you, and asks questions with you, but not because it does not know. Rather does it ask with you the question to which it knows the answer, so that in it you may find what you did not know. Anyone who wants to console someone else acts like this: unless he grieves with the other, he cannot lift him up. First of all he grieves with him, and then he strengthens him with a consoling word. If he laughs at the other's sorrow when he comes in to see him, he is not heeding the advice given by the apostle in the passage we read just now, that we should *rejoice with those who rejoice, and weep with those who weep* (Rom 12:15). You first weep with him so that afterward he may rejoice with you; you share his sorrow in order to refresh him. So too the psalm, and

30. See Acts 2:44-45.
31. See Acts 4:32.

indeed the Spirit of God, though knowing everything, ask questions with you, as though putting your own thoughts into words.[32]

How long will sinners gloat, O Lord, how long? They are ready with answers, but all they will say is iniquitous. So will they speak, all those who commit iniquity. What will they say, those folk who ask, "What use is it to us to live in the way we do?" What else will they utter, except objections against God? And what will you say, when they ask, "Does God really take any notice of what we do?" Sinners take the fact that they go on living to mean that God cannot know what they are up to. Consider: does anything bad happen to them? If any police officer[33] knew of their doings he would apprehend them; so they keep out of the officer's sight to avoid instant arrest. But no one can keep out of God's sight, for he not only sees you in your private room,[34] he sees even the innermost places of your heart. Some sinners realize that nothing can be hidden from God. Yet they know what they have done, and that they continue to live although God also knows it, and that they would not be left alive if the police knew. So they tell themselves, "These actions of ours must please God! It's quite obvious that if our deeds were as offensive to him as they are to judges, and kings, and emperors, and notaries,[35] we would not be able to escape God's scrutiny as we escape theirs, would we? So our activities must be acceptable to God."

To refute this theory a sinner is warned in another psalm, *All this you did, and I was silent; but you were wrong to think that I will be like you* (Ps 49(50):21). What does it mean—*that I will be like you*? It means, "You imagine that because your bad deed pleases you, it will please me as well." And the last word is *I will rebuke you*. So he who said, *I was silent*, is not silent now. In that psalm he said, *All this you did, and I was silent; but you were wrong to think that I will be like you*; but he has not altogether kept silence, for when we speak, he is not silent, when the reader proclaims the reading, he is not silent, and when the psalm sings of these truths, he is not silent. All these voices are God's voice, resounding all round the world. In what sense, then, does he keep silence, and in what sense is he not silent? He is not silent as to speech, but he is silent with regard to punishment. How are we to take *All this you did, and I was silent*? "You did all this, and I did not punish you; but *you were wrong to think that I will be like you*." He speaks in another place of this silence with regard to punishment, this delaying

---

32. These lines are a good example of Augustine's conviction that the prayer of the psalms can be therapeutic.
33. *Stationarius*. The *stationarii* were detachments of soldiers on police duty, stationed in various places throughout the provinces and answerable to the governors. Their duty was to inform the magistrates of notorious offenses.
34. See Mt 6:6.
35. *Commentariensibus*. The Maurists note that the *commentarienses* were prison governors and notaries whose duty it was to keep records of imprisonments and offenders, and to handle indictments.

of vengeance: *I have long been silent and patient, but shall I be silent for ever?* (Is 42:14, LXX).

How long will sinners gloat, O Lord, how long? They are ready with answers, but all they will say is iniquitous. So will they speak, all those who commit iniquity. And it means sins of all kinds. *They are ready with answers, but all they will say is iniquitous*. Answers? What does that suggest? That they have some retort when a righteous person confronts them. Some good person comes along and says to a sinner, "Don't commit that sin." "Why not?" "Because you may die." "But I have committed the sin, so why don't I die? And that other fellow lived a righteous life, and he did die. How did that happen? I sinned, yet God has not done away with me. Why not? You can see for yourself that that man acted justly, so why did God punish him like that? And why does that other person have such a hard time of it?" They are ready with answers, you see; they have plenty to say; and because God spares them they find in his divine patience a basis for their argument.

But God's reason for sparing them is quite different from what they assume it to be when they argue from the fact that they are allowed to live. The apostle tells us why God holds back, explaining how God's plan is served by his patience: *Do you, who behave so, suppose that you will escape the judgment of God? Do you despise his generous kindness and forbearance, not realizing that God is patient only to lead you to repentance? But you*—he means the person who argues, "If God were not pleased with me, he would not be sparing me"; and now look what such a person is storing up, according to the apostle: *but you with your hard and impenitent heart are storing up against yourself anger that will be manifest on the day of God's just judgment, for he will render to each and all as their deeds deserve* (Rom 2:3-4.5-6). God is stretching his forbearance while you are heaping up your sin. The treasure stored up for those who have not scorned mercy will be everlasting mercy; but the treasure stored up for you will be one of wrath. Day by day you add a little, but later you will find a heap; you add to it in minute quantities, but what you will find is a towering mass. Do not regard your daily sins as tiny, for it is from tiny drops that rivers are filled.

Verses 5-7. Two deluded assessments

10. How do they react, those people who are ready with their answers? All they will say is iniquitous, but what do they do, seeing that they are spared, in spite of their wicked deeds? *They have humiliated your people, O Lord*, which means those well-intentioned persons over whom all bad people try to domineer. *They have humiliated your people, O Lord; they have harassed your heritage, killed widow and orphan, and slain the proselyte*. This last refers to any pilgrim,

foreigner, or stranger, whom the psalm calls a proselyte.[36] These points are all perfectly clear, so we need not delay over them.

11. *And they have claimed, The Lord will not see.* "He takes no notice of such things," they say. "He ignores them. He has other matters to take care of, he knows nothing about it." So we hear about two positions adopted by the wicked. One we have discussed already: *all this you did, and I was silent; but you were wrong to think that I will be like you.* What is implied by *that I will be like you*? You think that I see your actions, but find them acceptable, since I do not punish you. The other position taken by the wicked is this: "God takes no notice of such things; he does not look to see how I am leading my life. God does not care about me. Among all the things he has to attend to, does he have time for me? Do I really count with him? Does he take account of men and women at all?" Wretched doubter, he cared enough to give you existence, and does he not care whether you live your life in the right way? But these unhappy folk think, *The Lord will not see, nor will the God of Jacob understand.*

Verses 8-11. The all-wise Lord is instructing you, and offering you understanding

12. *Understand now, you stupid ones among the people; fools, learn wisdom at last.* God is educating his people; he knows that the steps of a man or woman may begin to slide when we see the prosperity enjoyed by sinners.[37] A person may be living a good life as one of God's saints—among the children of the Church, I mean. But then he observes how the wicked flourish in spite of their iniquity; so he is jealous of them and tempted to imitate their conduct, for he sees that as long as he lives a good, humble life, hoping for a reward in this world, he is getting nowhere.

If such a person hopes for a reward in the future, however, he or she will certainly not be disappointed; it is just that the time for receiving it has not yet come. You are at work in the vineyard, so do your work, and you will get your wages. You would not demand your pay from a human employer before the job was done, so why demand it of God before you do the job? But that is not all: this patience is itself part of your work, and it will enhance your reward. If you are unwilling to hold out patiently, you are opting to do less in the vineyard, because patient endurance is part of the work, and therefore necessary if you are to earn your wages. If, on the contrary, you are a grudging worker, you must be careful lest you not only lose your reward, but even incur punishment for choosing to be a grumbler. A worker of that type keeps an eye on the householder who hired

---

36. Strictly, one who had come from the Gentiles to embrace the Jewish faith, but more loosely any traveler or foreigner. Compare note at Exposition of Psalm 69,7.

37. See Ps 72(73):2-3.

him to work in the vineyard; he waits for the moment when the employer is not looking so that he can begin to loiter and not do his work properly. When the employer looks his way again, the hired man works busily. But God hired you, and he does not turn his eyes away. You are not allowed to do your work in a grudging spirit. The eyes of the householder are on you all the time. Look for a chance to trick him and slacken off, if you can.[38]

So then, if any of you were perhaps harboring jealous thoughts when you observed the successes of the wicked, and if those thoughts had begun to set your feet a-slither from God's path, this psalm is speaking to you. But if none of you were in that state, it speaks to others through you when it says, *Understand now*. Those others said, *The Lord will not see, nor will the God of Jacob understand*; and so to them the psalm now appeals: *Understand now, you stupid ones among the people; fools, learn wisdom at last*.

13. *Will he who implanted the ear not hear?* Has he no means of hearing, he who created the means of hearing for you? *Will he who implanted the ear, not hear? Or will he who fashioned the eye not observe? Will he who educates the nations not rebuke them?* This last phrase demands your most careful attention, my brothers and sisters. *Will he who educates the nations not rebuke them?* This is what God is doing at present—educating the nations. This is why he sent his word to people all over the world. He sent it through angels, through patriarchs, through prophets, through his servants, through countless heralds who ran ahead of the judge. Then he sent his Word in person. He sent his only Son; and he sent the servants of his Son, and in those servants he sent the Son himself. Everywhere, all over the world, God's word is preached. Is there any place where people are not admonished, "Leave your former iniquities behind, and turn your steps into straight paths. God is sparing you only to give you a chance to correct yourselves; the only reason why he did not punish you yesterday was that he wants you to lead better lives today"? He is instructing the nations, then; so is he likely to hold back from reproof? Will he not listen for the response of those whom he is teaching? Will he not judge those to whom he has already sent his word, those among whom it has already been sown? If you were in school, would you just take in what you were taught, but never expect to reproduce it? Obviously if you are listening to a master's lesson you are being educated; but does the teacher simply hand out knowledge to you, and never expect you to play it back to him? And when you begin to recite it back, will you be without any fear of being beaten?[39]

Now is the time for taking in what is given to us, but later we shall stand before our teacher and rehearse our whole past. We shall be asked to give an

---

38. In the preceding sentences Augustine has been addressing a single "you." In the next paragraph the verbs become plural as he speaks more generally to the congregation.

39. This seems to echo Augustine's own miseries as a small boy terrified of thrashings; compare his *Confessions* I,9,14-15.

account of all that is being imparted to us now. Listen to the apostle's testimony: *We will all have to stand before Christ's judgment seat, that each of us may receive due recompense for what we have done in the body, good or bad* (2 Cor 5:10; Rom 14:10). *Will he who educates the nations not rebuke them, he who teaches human beings knowledge?*[40] If he causes you to know, must he not know himself, *he who teaches human beings knowledge?*

14. *The Lord knows human thoughts, and knows them as empty.* Even if you are unaware of God's thoughts, and do not know them as just, he *knows human thoughts, and knows them as empty.* There have been people who know God's thoughts, the ones to whom he discloses his plan because he has already become their friend.[41] As for you, my brothers and sisters, you must not underrate yourselves; if you too draw near to God with faith, you too hear what he is thinking. You are learning about his thoughts at this very moment. You are being informed and instructed why God spares wicked people for the present, so that you may not be tempted to murmur against the God who *teaches human beings knowledge. The Lord knows human thoughts, and knows them as empty.* Abandon those empty human thoughts, then, so that you may comprehend the thoughts of God, wise thoughts. But who comprehends God's thoughts? Only the person whose place is in the firmament of heaven. We sang about this earlier, and we have discussed and explained it already.[42]

Verses 12-13. The humility of a sinner is more acceptable to God than the complacency of one who lives virtuously

15. *Blessed is the person whom you train, O Lord; from your law you will have instructed him, to make him gentle through days of misery, until a pit is dug for the sinner.* Here you have the logic of God's plan, whereby he spares wrongdoers: a pit is being dug for the sinner. You want him buried straightaway, but don't be in too much of a hurry to see his funeral: the pit is still being dug for him. Yet what does the psalm mean by *until a pit is dug for the sinner?* Or, rather, whom does it call a sinner? Some particular individual? No. What does it have in mind, then? The whole human race of sinners? No, sinners who are proud; for it said earlier, *Give the proud their just deserts.* After all, the tax collector in the gospel was a sinner. He had cast his eyes to the ground and was beating his breast, saying, *O God, be merciful to me, a sinner* (Lk 18:13); but because this man was not proud, and it is to the proud that God gives their just deserts, the pit is being dug not for those like him but for proud sinners, in anticipation of the day when God will give them what they deserve. When you hear the psalm say, *Until a pit is dug for the sinner*, you must understand that it refers to the proud.

40. Variant: "wisdom."
41. See Amos 3:7.
42. See section 5 above.

Now who is proud? One who does not repent by confessing his sins, in order to be healed by humility. Who is proud? A person who tries to arrogate to himself the few good deeds he seems to have, and thereby detracts from God's mercy. Who is proud? One who, though ascribing his good actions to God, insults others who do not perform similarly, and exalts himself above them. The Pharisee in the story did go so far as to say, *O God, I thank you* (Lk 18:11); he did not say, "I achieve all this by myself." He was thanking God for his achievements, so he was aware both that he did good things, and that he did them with God's help. So why was he rebuked? Because he was insulting the tax collector.

Pay close attention now, so that you may grow to maturity. The first thing for any man or any woman is confession of sins. This is the salutary repentance which is powerful for correcting a sinner without mocking God. After repentance, when such a person has begun to lead a good life, he still needs to be careful not to attribute that good conduct to his own strength, but to give thanks to God, by whose grace it has come about that he should live virtuously; for it is God who calls him and God who has enlightened him. Is this person perfect now? No, not yet; something is still missing. What does he still need? He needs to beware of arrogance with regard to others who do not yet live as he does. Anyone who avoids this can be without anxiety; not for such a person will be the retribution demanded by the psalm: *Give the proud their just deserts*. This one is not among those for whom the pit is being dug.

How different was the Pharisee who kept on saying, *I thank you that I am not like other people: frauds, robbers, adulterers, like that tax collector there*! How he glorified himself by saying, *I am not like that tax collector there* (Lk 18:11)! But the other, hanging his head, would only strike his breast, saying, *O God, be merciful to me, a sinner*. The one was proud about his good deeds, the other humble in his bad deeds. And mark well, brothers and sisters, humility over bad deeds was more acceptable to God than pride in good deeds, so hateful are the proud to God. This is why the parable ends, *Truly I tell you, that tax collector went down to his house at rights with God, rather than the Pharisee*. And the reason is added: *for anyone who exalts himself will be humbled, but the one who humbles himself will be exalted* (Lk 18:14).

My brothers and sisters, we learn that Christ has taught us humility even from[43] this fact alone, that God became human. This is the humility that pagans find offensive, and provokes the insults they fling at us: "What kind of God do you worship? A God who was born! What kind of God do you worship? A God who was crucified!" The humility of Christ is offensive to the proud; but if it is beautiful in your sight, Christian, imitate it. If you imitate it you will not find it laborious, because he himself invited us, *Come to me, all you who labor and are heavily burdened, and learn from me, for I am gentle and humble of heart* (Mt

---

43. Variant: "…we do not say that Christ has taught us humility from…."

11:28.29). This is what Christian learning is about: no one does anything good, except by Christ's grace. When a person acts wrongly, the wrong is his own doing; when well, the good he does is done by God's gift. When someone begins to behave well, let such a one not attribute it to himself or herself; and when the good is not claimed for self, let the doer give thanks to the one whose gift has made it possible. But when we do act well, let us not insult anyone else who does not act so, or exalt ourselves above others; for God's grace is not used up on us, leaving none to reach those other folk.

16. *To make him gentle through days of misery, until a pit is dug for the sinner.* This means that you, who are a Christian, must be gentle during the days of misery; for miserable indeed are the days when sinners seem to flourish and the just struggle. But the struggles of the righteous are the chastisement imposed by their Father, while the prosperity of sinners is the pit of their downfall. Now, when you are told that God makes you gentle through days of misery, until a pit is dug for the sinner, you must not imagine that even now angels are stationed somewhere, equipped with mattocks, busy digging a huge pit to hold the entire race of evildoers. You might think in carnal terms, seeing how many bad people there are, and wonder to yourselves, "What pit can be big enough to hold such a multitude of rascals, such an enormous crowd of sinners? How long will it take to dig it deep enough to contain them all? Surely it will never be finished? That must be why God spares sinners." No, that is not right. The pit prepared for sinners is the very prosperity they enjoy; they fall into it as into a pit. You must think clearly about this, brothers and sisters, because it is a daring thing to assert that prosperity is a pit, the pit being dug for the sinner. But so it is: in his own mysterious justice God spares a person he knows to be a sinner, and the sinner is made more smug and arrogant by the very fact of being spared by God. So he thinks he is in a lofty place, and he falls: he falls simply by thinking himself exalted. The sinner regards his elevated position as a mark of grandeur, but God calls it a pit. A pit is sunk deep, not lifted toward the sky; yet proud sinners who seem to raise themselves skyward are really sinking into the earth. Humble people, on the contrary, by abasing themselves toward the earth, ascend to heaven.

Grow gentle, then, believer, if you have been trained by God's law. Then your heart will be established in the firmament of heaven; for God made the great lights on the fourth day, the fourth of the week, from which this psalm took its title. As you watch those luminaries patiently pursuing their courses, heedless of what human beings say about them, so must you too disregard whatever flesh and blood may do to you. Every human being is, after all, flesh and blood, and you are in no way inferior to the fleshly creature who seems to be treading you down, because he who will one day bring both you and your persecutor to trial[44]

---

44. Some codices omit "who will ... trial."

himself took flesh for your sake, and for you poured out his own blood. If he paid so high a price for you in advance, when you were an infidel, what must he be keeping for you now that you are a believer? Let this thought make you gentle and humble.

How ought your gentle humility to show itself? It should inspire you to reflect, "The wicked flourish because[45] God wills it so. He wills to spare bad people, and by sparing them he leads some to repentance. As for those who are not corrected, he knows how to judge them." But if anyone tries to call into question either the goodness, or the patience, or the power of the Lord, or the justice of the judge, such a person is anything but gentle and meek. He is rearing up against God in pride, and God thrusts him down. His very act of rising against God plunges him into the deep, for another psalm attests, *You threw them down even as they were lifting themselves up* (Ps 72(73):18). Notice that it does not say, "You threw them down because they were lifting themselves up," or "You threw them down after they had lifted themselves up," implying that their self-exaltation and their overthrow were separated in time. It says that in the very moment when they lifted themselves up they were being overthrown. In the measure that the heart of a man or a woman grows proud, in that same measure it moves away from God, and if it withdraws from God it plunges into the depths. A humble heart, on the contrary, draws God down from heaven to be very near it. God is on high, certainly; God is above the highest heavens, he transcends all the angels. How high would you have to reach to touch that sublime majesty? I would not like you to overstrain yourself by stretching so far. No, I have better advice for you, a plan that will save you from possible injury through your proud effort at over-extension. God is most high, to be sure; but humble yourself, and he will stoop down to you.

Verse 14. Temporary suffering is chastisement, not rejection

17. We have heard why he spares the wicked, and in what sense this forbearance can itself be their downfall. But God says to you, "It is not for you to know how or why the pit is dug for them; your business is to learn from my law how to be patient *until a pit is dug for the sinner.*" Yet you protest, "What about me? I am having a hard time, and struggling amid these same sinners." You will get your answer in the next line of the psalm: *the Lord will not cast off his people.* He puts them through their paces, but he does not cast them off. What does another text of scripture have to say? *Those whom the Lord loves, he corrects, and he whips every child whom he accepts* (Heb 12:6). He accepts those he whips: are you so presumptuous as to say he casts them off? We see human fathers behave in the same way toward their children. They sometimes wash their hands of

---

45. Some codices omit these first four words.

those children of whom they have no hope, leaving them to live as they choose; but they chastise the ones of whom their hopes are high. It is the ones they regard as hopeless and ungovernable whom they allow to go off and act as they please. But when a father allows his child to depart and behave without restraint, he does not intend to admit that child to the inheritance. He reserves the inheritance for the child he whips.

When God whips his child, that child should run beneath the hand of our severe Father, because in chastising us he is educating us with a view to our inheritance. A child under the lash is being educated and prepared to inherit, not being rejected. The chastisement has no other purpose. He or she must not be so silly and childish as to say, "Father must love my brother more, because he allows him to do whatever he likes, whereas if I make any move against my father's orders, the whip descends on me." You, for your part, should rejoice under the chastisement, because it means that an inheritance is saved up for you, for *the Lord will not cast off his people.* He corrects you for a time, but does not condemn you for eternity; he spares those others for a time, but will condemn them for eternity. Take your choice: do you prefer temporal hardship, or eternal punishment? Temporal prosperity, or eternal life? What does God threaten us with? Punishment that will last for ever. What does God promise? Everlasting rest. His policy of chastising good people lasts only for a time; his forbearance with the wicked lasts only for a time; because *the Lord will not cast off his people, nor will he abandon his inheritance.*

Verse 15. Rectitude of heart: Christ prefigured our weakness in his agony

18. The psalm continues, *Until justice is changed into judgment; all who have justice are right of heart.* Think about this, and make sure that you have justice, since you cannot have judgment yet. You need to have justice first, but later this very justice of yours will be converted into judgment. Here on earth the apostles had justice and they endured wrongdoers; but what were they promised? *You will sit upon twelve thrones, judging the twelve tribes of Israel* (Mt 19:28). Their justice is to be converted into judgment, it seems. If anyone is just now, that justice enables him or her to suffer evils and bear up under them; the time of suffering must be endured, but the day for judging will come. But why should I speak only of God's servants? The Lord himself is judge of all the living and the dead, yet he willed first to submit to judgment, and only so to come to his act of judging.

Until justice is changed into judgment; all who have justice are right of heart. Those who have justice now do not judge yet, for it is necessary to have justice first, and to judge afterward. Justice first of all puts up with the wicked, and later judges the wicked. Let justice abound now, and it will be converted into judgment later. Justice endures bad people for as long as God wills, and for as long as

God's Church goes on bearing with them, that it may be exercised through their malice. But for all that, God will not reject his people. These things will last only *until justice is changed into judgment.*

All who have justice are right of heart. Who are the right of heart? Those who want what God wants. God spares sinners, but you want him to destroy sinners straightaway. If you want one thing when God wants something else, you are a person of twisted heart and depraved will. God wants to spare the wicked, and you want no forbearance to be shown them; God is patier: with sinners, and you are unwilling to tolerate them. As I was saying, if you want one thing when God wants something different, it is for you to turn your heart around and direct it toward God, for the Lord has shown compassion on the weak. In his body, the Church, he saw weak people who at first would attempt to follow their own wills, but on seeing that God willed differently would redirect themselves and their hearts to accept God's will and follow it. Do not try to twist God's will to fit your own, but correct your will by aligning it with God's. God's will then serves as a kind of ruler for you. But if you have bent your ruler, how will you be straightened? In fact God's will cannot be bent out of true; it is an unchangeable norm. As long as you have this absolutely true rule you can convert yourself and correct your crookedness; you have the means to straighten out whatever is twisted in you.

But what do people try to do? It is less important that their own wills are twisted: what is worse is that they even try to twist God's will to fit in with their own hearts, so that God may do what they want, when they ought to be doing what God wants.

19. How did our Lord marry two wills so that they became one in the humanity he bore? In his body, the Church, there would be some people who, after wanting to do their own will, would later follow the will of God. The Lord prefigured these people in himself. He wanted to show that though they are weak, they still belong to him, and so he represented them in advance in his own person.[46] He sweated blood from his whole body, as a sign that the blood of martyrs would gush from his body, the Church. The blood burst from every pore of his body because that was how the Church would have its martyrs: the blood covered his body entirely. He prefigured certain weak persons in himself, in his own body; and because he felt compassion for them he cried out in the name of these weak members, *Father, if it is possible, let this cup pass from me.* He revealed the human will that was in him, but if he had continued to insist on that will, he would have seemed to display perversity of heart. If you recognize that he has had compassion on you, and is setting you free in himself, imitate the next prayer he made: *Yet not what I will, but what you will be done, Father* (Mt 26:39). If some human impulse begins to invade your mind, and you find your-

---

46. *Eos praefiguravit in se*, twice repeated in this sentence, a key phrase in Augustine's Christology.

self wishing, "If only God would kill that enemy of mine, so that I could be rid of his harassment! Oh, if only things could be different, so that I did not have to put up with so much from him!" then if you keep to that line, and find the idea pleasing, although you see that God does not will it, you are crooked of heart. And this means that you lack the justice which is destined to be changed into judgment, because all who have this justice *are right of heart*.

Who are *right of heart?* Those who prove themselves to be like Job, who said, *The Lord gave, and the Lord has taken away. This has happened as the Lord willed: may the Lord's name be blessed* (Jb 1:21). There is rightness of heart for you. The devil had left Job his wife, not killing her along with all the rest, but left her not as a consoler for her husband but as an accomplice for himself. So what did Job, in his gravely wounded condition, say to her? The devil remembered that Adam had been beguiled by Eve, so he thought that this Eve would further his purposes. She approached Job, playing the role of Eve; but this Adam on his dunghill won a nobler victory than did the Adam who had been vanquished in paradise. What reply did he make to the woman? Observe a heart well prepared, a straightforward heart. Was he not suffering persecutions, and grievous ones at that? He was; and so do all Christians. Even if human beings are not on the rampage, the devil is prowling, full of ferocity; even if emperors have embraced Christianity, has the devil become a Christian? Look closely, holy brethren,[47] and see what rectitude of heart is. The woman approached Job, and urged, *Curse God, and die* (Jb 2:9). But he recognized Eve in her, and willed to regain the place whence he[48] had fallen. His heart was fixed in God like a star in the firmament, because in his heart he dwelt in God's book.[49] *You have spoken like the silly woman you are*, he replied. *If we have received good things from the Lord's hands*, should we not endure the bad too? (Jb 2:10). His heart was right and straight because it was fixed in God. God is right and straight, so when you fix your heart in him he becomes a pattern for you, on which you can straighten your heart. Establish your heart in him, then, and it will be straight.

But perhaps human desire has been sidling up to you, and some kind of carnal weakness cajoling[50] your mind? Do not despair. The Lord in his weakness prefigured you, rather than speaking for himself; for the Lord, who was to rise again on the third day, was not afraid to suffer. We could go further, and say that if he had been no more than a man confronted with suffering (rather than one who as God had come on purpose to suffer) who yet knew that he would rise again after three days, he could not possibly have dreaded death; for Paul did not

---

47. *Sanctitas vestra.*
48. Adam.
49. For the imagery of the saints on earth dwelling like stars in God's firmament, see section 5 above; for the imagery of the scriptures as a skin (tent) stretched out like the sky, see section 6.
50. Reading *lactabat* with the CCL editors, from *lacto*, "allure, beguile, dupe, cajole"; but most codices have *iactabat*, "shake, toss."

dread it, even though his resurrection would take place only at the end of the world. He declared, *I am hard pressed on both sides. I long to die and to be with Christ, for that is much the best; but it is necessary for you that I remain in the flesh* (Phil 1:23-24). To remain in the flesh would be wearisome for him, and caught between the two he suffered ardent longing, for to die and be with Christ would be the better option by far. Indeed, how he leapt for joy as his passion drew near! *I have fought the good fight, I have run the whole course, I have kept the faith; all that remains for me now is the crown of righteousness which the just judge will award me on that day*, he exclaims (2 Tm 4:7-8). Paul rejoices at the prospect of being crowned, yet Christ, who is to crown him, is saddened. The apostle is jubilant, while Christ our Lord is praying, *Father, if it is possible, let this cup pass from me* (Mt 26:39). But he had taken that sadness upon himself in the same way as he had taken flesh. I do not mean that the Lord was not truly sad: do not take my words in that way. If we were to say that his sadness was not real, when the gospel testifies, *My soul is sorrowful to the point of death* (Mt 26:38), we would have to assert likewise that when the gospel says, "Jesus slept,"[51] he did not really sleep, and when it says, "Jesus ate,"[52] he did not really eat. Then a little worm of rottenness wriggles in, leaving nothing sound, for we should be saying that his body was not real, and that he did not have true flesh.

So was he sad? Certainly he was sad, but he voluntarily accepted sadness as he had voluntarily accepted flesh; and just as he freely took on real flesh, so he freely took on real sadness. He chose to manifest it in himself for your sake, because human weakness may creep up on you, and you may begin to will something that God does not will. Then you will see that your crooked heart is not lying true with the ruler, and you can align it with the ruler, directing to God that heart of yours which by following its human bent had begun to go crooked. The Lord was displaying your inclination when he said, *My soul is sorrowful to the point of death* and *Father, if it is possible, let this cup pass from me*. But in order to teach you, he added, *Yet not what I will, but what you will be done* (Mt 26:39); and you must immediately do the same.

If you do this, you will have justice, and if you have justice, you have rectitude of heart. If your heart is right, that justice which at present must practice endurance will be converted into judgment; and later on, when your Lord comes to judge, you will not only be without fear of doom, but will even glory in the crown you have won. Then you will see how God's patience has achieved its ends, both in the punishment of the wicked and in awarding you your crown. You do not see this yet; but believe in what you do not yet see, so that you may have no occasion to blush when you do see it, *until justice is changed into judgment; all who have justice are right of heart.*

---

51. See Mk 4:38.
52. See Lk 14:1.

Verses 16-17. The just person, beset by temptation, finds help in the Lord

20. *Who will arise to help me against people of ill-will? Or who will stand by me against those who commit iniquity?* Many people urge you to many evil deeds, and the snake never tires of whispering suggestions to lure you to iniquity. If you have perhaps made some progress, then whichever way you turn, looking for someone in whose company you may live a holy life, you will scarcely find one. But there are plenty of bad people all round you, because though the grains are few, the chaff is abundant. The threshing floor certainly does contain the grains you seek, but they are still in difficulties. Once they are separated from the chaff they will form a big heap; the grains seem few now, but only when compared with the straw, for in themselves they are numerous. Mean-while, the bad people all around you raise their din, demanding, "Why do you live so unconventionally? Do you think you're the only Christian around? Why can't you behave like other people? Why don't you watch shows and fights[53] along with the rest of us? Why don't you make use of spells and lucky charms? Why not consult astrologers and soothsayers, like everyone else?" You make the sign of the cross, and reply, "I am a Christian," and so you fend off these challengers; but the enemy is still pressing you hard and harassing you. What is worse, he chokes Christians with the example set by other Christians. And so the Christian soul sweats and gasps and is sorely disturbed. It has the means of conquering; but will it find the power within itself? Hardly. Listen to what it says, for it has an answer ready: "What good would it do me if I were to resort to spells for a cure, and so win a few extra days? Then I would depart from this world and go to meet my Lord, and he would cast me into the fire. Because I reckoned those few days better than eternal life, he would send me to hell." "Hell? What do you mean?" "The hell of God's eternal condemnation." "But would that really happen? You surely don't think God cares how human beings live their lives, do you?"

Furthermore, it may not be only your friend who talks to you like this in the street; it may be your wife at home. Or it may be a husband who plays the role of seducer to a good, faithful, holy wife. If the wife beguiles her husband, she plays Eve to him; if the husband beguiles his wife, he plays the devil to her. Either she is Eve to you, or you are the snake to her. Again, sometimes a father tries to reach an amicable agreement even with his own son,[54] yet finds him wicked and thoroughly depraved. The father is agitated, he wavers, he casts about for a means to

---

53. *Quare non spectas?* The *spectacula* on offer included plays, to which Augustine had himself been addicted in his student days (see his *Confessions* III,2,2), gladiatorial contests, which had nearly been the undoing of his close friend Alypius (see *Confessions* VI,8,13), and chariot races.

54. Or, perhaps, "tries to imbue his son with his own principles."

prevail, he is almost drowning, almost ready to acquiesce—but may God stand by him. Listen to the psalm: *Who will arise to help me against people of ill-will?* There are so many of them. Wherever I look, they are rushing at me. Who will confront the devil, the prince of ill-will, and his angels, and the men and women seduced by him?

21. *If the Lord had not come to my aid, my soul would soon have made its home in hell.* "I had almost fallen headlong into the pit dug for sinners": this is what is meant by *my soul would soon have made its home in hell.* The psalmist was already staggering, already almost consenting; but he looked to the Lord. Suppose, for example, he was being insulted by those who were tempting him to sin. Sometimes a gang of wicked people make fun of the good, especially if they are many, and they try it on with a good person who is all alone. They are like the wads of chaff that surround a solitary grain, though they will not stick together when the whole crop is threshed. This lone person is caught by the gang of wrongdoers, insulted and surrounded. They attempt to beat him down, they harass him because he is just, and make his very justice the butt of their mockery. "What a mighty apostle!" they say. "Have you flown off to heaven, like Elijah?" Under treatment like this a good man or woman is sometimes so far influenced by human tongues as to be ashamed of being good among bad people. Let such a one resist the wicked, but not by relying on his or her own powers, lest by trying to escape proud people a good person become proud likewise; for then the number of the proud would increase. What should the oppressed say? *Who will arise to help me against people of ill-will? Or who will stand by me against those who commit iniquity? If the Lord had not come to my aid, my soul would soon have made its home in hell.*

Verses 18-19. Confess your instability, and you will walk triumphant

22. *Whenever I said, "My foot has slipped," your mercy, Lord, always supported me.* See how much God loves our confession! If your foot slips and you do not admit it, but instead claim to be standing firm when you are already tumbling, that is not the right way. If you have begun to slip, if you are already beginning to waver, confess your instability so as not to find yourself bewailing your complete downfall. Confess it, so that he may help you, and keep your soul from hell. God wants our confession; he wants humility. As a human creature you have slipped; as God he helps you. But all the same you must admit, "My foot slipped." Why say, "I am on my feet," when you are already slipping?

Whenever I said, "My foot has slipped," your mercy, Lord, always supported me. You must say this as bravely as Peter did, not presuming on his own strength. The Lord appeared to the apostles walking on the sea, trampling on the heads of all the proud folk in this world; for his walk over the swollen waves was a sign of his treading down of the heads of the proud. The Church tramples on them too, because the Church is Peter. Yet Peter did not dare to walk on the waves by his own power. What did he say? *Lord, if it is you, tell me to come to you over the water* (Mt 14:28). Christ walked by his own power; Peter walked at Christ's command. *Tell me to come to you*, he begged; and Christ responded, *Come.* The Church likewise treads on the heads of the arrogant; but the Church is Church, and comprises human weakness. As a counterpart, therefore, to the psalm's avowal, *My foot has slipped*, Peter faltered in the sea, and cried, *Lord, I'm sinking!* The psalm had said, *My foot has slipped*, and corresponding to this avowal is Peter's shout in the gospel, *Lord, I'm sinking!* And just as the psalm had said, *Your mercy, Lord, always supported me*, so too the gospel has *Jesus stretched out a hand to him, and said, "You man of feeble faith, why did you doubt?"*

It is wonderful how God tests human beings:[55] the very dangers that threaten us make our deliverer seem all the more welcome; for notice how the psalm continues. Having confessed, *Whenever I said, "My foot has slipped," your mercy, Lord, always supported me*, the psalmist found that the Lord who had snatched him from danger had become delightful to him; and he drew attention to this sweetness of the Lord by exclaiming, *In the measure that sorrows abounded in my heart, O Lord, did your exhortations[56] cheer my soul.* Many are the sorrows, but many the consolations; harsh are the wounds, but gentle their healing.

Verses 20-21. The labors and suffering of the righteous are God's educative tools. Labor is the price of rest

23. *Will any iniquitous ruler form an alliance with you, who fashion our pain as our precept?* This means that no one who is wicked will reign[57] with you, O Lord, nor will you yourself be enthroned in any place of iniquity. The psalm then elucidates what has been said in the second part of the verse: *you who fashion our pain as our precept.* I know that no iniquitous ruler will find an ally in you, because you have not spared even us. The same idea occurs in the letter of the apostle Peter, who reinforced his teaching from scripture: *It is time for judgment to take place, beginning from the house of the Lord*, he warns; that is to say, now is the time for those who belong to the Lord's house to face judgment. If the children are whipped, what must exceedingly wicked servants expect? Accordingly

---

55. Variant: "It is wonderful, what God proves to human beings."
56. *Exhortationes tuae* is the reading of most codices here, and is preferred by the CCL editors; but the Septuagint's παρακλήσεις, together with other works of Augustine (see *Continence* XI,25,4; *The City of God* XVIII,51,28), suggests that *consolationes* is the better reading. Augustine's comments in the following sentence and in section 24 below seem to reflect the latter.
57. Or perhaps merely "sit."

he adds, *If it originates with us, what will be the outcome for those who do not believe in the gospel of God?* Then he supports what has been said with the testimony of scripture: *what will become of the wicked and the sinner if the righteous will scarcely be saved?* (1 Pt 4:17-18; Prv 11:31). How can the iniquitous possibly be with you, if you do not spare even your believers, but exercise and train them? However, the psalmist wants to make it clear that God's severity toward the faithful is for the purpose of education, so he adds, *You fashion*[58] *our pain as our precept.* We must take this word *fingis* to mean "shape" or "give form to"; so we speak of a potter,[59] and of what he makes as a fictile vessel. We are not to associate *fingis* with anything fictitious, like lying, but with what is carefully fashioned to exist and have a certain form. So the psalm asked earlier, *Will he who fashioned the eye not observe?* His fashioning of our eyes was no lie, was it? The psalm clearly means to suggest, "He shaped the eye, he made the eye." And is God not a potter[60] who makes fragile, weak creatures of earth? Listen to the apostle's teaching: *We carry our treasure in earthen vessels* (2 Cor 4:7). Was it anyone other than God who made these vessels for us? Listen again: *who are you, a mere mortal, to answer back to God? Does the vessel that is fashioned demand of its fashioner, "Why did you make me like this?" Does the potter not have power over the clay, to make from the same lump one vessel for honorable use, and another for lowly purposes?* (Rom 9:20-21). Consider Christ our Lord himself, for he showed himself to be a potter. He had made man from mud in the beginning,[61] and he smeared mud on someone whose eyes he had not fully formed in the womb.[62]

Therefore when the psalm asks, *Will any iniquitous ruler form an alliance with you, who fashion our pain as our precept?* we should take it in this way: will any iniquitous ruler form an alliance with you, who shape our pain into a precept for us? You make pain your precision tool to teach us our lesson; you arrange that the pain itself shall teach us. When and how can pain be a lesson for us? This happens when he who died for you chastises you, not promising[63] you happiness in this life. Although he cannot deceive you, he does not give you here what you are seeking. What will he give? Where will he give it? How much will he give you, this God who does not give it to you here, but only trains you here, shaping your pain into a lesson for you? Your lot here is labor, yet what you are promised is rest. You are well aware that what you have here is labor, but see too what kind of rest he promises. Can you encompass it in your thoughts? If you could, you would think all your labor counted for nothing. Listen to the testimony of one

---

58. *Fingis.*
59. *Figulus.*
60. *Figulus.*
61. See Gn 2:7.
62. See Jn 9:6.
63. Variant: "permitting."

who discerned it in part, who claimed, *Now I know only in part* (1 Cor 13:12). What does this same apostle say of it? *The slight momentary thing that distresses us now is working in us*, in a measure and in a way that we cannot conceive, *towards an eternal glory in heaven that far outweighs it*. What does that mean—that it is *working in us towards an eternal glory in heaven that far outweighs* our present suffering? For whom is this work going forward? *For us who keep our eyes not on things that are seen, but on those which are not seen; for things which are seen are temporal, but things unseen are eternal* (2 Cor 4:17-18). Do not be lazy about your brief labor, and you will be joyful without end. God is to give you eternal life; consider how much labor you are prepared to spend to get it.

24. Listen, brothers and sisters: it is for sale! "What I have is for sale," God tells you. "Buy it." What is this commodity that he has to sell? "I have rest for sale; buy it with your labor." Concentrate now, so that in Christ's name we may be valiant Christians;[64] there is not much left of the psalm, so let us not flag. How can anyone who is too tired to listen be valiant in action? The Lord will be with us, and enable us to expound to you the little that remains.

Well now, think hard. God in a sense offers to sell us the kingdom of heaven. You ask him, "How much does it cost?" It costs labor. If he had told you the price was in gold, it would not have been enough just to say, "Gold," because you would have wanted to know how much gold. A solidus[65] is gold, so is a semiuncia,[66] and so is a libra,[67] and other similar coins. So God quoted a price to you, to save you the trouble of wondering how you could ever get it. The price of this valuable possession is labor. How much labor? You must ask how hard you will have to labor. But you are not yet told what it will amount to, how much labor will be required from you.[68] No, what God says to you is this: "I will show you what a fine thing the rest is, and then it is for you to judge how much labor is worth expending to buy it." All right, then; let God tell us how valuable a thing is that rest that awaits us. *Blessed are they who dwell in your house; they will praise you for ever and ever* (Ps 83:5(84:4)). This is everlasting rest: a rest that will never end, a joy without end, gladness without end, incorruptibility without end. You will own eternal life, a rest that knows no end. How much labor is that worth? If you wanted to make a true comparison, and fairly weigh one against the other, you would have to say that the proper price of eternal rest is eternal labor. That is the true answer; but don't worry, because God is merciful. If you undertook eternal labor, you would never arrive at eternal peace. If you

---

64. Variant: "… may be Christian brethren."
65. A gold coin originally called an aureus; it had been worth 25 denarii, but was later devalued.
66. Half an ounce in the Roman system of weights.
67. The Roman pound, consisting of twelve ounces.
68. The point is in fact being labored. This passage seems to reveal Augustine deliberately playing with his hearers, some of whom may have been persons of keen commercial sense.

contracted to labor unceasingly, so paying a just price for everlasting rest, how would you ever attain it? Compare the price with the goods: eternal rest is certainly worthy to be balanced against eternal labor; but if you were to be always laboring you would never reach that rest. So you are not required to labor for ever, not because the object of your desire is not worth it, but so that you may eventually receive what you are purchasing, and possess it as duly bought. It is worth buying with eternal labor, but it is of necessity bought by labor that is limited in duration. Everlasting labor ought to have been the price of everlasting rest. What is ten times a hundred thousand years' labor worth? "What I am going to give you has no end," says God. How merciful God is! He does not say, "Work for ten times a hundred thousand years," nor does he say, "Labor for just a thousand years," nor even, "Labor for five hundred years." All you have to do is to labor for your own lifetime, just these few years, and then there will be rest for you, rest that has no end.

Nor is that all: listen to what follows. *In the measure that sorrows abounded in my heart, O Lord, did your exhortations cheer my soul.* Not only are your years of labor so few; even amid your labors you do not want for consolation, you do not lack daily joys. Only do not find your joy in the world: rejoice in Christ, rejoice in his word, rejoice in his law. What we are saying to you, what you are hearing, is all about these joys. So then, what do the consolations amount to, amid these grueling labors? The apostle truly summed it up: *the slight momentary thing that distresses us now is working in us*, in a measure and in a way that we cannot conceive, *towards an eternal glory in heaven that far outweighs it* (2 Cor 4:17). Look at the price we pay—a penny[69] to gain everlasting treasures, a paltry mite of labor to win unbelievable rest, as scripture says: in a measure and in a way that we cannot conceive, it is working toward an eternal glory that far outweighs it.

You are joyful for a time, but do not set your hope on that. You are sad for a time, but do not despair. Do not allow prosperity to corrupt you; but do not allow adversity to crush you, either, for then you might say in your mind, "It is not possible for God to admit wicked people like me to his presence." He chastises the just themselves, in order to save them; the purpose of his chastisement is to train them. *What will become of the wicked and the sinner if the righteous will scarcely be saved?* (1 Pt 4:18; Prv 11:31). When the psalm asks God, *Will any iniquitous ruler form an alliance with you?* it means, "You surely will not admit the impious to your fellowship, if you fashion our pain into a precept for us? You have willed so to train and educate your children, so to instruct them, that they may not be without fear, nor fall in love with anything else, and forget you, their

---

69. *Siliqua*: a pod or husk, or the fruit of the carob tree, or the plant fenugreek; but the word was also used for a very small weight or coin, the twenty-fourth part of a solidus.

true good." God is good. If he let us be, and did not mix bitterness into worldly prosperity, we might forget him.

25. But when vexation and trouble whip up waves in your soul, let your faith, which has fallen asleep, be awakened. The weather was calm when Christ went to sleep at sea, but while he slept a storm arose, and they were faced with danger. In the same way there can be calm conditions in a Christian heart, and all may be peaceful, but only as long as faith is wide awake. If it falls asleep, we are in peril. This is what the sleeping Christ signifies: some people are unmindful of their faith, and they are at risk. But when the boat was being battered Christ was awakened by the storm-bound sailors, who appealed to him, *Lord, we're sinking!* (Mt 8:25). He stood up and commanded the tempestuous winds, and tranquillity was restored. So it will be with you. When evil concupiscence and wicked suggestions disturb you, these are only waves, and they will be calmed. You are in despair, and think that you do not belong to the Lord; but let your faith wake up. Awaken Christ in your heart, and as faith arises, you realize where you are. If the waves of concupiscence tempt you, you can fix your eyes on what God has promised. Then will the delights of what has been promised instill in you contempt for the delights of the world. Or perhaps repeated threats from powerful, wicked people are harassing you and driving you off the righteous course. Then you are reminded of what God threatens: *Depart from me into the eternal fire which was prepared for the devil and his angels* (Mt 25:41), and you do not veer away from righteousness. If you fear everlasting fire you make light of temporal pains, and when you recall what God has promised, you make light of temporal happiness. He has promised you rest, so endure hardship; he has threatened eternal fire, so despise temporal pain. As Christ awakes, your heart will be restored to tranquillity, so that you may come safely into port. He who prepared the ship for you would not have neglected to prepare for you a harbor.

Will any iniquitous ruler form an alliance with you, who fashion our pain as our precept? He uses bad people to put us through our paces, and trains us through their pestering. A good person is scourged with the malice of a bad one, and a son or daughter is corrected through the misbehavior of a slave. Thus does God fashion our pain into a lesson for us. Bad people do only as much harm as God allows them to, in the time during which he spares them.

26. For what does the next verse say? *They will seek to entrap the soul of the just person.* Why will they seek to entrap it? Because they find no real charge they can bring. What did they prove against the Lord? They concocted false charges because they could find no true ones. *And they will condemn innocent blood.* The following verses will explain why all this happens.

Verse 22. The positive effect of the discipline begins to appear

27. *The Lord has become a refuge for me*, says the psalm. You would not be seeking a refuge of this kind if you were not in danger; you were allowed to run into danger precisely so that you might seek it, for God fashions our pain into a lesson for us. He caused me to suffer distress from the malice of bad people; then, when I was wounded by it, I began to look for a refuge, one that I had stopped looking for when I enjoyed worldly fortune. When we are habitually prosperous, and find our joy in a hope focused on the present, are we likely to be mindful of God? Let the hope fixed on this world fade away, and hope focused on God take its place, so that you may say, "*The Lord has become a refuge for me*; my grief has no other purpose than to make me find my refuge in him."

And my God is my helper in this time of my hope. The Lord is our hope as long as we are here, for we live in hope, and not yet in the reality.[70] But to make sure we do not slacken in our hope, he who made the promise stands by us and lifts us up, tempering even the woes we endure. With good reason was it said, *God is faithful, and he does not allow you to be tempted more fiercely than you can bear, but along with the temptation ordains the outcome, so that you may withstand it* (1 Cor 10:13). May he plunge you into the furnace of tribulation only as long as it takes for the vessel to be fired, not so as to break it. *The Lord has become a refuge for me, and my God is my helper in this time of my hope*.

Why, then, did it seem to you that God was unjust in his policy of sparing bad people? Look how the psalm corrects itself now, and allow yourself to be corrected along with it. It was to that end that the psalm adopted your complaint. What did you say? *How long will sinners gloat, O Lord, how long?* The psalm took on your words, so now you take on the words of the psalm. And what does the psalm say? *The Lord has become a refuge for me*.

Verse 23. God brings good results from the actions of bad people, but the wicked are requited according to their intentions

28. *The Lord will requite them in accordance with their works, and according to their malice will the Lord our God destroy them*. The phrase, *according to their malice*, is significant. I am enriched through them, and yet the psalm speaks of their malice, not their kindness. The Lord certainly makes use of bad people to train us and whip us. To what end does he whip us? Undoubtedly for the kingdom of heaven, for *he whips every child whom he accepts. What child is there whom its father does not discipline?* (Heb 12:6-7). When God acts so, he is educating us for an eternal inheritance, and often he confers this benefit on us through bad people, for he uses them to develop and perfect our love, which he

---

70. *In spe sumus, nondum in re.*

wishes to be extended even to our enemies. No Christian is perfect in love except by fulfilling Christ's command, *Love your enemies, do good to people who hate you, and pray for those who persecute you* (Mt 5:44). This is the way the devil is vanquished; this is the way in which our crown of victory is won.

You see, then, how much good God does for us through bad people; but he will requite them not in accordance with the good things he gives us through them but according to their malice. Think what enormous benefits he has conferred on us by means of the most heinous crime of the traitor Judas. Judas delivered the Son of God to his passion, and through the passion of the Son of God all nations have been redeemed and brought to salvation. Yet no reward was given to Judas on account of the salvation of the nations; rather was due punishment visited upon him for his malice. If we consider only the action of delivering Christ up, as opposed to the intention of the one who delivered him, Judas did the same thing as God the Father; for of the Father it is written that *he did not spare even his own Son, but delivered him up for us all* (Rom 8:32). Judas also did the same things as Christ our Lord did himself, for of Christ it is written that *he loved us, and delivered himself up for us as an offering and sacrifice to God for a sweet fragrance*, and again *Christ loved the Church, and delivered himself up for her* (Eph 5:2.25). And yet we give thanks to God the Father who did not even spare his own Son, but delivered him up for us; we give thanks to the Son, who delivered himself for us and in so doing fully carried out his Father's will; but we loath Judas, through whose act God has bestowed on us so great a gift. We rightly say, "The Lord has requited him in accordance with his iniquity,[71] and according to his malice has he destroyed him"; for he delivered Christ up not for our sake, but with an eye to the money for which he sold him, although the delivering up of Christ meant acceptance for us, and the selling of Christ meant our redemption.

The case is similar for those who persecuted the martyrs. By persecuting them on earth they dispatched them to heaven; they knowingly brought upon the martyrs the loss of this present life, but unknowingly enabled them to win the life to come. Nonetheless, those who obstinately hated the just will be requited by the Lord in accordance with their iniquities; he will destroy them according to their malice. As the goodness of righteous people can be an obstacle to the wicked, so can the iniquity of the godless be a help to good people. The Lord himself declared, *I came so that they who do not see may see, and those who see may become blind* (Jn 9:39); and the apostle testified, *For some we are the scent of life, leading to life, but for others the stench of death unto death* (2 Cor 2:16). The malice of wicked people furnishes the just with weapons for their left hands, as the same apostle pointed out: we have *the weapons of righteousness in right hand and left*; that is to say, *in high renown and ignominy* (2 Cor 6:7.8). He went on to display them. The weapons in their right hands were the glory of God; their

71. Variant: "his works."

own good reputation; and the truth by which they were recognized as alive, not done to death, always rejoicing, enriching many, and possessing all things. The weapons in their left hands were the denunciations uttered against them as ignoble men of ill repute; their being regarded as seducers and ignorant folk, being killed and hounded and afflicted, being in want, and seeming to own nothing.[72] Is it any wonder that Christ's soldiers wage war against the devil with weapons in both right hands and left? Peace is proclaimed for men and women of good will,[73] yet they can sometimes be *the stench of death unto death* for certain others; so too though ruin is decreed for men and women of bad will, they can sometimes provide weapons for the left hands of the just in the fight for salvation. God will requite them not in view of the profit that comes to us through their agency, but in conformity with their sins, for by loving iniquity they hate their own souls.[74] He does not honor them for the kindness he himself confers on us by means of them, using even the wicked to good purpose; but *according to their malice will the Lord our God destroy them.*

Augustine sums up his reflections and concludes the sermon

29. Let the just person tolerate the unjust, then. Let the time-bound labor of a just person tolerate the temporal impunity of the unjust; for there is no other justice for men and women in this life but to live by faith,[75] a faith that works through charity.[76] But any just person who lives by faith believes both in the rest that awaits us after our present labor, and in the everlasting torments reserved for malefactors after their short-lived glee. Moreover, if our faith works through charity we must love our enemies, and, insofar as we can, desire to help them; for by so doing we can thwart them in any harm they try to do us. If perhaps they have obtained power to hurt and tyrannize, we should lift up our heart[77] to the place where no one can hurt us. There, instructed and well versed in the law of God, may we be rendered patient and gentle through days of misery, until a pit is dug for the sinner. If Christians steady their wills in the law of God, meditating on it day and night[78] because their citizenship[79] is in heaven, they are like stars shedding radiance over the earth from the firmament. Our psalm took its title from them by mentioning *the fourth day of the week*, since it was on that day that the luminaries were created. Thus they are able to do everything without grum-

---

72. See 2 Cor 6:7-10.
73. See Lk 2:14.
74. See Ps 10:6(11:5).
75. See Hkk 2:4; Rom 1:17.
76. See Gal 5:6.
77. *Sursum cor*; see note at Exposition of Psalm 10,3.
78. See Ps 1:2.
79. *Conversatio*; see Phil 3:20, and section 4 above, with note there.

bling, holding fast to the word of life amid a crooked and perverse race.[80] Night does not extinguish the stars, and neither does iniquity overcome the minds of the faithful when they dwell in the firmament of God's scripture. If it sometimes happens that our earthly lives are subjected to the dominance of evil people, this not only serves to educate us, inasmuch as the Lord becomes a refuge for us and our God a helper in this time of our hope; it also furthers the digging of that pit for the sinner, of whom it is said in another psalm, *He will bow down and fall, when he exercises dominion over the poor* (Ps 9B:10(10:10)).

30. The length of this sermon may have been hard for you to bear, though your alacrity and eagerness do not suggest that this is the case. But if it is, you must forgive me; first, because I am speaking under orders, for the Lord our God commanded me through the brethren in whom he dwells. God issues his commands only from the place where he is enthroned. And, secondly, we must confess that because you are so avid to hear us, we are equally avid for you.

May our God comfort us, then, after all our hard work; and may the effort that cost us sweat be a furtherance of salvation for you, and not a ground of reproach against us. I am saying this, brothers and sisters, so that you may profit from what you have heard, and ruminate on it afterwards. Make sure that you do not forget it: make sure not only by thinking it over and discussing it among yourselves, but also by ordering your lives in conformity with it. A good life, conducted according to the commandments of God, is like a pen that writes on the heart what has been heard. If it were written on wax it could easily be rubbed out. Write it rather on your hearts and in your conduct, and it will never be effaced.

---

80. See Phil 2:14-16 and section 3 above.

Exposition of Psalm 94

A Sermon

Verse 1. Approaching the Lord through the renewal of his image in us

1. If it had been up to me, brothers and sisters, I would have preferred that we listen to our father.[1] But to obey our father is also a good thing. Since he has commanded us, and graciously agreed to pray for us, I will speak to you about the present psalm, beloved, as the Lord, who is God of us all, enables me.

The title of this psalm is *A song of praise, for David himself.* Now the designation, *song of praise*, connotes both cheerfulness, since this is a song, and devotion, since it expresses praise. What is more worthy of human praise than an object which is so delightful to us that nothing displeasing can be found in it? Evidently, then, praise offered to God is the only praise that can be entirely unqualified. Anyone who praises God can be wholly free from anxiety, because there is no possibility that we shall ever be ashamed of the one we have praised. Let us praise him, and sing as we do so; let us praise him, I mean, cheerfully and with joy. What we are to praise him for is made clear in the subsequent verses of the psalm.

2. *Come, let us rejoice exceedingly to the Lord.* The psalm invites us to a great banquet of joy, but it is joy in the Lord, not in the world. It would have been enough to say, *Let us rejoice exceedingly*, without adding, *to the Lord*, but for the fact that there is a bad kind of rejoicing: rejoicing over this world. This had to be distinguished from good rejoicing, so the psalm indicated the distinction briefly. What does the right kind of rejoicing consist of? Finding joy in the Lord. The wrong kind is rejoicing with the world; the right kind is rejoicing to the Lord. You need to laugh devoutly with the Lord if you want to laugh safely at the world.[2]

But what does the invitation, *Come*, suggest? How can these people who are to rejoice in the Lord be summoned to "come"? Clearly they must be far away if they are invited to travel nearer by this coming, and to approach God by traveling nearer, so that as they approach him they may rejoice in him. But in what sense are they far away? Is it possible for anyone to be in a different place from him

---

1. Presumably Aurelius, Bishop of Carthage from about A.D. 341. He frequently took advantage of Augustine's presence at Church councils held at Carthage to persuade him to preach. This may have been the occasion of the present sermon.
2. The pun comes out better in Latin: *exsultare ... insultare.*

who is present everywhere? Suppose you want to go far away from him: where will you go, to get away? Remember the words of someone who, though a sinner, was repentant and hopeful of salvation, someone who bewailed his sins and dreaded God's wrath, and sought to appease him. In another psalm this person asks, *Whither shall I go from your spirit, and whither flee from your face? If I mount to heaven, you are there.* Is anywhere else left? If he climbs up to heaven, he finds God there; so where can he go to get away from God? See what he tries next: *If I sink down to hell, even there you are present* (Ps 138(139):7-8). Ascending to heaven only brings him to God, and going down to the underworld affords him no escape from God, so where else is he to go? Where can he flee to escape his wrathful God, except to God appeased?

Yet even though no one can escape from him who is everywhere present, there are people who are far from God. Otherwise scripture would not have said, *This people honors me with its lips, but its heart is far from me* (Is 29:13). A person can be far away from God, not geographically, but by being unlike him. What form would such unlikeness take? A bad life and corrupt morals, for if we draw near to God by good morals, inevitably we distance ourselves from him by bad ones. One and the same man or woman, while standing in the same spot, may approach God by loving him, or withdraw from him by loving iniquity. The feet do not move at all, yet the person can either approach or withdraw. Now the feet that carry us on our journey are our intentions.[3] Each of us draws nearer to God, or moves further from him, in accordance with the intention we have, the love that is in us. When we are looking at two very dissimilar things, we commonly say, don't we, "This one is far removed from that"? Or suppose we are comparing two people, or perhaps two horses, or two coats, and someone says, "This coat is very much like that other one," or "This person closely resembles that other"; what does someone else say, to register disagreement? "Oh, no; they are miles apart." What does that expression mean: "miles apart"? It means, "This one is unlike the other." The two may be standing side by side, yet be far apart. You might find two wicked people, two of a kind as to their way of life and morals, and even though one is in the East and the other in the West, they are shoulder to shoulder. Or again, think of two righteous persons: one is in the East, the other in the West, yet they are close to each other because they are in God. But suppose, on the contrary, one is righteous and the other wicked; then, even if they are shackled with the same chain, they are widely separated from each other.

If, therefore, we move away from God by being unlike him, we also approach him by likeness to him. What sort of likeness is this? It is the likeness to God in which we were created, which we had spoiled by sin, which we receive afresh when our sins are forgiven, which is renewed in us inwardly, in our minds. Thus the image of our God is engraved anew on his coin, which is our soul, so that we

---

3. *Affectus.*

may return to his coffers. Why did our Lord Jesus Christ choose a coin to demon-strate to his challengers what God seeks in us, brothers and sisters? Why a coin? They were seeking some ground of accusation against him, and they decided to consult the teacher of truth about the tribute exacted by Caesar: they wished to ask him whether it was lawful to pay this tax. And what did he say? *Why are you putting me to the test, you hypocrites?* Then he asked for a coin, and one was brought. *Whose image does it bear?* he demanded. They replied, *Caesar's,* and he took them up on that: *Then render to Caesar what is Caesar's, and to God what is God's* (Mt 22:18.20-21). This was his way of saying, "If Caesar claims his own image in this coin, does not God likewise claim his image in human beings?"

Moreover, our Lord Jesus Christ invites us to live in harmony with our like-ness to God when he commands us to love even our enemies, for he presents God himself as our model: you are to be *like your Father in heaven,* he says, *who causes his sun to rise over the good and the wicked, and sends rain upon the just and unjust alike. Be perfect, like your Father in heaven* (Mt 5:45.48). By saying, *Be perfect, like your Father in heaven,* he invites us to make the likeness real. But if he needs to invite us to it, we must conclude that by becoming unlike God we had distanced ourselves from him. We had gone far away in our loss of like-ness, but we are brought near by being like him, so that the scriptural word may be verified in us: *Draw near to God, and receive his light* (Ps 33:6(34:5)).

When our psalm says, *Come, let us rejoice exceedingly to the Lord,* it is addressing people who have taken up a position far from the Lord and are leading bad lives. "Where are you going? What hiding place are you looking for? Where are you off to? Where do you think to escape, by rejoicing with this world? *Come, let us rejoice exceedingly to the Lord.* Why seek your enjoyment in a place where you will certainly come to grief? Come on, let us exult rather in him by whom we were created." *Come, let us rejoice exceedingly to the Lord.*

3. *Let us shout for joy to God, our salvation.* What is shouting for joy?[4] When we cannot express our joy in words, and yet we want to use our voices to give proof of what we have conceived within but cannot articulate, that is shouting for joy. Consider, beloved ones,[5] how people sing songs when they are making merry, vying with each other in celebrating worldly happiness. You know how sometimes, in between songs with words, the singers seem to overflow with a joy that the tongue is inadequate to express verbally; you know how then they let out wild whoops to give utterance to a gladness of spirit, since they are unable to put into words what the heart has conceived. Well then, if they shout for joy over earthly happiness, ought not we to shout for joy over heavenly happiness, which certainly cannot be spelled out in words?

---

4. *Iubilare*: to let out wild whoops of joy. The verb often had rustic or bucolic overtones.
5. *Caritas vestra.*

Verse 2. Confession of sins, confession of God's glory

4. *Let us forestall him by coming into his presence confessing.* "Confession"
is understood by scripture in two senses: there is the confession of one who
praises, and the confession of one who groans. The confession of one who
praises is concerned with the honor of him who is praised; the confession of one
who groans belongs to the repentance of the one who is confessing. Men and
women confess when they praise God, and they confess when they accuse themselves; and the tongue has no nobler function. Indeed, I think these confessions
are the vows of which another psalm declares, *I will pay my vows to you, the
vows my lips have uttered with discernment* (Ps 65(66):13-14). Nothing is more
sublime than this discernment, and nothing more necessary with regard both to
understanding and to action.

How, then, are you to practice discernment in the vows you pay to God? You
must accuse yourself in order to praise him, for to him belongs the mercy that
forgives our sins. If he chose to act only on the basis of our merits he would find
only people deserving of condemnation. This is why he said, *Come,* inviting us
to leave our sins behind at last, so that he need not demand of us an account of
past deeds. Thus new, clean records may come into being, on which the tally of
our debts is no longer registered. Let us confess how worthy of praise he is, and
how great his mercy, and let us confess this always in a spirit of praise. If
"confession" always meant repentance, the gospel could not have said of the
Lord himself, *At that hour Jesus exulted in the Holy Spirit, and said, I give
thanks to you, Father, Lord of heaven and earth, because you have hidden these
things from the wise and clever, and revealed them to little ones* (Lk 10:21). This
cannot mean that Christ was confessing as a penitent, can it? Nothing could lead
him to repent, because he had done nothing worthy of blame; his confession was
a confession of praise to the Father. Now, since the present context is also one of
rejoicing, perhaps we should understand the confession to which the psalm
invites us to be likewise one of praise. This would be why the psalm is entitled, *A
song of praise*, plainly indicating that we are to take it as the confession not of
penitents but of praise-singers.

And yet, what kind of confession does it immediately enjoin upon us, when it
says, *Let us forestall him by coming into his presence confessing*? What does
that mean? He will come himself, one day, so let us forestall him. Before he
comes, let us condemn what we have done by making our confession, so that he
may find only deeds to crown, and nothing to condemn. But does this too not
redound to God's glory, when you confess your sins? Yes, indeed; it is very
much part of the praise you give to God. Why is that? Because the more
desperate was the patient's case, the more credit is due to the healer; so the more
hopeless you were about yourself, the more readily should you confess your
sins. The higher the heap of sins on the part of one who confesses, the higher the

praise to him who forgives. Let us not think, then, that we have strayed away from the song of praise if we understand the invitation to be concerned with the confession of our sins, because this too is part of the praise offered to God. When we recognize our sins, we acknowledge God's glory. *Let us forestall him by coming into his presence confessing.*

Verses 3-5. Reasons for joyful shouting: the sovereignty of God

5. *And let us shout for joy to him with psalms.* We have already explained what shouting for joy is, but the phrase is repeated so that the shouting may be put into effect; for the repetition is a summons to action. It is not that we have forgotten already, or need to be reminded, how we were told just now to shout for joy. No, but where strong feelings are expressed it is quite usual for a word to be repeated, not as imparting new information but to give emphasis by reiterating it. By the repetition, the speaker makes his earnestness clear. That is why the Lord says, *Truly, truly, I tell you* (Jn 1:51). It would have sufficed to say a single "Truly"; so why say, *Truly, truly*? It can only be because the repetition strengthens the accompanying statement. Similarly our psalm repeats, *Let us shout for joy to him with psalms.*

And what are we to say in our psalms—or, rather, what are we to have in our minds as we shout for joy? What are the perspectives of this song of praise? Listen: *Because the Lord is the great God, mighty king over all gods*, let us shout with joy to him. *Because the Lord will not reject his people*, let us shout for joy to him. *Because all the ends of the earth are in his hand, and his are the mountain peaks*, let us shout for joy to him for all of them. *Because the sea is his, for he made it, and his hands laid down the dry land*, let us shout to him with joy.

If we were to discuss the meaning of all these separate declarations with proper care we should probably run out of time; but, on the other hand, if we neglect them altogether we shall remain in your debt.[6] Take in such brief explanation as we can give you, then. We will condense it as far as possible, and use what time we have; for even a few seeds can yield a plentiful harvest if the ground is fertile.

6. The first reason it gave us for shouting with joy and praising God was this: *the Lord is the great God, mighty king over all gods.* So it seems there are gods over whom our God is superior, our God to whom we joyfully shout, in whom we rejoice, to whom we offer songs of praise. Yes, other gods there are, but not for us. The apostle says, *Even if there are beings called gods in the sky or on earth (as in fact there are gods and lords aplenty), still, for us there is one God*

---

6. That is, Augustine will have cheated his hearers of what they have a right to expect. He frequently mentions the debt he owes them as their preacher, and their demands that he discharge it to the full.

from whom all things come, and through whom we exist; and one Lord, our Lord Jesus Christ, through whom all things come, and in whom we exist (1 Cor 8:5-6). So if those beings are not our gods, whose are they? Another psalm gives the answer: *the gods of the heathen are demons, but the Lord made the heavens* (Ps 95(96):5). The Holy Spirit could hardly have given you a more splendid or more succinct reminder through the prophet of your God, your Lord; for it would not have amounted to much if that psalm had merely said that God is more to be feared than any demons. Is it anything glorious to be superior to all demons? For *the gods of the heathen are demons*. But where is your God? *The Lord made the heavens.* Your Lord made a realm where demons cannot live, for the demons were thrown down from heaven. The heavens are therefore more honorable than the demons, and your Lord is more honorable than the heavens, since he created even them. How much loftier must he be than the demons who are held to be gods by the pagans, if he is loftier than the heavens from which angels fell, to be turned into demons?

And yet all the pagans were under the power of demons. Temples were built to demons, altars were set up to demons, priests ordained for the service of demons, sacrifices offered to demons, and ecstatic ravers were brought in as prophets for demons. All these things the pagans did for demons, although all these things are rightly owed to the one God alone. Pagans built a temple to demons, but God has his temple; pagans ordained priests for demons, but God has his priest; pagans offered sacrifice to demons, but God has his sacrifice. Those demons wanted to pass themselves off as gods, so they demanded that all those services should be rendered to them in order to deceive people, because they know that such services are due to the true God. This is what customarily happens: what a false god exacts is something owed to the true God. We recognize the real temple of God: *God's temple is holy*, says scripture, *and that temple is yourselves* (1 Cor 3:17). If we are God's temple, his altar is our soul. And what is God's sacrifice? Perhaps it is exactly what we are doing at this moment. We lay a sacrifice on the altar when we praise God, for another psalm teaches, *By a sacrifice of praise I shall be honored, and that is the way where I will show him the salvation of God* (Ps 49(50):23). If you look for the priest, you will find him above the heavens, for he who died for you on earth now intercedes for you there.[7]

The Lord is the great God, mighty king over all gods. Let us now take *gods* to mean human beings, for the Lord is not king over demons. Such an interpretation is justified by scripture: *God has taken his stand in the synagogue of the gods, to make a distinction among them* (Ps 81(82):1). He calls them *gods* in virtue of participation, not nature; they are gods by the grace through which he willed to deify them. How great must our God be, if he makes us gods? What sort of gods are they that men and women make? As he is so great in making us gods, so are

---

7. See Rom 8:34.

those gods mere nothings which are made by human beings. The true God makes gods of those who believe in him, for he has given them power to become children of God.[8] He is the real God, because God is not made; we who are made are not true gods, yet we are nobler than the gods made by humans. The idols made by pagans are of silver and gold, the products of human hands; they have mouths but they will never speak; eyes, but they will never see.[9] But our God made for us eyes that do see. Yet it was not by creating our seeing eyes that he made us into gods, for he did the same for cattle. He made us into gods because he shed his light upon our inner eyes.

Praise be to him, then; confession be made to him; shouts of joy resound to him, *because the Lord is the great God, mighty king over all gods.*

Further reasons for shouting with joy: mercy to Jews and Gentiles

7. *The Lord will not reject his people,*[10] and therefore let praise be given him, and shouts of joy be raised to him. What people is this, that he will not cast off? We have no authority to impose any meaning on the text, because these words have been commented on in advance by the apostle, who has explained what the statement means. There stood the Jewish people: within that people were the prophets; within that people were the patriarchs; it was the people sprung from Abraham's stock according to the flesh. In that people all the sacred signs had been instituted which preceded and promised our Savior; for it was the people within which the temple had been established, and the anointing, and a figurative priest,[11] so that when all the shadows should have passed away, the light itself might come. This, then, was the people of God. Prophets were sent to it, prophets who had themselves been born within it. To it were delivered and entrusted the words of God. So what became of this people? Was it condemned in its entirety? Certainly not. It was called an olive-tree by the apostle, for the tree was rooted in the patriarchs. But some of its branches dried up, because they had reached too high in their pride; so they were found to be sterile and were lopped off, and a wild olive was grafted in, because it was humble. All the same, dearly beloved, the engrafted oleaster also needed to beware of pride. So what had the apostle to say to it? *If you were cut out of the wild olive and unnaturally grafted into the true olive, how much easier will it be for those who belong to it by nature to be grafted back into the olive where they naturally belong?* (Rom 11:24). The apostle is telling them, "Just as you Gentiles by not persisting in unbelief deserved to be grafted in, even though you were only a wild olive, so will it be

8. See Jn 1:12.
9. See Ps 113B(115):4-5.
10. These words, found in the Septuagint and in Augustine's Old Latin version, do not occur in the Hebrew.
11. Variant: "the anointing of a priest as a figure."

natural, and much easier, for those others to be regrafted once they have been brought to a better mind."

There stands the tree, then. Some of its branches have been broken off, but not all. If all the branches had been removed, where would Peter have come from? Or John? Or Thomas? Or Matthew? Or Andrew? Or any of the apostles? Where would the apostle Paul himself have sprung from, he who was speaking in these passages and bore witness to the good olive tree by his fruit? Were not all these branches of the same tree? And where did the five hundred brethren come from, the ones to whom the Lord appeared after his resurrection?[12] What about those many thousands who were converted by Peter's address when the apostles, filled with the Holy Spirit, spoke in the tongues of all nations—those who at their conversion were so eager to praise God and accuse themselves?[13] Where had they come from, those converts who in their savagery had shed the Lord's blood, but now in their new faith learned to drink it? All these thousands of people were so thoroughly converted that they sold their goods and laid the proceeds at the feet of the apostles. One rich man had been unable to do this, though he had heard the invitation from the lips of the Lord himself; he had been saddened and had left the Lord.[14] Yet now these thousands did it unhesitatingly, the very people at whose hands Christ had been crucified. As they were the more grievously wounded in their hearts, so were they all the more eager to seek the doctor.

All these believers were Jews, and it must be of them that the psalm now testifies, *The Lord will not reject his people*; for the apostle appealed to this psalm's testimony when he said, *What are we to think, brethren? Surely God has not cast off his people, whom he knew of old? By no means. For I am myself sprung from the race of Israel, from the stock of Abraham, of the tribe of Benjamin. God has not cast off his own people, whom he foreknew* (Rom 11:1-2). This is quite clear, because if the Lord had cast off his people, there would not have been any stock from which the apostle himself could spring. But from that same stock that produced him, all the rest sprang too. In them was the Lord's people to be found, but not in all of them; for, as scripture says, *A remnant shall be saved* (Is 10:22; Rom 9:27). Not in all of them; for when the threshing had been carried out, the grain was extracted and the chaff left lying. All the Jews whom you see to have been rejected, you see as chaff; but from this place where you now view the chaff, there has already been a collection of grain, and the grain is stored away in the barn. Let us observe both, and distinguish them from each other.

8. What does the psalm add to this? *Because all the ends of the earth are in his hand.* Here we recognize the cornerstone: the cornerstone is Christ. He can be the corner only because he has tied two walls together in himself; they come

---

12. See 1 Cor 15:6.
13. See Acts 2:37-41.
14. See Mk 10:22.

from different directions, but in the corner they are not opposed to each other. The circumcised come from one direction, the uncircumcised from another, but in Christ the two peoples are at peace, because he has become the cornerstone, he of whom it was written, *The stone rejected by the builders has become the head-stone of the corner* (Ps 117(118):22). If Christ has become the cornerstone, let us have regard not to the diversity of these peoples whose origins were so far apart, but to their close kinship as they embrace in Christ. And in them the prophecy comes true. In them let us observe the fulfillment of the promise that *the Lord will not reject his people*. Look at the first wall. Here it is true, as we have pointed out, that *the Lord has not cast off his people*, because from here came the apostles, and all the Israelites who believed and laid the price of the property they sold at the apostles' feet; they were poor people by their own choice, but enriched by God. So we have examined one wall, and found fulfilled in it the promise that *the Lord will not reject his people*. Now let us take a look at the other. *All the ends of the earth are in his hand*. The Gentiles too have come to the cornerstone, there to receive the kiss of peace; they have come to this one Christ who has made one people out of two, not like the heretics who have made two out of one. This is exactly what the apostle says about Christ our Lord: *He is himself our peace, since he united the two* (Eph 2:14).

Let us shout for joy to him. Why? Because *the Lord will not reject his people*. And is there another reason? Yes, *because all the ends of the earth are in his hand, and his are the mountain peaks*. The mountain peaks are the grandees of the earth. Time was when these high and mighty folk, earthly potentates, were hostile to the Church. They promulgated anti-Church laws and tried to blot out the Christian name from the earth.[15] But later another prophecy found fulfillment: *All the kings of the earth will worship him* (Ps 71(72):11). And so our psalm's statement was proved true, that *his are the mountain peaks*.

Even temptations serve God's benign purpose

9. You are beset by trials, are you, and shaken by all the things in this world that offend you, even though you have taken your stand on God's gracious promises? But even these troubles can do you no harm. Their limits have been imposed on them by the Lord, because *the sea is his*. This world is a sea, but God made the sea too, and its waves can rage only as far as the shore, which he has assigned to it as its boundary. There is no temptation to which the Lord has not set a limit. Let temptations come, then; let troubles come: you are being finely wrought by them, not wrecked.[16] Listen, and you will understand how useful

---

15. On persecution on account of the name, see notes at Exposition 2 of Psalm 68,4; Exposition 1 of Psalm 90,8.
16. *Consummaris ... non consumeris.*

temptations can be. Mark the apostle's words: *God is faithful, and he does not allow you to be tempted more fiercely than you can bear, but along with the temptation ordains the outcome, so that you may withstand it* (1 Cor 10:13). He does not say, "God will not allow you to be tempted at all." If you could dodge temptation, you would miss the refashioning. But you are being refashioned, and if that is your situation, you must be in the craftsman's hands. He chips something off you here, and straightens something there; he smooths something else, and cleanses another part. He works with his own tools, and these tools are the troubles of this world. Just make sure that you do not fall out of the craftsman's hand. No temptation will try you beyond your strength. God allows it for your profit, because he wants you to make progress. Listen to the apostle's clear affirmation: *Along with the temptation he ordains the outcome, so that you may withstand it*. Did the surging sea terrify you? Do not be afraid, because *the sea is his, for he made it*. Do you fear trouble from the nations?[17] But he himself made the nations, and he will not permit them to wreak havoc beyond the measure he has determined with a view to your progress. Does another psalm not predict, *All the nations you have created will come and worship before you, O Lord* (Ps 85(86):9)? If it can speak of *all the nations you have created*, it is obvious that he did indeed create the nations, and so we profess, *The sea is his, for he made it, and his hands laid down the dry land*. You have to be this dry land. Thirst for God's grace, so that a refreshing shower may fall upon you, and God find you bearing fruit. He does not allow the waves to cover what he has planted;[18] for *his hands laid down the dry land*. For this too let us shout with joy to him.

Verses 6-7. An invitation to repent. God's flock

10. We have recounted a good many reasons for praising God; so with all this in mind come back now to the invitation with which the psalm began: *Come, let us worship, and fall down before him. Let us weep before the Lord who made us.* Let us rejoice exceedingly because he made this, made that—the psalm has enumerated many of the things he made. But now it returns to its exhortation: *Come, let us worship, and fall down before him. Let us weep before the Lord who made us.* I have reminded you about the praises of God, so now do not be lazy or let your way of life and conduct keep you far away. *Come, let us worship, and fall down before him.* Perhaps you are anxious about your sins, and they have been keeping you far from God. In that case, let us accept the next part of the invitation: *Let us weep in the presence of the Lord who made us.* Perhaps you have a conscience on fire because of some offense. Put out the flame with your tears; weep before the Lord. Weep without fear in the presence of the God who

17. Possibly he has the Vandals in mind.
18. Variant: "to cover those whom he preserves."

made you, for he does not despise in you the work of his own hands. Do not suppose that you can make good the damage yourself. You can collapse by yourself, but not restore yourself; only he who made you can remake you. *Let us weep before the Lord who made us.* Shed tears before him, confess to him, forestall him by coming into his presence confessing; for who are you, you who weep before him and confess to him? You are the person he made. A thing that is made can be very confident in approaching its maker, and in this case it is no ordinary product but one made in his own image and likeness. *Come, let us worship, and fall down before him. Let us weep before the Lord who made us.*

11. *For he is the Lord our God.* And what are we? We need to know, if we are to fall down before him without fear. *We are the people of his pasture, the sheep of his hands.*[19] Notice how elegantly the psalm has inverted the order of the words, seeming to pair the phrases in a way we would not have expected. It does so to make sure we understand that *sheep* and *people* are the same thing. It might have seemed more appropriate to say, "The sheep of his pasture and the people of his hands," since sheep and pasture belong together; but it did not say that. Instead it spoke of *the people of his pasture.* The sheep are the people itself. Moreover, there is good reason to say, *the sheep of his hands,* because just before this the psalm has exhorted us, *Let us fall down before the Lord who made us.* He made us, his sheep. We do not make our sheep: we buy them. No farmer makes sheep for himself. He may buy them, or they may be given to him, or he may find them and add them to his flock, or he may even steal them; but he cannot make them. Our Lord did make us, and therefore we are *the people of his pasture and the sheep of his hands.* These sheep are the ones he has deigned to make for himself by his grace.

He extols these sheep in the Song of Songs, calling them flawless and comparing them to the teeth of his bride, holy Church: *your teeth are like newly-shorn flocks, coming up from their washing. All of them bear twins; there is never a barren one among them* (Sg 4:2; 6:5). Why teeth? Because you speak through them. They are the Church's teeth because through them the Church speaks. And what are these teeth like? *Newly-shorn flocks.* Why newly-shorn? Because they have shed the burdens of the world. Remember those people I was talking about earlier: they were like shorn sheep, shorn by God's command, *Go and sell all you possess and give the money to the poor: you will have treasure in heaven. Then come, follow me* (Mk 10:21). They were like shorn sheep, weren't they? They obeyed the command, and emerged from their shearing. Moreover, they had believed in Christ, and had been baptized; so what else are you told about them? They were *coming up from their washing,* from the bath that had cleansed them. And *all of them bear twins.* Twins? Yes, it means the twin

---

19. Variant: "hand."

precepts on which the whole law and the prophets depend.[20] We, then, are *the people of his pasture, the sheep of his hands.*

Verses 8-11. The testing in the desert; the prospect of entering God's rest

12. Accordingly the psalm urges, *If you hear his voice today....* O my people, O people of God! God is addressing his people: not just that primordial people that he will never cast off, but all his people. In the cornerstone he speaks to both walls, for in Christ the prophetic voice speaks to both the Jewish people and the Gentiles. *If you hear his voice today, do not harden your hearts.* Long ago you heard his voice through Moses, and you hardened your hearts. He spoke again through his herald, and you hardened your hearts. Now at last, when he speaks with his own lips, let your hearts become tender. He sent heralds ahead of him, time and time again, but now he graciously comes himself. He who used to speak through the mouths of the prophets speaks here with his own. *If you hear his voice today, do not harden your hearts.*

13. Why did you say this, Lord, *do not harden your hearts*? "Because you remember how your fathers are accustomed to behave. *Do not harden your hearts, as they did when they provoked me, as they did on the day of temptation in the desert.*" Brothers and sisters, you undoubtedly recall how that people did put God to the test, how it was subjected to discipline, and was controlled in the wilderness like a horse by an expert rider with the reins of his laws, the harness of his commands. You recall how in spite of its unruly conduct God did not abandon it, but never ceased to surround it with timely benefits and to correct it with his rod. So for your own part, the Lord says, *Do not harden your hearts, as they did on the day of temptation in the desert, when your fathers put me to the test.* Do not let people like that be your fathers anymore; do not imitate them. They were your fathers, but if you refuse to model your conduct on theirs they will not be your fathers in the future, although they used to be, since you were born from them. Jeremiah speaks of Gentiles coming from the most distant lands: *Gentiles will come to you from the furthest parts of the earth, and they will say, Truly our ancestors worshiped a lie, a futile thing that could not help them* (Jer 16:19). If those Gentiles could discard their idols in order to approach the God of Israel, should his own people desert their God, the God who brought them out of Egypt through the Red Sea, who drowned their pursuing enemies in it, who led them out into the desert and fed them there with manna, who never withheld his rod from training them or deprived them of his merciful gifts? Should they forsake him, their own God, when even Gentiles came to him?

---

20. See Mt 22:40.

There, in the desert, God reminds them, *your fathers put me to the test; they tried me, though they saw what I had done.*[21] They witnessed my works for forty years, and for forty years they provoked me. I worked miracles before them by the hand of Moses, but they went on hardening their hearts more and more.

14. *For forty years I stayed very close to this generation.* What is meant by *I stayed very close*? I demonstrated my presence by the signs and acts of power I showed them. Not on one day, or two, but *for forty years I stayed very close to this generation, but I said, They are always astray in their hearts.* The *forty years* mean the same as *always.* The number forty stands for the whole course of the ages, as though time reached its fullness at the number forty. That is why the Lord fasted for forty days, and was for forty days tempted in the wilderness, and was with his disciples for forty days after his resurrection. He made the first span of forty days a symbol of temptation, but the later period of forty days a sign of consolation, because when we are tempted we are certainly consoled as well. It is necessary for his body, the Church, to endure temptations in this world, but its consoler is never absent. He has promised, *Lo, I am with you throughout all days, even to the end of the ages* (Mt 28:20).

But I said, They are always astray in their hearts. I stayed with them for forty years in order to show them up as the sort of people they were, the sort who go on provoking me all the time, even to the end of the ages. God willed to make those forty years a sign of the whole stretch of time.

15. What will be the outcome? Will there not be others who will enter God's rest instead of them? Those who scorned God's mercy, who rebelled against God with their hardened hearts, were disqualified. But did their repudiation mean that God had lost his people? Assuredly not. Will it not be proved true that *God is able to raise up children to Abraham even from these stones* (Mt 3:9)?

Yet the psalm records his words, *I said, They are always astray in their hearts. These people do not know my ways, and to them I have sworn in my anger, They shall never enter my rest.* We began with intense joy, yet the psalm closes on a note of sheer terror: *to them I have sworn in my anger, They shall never enter my rest.* It is already a great matter that God should speak to us; how much greater if God should swear? You need to be careful of a human being who swears an oath, for he may on account of his oath do something he does not really want to do. How much more fearful should you be of God, who is incapable of taking any oath rashly? Yet he chose to swear this oath, as a confirmation of what he said. And by whom does God swear? By himself, for there is no one greater whom he could invoke.[22] In his own name he confirms his promises, and in his own name he confirms his threats. None of us must say in our hearts, "His promises are true, but his threats are empty." Just as what he promises is real, so is

---

21. Variant: "…they put me to the test, though they had proof of my works and had seen them."
22. See Heb 6:13.

what he threatens certain. As you must be utterly sure about gaining rest, happiness, eternity and immortality, if you have kept his commandments, so must you be equally sure of perdition, the heat of eternal fire, and damnation with the devil, if you have despised his commandments.

So, then, God swore in his anger that they will not enter his rest; yet there must be some who will enter it, for it is impossible that his rest will be granted to no one. They have been disqualified, but we shall enter it. Some of the branches were broken off because they had lost their likeness to God[23] and were unfaithful, but let us be grafted in through faith and humility. Let us enter into his rest.

But why have they entered it—the people who are there, the ones who have been chosen, who did not harden their hearts and resist God? Because *the Lord will not reject his people*.

---

23. *Propter dissimilitudinem*. At the end of the sermon Augustine returns to the thought of section 1: being close to God means being like him.

Exposition of Psalm 95

A Sermon[1]

Verse 1. The new song, charity; the building of the Lord's house

1. My lord and brother, Severus,[2] is still making us wait for the pleasure we expect to have in the sermon he owes us, though he does recognize that we hold him our debtor in this respect. Wherever he has traveled, the Lord has given joy to all the churches through his eloquence; so how much more should this church expect to enjoy his preaching, since it was from here that the Lord made him widely available for others? But what are we to do, except yield to his wishes? I have told you that he is only deferring his sermon, brothers and sisters, not defrauding us of it. Hold him to be your debtor, then, and do not let him off until he has discharged his debt.

Well then, beloved friends,[3] let us have your attention, so that we can say something about this psalm, in the measure that the Lord allows us. What we shall say is already familiar to you; but no matter, for it is pleasant to be reminded of the truth. When the title was read out some of you may possibly have been surprised, for over the psalm is the superscription, *When the house was being built after the captivity*. On hearing that you perhaps expected that the psalm would relate what stones were hewn out of the mountains, what heavy masses of them were dragged along, what foundations were laid, what beams set in place, and what pillars erected. But the psalm sings of none of these things. Does that mean, then, that when it sings of something else the psalm is out of harmony with its title, that it carries one indication on its forehead[4] and a different one in its wording? No, certainly not; but it does demand insight in its hearers.

The psalm speaks about the building of a house, and all the stones that make up the house need to understand[5] what they have sung. A house is being constructed for the Lord, but not in the place where Solomon built. He raised up

---

1. According to Perler, probably preached at Hippo, in winter or spring 406-407. From section 5 below it appears that this sermon was delivered on the day after Augustine's Exposition of Psalm 131.
2. Probably the bishop of Milevis whom Augustine had mentioned in an earlier sermon as being reluctant to preach to this same congregation until after Augustine himself had done so; see the Exposition of Psalm 131,1.
3. *Caritas vestra.*
4. Or perhaps "on its facade."
5. Variant: "…that make up the house understand."

the temple, and you have just heard what our Lord said about that temple.[6] The disciples were admiring the great stones of the temple and its massive bulk, and they expressed their admiration and wonder to the Lord. But he answered, *Truly I tell you, there shall not be left here one stone upon another that will escape destruction* (Mk 13:2). The house we are concerned with cannot be of this kind. Look what the psalm says about where it is built: not in a single place, not in one region only, for the opening verse invites us:

2. *Sing a new song to the Lord, sing to the Lord, all the earth.* If all the earth is singing a new song, it is being built up even as it sings, for to sing is to build—provided, that is, that its song is not the old one. The desires of the flesh sing an old song, but the charity of God sings a song that is new. If your song springs from earthly lust, you are singing an old tune; and even if the words in your mouth are those of the new song, praise is unseemly in the mouth of a sinner.[7] It is better to be a new person and keep quiet than to sing that old ditty, because if you are new in yourself, then even if you remain silent and human ears catch no sound from you, your heart is not silent. The new song your heart is singing reaches the ears of God who made you a new person. You love, and you are silent, but your love is itself a voice that sings to God; your love itself is the new song. Do you want proof of this? The Lord tells us, *A new commandment I give you: that you love one another* (Jn 13:34).

It is the whole earth that sings this new song, for that is where the house is under construction. The entire earth is God's house. But if this is the case, anyone who does not cling to fellowship with the whole earth is not the house, but a ruin—an ancient ruin, foreshadowed by that ancient temple. In that temple the old order was in process of being demolished so that the new order might be built. What sign is there that the old edifice is being dismantled? *Truly I tell you, there shall not be left here one stone upon another that will escape destruction.* Now Christ is a stone; but the apostle tells us, *As many of you as have been baptized in Christ have clothed yourselves in Christ* (Gal 3:27). If anyone who is baptized in Christ puts on Christ, then who is engaged in putting one stone upon another? Surely the person who piles baptism upon existing baptism?[8]

But do not let this worry you, because *there shall not be left one stone upon another that will escape destruction.* The stones destined for the new edifice, the one built after the captivity, are assembled in such fashion that charity binds them together into one. There is no stone resting upon another stone, because all the stones form one single stone. This should not surprise you, for it is the effect produced by the new song, the work of the charity that makes us new. The

---

6. From various allusions in the sermon, it appears that the gospel reading had been from Mark 13.
7. See Sir 15:9.
8. A sore point, since this was Donatist practice.

apostle joins us to one another and builds us in; or, rather, more than that: he binds us tightly together in that union and fits us into the whole when he says, *Bear with each other in love, careful to maintain the unity forged by the Spirit in the bond of peace* (Eph 4:2-3). Where the unity given by the Spirit reigns, there can be only one stone, but it is the one stone made out of many. How is the one made out of the many? By their bearing with one another in love.

The house of the Lord our God is a-building; it is happening all the time; the work is going forward. This is the work our voices are doing, and the readings, and the preaching of the gospel throughout the world: all of them are engaged continuously on the building of the house. Already it has grown large and extended through many nations. True, it has not yet occupied the territories of all of them, but as it grows it has taken hold in many lands and is destined to embrace all. Certain people who boast of belonging to the household belittle it by alleging, "It has shrunk nowadays."[9] Not at all: it is still growing, and all those nations which have not yet come to faith will believe in time. Let no one ask, "Is that uncouth language ever to be the language of faith? Will the barbarians ever believe?" What is the significance of the appearing of the Spirit in fiery tongues,[10] if not that there is no tongue so fire-resistant that the Spirit cannot melt it? It is not as though we had no barbarous peoples believing in Christ yet. There are regions where Roman rule has not reached, yet Christ has already claimed them; places still closed to those who fight with the sword are not closed against him who fights with wood. The Lord has established his sovereignty from a tree. Who is it who fights with wood? Christ. From his cross he has conquered kings, brought them into subjection and affixed his cross to their foreheads, so that now they glory in it, knowing that in it lies their salvation.

This is the work in progress, this is how the house grows, this is how the building goes forward. Listen to the rest of the psalm to assure yourselves of this; see in the psalm the builders at work, framing the house. *Sing a new song to the Lord, sing to the Lord, all the earth.*

Verses 2-3. The Church is universal

3. *Sing to the Lord, bless his name, worthily declare his salvation from day to day.*[11] How does the building grow? *Worthily declare his salvation from day to day*, the psalm exhorts us. Let it be preached from day to day, let the building go

---

9. A reference to the parochial mentality of the Donatists, who by regarding themselves as the only authentic Christians were implicitly confining the true Church to Africa. Augustine frequently refutes this narrow theory by appealing to the universalist perspectives of the psalms and the New Testament. Later in this sermon (section 5) he emphasizes that the ransom poured out by Christ was more than enough to redeem the whole world.
10. See Acts 2:3.
11. Variant: "proclaim his salvation as day succeeding day."

on from day to day; let my house grow from day to day, says the Lord. Then the
psalm seems to represent the laborers as inquiring, "Where are you ordering us
to build? Where do you wish your house to rise? Choose a level site for us, a site
where there is plenty of room, if you want a spacious house built for you. Where
are you telling us to make worthy proclamation from day to day?" The psalm
points out the place: *Proclaim his glory among the nations*. Notice that what is to
be proclaimed among the nations is *his glory*, not your own. Make a good job of
declaring his glory among the Gentiles, all you construction workers. If you try
to proclaim your own glory you will fall; if you proclaim his, you will be built up
yourselves even as you build.

We infer, then, that those who have attempted to proclaim their own glory
have chosen not to be part of the house, and therefore they do not sing the new
song in harmony with all the earth. They are not in communion with the whole
earth, and therefore they are not within the house, sharing in the work of
building, but instead have erected a whitewashed wall. And how stern are God's
threats against whitened walls, how innumerable the testimonies of the
prophets, through which God's curse upon every whitewashed wall is uttered![12]
What is a whitewashed wall? What else but hypocrisy and pretense? On the
outside it gleams white, but inside it is nothing but mud.

What I am about to say is no more than what has been said before; but we
speak because the Lord has graciously imparted to us the same Spirit who
inspired those who spoke before us, and whatever we say now we say under the
influence of the same Spirit who prompted our predecessors. We cannot omit to
say it, therefore; it must be said, since it has always been said through the gift of
God. A certain person[13] who mentioned this whitewashed wall said this about it:
if you build a wall that is not connected to other walls, but free-standing, and then
you make a door in it, anyone who enters by this door will still be out of doors! So
it is with that sect which has refused to sing the new song along with the house,
but preferred to build a wall, and a whitewashed, rickety wall at that. What use is
a door in it? If you pass through, you find yourself still outside. Since they have
not gone through the real door themselves, even the door they make does not
admit anyone to anything. The Lord says, *I am the door; through me they will
come in*. Who are they, who come in by the door? Those who seek the Lord's
glory, not their own. Who come in by the door? Those who obey the injunction,
Worthily proclaim his glory among the nations; for, as the Lord points out, *the*

---

12. See Ezek 13:10-15; Acts 23:3. Variant: "how many are the testimonies of the prophets, where
God says he will soon deal with every whitewashed wall."

13. Optatus of Milevis, in North Africa, flourished c. 370. In his book *On the Donatist Schism* 3,10,
he says, "False prophets are to be regarded as builders of a wall. Even if a door is constructed in
it, anyone who enters is still outside. Nor can a single wall accommodate a cornerstone, the
stone which is Christ." He goes on to contrast the warm safety of a house which shelters its
children (the Catholic Church) with the discomforts and dangers of living with only a wall.

one who enters by the door is the shepherd of the sheep, but the one who climbs up by another route is a thief and a brigand (Jn 10:9.2.1). Anyone who enters by the door is a humble person, but the one who climbs up by another route is proud. This is why the Lord describes the one as entering, but the other as climbing up. The former is welcomed on entering, but the climber is thrown down.

Proclaim his glory among the nations. What does *among the nations* suggest? Can it mean just a few favored nations, so that the sect that built the whitewashed wall can still make out its case? "What about Getulia, Numidia, Mauretania and Byzacena?"[14] they say. "Are these not nations? Provinces can be nations." But may that excuse be snatched away from hypocrisy, from the white-washed wall, by the word of God that is building the house all over the world. It is not explicit enough to say, as the psalm has done, *Proclaim his glory among the nations*, for you might think that some nations were excluded; so it continues, *and his marvels among all peoples.*

*Verse 4. The unutterable greatness of God. Our redemption
from captivity to demons*

4. *For great is the Lord, and exceedingly worthy of praise.* Who is this Lord, who is so great, so exceedingly worthy of praise? Who else but Jesus Christ? You know very well that he appeared as a man; you know that he was conceived in the womb of a woman; you know that he was born, that he was suckled, that he was carried in his mother's arms, that he was circumcised, that an offering was made for him, and that he grew up. You know too that in the end he was slapped, spat upon, crowned with thorns, crucified, killed, and pierced with a lance. You know that he suffered all these things; yet he is *great, and exceedingly worthy of praise*. Do not despise him because he was made little; rather understand him to be great. He was made little because all of you were little; let him be great in your estimation, and then you will be great in him. When the stones carried to the building are growing great in this way, the house itself is built up, and its mighty fabric rises. Grow, then; understand how great Christ is. Even when small he is great, exceedingly great.

The psalm leaves it at that, saying nothing further. It wanted to tell us how great the Lord is, but even were it to go on saying all day, "Great ... great...," what would it be saying? One who goes on repeating "great" all day long must stop some time, because the day itself comes to an end; but the Lord's greatness exists before all days and beyond all days, and has no "day" to confine it. What should the psalm say, then? Simply that *great is the Lord, and exceedingly worthy of praise*; for what can a little tongue say to praise him who is great? By saying *exceedingly* he articulated something, and commended to our reflection

---

14. Provinces of Roman Africa where Donatism was entrenched.

the wisdom in his own mind. It is as though he had said, "You must reflect on what I cannot put into words, but when you have thought about it, it will still be too little." If no one's mind can comprehend it, will anyone's tongue have the power to expound it? *Great is the Lord, and exceedingly worthy of praise.* May he be praised, may he be preached, may his glory be declared, because then the house is being built.

5. *He is more to be feared than all the gods.* Does that mean that other gods really exist, over whom he could loom terrifyingly? Let us see what gods it means, and then we shall see why it says this.[15] But before we go on to that, dearly beloved, notice something else.[16] The Lord, who seemed to have been intimidated by human beings, is he who *is more to be feared than all the gods.* Did not the nations rage? Did the peoples not devise futile schemes against the Lord and against his Christ?[17] Did not bull-calves throng round him and fat bulls besiege him?[18] Did not a ravening lion roar against him and, entering the hearts of those savage people, shout, *Crucify! Crucify!* (Lk 23:21; Ps 21:14(22:13))? Did they think that he who is to be feared not only more than all human beings, but even more than all the gods, could be terrified by such rampaging?

More to be feared he is indeed *than all the gods.* The place where he intends to build his house is thickly forested, which is why we heard in yesterday's psalm, *We found it in the pastures and woodlands* (Ps 131(132):6). It was this same house that was being sought when the psalm spoke of *pastures and woodlands.* Why was the place forested? Men and women were worshipping idols, so it is small wonder that they were feeding pigs. There was once a son who forsook his father, and ran through all his money by extravagant living and frequenting prostitutes. He ended by feeding pigs,[19] which is a way of saying that he paid cult to demons. Through the superstition prevalent among the Gentiles the whole earth had become a thick wood. But the Lord who builds his house uprooted the forest, and this is why our psalm is entitled, *When the house was being built after the captivity*; for people certainly had been held captive under the devil, and had served demons, but they were redeemed from captivity. They had the power to sell themselves, but were powerless to buy themselves back. The redeemer came, and laid down the price. He poured out his blood and purchased the whole round world. Are you asking what he bought? Look what he paid, and from that infer what he bought. The price paid was Christ's blood. What is worth a price like that? What else but the entire world? What else but all nations? When certain people maintain either that the price was so low that it purchased Africans only, or that they are themselves so important that so high a price was justly

---

15. Variant: "we shall see what gods ... and then let us see why...."
16. Augustine returns in section 6 to the question just posed.
17. See Ps 2:1.2.
18. See Ps 21:13(22:12).
19. See Lk 15:13-15.

paid for them alone, they are either shockingly ungrateful for the generosity that ransomed them, or else exceedingly proud. Let them not triumph,[20] and let them not be arrogant; whatever Christ spent, he spent for all the world. He knows what he has bought, and he knows what he paid for it.

Only because we were ransomed from captivity is the house being built. And who were they, our former captors? We can ask this now, because preachers who are[21] ordered to *proclaim his glory* are the workers who will clear the forest. Their mission is to uproot the trees, free the land from captivity, and then lay the foundations and build by proclaiming the greatness of this house of the Lord. How is the demon-infested forest to be uprooted? By the proclamation of him who is superior to all demons. All the nations paid cult to demons as gods. What they called gods were in reality demons, as the apostle plainly teaches: *The sacrifices offered by pagans are offered to demons, not to God* (1 Cor 10:20). People accustomed to offering sacrifices to demons were obviously still in captivity, and in consequence the whole earth had continued to be overgrown with forests. The Lord therefore had to be preached as *great and exceedingly worthy of praise*.

Verse 5. The glory of the Lord who made the heavens

6. He came, then, to redeem a people held captive, and to eradicate the superstitions that enslaved them. He came, he who is *more to be feared than all the gods*. How is his greatness to be manifested? It is as though you inquired of the psalmist, "Why did you say, *More than all the gods*? Did you mean that other gods really exist?" The psalm replies, *All the gods of the heathen are demons*.

Now listen carefully, beloved.[22] The psalm said something about greatness a few minutes ago: it declared, *Great is the Lord*; and then, as though owning itself insufficient to praise him, it continued, *And exceedingly worthy of praise.* I pointed out to you then, didn't I, that the psalmist left you to think about what he could not articulate? But now he does attempt to express it in words, and what does he say about the greatness of the Lord Jesus Christ? That he is superior to all demons—is that all? It seems to be; for after declaring that the Lord is *more to be feared than all the gods*, he added, *For all the gods of the heathen are demons.* But it is no great thing to be sovereign over demons; you can be so yourself, if you wish—but only if you believe in Christ, of course. So is this all it amounts to, is this the great praise due to him of whom it is said that *great is the Lord, and exceedingly worthy of praise*? The psalmist meant to explain, insofar as the human tongue had power to do so. The Holy Spirit is the great instrumentalist

20. Variant: "insult us."
21. Variant: "... our former captors? Who were they? Preachers who are...."
22. *Caritas vestra.*

who plays on that human organ, but he must make his music in syllables that can pass through the narrow human spirit. Nevertheless he does inspire our thoughts. What does the psalmist say, then, when he wants to express God's greatness with his human tongue? *Great is the Lord, and exceedingly worthy of praise.* Tell us, please tell us, how worthy of praise? Tell us, we beg. The psalmist replies, *He is more to be feared than all the gods.* Why did you say that, *more to be feared than all the gods*? Because *all the gods of the heathen are demons.* But is this all the praise we are to offer him who is exceedingly worthy of praise—that he is superior to all the gods of the heathen, gods who are nothing more than demons?

Wait a minute; the psalm has more to say. *But the Lord made the heavens.* So, you see, he is not just above the demons, but above all the heavens which he created. If the psalm had said only, "He is above all the gods, because all the other gods are demons," and the Lord's praise had amounted to no more than that, it would have said something less than we are accustomed to think of Christ. In fact it added, *But the Lord made the heavens*; so now consider what a distance there is between the heavens and the demons, and consider too what a distance there is between the heavens themselves and him who made the heavens. Then you will see how sublime the Lord is. The psalm did not say, "But the Lord sits enthroned above the heavens"; if it had, people might have imagined that someone else made those heavens for him to sit upon. No; it said, *But the Lord made the heavens.* And if he made the heavens, he made the angels as well; he it was who made the angels, and he it was who made the apostles, to whom the demons were subjected.[23] Yet the apostles themselves were heavens,[24] because they bore the Lord. And who was this Lord whom they carried? The Lord by whom they had been created. Scripture testifies that they were heavens when it declares, *The heavens proclaim God's glory* (Ps 18:2(19:1)).

To the heavens, then, the command is given: *Proclaim his glory among the nations, and his marvels among all the peoples, for great is the Lord and exceedingly worthy of praise, more to be feared than all the gods.* What gods? *All the gods of the heathen are demons.* More to be feared he certainly is than gods of that sort, but *the Lord made the heavens.* O you heavens whom he made, proclaim his glory among the nations! Let his house be built up all over the earth, and let the whole earth sing a new song.

---

23. See Lk 10:17.
24. A frequent metaphor in Augustine's preaching.

Verse 6. The order of priorities: confession before beauty

7. *Confession and beauty are fitting in his presence.* Are you in love with beauty? Do you want to be beautiful? Then confess. The psalm did not say, "Beauty and confession," but *confession and beauty.* You have been ugly, so confess and become beautiful. You were a sinner, but confess and become righteous. You were able to make yourself foul, but you cannot make yourself fair. What a bridegroom we have: one who loved a soiled bride in order to make her beautiful! "What do you mean?" someone asks. "In what sense did he love a soiled bride?" Remember what he told us: *I came to call not the just, but sinners* (Mt 9:13). But what about those sinners whom you call, Lord: do you mean them to remain sinners? "No," he replies. But how can they cease to be sinners? *Confession and beauty are fitting in his presence.* They confess their sins, they throw up the bad things they had greedily swallowed, and they do not return to their vomit like a filthy dog.[25] There you find confession and beauty. We are in love with beauty, so let us first opt for confession, that beauty may follow.

Perhaps now someone stands up who is in love with power, and in love with magnificence. Such a person aspires to be as great as the angels. There certainly is magnificence in the angels, and such mighty power that if angels were to do all they are capable of, we could not bear it. Everyone envies angelic power, but no one aspires to angelic justice. Set your love on justice first, and power will accrue to you. Even here, in the psalm, what follows? *Holiness and magnificence are in his holy place.* You were in too much of a hurry to seek magnificence: choose holiness as your love first, and when you have been sanctified, you will be magnificent as well. If you turn the proper order on its head and want to be magnificent first, you fall before you rise, for you are not truly rising but only exalting yourself. You will rise all the more surely if he who cannot fall lifts you up. He who cannot fall came down to you. You had fallen; he came down, and he stretched out his hand to you. You have no power to rise by yourself, so grasp the hand of him who stooped down to you, so that you may be uplifted by his strength.

Verses 7-10. The pure, humble offerings to be brought into the Lord's house

8. What, then, are the Gentiles required to do? The psalm has told us that *confession and beauty are fitting in his presence; holiness and magnificence are in his holy place*, and this is what we proclaim when we are building the house. This is what has already been proclaimed among the nations. When the uprooters of the forest proclaim the message to them, what must the nations do?

25. See Prv 26:11; 2 Pt 2:22.

To these same Gentiles the psalm now speaks: *Bring to the Lord, you Gentile countries, bring to the Lord glory and honor.* Do not claim glory and honor for yourselves. Those who proclaimed the news to you proclaimed not their own glory, but the Lord's; and you must do likewise. *Bring to the Lord glory and honor,* and say to him, *Not to us, Lord, not to us, but to your name give the glory* (Ps 113B:1(115:1)). Do not rest your hope in any merely human agent. If one of you is baptized, let that person acknowledge that "He is baptizing me, he of whom the bridegroom's friend testified, *He is the one who baptizes*" (Jn 1:33). If you speak so, you are bringing glory and honor to the Lord. *Bring to the Lord glory and honor.*

9. *Bring to the Lord the glory due to his name.* Not to the name of any men or women, not to your own name, but to his name bring glory. *Lift your offerings, and enter his courts.* You are bidden to pick up the victims for your sacrifice: what are you going to carry with you, to gain entrance to his courts? The house is getting bigger now, and its courts have been constructed; and those who bring victims for sacrifice are invited to enter them. Are we to bring bulls, goats, or sheep? By no means. *If you had wanted a sacrifice I would certainly have offered it.* God himself has indicated to us the sacrifice we must offer. May it not be that oblation of which the psalm has already spoken: *confession and beauty are fitting in his presence*? Confession is a sacrifice offered to God. Take care, then, you Gentiles, not to come empty-handed if you mean to enter his courts. *Lift your offerings.* What victims are we to carry with us? *A sacrifice to God is a troubled spirit. A contrite and humbled heart God does not scorn* (Ps 50:18.19(51:16.17)). If you enter God's house with a humble heart, you have entered with an oblation; but if you are proud, you are coming in empty-handed, for how is it possible for you to be proud, unless you are empty? If you were full, you could not be inflated. And how could you be full? By bringing a sacrifice with you and carrying it into the Lord's courts.

Let us run through the rest briefly, for we do not want to detain you too long. Contemplate the house as it rises, watch the building going on throughout the whole world. Be glad that you have entered its courts, be joyful that you are being built into the temple of God. Those who enter it are themselves built into its fabric; they are themselves the house of God. He it is who dwells in it, he for whom the house is constructed all over the world, after the captivity. *Lift your offerings, and enter his courts.*

10. *Worship the Lord in his holy court,* in the Catholic Church, for that is his holy court. Do not let anyone mislead you with *"Look, here is Christ!" or, "There he is!" for spurious prophets will arise* (Mk 13:21-22). Say this to them, *"There shall not be left here one stone upon another that will escape destruction* (Mk 13:2). You are enticing me toward a whitewashed wall, but I worship my God in his holy court."

11. *Let the whole earth be moved before his face. Publish among the nations: The Lord is king, he reigns from wood. Indeed he has set the round world to rights, and it will not be disturbed.* What magnificent testimonies these are to the building of God's house! The clouds of heaven thunder their witness that God's dwelling is being constructed throughout the world, and yet all the while frogs are croaking from the swamp, "We are the only Christians"![26] What proofs can I urge on you? Those of the psalter. I draw your attention to what you sing yourself, but as a deaf singer. Open your ears, you who sing these words. You sing with me, but you are not in tune with me; your tongue sings what mine sings, but your heart is not in harmony with mine. Do you not sing these same psalms? Look at the witness borne by all the world, then: *let the whole earth be moved before his face.* Can you deny that it is moved? *Publish among the nations: The Lord is king, he reigns from wood.*[27] But perhaps the Donatists will persist, and say that they too establish their rule from wood, since they dominate through the cudgels of the Circumcellions![28] Establish your power from Christ's cross, if you are determined to reign through wood. Your wooden weapon is making you wooden yourself; but on Christ's wood you sail across the sea. Listen to what the psalm says: *He has set the round world to rights, and it will not be disturbed*; yet you allege not only that it has been disturbed after being set to rights by the Lord, but even that it has dwindled.[29] Are you right, and is the psalm lying? Bogus prophets shout, *Look, here is Christ! There he is!* Are they telling the truth, while the prophet is a liar?

Brothers and sisters, at every street corner you hear the strident accusations, "He was a *traditor*, and that other fellow was a *traditor* too."[30] What are you saying? Are your statements more worth listening to than God's? *Indeed he has set the round world to rights, and it will not be disturbed.* I am showing you this whole world already a-building, so pick up your offering and enter the courts of the Lord. But you have no offerings, and so you refuse to enter. How is that? If God had required of you a bull, a goat, or a ram as a sacrifice, you would have found something to bring; but no, he demands of you a humble heart, and so you are unwilling to enter. You cannot find that offering in yourself, because you are

---

26. The Donatists, Augustine's target throughout the Exposition, and explicitly in the present section.
27. The words "from wood" or "from a tree" are found in neither the Hebrew nor the Septuagint, and may be a Christian interpolation. If so, it occurred early, for Justin quotes the psalm with these words included in his *First Apology* 41 (c. A.D. 155), and in his *Dialogue with Trypho* 73 (c.A.D. 135) he accuses the Jews of excising them. They influenced the sixth-century hymn to the cross, *Vexilla Regis*, by Venantius Fortunatus.
28. On the Circumcellions, see note at Exposition of Psalm 10,5.
29. Because, according to the Donatists, the true Church was now to be found only in Africa.
30. A reference to the events that had initiated the schism, the surrendering of the sacred books to the persecutors in the reign of Diocletian; see note at Exposition of Psalm 10,1. The double meaning of the Latin word, *trado* ("hand over" but also "betray") helped to inflame the controversy.

swollen with pride. *Indeed he has set the round world to rights, and it will not be disturbed. He will judge the peoples with justice*, and then will they mourn, those who refuse to love[31] justice now.

Verses 11-13. The new creation exults at the prospect of God's coming to judge

12. *Let the heavens rejoice and earth be glad.* Let the heavens, which proclaim God's glory, rejoice; let the heavens which the Lord has made rejoice; let the earth, as it drinks in the abundant rain from heaven, be glad. The heavens are preachers, the earth is those who listen. *Let the sea and all that dwell in it heave and rage.* What sea is meant here? The world. The sea was whipped up in all its fullness, for the whole world was aroused against the Church as it began to be extended and built up all over the earth. You heard about its uproar in the gospel: *They will hand you over to judgment* (Mk 13:9). The sea raged, but what chance had it of overpowering him who created the heavens?

13. *The fields and everything in them will make merry.* All gentle people, all kindly people, all even-tempered people, are God's fields. *All the trees of the forest will shout for joy.* These forest trees are the pagans. Why are they now shouting for joy? Because they have been cut away from the oleaster and grafted into the true olive tree.[32] *All the trees of the forest will shout for joy*, because huge cedars and cypresses and timbers resistant to decay have been brought in for the construction of the house.[33] They were forest trees, but only before they were set into their places in the building; they used to be forest trees, but only before they bore the olive.

14. *All the trees of the forest will shout for joy before the Lord, for he is coming, he is coming to judge the earth.* He came once, the first time, and he will come again. At his first coming he came in his Church, upon the clouds. What are the clouds on which he rode? The apostles who preached Christ; you heard about them when the passage from the apostle was read: *We function as Christ's ambassadors, and we beg you in Christ's name, be reconciled to God* (2 Cor 5:20). These are the clouds on which he came, if we are not referring to his final coming, when he will come to judge the living and the dead. His first coming is on the clouds. His own words trumpeted this first coming in the gospel: *Henceforth you shall see the Son of Man coming in the clouds.*[34] What does *henceforth* suggest? Does it refer to the time when the Lord will come at the end, when all

---

31. Variant: "choose."
32. See Rom 11:17.
33. See 1 Kgs 5:6, though the building there referred to is that of the first temple by Solomon, not "the house built after the captivity."
34. The quotation seems to be more directly from Mt 26:64; but Augustine may be thinking of Mk 13:26, "... they will see...."

the tribes of the earth will mourn?[35] No; he has come first in his preachers, and filled the whole earth. Let us not resist him in this, his first coming, if we hope not to be terrified at his second.

Woe betide those who are pregnant, or suckling babies (Mk 13:17). You heard the warning just now in the gospel, *Beware, for you do not know at what hour he will come* (Mt 24:42; Mk 13:33), and the former saying is a figurative way of making the same point. Whom do the expectant mothers, and the nursing mothers, represent? Those souls who cherish hopes of this world are likened to pregnant women; souls who have already obtained what they were hoping for are represented by nursing mothers. Suppose, for instance, someone wants to buy a country house. The purchase is not concluded yet, so the prospective buyer is pregnant, as it were, with a womb swollen with hope. Then the deal is done. The buyer has now brought forth the hope, and is now feeding the house he or she has bought. But *woe betide those who are pregnant, or suckling babies*; woe to those whose hope is set on the world, woe to those who cling to the goods they have brought to birth through their worldly hope.

What should a Christian do? Make use of the world, but not be enslaved to it. How can this be done? By possessing things with detachment. This is the advice of one who does not wish his disciples to be found like pregnant or nursing mothers on that day; this is his recommendation: *What I mean, brethren, is this: time is short. What remains for us is that those who have wives should live as though they were unmarried, those who weep should be as though they wept not, those who rejoice be as though they were not rejoicing, those who buy things hold to them lightly,[36] and those who use the world do so as though they made no use of it; for the form of this world is passing away, and I want you to be free from preoccupation* (1 Cor 7:29-32). One who is free from preoccupation looks forward with confidence to the coming of his Lord; for what kind of love for Christ would it be, to be afraid of his coming? Are we not ashamed of such an attitude, brothers and sisters? We love him, and yet dread his coming? Are we sure, in that case, that we do love him? Do we perhaps not love our sins more? Let us rather hate the sins, and love him who will come to punish sins. He will come whether we like it or not; the fact that he is not coming at the present moment does not mean that he will not in the future. Come he will, and you do not know when; but if he finds you ready, your ignorance of the time will do you no harm.

Then will all the trees of the forest shout for joy before the Lord, for he is coming, coming for the first time. And later? *He is coming to judge the earth*: then he will find intense joy among those who at his first coming believed that he will come again.

---

35. See Rv 1:7.
36. Variants: "... buy things as though they had no use for them"; "... buy things as though they were not buying."

15. Of that we can be certain, because *he will judge the world with equity*; and not merely a part of it, for it was not a part that he purchased. He has the right to judge the whole, because he paid the price for the whole. You heard him say in the gospel that when he comes *he will gather his elect from the four winds* (Mk 13:27); and if he is to gather them from the four winds, that must mean that he will gather them from all round the world. The name "Adam" stands for the four quarters of the world in Greek, as I mentioned once before.[37] In this name we have four letters: A,D,A,M. But in Greek these are the initial letters of the words signifying the four quarters of the world: Greek-speakers call the east Ἀνατολή, the west Δύσις, the north Ἄρκτος, the south Μεσημβρία; so the initial letters spell ADAM. We could think of this as signifying that the original "Adam" was scattered all over the earth. He was at first in a single place; he fell; and he was somehow fragmented until he filled the earth. But God's mercy collected the shattered pieces, forged them together in the fire of charity, and made what was broken into a single whole once more. God is a craftsman who well knows how to do this, so let no one despair. It is a difficult task, certainly, but think who the craftsman is. He who made us has remade us; he who formed us has formed us anew.

He will judge the world with equity, the peoples in his truth. What is equity, and what is truth? He will assemble his elect to sit with him in judgment;[38] but he will divide all the rest into two groups, placing some of them at his right hand, others at his left. What could be more equitable, what more consonant with truth, than that people who have been unwilling to show mercy to others, before the coming of the judge, should be disappointed of any hope of mercy for themselves? But those who have tried to act mercifully will be judged with mercy. To these, the people on the Lord's right hand, it will be said, *Come, you who are blessed by my Father, take possession of the kingdom prepared for you since the creation of the world.* And the Lord recalls their merciful deeds: *I was hungry, and you fed me; I was thirsty, and you gave me a drink*, and so on. But what stands to the account of those placed at his left? Their failure to show mercy. Where then will they go? *Depart from me into eternal fire.* These woeful tidings will set them groaning bitterly; but what does another psalm say? *The just will be held in eternal remembrance; woeful tidings hold no terrors for them* (Ps 111(112):7). Anyone who will be rejoicing at good news on that day will have no fear of hearing bad news. What sort of good news will cause their joy? *Come, you who are blessed by my Father.* What sort of bad news will they not need to fear? *Depart from me into the eternal fire which was prepared for the devil and his angels* (Mt 25:34-35.41).

---

37. See his Homilies on the Gospel of John IX,14; X,12.
38. On Augustine's distinction between those who will sit beside the Lord as fellow-judges, and those who will be assembled before him to be judged, see his Exposition 1 of Psalm 90,9-10.

This is equity, this is truth. *He will judge the world with equity, the peoples in his truth.* You surely cannot think that because you are unjust, the judge will be unjust, or that because you do not have truth in you, Truth himself will not be true? Well then, if you hope to find him merciful in your regard, be merciful yourself before he comes; forgive any offense committed against you, and give alms out of your own plenty. In any case, whose goods are you giving away, if not the Lord's? If you were disbursing what is truly your own, that would be generosity on your part, but since you only give what belongs to God anyway, you are only making restitution. *What have you that you did not receive?* (1 Cor 4:7).

These are the oblations most pleasing to God: mercy, humility, confession, peace, and charity. Let us bring him these, and then we can await without anxiety the coming of the judge who *will judge the world with equity, the peoples in his truth.*

Exposition of Psalm 96

A Sermon to the People[1]

Finding joy in the prophecies

1. God provides glorious sights[2] for a Christian heart. Nothing could be found more delightful than these, assuming that the palate of our faith is truly discerning and capable of enjoying the full flavor of God's honey. It is our belief that all of you, who have put your wholehearted faith in our Savior, have his Spirit dwelling within you and filling you with delight when the prophecies are read. Those prophecies were uttered many years ago by the lips of holy men, and now, so many years later, they have been fulfilled in the acceptance of the faith by the Gentiles. These same prophets reaped a harvest of magnificent joy even in their own day, when they contemplated in spirit[3] realities not yet present but guaranteed for the future. Intense delight was theirs; yet they were afire with love for us, whom they had not seen but whose spiritual forbears they were. Their charity filled them with a longing to live with us, in our days, were that possible, and to see the fulfillment of what they were prophesying in the Spirit. This is why the Lord said to his disciples, as to people who were beginning to witness these events, *Many righteous people and prophets longed to see what you see, but never saw it, and to hear what you hear, but never heard it* (Mt 13:17); for although the prophets did see these things in spirit, they saw them somehow represented as future, whereas to the apostles they were revealed as already present. Think how the righteous old man Simeon was transported with delight when he saw the infant Jesus. In that tiny child he recognized the Great One; in that diminutive body he knew the creator of heaven and earth. He thrilled with joy because he had received an assurance that he would not depart this life before seeing God's salvation. He acknowledged him, he was glad, he was uplifted with happiness, and he said, *You give your servant his discharge in peace, now, Lord, for my eyes have seen your salvation* (Lk 2:29-30).

---

1. Preached at Carthage, possibly in April 399.
2. *Magna spectacula*. The word sometimes carried sinister overtones for Augustine, who had in his youth recognized *spectacula* ("shows") as a dangerous seduction; see notes at the Expositions of Psalms 39,8; 93,20. But as a bishop he liked to point out that the Christian faith has much better *spectacula* to delight us; see Exposition of Psalm 39,9. The thought is similar here.
3. Or "in the Spirit."

438

Such joy is intense, and it springs from charity. We too were delighted when this psalm was sung. Some parts of it were understood by everyone, but others, we suspect, by only a few, or at any rate not by all. Let us then consider it together in this sermon, which we offer you as our service, and let us see how graciously God has willed to gladden us by setting out his promises, and then proving his faithfulness to us by fulfilling them.

Verse 1. The restoration of the Lord's land: this includes both the conversion of Jews and Gentiles, and the resurrection of his flesh

2. The psalm is entitled, *For David himself, when his land was restored*. If we want to keep to the path of correct understanding we must apply the whole psalm to Christ; let us not let go of the cornerstone,[4] lest our interpretation collapse in ruins. May whatever was tottering in its own weakness be steadied in him, what was held in suspense between uncertainties lodge firmly on him. Whatever doubts anyone has in mind on hearing God's scriptures, let him not move away from Christ. When in those words Christ has been revealed to him, let him understand that he has understood; but before he attains to this understanding of Christ, let him not presume that he has understood, for *Christ is the end of the law, bringing justification to everyone who believes* (Rom 10:4).

Well then, what is the meaning of that phrase in the title, *when his land was restored*, and how is it to be applied to Christ? It is easy enough to see how David is to be understood as Christ, for Christ was born of Mary, who was of David's line; therefore Christ could aptly be spoken of in prophecy as "David," since he was to be David's descendant. "David" means "Christ." There is an additional reason for this: the name "David" means "Strong of hand," and who is as strong of hand as he who conquered the world from the cross? After his resurrection and ascension the apostles received the Holy Spirit and spoke with various tongues, whereupon the crowd was thrown into commotion—this same crowd of people who had crucified Christ. This great throng begged to be guided to salvation.[5] They received the advice they sought, and believed. They were forgiven, the guilt of shedding Christ's blood was remitted and the chalice of that blood was given them to drink. Those who had been his persecutors became his faithful followers. They believed in him whom they had crucified. They believed in the one before whom they had wagged their heads in derision, and now they chose to have him as their head. Thus was *his land restored*, as the title of the psalm has it, for Judea was his land. The whole of Judea had been lost when ignorant men crucified their Lord, like maddened patients fighting the doctor and in their delirium rejecting their chance of health. It seemed as though

---

4. See Eph 2:20.
5. See Acts 2:37.

the whole of Judea had perished. All of it? Yes, because even the apostles were frightened. Peter followed Jesus—rashly, though impelled by love—but then denied him three times in fear and confusion. Even when our Lord Jesus Christ had risen from the dead, and joined two travelers who were talking together about him, he found them in such a state of mind that they could answer his question about what they were discussing with their own question, *Are you the only stranger in Jerusalem? Do you not know about the things that have happened in these last days? He said to them, What things? They replied, What the leaders and chief priests did to Jesus of Nazareth, who was a prophet, so powerful in deed and word before God and all the people? How they condemned to death and crucified him? And we had been hoping that he was the one to redeem Israel* (Lk 24:18-21). They had lost hope in Christ; for what they said to him was not, "We hope he will redeem Israel," but *We had been hoping that he was the one to redeem Israel.* Christ was with them, but hope in Christ was not in them. He showed himself to them, he was manifested also to the rest of the disciples, he was handled, and found again by those to whom he had seemed dead. Fallen men and women regained their faith, and so *his land was restored.*

Finally he spent forty days with them, and then ascended into heaven. He sent his Holy Spirit to them, as I reminded you just now, and made these disciples of his, unlettered people, speak in the tongues of all nations. For his persecutors he had prayed, *Father, forgive them, for they do not know what they are doing* (Lk 23:34), and now the efficacy of that prayer was proved. The crowd was deeply troubled, as we have pointed out, and sought salvation, and was led to belief in him. In a single day three thousand of them came to believe, and on another day five thousand.[6] The Church of Christ began to burn with zeal throughout Judea, in that very land where hatred of Christ had burned fiercely; and so *his land was restored.*

But that was not enough, for Christ had said, *Other sheep I have, not counted in this fold; them too I must lead in, that there may be but one flock and one shepherd* (Jn 10:16); and so although the prophets had not been sent to the Gentiles, the apostles were sent to them now. Peoples who had never sought for him were themselves sought out; peoples were found who were expecting nothing;[7] many who had never known God as author of the promises now found him to be their redeemer. The Jews, on the contrary, had long held to God as author of the promises, for the prophets had preached Christ among them and promised that he would come; but though they had heard about him in promise they did not know him when he came. To the Gentiles nothing had been promised, yet their faith had been signaled in prophecy. It had not been foretold to them, but it had been foretold about them. To them also the message was sent now. You have heard

---

6. See Acts 2:41; 4:4.
7. See Is 65:1; Rom 10:20.

about God's dispensation in their regard, for the passage read just now from the Acts of the Apostles described how the centurion Cornelius received the faith.[8] Cornelius was not of the Jewish race, but he prayed, fasted and gave alms. God did not leave him forlorn, Gentile though he was, so an angel was sent to him to assure him that his almsgiving and prayers were acceptable to God. Having summoned Peter to his house, Cornelius believed. Was the angel not capable of instructing him? Surely, yes; but the angel referred him to Peter, for it was better that faith should come to him through human ministry. The Lord had deigned to visit human beings, and having graciously willed to become human himself he did not disdain to teach through a human agent.

In this manner *his land was restored*, for one wall came from the Jewish direction and the other from the Gentiles, so that Christ himself might be the cornerstone, in whom the two were to be united.[9]

3. Is there another way of interpreting the words, *when his land was restored*? Yes; it could mean, "when his flesh was raised up again." This is a different approach, but it is equally concerned to understand the psalm as referring to Christ, because it may strike us that a "restored land" symbolizes resurrected flesh; and it was after Christ's resurrection that all the events took place of which the psalm sings.

Let us listen now to a psalm filled with joy about this restoration of the land. May the Lord our God himself stir up in us the expectant delight proper to such a great matter. May he also adapt our discourse to your hearts, so that whatever exultation our heart feels at such sights may be communicated to our tongue, and thence to your ears, to your hearts, and eventually to your actions.

Lord of the islands

4. *The Lord is king.* This is sung of him who stood before a judge, was slapped, scourged, spat upon, crowned with thorns, punched, hung on a tree, and insulted as he hung there. It is sung of him who died on the cross, was pierced with a lance, was buried, and rose again. *The Lord is king*: let earthly kingdoms rage as viciously as they can. What will they achieve against the king of all kingdoms, the Lord of all kings, the creator of all worlds? Is he to be despised because he showed himself so submissive, so humble? That was mercy, not powerlessness; he appeared in humility so that we could receive him.

But let us look at the next words: *The Lord is king: let earth be glad and the many islands rejoice.* This is what is happening, for God's word has been preached not only in continental countries but also to islands in the oceans; even these are full of Christians, full of God's servants. The sea is no barrier to him

---

8. See Acts 10.
9. See Eph 2:20.

who made the sea. If ships can get there, can God's words not reach them? They can indeed, and the islands have been filled with them.

Alternatively, we can quite well take the islands to symbolize all the churches. Why should they be called islands? Because they are surrounded by the roaring waves of all kinds of trials. But an island may be lashed on every side by raging waves without being shattered; on the contrary, it breaks the waves that beat upon it. So too the churches of God springing up all over the earth have endured persecutions from enraged unbelievers, yet the islands stand there still, and the sea has grown calm. *Let the many islands rejoice.*

Verse 2. The Lord is obscure to some, a guide to others

5. *Cloud and darkness are round about him; justice and judgment guide his throne.* For whom are *cloud and darkness round about him*? And for whom do *justice and judgment guide his throne*? Cloud and darkness are for the godless who have not understood him, but justice and judgment are for believers who have put their faith in him; for while the former were prevented by their pride from seeing him, the latter deserved his guidance by their humility. Listen to an instance of this: of cloud and mist on the one hand, justice and judgment on the other. The Lord declared, *I came into this* world for judgment, so that they who do not see may see, and those who see may become blind (Jn 9:39). What can that mean—*those who see may become blind*? That those who think they can see, those who esteem themselves wise, those who think they need no remedy, may become blind and not understand. But the Lord came so that *those who do not see may see*, so that those who confess their blindness may deserve to be enlightened.

Let him seem to those who have not known him to be enveloped by cloud and darkness; but for those who confess and humble themselves, *justice and judgment guide his throne.* People who have believed in him form his throne. He has made them his seat because Wisdom is enthroned in them, that Wisdom who is the Son of God.[10] We have heard[11] in another passage of scripture an important teaching that supports this interpretation: *the soul of a just person is the throne of Wisdom* (Prv 12:23, LXX). Such persons have been made righteous by believing in him. They have been justified by faith and so have become his throne; he is seated within them, gives judgment from them, and guides them. Why does this happen? Because he found them gentle, like mild-mannered beasts that do not kick, or try to shake the yoke off their necks, or refuse the whip. They have become his docile mounts, and have deserved the reward indicated in another psalm: *He will guide the meek in judgment, he will teach his ways to the gentle*

---

10. See 1 Cor 1:24.
11. Variant: "Let us hear...."

(Ps 24(25):9). Accordingly he is *cloud and darkness* to the other kind of people, who lack probity;[12] but for the humble, *justice and judgment guide his throne.*

Verse 3. God's fire can even now be either destructive to the sinner, or redemptive to believers

6. *Fire will go before him, to burn up his enemies on all sides.* What fire is the psalm talking about, brothers and sisters, when it says, *Fire will go before him, to burn up his enemies on all sides*? I do not think it refers to the fire into which the wicked will be cast by the final sentence of the judge. From what we read in the gospel we remember that to those placed at his left hand he will say, *Depart from me, you accursed, into the eternal fire which was prepared for the devil and his angels* (Mt 25:41); but I do not think that fire is meant here. Why do I not think so? Because the psalm speaks about a fire that will go ahead of him, before he comes to judgment. It says this fire goes before him and sets alight his enemies round about: in other words, throughout the world. The fire mentioned in the gospel will burn after his coming, but the fire referred to in the psalm will go before him.

What, then, is the fire of which the psalm speaks? We can take it either as the punishment of the wicked, or as the salvation of the redeemed. In what sense is it a punishment for the wicked? When Christ was first preached the pagans were roused to anger and stirred up persecution; but their anger was a fire that devoured the persecutors more surely than the persecuted. Think how it is when we see two people, one angry, and the other patiently bearing the other's wrath. It is for you to judge which of them is on fire. The human race provides plenty of examples of this phenomenon for you to observe. Picture to yourselves a bad-tempered person, agitated in mind, ferocious of aspect, with flashing eyes and incandescent speech, being swept along toward murder, or plunder, or violence, or insulting others. He cannot control himself, cannot restrain his impulses. Now picture another person patiently accepting harsh words, blows, and whatever the aggressor chooses to inflict. When struck on one cheek the victim offers the other. On the one side you see fury, on the other calm; on one side anger, on the other patience; on one side sparks, on the other endurance. When you see all this, will you be in doubt as to which of them is on fire, and suffering the pain of it? Is it the one whose body is attacked, or the one whose mind is ravaged?

With this in mind the prophet Isaiah said, *Even now will fire devour your adversaries* (Is 26:11). What is the force of *even now*? Before the great day of judgment arrives, those who are destined later to burn in the torment of eternal flames are already on fire. You surely cannot think, brothers and sisters, that the

12. Variant: "are not oriented aright."

injustice which proceeds from one human being to hurt another damages its object, but leaves its initiator unharmed? How could that be the case? Sometimes a burning torch is applied to a damp, green branch. It fails to set the branch alight, but it burns itself. The same is true of your enemy. There may perhaps be some unjust person who is plotting to trap you, or otherwise scheming to do you harm. That person is unjust; but if you are a green branch, healthy and vigorous, with plenty of spiritual sap in you, you will prove yourself resistant to the flames of enmity by praying for your persecutor. He is on fire, but you are unimpaired; his injustice does damage to him, but none to you. You can hardly think, can you, that it is any disadvantage to you if he has inflicted some injury on your body, while your soul, patient and uncorrupted, has made its way to God, there to receive its crown? It would only be following the example of its Lord, who voluntarily suffered at the hands of the Jews. He could have avoided death, but he died, even as he had power never to be born, but was born. You were born as part of your human condition, but he by free choice; you will die in accordance with your human condition, but he dies in his mercy. And as the Jews did not ultimately harm him, so will no persecuting enemy harm you, if you have chosen to be a member of the body whereof he is the head.

7. Well now, we have understood how the fire that goes before him in this present era can be understood as punitive for unbelievers and wicked people. But we earlier suggested a double possibility: this fire can be either punitive or salutary. So let us now try to understand how it can work for the salvation of the redeemed. The Lord himself told us, *I have come to set fire to the earth* (Lk 12:49). "Fire" corresponds to "sword"; for in another place he said he had come to send not peace to the earth, but a sword.[13] He brought a sword for division and fire for burning, but both were salutary, because the sword of his word cuts us off from bad habits of life, and so furthers our salvation. He brought a sword that divided every one of the faithful from a father who had not believed in Christ, or from a mother who was likewise an unbeliever; or at least, in the case of those born from Christian parents, from earlier generations of their families. There is not one of us who did not have a grandparent, or a great-grandparent, or some remote ancestors among the Gentiles, sharing in their detestable unbelief in God. We have been separated from what we were, but the sword that intervened was a sword of discernment, not of slaying.

The same is true of Christ's fire: *I have come to set fire to the earth*, he said. People who believed in him caught the fire and allowed the flame of charity to possess them. This is the significance of the form taken by the Spirit who was sent to the apostles: *there appeared to them tongues as though of fire, distributed and settling on each one of them* (Acts 2:3). Kindled by that fire they began to travel throughout the world; they spread the fire and burned up his enemies on all

___
13. See Mt 10:34; compare Lk 12:51.

sides. Who were these enemies? People who had forsaken the God who made them, and were worshipping idols they had made themselves. They were set on fire, to be consumed entirely if they were bad, or to be transformed if they were good. Or we could understand it to mean that a person who refused to believe was burnt by that fire, because after hearing God's word he became even worse, and was completely burnt and consumed by his own ill-will. If he had been converted and become a believer, it does not follow, however, that it would have burnt nothing in him at all. It would have burnt the straw so that the gold could be purified. Faith is gold, and carnal concupiscence is straw, for, as Isaiah says, *All flesh is but grass, and human glory like the flower of grass* (Is 40:6). It is clear from this that whatever in a carnal person craves for empty, worldly things is mere straw. What crowds have gone to the theater! And perhaps some of our own brethren among them. It was their straw that drove them there. Should we not hope for their sake that this fire will fall upon them, to burn away their straw and purge the gold? There may be some faith in them, but it is smothered by straw. It would be good for them to burn in the holy fire, so that the straw may be consumed, and the precious metal Christ redeemed may shine out gloriously.

Fire will go before him, to burn up his enemies on all sides. Some people there are who have been burnt for their salvation, since they are Christ's faithful today. They used to be his enemies but now they are his faithful ones: you look for his enemies but they are not to be found; they have been burnt and destroyed in the fire. Charity has consumed in them what drove them to persecute Christ, and purified in them what led them to believe in Christ:[14] it *will burn up his enemies on all sides.*

Verses 4-5. Christ is revealed as light and fire

8. *His lightning flashed around the earth.* This is a cause of intense joy for us. Can we not see it? Is it not obvious? His lightning has flashed throughout the whole earth; God's enemies were kindled by it, and his enemies were burnt. Whatever withstood him caught fire; *his lightning flashed around the earth.* How did it flash? In such a way that the world might at last believe. Where does lightning come from? From clouds. But what are God's clouds? The preachers of the truth.

When you see a cloud it looks like an obscure, dark shape in the sky, but something is hiding within it. If lightning strikes from the cloud there is a gleam of brightness; from something you despised has leapt something that terrifies you. Our Lord Jesus Christ sent his apostles, his preachers, like clouds. They seemed like ordinary men and they were despised, just as clouds are despised

---

14. Variant: "Charity has consumed what it was in them that persecuted Christ, and purified that element in them which could believe in Christ."

until something that amazes you leaps out from them. The apostles were initially seen as weak people, encumbered with flesh; then as ignorant, uneducated and common; but they bore within them something that could strike like lightning and glow fiercely. Peter stepped forward, a fisherman. He prayed, and a dead person sat up.[15] Peter's human shape was a cloud; the glory of his miracle was a flash of lightning. The same is true of both their words and their deeds: when they told of wonderful things, and performed wonderful acts, *his lightning flashed around the earth; the earth saw it and trembled.* Is this not true? Does not the whole Christian earth shout, "Amen," trembling at the lightning that bursts from those clouds? *The earth saw it and trembled.*

9. *The mountains melted away like wax from the presence of the Lord.* Who are the mountains? The proud. Every high thing that exalts itself against God[16] shuddered at the deeds wrought by Christ and by Christians, and sank down. If I say this in the same words that the psalm used, it is because no better expression could be found: *the mountains melted away like wax from the presence of the Lord.* What has become of those towering authorities? Where now is the rock-like obstinacy of the unbelievers? *The mountains melted away like wax from the presence of the Lord.* The Lord came to them as fire, and they melted in his presence like wax; they were hard only until the fire was applied to them. Every hill has been levelled, and dare not blaspheme Christ nowadays. A pagan may not believe in him, but dare not blaspheme him. Even if such a person has not yet become a living stone, at least the stony mountain he or she once was has been brought low.

The mountains melted away like wax from the presence of the Lord, from the presence of the Lord of all the earth.[17] He is Lord not of the Jews alone, but of the Gentiles too; for God is God not only of Jews but also of Gentiles, as the apostle teaches.[18] As Lord of the whole earth the Lord Jesus Christ was born in Judea, but born not for Judea alone, because even before his birth he made us all, and he who made all has remade all. *From the presence of the Lord of all the earth.*

Verse 6. All Christians preach Christ

10. *The heavens have proclaimed his justice, and all nations have seen his glory.* What heavens are these that proclaim him? *The heavens proclaim God's glory* (Ps 18:2(19:1)). Who then are these heavens? Those same people who have become his throne. As God is enthroned in the heavens, so is he enthroned in the apostles, and so too is he enthroned in all who preach the gospel. And you

---

15. Presumaby the reference is to Acts 9:40, though Tabitha was a woman and Augustine uses the masculine, *mortuus.*
16. See 2 Th 2:4.
17. Variant: "and all the earth from before his face."
18. See Rom 3:29.

too can be a heaven, if you wish. Do you want to be a heaven? Then purify your heart of earth. If you do not harbor earthly desires, and mean what you say when you respond that your heart is lifted up,[19] you will be a heaven. To his faithful people the apostle says, *If you have risen with Christ, seek what is above, where Christ is seated at the right hand of God. Have a taste for the things that are above, not the things on earth* (Col 3:1-2). You have begun to acquire a taste for the things that are above, rather than those on earth, so you have already become a heaven, haven't you? You carry flesh, but in heart you are already a heaven, for your way of life will be heavenly.[20]

Because you are that sort of person, you too proclaim Christ. Is any one of the faithful silent about Christ? We want you to focus on this, beloved. Do you suppose it is only we who stand here who proclaim Christ, and that you yourselves do not? Where do they come from, then, the people who approach us wanting to become Christians—people we have never seen before, whom we do not know, to whom we have never preached? Can they possibly have come to believe without anyone telling them the news? The apostle asks, *How will they believe in him of whom they have not heard? And how will they hear without anyone to preach to them?* (Rom 10:14). The whole Church preaches Christ. The heavens proclaim his justice because all the faithful who try to win for God those who have not yet believed, and who do this out of charity, are heavens. From them God thunders forth his terrifying judgment; a person who was an unbeliever trembles, and grows fearful, and believes. Point out to people what the power of Christ has effected throughout the round world by speaking to them and leading them toward the love of Christ. How many there are today who have led their friends along to the pantomime[21] or to hear the flute player?[22] And why do they do so? Surely out of love for the performer. You must love Christ like that. He has provided great shows for us, shows in which nobody can claim to find anything objectionable; and he it is who has conquered the world.[23] Very different is it in the amphitheatre, for there one's favorite contestant may be beaten; but in Christ no one is beaten, so we have no occasion to blush. Seize your neighbors, lead them here, drag along as many as you can. Have no anxiety, for you are bringing them to him who cannot fail to please his spectators. Beg him to enlighten them,[24] so that they may get a good view. *The heavens have proclaimed his justice, and all nations have seen his glory.*

---

19. Probably an echo of the liturgical response to the invitation, "Lift up your hearts"; see note at Exposition of Psalm 10,3.
20. An echo of Phil 3:20. An alternative translation would be "you already have a citizen's rights in heaven."
21. See note at Exposition 4 of Psalm 30,11.
22. The *choraula* or *choraules* was a flute player who accompanied dances performed by a chorus.
23. See Jn 16:33.
24. Possibly a reference to baptism.

Verse 7. The futility of idolatry and the dangers of demon-worship

11. *Let all who worship graven images be put to shame.* Has this not happened? Have they not been put to shame? Are they not being shamed every day? Graven images are idols made by hand.[25] Now in what sense are all those who worship graven images being put to shame? Inasmuch as all nations have seen Christ's glory. All peoples confess Christ's glory now, so let those who worship stones be ashamed. Those stones were dead, but we have found the living stone. Or, rather, those stones cannot even be called dead, because they were never alive; but our stone is alive, and has always been alive with the Father. He died for us, but rose to life again, so now he is alive, and death will never more have dominion over him.[26] The nations have recognized this glory in him, so they are abandoning their temples and running to the churches. *Let all who worship graven images be put to shame.* Are they still trying to worship graven images? It is not so much that they have forsaken their idols; rather have their idols forsaken them. *Let all who worship graven images be put to shame, those who boast of their idols.*

But then some argumentative fellow stands up, someone who fancies himself learned, and objects, "I do not worship a stone, nor an image devoid of intelligence. If your prophet perceived that these things have eyes but see not,[27] how is it possible that I could have failed to realize that an image has no soul, and is incapable of seeing with its eyes or hearing with its ears? Of course I do not worship it. But I reverence what I see, and serve one whom I do not see." And who is that? "Some invisible deity who presides over the image," he replies. In attempting to justify their images in this way they think themselves sophisticated, because they do not worship idols. But in fact they worship demons; for remember, brothers and sisters, what the apostle says about this: *The sacrifices offered by pagans are offered to demons, not to God; and I do not want you to have any truck with demons,* for though *we know that an idol is nothing, the sacrifices offered by pagans are offered to demons, not to God*; and, he emphasizes, *I do not want you to have any truck with demons* (1 Cor 10:20; 8:4). Let them not try to excuse themselves by protesting that they are not dedicated to inanimate idols. They are dedicated to demons, which is more dangerous, because whereas mere idols could no more harm them than help them, if you worship and serve demons, they will have the mastery over you. And who will be your masters then? Beings who hate you. Inevitably they envy you your freedom, and they are always seeking to possess you and turn you into the kind of person they can drag along with them. In these evil spirits there is an ingrained

---

25. Variant: "are plainly idols."
26. See Rom 6:9.
27. See Ps 113B(115):5.

malevolence and a baneful will to hurt us. They exult in human misfortune, and if they manage to deceive us they feed on our delusions. And what are they seeking? Not subjects over whom they may domineer for ever, but companions with whom they will be damned for ever, just as a spiteful robber will often incriminate an innocent person. If one convict is burnt alive, will the fire be any less hot for him because two are burning? Will his death be any less real because two die? His pain is not eased, but his malevolence is fed. "Let that other fellow die with me," he says, not because he thinks to save himself from impending death but because someone else's suffering gratifies him. This is what the devil is like: he wants to seduce people so that they may be punished with him. He cannot deceive the divine judge by accusing an innocent at the tribunal, so he tries to persuade us to sin in order to have real charges to press against us. You see, then, what kind of masters the worshippers of idols and demons set up for themselves, for *the sacrifices offered by pagans are offered to demons, not to God; and I do not want you to have any truck with demons.*

12. But we—what kind of God have we? Listen to the rest of the verse. The psalm has said, *Let all who worship graven images be put to shame, those who boast of their idols*, and its next words refute those who might try to justify their cult of images by saying, "We worship not stones, but gods." What gods do you worship? Tell me: do you worship demons, or good spirits, such as angels? There are holy angels, and there are malign spirits. I am saying that in your temples only malign spirits are worshiped. In their pride they demand sacrifices and wish to be worshiped as gods. This proves that they are malevolent and proud.

Human beings who are not good behave similarly, seeking their own glory and belittling the glory of God. But notice how good people behave, human beings who are like angels. If you find a holy servant of God, and you try to worship and adore him in place of God, he will forbid you to do it; he does not want to arrogate God's honor to himself, or stand to you in God's place. He wants to be with you in subjection to God. This is how the saints Paul and Barnabas conducted themselves. They were preaching the word of God in Lycaonia. They wrought wonderful deeds there, and the inhabitants of the region brought victims along, intending to offer sacrifice to them. They called Barnabas Jove, and Paul Mercury. But the apostles were not pleased. Were they unwilling to have sacrifice offered to them simply because they loathed being compared with demons? No: they were horrified that divine honor should be paid to human beings. This is not our conjecture; it is plain from their own words. The book in which the story is related describes their reaction: *Then Paul and Barnabas tore their clothes, and cried, Men, brethren, what are you doing? We are frail human beings, like yourselves* (Acts 14:13-14).

Now think carefully. Good people forbid others to worship them as gods; they want the one God to be worshiped, the one God adored. They want sacrifice to be offered to the one God, not to themselves. It is the same with all the holy angels. They seek the glory of him whom they love. They strive to seize and enkindle all the humans whom they love, and to guide them to worship God, to adore him, to contemplate him. To humans they announce God, not themselves, because they are angels.[28] Because they are also soldiers they have no thought of seeking glory except that of their commander-in-chief, for if they seek their own glory they are condemned as usurpers.[29] Such were the rebellious devil and the angels who followed him, his demons. He arrogated divine honor to himself and all demons. He occupied the temples built by pagans, led the pagans to idolatry, and induced them to offer sacrifices to him. Would holy angels not have been a better object for their worship than demons?

The pagans retort, "We do not worship evil demons. The beings you call angels we too worship: the powers of the great God, the ministers of the great God." If only you would try to worship them! You would soon learn from them not to do it. Listen to what an angel has to teach you. In the Revelation of John an angel was teaching one of Christ's disciples, showing him many amazing feats. After a certain miracle had been revealed to him in a vision the seer was filled with awe and prostrated himself at the angel's feet. But the angel's whole concern was to seek the glory of his Lord. *Get up*, he said. *What are you doing? I am your fellow-servant, and the servant of your brethren* (Rv 19:10).

What are we to conclude, brothers and sisters? No one should say, "I am afraid an angel may be angry with me if I do not worship him as my god." It does indeed make him angry if you try to worship him; for he is good, and he loves God. As demons are angry if they are not worshiped, so are angels indignant if they are worshiped instead of God. But this does not mean that some weak, frightened heart should say to itself, "Well then, if demons are angry at not being worshiped, I had better take care not to offend them." Not at all. What can even the prince of demons do to you? If he had the power to do anything, none of us would survive. Are not plenty of things offensive to him spoken daily by Christians? Yet the harvest of Christians only increases. When you are angry with a particularly troublesome servant you call him by that name: "You Satan! You devil!" That is what you say to him. Perhaps you are wrong to do so, because it is to a human being that you are speaking, and your unbridled anger is driving you to revile the image of God. All the same, what you choose to call him is what you hate intensely. If the devil were able to take revenge for this, would he not do so? But he is not allowed to; he acts only as far as his permission extends. He wanted to tempt Job, and all he needed was the power to do it; he could have done nothing had the power not been given to him. Why then do you not worship God

---

28. The primary sense of the name, "angel," seems implied here: an angel is a messenger.

29. *Ut tyranni.* The word *tyrannus* was used of any ruler or monarch, but particularly of one who was absolute, oppressive or cruel, often with the connotation of ruling outside the law.

in peace? No one can hurt you unless he wills it; if he does permit it, you will not be wrecked but chastened. If it pleases the Lord your God to allow some human being to harm you, or even some spirit, God will only be chastening you so that you may cry to him, *The Lord chastened me, chastened me severely, but did not deliver me to death* (Ps 117(118):18).

So then, *Let all who worship graven images be put to shame, those who boast of their idols. Adore him, all you his angels.* Let the pagans learn to adore God. If they are inclined to worship angels, let them rather imitate the angels and adore him who is by the angels adored. *Adore him, all you his angels.* Let that angel who was sent to Cornelius worship God; indeed, it was because he worshiped God that he sent Cornelius to Peter. Let that angel, Peter's fellow-servant, worship Christ, who is Peter's Lord. *Adore him, all you his angels.*

Verses 8-9. The Jewish-Christian churches rejoice at the faith of the Gentiles

13. *Zion heard, and was glad.* What did Zion hear? That all God's angels worship him? Yes, to be sure; but what else did Zion hear? This is what it heard: *the heavens have proclaimed his justice, and all nations have seen his glory. Let all who worship graven images be put to shame, those who boast of their idols.* The Church had not yet extended to the Gentiles, you see. Some of the Jews in Judea had come to believe, but these Jews imagined that they alone belonged to Christ. Then the apostles were sent to the Gentiles, and the word was preached to Cornelius. He believed and was baptized, and his companions were baptized with him. You know what had happened to lead them to baptism. The reader did not get as far as that, but some of you will remember, and those who do not remember can listen to me as I recall it briefly. An angel was sent to Cornelius; the angel sent Cornelius to Peter, and Peter came to Cornelius' house. But Cornelius was from the Gentiles, so he and his friends were uncircumcised. In order, therefore, that Peter and his companions might have no hesitation about delivering the gospel to uncircumcised persons, the Holy Spirit came upon Cornelius and the others even before they were baptized; the Spirit filled them and they began to speak in tongues. Until this time the Holy Spirit had never fallen upon any unbaptized person; but he fell on these before their baptism. Peter might well have hesitated over whether to baptize the uncircumcised, but the Holy Spirit came, and they began to speak in tongues. The invisible gift was conferred, and removed any doubt about the visible sacrament; so they were all baptized.

Now you find it recorded in scripture that *the apostles and the brethren in Judea heard that the Gentiles too had accepted the word of God, and they glorified God* (Acts 11:1.18). It is this thanksgiving on their part which is mentioned in our psalm: *Zion heard and was glad, and the daughters of Judea*[30] *leapt for*

---

30. Variant: "of Judah."

joy. What did Zion hear, to inspire such gladness? *That the Gentiles too had accepted the word of God*. One wall had already been set in place, but as yet there was no corner. The Church in Judea is rightly called "Zion" in this context. *Zion heard and was glad, and the daughters of Judea leapt for joy*. Scripture records that *the apostles and the brethren in Judea heard*—does that not mean that *the daughters of Judea leapt for joy*? What did they hear? *That the Gentiles too had accepted the word of God*. And where did the psalm testify to the same event? *The heavens have proclaimed his justice, and all nations have seen his glory*. And since they were Gentiles who had come to believe, former idol-worshippers, the psalm continued, *Let all who worship graven images be put to shame, those who boast of their idols*. Rightly, then, is it said, *Zion heard, and was glad, and the daughters of Judea leapt for joy*.

Later some Christians from the circumcision wanted to put Peter in the wrong. They challenged him, *Why did you go into the house of uncircumcised Gentiles, and eat with them?* (Acts 11:3). He explained to them how a dish was shown to him while he was praying, let down from heaven by four linen cloths. This dish contained all kinds of living creatures, signifying all nations. The reason why it was suspended by four linen cloths was that there are four quarters of the world, from which people would come. This is also why four gospels preach Christ, so that his grace may be understood to reach all four regions of the earth. Peter explained to them that this vision had been granted to him, and he openly related to them the whole story of how Cornelius had come to believe, and how before this Gentile had been baptized the Holy Spirit had come upon him. When the others heard the whole story it silenced their criticism, and they glorified God, saying, *God has evidently granted to the Gentiles also the repentance that leads to life* (Acts 11:18).

You see, then, how *Zion heard, and was glad, and the daughters of Judea leapt for joy on account of your judgments, O Lord*. What does it mean by *judgments*? It means God's impartiality, for with him there is no favoritism. Peter himself, on seeing the centurion Cornelius and those who were with him filled with the Holy Spirit, exclaimed, *In truth I now understand that God has no favorites* (Acts 10:34). Accordingly *the daughters of Judea leapt for joy, on account of your judgments, O Lord*. What judgments are referred to here? His decision that *in every race and in every nation, whoever serves him is acceptable to him* (Acts 10:35); for he is the God not of the Jews alone, but of the Gentiles also.[31]

14. Look further, and you will see that this is why *the daughters of Judea leapt for joy, on account of your judgments, O Lord. For you are the Lord, most high over all the earth*. Not only over Judea, not only over Jerusalem, not only over Zion, but *over all the earth*. For this whole earth God's judgments have

31. See Rom 3:29.

prevailed in strength, calling the peoples together from every side. Those who have cut themselves off[32] are not in communion with the incoming nations. They neither hear the prophecy nor see its fulfillment; they do not see that *you are the Lord, most high over all the earth.*

You are glorified exceedingly, more than all gods. What is the force of *exceedingly*?[33] Remember that this is said of Christ. What else can *exceedingly* mean, except that you, O Christ, are understood to be equal to the Father? And why *more than all gods*? Who are they? Idols have no intelligence, and no life. Demons have intelligence, and they have life, but they are evil. Are we making any great assertion if we say that Christ is more glorious than idols? To be sure, he is glorified above the demons as well, but this is still too little to say of him. The demons are gods to the Gentiles, certainly,[34] but he is glorified exceedingly, more than all gods. Even human beings have been called gods: *I have spoken, and you are gods, sons of the Most High, all of you*, says scripture; and again, *God has taken his stand in the synagogue of the gods, to make a distinction among them* (Ps 81(82):6.1). Our Lord Jesus Christ is more gloriously exalted than everyone: not only more than idols, not only more than demons, but more than all righteous men and women as well. Yet still this is not enough: he is exalted more than all the angels too, or why would the psalm say, *Adore him, all you his angels*? Therefore *you are glorified exceedingly, more than all gods.*

Verse 10. *Love the Lord, hate the malevolent enemy, and do not be afraid*

15. All of us have rallied to him who is exceedingly glorious, more so than all gods; what then are we required to do? The psalm has given us a terse command: *You who love the Lord, hate the malevolent one.* Christ is too noble to share your love on an equal footing with avarice. If you love him, you have to hate what he hates. Think of someone who is your enemy. He is human like you: you and he were created by the one creator in the same human condition. And yet, if your son talks to your enemy, visits your enemy's house and is habitually in conversation with him, you have a mind to disinherit your son for consorting with your enemy. How can that be? Because you think you have a valid reason: "You are a friend to my enemy, and you think you are going to get any of my money?"

Think it over. You love Christ, and avarice is Christ's enemy. Why, then, do you consort with it? I should go further, and ask not merely why you hold conversations with it, but why you make yourself its slave. It is true, you know. Christ lays many commands on you, and you do not obey; but avarice dictates something, and you do it. Christ orders you to clothe a poor person, and you do not; avarice orders you to commit fraud, and you are very ready to do that.

---

32. Donatists.
33. *Nimis.*
34. See Ps 95(96):5.

If this is how things stand, if you are that sort of person, do not be too confident in promising yourself an inheritance from Christ. But you protest, "I love Christ!" Very well, *you who love the Lord, hate the malevolent one.* You prove that you love what is good by demonstrating that you hate what is evil. *You who love the Lord, hate the malevolent one.*

16. But as soon as we begin to hate the evil one, persecutions ensue. We hate the malevolent enemy, but some persecutor says to us, "Act dishonestly," or "Worship this idol," or "Offer incense to the demons." But we have heard the command, *You who love the Lord, hate the malevolent one.* Yes, we heard it; but if we do not act on the persecutor's suggestions, he turns savage. But how far will his cruelty go? What will he take away from you?

Tell me this: why are you a Christian? To win an eternal inheritance, or to secure earthly prosperity? Question your faith, hoist your soul onto the platform[35] of your conscience, torture yourself with the fear of judgment and then answer. In whom did you believe? Why did you believe? You tell me, "I believed in Christ." Very good, then; what did Christ promise you—anything different from what he exemplified in himself? What did his own life show you? He died, he rose from the dead, he ascended into heaven. Do you want to follow? Imitate his suffering, and then hope for what he promised. When you begin to hate the evil one because you love the Lord, what is the cruel oppressor going to take away from you? What will he seize? Your patrimony, perhaps; but not heaven, surely? In the end let him take everything God has given you. No one will take God from you, though you can deprive yourself of God by fleeing from him. In any case, the persecutor cannot take anything at all unless God wills it. If God does will it, he only takes what God has given, and thereby ensures that God may not take himself away from you.

17. You may reply, perhaps, "I don't care about my patrimony. *The Lord gave, and the Lord has taken away.* I can say, *This has happened as the Lord willed* (Jb 1:21). What I am afraid of is that he may kill me; that's all." But listen to the psalm's comforting assurance: *the Lord guards the souls of his righteous ones.*[36] It had commanded you just before this, *You who love the Lord, hate the malevolent one.* But you might have been afraid of this malevolent agent in case he killed you, so it immediately added, *The Lord guards the souls of his servants.* Listen to how he guards them: he told us, *Do not be afraid of those who kill the body, but cannot kill the soul* (Mt 10:28). The enemy may do his utmost to hurt you, even to the point of killing your body. But what has he done against you? No more than was done to the Lord your God. Why aim to have what Christ has, if you are afraid to suffer what Christ suffered? He came to bear your temporal life,

---

35. *Catasta*, a stage or platform on which slaves were exposed for sale, martyrs or criminals were burnt, or lectures were given.
36. Variant: "of his servants," as below.

a fragile life, liable to death. By all means fear death, if it is in your power to avoid it. But if you are powerless to avoid it because it is inherent in your nature, why not welcome it as inherent in your faith? Let the minatory foe take this life away from you; God gives you another life. Even the present life was his gift to you, and you will not be robbed of it unless he wills. If he does will it to be taken from you, he has something ready for you in exchange, so do not be afraid of being stripped of it to gain that other life. Are you reluctant to have that tattered garment taken off? He will give you a robe of glory.

"What is this glory you are talking about?" someone asks. *This corruptible body must put on incorruptibility, and this mortal body be clothed in immortality* (1 Cor 15:53). Even the flesh you carry will not perish. The enemy may do his savage worst, even to the point of killing you, but he has no further power; not over your soul, but not over your flesh either. Even if he scatters your members about, that is no impediment to your resurrection. When some people were fearful of losing their souls, what did the Lord say to them? *The very hairs on your head are numbered* (Mt 10:30). Can you be afraid that you may lose your soul, when you have been assured you will not lose so much as a hair? All things are counted in God's sight. He who created them all will make them all whole again. They did not exist; they were created; they existed; and will they not be restored?

Believe with your whole hearts, my brothers and sisters, and hate the malevolent one, you who love the Lord. Be valiant, not only in loving God, but in hating the evil one too. Do not let anyone[37] frighten you. He who has called you is more powerful; indeed, he is omnipotent. He is stronger than any strong man, and higher than anything exalted. The Son of God died for us; be confident that holding this pledge of his death you will receive his life. For whom, after all, did he die? For good people? No; ask Paul. *Christ died for the godless* (Rom 5:6). You were godless, and he died for you; now that you are justified, will he abandon you? Will he who justified the godless leave the godly forlorn? *You who love the Lord, hate the malevolent one.* Let nobody be afraid. *The Lord guards the souls of his servants, and he will deliver them from the hand of the sinner.*

Verse 11. True light for the just

18. Perhaps you will say, "But it's the light of day that I am losing!" What light do you fear to lose? Are you afraid of finding yourself in darkness? Do not fear to lose daylight; fear rather that in your care not to lose it you lose the true light. To what other creatures has it been given, this light you are worried about losing? It is obvious who shares it with you. Is it good people alone who behold

---

37. Variant: "Do not let more powerful people...."

the sun? God causes his sun to rise over good and evil alike, as he sends his rain on the just and unjust.[38] The wicked see this light as much as you do; robbers see it with you; lechers see it with you; animals see it with you, and flies, and little worms. What kind of light must God be reserving for a righteous person, if he bestows sunlight on all these?

The martyrs saw that other light in faith, and they deserved to, for they spurned this light of day, and having reckoned it so cheap they saw another light, the object of their desire. *Light has arisen for the just person, and good cheer for those of straightforward heart.* Do not suppose that they were really miserable when they walked in chains. For believers prison was a spacious place, for confessors the chains were light.[39] Those who preached Christ amid their torments found joy even on the scaffold.[40]

Light has arisen for the just person. What light is there for a just man or woman? A certain light that does not rise for the unjust, different from the light that dawns on good and bad alike. Another light rises on a righteous person, that light of which the unrighteous will confess at the end that it never dawned for them: *No doubt of it, we strayed from the path of truth. On us the light of righteousness did not shine, nor did the sun rise for us* (Wis 5:6). Revelling in the common sunlight, they lay in darkness of heart. What did it profit them to see daylight with their eyes, if their minds could not see the light beyond? Tobit was blind, yet he taught his son the way of God. You know this is true, because Tobit advised his son, *Give alms, my son, for almsdeeds save you from departing into darkness* (Tb 4:7.11); yet the speaker was in darkness himself. Do you see from this that it is a different light that rises for a just person, and good cheer for those of straightforward heart? Tobit had no eyesight, yet he told his son, *Give alms, my son, for almsdeeds save you from departing into darkness.* He had no fear that his son might say in his heart, "Did you not give alms yourself? Why, then, are you talking to me out of your blindness? Darkness is where almsgiving has evidently led you, so how can you advise me that *almsdeeds save you from departing into darkness?*" How could Tobit give that advice with such confidence? Only because he habitually saw another light. The son held his father's hand to help him walk, but the father taught his son the way, that he might live.

There is a different light, then, that dawns upon a just man or woman: *light has arisen for the just person, and good cheer for those of straightforward heart.* Do you want to perceive it? Be straightforward of heart. What does it mean, to make your heart straight? Do not be a person of twisted heart in relation to God, resisting his will, trying to bend him to yourself instead of straightening yourself to fit in with him. Then you will know that good cheer familiar to all the straight-

---

38. See Mt 5:45.
39. Variant: "gentle."
40. Literally "platform," *catasta*; see note at section 16 above.

forward of heart. *Light has arisen for the just person, and good cheer for those of straightforward heart.*

Verse 12. The promise of joy

19. *Make merry, you just.* Possibly when the faithful hear the invitation to *make merry* their minds turn to feasting, they prepare cups and look forward to the season of roses: all this because the psalm said, *Make merry, you just.* But notice the next words: *in the Lord.* It bids us, *Make merry, you just, in the Lord.* You are looking forward to the merrymaking of springtime; but you have the Lord as your gladness, and the Lord is with you all the year round, for there is no time with him... You have him at night, and you have him by day. Be straight of heart, and there will always be good cheer for you from the Lord. What the world calls good cheer does not merit the name. Listen to the prophet Isaiah: *There is no joy for the wicked, says the Lord* (Is 48:22, LXX; 57:21, LXX). What the impious call rejoicing is no true rejoicing. What kind of joy must he have experienced himself, the man who deprecated such joy? Let us believe him, brothers and sisters; he was only a man, but he had known both sorts of joy. He was certainly familiar with the joys of the cup, since he was human; he knew the joy of the table; he knew the joy of the bed; he knew all these worldly, sensuous joys. He knew them all, yet took it upon himself to declare, *There is no joy for the wicked, says the Lord.* This is not a man's statement: the Lord says it; from the Lord's truth we hear that *there is no joy for the wicked.* They think they are rejoicing, but the Lord—not man—says that *there is no joy for the wicked.* Observing what with them passes for joy, the prophet says, *I have never craved the human light of day, as you know.*[41] You show me a different light of day, you teach me about a different dawn, you flood me with a different gladness, you give me an inkling of something different in my inmost self, and so you have saved me from craving the human light of day. Isaiah was undoubtedly used to seeing people drinking, indulging themselves, frequenting theatres and shows; he saw his whole world abandoned to licentiousness and all kinds of frivolity; and yet he kept shouting, *There is no joy for the wicked, says the Lord.*

If this was not rejoicing, what kind of joy was before his eyes, in comparison with which this was no joy at all? Suppose you were familiar with sunlight, and someone was singing the praises of a lamp. You would say to him, "That isn't light!" Or again, suppose someone was admiring an ape; you might say, "But that is not beauty." The other person might be entranced by the arrangement of limbs in the animal, and full of admiration for its harmonious coordination; but if

---

41. Jer 17:16; it appears that Augustine, quoting from memory, thought this statement belonged in the Isaian context he was discussing.

you knew a different beauty you would deny that it was beautiful. "No, it isn't," you would say. Why? Because you knew beauty of a different order.

You may object, "But I don't see that beauty which Isaiah saw." Believe, and you will. Perhaps your trouble is that you have nothing to see it with, for a special eye is needed to see that beauty. As there is a bodily eye with which we see ordinary light, so is there an eye of the heart which is capable of seeing that gladness. This eye may be diseased in you, or begrimed, or out of focus because of anger, avarice, passion, or inordinate sexual desire. If your eye is out of sorts, it cannot see that light. Believe before you see; you will be healed, and then you will see. *Light has arisen for the just person, and good cheer for those of straightforward heart.*

20. *Make merry, you just, in the Lord*, it says, *and confess to his holy name.*[42] Already you have been gladdened in the Lord, already you are rejoicing in the Lord. Now confess to him, because we should not be rejoicing in him if he did not will it. Our Lord himself said, *I tell you these things so that in me you may have peace, but in the world you will have distress* (Jn 16:33). If you are Christians, look for distress in this world; do not hope for more tranquil times and better conditions. Brothers and sisters, you are deceiving yourselves: do not promise yourselves what the gospel does not promise you. You know what the gospel says; we are speaking to Christians. We must not play false to the faith. The gospel teaches that in the final days there will be many evils, many scandals, plenty of distress, and manifold iniquities; all these will multiply, but anyone who perseveres to the end will be saved. *The love of many will grow cold* (Mt 24:12), it warns us. But if anyone has perseveringly kept the fervor of the Spirit aglow, as the apostle exhorts us to do, telling us to be *ardent in the Spirit* (Rom 12:11), the charity of such a person will not grow cold, because the very charity of God has been poured out liberally in our hearts through the Holy Spirit who has been given to us.[43]

None of us must promise ourselves what the gospel does not promise: "Happier times are on the way; I'm going to do this, and buy that." No; it is better for you to pay attention to him who is not deceived,[44] and has never deceived anyone. He has promised you happiness, but happiness in himself, not here. When all these things have passed away, may you hope to reign with him for ever. Take care lest in wanting to reign here you neither enjoy good cheer in this world, nor find it in the next.

---

42. Literally "to the memory (or memorial) of his holiness"; but in Ex 3:15 it is the divine name, just revealed, that the Lord says will be his memorial to all generations.
43. See Rom 5:5.
44. Variant: "who does not deceive."

Exposition of Psalm 97

A Sermon to the People

Verse 1. The new song, sung by renewed humanity throughout the world

1. *Sing to the Lord a new song.*[1] The new person knows this song, but the old person does not. The old person is the old life, and the new person is the new life. The old life is derived from Adam, but the new life is brought to birth in Christ. In the present psalm the entire world is summoned to sing the new song: this is evident, because elsewhere a psalm says explicitly, *Sing a new song to the Lord, sing to the Lord, all the earth* (Ps 95(96):1). Those who cut themselves off from communion with the whole earth are thereby warned that they cannot sing the new song, for the new song is a universal song, not the property of some exclusive region.[2] Notice this point, and observe that it is reiterated here. Moreover, since the entire world is invited to sing this new song, it is implied that the singer of the new song is peace.

Sing to the Lord a new song, for the Lord has wrought wonderful deeds. What wonderful deeds are meant? Well, think of the gospel that was read just now: we heard there about some of the Lord's wonderful deeds. A dead man was being carried to his burial, the only son of a widowed mother. The Lord was stirred to pity and ordered the cortège to halt. The bearers put the body down, and the Lord commanded, *Young man, arise, I tell you* (Lk 7:14). The dead man sat up and began to speak, and he gave him back to his mother. There you have one of the Lord's wonderful deeds; but far greater than the resuscitation of a widow's only son are the wonderful deeds he has wrought in raising the entire world from everlasting death. *Sing to the Lord a new song*, then, *for the Lord has wrought wonderful deeds.*

What other wonderful deeds shall we sing about? Listen, for the psalm is going to tell us. *His right hand and his holy arm have worked healings for him.* What is meant by the Lord's holy arm? Nothing else but our Lord Jesus Christ. Hearken to Isaiah: *Who has believed our report, and to whom has the arm of the Lord been revealed?* (Is 53:1). His holy arm and his right hand are the same thing, and they are nothing other than himself. Our Lord Jesus Christ is God's arm, and God's right hand; and this is why the psalm says they *worked healings*

---

1. One manuscript prefixes the title, *A psalm for David himself*, which Augustine omits.
2. Aimed at the Donatists.

for him. It did not confine itself to saying that his right hand healed the whole world; it said specifically that the healings were *for him.* Plenty of people are healed for their own benefit, but not for him. Think how many long for bodily health, and from him they receive it; they are healed by him but not for him. Why can that be said—that they are healed by him but not for him? Because once they regain their health they lead dissolute lives. While ill they were chaste, but when healed they become adulterers. People who did no harm to anyone while they were sick trample on innocent folk and oppress them as soon as they get their strength back. Such persons are healed, but not for God.

Who, then, is healed for God? One who is healed inwardly. But who are the inwardly healed? Those who trust in God, certain that if they have been healed in their inmost being and transformed into new persons, even their mortal flesh will itself receive perfect health eventually, even though it now languishes for a time. Let us, then, be healed for God. And to this end let us believe in his right hand, for *his right hand and his holy arm have worked healings for him.*

Verses 2-3. Christ is the right hand, the arm, the salvation, and the justice of God. The true Israel

2. *The Lord has made his salvation known.* Our Lord Jesus Christ is God's right hand, God's holy arm, and also his salvation. All these are one and the same; for he it is of whom scripture promises, *All flesh shall see the salvation of God.* Simeon acknowledged him under this title when he took the baby in his arms, praying, *You give your servant his discharge in peace, now, Lord, for my eyes have seen your salvation* (Lk 2:29-30). *The Lord has made his salvation known.* To whom has he made it known—to a part only, or to the whole? Not to any part alone, certainly. Let no one deceive you, no one hoodwink you, no one tell you, *Look, here is Christ! or, There he is!* (Mk 13:21); for anyone who speaks in terms of "here" or "there" is directing you toward a sect. To whom has the Lord *made his salvation known?* Listen to the next line: *he has revealed his justice before the gaze of the Gentiles.* God's right hand, God's arm, God's salvation, and now God's justice: our Lord and Savior Jesus Christ is all these.

3. *He has remembered his mercy to Jacob, and his fidelity to the house of Israel.* What does this suggest: *he has remembered his mercy and fidelity?* It means that because he was merciful, his mercy impelled him to make the promise; and then what he had mercifully promised, his fidelity made good. Mercy preceded promise, and the fulfillment of the promise demonstrated his fidelity.

He has remembered his mercy to Jacob, and his fidelity to the house of Israel. Are we to conclude from this that they were shown to Jacob alone, or to the house of Israel alone? The Jewish nation and the descendants of Abraham according to the flesh are customarily called "Israel"; and Israel is another name for Jacob. Now Jacob was the son of Isaac, and Isaac the son of Abraham. Thus Jacob was Abraham's grandson. Jacob had twelve sons, and from these twelve sons sprang the whole race of the Jews. But was Christ promised to them only? To that we can say, "Yes," because if you examine the name "Israel" carefully, you see that Christ was promised to Israel, for "Israel" means "One who sees God."[3] If we see him now by faith, we shall see him in vision later. Only let our faith have eyes, and the reality which faith touches will be revealed; let us believe in the one we do not see, and we shall see him with joy; let us long for him whom we have not seen, and we shall enjoy him when he gives himself to our contemplation. We are "Israel" by faith now, but later we shall be "Israel" in face-to-face vision. Then we shall see him, not as in a mirror's puzzling reflection,[4] but in the way John foretells: *Dearly beloved, we are children of God already, but what we shall be has not yet appeared. We know that when he appears, we shall be like him, because we shall see him as he is* (1 Jn 3:2). Prepare your hearts for this vision, prepare your souls for this joy. If God wanted to show you the sun, he would warn you to prepare your bodily eyes; as it is, he graciously proposes to grant you the vision of his Wisdom, so make ready the eyes of your heart. *Blessed are the pure of heart, for they shall see God* (Mt 5:8).

He has remembered his mercy to Jacob, and his fidelity to the house of Israel. What "Israel" is this? You must not think it means a single race, that of the Jews. To save you from that mistake the psalm continues, *All the ends of the earth have beheld the salvation of our God.* Observe that it does not say, "All the earth," but *all the ends of the earth*, suggesting all of it, from furthest boundary to furthest boundary. Let no one tear it, no one fragment it, for our unity in Christ is strong. He who paid so high a price purchased no less than the whole. *All the ends of the earth have beheld the salvation of our God.*

Verses 4-5. Shouting for joy and playing psalms

4. And since they have beheld it, they are bidden, *Shout to God with joy, all the earth.* You already know what it means to shout for joy.[5] Rejoice, and speak of what makes you happy, if you can. But if you cannot find words for it, shout for joy. Let your shouting express your gladness if speech cannot; but one way or another, do not let your joy be dumb. Let your heart not be silent about its God, or silent about his gifts. If you talk only to yourself, it is a sign that you have been healed for yourself; but if God's right hand has healed you for him, speak to him for whose glory you received your healing. *All the ends of the earth have beheld the salvation of our God. Shout to God with joy, all the earth, sing and make merry and sound forth his praises.*

---

3. A popular etymology; see note at Exposition 1 of Psalm 21,4.
4. See 1 Cor 13:12.
5. See the Exposition of Psalm 94,3, and note there.

5. *Sing psalms to the Lord on the lyre, praise him with lyre and psalm.* Play psalms to him; do not be content with using only your voice. Take up good works, so that you are not merely singing, but working too. Anyone who both sings and works is playing psalms on the lyre and the psaltery.[6]

Verse 6. Trumpets and horns

6. Other musical instruments are mentioned for the sake of their symbolism; notice what kind they are: *with ductile trumpets and the sound of the horn.* What is the significance of these ductile trumpets and horns? Ductile trumpets are trumpets made of bronze, hammered out thin and long. If hammering is needed, it must represent whipping; you, then, will be ductile trumpets, drawn out into a long shape for the praise of God, if you improve when you suffer tribulations. Tribulation is the hammering, and your improvement is the lengthening.

Job was a ductile trumpet. He was suddenly struck by enormous losses and bereaved of his children, but through the hammer-blows of such great distress he was fashioned into a ductile trumpet that blew its note: *The Lord gave, and the Lord has taken away. This has happened as the Lord willed: may the Lord's name be blessed* (Jb 1:21). What a trumpet-blast that was! How sweet a sound he gave! But wait, this ductile trumpet is still being hammered. He has been so far delivered into the tempter's power that even his flesh is afflicted. He is smitten, and he begins to ooze pus and swarm with maggots. A surrogate Eve is presented to seduce him, for his wife has been preserved, not to comfort her husband, but to do the devil's work. She prompts Job to blasphemy, but he does not obey her. Adam in paradise did obey Eve, but Adam on the dunghill rebuffs Eve; for that was where Job was sitting as he oozed pus and rotted amid his maggots—on a dunghill. Yet Job, stinking on his dunghill, did better than the healthy Adam in paradise. But though Job was no Adam, his wife was still Eve, and he had an answer for this Eve who was so ready to deceive and tempt him. We have heard how this trumpet was hammered into shape. The devil had struck Job from head to foot with acute ulcers; he was swarming with maggots and seated on a dung-hill. Having heard how he was hammered, let us now listen to the sound he produces. You would like to hear the melodious note of this ductile trumpet, wouldn't you? Let us listen, then. *You have spoken like the silly woman you are*, he said. *If we have received good things from the Lord's hands, should we not endure the bad too?* (Jb 2:10). What a ringing sound! What a pure note! Is anyone so fast asleep as not to be wakened by a sound like this? Could anyone fail to be heartened by such confidence in God, and emboldened to plunge

---

6. For Augustine's ideas on the symbolism of these two instruments see his Exposition 2 of Psalm 32; Exposition of Psalm 42,5; Exposition of Psalm 56,16; Exposition 2 of Psalm 70,11; Exposition of Psalm 80,5.

without fear into battle against the devil, there to prevail not by his own strength, but in the power of God who is testing him? It is indeed God who beats us into shape; the hammer could not act on its own.[7] This is why a prophet refers to the future punishment of the devil in these terms: *The hammer of the whole earth has been shattered* (Jer 50:23). He meant us to recognize the devil under this image, *the hammer of the whole earth.* But the hammer is in God's hand, under God's power; and with it the ductile trumpets are beaten to shape them for offering resonant praise to God.

I would dare to go further, my brothers and sisters, and invite you to see how even the apostle was beaten with this same hammer. *To make sure that I would not grow conceited over these great revelations,* he tells us, a sting of the flesh was sent to me, a messenger of Satan to buffet me. He is being hammered, evidently, so let us now find out how he sounds. *Three times I begged the Lord to take it away from me, but he said to me, My grace is sufficient for you, for my power is fully deployed in weakness.* "I want to bring my trumpet to perfection," says the maker, "and I can do so only by beating it. *My power finds complete scope in weakness.*" Now listen to the fine notes from this hammered trumpet: *When I am weak, then I am strong* (2 Cor 12:7-10).

Now the apostle was very close to Christ, and he clung tightly to that right hand which held the hammer needed for shaping the trumpet. This is why the apostle, from his position in God's right hand, wields the hammer himself. Concerning certain wrongdoers he says, *I have delivered them to Satan, that they may learn not to blaspheme* (1 Tm 1:20). He subjected them to the hammer, to be beaten. Before the lengthening process they had emitted discordant sounds, but perhaps after being hammered out and turned into ductile trumpets they were rid of their blasphemy and sounded forth the praises of the Lord. So much for the ductile trumpets.

7. But what about the sound of the horn? A horn is something that thrusts out from the flesh. Evidently, then, a horn is firm enough to overcome the flesh; it is strong and durable, and capable of emitting a sound. Why is this so? Because it has proved itself tougher than flesh. Anyone who wants to be a melodious horn must overcome the flesh. What does overcoming the flesh entail? It means that we must transcend carnal affections and subdue carnal desires. Listen to the music of horns: *If you have risen with Christ, seek what is above, where Christ is seated at the right hand of God. Have a taste for the things that are above, not the things on earth* (Col 3:1-2). What is the implication of the words, *seek what is above*? The apostle means, "Go beyond your flesh, do not let your minds run on carnal things." They were not yet ductile trumpets, the Christians to whom he still had to say, *Not as spiritual persons could I speak to you, but only as carnal.*

---

7. Variant in some codices: "Even though God himself beats us into shape, he would not of himself make the hammer."

As if to little children in Christ I gave you milk to drink, rather than solid food. You were not capable of it then, nor are you even now, for are you not carnal still? (1 Cor 3:1-2). They were not tuneful horns, because they had not yet protruded beyond the flesh. A horn is attached to the flesh, but thrusts out beyond the flesh; although it erupts from the flesh, it proves itself stronger than the flesh. If you have been transformed from a carnal into a spiritual person, you still tread the earth in your flesh, but in your spirit you are bursting forth into heaven; as the apostle says, *Though we live in the flesh, our weapons are not those of the flesh* (2 Cor 10:3). We should not omit to notice who those people were to whom the apostle spoke, brothers and sisters. What else had he to say to them, as evidence that they were carnal folk with carnal ways of thinking, and not yet fashioned into horns? *When one says, "I belong to Paul," and another, "I belong to Apollos," and another, "I belong to Cephas," are you not carnal still, conducting yourselves in a merely human way? What is Apollos, in any case, and what is Paul? God's servants, through whom you came to believe. I planted, Apollos watered, but God gave the growth* (1 Cor 3:3-6). He wanted them to rise above these hopes they had placed in human agents, and make contact with the spiritual powers of Christ, so that having overcome the flesh they might be tuneful horns.

Nonetheless, brothers and sisters, you must not mock any of our brethren whom God's mercy has not yet converted, for you know that as long as you do you still smack of the flesh yourselves. No such trumpet produces a note pleasing to God's ears; a trumpet that sends out a blare of mockery does not lead to victory in the war. Let the bugle blast you into battle against the devil, but not fleshly folly into fighting your friends.[8] *With ductile trumpets and the sound of the horn shout with joy in the presence of the Lord, our king.*

Verses 7-9. Joy amid persecution; the coming of the judge

8. Now you are shouting with gladness and making joyful sounds on ductile trumpets and horns; so what comes next? *Let the sea roar and all the multitude of creatures in it.* This indeed happened, brothers and sisters, for when the apostles were trumpeting the truth and blaring it on their horns the sea grew rough, the waves surged high, and storms arose: persecutions raged against the Church. What whipped up the sea? When people were shouting with gladness and playing psalms to God these pleasant sounds delighted God's ears, but the waves of the sea were troubled. But *let the sea roar and all the multitude of creatures in it, the round world and all that live therein.* Let the sea be whipped up to persecute.

---

8. A free translation of an Augustinian pun: *tuba cornea te erigat adversus diabolum, non tuba carnea adversus fratrem tuum.*

Let the rivers clap their hands to the selfsame.[9] Persecutions arise, but the saints rejoice to God. How can rivers clap their hands? Well, what is clapping? To clap is to express joy by our actions; to clap is to rejoice with our hands, with our works. And what rivers are referred to here? People whom God has made into rivers by giving them the water which is the Holy Spirit. *Let anyone who is thirsty come to me and drink*, he said. *If anyone believes in me, rivers of living water shall flow from within that person* (Jn 7:37-38). These rivers were clapping their hands all the while; these rivers were rejoicing with their actions and blessing God.

9. *The mountains will leap for joy in the presence of the Lord, for he is coming, he is coming to judge the earth.* The mountains represent great men and women. God is coming to judge the earth, and at this they rejoice. But there are other mountains who will shudder at the prospect of the Lord's coming to judge the earth. What I mean is that there are good mountains and bad mountains. Good mountains are people of great spiritual stature; bad ones are puffed up with pride. *The mountains will leap for joy in the presence of the Lord, for he is coming, he is coming to judge the earth.* Why will he come, and how will he come? *He is coming to judge the earth. He will judge the round earth in justice, and the peoples with fairness.* Let the mountains rejoice at this, for the Lord will not judge unjustly. If people are anticipating the arrival of some human judge, one who cannot read consciences, it may well happen that even the innocent will be apprehensive, if they are either hoping for praise or dreading condemnation. But the Lord who is coming cannot be deceived. Let the mountains rejoice, therefore, and rejoice with confidence, for they will be flooded with his light, not condemned. Let them rejoice, because the Lord will come to judge the whole earth fairly. But while these righteous mountains rejoice, let the unjust tremble.

He has not come yet, so why need they tremble? Let them be corrected, and then rejoice. How you look forward to Christ's coming depends on you. He defers his coming so that when he comes he will find nothing in you to condemn. Think about this. He is in heaven, and you are on earth; he is postponing his arrival, but you must not postpone your decision. His coming will be hard for hard-hearted people, but gentle for the devout. Take thought, then, for which sort you are. If you are hard, you still have the chance to become gentle; if you are gentle, be happy even now at the prospect of his coming. Why? Because you are a Christian. "Yes," you say, "what about it?" I believe that when you pray, you ask, "Your kingdom come"; and if you pray so, you hope for his coming. Yet all the while you dread it! Correct yourself, so that you may no longer pray against yourself.

---

9. *In idipsum*: we should probably take this to mean "all together," but Augustine hears in it a reference to the divine name. Compare Exposition of Psalm 4,9; Exposition 2 of Psalm 18,10, and notes at both places.

Exposition of Psalm 98

A Sermon to the People[1]

Introduction: many prophets spoke of Christ before he came

1. You are the children of the Church, beloved ones, and well instructed in the school of Christ by means of all the writings of our fathers from ancient times. These men recorded God's words and wrote of his wonderful deeds. Being so well instructed you ought to know that by their writings they were seeking the welfare of all of us, who were destined to believe in Christ today. At the proper time he came to us, humbly at first; but later he will come in majesty. He came the first time to stand before a judge; but at the end he will come to sit as judge, and he will summon the whole human race to stand before him and answer for its deeds. Since he is so august a judge, many heralds preceded him, even before his first coming in humility. When he was still to be born of the virgin Mary, still destined to be an infant sucking milk, even then a succession of heralds went ahead of him. Many a herald went in advance of the Word of God, the Word through whom all things were made, who yet was to be an infant.[2] These many heralds foretold the times that were to come, but they spoke in such a way as to conceal their meaning under certain figurative signs. The veil which covered the truth in the books of the ancient writers was to be stripped away only when truth in person should spring up from the earth. That is how another psalm speaks of his coming: *truth has sprung up from the earth, and righteousness has looked down from heaven* (Ps 84:12(85:11)).

When we listen to a psalm, or to a prophet, or to the law, all of which were set down in writing before our Lord Jesus Christ came in the flesh, our whole endeavor must therefore be to find Christ in what we hear, and to discern his presence in it. Listen to this psalm together with us, beloved, and let us seek Christ as we listen. He will certainly show himself to those who seek him, for he first showed himself to people who were not seeking him. He will not abandon us who long for him, since he redeemed those who were careless about him. The psalm begins by speaking about Christ, for it is of him that it proclaims:

---

1. Preached at Carthage, possibly in 411.
2. *Infantem* in the exact sense of one who cannot speak, as often in Augustine. Here it is contrasted with the divine Word.

Verse 1. God's enthronement in the souls of the just

2. *The Lord has become king; let the peoples be angry.*[3] Our Lord Jesus Christ has begun his reign, because preaching about him began after he had risen from the dead and ascended into heaven; it began after he had filled his disciples with such courage from the Holy Spirit that they had no fear of death, which Christ had already slain in himself. Christ the Lord began to be proclaimed so that all who desired salvation might believe in him; and this enraged the nations who were accustomed to worship idols. People who paid cult to what they had made were angry because he by whom they themselves were made was being proclaimed. This was exactly the situation, for through his disciples Christ was spreading the news about himself, wanting people to turn to him by whom they were made, and to turn away from gods of their own making.

The pagans, however, were angry with their Lord out of consideration for their idol, though they would already have been culpable if for the sake of an idol they had been angry even with one of their slaves, for the slave was at least more honorable than the idol, since their God had made the slave, whereas a workman made the idol. Yet they were so angry at the slighting of their idol that they dared to be angry with their Lord. But when the psalm said, *Let them be angry,* this was a prediction, not a command. The statement that *the Lord has become king; let the peoples be angry* was prophetic.

Some good purpose can be served by these angry peoples: let them be angry, and through their rage let martyrs be crowned. What did the pagans do to the preachers of the word of truth, to those clouds of Christ who enriched the world and poured down rain upon God's field? What did the furious peoples do to them? They made sure that the flesh of Christ's preachers should suffer at their hands, so that the spirit might be crowned at the hands of Christ. Yet not even the flesh which the persecutors had power to kill died so finally as to perish for ever; the flesh too will have its season for resurrection, because the Lord has already given proof of the resurrection of our flesh in himself. He took flesh from us in order to show us that we need not despair about the ultimate fate of our own. We can be sure, then, brothers and sisters, that the flesh of his servants, slain by idol-worshippers, will rise again at its own time; but no workman will ever put together again the idols smashed by Christ. If you were listening attentively to the passage from Jeremiah that preceded the reading from the apostle, you will have seen in it a prophecy of the period through which we are living now. *The gods that did not make heaven or earth must perish from the earth, and from under heaven* (Jer 10:11), it said. Notice that the text did not say, "Let the gods who did not make heaven or earth perish from heaven and earth"; that could not be said because they never were in heaven. What did it say? *The gods that did not*

---

3. One manuscript prefixes the title, *A psalm for David himself*, which Augustine omits.

make heaven or earth must perish from the earth, and from under heaven. It took up the allusion to the earth, but it could not go on to say, "perish from heaven," about beings which had not been in heaven. Instead it mentioned "earth" twice, equivalently, for earth is "under heaven." *Let them perish from the earth and from under heaven*, that is to say, from their temples. Think now: is this not what is happening? Has it not already come about to a large extent? What is left of them; how much is left? The idols have kept their places in the hearts of pagans more successfully than on their pedestals in the temples.

3. *The Lord has become king, let the peoples be angry; he who is seated upon the cherubim* (here you understand "has become king"), *let the earth quake.* This last phrase is a repetition of *let the peoples be angry.* The subject in the first line, *the Lord,* is echoed in the second line by *he who is seated upon the cherubim.* The idea, *has become king,* is understood in both lines. Finally the phrase in the first, *let the peoples be angry,* is matched in the second by *let the earth quake*; for what else are the peoples but earth? Let the earth be as angry as it can be with him who is already seated in heaven. Time was, when the Lord was also on earth, for he took to himself the earthy substance that would enable him to live on earth. He clothed himself in flesh, and chose to be the first to confront the angry peoples. He willed to be the first to suffer that anger, so that it would hold no terrors for his servants later. The anger of the peoples would be something necessary for his servants, for through it they would be cured of all their sins through tribulations, and be completely healed. Knowing this, the physician drank the medicine first, that the patient might not fear to drink it too. *The Lord has become king; let the peoples be angry.* Yes, let the peoples rage, because God brings about much good through their fury. They vent their anger, and God's servants are purged thereby. After being put to the test, God's servants are crowned, so *let the peoples be angry.*

He who is seated upon the cherubim has become king; *let the earth quake.* Scripture teaches us that the cherubim are God's seat, a sublime, heavenly seat which we cannot see. But the Word of God knows it, knows it as his own seat; and this Word of God, together with the Spirit of God, has told his servants where God sits. Not that God is seated in the same way as a human being sits down; no, but you can have God seated within you if you want to, because if you are a good person you will be God's throne. As scripture says, *the soul of a just person is the throne of Wisdom* (Prv 12:23, LXX). A throne is called a "seat" in English.[4] Certain interpreters familiar with the Hebrew tongue have also explained what the name, "cherubim," means. The word is Hebrew, but in English it means "the fullness of knowledge." Thus God is said to be seated above the fullness of knowledge, because God surpasses all knowledge. Let the fullness of knowledge be found in you, then, and you too will be God's seat.

---

4. He says, "in Latin," of course, here and in the following lines.

Perhaps you will object, "And when is the fullness of knowledge going to be in me? Who can rise to such heights[5] as to contain knowledge in all its fullness?" But you do not really think, do you, that God wills us to possess such a plenitude of knowledge that we could know the number of the stars, or how many grains there are—even grains of wheat, to say nothing of sand—or how many apples hanging from a tree? No. He knows all this, for even the hairs on our heads are counted in God's sight.[6] The fullness of knowledge that he wills human beings to have is of a different kind: the knowledge he wants you to make your own is concerned with God's law. Still you complain, "But who can know the law so perfectly as to possess the fullness of knowledge in its regard, and become the seat of God?" Do not worry. You are given the briefest of instruction as to what you must have if you aspire to gain the fullness of knowledge and become the throne of God. The apostle tells you, *The fullness of the law is charity* (Rom 13:10). What have you to say to that? You are bereft of all excuse. Question your heart, and find out whether it has charity. If charity is there, the fullness of the law is there, and therefore God already dwells in you, and you have become God's seat.

Let the peoples be angry. What will angry peoples do to anyone who has become the throne of God? You are bedazzled by those who rage against you, and you forget who is enthroned within you. You have become heaven; can you be frightened of earth? In another passage of scripture the Lord our God declares, *Heaven is my throne* (Is 66:1). If, then, you have attained to the fullness of knowledge by possessing charity, and have thereby become God's throne, you have become a heaven. The heaven to which we look up with our bodily eyes is not all that important to God. Saintly souls are God's heaven; the minds of the angels and all the minds of his servants are God's heaven. *Let the peoples be angry*, and *let the earth quake*. What damage are the peoples going to do, what damage is the earth going to do, to God's seat, or to the heaven where he is enthroned?

Verse 2. Zion is the Church, God's holy city, praying and fasting for its persecutors

4. *The Lord is great in Zion, most high over all the peoples.* The Lord is great and exalted in Zion. Remember how you found it difficult to understand when God was said to be *seated upon the cherubim*. You did not know what *cherubim* meant, and perhaps you formed for yourself a mental image of a huge, lofty throne studded with jewels; perhaps you allowed your carnal imagination free flight, and thought that was the cherubim. But you were corrected by being told

---

5. Variant: "rise to so much knowledge."
6. See Mt 10:30.

that "cherubim" means "fullness of knowledge"; then you were further instructed about this plenitude of knowledge, and understood that it is not knowledge of any and every kind, but that which is profitable to men and women, namely full knowledge of the law. Finally you were saved from despair of attaining even knowledge of the law, for you were succinctly told, *The fullness of the law is charity*. Try to have charity for God and for your neighbor, and then you will be God's throne; you will have fellowship with the cherubim.

Do you still find this difficult to understand? Listen, then, to the next line: *the Lord is great in Zion*. He who is above the cherubim, as I told you, is great in Zion. Now you need to find out what Zion is. We know that Zion is the city of God. The city of Jerusalem was called Zion, but it was so called because of a particular interpretation of this name, for "Zion" means "a lookout post," which suggests vision and contemplation. To be on the lookout for something means to keep watch, or to descry it, or to strain the eyes to see. Every soul is Zion, if it focuses its gaze in order to see the light which it is meant to see.[7] If it concentrates on any light of its own it is darkened, but if it concentrates on God's light it is illumined.

However, it is very clear that Zion is the city of God; and what is God's city, if not holy Church? When people love one another, and love their God who dwells in them, they form a city for God. Every city is held together by some law, and the law of this city is charity. But God himself is this charity, for scripture says unambiguously, *God is charity* (1 Jn 4:8). Any person who is full of charity is therefore full of God, and when many persons are full of charity, they make a city for God. That city of God is called Zion, and so the Church is Zion. In this city, Zion, the Lord is great.

Make your home in it, and God will not be far from you. When God is established in you, because you belong to Zion, because you are a member of Zion, a citizen of Zion and part of the fellowship of God's people, then in you God will be *most high over all the peoples*—over those who are still angry, and over those who used to be angry in earlier days. You do not suppose, do you, that their anger is only something past, that they are angry no longer? They used to be angry in open fashion in earlier times because then they were numerous; but now that they have dwindled to so few they are angry in secret. For the time being it is only their effrontery that has been battered, but their fury too will soon be brought to an end.

5. Do you not realize, brothers and sisters, that the people whose musical instruments made such a din yesterday are angry about our fasting? We are not angry with them, but we fast for them. The Lord our God who has set his throne within us expressly commanded us to pray for our enemies, to pray for those who persecute us;[8] and while the Church is doing this, the persecutors have been all

---

7. Variant: "in order to see what must be seen."
8. See Mt 5:44.

but eliminated. The Church was heard when it prayed so, and is still heard when it prays so. The persecutors who had prevailed in their wickedness were defeated for their good. Do you want to hear how they were finished off? I will tell you: they were eaten by the Church. You look for them in themselves, and you do not find them; look for them in the Church which has eaten them, and there they are, in the Church's gut;[9] for when they passed over to the Church and became Christians, the persecutors perished and preachers grew up instead.

When we watch the few who remain still going crazy in their foul, perverted pleasures on their festivals, we pray to God for them, that those who delight in listening to a musical instrument may find even more delight in hearkening to God's voice. It cannot be that if an irrational sound delights the ear, the word of God can fail to delight the heart. Our motive in fasting for them on their festivals is to pray for them, that they may find in themselves a more eye-catching spectacle. When they have caught sight of themselves they will find the sight repulsive, for the only reason they do not perceive their own ugliness is that they are not really looking at themselves. A drunken man does not find himself disgusting, but a sober person is revolted by the sight. Take a person who is already experiencing joy in God, one of serious life[10] who already longs for the eternal peace God has promised: when such an observer sees someone dancing to a musical accompaniment, he or she is more grieved over the fellow's idiocy than over the delirium of a madman.

For our part, let us grieve over them when we see their evil ways, well known to us because we were freed from the same evil ways ourselves. If we are sorry for them, let us pray for them; and in the hope of being heard let us fast for them. I do not mean that we should make their festivals the occasion for celebrating our fasts. The fasts we shall celebrate through the coming paschal days are quite different, as are the many other solemn occasions we mark in our Christian life by fasting. On the days I mean we fast with a particular purpose, for while they are making merry, we groan on their behalf. By their jollity they provoke our grief, and remind us how wretched they still are. But since we see many of them now freed from those evils in which we once participated ourselves, we must not despair even of the rest. If they are still angry with us, let us pray; if the tiny portion of earth that is left is still quaking, let us persevere in our groaning for them, that God may grant understanding to them as well, and bring them to hear together with us the words which afford us such joy. *The Lord is great in Zion, most high over all the peoples.*

---

9. This image, originally inspired by the command to Peter, "Slaughter and eat" (Acts 11:7), is for Augustine a favorite way of expressing the reality of the body of Christ.

10. *Vivit graviter*, an echo of the virtue *gravitas*, greatly admired in classical Roman culture: a weighty, serious, dignified temper of mind.

Verses 3-4. God's name is terrible and holy. Judgment and justice in human beings are his creation

6. *Let them confess*[11] *to your great name*. Let all those peoples, over whom he is acknowledged to be great in Zion, now confess to your great name. Your name was quite insignificant when the nations were angry; but now that it has become so great, let them confess it. How can we say that his name was without significance, before Christ was preached abroad in all his glory? We can say it because by his name is meant his renown. His name was insignificant once, but now it has become great and famous. Is there any nation that has not heard the name of Christ? Let the peoples who in earlier days were angry at an insignificant name now confess to a name that has become great: *let them confess to your great name*. Why should they confess? *Because it is terrible and holy*. Terrible and holy is your very name. The man who was crucified, the man who was humbled, the man who was subjected to judgment, is preached as the one who is to come, sublime, living, and ready to judge in his strength. For the present he spares blaspheming nations, because God's patience is leading them to repentance.[12] He who spares them now has no intention of sparing them for ever; he is preached today as one to be feared, but we must not deceive ourselves and think that he will never come to judge us. Come he will, brothers and sisters, come he will indeed; so let us fear him, and so conduct our lives that we may find our station at his right hand. He will come and he will judge, placing some at his left hand and others at his right. He does not do this capriciously, as though muddling people, putting at his left hand someone who deserves to be at his right, or at his right hand someone who ought to stand at his left, as though God could make mistakes. He cannot get it wrong, placing a bad person where a good person should be, or a good one in a position he should assign to a villain. He cannot make mistakes; but that means that we make a grave mistake if we do not stand in awe of him. If we have feared him in this present life we shall have nothing to fear hereafter.

Your name is terrible and holy, and the honor of the king loves judgment. Let the peoples so fear him as to correct their ways. They must not presume so far on his mercy as to make excuses for themselves and continue to live in wickedness, for though he loves mercy, he also loves judgment. In what does his mercy consist? In preaching the truth to you now, and sending to you now his resounding summons to conversion. Has he been niggardly in his mercy toward you? You lived an evil life, yet he did not snatch you away in your sins; he spared you so that he could forgive your sins now that you are a believer. That is no slight mercy, is it? But do you suppose that his mercy will be there always, and

11. Variant: "Let them all confess."
12. See Rom 2:4.

that he will never punish anyone? Do not so delude yourself. His name is *terrible and holy, and the honor of the king loves judgment.* Judgment is not just—indeed, it is not judgment at all—unless all are given their deserts, according to what each has done in the body, whether good or evil;[13] and *the honor of the king loves judgment.* Let us therefore fear him, and deal justly, and conduct our affairs with equity.

7. But who deals justly? Who practices justice? A sinful human being, an unjust person, a perverted man or woman, one turned away from the light of truth? Let us rather turn to God so that he may form this fairness in us, for of ourselves we cannot form it, but only deform it. Anyone is capable of wounding himself, but can he heal himself? He can be ill whenever he likes, but cannot rise from his sickbed whenever he likes. Let him live without moderation in cold or in heat, if he chooses; he will fall ill on the day of his own choosing. But if he has fallen ill through intemperate habits, let him try to rise from illness when he wishes. He fell ill when he chose; let him rise up when he chooses, if he can. All he needed to lay him low in sickness was his own intemperance, but in order to recover he needs the doctor's skill. Similarly we have it in our own power to sin, but to be justified is not within our power: we can only be justified by him who alone is just.

This psalm sets out to persuade men and women to give themselves to God, that he may form them to justice. It had struck fear into the peoples with its admonition, *Let them confess to your great name, because it is terrible and holy, and the honor of the king loves judgment.* Now it seems that these terrified peoples were asking how they should live justly, since they had no capacity for justice within themselves. The psalm therefore drew their attention to him who would shape justice in them. It continued by saying to God, *You have prepared fairness, you have created judgment and justice in Jacob.* We too are obliged to have judgment, and we are obliged to have justice, but God creates judgment and justice in us: God who formed us in order to form them in us.

How, then, should judgment and justice work out in us? You exercise judgment when you distinguish evil from good; you practice justice when you pursue the good and turn away from the evil. Judgment is yours in discerning, justice is yours in acting. *Turn away from evil and do good,* says another psalm. *Seek peace and pursue it* (Ps 33:15(34:14)). You must have judgment first, and then justice. What kind of judgment do you need? You must begin by judging what is evil, and what is good. And what kind of justice must you practice? You are to turn away from evil, and do good. But you have no power in yourself to do this. Look what the psalm said to God: *You have created judgment and justice in Jacob.*

---

13. See 2 Cor 5:10.

Verse 5. How can we worship the Lord's footstool? Christ's flesh is meant

8. *Exalt the Lord our God.* Exalt him with sincerity, exalt him with all your might. Let us praise him, let us exalt him who made the justice we possess, let us exalt him who created it in us. Who else created justice in us, if not he who justified us? But of Christ it was said, *He justifies the impious* (Rom 4:5). We are the impious, he the justifier, since it is he who has created in us the very justice through which we are pleasing to him—pleasing enough for him to place us at his right hand, not his left, and to say to those at his right hand, *Come, you who are blessed by my Father, take possession of the kingdom prepared for you since the creation of the world* (Mt 25:34). God grant that he may not assign us to a place at his left, among those to whom he will say, *Depart from me into the eternal fire which was prepared for the devil and his angels* (Mt 25:41). How greatly should he be exalted, he who will crown in us not our merits, but his own gifts![14] *Exalt the Lord our God.*

9. *And worship his footstool, because he[15] is holy.* What are we to worship? *His footstool.* A footstool[16] is something beneath one's feet. The Greeks called it ὑποπόδιον, the Latins translated it *scabellum* or *suppedaneum*.[17]

But reflect on what the psalm is commanding us to adore, brothers and sisters. In another passage of scripture God says, *Heaven is my throne, but the earth is my footstool* (Is 66:1). Is the psalm ordering us to worship the earth, then? It seems like it, since scripture tells us what God's footstool is. But how can we worship the earth, when scripture plainly instructs us, *The Lord your God you shall adore* (Mt 4:10; Lk 4:8; Dt 6:13)? Yet here it commands, *Worship his footstool*, and explains to me elsewhere what this footstool is by saying, *The earth is my footstool.* I am in a dilemma: I shrink from adoring the earth, lest I be condemned by the Lord who made heaven and earth; on the other hand, I am afraid to hold back from adoring the footstool of my Lord when the psalm tells me, *Worship his footstool*; and when I ask what that is, scripture informs me, *The earth is my footstool.*

In my uncertainty I turn to Christ, for he it is whom I am seeking in this psalm; and then I discover how, without idolatry, the earth may be worshiped, how God's footstool may be adored without impiety. He took earth from earth, because flesh comes from the earth, and he received his flesh from the flesh of Mary. He walked here below in that flesh, and even gave us that same flesh to eat for our salvation. But since no one eats it without first worshipping it, we can

---

14. Compare Exposition 2 of Psalm 70,5; Letter 194,19. The phrase became classical.
15. *Sanctus* is the reading of the best codices, and follows that of the Septuagint. The Vulgate has *sanctum*: "because it is holy."
16. *Scabellum.*
17. The words usually meant footstool, though they could also refer to a clapper beneath the foot, like a castanet.

plainly see how the Lord's footstool is rightly worshiped. Not only do we commit no sin in worshipping it; we should sin if we did not.

However, is it the flesh that gives life? No, for the Lord himself, after speaking of this very earth, declared, *It is the spirit that gives life; the flesh is of no avail* (Jn 6:64). When you bow down to the earth somewhere, and prostrate yourself upon it, you must not look at the earth, but at the Holy One whom you are worshipping, whose footstool is the earth. It is adored for his sake, as the psalm immediately makes clear by adding the reason: *Worship his footstool, because he is holy.* Who is holy? He in whose honor you worship that footstool. So too he does not want your thoughts to remain fixed on the flesh when you worship him; he wills you to be given life by the spirit. That is why he says, *It is the spirit that gives life; the flesh is of no avail.* Yet when the Lord pointed this out, he had been speaking directly about his flesh. He had said, *Unless you eat my flesh and drink my blood, you will not have life in you* (Jn 6:54). Some of his disciples—about seventy of them—were scandalized, protesting, *This is a hard saying; who can understand it?* (Jn 6:61). They left him, and walked with him no more. What he said seemed hard to them: *Unless you eat my flesh and drink my blood, you will not have life in you.* It seemed to them a stupid idea, for they took it in a carnal sense, supposing that the Lord meant to hack off small pieces of his body to give them; so they objected, *This is a hard saying.* It was they who were hard, not the saying. If instead of being hard they had been docile, they would have said to themselves, "There must be some holy mystery[18] here." Then they would have stayed with him, not hard but flexible and receptive, and would have learned from him what those others learned, while they themselves went away.

This is clearly so, because when the objectors departed, the twelve disciples who had stayed with the Lord mourned over them as though over the dead, and hinted to the Lord that those who had gone had been scandalized by his teaching. But the Lord insisted: *It is the spirit that gives life; the flesh is of no avail. The words I have spoken to you are spirit and life* (Jn 6:54). "Understand what I have told you in a spiritual way. You are not asked to eat this body that you can see, nor to drink the blood that will be shed by those who will crucify me. What I have revealed to you is something mysterious,[19] something which when understood spiritually will mean life for you. Although it is to be celebrated in a visible manner, you must understand it in a way that transcends bodily sight." *Exalt the Lord our God, and worship his footstool, because he is holy.*

---

18. *Sacramentum.*
19. *Sacramentum.*

Verses 6-8. The privileges of Moses, Aaron and Samuel, who prophesied of Christ

10. *Moses and Aaron were among his priests, and Samuel among those who invoked his name. They constantly invoked the Lord, and he heard them; he spoke to them in a pillar of cloud.* These men of old, Moses and Aaron and Samuel, were servants of God, and of high standing among the ancients. You know how Moses led the people of Israel out of Egypt and through the Red Sea in the power of God, and guided them in the desert. You know what wonderful works were wrought by God through the agency of Moses at that time. All of you who listen eagerly to the scriptures in church, or read them privately, or learn about them in any other way, are familiar with these stories. Aaron was the brother of Moses, and was ordained a priest by him.[20] In those passages it does not appear that anyone other than Aaron was a priest. Aaron is clearly depicted there as a priest of God, but Moses is not said to have been a priest. But if he was not, what was he? He could not have been greater than one who was a priest, surely? In fact our psalm does portray Moses as a priest, for it says, *Moses and Aaron were among his priests.* So both of them were priests of the Lord.

Samuel came later; we read about him in the Books of the Kingdoms.[21] Samuel lived in David's time, for he it was who anointed holy David.[22] From early childhood Samuel grew up in the temple. His mother had been sterile, but in her longing for a son she prayed to the Lord in bitter grief, begging that God would send a son to her. But she proved that her motive was not carnal by dedicating the child to God, by whose will he came to exist. She had made a vow to the Lord God: "If a male child is born to me, he shall serve in your temple,"[23] and she carried it out. After his birth holy Samuel stayed with his mother as long as he was being suckled; but as soon as she had weaned him she handed him over to the temple to grow up there, and to be strengthened in spirit,[24] and to serve God. So he became a great priest, the holy priest of that era.

The psalm mentions these three, but it means us to regard them as representative of all holy people. Why does it name these three in particular? Because, as we have pointed out, we must recognize Christ in this psalm.[25] You need to concentrate now, holy brethren.[26] The previous verse commanded, *Exalt the Lord our God, and worship his footstool, because he is holy*, and by these words it pointed toward someone, namely our Lord Jesus Christ. His footstool is

---

20. See Ex 28:1.41.
21. 1 and 2 Samuel, in our usage.
22. See 1 Sm 16:13.
23. See 1 Sm 1:11. The temple was not yet built, but Shiloh was the central sanctuary of the tribes, and the home of the Ark.
24. Variant: "be spiritually tested."
25. See section 1 above.
26. *Sanctitas vestra.*

worthy of adoration because he took to himself the flesh in which he would appear to the human race. But the psalm wished to show us that the ancient fathers also foreshadowed him, prophesying that our Lord Jesus Christ is the true priest. This is why it mentioned them in particular, recalling that God spoke to them in a pillar of cloud.

What does this *pillar of cloud* signify? It means that God used to speak to them in figures. If he had literally spoken through some wispy cloud, the obscure things he said might have prefigured the manifestation of someone or other, but I do not know whom. But this unknown "someone" is an unknown "someone" no longer; he is someone well known to us, our Lord Jesus Christ. *Moses and Aaron were among his priests, and Samuel among those who invoked his name. They constantly invoked the Lord, and he heard them; he spoke to them in a pillar of cloud.* He who of old used to speak in a pillar of cloud has spoken to us now in his footstool: that is, in the earth which is the flesh he assumed. That is why we worship his footstool, for he is holy. He spoke of old from the cloud, and what he said was not understood at the time; now he has spoken in his footstool, and the cloudy words of old have been made clear. *He spoke to them in a pillar of cloud.*

Moses, Aaron, and Samuel were nonetheless punished, and in this they foreshadowed all faithful disciples

11. We must investigate carefully, brothers and sisters, to see what sort of holy people these were who have been named. *They were accustomed to keep his testimonies and the commandments he gave them.* They did keep them, certainly; be sure of that. *They were accustomed to keep his testimonies, and the commandments he gave them.* This is what it says, and it cannot be contradicted. Does it mean that they committed no sins? How can that be true? It is true only insofar as they kept his commandments and his testimonies. But observe how the psalm forms us into the kind of people we ought to be, and warns us against assuming that we are perfect in righteousness. Consider this: Moses and Aaron were among his priests, and Samuel among those who called upon his name; he was accustomed to speak to them from the pillar of cloud, and it is quite obvious that he listened to these people who habitually kept his testimonies and the commandments he gave them. *O Lord our God, you heard them*, says the psalm. But it continues, *O God, you were propitious toward them.* God is described as propitious only where sins are concerned, for he is said to be propitious when he grants pardon. What did he find in them that deserved punishment, what did he find that he could mercifully forgive?

He was propitious in forgiving their sins, but propitious too in punishing them; for what does the psalm say next? *You were propitious toward them, and punished them in all the things they cared about.* Even in punishing you were propitious. Not only in forgiving sins were you propitious, but in punishing them too. Look what the psalm is telling us here, my brothers and sisters; take careful note of it. When people are not scourged for their sins, it is because God is truly angry with them. But he is propitious toward us when he is not content simply to forgive our sins, so that they may not debar us from the world to come, but he also chastises us, lest we go on enjoying them.

12. Let me have your attention now, brothers and sisters. If we seek to understand how they were punished, God will help me to explain it. Let us consider these three persons—Moses, Aaron, and Samuel—and in what their punishment consisted, since the psalm has stated, *You punished them in all the things they cared about.* It must refer to disordered affections which the Lord saw in their hearts, inclinations unknown to other men and women, for they conducted themselves in the midst of God's people without incurring any human reproach. What are we saying, then? That Moses, perhaps, had lived a sinful life in earlier days? He struck a man, and then fled from Egypt.[27] Aaron too had lived previously in a way that displeased God, for he allowed a headstrong, maddened people to make an idol, and so it came about that an idol was fashioned for God's people, for their worship.[28] But what had Samuel done? He had been dedicated to the temple from infancy. Through all the stages of his growing up he lived amid God's sacred symbols; he was God's servant from childhood. Nothing was ever alleged against Samuel, or at any rate not by human critics. Possibly God knew of something that demanded purification, for even what seems perfect to human eyes is imperfect in the face of the holiness of God. Craftsmen make plenty of artefacts that are displayed to ignorant beholders, but after the viewers have judged the products to be perfect, the craftsmen polish them further, because they know the flaws. People are amazed that extra refinement should be applied to things they had themselves pronounced perfect. This happens with buildings, paintings, garments, with almost every type of art and craft. To begin with, people judge an object to be perfect, leaving nothing to be desired; but the untutored eye judges differently from the canons of art. So too the holy men we are considering lived under God's scrutiny: they seemed to be faultless and perfect, like angels; but God knew their shortcomings and punished their wayward affections. In punishing he was not angry with them, but propitious. He punished in order to make perfect one whom he had accepted, not to condemn an outcast.

God was careful, then, to punish all their wayward inclinations. How did he punish Samuel? In what did that punishment consist? What I am going to say is for the enlightenment of Christians, of those who have already come to know Christ, those to whom he came in the guise of his footstool, whom he so loved and for whom he shed his blood. They need to know how, having made good progress, they will yet be chastised. We look for the punishment visited upon

27. See Ex 2:12.15.
28. See Ex 32:1-4.

Moses. It seems that he suffered hardly any, unless we count God's command to him at the very end, *Go up onto the mountain, and die* (Dt 32:49). To an old man God said, *Die*. He had already attained a ripe old age, and was he not going to die sometime in any case? What kind of punishment was that? Perhaps, though, God was indicating his intention to punish when he told Moses, *You shall not enter the promised land* (Dt 32:52; 34:4), the land into which the people was about to cross? No; more probably Moses was simply a representative of a certain class of people; for is it any great punishment for one who has entered the kingdom of heaven to be debarred from that land which was promised for a time only, to serve as a foreshadowing, and then pass away? Did not many unbelievers enter that country? Were there not also some who while living in the land committed many evils, and offended God? Did they not give themselves up to idolatry in that country? Was it, then, such a harsh sentence when God did not confer the land on Moses? No, but Moses served as a type of those who were under the law, for *the law was given through Moses* (Jn 1:17). What his exclusion signified was that people who wanted to be under the law, and refused to be under grace, would not enter the land of promise. What happened to Moses was a sign, not a penalty. Is death a penalty to an old man? Was it a punishment to be forbidden entry into the country which many unworthy persons entered?

Now, what is said about Aaron? He too died as an old man, leaving sons to succeed him in the priesthood.[29] His son exercised the priestly ministry after him. How was he punished, then? Samuel likewise died as an old man, leaving sons to succeed him.[30] I ask, then, what punishment these men underwent, and in human terms I find none. But from the perspective of what I know about God's servants, I can say that they endured punishment every day. Read about them, and see their punishments; and you, who are making progress, be prepared to bear the same yourselves. Every day they had to put up with people who argued with them, every day they had to tolerate those who led wicked lives, and they were forced to live among people whose conduct they had to rebuke day after day. That was their punishment.

Anyone who regards that as a light matter has not advanced very far. The iniquity of other people is a torment to you in the measure that you have left your own behind. When you have become wheat—healthy growth, I mean, from good seed—when you have become a son or daughter of the kingdom and have begun to yield fruit, then will the tares appear, for *when the shoots had grown up and come into ear, then the tares became apparent* (Mt 13:26). When weeds are rampant, you will see that you are surrounded by bad people. You may be conscious of a desire to keep the bad people at a distance from yourself, and to exclude all wrongdoers from the Church; but the Lord's view of the matter gives

29. See Nm 20:24-28; 33:38.
30. See 1 Sm 8:1.

you your answer: *Let them both grow together until harvest time. In trying to uproot the tares, you may uproot the wheat as well* (Mt 13:30). By the Lord's decree the tares must be tolerated, and from your condition as his servant arises the necessity of living amid the tares. You cannot remove them to a distance; you have to put up with them.

Even though you enjoy bodily health as you live out your days among bad people, see what grave injuries you suffer in your heart. All of you who are destined to make progress will experience the truth of what I say, as you who are advanced have verified it already. These things have to be borne, and perhaps another text is relevant here: *a servant who knows his master's will, yet does not behave worthily, will be severely flogged* (Lk 12:47). This is a matter of common experience. In the measure that God's will makes itself known to us, in that same measure does our own guilt confront us; and the more conscious we are of our guilt, the more we are driven to mourning and tears. We recognize the justice of whatever it is that God demands of us, and how great is the imperfection in which we still languish. The saying comes true in us, that *anyone who increases knowledge increases sorrow* (Eccl 1:18). As charity grows strong in you, you will suffer all the more over a sinner. The greater your charity, the more agonizing will your pain be over the sinner you must tolerate, though he will provoke you not to anger, but to pity for him.

13. Consider the apostle Paul, and what he endured. Think who was in pain, and what his sufferings were. *Quite apart from external things*, he says (for he has been enumerating many hardships, and is about to begin speaking about the interior distress that was his lot, over and above the external afflictions imposed on him by the wicked persecutors of Christ)—*quite apart from external things, there are the daily inroads made in me by my anxiety for all the churches* (2 Cor 11:28). Imagine what an anxiety it was: the anxiety of a father, and that of a mother too. And now observe how he was castigated, for God punished him in all the things he most cared about. We will tell you what he cared about, and how God used these same things to punish him. *Is anyone weak*, he cries, *and I am not weak too? Is anyone tripped up, without my being afire with indignation?* (2 Cor 11:29). The more ardent your charity, the more deeply you are wounded by other people's sins. Paul had been given a sting of the flesh, Satan's envoy, whose job it was to belabor him. See how propitious God was, punishing him in the things he cared about most! But what were these dearest concerns of his? *To make sure that I would not grow conceited over these great revelations*, he tells us, *a sting of the flesh was sent to me, a messenger of Satan to buffet me*. So perfect was he that there must have been some danger of vainglory, for God would not have applied a remedy where there was no wound. Paul begged to be relieved of it; the patient begged for the means of healing to be taken away: *three times I begged the Lord to take it away from me*, this sting of the flesh that buffeted him—some bodily ailment, perhaps—*I begged the Lord to take it away from me, but he said*

to me, "My grace is sufficient for you, for my power is fully deployed in weakness (2 Cor 12:7-9). I know the sick man I am treating, and it is not the patient's business to give me advice. A caustic dressing burns, but it heals you." Paul begs the doctor to remove the dressing, but he will not take it off until the wound has healed. *My power is fully deployed in weakness.*

You see, then, brothers and sisters, that any of us who are making progress in Christ must not look to be exempt from chastisement. However far we may have advanced, God knows our sins. Sometimes he also shows them to us, and then our sins are clear to our own eyes. Even if we pass our lives among the kind of people who find nothing in us deserving of censure, he who knows all things does censure us, and he punishes us in all the things we care about, because he is propitious toward us. If instead of punishing he abandons us, we perish. *O God; you were propitious toward them, and punished them in all the things they cared about.*

Verse 9. The stone hewn from the mountain fills the earth

14. *Exalt the Lord our God.* Yet again we exalt him, for how sincerely must he be praised and how highly exalted, he who is good even when he beats us! Can you treat your son like that, yet deny God the right to do so? It is not true that you are good when caressing your child, and bad when you strike him. When you caress him, you are his father, and when you strike him, you are his father still. You caress him lest he become discouraged, and you beat him lest he go to ruin.

Exalt the Lord our God, and worship him on his holy mountain, for the Lord our God is holy. An earlier verse of this psalm invited us, *Exalt the Lord our God, and worship his footstool*; we understood then what worshipping his footstool meant. Similarly now, after proclaiming that the Lord our God is to be exalted, the psalm mentions his mountain, to make sure that no one tries to exalt him anywhere else. What is his mountain? We read about the mountain in another part of scripture, and how a stone was hewn out of it without hands, a stone which grew great after smashing all the kingdoms of the earth. It is Daniel's vision that I am describing.[31] The stone hewn out of the mountain without hands grew enormous; as scripture says, *It grew into a lofty mountain which filled the whole earth* (Dn 2:35). Let us worship him on this great mountain, if we hope to be heard. Heretics do not worship on this mountain, for this is a mountain that has filled the whole earth, whereas the heretics have stuck fast in a part, and lost the whole. If they come to acknowledge the Catholic Church, they will worship on this mountain with us. We see already how great it has grown,

---

31. See Dn 2:34-35.

this stone hewn without hands from the mountain, what vast regions of the earth it has conquered and how many nations it has reached.

What is the mountain from which the stone was cut without hands? In the first place it is the kingdom of the Jews, which from of old gave its allegiance to the one God. From it was hewn the stone, our Lord Jesus Christ, he of whom it was said, *The stone rejected by the builders has become the headstone of the corner* (Ps 117(118):22; Acts 4:11). He was the stone hewn out of the mountain without hands, and he has shattered all the kingdoms of the earth. Indeed, we see that all earthly sovereignties have been broken by this stone. What were the kingdoms of the earth? The realms of idols, the domains of demons, now broken. Saturn used to hold sway over many people, but where is his sovereignty now? Mercury reigned over many, but where is his domain? It has been broken, and those who used to be his subjects have been brought into the kingdom of Christ. Think what a reign the "Heavenly One" used to enjoy at Carthage![32] But where is the Heavenly One's dominion now? The stone hewn from the mountain without hands has shattered all the kingdoms of the earth. In what sense was it hewn without hands? Christ was born from the Jewish race without human intervention. All others who are born are the fruit of sexual union, but he was born of a virgin, and therefore is said to have been born without hands, because hands symbolize human work. Where there were no human hands involved, where no marital intercourse took place, there was nonetheless the birth of a child. This stone was therefore born from the mountain without hands. The stone grew very big, and as it grew it smashed all the kingdoms of the earth.

It became a mighty mountain, and filled the earth's entire surface. This is the Catholic Church,[33] and you should rejoice to be in communion with it. Those who are not in communion with it, people who worship and praise God somewhere other than on this mountain, are not heard when they pray, or at any rate are not heard in a way that will lead them to eternal life, even if they are granted some temporal benefits. Let them not congratulate themselves because God has heard some of their petitions, for he hears the pagans too in certain matters. Do the pagans not cry to God for rain, and get it? Why? Because God makes his sun rise over both good and bad people, and sends rain on just and unjust alike.[34] You have nothing to boast about, you pagan, because God sends rain when you cry to him, for he pours rain on just and unjust without distinction. He has heard you with regard to temporal needs, but he does not hear you with a view to eternal life unless you worship on his holy mountain. *Worship the Lord on his holy mountain, for the Lord our God is holy.*

---

32. *Caelestis* was a female deity venerated especially at Carthage, where, probably, this sermon was preached. See Exposition of Psalm 62,7, and note there; also *The City of God* II,4.

33. Typically, Augustine passes without more ado from identifying the mountain with Christ to identifying it with the Church.

34. See Mt 5:45.

Conclusion: the life-giving rain must find receptive soil

15. These comments on the psalm must suffice, beloved friends.[35] Insofar as the Lord enabled us, we have spoken; and whatever we say in the name of God is for you a shower of God's rain, for God is speaking through us. But you must take care to be the right kind of soil. When rain falls on the earth, the soil brings forth a good crop if it is good soil; but if it is bad soil it produces thorns. Whether it falls on healthy crops or on thorns, the rain is sweet and wholesome. Anyone who becomes worse after hearing these words, and produces thorns after the rain, can hope for nothing but the bonfire, and must not blame the rain. But anyone who is improved by listening, and brings forth fruit from good earth, can look forward to the barn and must give credit to the rain. But what are the clouds? What is the rain? What else but the mercy of God, who lavishes all care on those whom he loves? He has forgiven them so that he may in turn be loved by them.

---

35. *Caritati vestrae.*

Index of Scripture

(prepared by Michael Dolan)

(The numbers after the scriptural reference refer to the section of the work)

Old Testament

Genesis

1:20	80, 2
2:2	92, 1
2:7	89, 3
2:24	74, 4
3:19	81, 5; 82, 14; 84, 14
3:22	73, 17
21:12	77, 44
25:23	78, 10
25:33	II, 88, 6
32:26	79, 3
48:5.6	75, 1
49:9	II, 88, 7
49:10	75, 1

Exodus

3:14	82, 14; 89, 3
4:6	73, 13
4:7	73, 13
19:8	77, 10; 77, 33
20:3	77, 34
32:10	77, 22
33:23	73, 5

Leviticus

19:2	85, 4

Deuteronomy

6:13	98, 9
6:16	II, 90, 7
8:3	II, 90, 6
21:23	87, 7
32:49	98, 12
32:52	98, 12
34:4	98, 12

2 Samuel

7:27	85, 7
12:13	75, 15

2 Kings

2:23-24	83, 2

Tobit

4:7.11	96, 18

Job

1:16.21	77, 28
1:21	76, 2; 93, 19; 96, 17; 97, 6
2:9	93, 19
2:9-10	I, 90, 2
2:10	93, 19
7:1	74, 1; 76, 4

Psalms

1:1-2	93, 6
2:10	I, 88, 27
2:11	75, 17; 85, 15

485

72:24(73:23-24)	73, 19
73(74):6	79, 10
77(78):8	77, 1; 79, 14
77(78):51-54	77, 23
78(79):6	86, 6
79:6(80:5)	78, 8
81(82):1	94, 6
81(82):6	83, 11; 84, 9; 85, 12
81(82):6.1	96, 14
83:5(84:4)	85, 23; 86, 9; 93, 24
85(86):9	94, 9
93(94):3.4	75, 11
93(94):14	78, 2
95(96):1	97, 1
95(96):5	76, 15; 85, 12; 94, 6
95(96):12	79, 11
100(101):1	74, 5
101:8(102:7)	83, 7
101:27-28 (102:26-27)	89, 3
101:28(102:27)	76, 8; 77, 19; I, 88, 29; 89, 15
102(103):14	75, 18
103(104):26	I, 88, 11
103(104):29-30	75, 18
105(106):1	74, 3
105(106):47	77, 3
106(107):1	74, 3
107(108):1	74, 3
110(111):10	77, 7
111(112):7	95, 15
111:7(112:6-7)	91, 12
113(114):4	93, 4
113B:1(115:1)	95, 8
113B(115):1.2	I, 88, 13
113B(115):4	80, 13
114(116):3-4	83, 5
114(116):8-9	85, 23
115(116):11	91, 6
117(118):18	78, 8; 96, 12
117(118):19	85, 5
117(118):22	78, 3; 94, 8; 98, 14
118(119):18	89, 17
118(119):34	77, 45
118(119):53	76, 5
118(119):133	77, 13
120(121):1	75, 7
120(121):2	75, 7
125(126):6	83, 10
128(129):1	87, 15
129(130):3	78, 12
131(132):6	95, 5
131(132):11	II, 88, 6
137(138):6	74, 2
138(139):7	I, 88, 24
138(139):7-8	94, 2
138(139):8	81, 2
142(143):2	78, 12
144(145):3	I, 88, 8
146(147):7	75, 3
148:5	89, 3

Proverbs

1:28	85, 8
2:19	77, 24
4:17	77, 13
11:31	93, 23; 93, 24
12:23, LXX	96, 5; 98, 3
14:28	85, 14
16:32, LXX	92, 4
22:17	77, 3

Ecclesiastes

1:18	98, 12

Song of Songs

1:3	II, 90, 13
1:4	73, 16
2:15	80, 14
4:2	77, 44; 94, 11
6:5	94, 11
8:5, LXX	73, 16

Wisdom

1:7-8	74, 9
1:11	79, 13; 80, 21
3:1	87, 5
5:3	75, 11
5:3-5.8	85, 23
5:3.8-9	74, 1
5:6	75, 11; 80, 14; 96, 18
5:6.8.9	75, 11
5:8-9	85, 23
7:24	75, 17
12:18	78, 8

Sirach

2:1	79, 5; 83, 1
2:15	77, 10
6:25	78, 15; 89, 13
10:9	82, 14
10:15	73, 16
17:26	87, 10
24:29	85, 23

1 Corinthians

Index

(prepared by Joseph Sprug)

The first number in the Index is the Psalm number.
More than one Exposition is cited by the number in parentheses, for example (2)
The number after the colon is a paragraph number.
Different expositions in the same heading are separated by a semi-colon.
Biblical texts/words are in italics.

inheritance (God's people), 78:2,3,10,11; 79:10; 81:7; 85:14; 96:15
iniquity, 84:5; 89:8; 92:5; 93:1,20; 98:12
injustice: damage to author of, 96:6
innocence, 77:45; 93:1
   possession of good things and, 83:17
insult, 88(2):12; 92:4
intelligence, 77:45
invoking God, 85:8
irreligion: far away from God, 94:2
Isaiah, 96:19
Ishmaelites, 82:7
islands: churches as, 96:4
Israel, 75:2,3; 76:17; 77:1,2,7,33,35,44; 78:3; 79:9; 80:18; 81:1; 82:5,9; 83:12; 84:3; 86:5; 88(1):3,7; 88(2):7; 97:3
Israelites, 73:1,16; 76:22; 77:3,10,12; 81:1; 83:3; 87:3
   belief in Christ, 78:2
   true: *no guile*, 75:2

Jabin, 82:9
Jacob, 77:7,9,41,44; 78:10; 80:3; 82:6; 83:12; 84:4; 86:5; 97:3
   See also Esau; Israel
   thigh, 76:22; 79:3
   twelve sons of, 75:1
Jericho, 86:6; 88(2):5
Jerusalem, 73:7,8; 85:14; 78:4,6,7; 83:8; 84:4; 86:6,7; 90(1):5; 93:6
   destruction of, 78:2
   heavenly, 86:2
   twelve gates, 86:4
Jesus Christ, 73:2,6,16; 77:8,9,13,26,41,43; 83:13; 84:9; 86:4,8
   See also Incarnation; Second Coming of Christ; Son of God; Word of God
   accused of sin, 73:21
   ascension; hands of angels, 90(2):8
   baptized, 90(2):6
   beauty and strength = his raiment, 92:2
   Before Abraham came..., 92:6
   bridegroom, 84:2; 90(2):5,13
   burial: *three days and nights*, 87:9
   Church and, *See* Church.
   confess to your great name, 98:6
   cornerstone, 86:2,3,5; 94:8; 96:2; 98:14
   covenant and, 88(1):28
   crucified: *Stir up your power*, 79:3
   crucifixion; belief, 90(2):13
   David and, 75:1; 85:1; 88(2):6
   death of, *See below:* passion and death.
   destroy this temple..., 85:22

divinity hidden, 87:8
divinity; humility, 85:1
door; shepherd, 86:3,4; 90(1):1; 95:3
end of the law, 76:1; 77:7; 79:1; 84:2
enemies enumerated, 82:7
feet of the Lord, 90(2):8
figures of
   bald man, 83:2; 84:2
   Rahab, 86:6
   Samson, 80:11,14
food to be consumed, 73:16
footprints not recognized by Jews, 76:22
free among the dead, 87:5
gentle and humble of heart, 90(1):1; 93:15
Giant of giants, 87:10
gifts to the poor and, 75:9
glorified exceedingly, 96:14
God dispelling his mercy from, 88(2):3
God of gods, 83:11
God's arm, and right hand, 97:1,2
God's inheritance, 78:3; 79:10; 81:7; 85:14; 88(2):3
God's Way found in, 76:15
good works "all day long," 87:9
handmaiden's son, 85:22
harsh words spoken against, 90(1):4
hen gathers her chicks, 88(2):14; 90(1):5
humanity, 88(1):22; 90(2):1
   true flesh, 93:19
humility, 81:6; 88(1):11
I am the light of the world, 84:8
I am the living bread, 84:9; 90(2):6
I and the Father are one, 76:1
I have come to set fire..., 96:7
I was hungry..., 86:5
I will show myself..., 89:15
Israelite belief in, 78:2
Joseph of Egypt and, 76:17; 80:7
judge, 81:7; 85:21; 93:8
judgment, 80:7
justice of God, 97:2
king of kings, 88(1):27
King of the Jews, 80:11
kingship, 96:4
leader in song and suffering, 87:1
Learn of me..., 81:3
light of the world, 88(1):13
mediator, 90(2):1
miracles, 90(2):6
   Young man, arise..., 97:1
My soul is sorrowful..., 87:3
Old Testament goods and, 77:7
our king and our God, 75:1
our root, ascended, 91:13

motive for refraining from, 93:2
ownership of, 84:15
punishment for, 78:11
as pursuing Egyptians, 80:8
reigning in the body, 75:5
renouncing, 80:19
slave of, 87:5
two sources: desire and fear, 79:13
sing (-er; -ing)
  body of Christ, 83:5,6,7
  precentor and succentor, 87:1
  to sing is to build, 95:2
sinner(-s), 73:1,19; 74:2,12,14; 75:14,15; 76:7;
    77:7,24; 83:16; 85:9; 88(2):3; 88(2):7;
    89:11; 90(1):11; 90(2):2; 91:7,9;
    93:5,23,27; 95:7
  attitude towards God and sin, 93:11
  evildoers, 93:7,11
  gloat: God ignores our sins, 93:9,11
  God holds back vengeance, 74:9
  God wants to spare the wicked, 93:18
  Lord, be merciful to me..., 90(1):6
  no joy for the wicked, 96:19
  pit is dug for, 93:15,16,17,29
  prosperity, *See* temporal goods.
  proud, 93:15
  putting up with, as punishment, 98:12
  toleration; pity, 98:12,13
  wrongdoers, 93:7,15
          Sisera, 82:9
skin: whiteness, 73:13
snake, 90(2):9
  death and, 73:5
  healed by gazing at, 73:5
  staff turned into, 73:5
Sodom, 77:29; 83:3
soldiers, 90(1):10
Solomon, 77:26; 83:10; 88(2):6; 95:1
Son of God, 84:13
  form of a servant, 77:43; 85:1,4; 87:2
  hidden in the crucified Christ, 79:4
  omnipresence, 75:17
  time and, 74:5
  unique, 88(1):7
Son of Man, 79:12
song, 94:3
  Sing a new song..., 97:1
  song of ascents, 83:10
sorrow, 76:6
  sharing, 93:9
soul: *See also* body and soul
  dead, 87:11
  filled with evils, 87:3
  God contained in peaceful soul, 92:6

harmed by iniquity, 93:1
  lie in the mouth kills, 79:13
sower, 90(1):8
sparrow, 83:7
speaking in tongues, 96:13
spirit, 77:10; 79:14
  gives life, 98:9
  searching one's own, 76:9,13,14
spiritual life
  See also Christian life; grace; heart
  change wrought in me, 76:12,13
  likeness to God, 94:2
  looking back, 83:4
  miracles wrought in souls, 76:16
  prepare self for trials, 83:1
  weapons; flesh, 97:7
  weariness, 91:1
spiritual warfare, 75:4; 76:7; 80:11; 83:9; 84:10
squabs, 83:7
staff: turned into snake, 73:5,16
stars, 93:3,5,6,29
Stephen, Saint, 78:2
stones, 95:2; 96:11
storm, 80:11
straw, 96:7
strength, 73:18; 89:10; 92:2,3,4,6
suffering, 83:6; 85:19; 86:5; 87:3; 89:11,14;
    92:8,19
  God accused of being unjust, 74:8
  as test, 77:29
summer, 73:20
sun, 73:19; 77:22; 80:14; 88(2):5; 90(1):8;
    93:4,5; 98:14
sunlight, 96:18,19
sweetness, 84:15; 85:11,24; 85:7
sword: fire and, 96:7
syllables, 76:8
symbols, 77:3,26,27
synagogue, 73:1; 77:2,3; 81:1,2; 82:1

Tabor (mountain) , 88(1):13,17
talking, 76:7
tares and wheat, 98:12
tax collector, 74:10,12; 85:2
  Lord, be merciful to me..., 84:14; 93:15
teaching, 93:13
tears, 83:10
teeth, 77:44
temperance, 83:11
temple, 73:11; 74:2; 78:4,10; 82:10; 92:6;
    95:1,2